PAINTING
& DRAWING

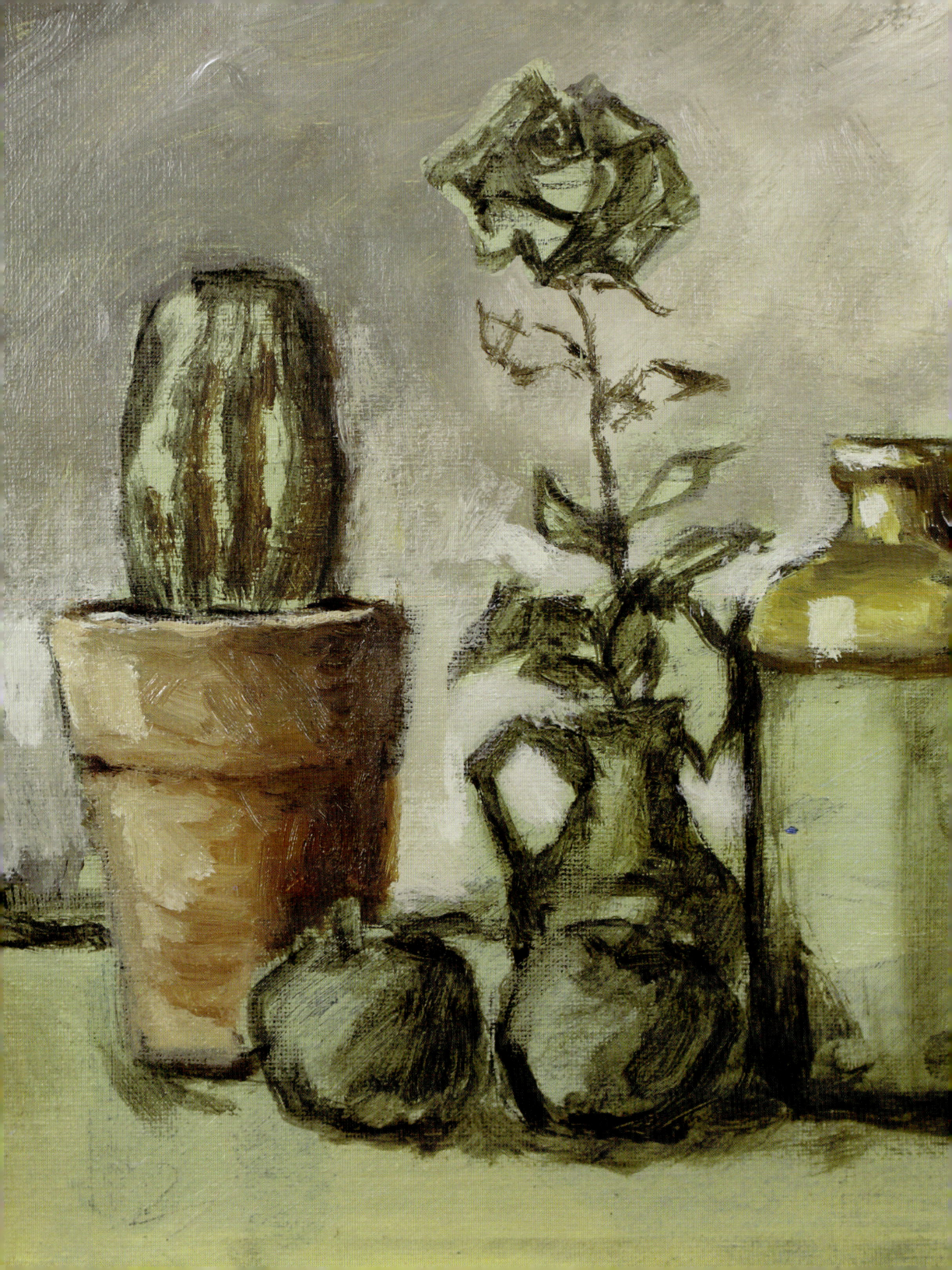

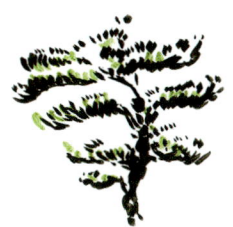

PAINTING & DRAWING

TECHNIQUES AND TUTORIALS FOR THE COMPLETE BEGINNER

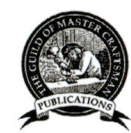

Contents

Colour Pencils

Charcoal

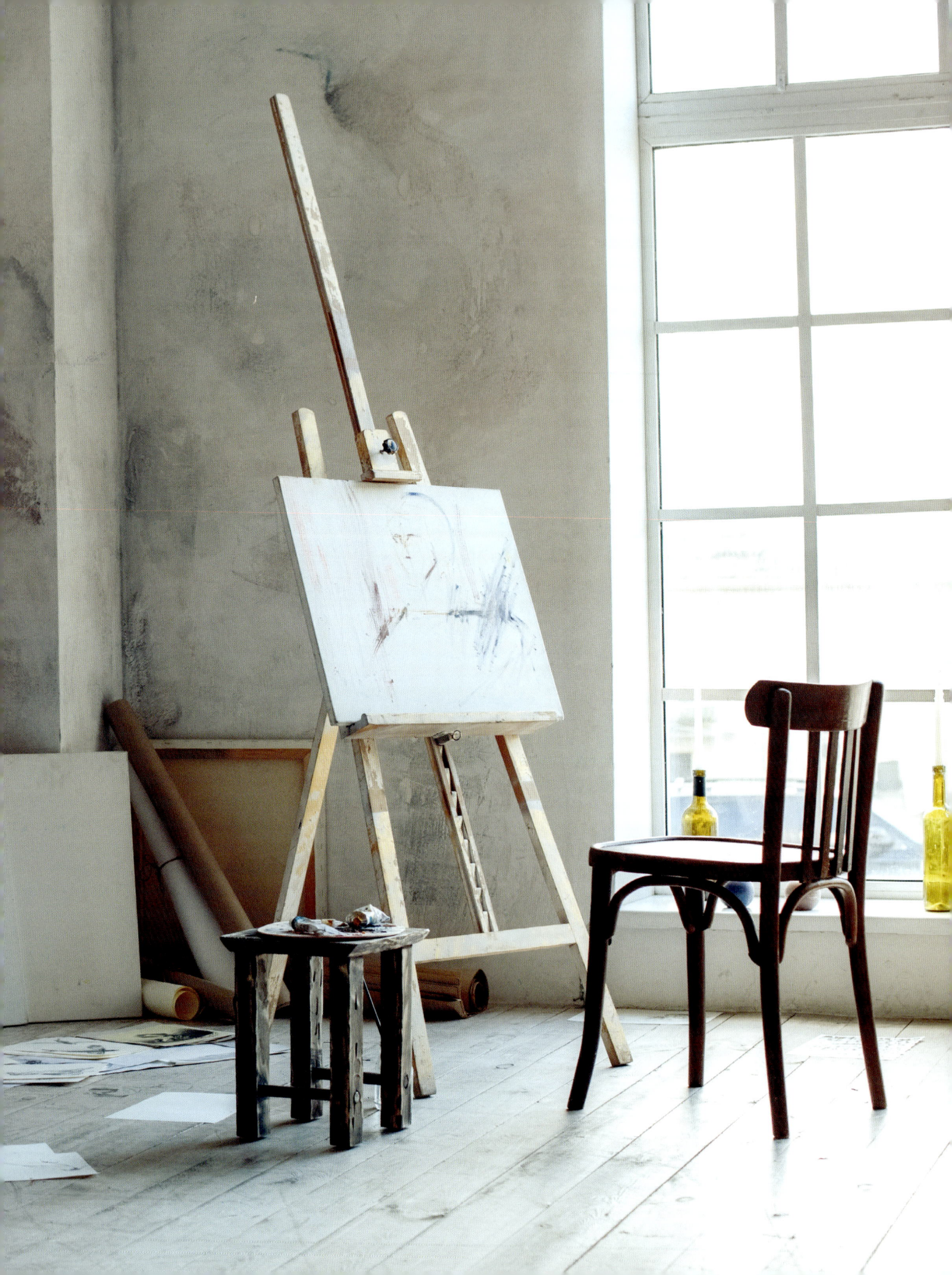

Preface

'If you hear a voice within you saying, "You are not a painter," then by all means paint… and that voice will be silenced,' Vincent van Gogh once proclaimed. And the same principle applies to whichever creative medium you prefer.

Nevertheless, the blank page can be a daunting thing and for the self-trained, the advice of those who have spent years honing their crafts can be invaluable. Gathered together here is the guidance of five artists who are each expert in their particular field. This presents the added opportunity to compare and contrast the way each medium is approached and executed. While each has equipment and techniques unique to it, many of the principles are shared. But the particular prism through which the artist creates his or her work can give us food for thought, even if we are already committed to one channel. Alongside this, surprising and inspiring 'tricks' are shared, including the unexpected uses for salt, credit cards, mirrors and more that form part of these experts' artistic arsenal.

Balancing practical, easy-to-follow exercises with insightful advice and tips honed from years of experience, each section gives the reader the tools needed to either begin from scratch or improve their practice. Not only will you discover what each piece of equipment can achieve but the mysteries of the more subtle arts such as perspective and tonal values will be solved. Scale and composition, measuring and arrangement, colour and tone are all discussed from the perspective of the watercolour, acrylics, oil, pencil and charcoal artist. From the oldest medium (oils became popular in the 15th century) to the newest – acrylic paints have only been around for 70 years or so – we find out why certain methods are preferred and what might happen if we stray too far from the accepted path (although all artists inevitably have a rebellious, experimental streak, it is acknowledged).

Common across each teacher's advice is that it is impossible not to bring your own personal interpretation to whatever you are trying to capture. Which means, the extension, that nothing is 'wrong'. Don't aim to replicate but to render your individual version of what you either see before you or imagine – that is all that is required. Make your mark, be bold and, above all, enjoy.

By picking up this book, these experts argue, you are already an artist. Even if you can't draw a straight line.

WATERCOLOUR

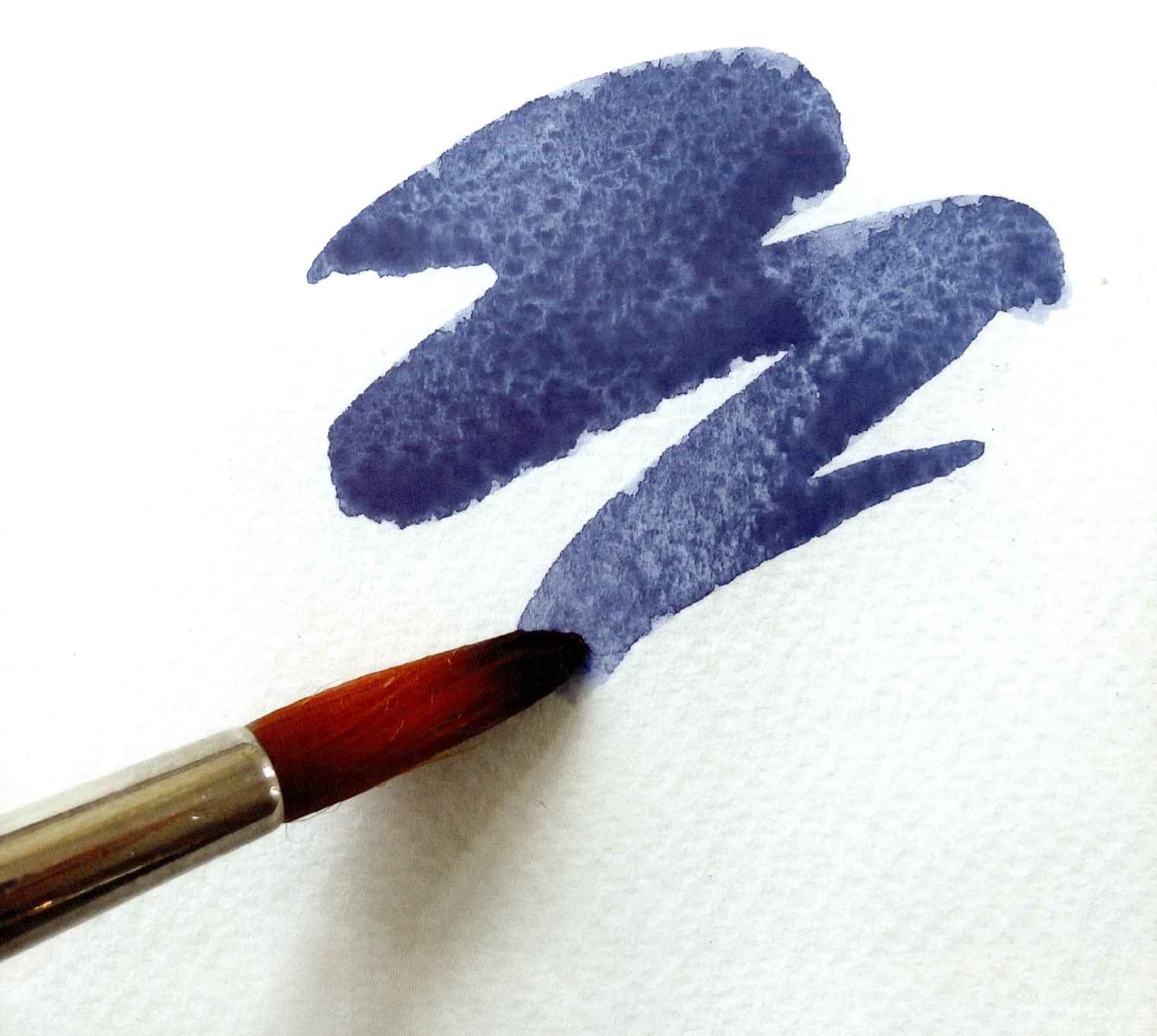

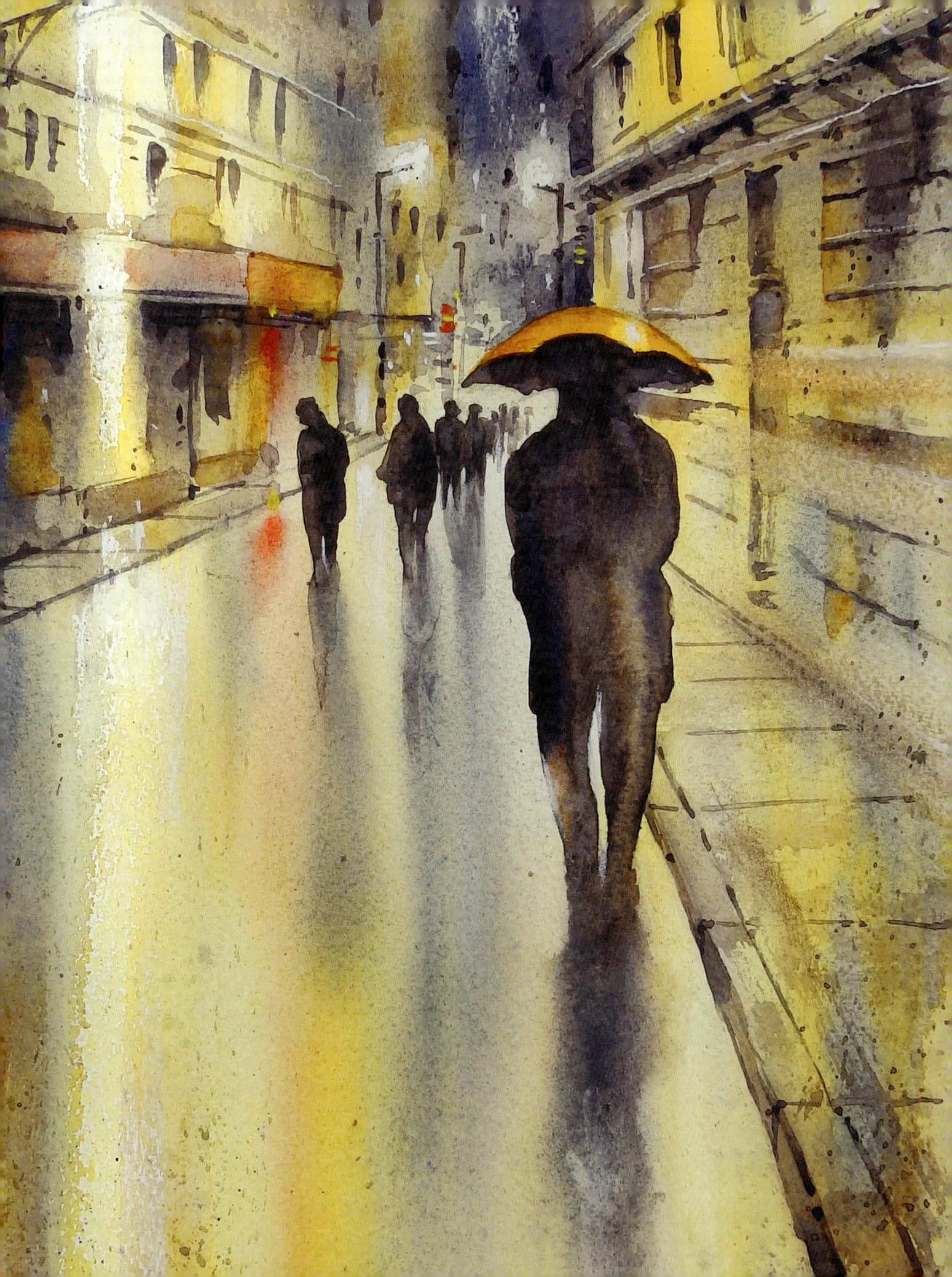

Introduction

Watercolour is an incredibly beautiful painting media. Its vibrancy and spontaneity can give the impression of effortlessness, but it is these very qualities that also present the biggest challenge, particularly for those starting out.

I have been teaching adults to paint using watercolour for more than 25 years. Unlike other books that teach watercolour I would like you, the reader, to feel as though you are taking part in one of my painting classes; the lessons set out in the following pages replicate those I run in my studios. Teaching is my passion and I never fail to get a buzz from seeing students become excited by the magic spell that watercolour weaves when painted in a free and uninhibited way.

Its very unpredictability makes watercolour both an exhilarating and a frustrating medium, but I firmly believe that you learn just as much from your failures as from your successes. And the wonderful thing is that you will never stop learning. Even after all these years I still find I am learning something new all the time.

I have often felt that the teaching of watercolour can be overly complicated. My basic approach is to make the process as easy as possible, and my whole ethos throughout the tutorials on the following pages is to keep it simple!

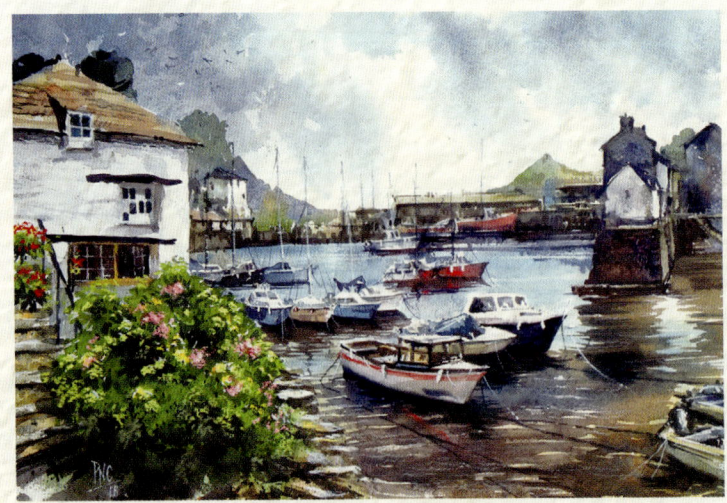

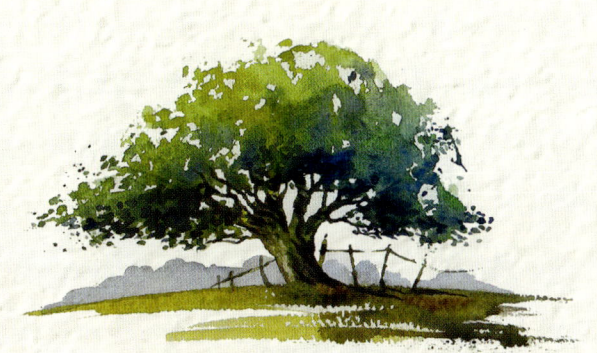

My students often hear me use the phrase: 'Let the paint paint itself!' The alchemy of watercolour only comes alive by letting the colours flow and move together freely without unnecessary fiddling. This is when those surprising 'happy accidents' happen, when what might be considered a mistake actually improves the final result and the painting evolves, helped by the laws of physics.

For those of you who haven't painted since schooldays, getting to grips with painting with watercolour can be quite a challenge. Unlike the art room's poster paints where solid colour is applied to cover the paper, watercolour is all about transparency, allowing the white of the paper to shine through. I can't stress enough how important it is to get to know the paint and the way it reacts in different situations, and this comes about only through practice.

When you start, don't expect to paint a 'masterpiece' straight away. Too often I have seen students becoming frustrated and disappointed with their first attempt at a finished piece. I begin with a number of basic techniques for you to practise and I strongly advise you to master these before embarking on the projects that follow. It is also very important that you paint in a relaxed and comfortable place and that you give yourself enough time to make reasonable progress. But most important of all, enjoy the experience, as it will always show in your work.

Paul Clark

Materials and Equipment

The subject of the tools and materials to be used in watercolour painting has the potential to become vast and confusing. In fact, it would be quite easy to write a whole book on it alone. So I'll keep this simple and only refer to the absolute basics a beginner will need to start painting.

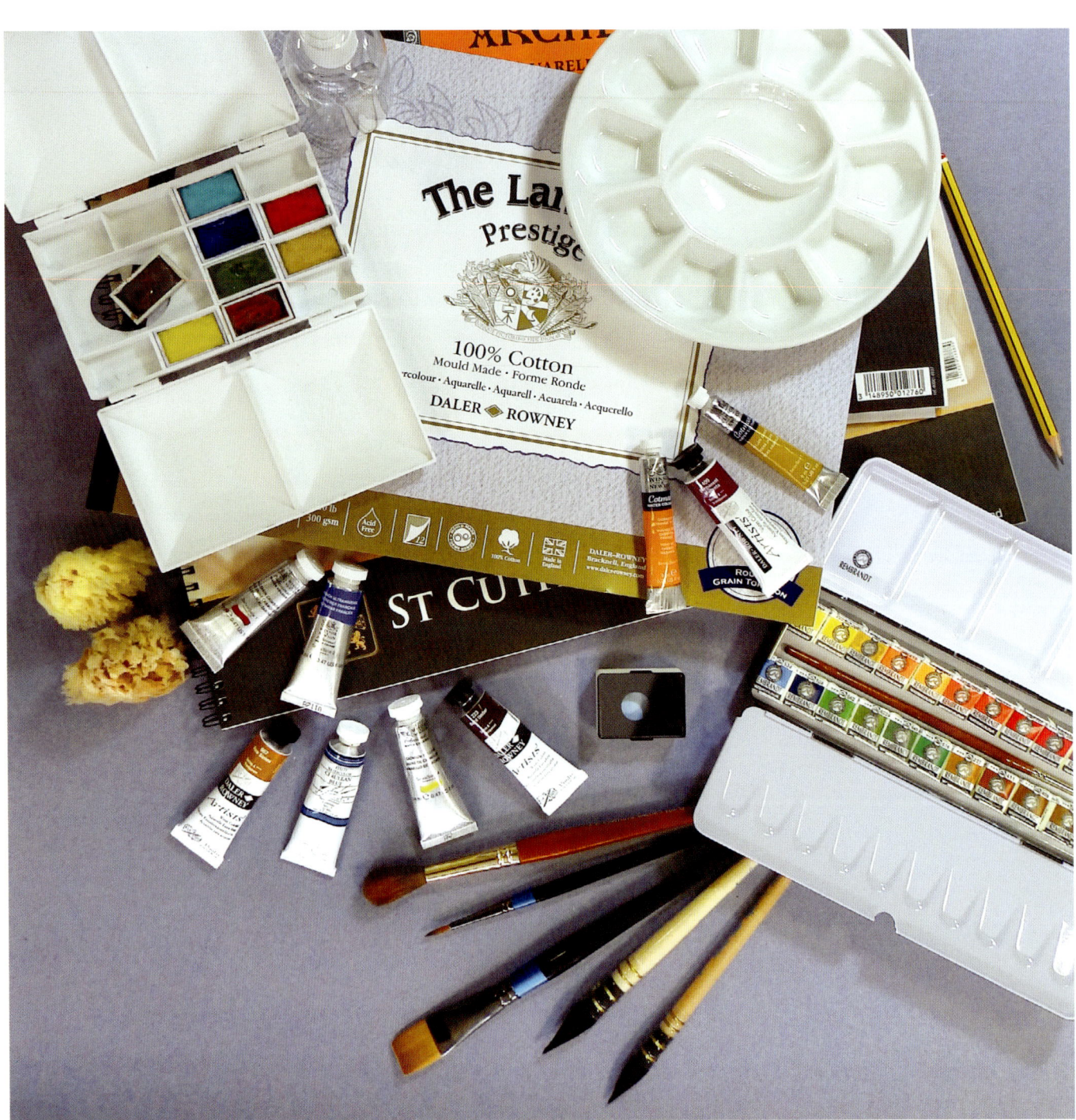

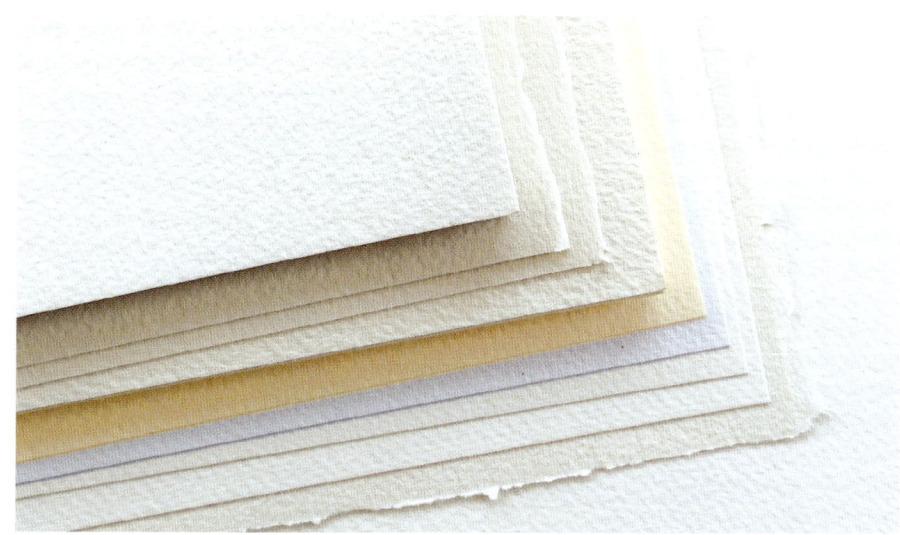

I often hear the phrase 'Buy the best you can afford', and while this is perfectly true, I'm a firm believer in not paying a fortune for 'artist quality' materials when more affordable ranges are readily available, especially for the beginner. Having said that, beware: there are art and craft shops that sell ranges of cheap, poor-quality products.

Paper

Out of all the main materials, I consider that paper is the most important. In my experience, when a student is disappointed with their work, in the majority of cases the cause can be attributed to the use of cheap paper.

Watercolour paper can be either pulp- or cotton-based and is available in a variety of finishes, sizes, colours and weights. It is usually made by one of three processes: handmade, mould-made or machine-made.

Many of the leading paper-makers produce paper in three finishes:
• Hot press, as the name suggests, has a flat, smooth finish and is ideal for painting fine detail.
• Cold press (sometimes referred to as NOT, as in not hot-pressed!) has a texture or 'tooth' and is the most widely

used watercolour paper available. This is the type of paper I have used for the projects in this chapter and I would recommend it for the beginner.
• Rough has a highly textured surface, which is more suitable for experienced painters.

For a beginner, I would recommend plain white paper in a pad of 10 x 14in (260 x 360mm) cold press (NOT), 140lb (300gsm). Look for paper from manufacturers such as Saunders Waterford and Bockingford, both made by St Cuthberts Mill, Winsor & Newton, Langton (Daler Rowney), Fabriano, Canson and, probably the best of all, Arches, where they have been making watercolour paper in the same French village since 1492! It's good to try out a variety of paper manufacturers and, once you find one you like, to stick to it, so you get to know its unique properties as you build up your experience.

STRETCHING YOUR PAPER
This may sound obvious but the use of water plays a key role in watercolour painting. It is therefore important to stretch your paper before starting your finished painting; otherwise, the water in the paint will cause the paper to buckle.

In addition, when your paper becomes very wet it will ripple, causing the paint to dry at different times, which will result in unsightly staining.

There are several ways to avoid this buckling and staining. The expensive option is to buy much thicker paper. You can get paper weighing up to 300lb (600gsm), which is almost like card and will remain flat regardless of the amount of water on its surface.

Another, cheaper, alternative is to buy a watercolour 'block', which is a pre-stretched paper that has been gummed on all four sides with a strong backing board. When the painting is dry, just run a palette knife around the edges to free the paper from the block. This type of paper is ideal for painting *en plein air* (outdoors).

Finally, you can stretch your paper yourself, as follows. Completely submerge the paper in water. Allow it to soak for thirty seconds then drain off any excess water. Moisten a length of gummed tape and stick all four sides of the paper to a wooden drawing board and leave it to dry for at least three hours. The paper will buckle to start with, but as it dries it will stretch and you will be left with a wonderful flat sheet of paper that will be able to handle plenty of wet washes.

BELOW *Make sure you use gummed brown paper tape as opposed to self-adhesive parcel tape.*

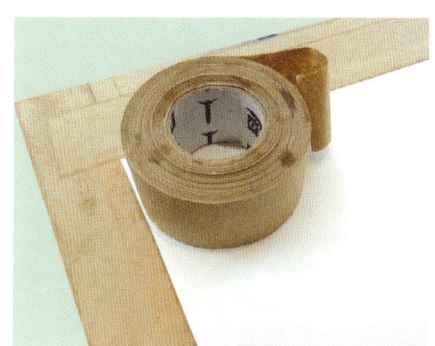

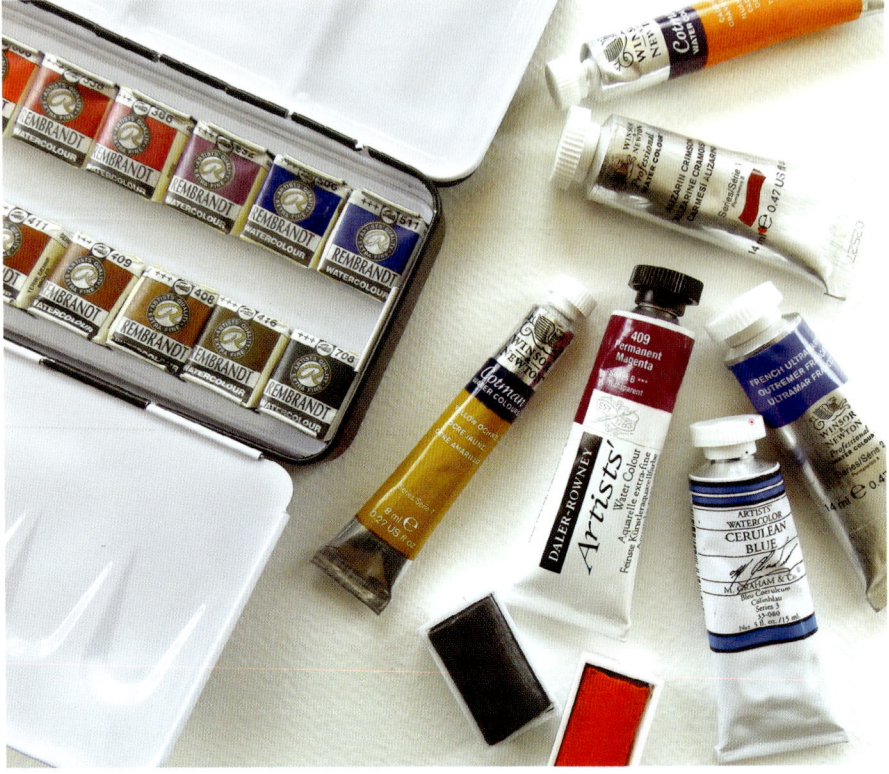

A The 1in (25mm) flat brush is great for laying down large washes quickly and is perfect for painting skies. I also use this brush when I just want to wet the paper to create soft edges to large washes.

B The most important is the No. 10 or 12 round brush. This will be your 'workhorse' brush, which you will use for most of your painting. Its point, together with its capacity to hold a lot of wet paint, means that you can use it for fine detail as well as large washes. The price range is huge. You can buy a decent quality synthetic brush for the price of a paperback, whereas a top of the range Kolinsky Sable could cost you the equivalent of a Shakespeare first edition! A good guide is to stick to the recognized brands, such as Winsor & Newton, Pro Arte, Daler Rowney, Da Vinci and Escoda.

C Finally, there's the No. 6 brush, or 'rigger', which is used for finer detail. The rigger has a lovely long bristle length and is great for details like fine branches and grass. It gets its name from the marine artists who used it for painting rigging on ships.

There are a whole host of other brushes that the more experienced artist would use including filberts, mops, sword liners, fans and hakes, but for the projects covered in this chapter these three are all you will need.

Paint

Watercolour paint is available in two main forms: pans and tubes. The make-up of the paint is exactly the same but the consistency of paint in the pans is more solid, while in a tube it remains moist. I am often asked which is the best and my response is that the pans are more convenient to take with you on holiday when you will probably be working with a sketch pad, whereas I prefer tubes for everyday use because you can squeeze out lots of colour quickly, especially when you are working on large washes.

Again, quality is important so avoid cheap paint sets that include a large range of colours. Leading manufactures such as Winsor & Newton and Daler Rowney offer both 'artist' and 'student' quality ranges. In the case of Winsor & Newton, I find that their 'Cotman' range represents good value and is perfectly adequate for the beginner.

The two principal ingredients in watercolour paint are the pigment and the all-important binder, which in watercolour paint is gum arabic. This is the key ingredient that helps the paint flow and creates its transparency. Some manufacturers such as M. Graham also add honey to their paint. Cheap watercolour paints invariably contain inferior ingredients and you will always find the results disappointing.

My advice, again, is to stick to the recognized brands and I would include in this list those mentioned above as well as Rembrandt, Daniel Smith, Sennelier and Schmincke. I will go into more detail on the colours you need in the Colour Theory section (see pages 16–17).

Brushes

I keep my selection to a minimum and work with just three brushes for most of my watercolour paintings:

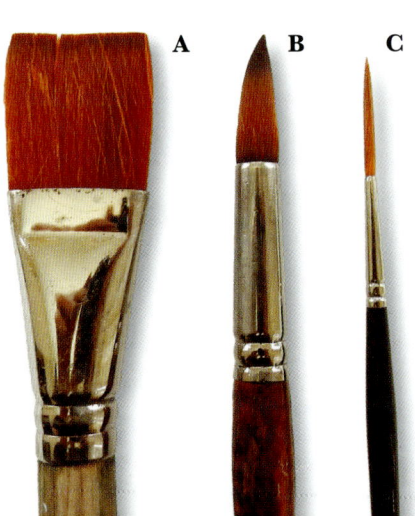

Palettes

Ceramic palettes are probably the best, as they tend to stain less than their plastic counterparts. I use a palette with a large mixing area and plenty of compartments for my paints. I always place my colours in the same compartments, so I instinctively know where each colour is almost without looking. As you become more experienced you will begin to value any technique that helps you to work quickly when you need to.

If you do decide on a plastic palette and buy a brand-new one you may find that its super-shiny surface will cause the paint to separate. This is known as 'beading'. A tip is to put the palette through a dishwasher before you use it. This will take the edge off the surface, allowing it to accept the paint without encountering this problem.

BELOW *Always keep the mixing area of your palette clean. Unlike acrylic paint, once it has dried out you can re-use your watercolours – adding water will bring them back to life.*

Other useful items

A handy addition to your kit is a box to contain everything safely. I find that an inexpensive plastic toolbox available from a DIY store is ideal, as it contains many small compartments for storing all your bits and pieces.

You will also need a drawing board – a good piece of plywood or MDF is ideal but it is important that it has a slope of approximately 10 degrees. You can make this yourself or you can simply place a book under the top edge. This allows for the paint to move slowly across the paper. Some artists like to work with a much steeper angle, but for beginners I would suggest a 10-degree angle gives you the best level of control.

And, of course, you need a glass, jug or cup of water. There are may containers on the market – from lightweight collapsible plastic ones which are ideal for using outdoors to a simple jam jar. When working at home in my studio I like to use a large glass bowl as this means that I am not constantly changing my water.

There are other, less important, materials that you will need, but I will mention these as we go along and work through the chapter.

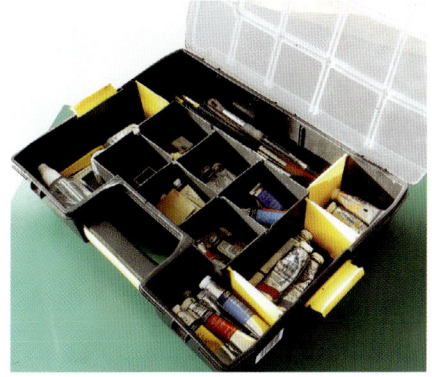

ABOVE *A plastic toolbox is a cheap solution for keeping painting materials secure and organized in one place.*

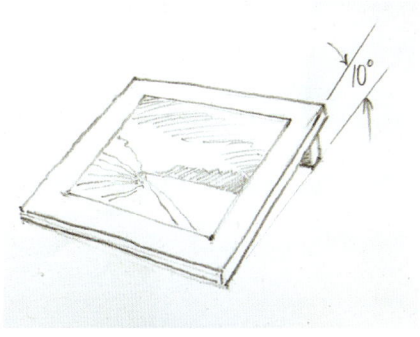

ABOVE *A slightly angled drawing board will enable you to best control the flow of paint across your paper.*

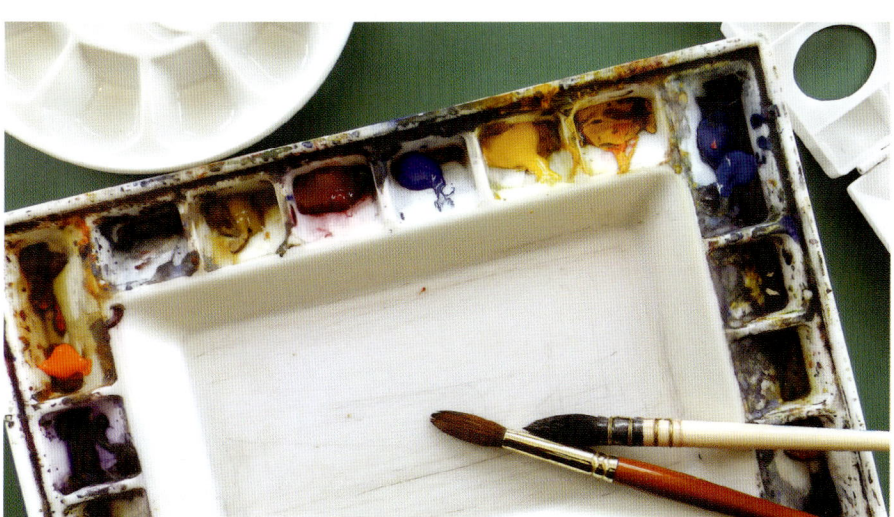

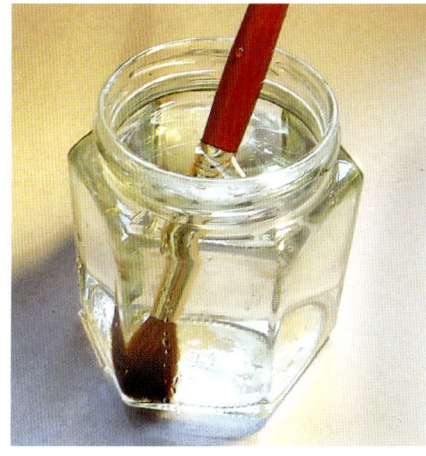

ABOVE *Use a clear container so that you can see how murky the water is and change it regularly.*

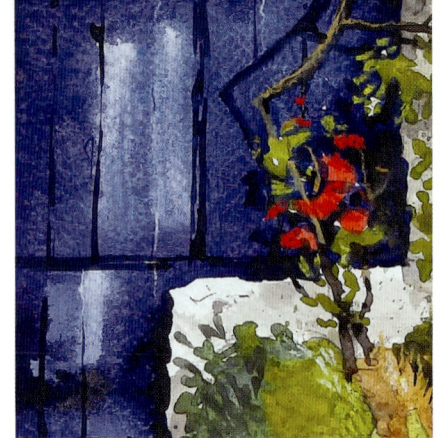

Colour Theory

The subject of colour and what paints to buy can be, for the beginner, the most confusing of all. There are countless colours available from many different manufacturers. For this reason I will try to make the theory of colour as simple as possible.

Three primaries

1

2

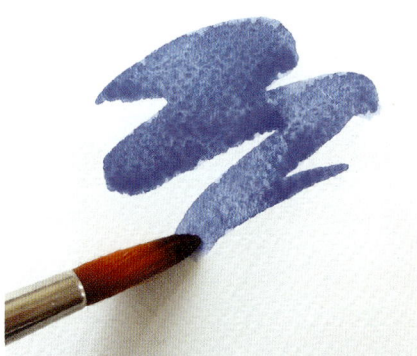

3

One of the most useful things I ever learned when I started watercolour painting was the three-colour theory and this has stood me in good stead throughout my painting career. Theoretically it is possible to mix any colour that you need from the three primary colours: red, yellow and blue. Think about an inkjet printer – if you disregard the black, you can print out full-colour photographs from the yellow, cyan and magenta ink cartridges. This principle also applies to painting.

In this chapter you will learn to paint using just three colours for most of the projects. Not only will this be an excellent grounding in understanding the theory of colour, it will also give your pictures harmony and balance. Every time I demonstrate this in class, students are amazed at the endless range of colours you can get when you learn to mix from these three primaries – you can even mix a black! And the good news is that there is no better medium than watercolour paints for mixing – they are simply made for it.

The three primaries I have chosen are Cadmium Yellow (1), Cobalt Blue (2) and Alizarin Crimson (3), so when I refer to yellow, blue and red in the instructions for the projects, these are the colours I would like you to use. They are all well known, available from most paint manufacturers, and have been chosen to give you the maximum range of colours when mixed. If you do use other variants for your primaries, for example, Lemon Yellow rather than Cadmium Yellow, your finished colours will be slightly different from those shown in this book.

In some of the projects, we will be adding two extra colours: Payne's Grey (4) and Cobalt Violet (5). You will find as you progress as an artist you will add your own favourites, but it is worth persevering with the discipline of learning to mix from just the three primary colours.

4

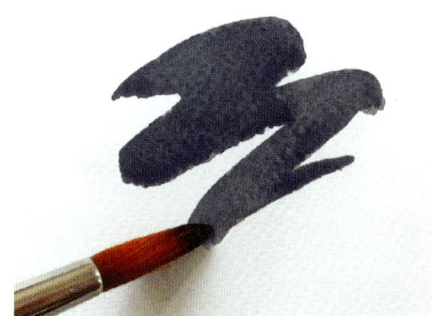

5

Colour wheel

The next stage is to reproduce the colour wheel illustrated below. Start by drawing a circle in pencil. You can use a compass or draw around a plate or saucer for this purpose. Mix a pure wash with your blue and paint a blob directly at the top at point A. It is important that you keep the ratio of paint to water consistent and that the colour remains transparent so that you can see your pencil line through the wash. Next, use a pure wash of red and paint a blob of that at point B. It is vital that you keep your brush and water clean so as not to contaminate the colours. I suggest you change your water regularly! Next, use a pure wash of yellow and paint a blob of that at point C on the colour wheel.

Now we come to the mixing! Start by mixing together a 50/50 ratio of red and blue, which should give you purple, and paint this exactly halfway between the red and blue at position D. Next do the same with the red and yellow: mix a 50/50 ratio, making orange, and paint this exactly halfway at position E. Then mix a 50/50 ratio of blue and yellow, making green, and paint this exactly halfway at position F.

Form the complete wheel by adding at least three further colours between each of the points. The easiest way to do this is to start from the pure colour point (A, B, C) and work round to the 50/50 mix. For example, if you start with the blue at point A, just add in a tiny amount of red each time until you reach the purple, creating a smooth transition of colour. Once you have

completed the wheel you will see the broad range of colours produced by just mixing two colours together. By adding a third colour into the mix, the range becomes infinite.

To simplify the three-colour mixes I have added three important colours in the centre. Point G is brown, which is produced by mixing equal amounts of all three. Point H is grey, produced by adding a fair amount of blue into the brown you have just mixed. And finally we have black at point I, which is created by simply adding more paint into the grey you have already mixed. Black is a controversial colour in watercolour painting and I would always recommend getting your black by mixing three colours rather than using a tube of ready-mixed black, which will always be dull and lifeless.

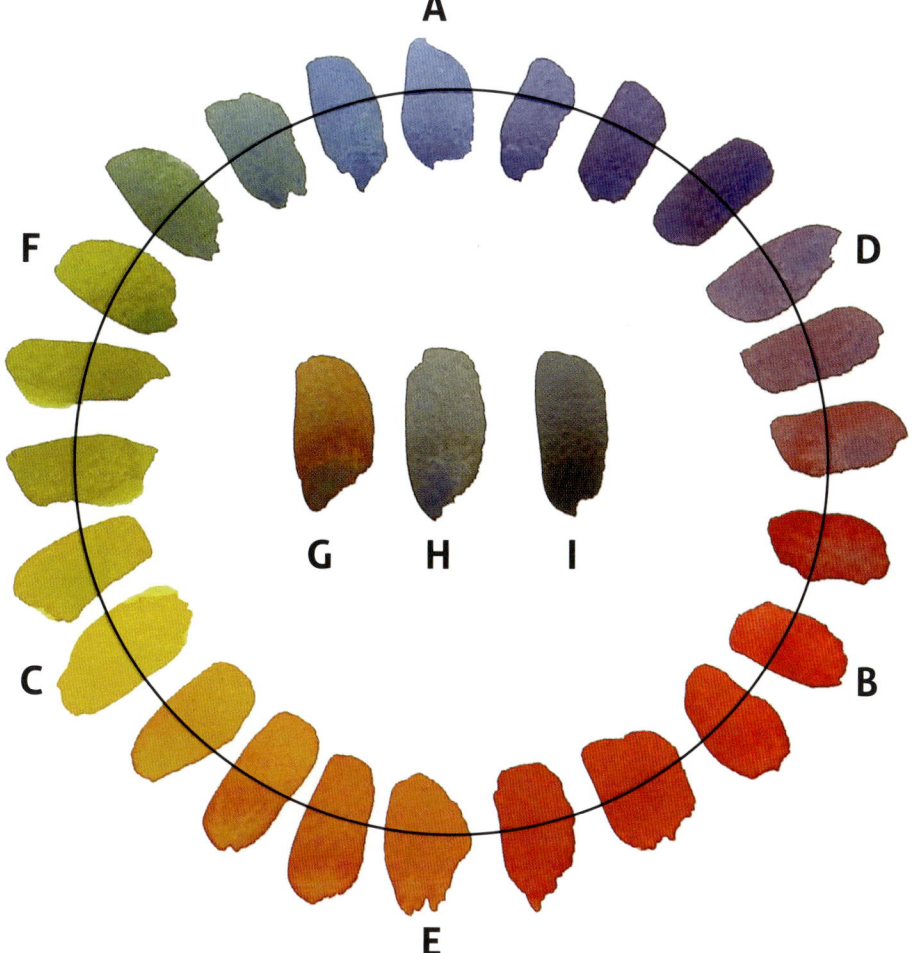

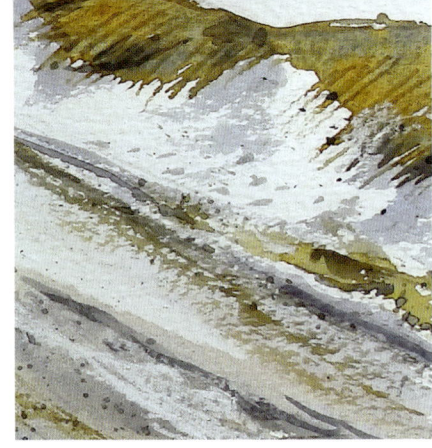

Brushstrokes

To paint well, you have to be able to transfer what is in your mind to your hand, and learning to have total control over your brush is a vital part of this process. These simple exercises will help you take command of your paintbrush.

Beginners will automatically hold the brush as they would a pen, as close to the point as possible. Try to get used to holding your brush at least halfway up the shaft. This will allow more free-flowing movement in your wrist and arm, making your brushstrokes less contrived and more natural.

For the brushstroke exercises use only your No. 12 brush and learn how versatile it is. To become an expert at anything you must practise, practise, practise. Make these exercises a part of your learning regime.

Broad to narrow stroke

Using a single colour, press down hard with your brush to create a broad stroke but then take the pressure off to create a narrow stroke without ever lifting your brush off the paper (1).

The flick

This is simply a case of pressing down hard with your brush and quickly lifting the brush off the paper, leaving a fine taper to the stroke. The flick technique is perfect for creating leaves, stems and grasses (2).

Dry brush

This technique is brilliant for creating a lovely texture and I often use this when painting trees and glistening water. As its name suggests, there shouldn't be too much water in the wash. However, this technique only works when using textured watercolour paper as we take advantage of its 'tooth' to create the texture. The trick is to hold the brush between your thumb and forefinger, keeping your hand above the brush while allowing it to be totally flat to the paper. Then drag the brush hairs lightly over the paper's surface, leaving the 'valleys' unpainted (3).

Scoring into paint

For this mark-making technique you can use a wooden stick but I like to use the end of my brush by sharpening it with a pencil sharpener then blunting it on a rough surface. I find that having this on the end of my brush means that it is always at hand and impossible to lose! Once you have applied the paint, simply score into the paper with the wooden point, making a groove into which the paint travels, creating a darker line of the same colour. Again, this is great for grasses and foliage (4).

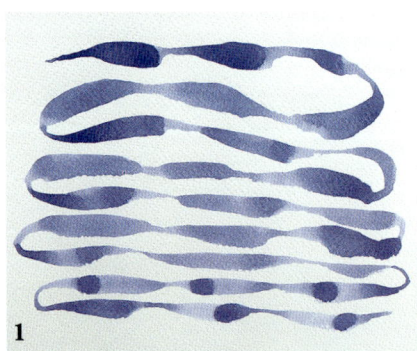

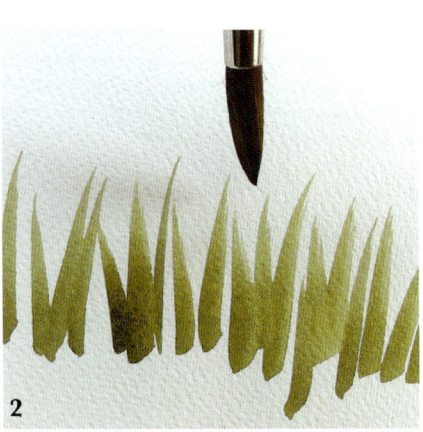

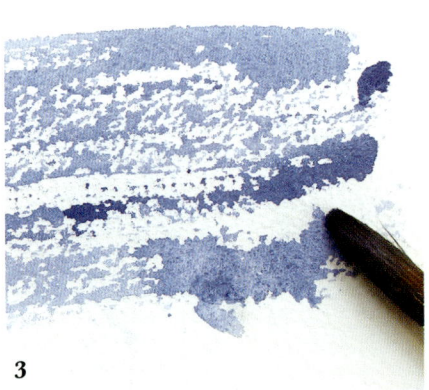

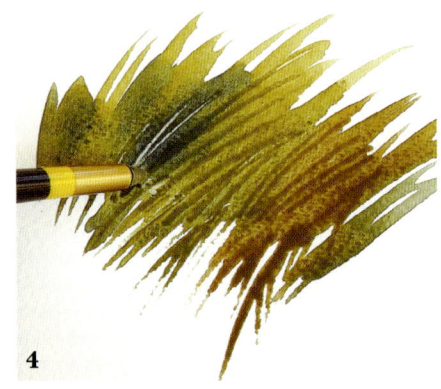

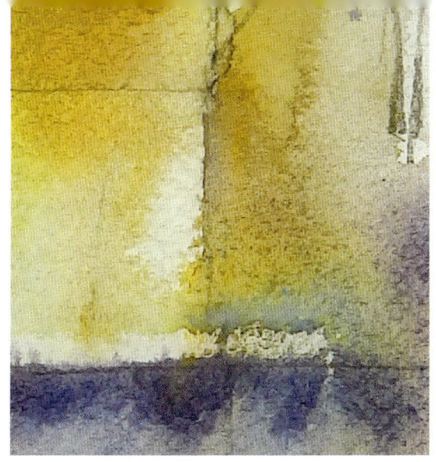

Washes

Getting the ratio between water and paint correct is the key to good watercolour painting. There is no magic formula: the amount of paint to use depends on the strength of colour you want to create. But these exercises are a great starting point.

Wet-in-wet

Exercise A First, mix up two washes, a yellow and a blue, to about a 60% water to 40% paint ratio. Start by painting a blue blob then paint a yellow blob next to it and slowly join the two washes together, allowing the colours to merge into each other. You should see a lovely blend of the two colours, as well as the texture of the paper showing through to indicate that your paint has not been applied too thickly.

Exercise B A similar exercise is to paint another single blob of colour, but this time, using only clean water, apply a wash up to the colour's edge and watch the paint flow into the clear water.

Exercise C This exercise requires you to splash around with the paint and see what happens when you mix lots of colours and water together. Just have fun with this by experimenting with different ratios of water to paint without painting anything in particular. There is no better way of learning what the paint can do when applied in such an uninhibited way, and this is probably the foundation stone to mastering what is achievable with watercolours. It's not until your washes are dry that the paint stops evolving. You will be amazed at what happens as the paint 'paints itself'.

Tip
Make sure you always clean your brush thoroughly between mixes to avoid colour contamination.

Backwashes and cauliflowers

A backwash, or cauliflower, occurs when a wash begins to dry and a wetter area pushes back into the wash, creating a strange cellular effect (below). These can look stunning and enhance your work, but many artists try to avoid them, seeing them as mistakes. I love these 'happy accidents' and encourage them by dropping either clean water or a diluted colour into a drying wash and watching it evolve. This technique is especially good in flower painting.

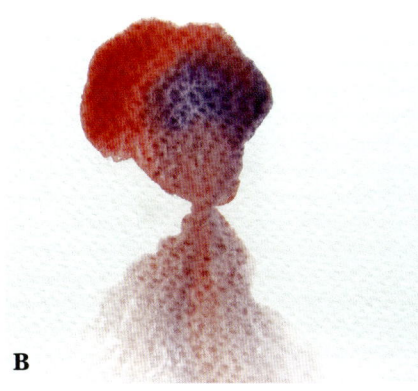

B

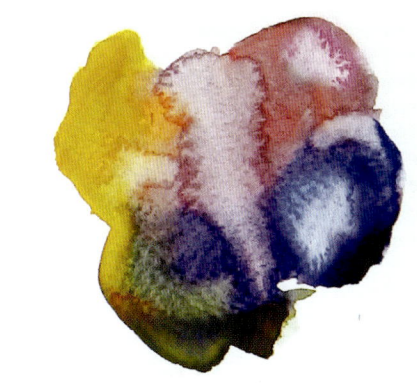

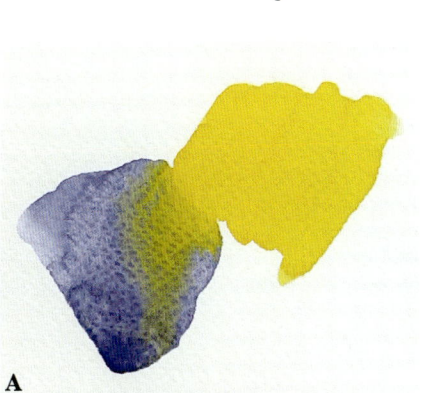

A

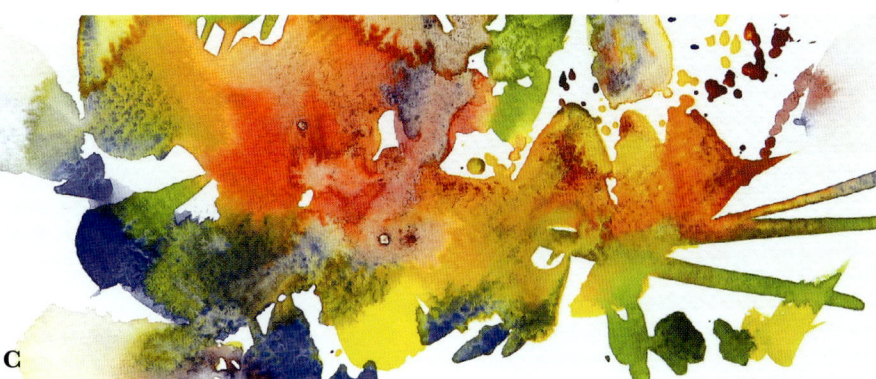

C

Wet-on-dry

We have already looked at the spontaneity of using the wet-in-wet technique, but with this simple exercise you will learn the effect of applying several layers of transparent paint to a wash that has completely dried.

    You will see how the same tonal value can be deepened by applying further layers of paint. You will also see how to achieve a hard-edged outline to your washes because each wash has been allowed to dry completely, stopping the bleeding of colour that you get with a wet or damp wash. The drying process can be speeded up by using a hairdryer, but let the paint dry naturally for at least five minutes first to allow the paint to flow.

    This exercise also demonstrates that you have to paint darker colours onto lighter tones. For those of you who have always painted with solid pigment paint, such as acrylics, oils and poster paint from your school days, this is one of watercolour's biggest challenges. Because of the translucency of watercolour, you can clearly see that you can't paint a lighter tone on top of a darker area as you can with solid paint, which does make watercolour more difficult to correct. But never fear – as you progress you will find that mistakes can often be turned into successes!

Tip

To apply a flat wash of paint that dries evenly, paint across the paper in one continuous stroke. Reload your brush and slightly overlap the previous brushstroke. This helps your strokes to blend. Repeat until you have covered the whole area.

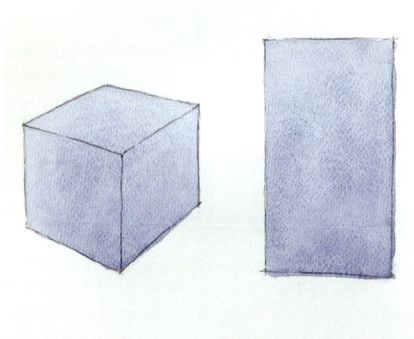 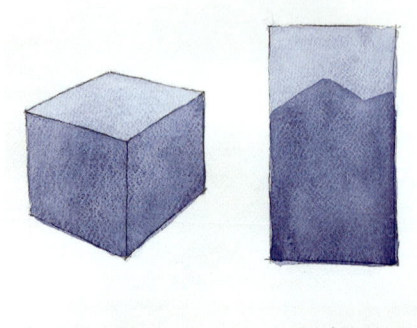

STAGE 1

Using a pencil, draw a cube showing the top and two sides, and a rectangle next to it. Mix a very watery blue and paint a flat wash over both drawings. It is important that this wash is light and the texture of the paper is still visible. Now allow the wash to dry completely.

STAGE 2

Using the same strength of wash as you did in stage 1, paint the two front faces of the cube, then paint two thirds of the rectangle with a 'hilly' outline. Once again, allow the wash to dry completely.

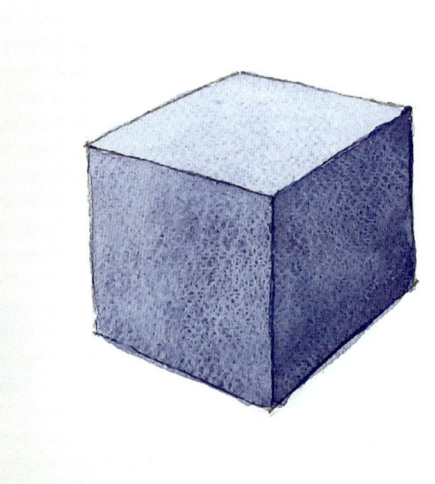 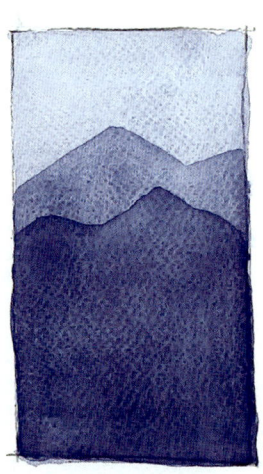

STAGE 3

Apply the final layer just to the right-hand side of the cube and another 'hilly' outline wash to the bottom third of the rectangle. What is important here is that the two areas that have had three layers remain transparent and the texture of the paper is still visible. You will see that the strength of colour is three times darker than your first wash. The cube now has a sense of volume, while the rectangle has a feeling of recession and distance echoing a mountain range.

Practice painting: Woodland reflections

Here's an exercise in which you can put into practice the techniques discussed in the sections on Wet-in-Wet and Wet-on-Dry (see pages 19–20) to create the effect of a reflection on water.

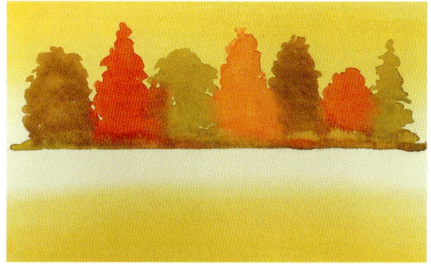

STAGE 1

Prepare a mix of warm yellow using roughly 80% yellow and 20% red. Always make sure you mix up enough paint to cover the entire paper. I tell my students to mix more than they think they are going to need as there is nothing worse than running out of a colour halfway through, and your original wash will start to dry as you struggle to mix the same colour again.

Using a full sheet of paper, with your largest brush entirely cover it with clean water and allow a few moments for it to soak in. Starting at the top, paint in a graduated wash: lay the wash down in bands that are diluted with more and more water to gradually lighten the paint and let it run down the paper. Turn your sheet upside down and do the same from the other edge. Leave it to dry completely.

STAGE 2

Wet-on-dry: Mix up several colours that you associate with autumn. I will leave the choice up to you. Just have fun and experiment with various colour mixes but make sure you have made enough to use when painting the reflections in the water during stage 3.

At roughly the centre of the paper, paint in some blob-like tree shapes across its width, keeping the base line straight, creating the water's edge. Make sure you don't paint two trees next to each other in the same colour. Again, leave this to dry.

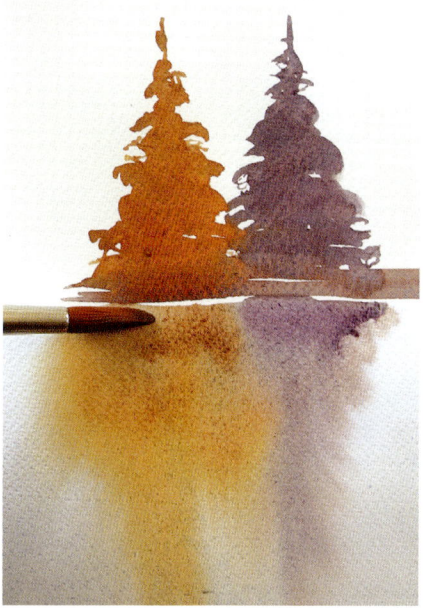

ABOVE *Here the out of focus wet-in-wet technique creates the illusion of reflection. With the board nearly vertical, you can still drop in some darker tones at the top to continue to run into the wet wash.*

Tip

Remember: when your washes are completely dry they will always look about 10% lighter than they do when wet.

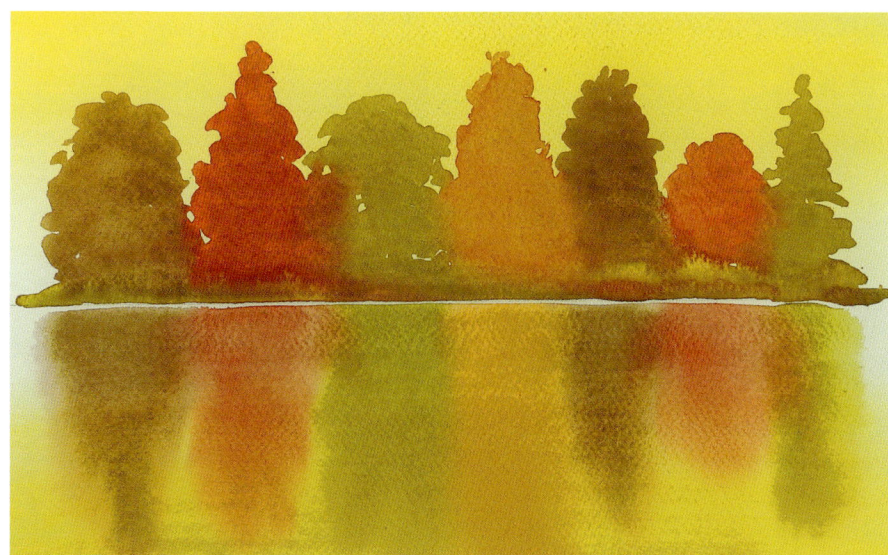

STAGE 3

Wet-in-wet: Using your large brush, apply a clean water wash on to the entire bottom half of your picture, leaving a small gap at the water's edge. Again, let this soak in for a few moments. Now drop in a large blob of the corresponding colour underneath each tree, then tilt the angle of your board to about 45 degrees and let the paint run down into the wet wash. This will create a soft wet-in-wet feel, giving the illusion of a reflection in the water.

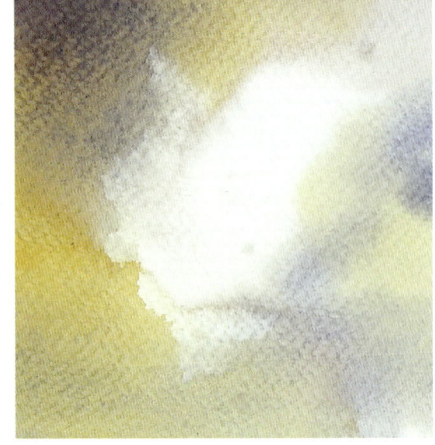

Lifting Out

It is often said that a traditional watercolourist will never use white paint, as whiteness is provided by the paper itself. In this section we look at a number of different ways to 'lift out' paint to create the white areas you need in your painting.

Masking fluid

Masking fluid is a rubbery solution that is applied to the areas you want to remain unpainted. Once your paint has totally dried you can then remove the masking fluid by rubbing your fingers over the area. You can also apply masking fluid to areas that have already been painted to create contrasting shades. It is worth experimenting with, but personally I find it gives an over-defined edge to my style of painting.

Kitchen paper or tissue

This is an excellent way to absorb paint quickly and is fantastic for creating cloud effects. Paint an area of sky with a watery blue and, with a scrunched-up piece of kitchen paper, immediately lift out some cloud shapes. It is important to roll the tissue as you move to avoid a 'step and repeat' pattern. Remember, no two clouds are ever the same!

Tip

The harder you press the paper, the more colour will be lifted out and the whiter the clouds will look. Less pressure on the paper will create a lighter, more wispy effect.

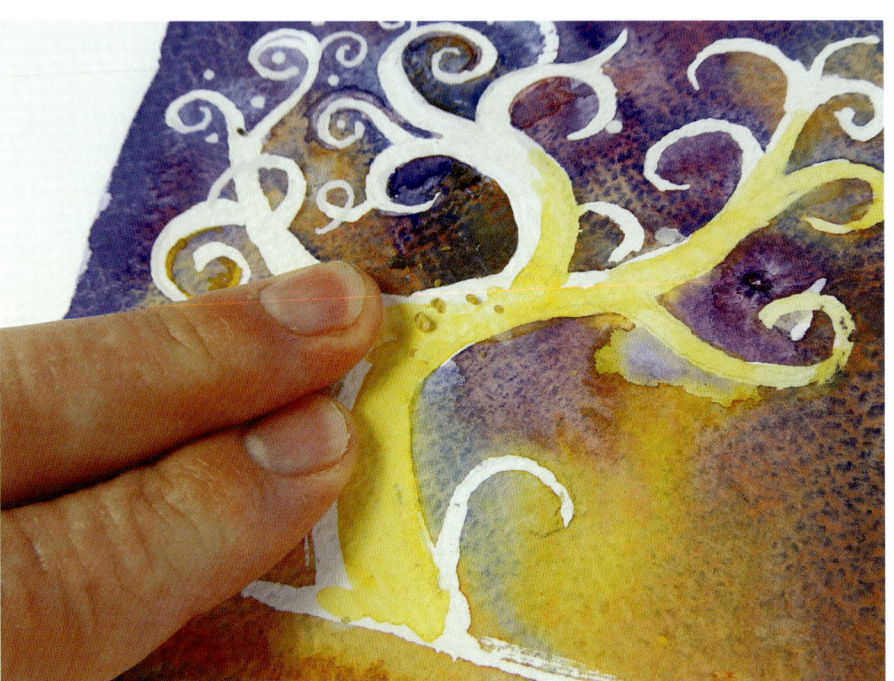

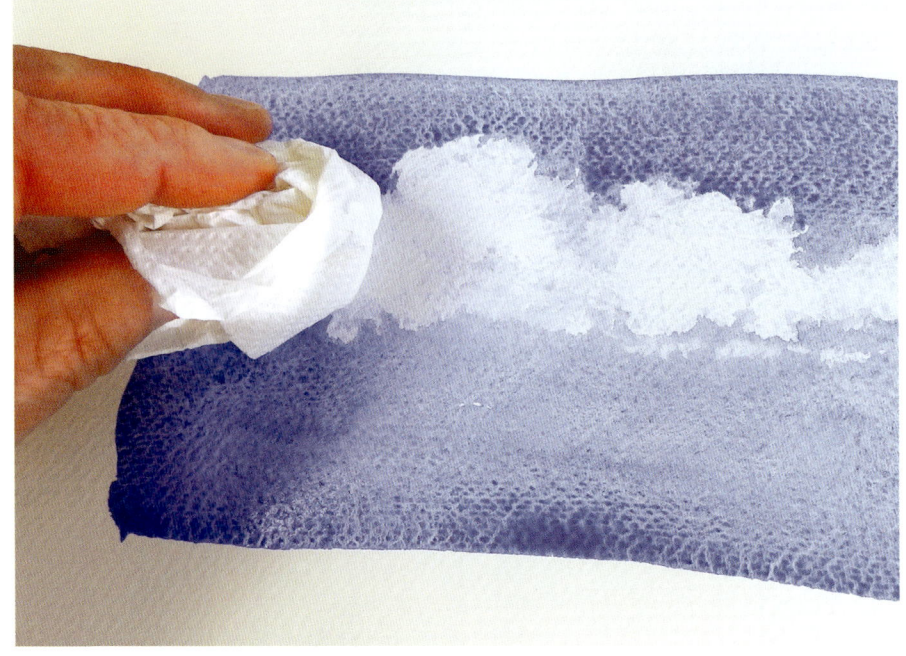

Lifting out with a brush

Exercise A Apple: A No. 12 brush is a wonderful way to lift out highlights in wet washes. Start by pre-mixing three colours: a watery yellow, a green using a 50/50 mix of yellow and blue, and a pure red. Begin by painting a yellow circle and while this is still wet, drop in the green to the left-hand side and the red to the right. Then watch the colours merge. If they don't, it means that the yellow isn't wet enough. The highlight is created by taking the No. 12 brush, making sure that it is clean but slightly damp, and lifting out the paint. You need to work quickly before the paint dries and you may find that you have to repeat the lifting-out process several times to avoid the wash closing up.

Exercise B Bush: This example is treated in exactly the same way as exercise A. Pre-mix two greens: one with a 50/50 mix of yellow and blue and one slightly darker by adding in more blue and a touch of red. Paint a bush shape using the lighter of the greens. While this is still wet, drop in the darker green to the right-hand side. Then quickly take your damp brush and create the light side by lifting out the highlights.

Exercise C Tree: Pre-mix a brown by using all three colours with slightly more blue. Paint a simple tree shape with your No. 12 brush and use your No. 6 brush to create some of the finer branches. Again, while this is still wet, use your brush to lift out the paint to create the highlight on the right-hand side of the trunk.

A

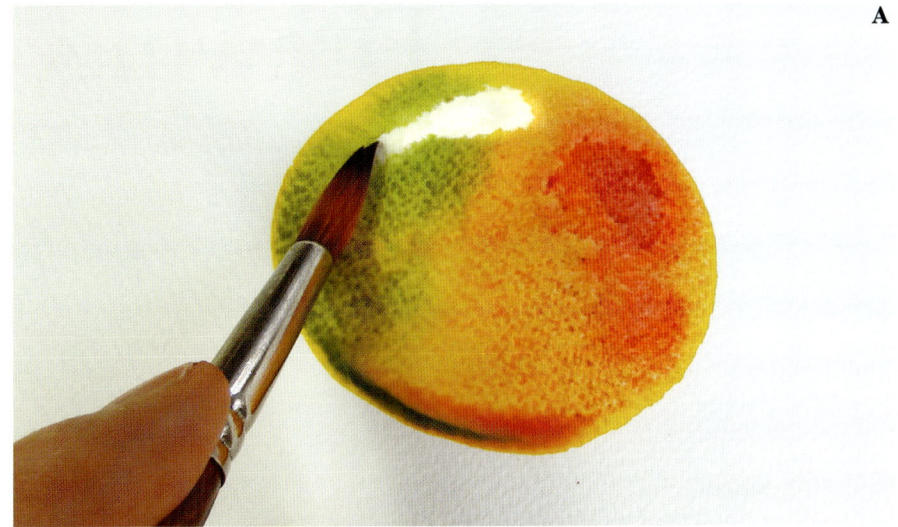

B

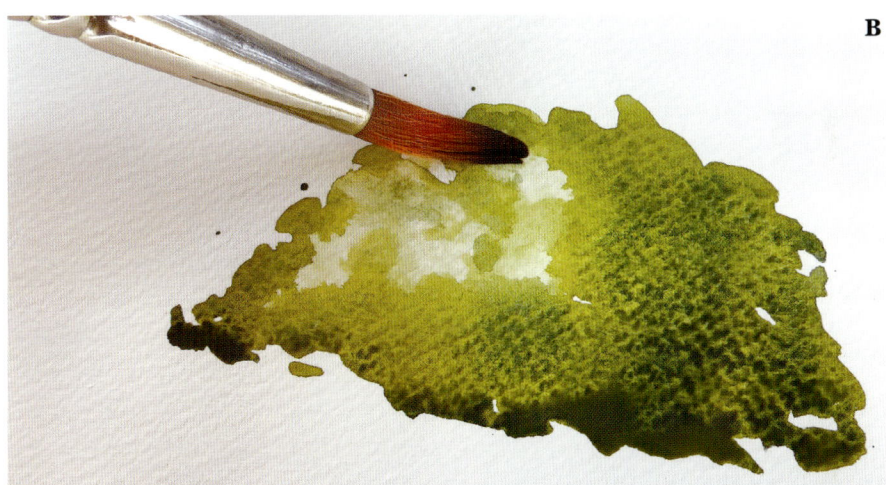

C

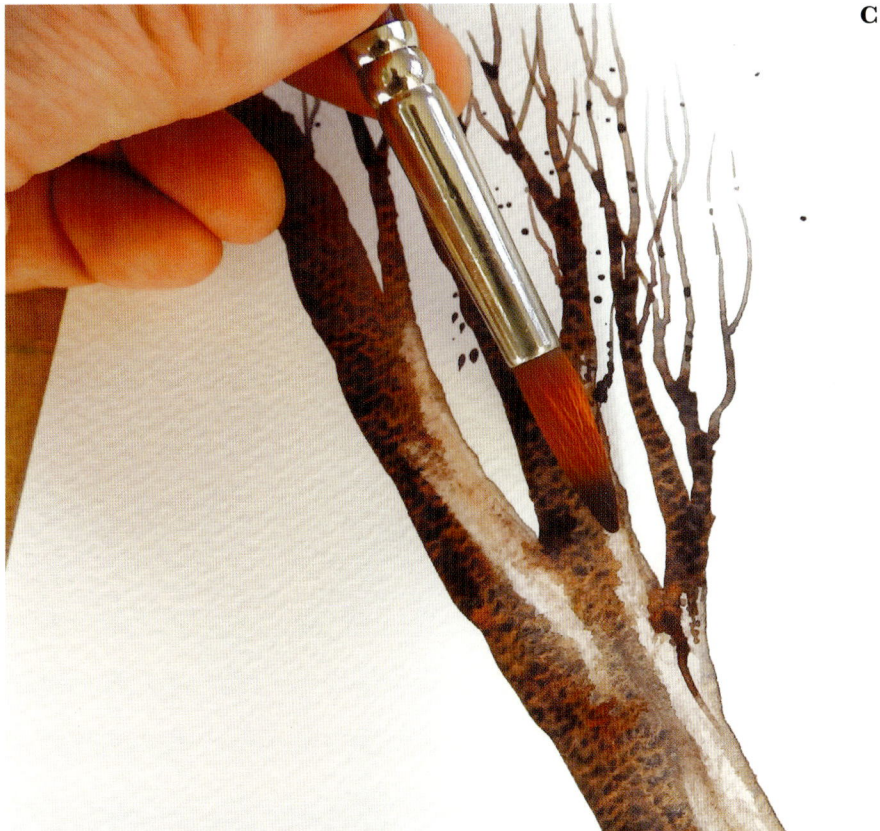

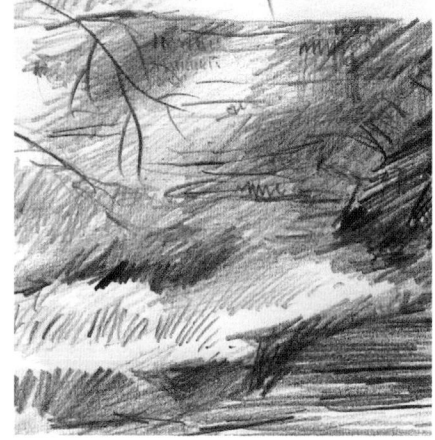

Drawing

No matter what style of painting you wish to produce, it is vitally important that you understand the basic principles of drawing if you are going to flourish as a painter. The essentials, which will enable you to tackle the projects, are outlined below.

Tonal values

In many ways, the light and shade or tonal values of a painting can be more important than colour. Finding your darks, lights and contrast points in a composition is important to create the suggestion of dimension and depth.

I call these the three tonal values: the lights, the mid-tones and, of course, the darks. I have shown a simple cube with the three tones (see A, below) and these are what I look for in my finished work. An excellent way to establish the tonal values of any picture is to remove all colour and turn it into a black and white image (see the *Roman Bridge* project on pages 26–31 for more detail).

'Don't be afraid of the dark' is something I often say to my students –this is the tone that most beginners feel apprehensive about. Remember, the only way to achieve the sense of light is to surround it with dark. I ask my students to place their finished work at the other end of the room then see if they can detect the darks and the lights rather than a blend of mid-tone grey.

Perspective

Understanding perspective is probably the most important principle of being able to draw well, as it is present in practically everything we see. Always remember the golden rule: the further away objects are, the smaller they appear. We don't stop to consider this as we walk around our three-dimensional world, but we must understand the basic principles when transferring it to our two-dimensional paper. There is no better lesson than observation – just look down a street and see all the lamp-posts getting smaller and closer together as they recede into the distance. Even looking at a square table in front of you, you will be able to see the converging of the sides as they move away from your line of sight, as drawing B (below) shows.

VANISHING POINTS WITH ONE- AND TWO-POINT PERSPECTIVE

A vanishing point is the place where receding parallel lines appear to converge. With any drawing, the first thing to consider is your line of sight or eye level because that is always where your vanishing points will meet. Drawing C (top right) is a typical one-point perspective because we are standing directly in the centre of the road and as you can see, all the lines of each building are receding to the same vanishing point at the centre.

Drawing D (right) is a typical two-point perspective as we are standing on the corner of the street, allowing us to see both the front and the sides of the buildings, which gives us the two vanishing points, again positioned at our eye level.

One final perspective point to mention is that of height, especially when drawing tall buildings such as cathedrals and skyscrapers. That simple golden rule still applies. As the building reaches skywards it becomes further away, appearing smaller at the top and eventually converging at a vanishing point in the heavens (E, far right).

Tip
Tone and perspective add depth to your work. Practise these basic principles of drawing so that you can incorporate them into your painting.

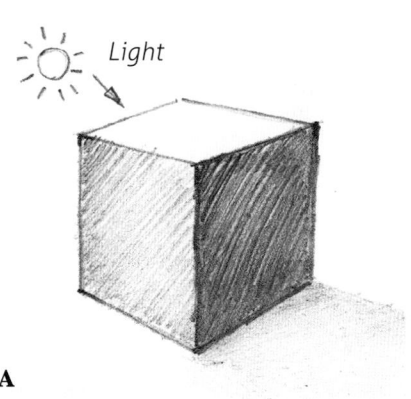

Light

A

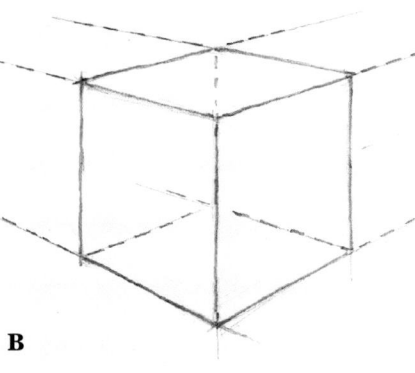

B

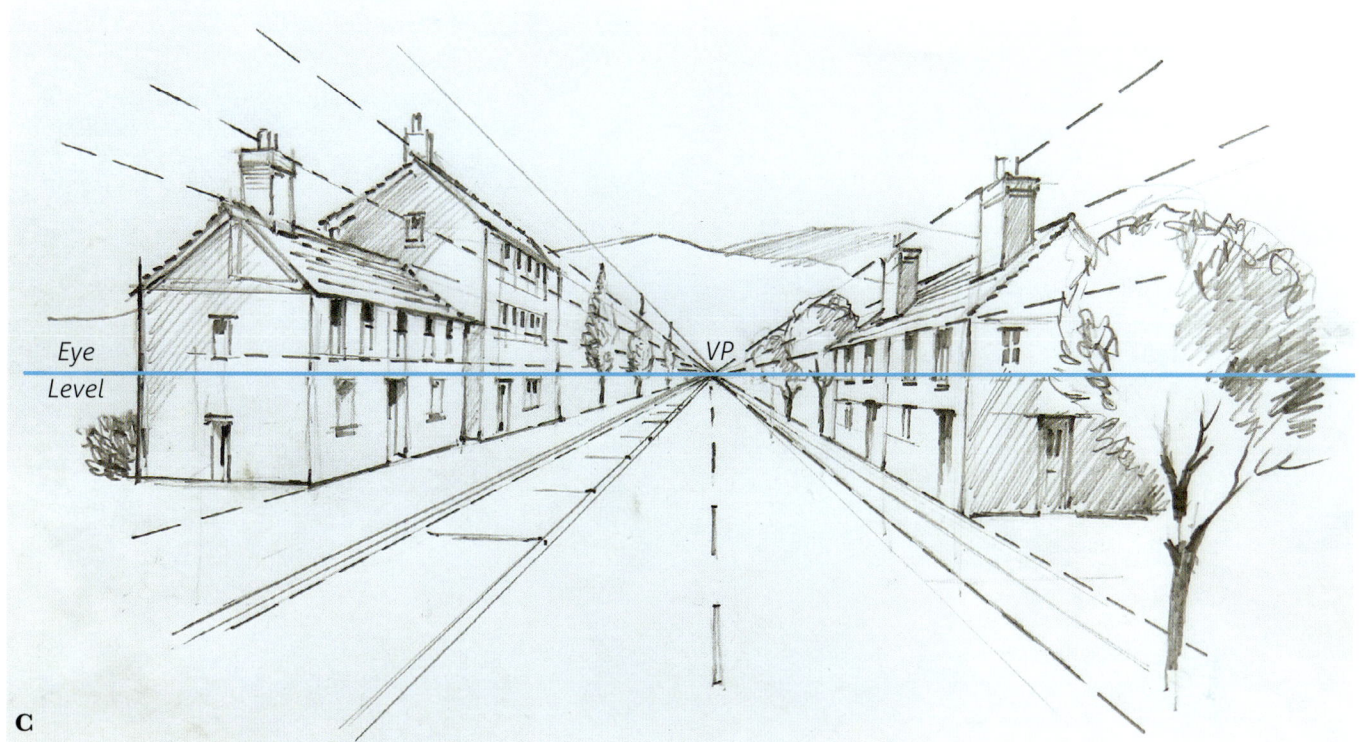

C

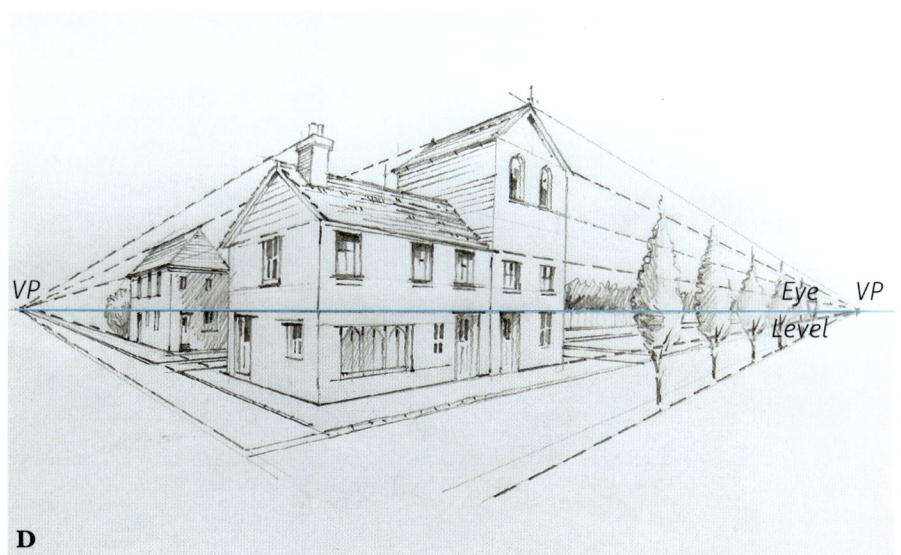

D

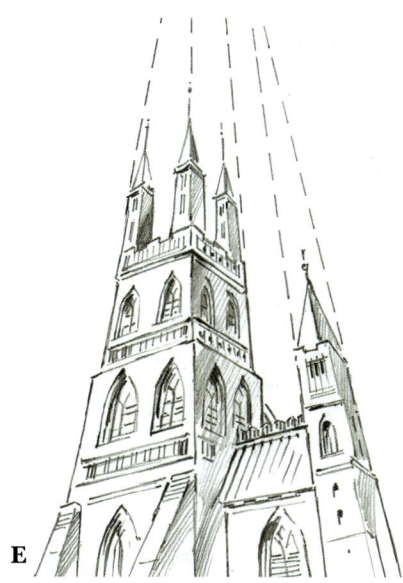

E

Tip

A good drawer is a good observer and nothing can match the art of simply looking. Always take a sketch pad with you, especially on holiday, and enjoy the thrill of drawing new, exciting subjects while constantly training your artist's eye.

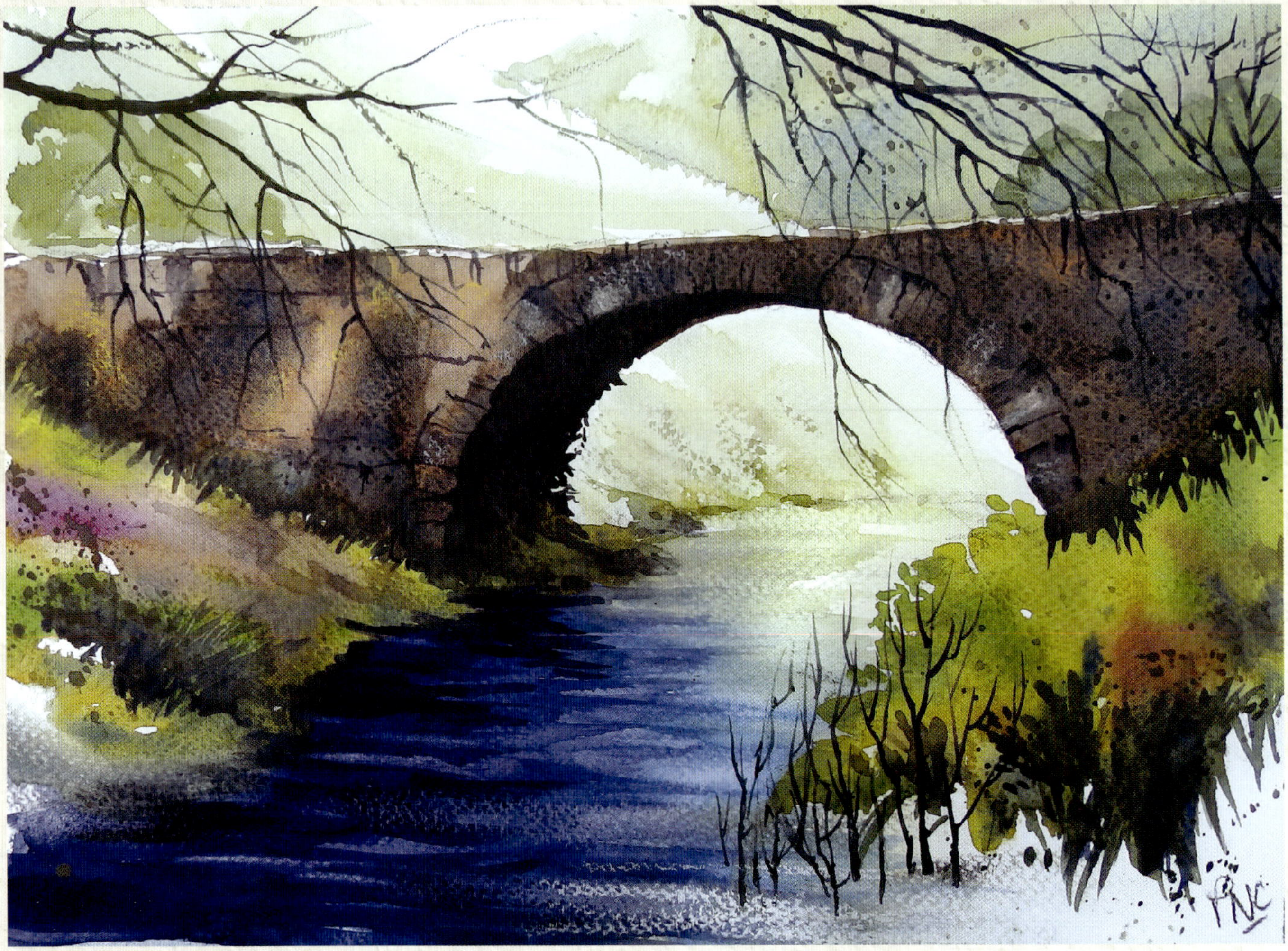

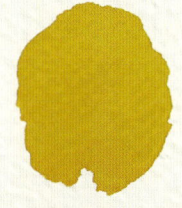

Roman Bridge

This project is about working from a photo then simplifying the scene, while bringing your own artistic interpretation to make the finished painting more pleasing and personal.

COLOURS NEEDED

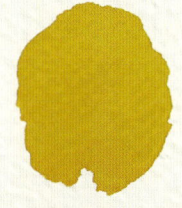

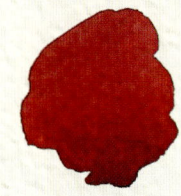

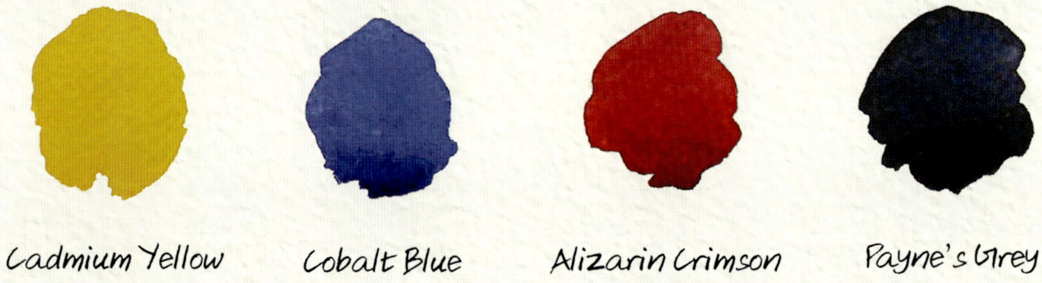

Cadmium Yellow   Cobalt Blue   Alizarin Crimson   Payne's Grey

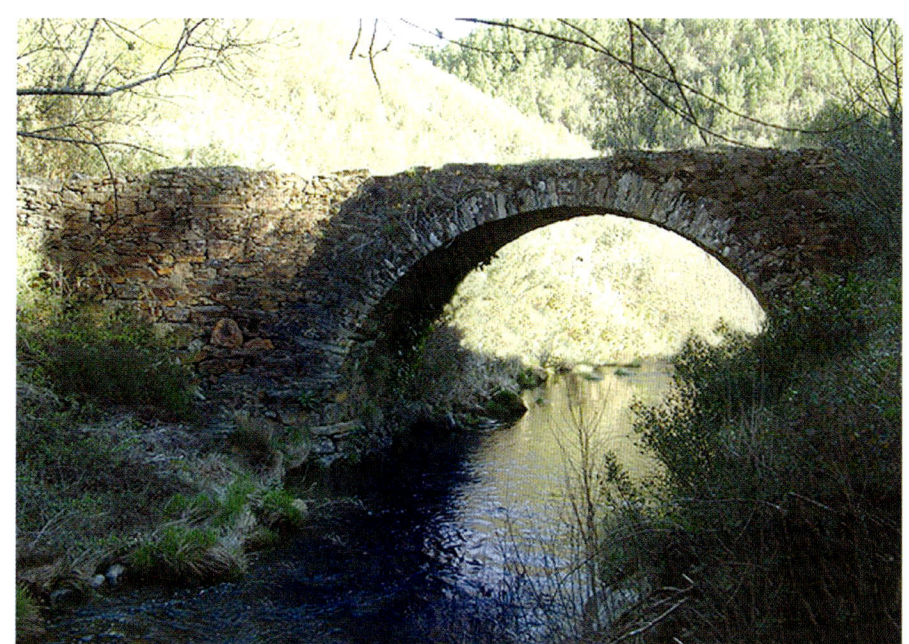

When working from a photographic reference it can become all too easy to focus on replicating exactly what you see rather than using your imagination to enhance it. Don't be a 'slave to the picture'. Keep in mind the fact that the viewer will never see the original photo, only your finished piece, so no one is going to worry about anything that's been added or isn't included. If your aim is to achieve an exact reproduction of the photo you could simply photocopy it!

If you look at the finished painting of this Roman bridge, you will see that it has quite a different feel to the original photograph (above). I've added a lot more branches at the top but taken out most of the detail in the grass banks in the foreground. The distant hills have been suggested by simple washes while leaving out the fine detail of the trees in the middle distance.

Always remember as you progress through the stages that they are only there as a guide, so don't feel frustrated if your version doesn't match exactly the colours and proportions of my painting. Most importantly, enjoy the experience.

REFERENCE PHOTO

This photograph is an old snapshot taken on holiday in Yorkshire, England, many years ago (before the time of digital cameras, so the quality isn't that good). When choosing a subject to paint, I will start by studying the picture and decide on the elements I like and those that I can improve on. In this photo, I love the way the sun is illuminating the near hillside, showing through the arch of the bridge and reflecting into the water. The way the dappled light is cast across the bridge, leaving the right side in shadow, and the strong dark under the arch are important features that need to be included.

PENCIL SKETCH

I often start by doing a simple pencil sketch that helps me to see where the highlights and shadows are. Changing a scene into a monochromatic image is an excellent way to see where the tonal values are without the colours getting in the way (see pages 24–5 for more on drawing techniques). You can also do this by taking a black-and-white photograph of your image. Most smartphones have the option to take a photo in 'mono', which is a quick and easy way of seeing where your darks and lights are.

Tip

Don't be afraid to add interesting colours, take out things you don't like and exaggerate pleasing features.

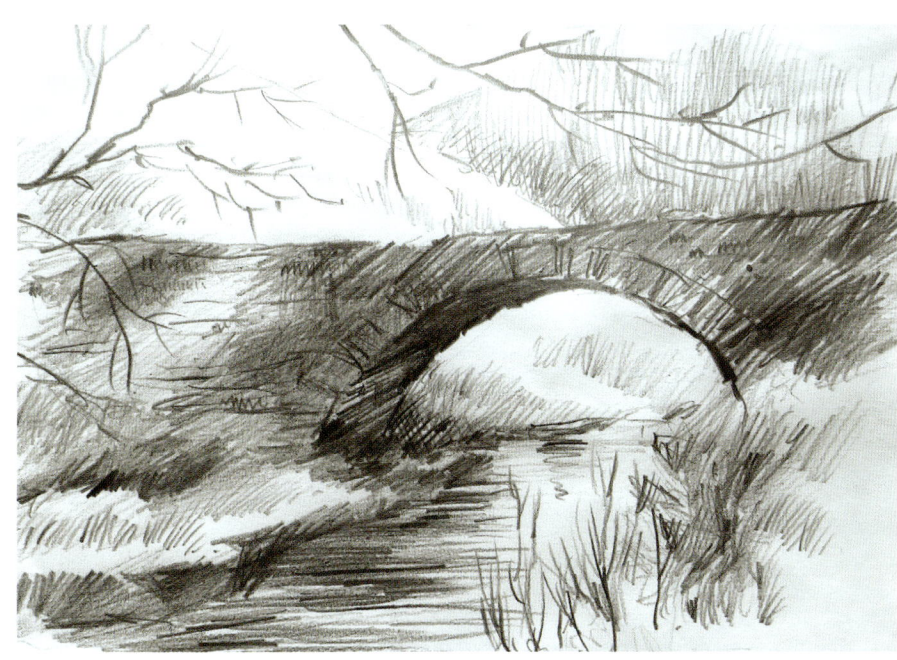

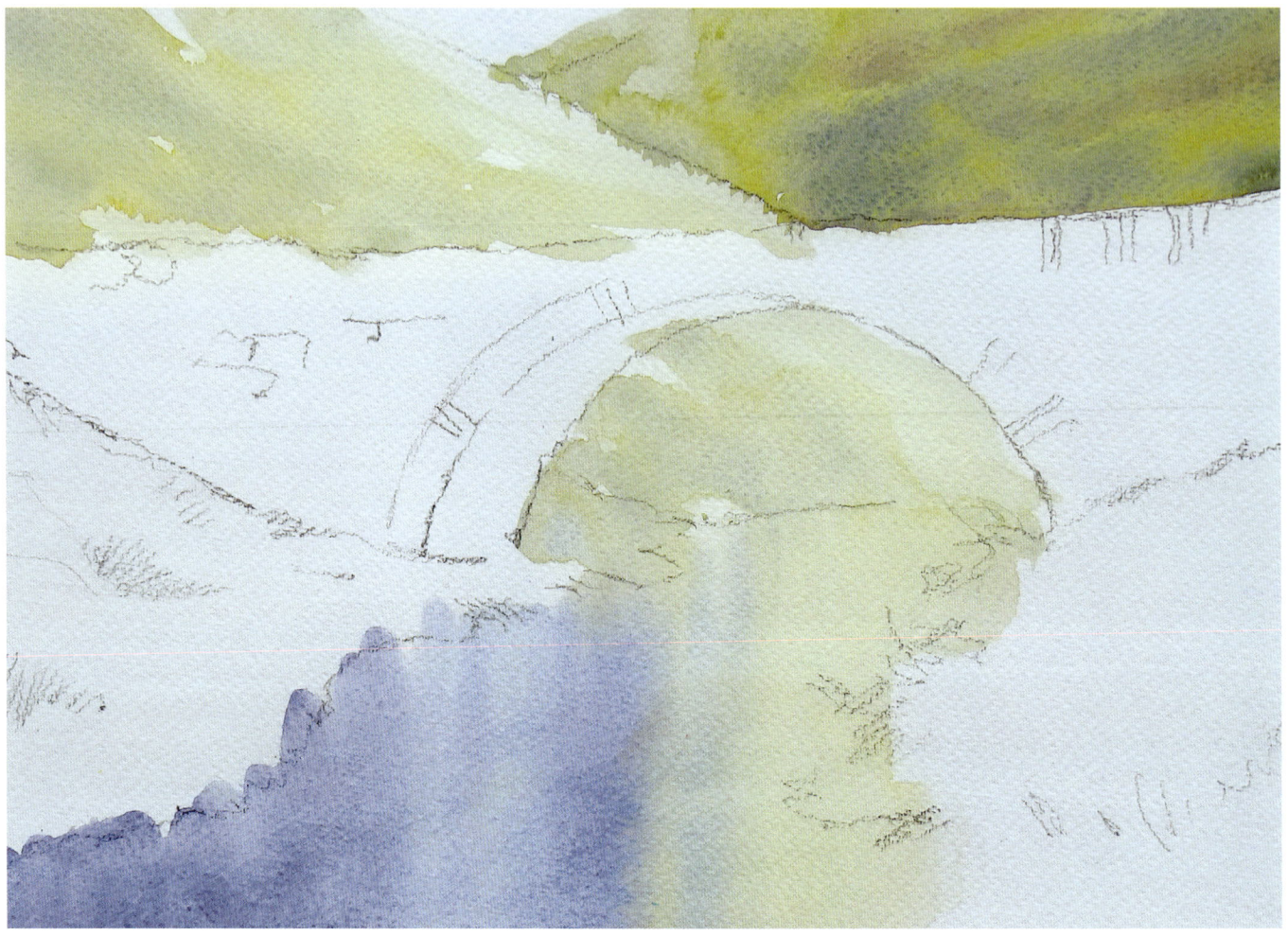

Tip

Keep your pencilwork to a minimum. Too much drawing can inhibit what you do with the brush.

STAGE 1

Start by making a watery mix of yellow with a touch of blue, and lightly paint the sunlit bank on the left using a No. 12 brush. Keep your brush-strokes moving at the same angle as the hill, making sure you continue right down to the waterline through the bridge but not into the river area.

Now dry your brush with tissue and lift out some of the wet paint to create a few highlights in the bank.

Next, paint the river area using only clean water. Let it soak into the paper for about a minute and drop in at the top the same mix of colour used in the bank, adding some blue. Tilt the paper to an angle of about 45 degrees, letting the paint run down and merge for 30 seconds, then lay it flat again.

Let everything dry and then paint the darker bank on the right at the top. Use a slightly stronger mix of yellow and blue but this time, after you've painted the bank, add a little red to the mix and drop a few strokes into the wet wash.

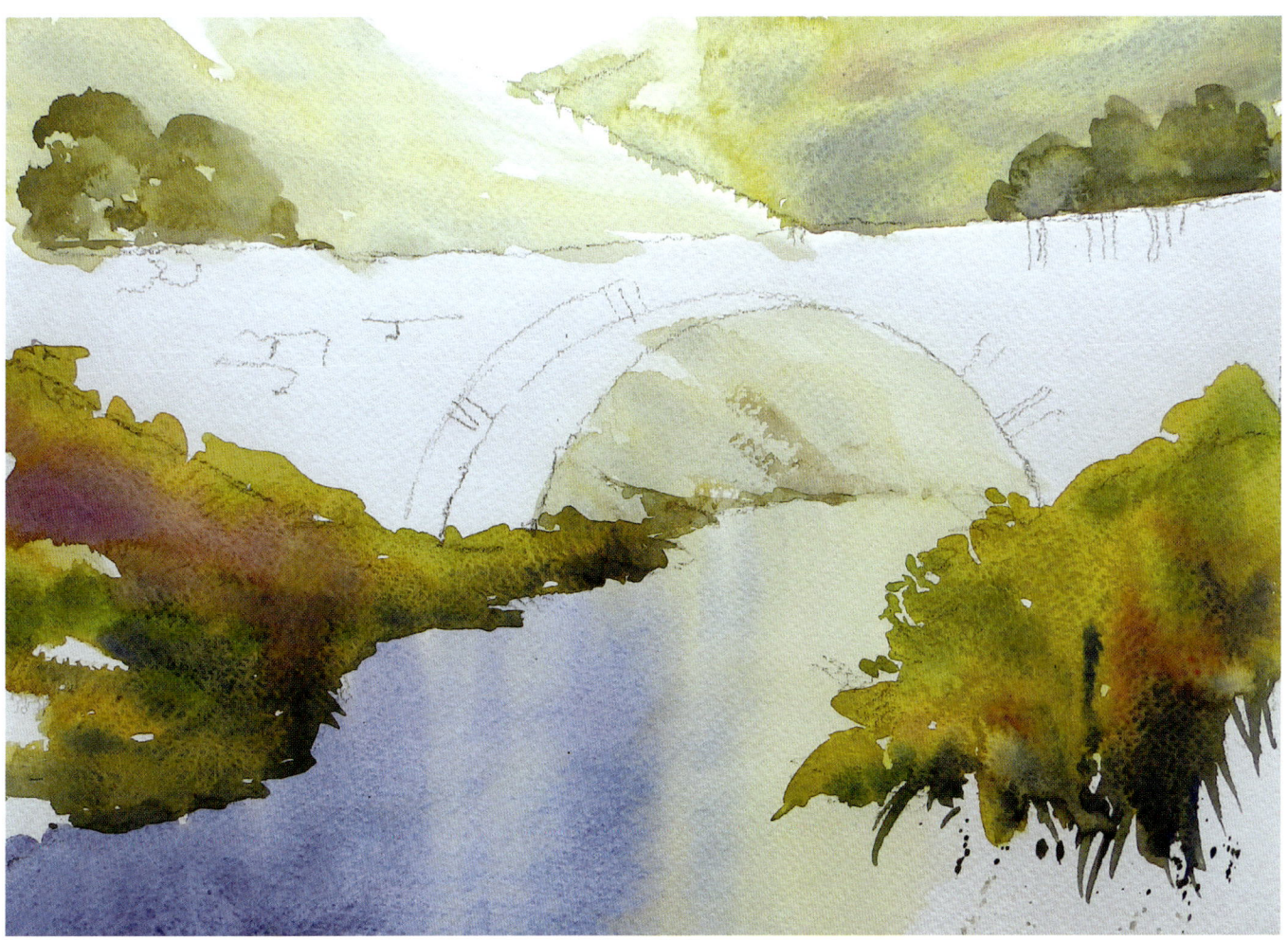

Tip

Don't worry if you have left some areas of white paper as this can give a sparkle to your painting. Leaving an area unfinished, as I have done in the bottom right-hand corner, can give an 'arty' feel to a painting.

STAGE 2

You can now move on to the left and right banks in the foreground. Mix a strong green using mostly yellow with a touch of blue and paint in both banks.

While this is still very wet, drop some pre-mixed colours such as browns, pinks and blueish greens into the wash and let the colours merge. Leave the colours to move and blend on their own without fiddling! While the paint is still wet, use the end of your brush to create some grassy detail to the edges of your washes.

Now paint in the trees at the top of the bridge in a blueish green as simple blob-like shapes. Leave some gaps so the hill behind comes through. Then add a little bit of detail with a dry brush at the waterline through the bridge. Allow to dry for at least 15 minutes before moving on to the next stage.

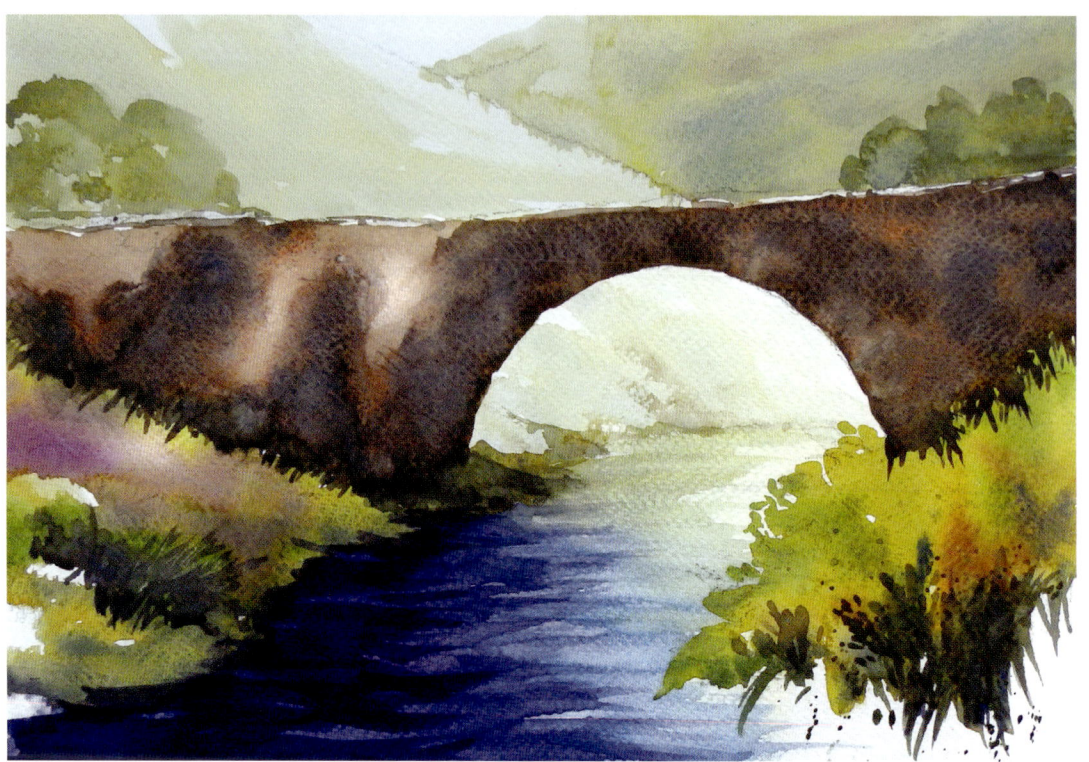

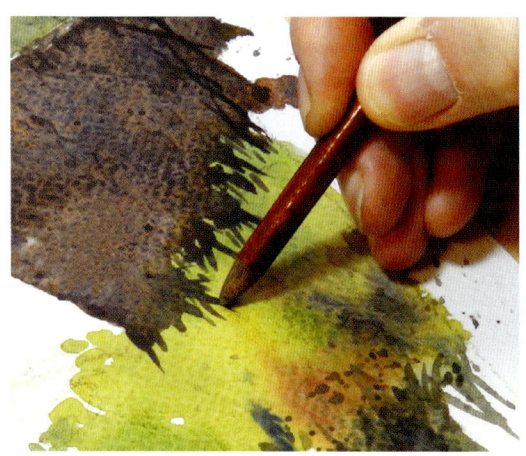

Use the end of your brush to 'push in' the very dark tone into the riverbank to create the impression of a grassy edge.

STAGE 3

First, make two mixes: a mid-brown using all three colours and a darker brown by adding more blue. Paint the entire bridge in the mid-brown and let that soak into the paper for about 30 seconds. While it's still wet, drop in the darker brown on the right side, across the top of the arch and the shaded areas on the left of the bridge. Then with a dry brush lift out the sunlit areas on the left side.

Define the top edges of the grass bank where it meets the bridge using the end of your brush (see inset). Follow this by mixing a dark green, using yellow and blue with a hint of red, and paint the darker detail into both foreground banks. Leave to dry for about 10 minutes.

Paint the river in three stages, starting with a light watery blue, keeping your brushstrokes horizontal to suggest the flow of the water. Once dry, paint a second wash of slightly darker blue by adding in a touch of red and making sure the brushstrokes only cover two thirds of the width of the river. Finally, mix a very dark blue using lots of pigment, and paint in the edge of the bank out into the river.

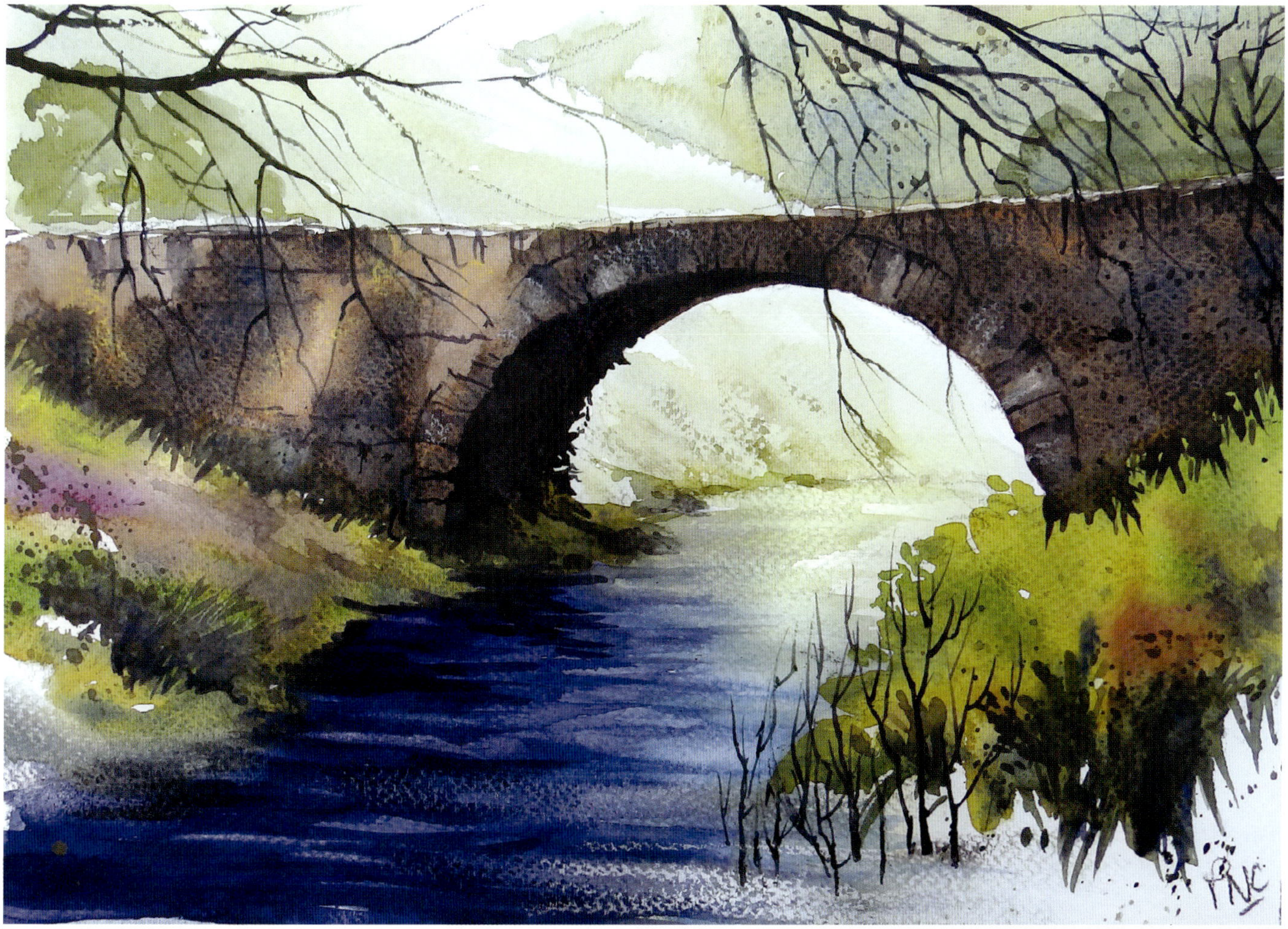

STAGE 4

The final stage is where you add in the detail. First, create the glistening on the water by rubbing a damp tissue horizontally across the river in the foreground and on the left bank (see inset). Next, mix a very dark wash using all three colours but slightly more blue for the branches and the details on the bridge. If you feel your mix isn't dark enough, this is where you can add some Payne's Grey to your mix to give it some extra strength.

Paint in the dark arch under the bridge. Then with your No. 6 brush put in a few lines to suggest some shapes in the stonework. Using the same colour, paint in the trees at the top and bring some of the branches down over the bridge. Finally, paint the twigs and reeds in the foreground and finish off with a bit of texture by splattering some spots of paint into the bridge, trees and bank on the left.

Let your painting dry, then sign and frame it!

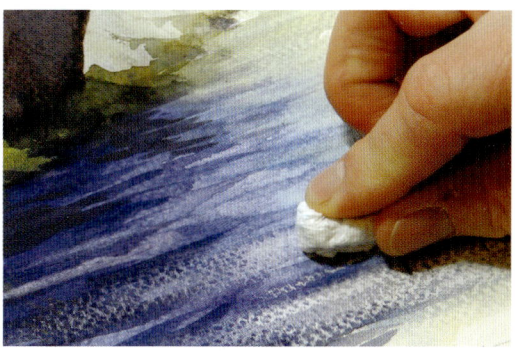

ABOVE *Use a damp tissue to lift out some of the paint to create a glistening effect.*

Tip

I often use the phrase 'Less is more,' and that certainly is the case when it comes to finishing off your painting, so keep the detail to a minimum.

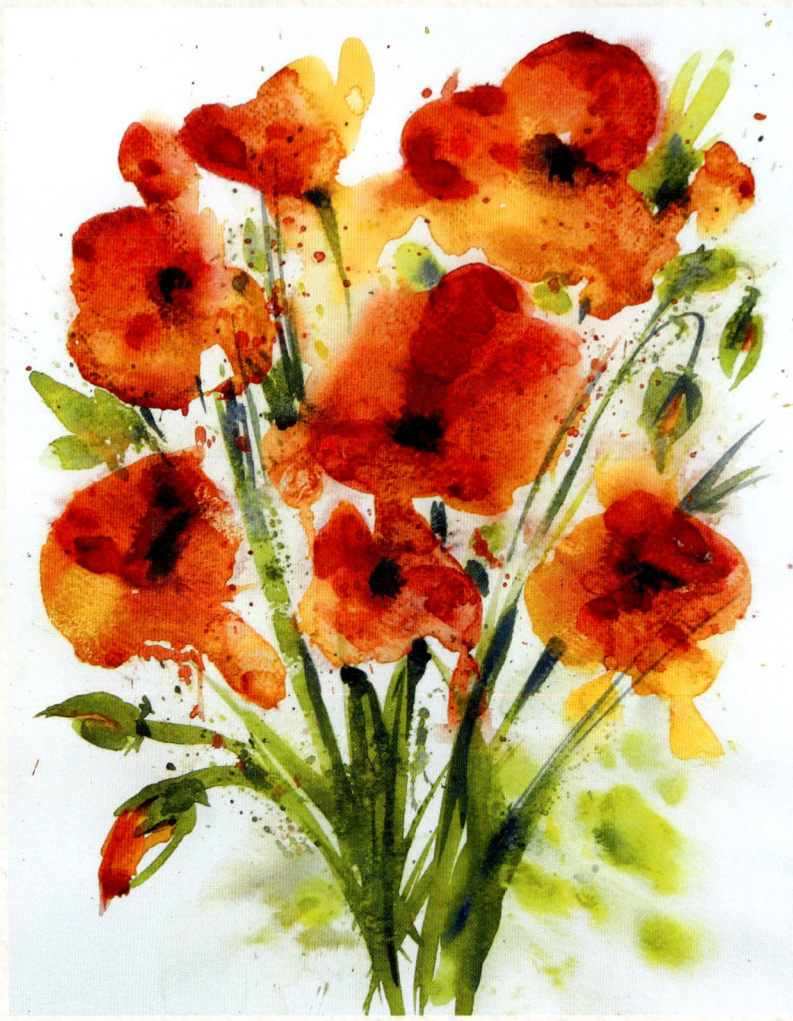

Flowers

Flowers are an ideal subject to paint in watercolour. Their free-flowing forms and delicate, translucent petals in a stunning array of myriad shades lend themselves to a loose, experimental approach to your painting.

COLOURS NEEDED

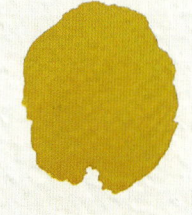  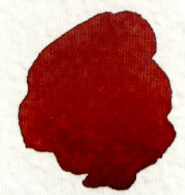  

Cadmium Yellow   Cobalt Blue   Alizarin Crimson   Payne's Grey   Cobalt Violet

The wet-in-wet technique is perfect for achieving a lot of the lovely blends and colour changes that we see in nature. The patterns and textures noticeable in flowers, and the patterns and textures produced as the watercolour paint moves on the paper, are governed by the same laws of capillarity and osmosis.

In this project, I would like you to experiment with the paint and have a go at splashing around with colour. It's important to understand that you will never exactly replicate the images shown here because of the unpredictability of the paint when combined with lots of water. I have painted a version of the poppies many times and have never painted two that look remotely the same.

Before you start painting the poppies, I suggest you try an exercise in painting petals, which involves experimenting with colour and lifting out (see pages 22–3) to create highlights and patterns. By focusing in on a detail before starting a whole picture, you will gain confidence in the type of subject matter you are about to approach. This will stand you in good stead for the main project.

Tip
Think of your final piece as a semi-abstract work and try not to be too concerned about realism – here is your chance to express yourself!

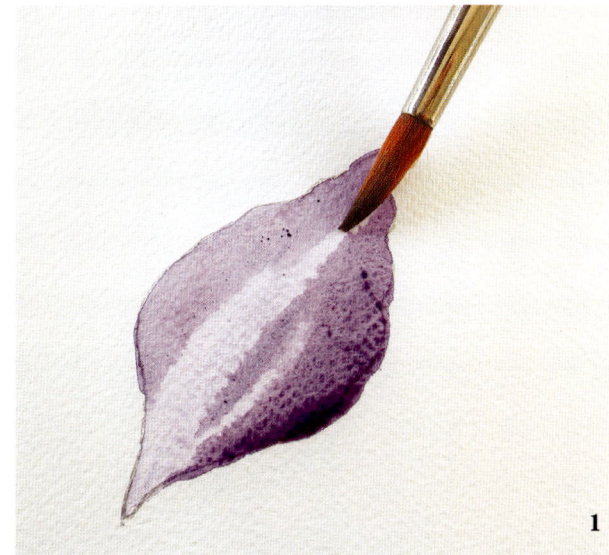

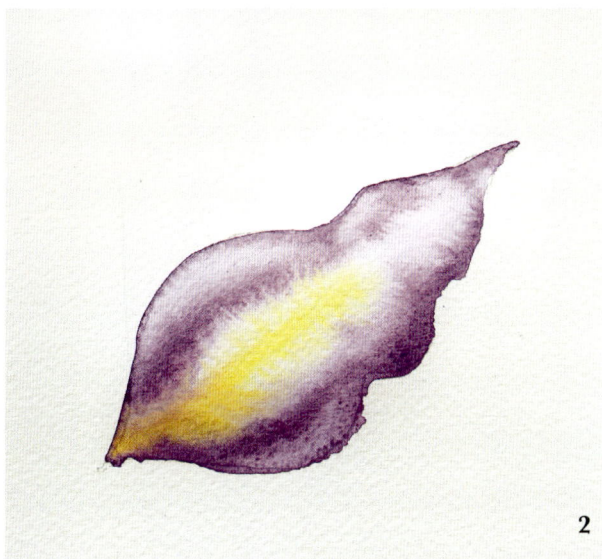

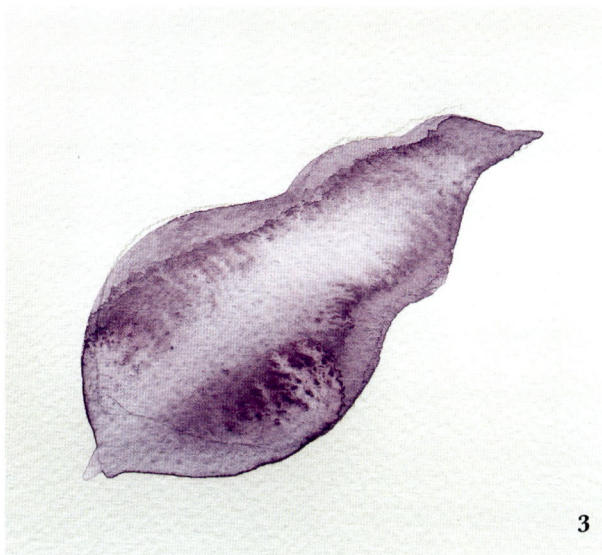

Petals

1 Sketch out a simple petal shape and paint in the entire area in purple, allowing the wash to run down and gather to a darker tone at the bottom edge. Before it dries, take your No. 12 brush and lift out to create a highlight in the centre. You may have to do this several times if the wash closes up.

2 Draw another petal shape and paint in purple, as in step 1. This time, while it is still wet, take your No. 12 brush and run a stripe of yellow across the centre, allowing both the colours to merge together.

3 Draw another petal shape and again paint the entire area in purple but this time, before it dries, run a line of clean water into the drying wash. This will create a backwash resembling the petal's veins.

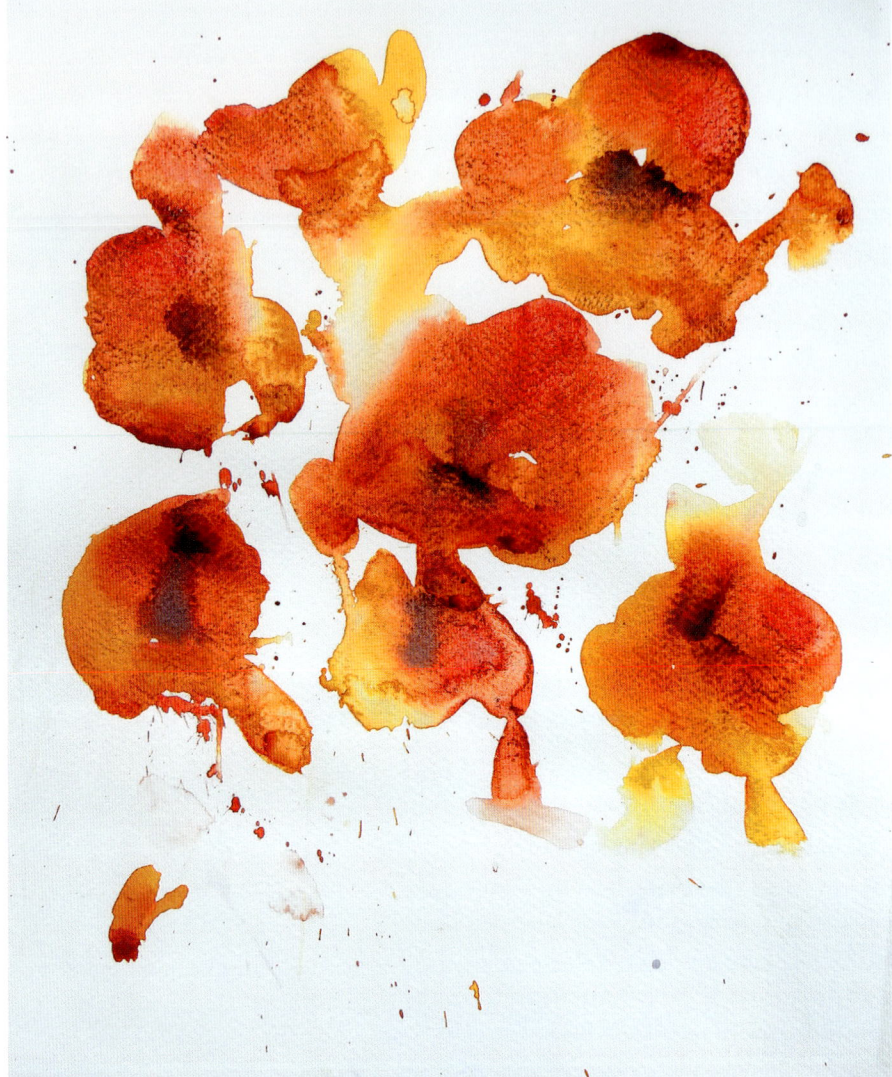

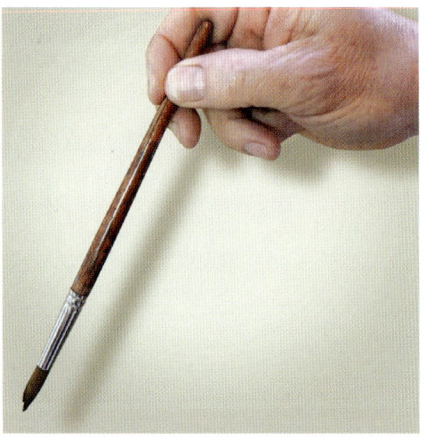

ABOVE *Hold your paintbrush at the very end to create a much looser and free-flowing brushstroke. This will allow your wrist to have much more movement.*

STAGE 1

Make a 50/50 mix of yellow and red to create a bright orange, and a further mix of red using 95% red and 5% blue. Using your No. 12 brush, randomly splash in droplets of clean water across your paper. Then paint in some simple poppy shapes using orange and, while this is still wet, on the right-hand side drop in your red mix. When the paint touches the water droplet you will notice some bleeding but this is all part of the effect you want to achieve. Next, drop a little Payne's Grey into the centre of each poppy, making sure that the washes are still wet. Finally, with your No. 12 brush, splatter some red spots randomly over the paper.

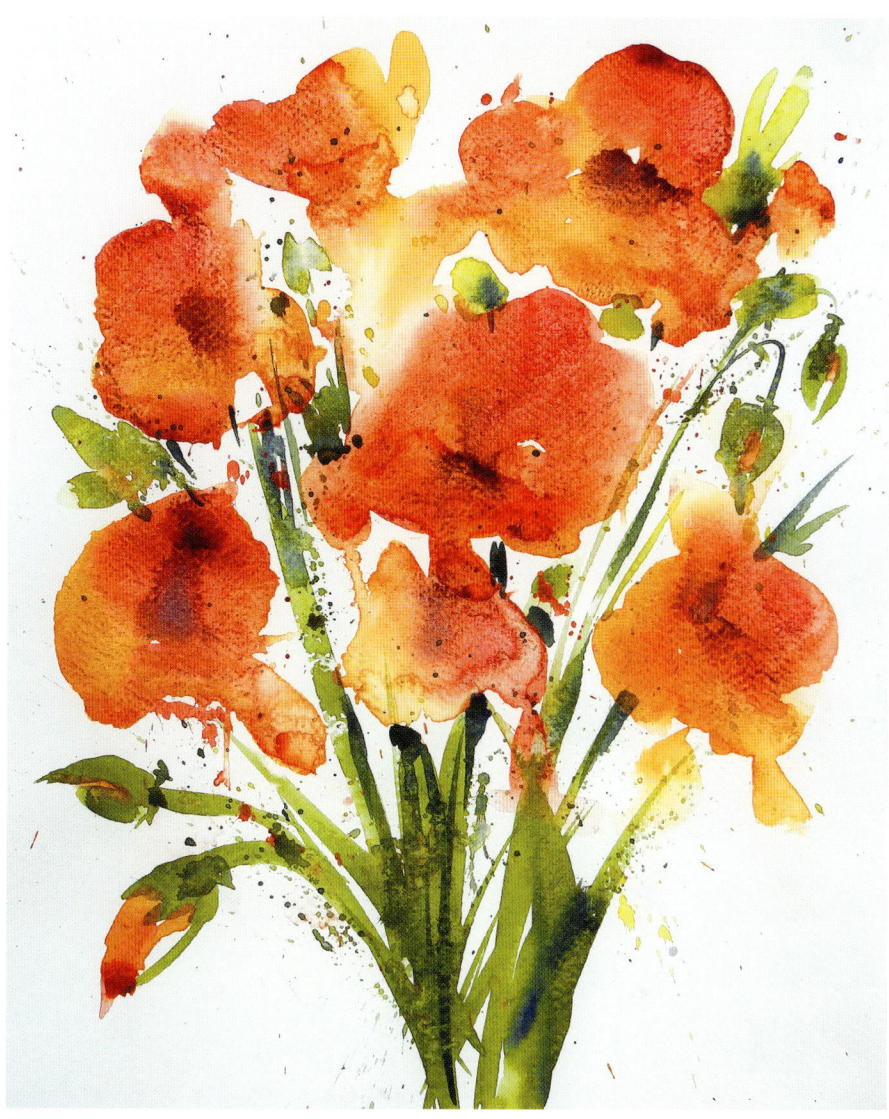

Tip

It's not necessary to do any preliminary sketching for this exercise. Simply pick up your brush and start painting.

STAGE 2

Mix up two shades of green, one with a 50% mix of yellow and blue and one with the same mix, but adding a touch of red to darken it. Paint in the stems quickly and loosely by holding your brush right at the end to give you less control and a more spontaneous stroke. While this is still wet, paint in the darker green right through the stems and underneath the poppies to create a shadow. Allow to dry.

Finally, paint in a little more detail with the darker green onto the dry paint to create some clearly defined shadows. Don't be tempted to use a hairdryer to speed up the drying process, as letting the paint dry naturally can create some interesting backwashes. Always keep your brushstrokes to a minimum. Overworking can cause your washes to become muddy: remember, don't fiddle and let the paint do the work!

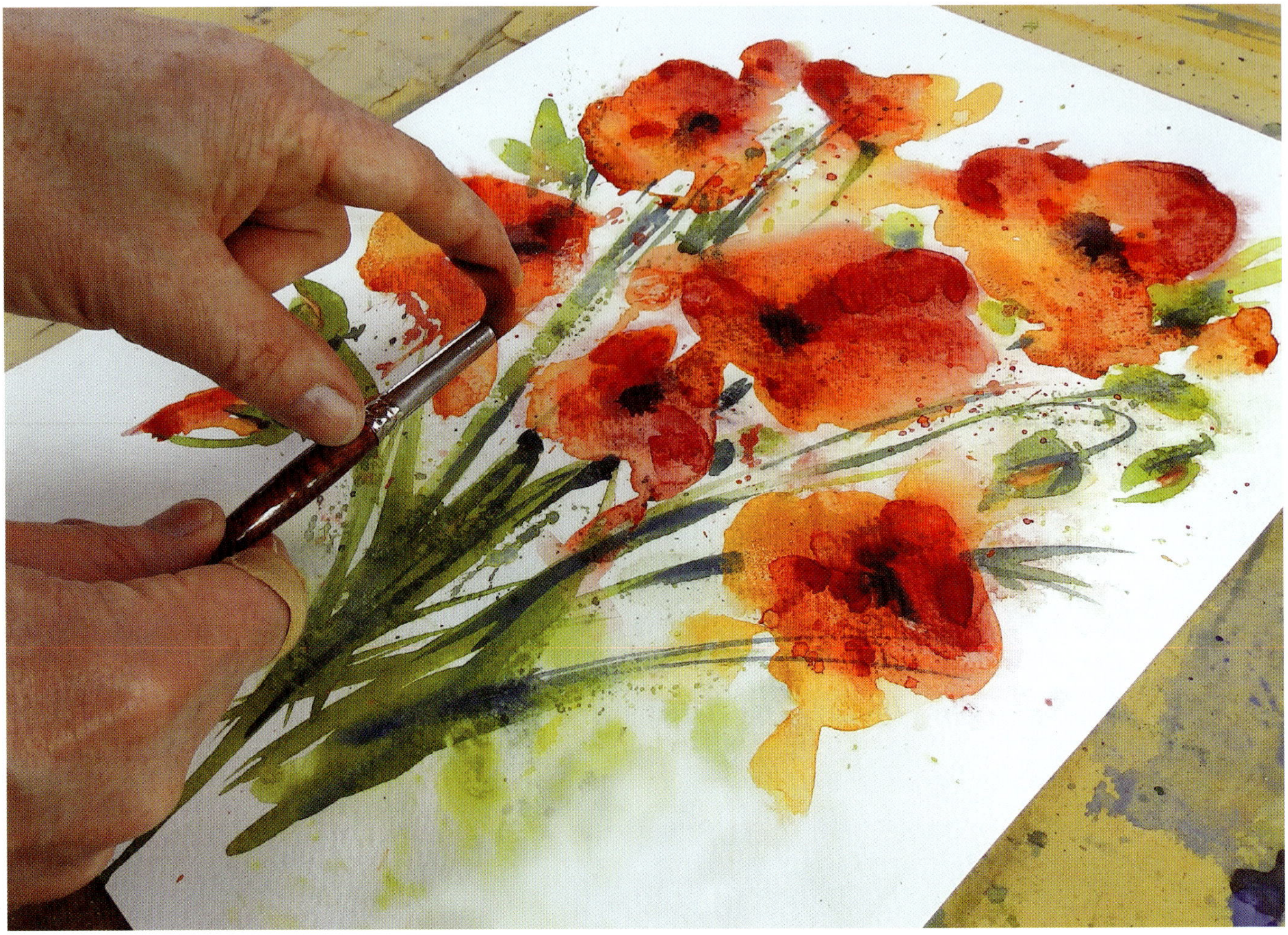

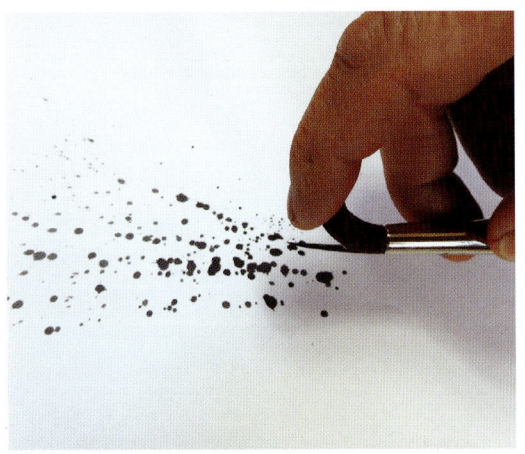

STAGE 3

Using your No. 12 brush, splatter in some red across the poppies and some green across the stems using the flick technique to add a bit of impact. To avoid the green splattering across the red of the poppies, you can mask them out using either some cheap paper or scrunched-up tissue.

ABOVE *Before applying your splats directly to your painting, it's worth a few trial runs on a piece of scrap paper to get the right consistency.*

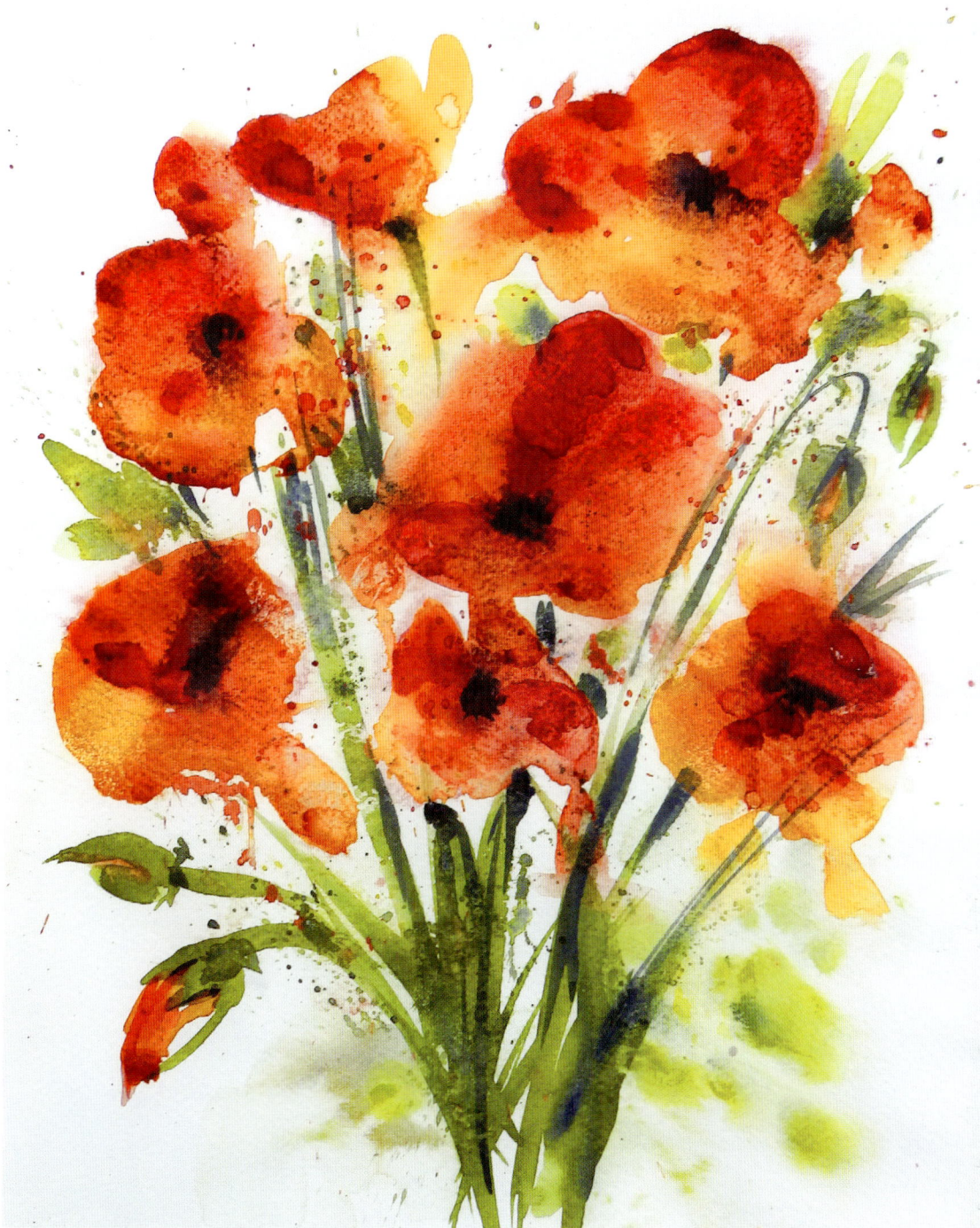

Tip

Flowers don't always need to be part of a finished scene. Painting flowers standing alone, surrounded only by white paper, is often enough to show their beautiful shapes and colours.

STAGE 4

Finally, paint in the dark stamens by re-wetting each poppy with clean water and allowing it to soak in for about 30 seconds. Then, in the centre of each poppy, drop in a blob of Payne's Grey. This should create dark centres with natural soft edges. Mix another green made up of 70% yellow and 30% blue. Then re-wet the bottom right-hand corner of the paper with clean water and drop the green onto the damp paper to create the suggestion of some out-of-focus foliage.

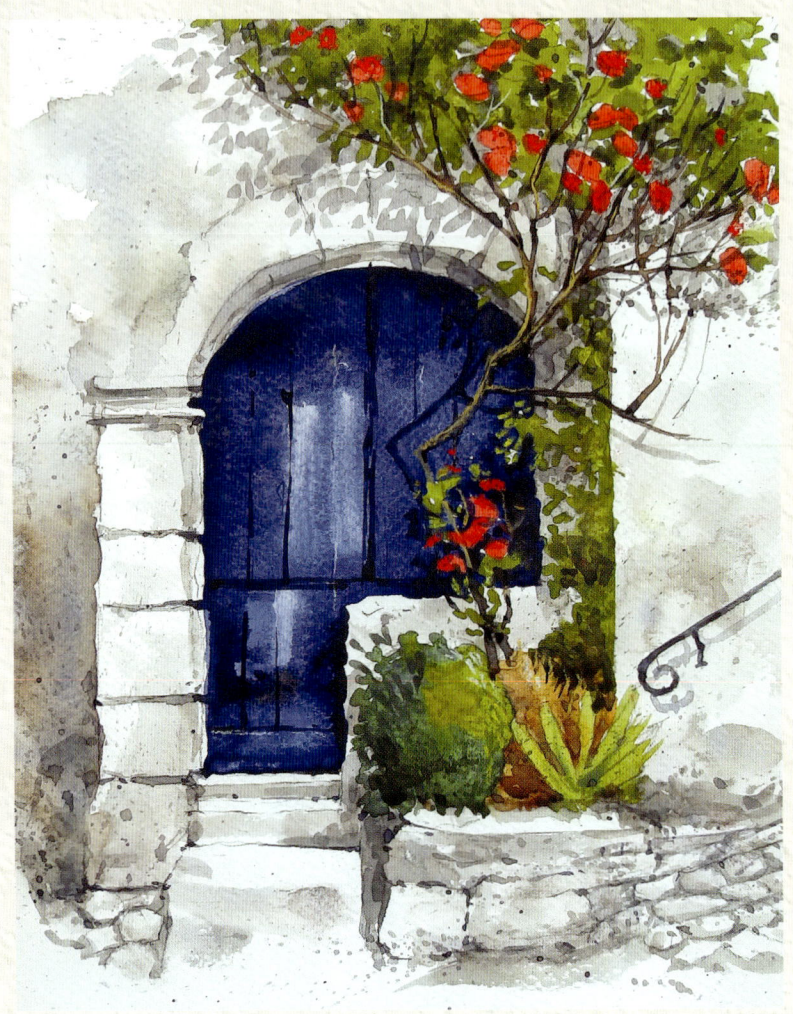

Blue Door

*Here we look at how a quick sketch of a very simple feature,
in this instance a doorway, can become an attractive watercolour painting.*

COLOURS NEEDED

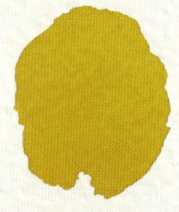

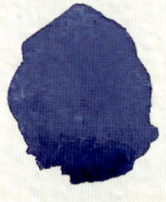

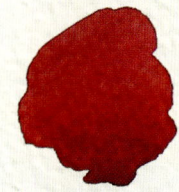

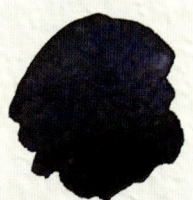

Cadmium Yellow   Cobalt Blue   Alizarin Crimson   Payne's Grey

I came across this view, purely by chance, on a holiday in Sarlat in the Dordogne, France. I just happened to peer up a side street while at the market and instantly thought there was a painting to be had.

I could have taken a photograph for reference and painted it back at the studio, but sometimes it is better to paint a quick sketch so as to avoid trying to copy the photograph too realistically; this allows you to put your own interpretation on it. It was also such a beautiful day and I wanted to soak up the atmosphere.

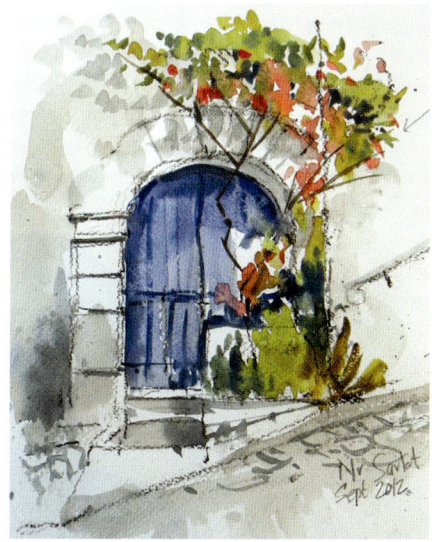

Instead of painting a sketch, many prefer to carry a pencil and pad with them and sketch a line drawing that they can fill with paint later. I am often asked how important it is to see the pencil line in your finished painting and I always say it is entirely up to the individual. Some artists, who paint in a more realistic way, use their pencilwork purely as a guide to lay down their washes, whereas others prefer to see the line work as part of the painting. The pencilwork can be as prominent as you wish. Personally, I like to see some of the pencil lines showing through as I feel it can add character to the piece.

PEN AND WASH

You can take this a step further by painting in a 'pen and wash' style, introducing black ink. There are various ways to achieve this, using a permanent black marker or pen. Some artists like to put in the watercolour first then add the drawing work in black ink afterwards. I personally like to finish my drawing work so it stands alone as a finished monochromatic piece, introducing all the tonal values of light and shade with various short hatching

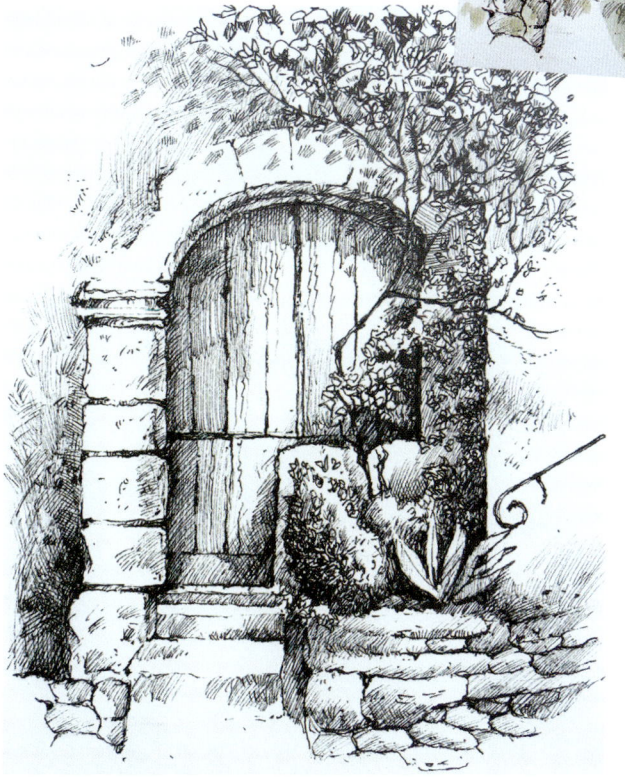

strokes (closely spaced parallel lines). See pages 24–5 for more on drawing techniques. Once I have completed the hard work, I can sit back and relax, and simply paint in the watercolour. Some of my students have enjoyed working in this way to such a degree that they have continued using this as their preferred method of painting.

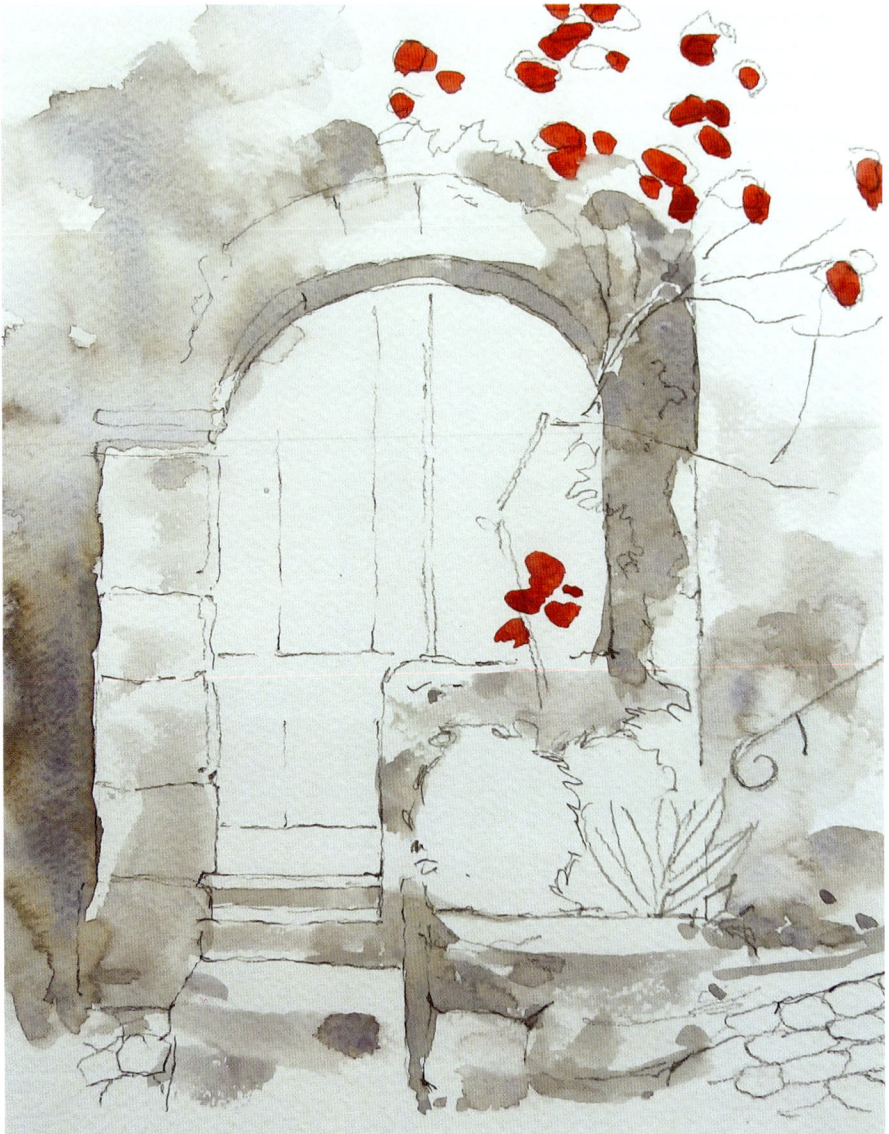

Tip
Always keep your drawing work simple, allowing your paintbrush to do most of the work.

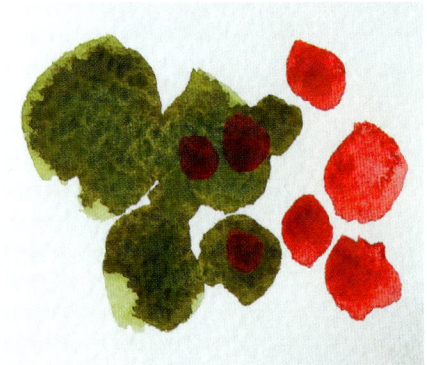

ABOVE *You can see how important it is to paint your red onto white paper. Because of the transparency of the paint, the red looks much duller when painted on top of a green wash.*

STAGE 1

Start by doing a little loose drawing. Keeping your drawing work quite sketchy stops you being too precise with your painting and avoids the 'paint-by-numbers' feel. Next, using your No. 12 brush, paint a few simple red blobs for the flowers. It's important these are painted first as we need to have bright white paper for the red to be strong. Then mix a grey, starting with a 50/50 mix of blue and red then mixing in a small amount of yellow. Paint this into the wall areas, using more colour in the shadow areas. While still wet, drop some clean water into the wash in a few small areas to create some interesting texture. Because you mixed the grey from the three colours, you can see the paint has separated, which gives a lovely granulation to the washes.

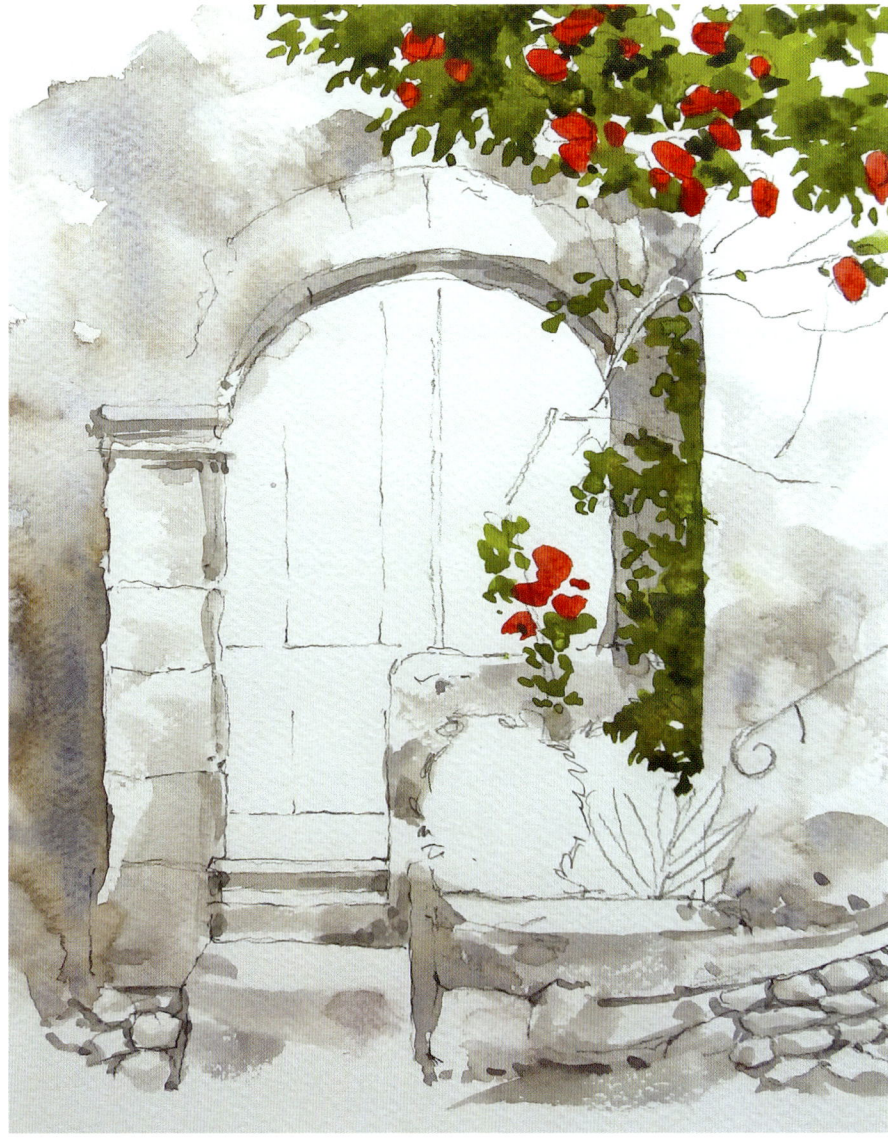

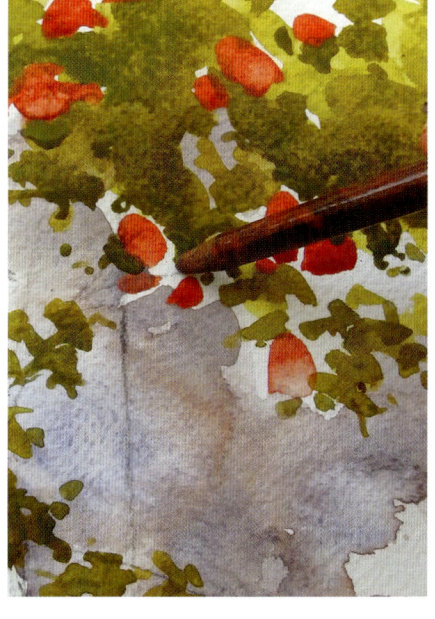

ABOVE *Use the end of your brush and work into the wet paint to create some harder edge details.*

STAGE 2

Next, mix a bright green using a 50/50 mix of blue and yellow and paint in the leaves and ivy. Using this same colour, mix into it some more blue and a touch of red to darken it and paint this into the wash before it has a chance to dry totally, to create some shadows in the foliage. Mix another grey (as in stage 1), but this time a little darker and, with your No. 6 brush, paint in some of the cobble details and shadows under the arch and on the steps.

Make sure you don't over-paint. Always leave areas of white paper showing through to give some extra sparkle.

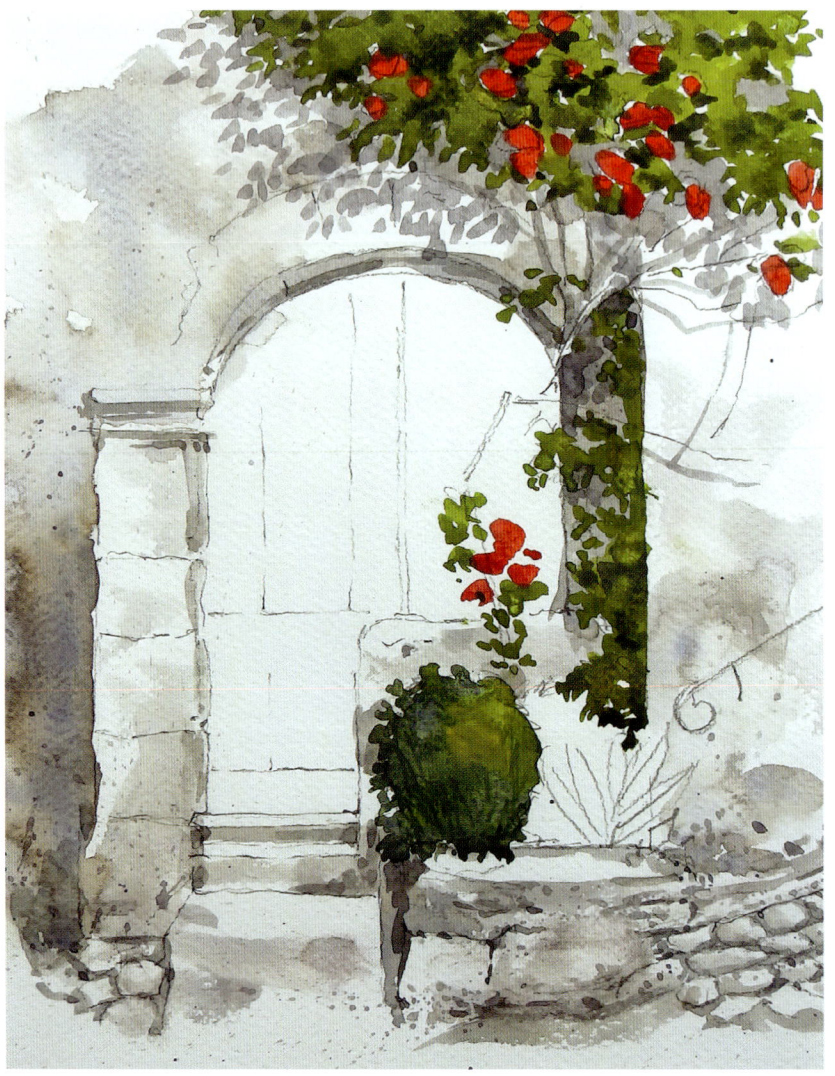

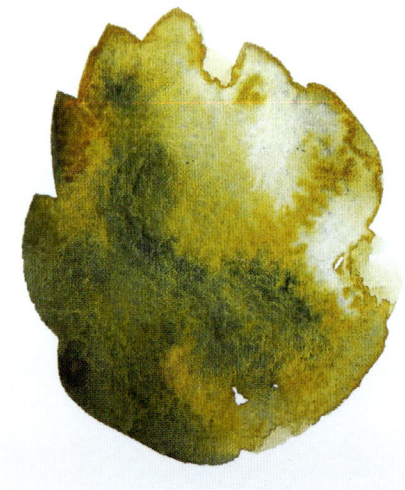

ABOVE *Dropping clean water directly into the wet wash will add interesting texture to the foreground foliage.*

STAGE 3

Making sure all your washes are dry after stage 2, use grey again to paint in the shadow of the tree foliage and add some detail to the stones at the bottom. I also used the same colour to splatter some texture into the foreground and left-hand wall. Next, mix up another green but this time use more blue, and then paint in the bush in the centre. While still wet, I dropped in a more yellowy green to the right and with the end of my brush scored in some lines to create a bit of bush texture.

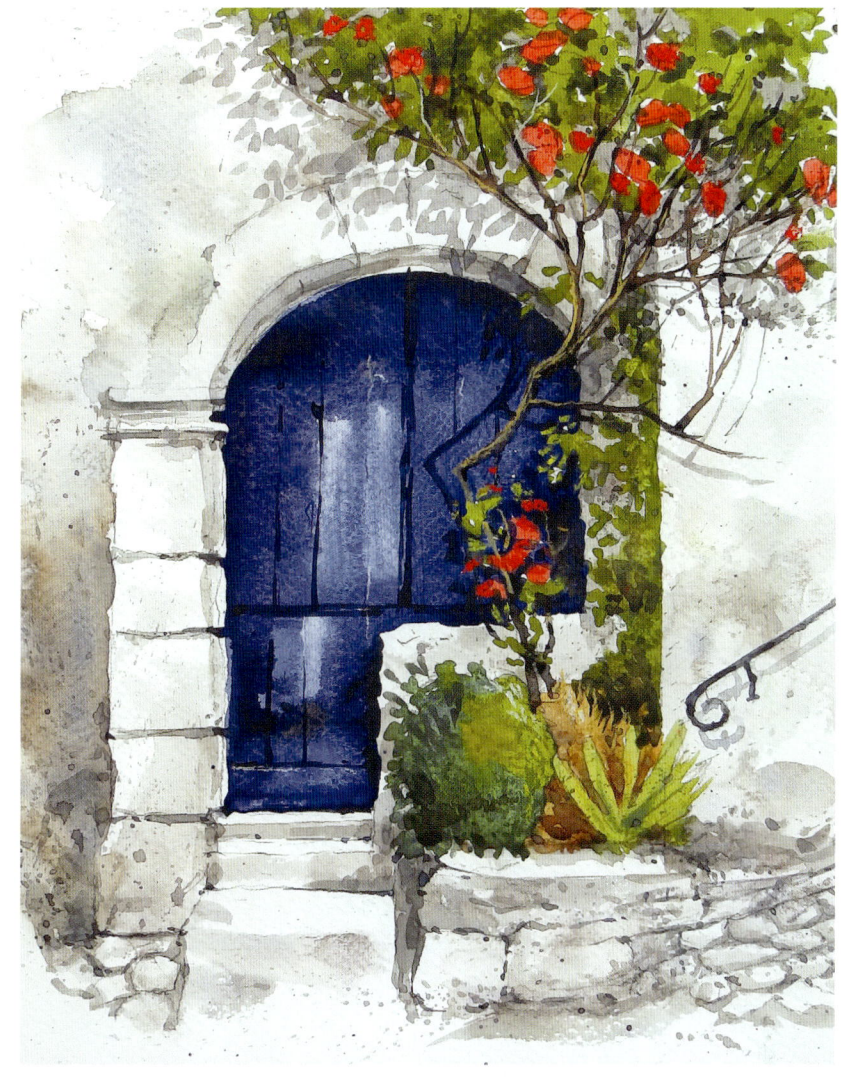

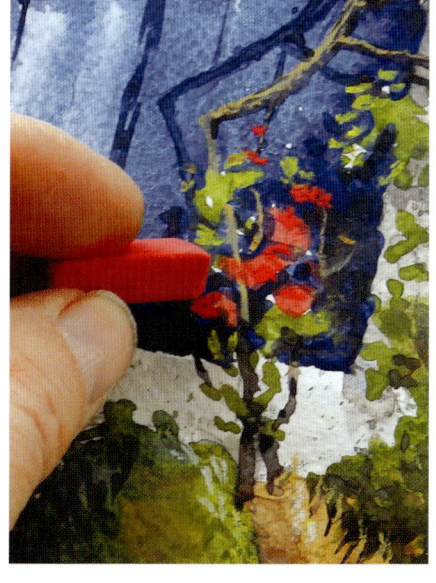

ABOVE *If some of your flowers have become overpainted by the blue paint of the door, you can use a soft pastel to bring back the red detail.*

STAGE 4

Pre-mix two colours for the door: a bright blue using lots of blue with a small touch of yellow, and a dark blue using blue, red and a touch of Payne's Grey to give it strength. Paint in the brighter blue, carefully working around the arch and foliage. While this is still wet, quickly paint in the darker blue along the top and sides of the door to create a shadow and then with a clean damp brush lift out the highlights in the door panels. Then mix a sandy colour using yellow and red with a tiny hint of blue to paint the second bush but leaving the paper white where the palm leaves are to be painted. When this is dry, paint in the small palm with a mix of mainly yellow but with a hint of blue. Paint in the branches using a dark brown mixed with all three colours, making sure you keep this to a minimum in the area where the leaves are. To finish off, mix a dark grey and paint the details in the door panels, the shadow of the tree on the door, the handrail and a few bits of foliage detail.

It's so easy to overwork this final stage, so keep the details fresh and loose and to a minimum – always remember, less is more!

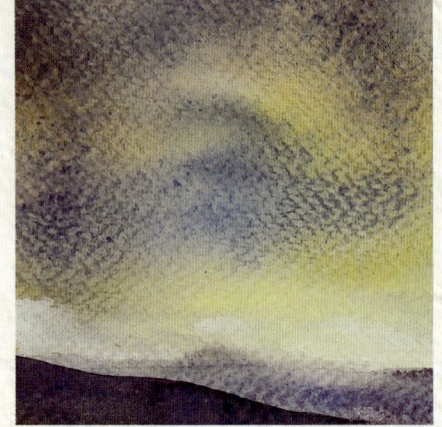

FOCUS ON
Skies

We are all moved by the beauty of the sky as it appears at different times of the day and in different weather conditions. Watercolour paints can help you capture every subtle yet stunning variation to great effect.

Cloudy sky

1A Mix a large quantity of strong blue. Wet the paper thoroughly with your 1in (25mm) flat brush and clean water and let it soak in for 30 seconds. With the same brush, paint in a graduated wash across the paper. Before this dries, form clouds by lifting out the paint with a piece of scrunched-up kitchen paper. With a (clean and fairly dry) No. 10 or 12 brush, lift out the paint to form wispy clouds at the bottom. Let dry for half an hour.

1B Make sure your first wash is completely dry. Mix up a very pale grey using mostly blue with a touch of red and yellow. Soak the paper with a large brush using clean water. While still wet, paint in the grey on the bottom edges of all the clouds to create a subtle shadow.

Summer sky

2A Make up a soft, watery yellow by mixing yellow with a hint of red, then a soft purple of red and blue. It

is important the yellow is very pale. Use a 1in flat brush to wet the paper with clean water and allow to soak in for 30 seconds. With a No. 12 brush, paint in some purple blobs and then immediately paint in the yellow along the top edge. Lift up your board and tilt it diagonally, letting the paint run through the damp paper. Leave to dry.

2B Make sure your first wash is completely dry (leave for half an hour) then re-wet the whole surface of the

1A

2A

1B

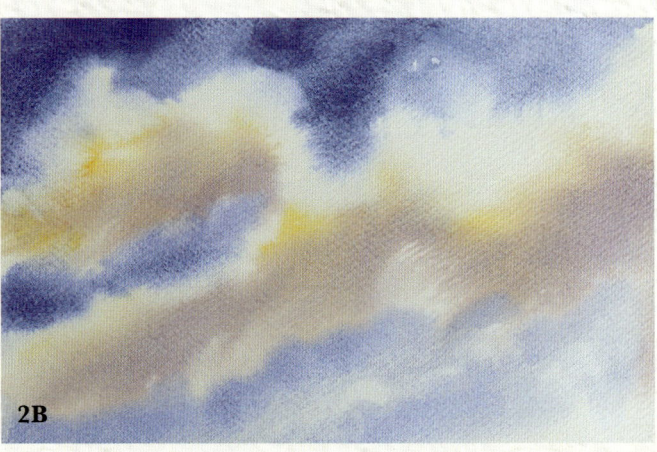

2B

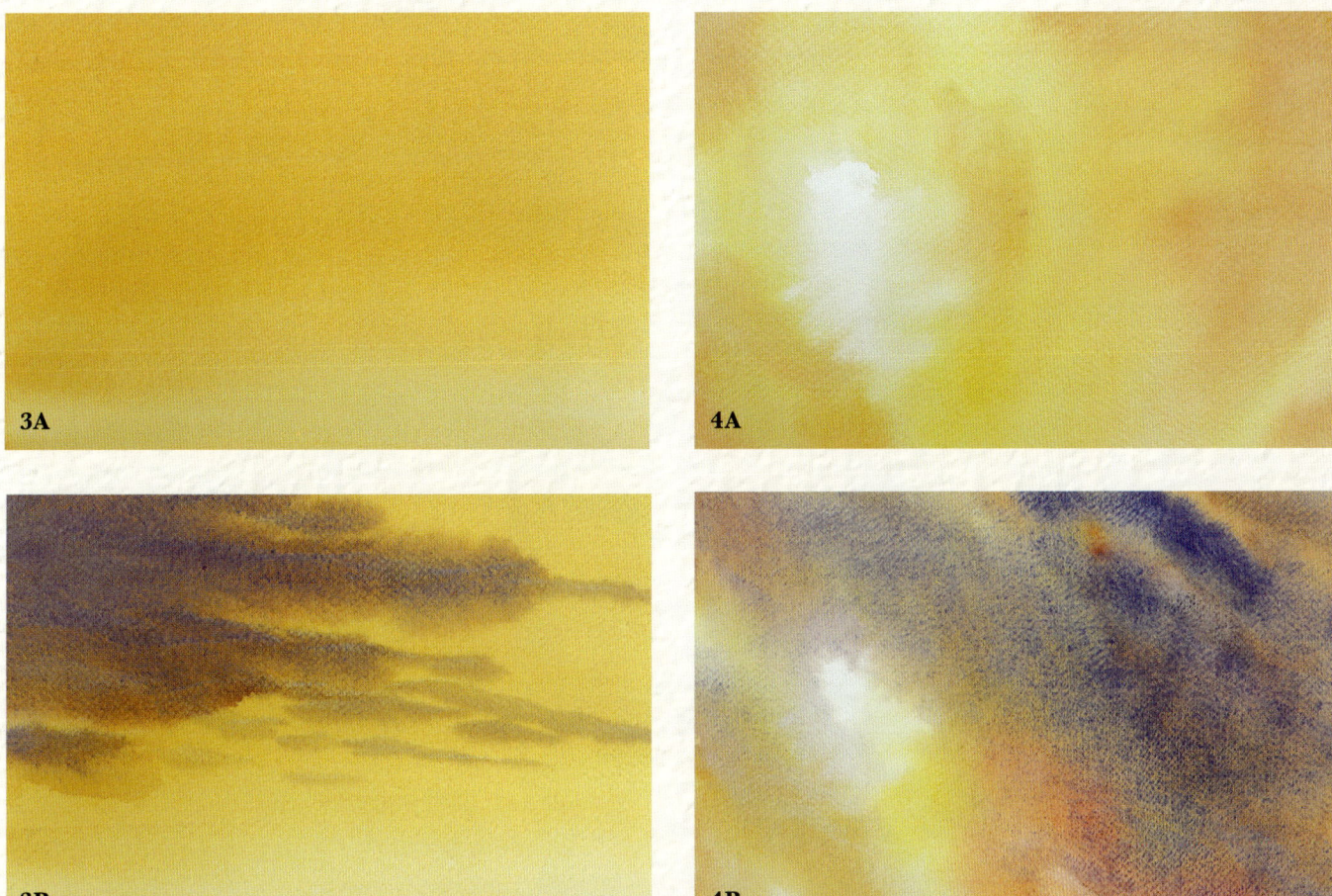

3A

4A

3B

4B

paper with clean water using your 1in flat brush. Make up a mixture of mainly blue with a hint of red. While the paper is still wet, paint around the existing cloud shadows with a No. 12 brush, making sure you leave white space to create the shape of the clouds, especially around the top edges. Use a stronger blue above the clouds and a more diluted blue below.

Evening sky

3A Mix up a large quantity of warm yellow, about 95% yellow and 5% red. Wet your paper thoroughly with the 1in flat brush using clean water and let it soak into the paper for about 30 seconds. Using the same brush, paint in a graduated wash across the paper. Leave to dry for half an hour.

3B Make sure your first wash is completely dry, then re-wet the whole surface with clean water using the 1in flat brush. Mix up a strong wash of 60% blue and 40% red to make a darkish purple. Paint in the solid areas in the top left and then streak your brush across the surface to create the cloud shapes. Use a lighter version of the same colour by adding more water to create the lighter, wispy clouds at the edges. Lift up your board at the left-hand side to about 45 degrees and let the colour slowly run across the surface.

Stormy sky

4A Mix a large amount of warm yellow, about 95% yellow and 5% red. Wet the paper thoroughly with the 1in flat brush using clean water and

let it soak into the paper for about 30 seconds. With the same brush, paint the yellow over the whole paper but leave an area to the left unpainted to create a glow effect. Mix some more red into your wash to create an orange and paint this into the wet wash around the edges. Let it dry for half an hour.

4B Make sure your first wash is completely dry before again wetting the whole surface with clean water. Mix up various tones of blues, oranges and purples, and paint into the still-wet wash large blobs of each colour, which can overlap. Lift up and tilt your board diagonally, letting the paint run through the damp paper, but make sure it does not run into the glow area created at stage 4A. Let the colours run naturally together.

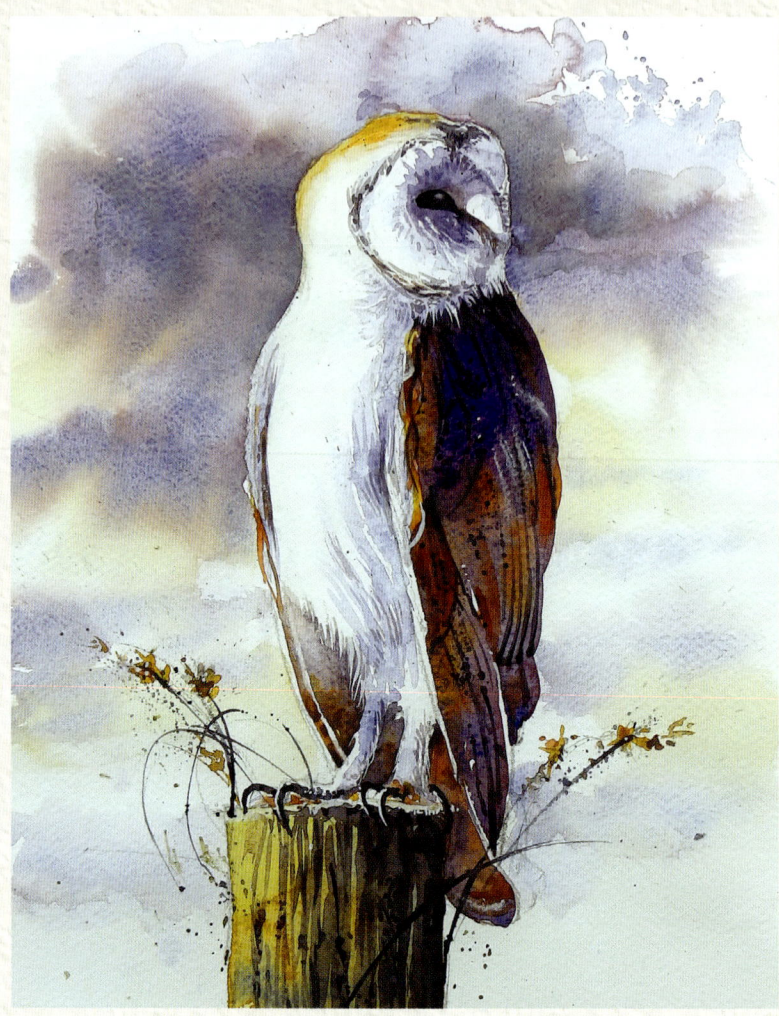

Birds

Birds can provide the artist with such a wealth of visual inspiration.
Whether studied in fine detail, at close distance, or in flight,
they make a fascinating and striking subject to paint.

COLOURS NEEDED

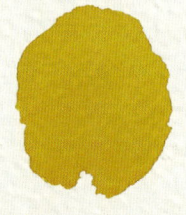 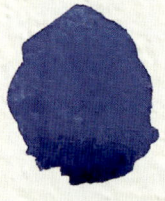 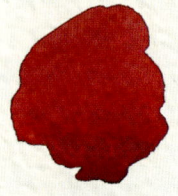 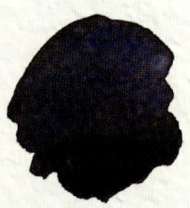

Cadmium Yellow   Cobalt Blue   Alizarin Crimson   Payne's Grey

1A

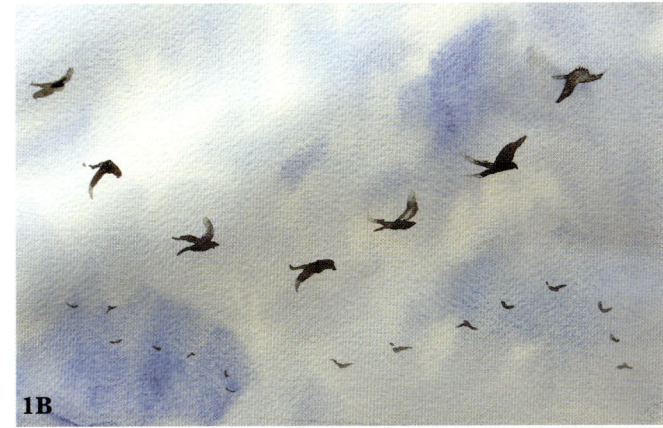

1B

In this tutorial we are going to focus on painting a beautiful, arresting barn owl. But first there are a couple of brief exercises you can try that demonstrate a simple method of depicting birds in flight and creating the fine detail of a hawk's feather. These will give you a good basis from which to continue exploring this fabulous subject matter.

Birds in flight

Although simplifying a bird's shape is key, especially for birds that are in the distance, I have seen many a landscape ruined by badly painted birds resembling the McDonald's 'M' that we painted as children. To make sure you don't fall into this trap, try this method instead:

1A Prepare a mix of blue with a tiny amount of red. Completely wet your paper with clean water and let it soak in for a few moments. Randomly drop blobs of blue into the wet paper, leaving some areas of white to suggest clouds. Let this wash dry without fiddling and you will see clouds naturally appear.

1B Allow to totally dry then, using your Payne's Grey, paint in some simple bird shapes. While still wet, you can create the suggestion of movement by lightly dabbing out with tissue some of

the colour on the wing tips. The birds in the distance only need to be simple little blobs and V-shapes rather than proper depictions of birds.

It's best to practise several bird shapes on a spare sheet of paper before committing them to your final piece. Also, try to avoid painting too many on your final piece, as less is always more.

Hawk's wing

Now we move closer to the birds, in preparation for the project that follows. This exercise will help you to practise creating the texture of a bird's wing.

2A Mix a warm gold colour using 80% yellow, 15% red and 5% blue. Next, mix a brown using all three colours, and a dark red using 75% red and 25% blue. Sketch out the shape of a wing made up of at least five feathers as shown, and paint in using the gold. While this is still wet, add in a stripe of brown along the pencil dividing lines and then a stripe of red in the centre of each feather.

2B After allowing your painting to dry, with the same dark red add a second stripe halfway down the length of the wing. Leave to dry.

2C Using your No. 6 brush and some Payne's Grey, carefully paint in the dark details on each feather, making sure they form a V-shape to the centre. Finally, using a white pastel pencil or white gouache, pick out the ridge on the spine of each feather.

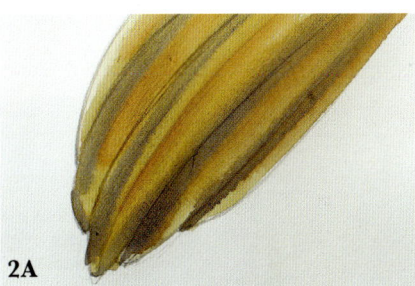

2A

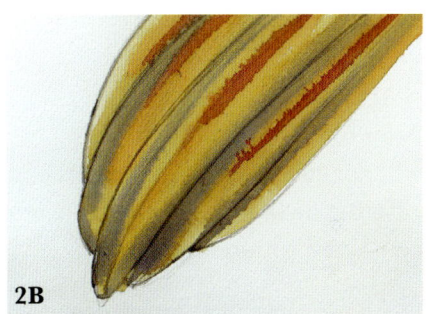

2B

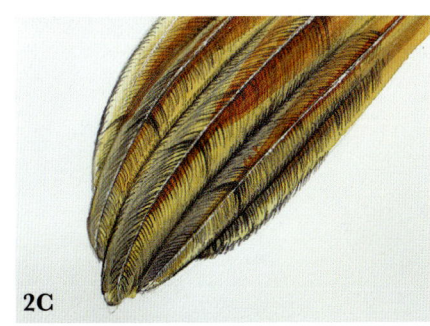

2C

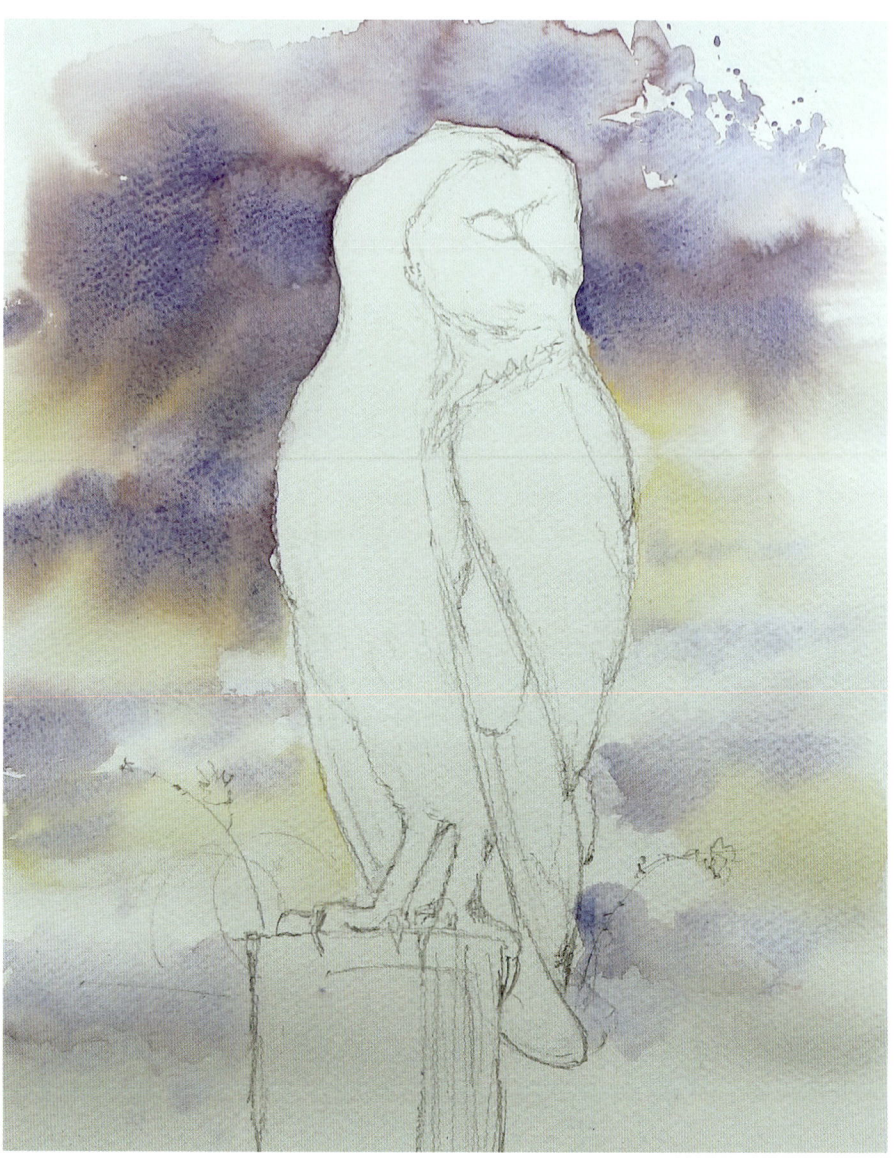

Tip
Paint travelling across the paper will not colour dry areas (in this case the owl); it will always stay contained within the wet wash.

STAGE 1

Sketch out the owl in pencil, being careful not to add in too much detail. Pre-mix a purple using 50/50 blue and red, and also a warm yellow using mainly yellow with a tiny hint of red. Using your biggest brush, paint with clean water the entire background, making sure that you neatly paint around the shape of the owl and not within it. While this is still wet, use your No. 12 brush to drop in random blobs of both purple and yellow to suggest a blurry background. As the wash begins to dry, tilt your board at an angle and let the paint travel diagonally across the paper without worrying about it moving across the owl.

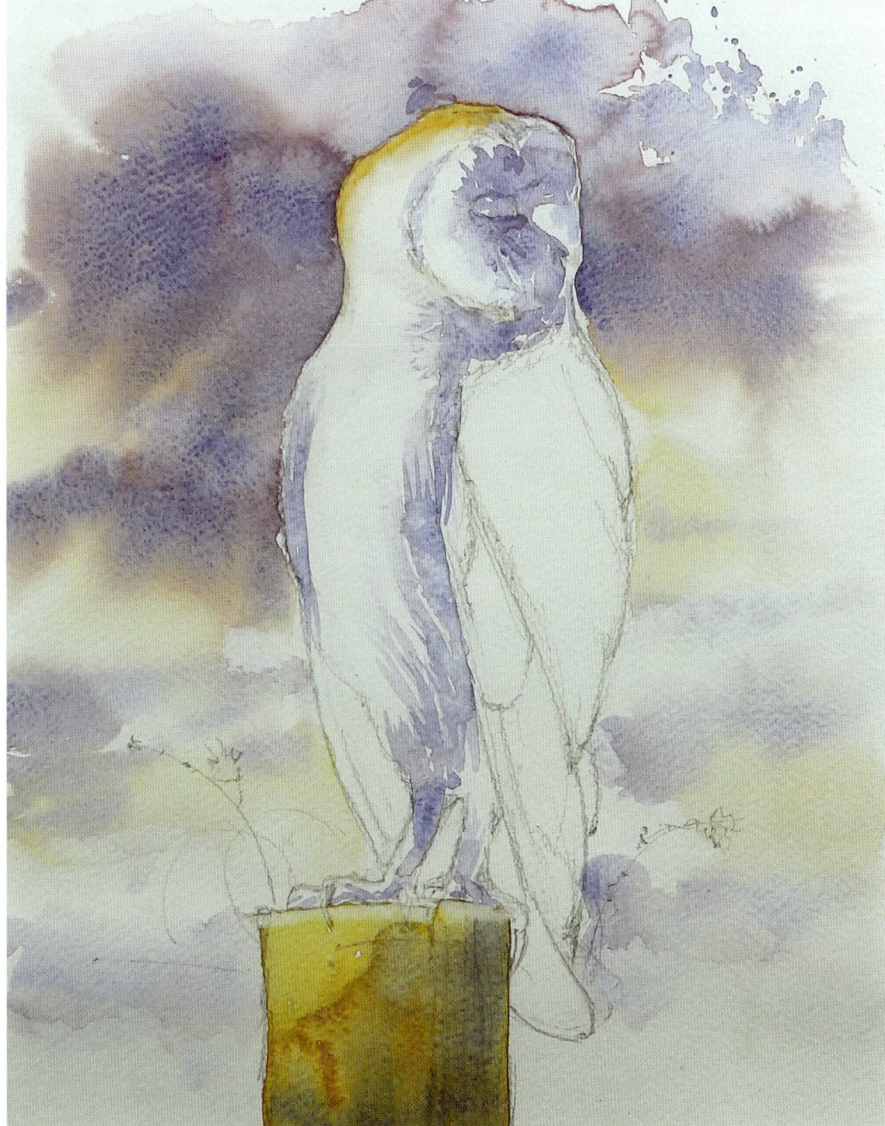

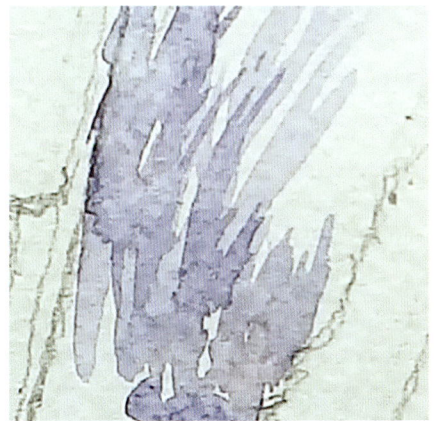

ABOVE *When painting shadows on feathers, lift your brush off the paper as you paint each upward stroke to create a tapering effect.*

STAGE 2

Mix a sandy colour made up of 50/50 yellow and red with a touch of blue. Use this to paint in the wooden post and the top of the owl's head. You can soften the outline of colour on the owl's head by simply painting in a little bit of clean water. Next, mix a darker brown using all three colours – red, yellow and blue but with a touch more blue – and while the post is still wet, drop some colour into the left-hand side. Then with the purple you mixed in stage 1, paint in the shadows on the owl's head and body; then allow your painting to dry.

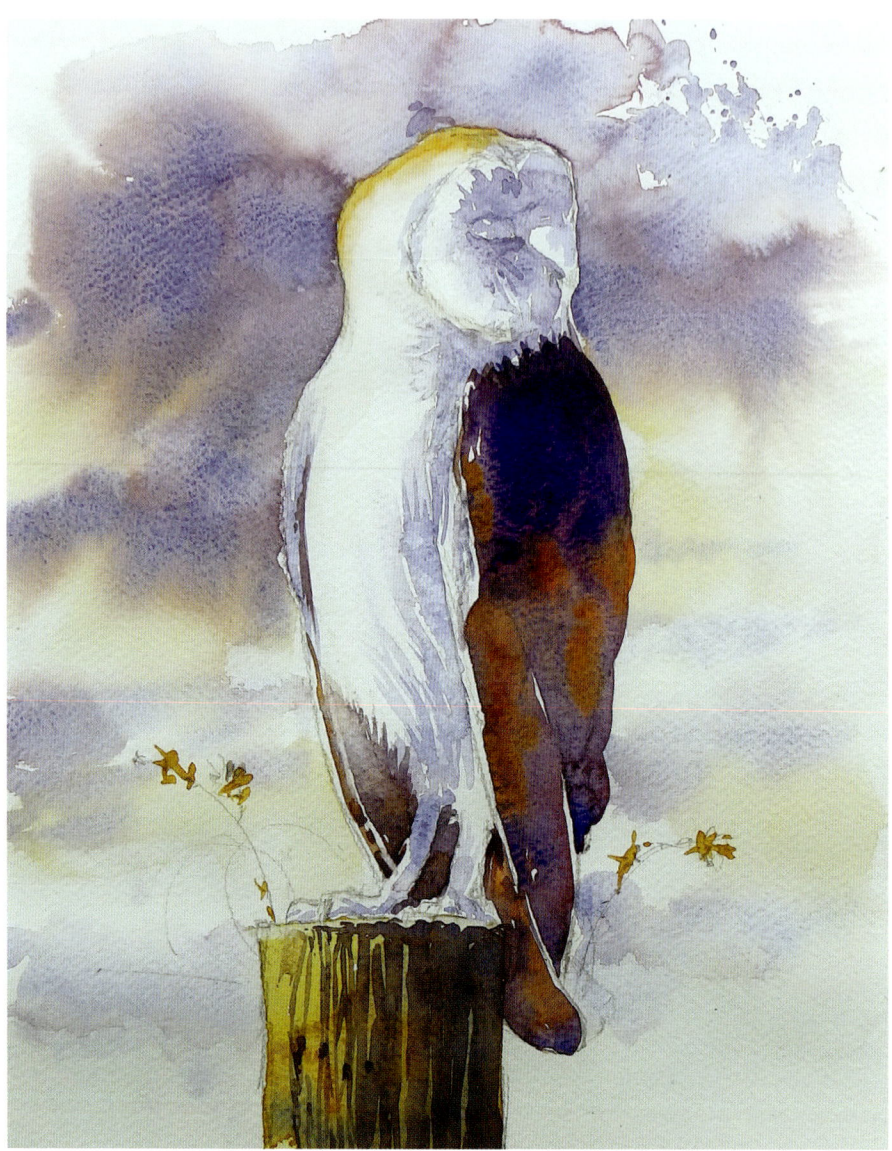

STAGE 3

Mix up a dark purple using a 50/50 mix of blue and red, this time adding in a very small touch of yellow. Then mix an orange using 50/50 yellow and red. Using the purple, paint in the owl's wing and, while still wet, drop in a few blobs of orange. Add a little Payne's Grey into your purple and paint this darker tone into the wing at the top to create some contrast. To complete the post, mix a brown using equal amounts of all three colours and paint in from the left vertical stripes to give the illusion of grain in the wood, leaving a few gaps. With your No. 6 brush, paint in the seed heads either side of the owl. Allow to dry.

Tip
When painting the stripes on the post, make sure you leave a few gaps for the lighter colour to come through.

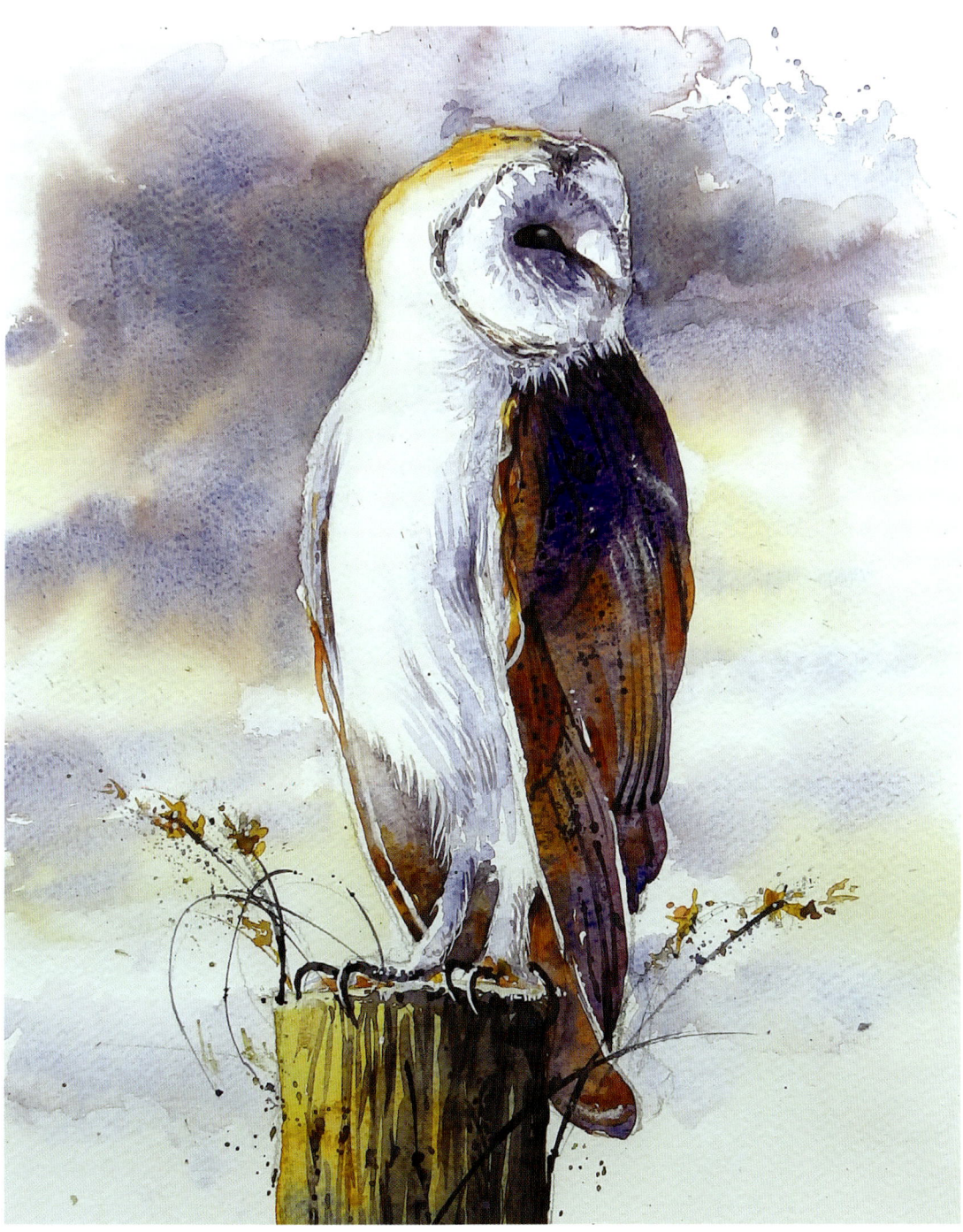

STAGE 4

Now it's time to add the finer details. Again with your No. 6 brush and using the pre-mixed purple from stage 3, paint some of the feathers onto the owl's body and head. Darken this colour by adding in a little yellow and paint in the outline of the owl's face, details in the wing (see the Hawk's wing exercise on page 47), its claws and the stalks of the seed heads. Darken this colour even further by adding a little more blue and carefully paint in the owl's eye, making sure you leave a small white dot in the centre. To finish, use a white pastel pencil or some white gouache to pick out a few details on the owl's wing.

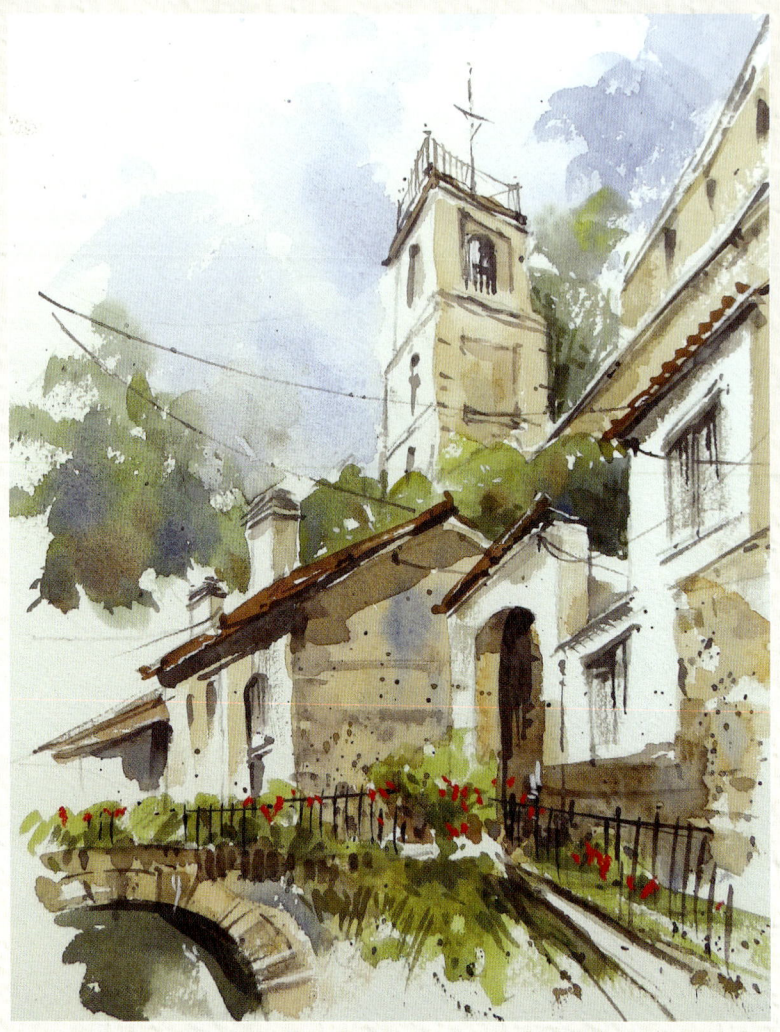

En Plein Air

Painting from photographs is an excellent way to learn and shouldn't be dismissed, but there is nothing like the sensation of painting in the great outdoors, or 'en plein air', as it is known. Painting outdoors is one of the most enjoyable but challenging activities you can do as an artist.

COLOURS NEEDED

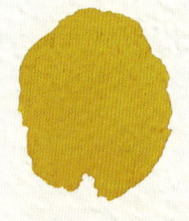

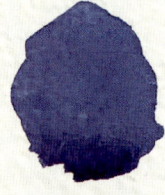

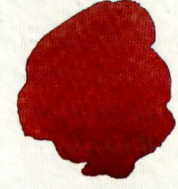

Cadmium Yellow   Cobalt Blue   Alizarin Crimson

The painting shown opposite, which we will be looking at in depth on the following pages, was a work I produced while on a painting holiday in Tuscany, Italy. One of the most gratifying things I find with looking at a painting I have done *en plein air* is that I am immediately transported back to the day I painted it – revisiting the sounds, smells and atmosphere of the day.

Not everybody is lucky enough to have Tuscany on their doorstep, but you can paint equally satisfying pictures in your garden or the local park. Use your artist's eye to look for interesting subjects in everyday spaces. 'Interesting' needn't be beautiful, and you don't have to have a stunning scene to make an interesting watercolour. A good example of this is the American artist Edward Hopper, who would often paint subjects that others might view as fairly mundane (see *House of the Fog Horn, No. 3*, right).

Equipment

Once you have chosen your subject, make sure that you have all the right equipment with you. However, don't feel that you must take along the contents of your studio! All I take is a lightweight folding chair and a small folding stool for my paints and water. I find this easier than placing them on the ground as it avoids having to constantly bend to reach your materials. A watercolour paper pad is ideal as the stiff back cover doubles up as a drawing board. I also take my usual three brushes, my three tubes of colour, a plastic mixing palette, a lightweight water pot, some water – and, of course, don't forget your straw hat to look the part!

RIGHT *The author painting outdoors in the sunshine in Chalimont, France.*

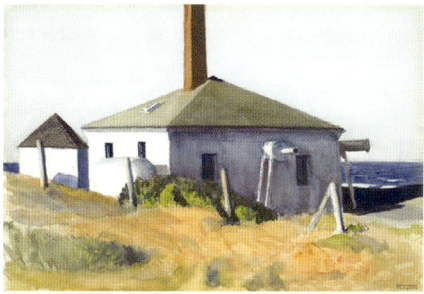

ABOVE House of the Fog Horn, No. 3 *by Edward Hopper, 1929.*

Light conditions

The challenge that is faced when painting a landscape outdoors is the ever-changing light. For that reason, I often do a quick pencil sketch first and roughly shade in my shadows in a fixed position so they remain constant when I come to paint. I also like to paint quickly and very loosely with almost a sketch-like quality and keep my pencilwork to a minimum so as not to inhibit my brushwork.

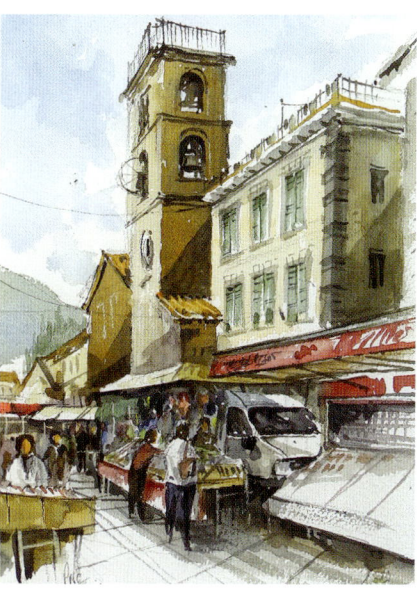

ABOVE *A painting done outdoors takes me straight back to the time and place where it was painted – here, Piazza Medicea, Fivizzano.*

Tip

Try not to worry about passers-by looking at your work. I have had many an interesting conversation with wannabe art critics; most are usually very encouraging.

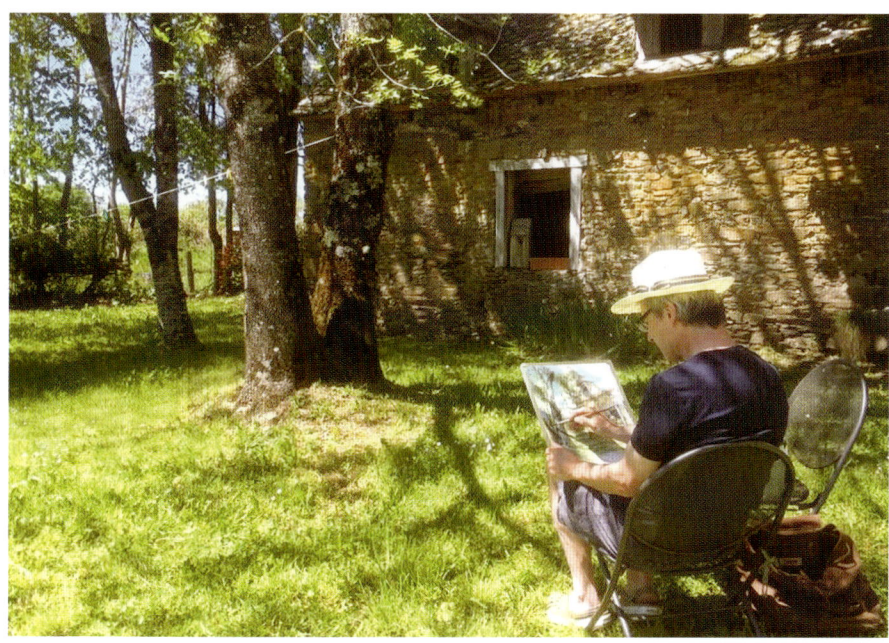

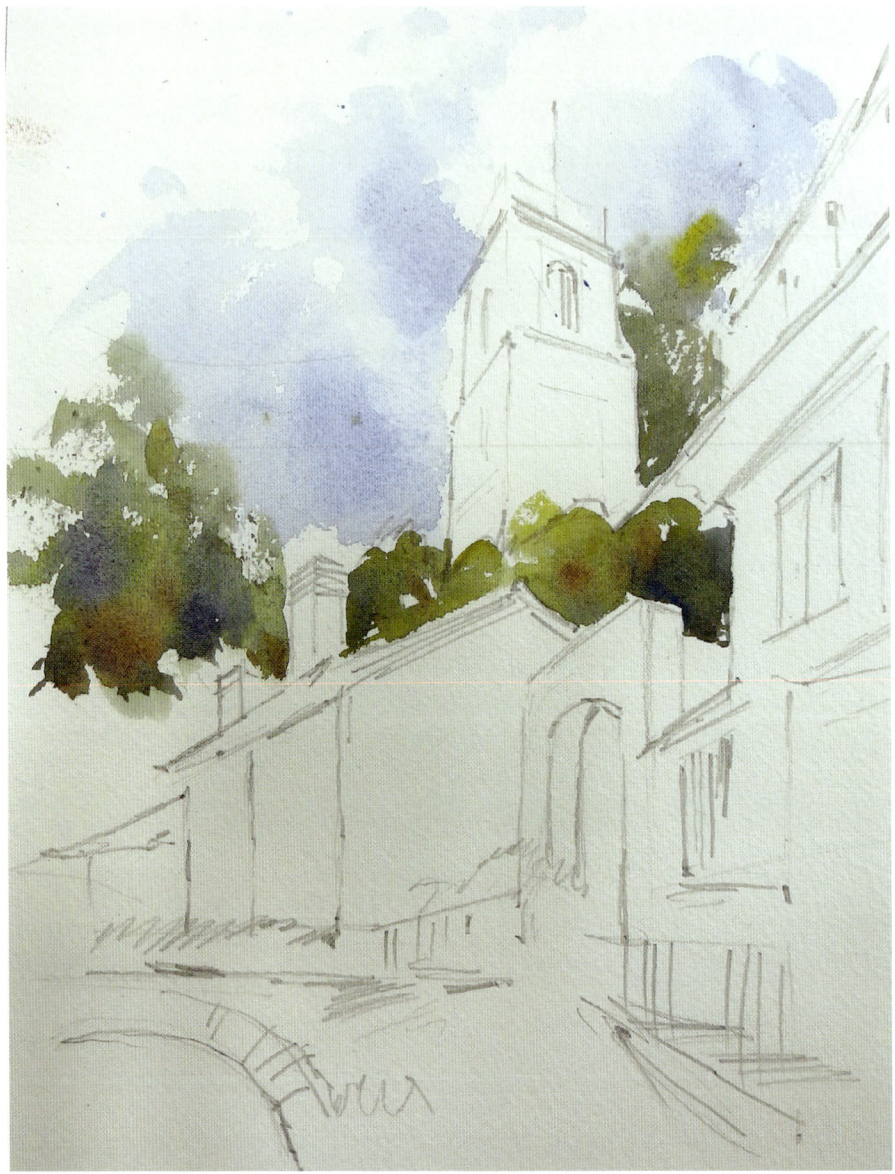

Tip

Leaving white areas in your wash of blue is a good way of representing the clouds in the sky.

STAGE 1

Imagine you are with me in the medieval streets of the village of Verrucola in Tuscany, which is where I painted this picture. We are sitting in a garden looking towards the church with its campanile. Start with a quick pencil sketch and then, using your No. 12 brush, paint a simple wash of blue into the sky, leaving white areas for a few summery clouds. Next, prepare a green wash of 50/50 yellow and blue and quickly paint the trees in the middle distance and to the right of the tower. While this is still wet, drop in a few blue and red tints to give the trees a bit of interest, then leave to dry. To create a looser and impressionistic style to this scene, I have deliberately left a lot of areas unpainted.

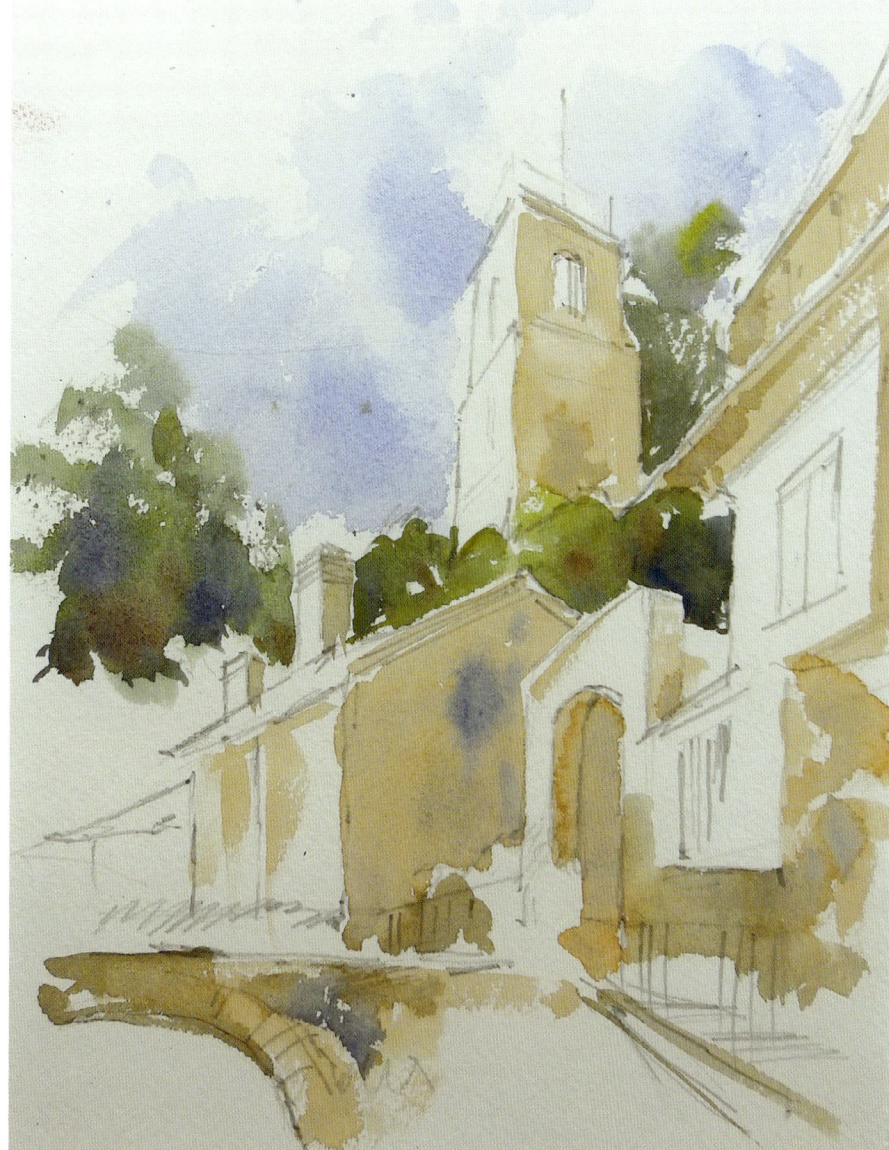

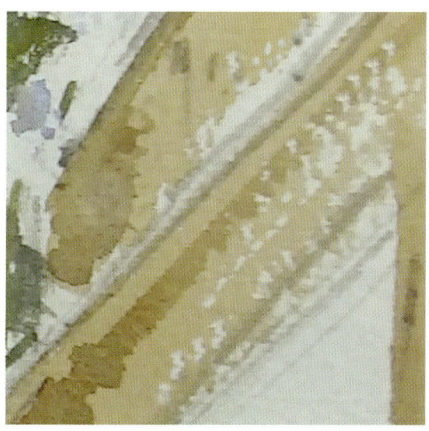

ABOVE *By painting quickly, some of your brushstrokes will naturally acquire a dry-brush effect, which always helps to create some extra texture. This can be seen clearly in the tops of the buildings on the right.*

STAGE 2

Prepare a sandy colour mix of mainly yellow with a small amount of red and blue. Using your No. 12 brush, paint in the shadow areas of the buildings as shown. Then add some blue into your mix and drop this randomly into the stonework to create some texture. All the walls facing the light to the left can simply remain unpainted. You can see that I have used the very dark areas of the trees over the roofs and the right side of the campanile to create contrast.

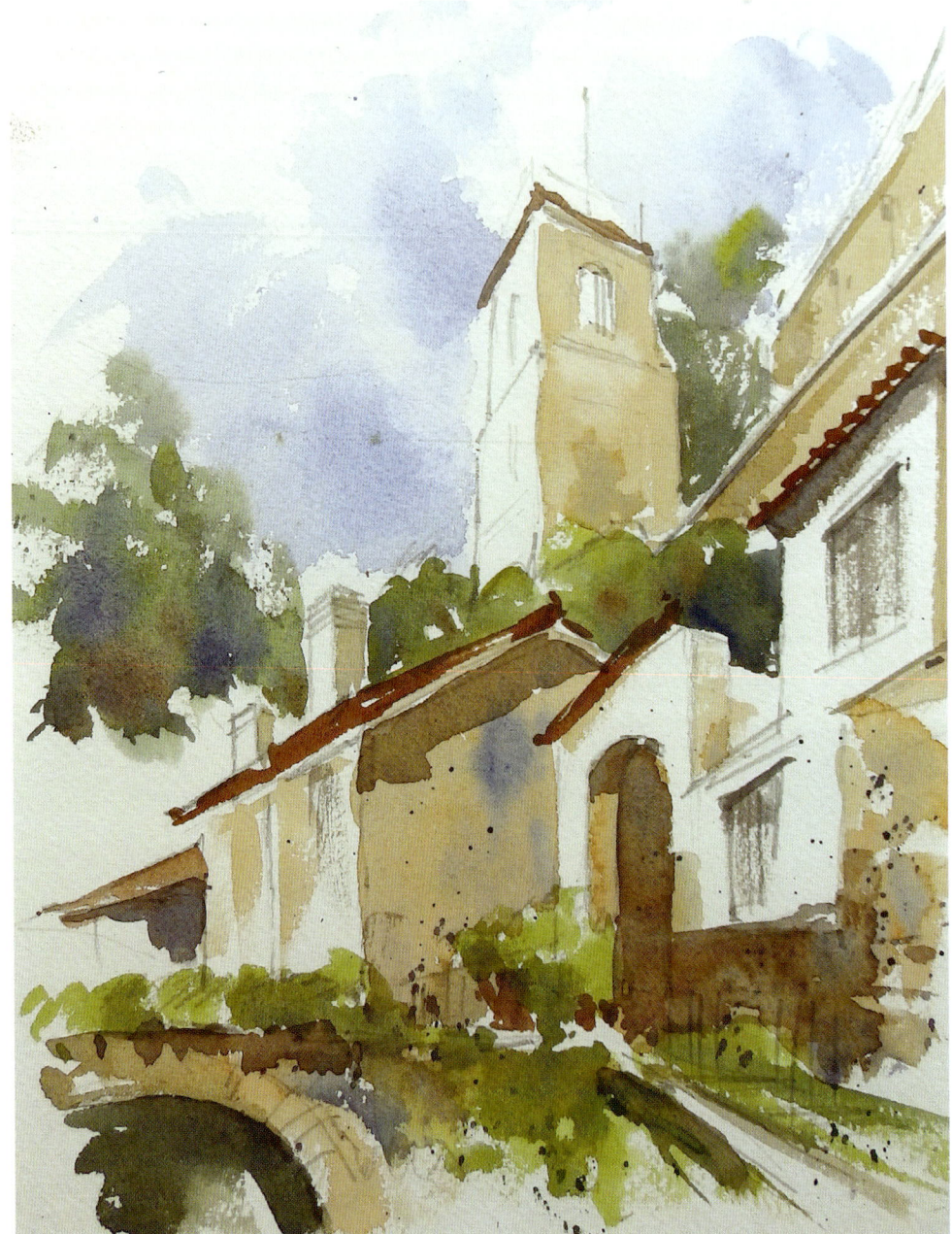

Tip

I sometimes find it more comfortable to stand up to paint. This can help me be more expressive, especially when painting in a loose way.

STAGE 3

Mix a brown wash using equal amounts of all three colours and use this to pick out the areas in deep shadow, especially through the arch and under the bridge. Then add a little extra red into this wash and paint the three roof angles across the centre. Use your green wash to very loosely paint in the foreground area around the bridge. To create the illusion of curtains in the foreground windows, use your brown and lightly drag your No. 12 brush across the surface of the paper, again creating a dry-brush effect.

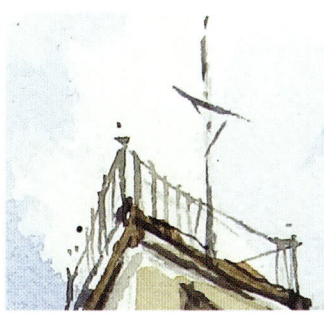

ABOVE *When painting in details such as railings and ironwork, I always leave gaps or even omit whole sections. This will help the painting to have a more artistic, as opposed to photographic, feel.*

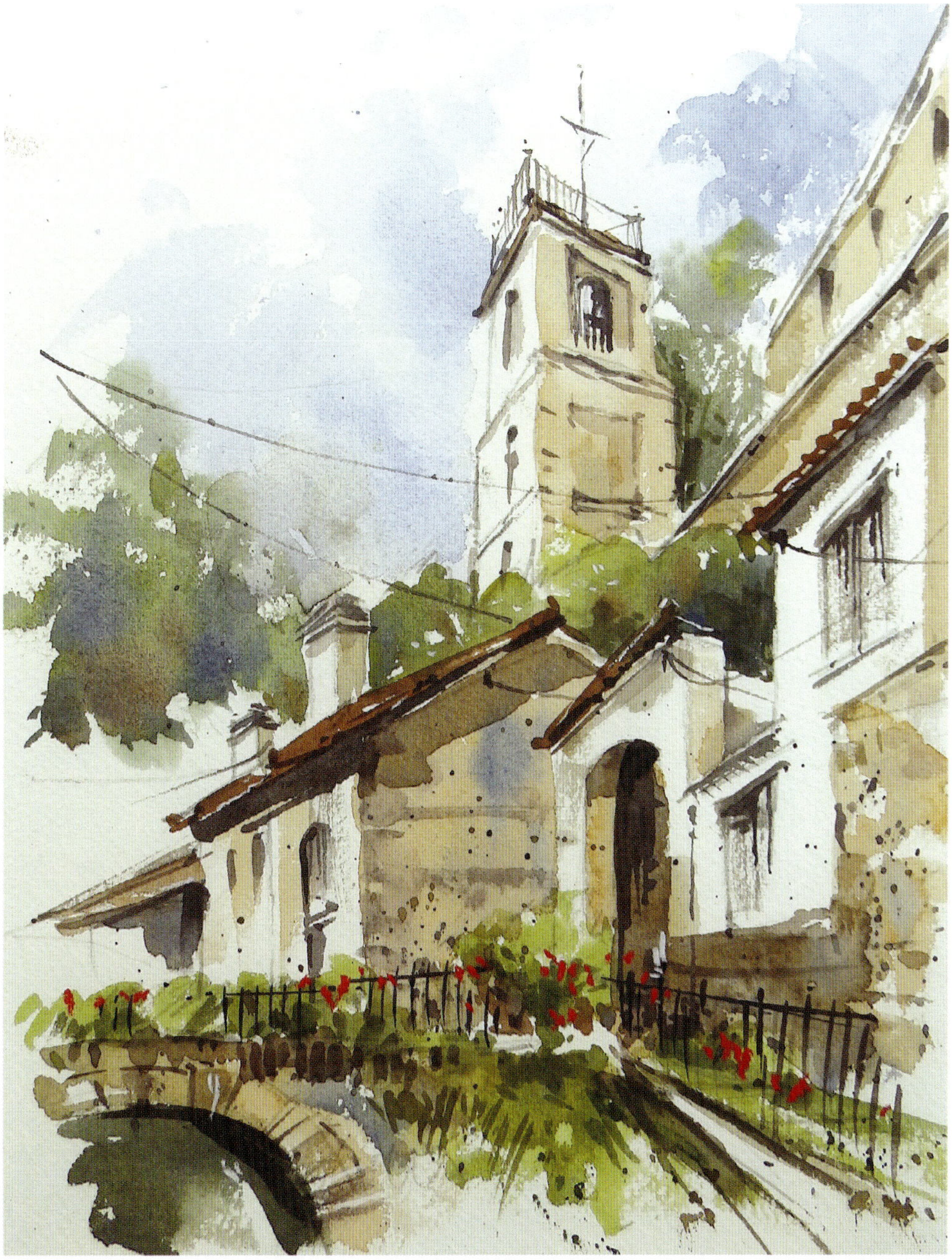

STAGE 4

Now it's time to add in the detail. Mix two washes, one brown as before and one made much darker by adding some more blue. Start by splattering with your No. 12 brush some of the lighter brown into the foreground walls and pick out details around the archway and the tower. Now use your No. 6 brush and, with the darker brown, paint in all the fine details in the tower, the wires and the railings in the foreground. When adding details such as cables and wires, paint in one swift stroke. Don't worry if the paint breaks up as it travels across the surface of the paper as this helps it to look less contrived and more naturalistic.

Now it's time for a well-earned limoncello!

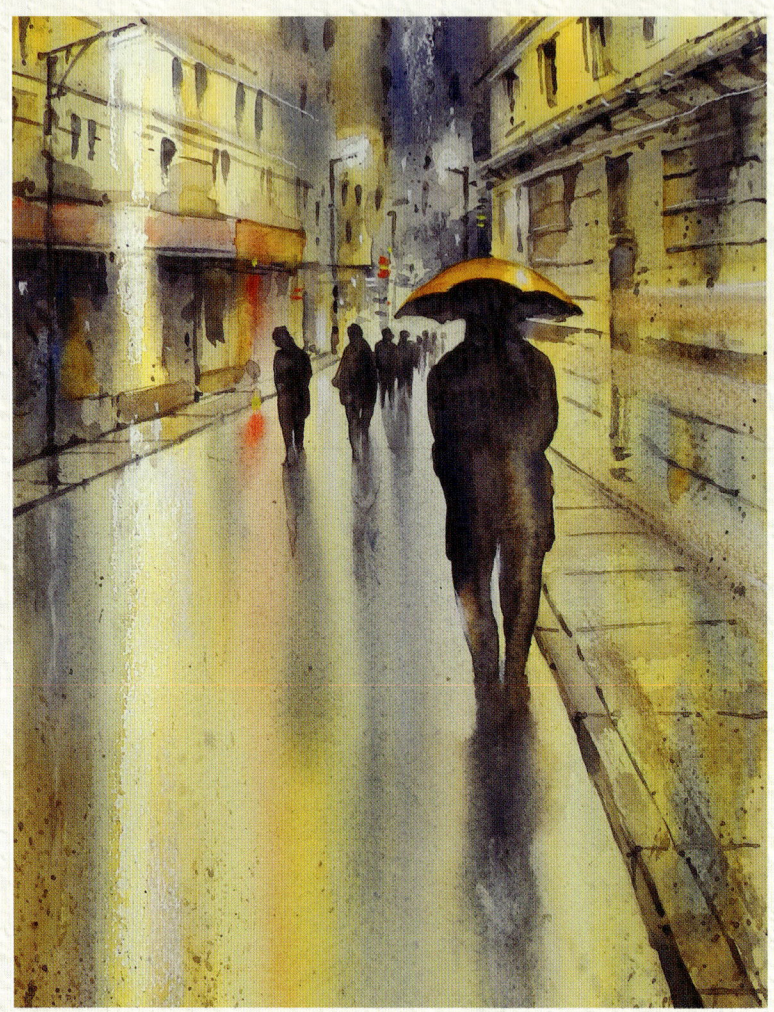

Figures

Figures can bring character and scale to your landscapes. Here we will explore ways to simplify the human form so that it doesn't become the main focal point.

COLOURS NEEDED

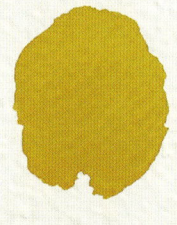

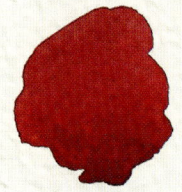

Cadmium Yellow   Cobalt Blue   Alizarin Crimson   Payne's Grey

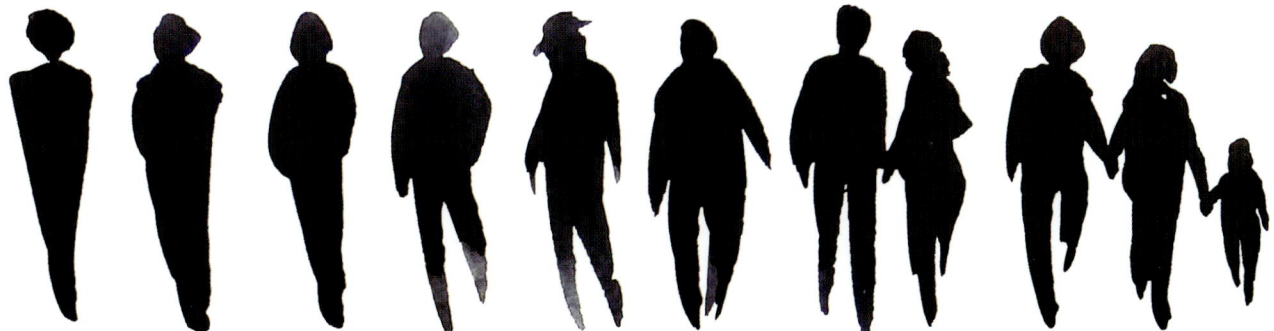

Closer figures

As we paint figures closer to us we need to think about adding more detail and colour. Start by mixing a warm yellow, made up of 70% yellow, 20% red and 10% blue, and paint a simple shape to represent the couple as shown (right). While this is still wet, drop your own chosen colours into the torso and leg areas, trying to avoid the heads.

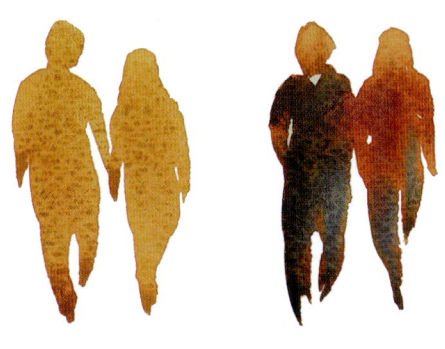

Before you embark on the main project, which is a wet street scene featuring a simple rendition of figures, try the following quick exercises to get used to this way of approaching figure painting.

Stationary figures

Using Payne's Grey, paint a line of figures as shown (top), starting with a simple blob for the head and a carrot shape for the body. As you paint the next figure, add a little more form and shape each time but try to complete the task with a minimum of brushstrokes. I often find that beginners tend to paint heads too big, so always consider proportion. A head will usually fit seven to eight times into the height of the body. As you can see, I don't include any feet as they add unnecessary detail.

Moving figures

With these figures (bottom right) I have tried to get a sense of movement, achieved by using the dry-brush technique on the ends of the arms and legs. Use the paint a little more thickly to help you achieve this.

Adding detail

Carry out this exercise (right) in the same way as above (I have added a child), but this time allow the figures to dry totally. Then, to give your group a sense of form, paint some shadows to the right-hand side using darker versions of the same colours. I have also painted in a pale grey background, making sure that I have left a white edge around the left-hand side of all three figures to give the impression of the sun shining on the group. Finally, paint a shadow on the ground, making sure it touches the bottom of their legs.

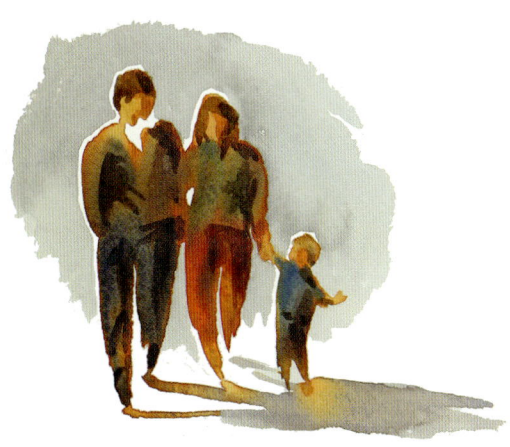

Tip

The human form is highly complex to paint and I recommend you attend a life drawing class if you want to make it your main subject.

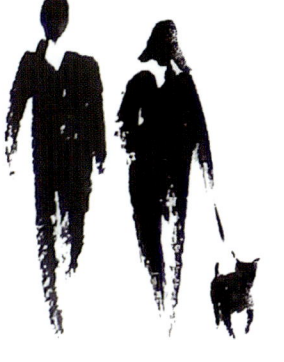

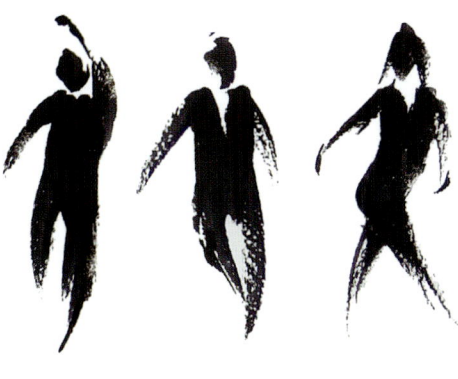

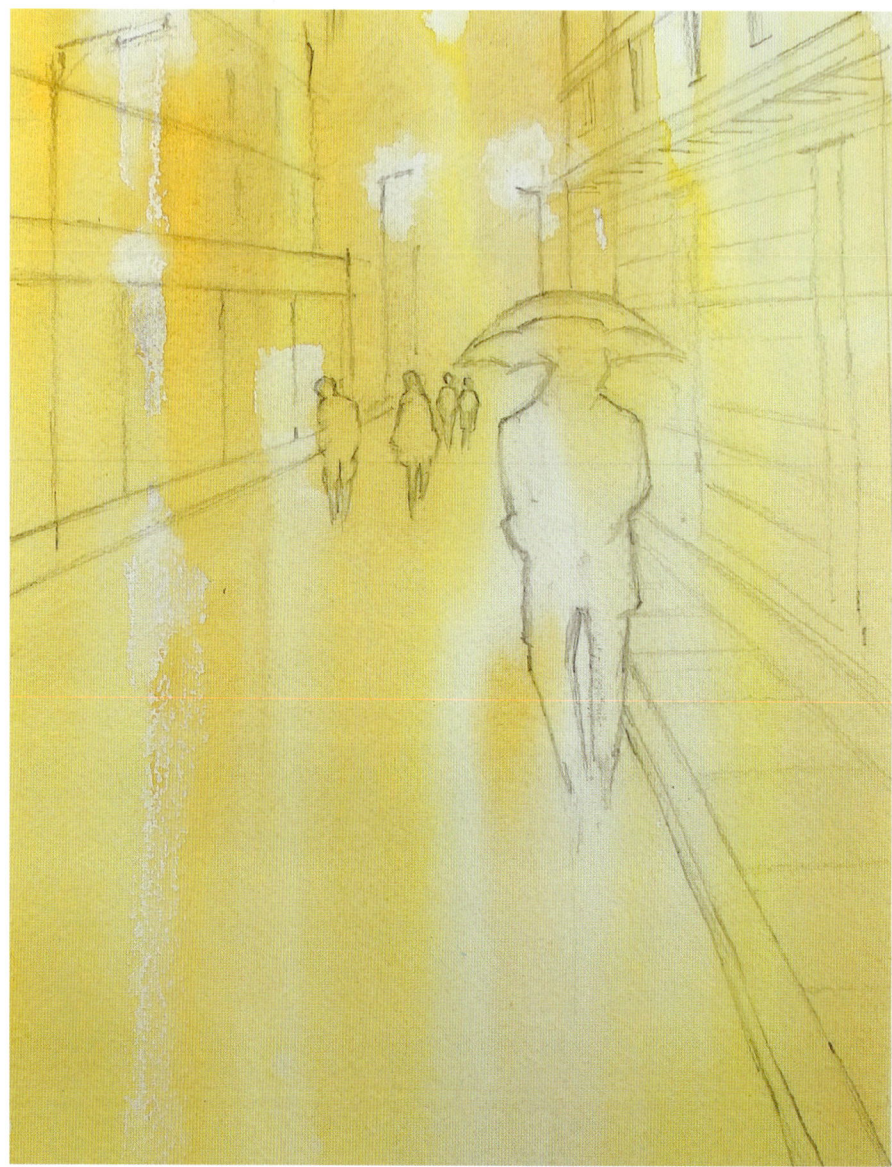

Tip

If your wash is not totally dry when you move on to stage 2, you will pull off some of the colour with your brush when you re-wet your paper.

STAGE 1

Roughly sketch out the shapes of the figures and the buildings, making sure that you get the correct perspective on the road and the shops. Wet the whole surface of the paper with clean water and allow it to soak in for a few moments. Mix a large wash of 90% yellow and 10% red and paint this in streaks over the entire surface. Tilt your board to about 45 degrees and let the colour run down. With your No. 12 brush, lift out a few areas around the street lights to create a glow effect. It is vitally important that your sheet is completely dry before you attempt stage 2.

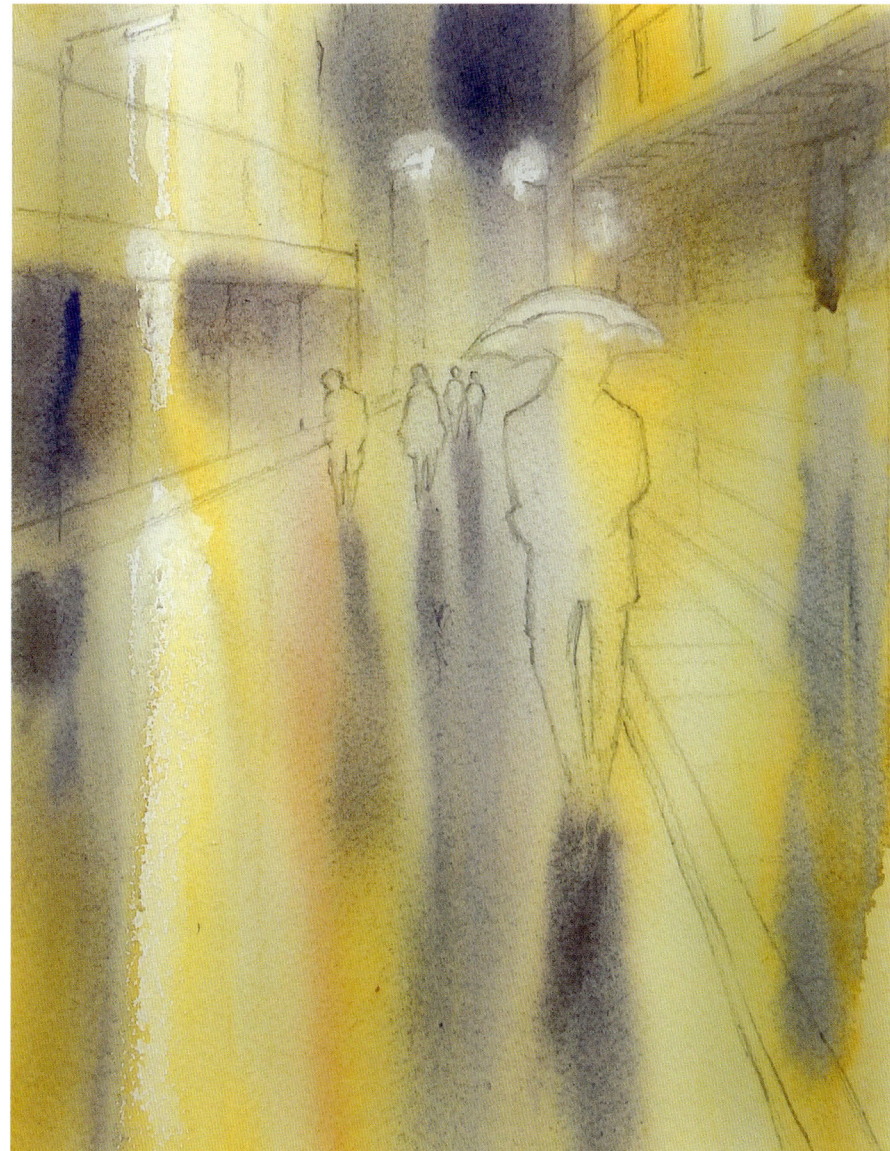

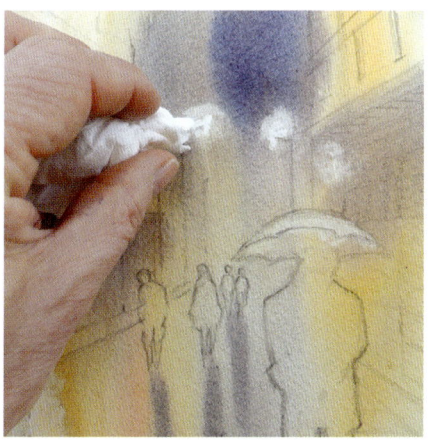

ABOVE *Before the paint has the chance to dry, use a tissue to lift out the highlights around the street lights.*

STAGE 2

Mix up various tones of orange, grey and blue. I will leave you to mix your own but keep them fairly muted. Re-wet the entire sheet again with clean water (again, making sure it's dry first). Let the water soak into the paper for a few moments then drop large blobs of grey into the middle distance, the shops and the reflections under the figures. Use some of the other colours you have mixed and drop them in randomly across the sheet. Now tilt your board almost vertically to allow the paint to run down the page. Lift out the highlights (see inset) and then take your No. 12 brush and lift out the colour on the top side of the umbrella.

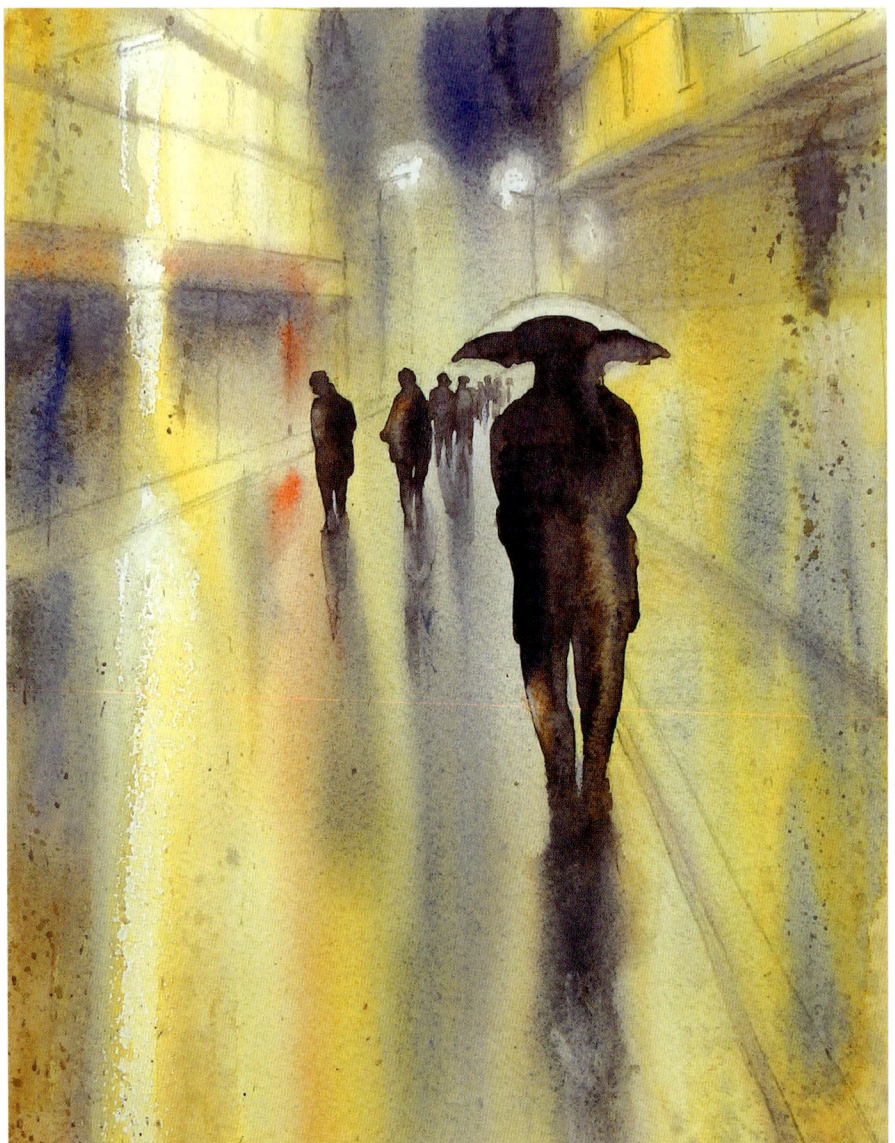

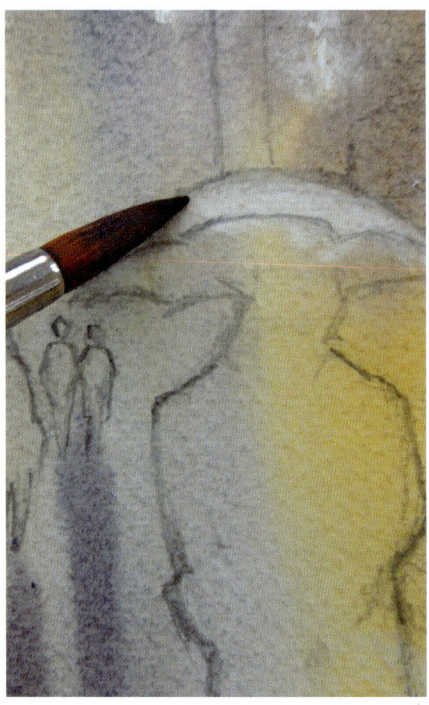

STAGE 3

Make a very dark mix of grey with all three colours but using more blue and then add a touch of Payne's Grey to strengthen it. Paint in the silhouettes, making sure that the ones in the distance are slightly lighter to give a sense of depth. While the main figure is still wet, use your damp brush to pull out a little paint to create a touch of contrast. Then use the same colour and add a few random splats on the walls of the building. Also, use a little diluted red to put some details in the shop fascias and the reflected shop sign. Allow to dry.

ABOVE *With a damp brush, lift out the colour in the space where the umbrella is to be painted. This will ensure that when the orange is applied it will be brighter because it is painted on a lighter background.*

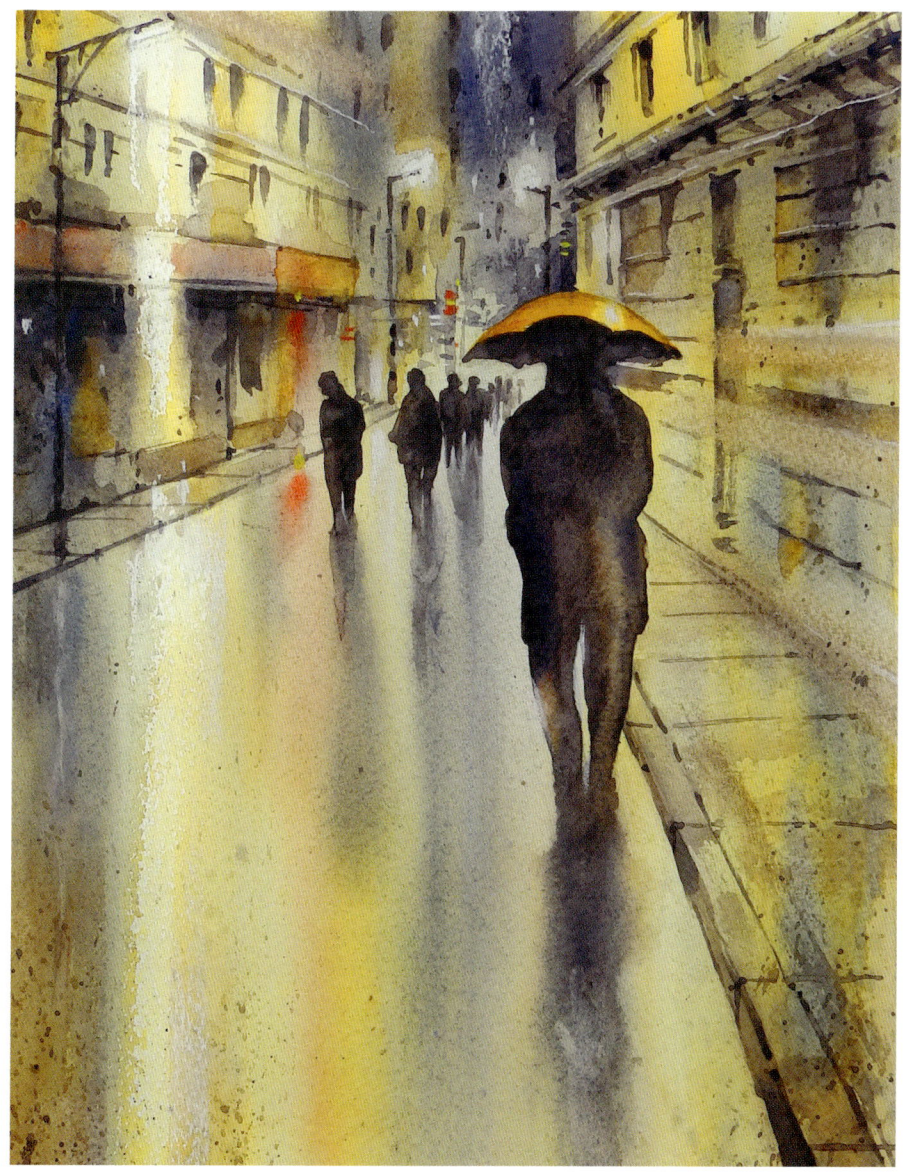

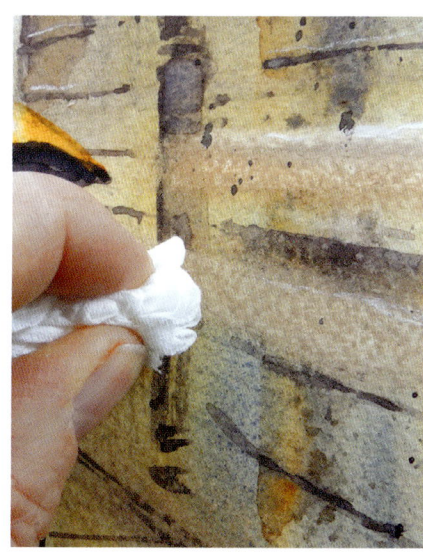

ABOVE *Once your painting is completely dry, create a sense of texture and movement by dragging a damp tissue along the edge of the buildings on the right.*

STAGE 4

The final stage is all about adding the detail, but be very careful that you don't overwork it. Leave your viewers something to interpret for themselves: it will always make your paintings more interesting. With your No. 6 brush and some Payne's Grey, paint in some simple shapes for the street lights and lines in the pavement and buildings, leaving small gaps in between your brushstrokes. When it comes to painting the windows, try to do this with one brushstroke and avoid the temptation to square them up. Always try to make your brushstrokes look spontaneous and fluent rather than laboured.

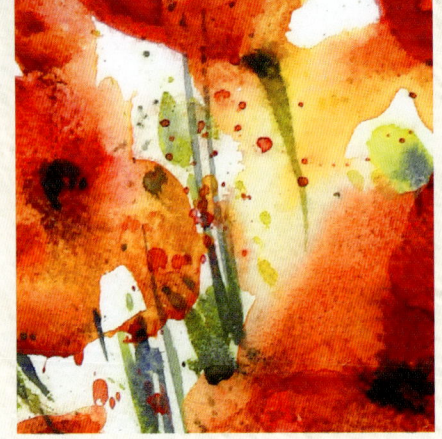

FOCUS ON
Special Effects

By adding ingredients to your watercolour painting and working with unconventional tools you will be able to create some surprising and dramatic effects. It still amuses me to hear my students say, 'Would you pass the salt, please?'

Splattering effects

The splattering technique is a great way of creating random texture.

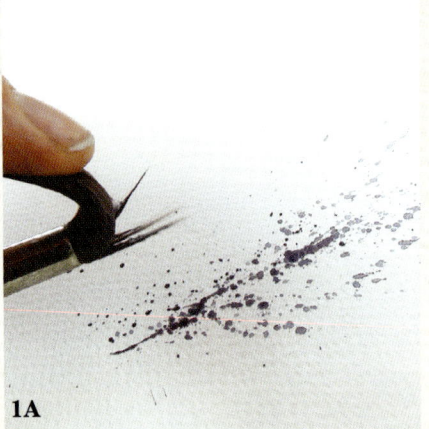

1A

1A Load up a No. 12 brush with colour and hold it horizontally about 1in (25mm) above the surface of the page. Use the forefinger of your other hand to pull back the bristles. Slowly release the bristles, allowing the paint to splatter across the page.

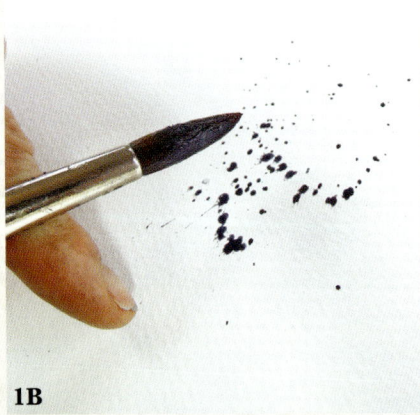

1B

1B This effect can be used for creating a larger dot texture and is ideal for paths and wall textures. Fill a No. 12 brush with paint and this time rest your hand on the surface of the paper with your forefinger extended. With the brush in your other hand, knock it against the extended finger to create a dapple effect.

Using salt

Ordinary table salt can create fantastic effects, especially when painting flowers.

TECHNIQUE 1

2A Mix up a watery purple and various shades of green using yellow and blue. Using a No. 12 brush, paint a rectangle of clean water and let it soak in. Drop colours onto the paper and let them merge and blend. While still wet, using your finger and thumb, sprinkle some salt evenly into a few areas of wash. The salt will begin to absorb the moisture, creating a wonderful feathery texture. Allow to dry.

2B Mix up some more purple and paint in a few blob-like shapes to suggest flower heads, making sure the wash remains transparent. Mix up some more green, but this time darken it slightly by adding a touch of red. Loosely paint in some random strokes to suggest leaves and stems, then splatter in the same colour to create a texture. Finally, with a little bit of yellow gouache or soft pastel, dab in the centres of the flowers.

Tip
Adding salt to your wash slows down the drying process. If there are salt granules left once your wash has dried, brush off with your fingers.

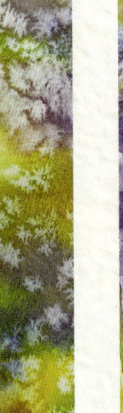

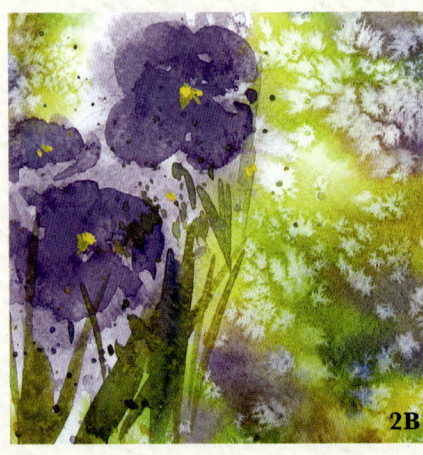

2A

2B

TECHNIQUE 2

This is another technique using salt to create some fantastic stone textures.

3A Draw out a simple dry-stone wall in pencil.

3B Mix up a wash of brown using all three primary colours and quickly paint in the wall. Add some more blue to the mix and, while this is still wet, drop this colour into the wash and let it soak in for a few moments. While this is still wet, using your forefinger and thumb, sprinkle some salt evenly into a few areas of the wash.

3C Because your colours were mixed from the three primaries, the addition of salt causes them to separate, creating a granulated texture. This gives a very realistic stone effect.

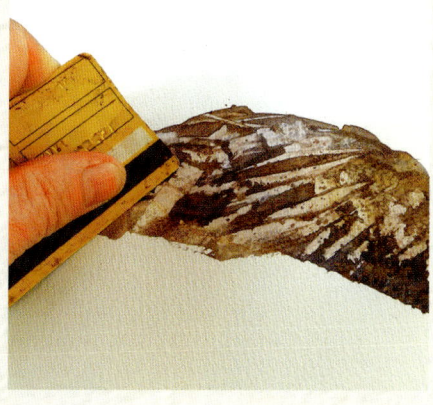

Plastic credit card

This technique (above) is great for creating rock and cliff textures. Paint a small wash in the shape of a rock and let it soak into the paper for a few moments. With an old credit card, push the paint across the surface in different directions to give interesting edges and texture as it scores into the paper.

Tip

Special effects can greatly enhance your painting, but don't overdo them or they'll dominate your work.

Plastic wrap

Out of all the special effects, this is probably the most spectacular, perfect for rock and wall textures (below), but can also be the most hit and miss. Mix a variety of colours together and paint a fairly large blob on your paper. While this is still wet, screw up a ball of plastic wrap and let it unravel a little before placing it over the entire painted area. Immediately place a heavy book on top and leave for at least five minutes. Slowly lift off the book and plastic wrap to reveal your work of art.

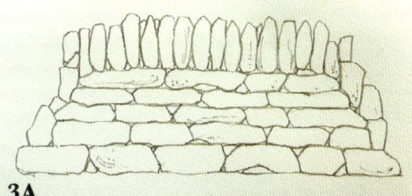

3A

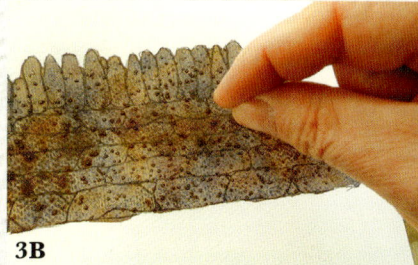

3B

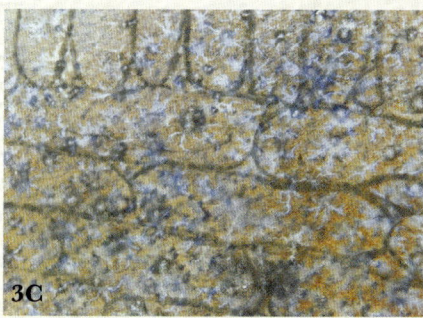

3C

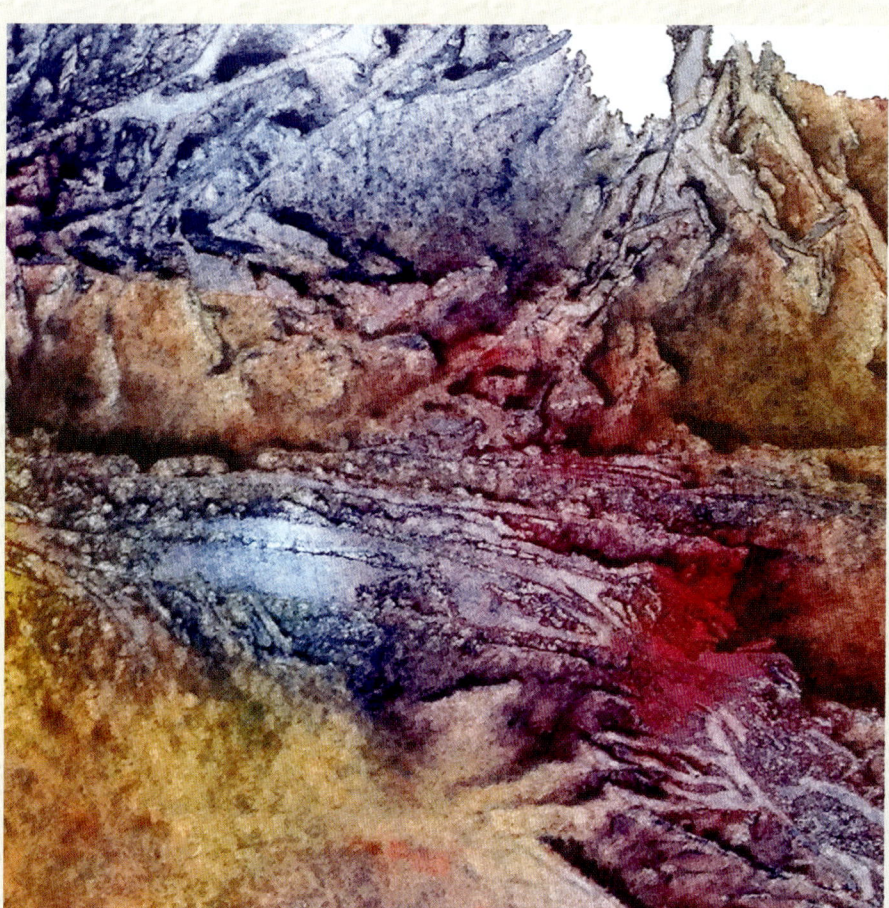

ACRYLICS

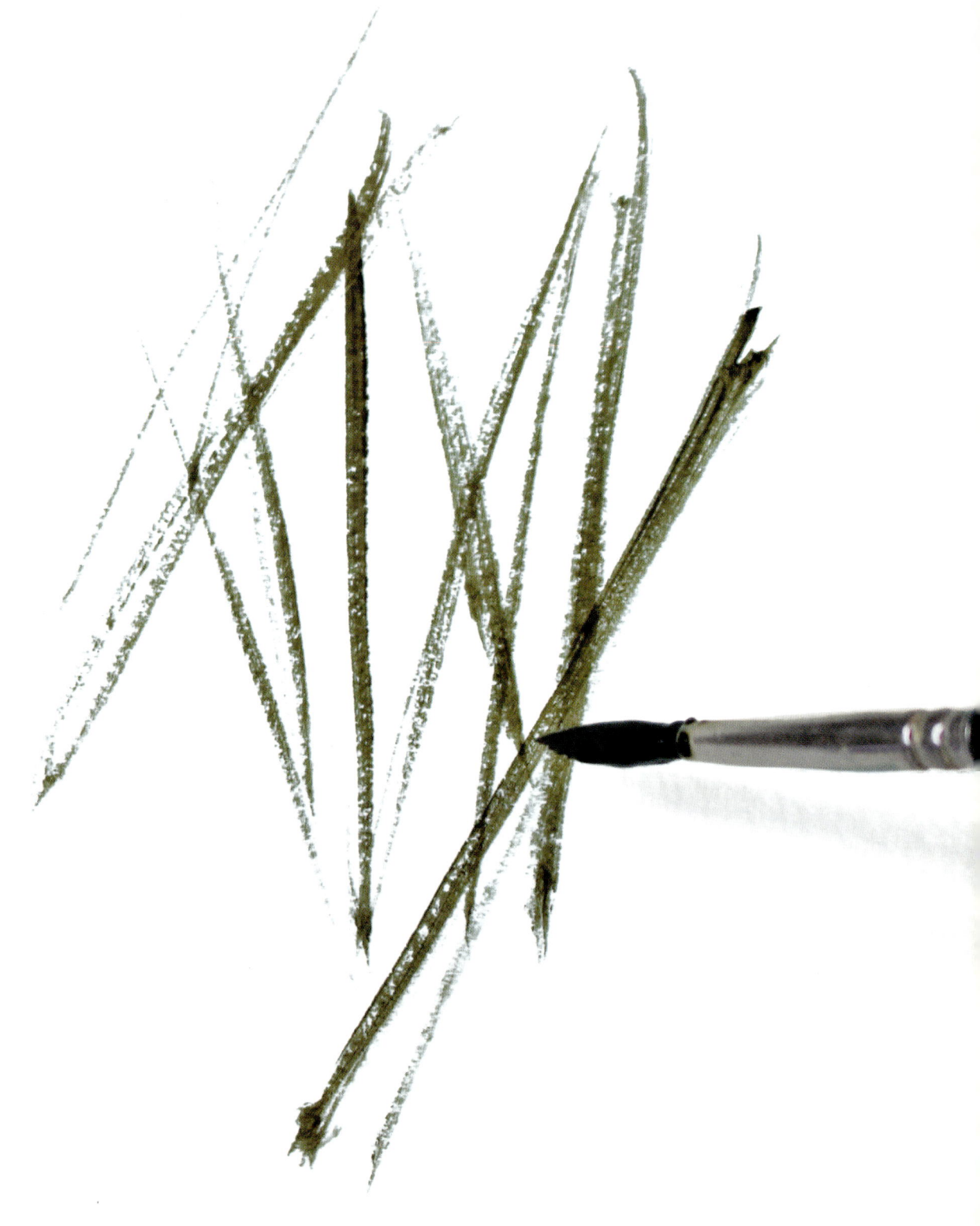

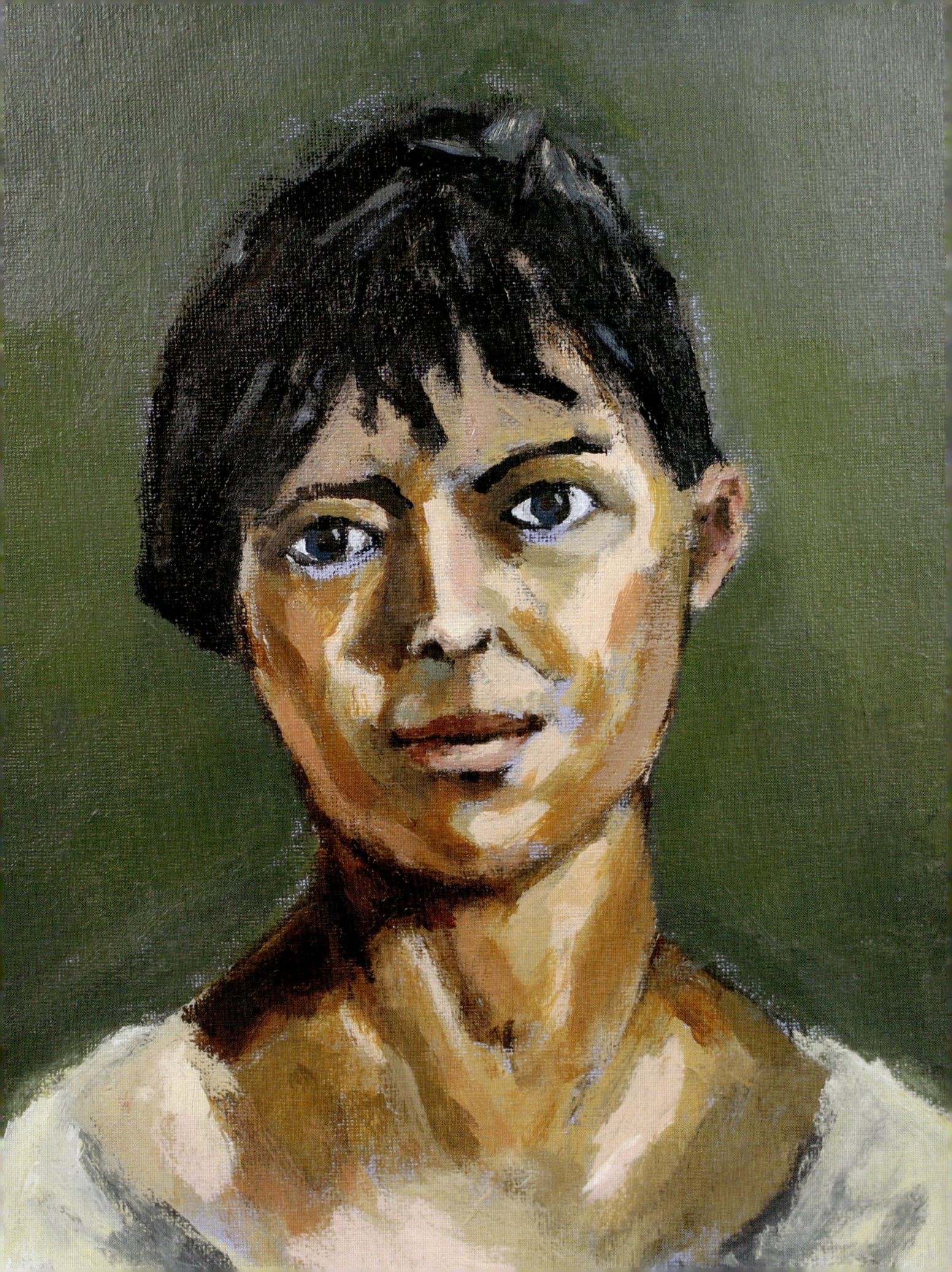

Introduction

Acrylics can be a very satisfying and uplifting medium as the colours are so vibrant and fresh. You could say that acrylics bridge the gap between oils and watercolour as they exhibit characteristics of both these mediums. They are simple to use and have the added benefits of being odourless and easy to clean.

Acrylics are water-soluble and extremely versatile. They can be used to stain the canvas or, by using heavy body acrylics or gel mediums, they can be put down in very thick layers of paint. When used straight from the tube, the marks you make seem more like drawing than painting. Watercolour effects are easily achievable since water is the base for the pigment.

I will show you how to paint effectively with acrylics, but the main aim is to keep things simple. A lot can be achieved through the interpretation of a scene, figure or object by getting into the *spirit* of what you see in front of you rather than trying to copy it or adopting a false idea of what a painting should look like.

For the purposes of this book, I will demonstrate techniques based on photographic reference and sketches from life. However, the imagination is a powerful ally, so it is perfectly acceptable to edit your painting to remove or add features that might improve your composition. You can even work entirely from your imagination.

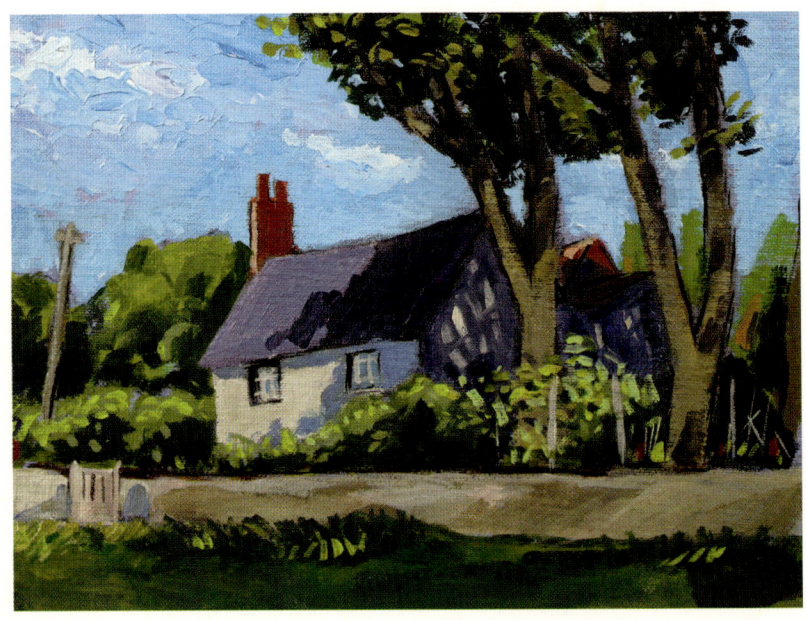

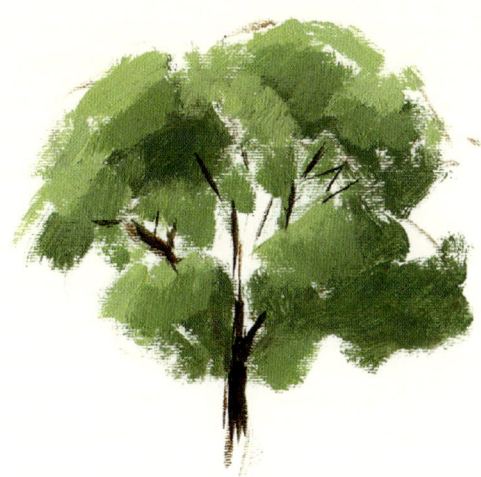

In the demonstrations, I only want to show what is achievable for the beginner: I don't want to show virtuoso performances that are not relevant to the student. But there are some basics that have to be observed.

Drawing skills, while not essential in every painting, do tend to convince the viewer that the artist has understood what he or she has seen. Also, there are acknowledged steps that can be said to have a certain artistic pedigree. You may have heard of underpainting, blocking in, complementary colours and so on. All these techniques are tools to help you to express what you have in mind.

For this book, I have made the creation of a picture fit into stages. This approach is useful as it shows the thought processes of the artist. Yet a lot goes on that can't be shoehorned into stages. Some artists paint from painstaking preparatory drawings and then go back and re-paint whole passages, while Caravaggio, Van Gogh and Velázquez, for instance, went straight into a painting with little or no preparation.

I begin with a series of techniques that I would advise you to practise before embarking on the projects. The six projects are exercises that demonstrate the versatility of acrylics and each study is only intended as an inspiration for the beginner. I suggest that you work on them in sequence, taking your time to develop and improve your skills. I hope that you take pleasure in your first steps with acrylics and are proud of your achievements.

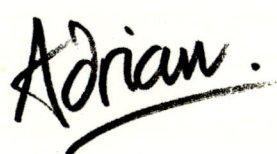

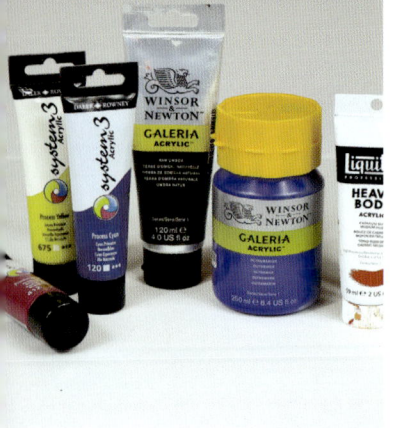

Materials and Equipment

On entering an art shop you may be both impressed and slightly intimidated by the sheer volume and variety of materials and equipment before you. This section lists the basic items you need to start with: paint, something to paint on, something to paint with, and a few other essentials.

Paint

Acrylic paint was developed in the 1950s and has been popular ever since. It can be bought in ranges of various qualities but you can reduce all of them down to two basic types: 'student' and 'professional'. The student paints are usually cheaper than the professional ones, and a good brand of student paint is perfectly adequate for the beginner.

For the paintings in this chapter I have used Liquitex heavy body paint but mainly Winsor & Newton's Galeria paint. For the primaries in the colour feature (see page 74) I used System 3 Acrylic from Daler-Rowney.

COLOURS

How do you decide which colours to choose? Well, you might be familiar with the term 'limited palette'. This means that instead of using the vast range of pre-mixed colours on the market, you limit your colours to just a few essentials that can produce a relatively broad range when mixed together. All the paintings in this chapter were created from a limited palette of:

- Ultramarine Blue
- Winsor Blue
- Cadmium Yellow
- Yellow Ochre
- Burnt Sienna
- Raw Umber
- Cadmium Red
- Mars Black
- Titanium White

What to paint on

The most common surfaces associated with acrylic painting are stretched canvas, canvas boards, canvas-textured paper, cardboard and wood. You can also paint on glass and concrete and many other surfaces, but here we will stick with the most conventional surfaces.

STRETCHED CANVAS

Nowadays, you can buy ready-primed stretched canvas from scores of outlets. These are covered with gesso, a hard compound of plaster of Paris in glue, which acts as a stable surface on which to paint. You can buy gesso and apply more layers of priming to your canvas, or prime less robust papers and card to make them tougher.

CANVAS BOARDS

These boards have the same surface as pre-stretched canvases except the canvas is glued on to a stiff backing.

CANVAS-TEXTURED PAPER

This is a specially made paper that comes in pads and in various sizes. It has a stippled surface and exhibits some of the qualities of canvas. It is not as stable as stretched canvas and tends to cockle and warp if there is extra water in your paint mix. Priming it with gesso can help prevent these problems.

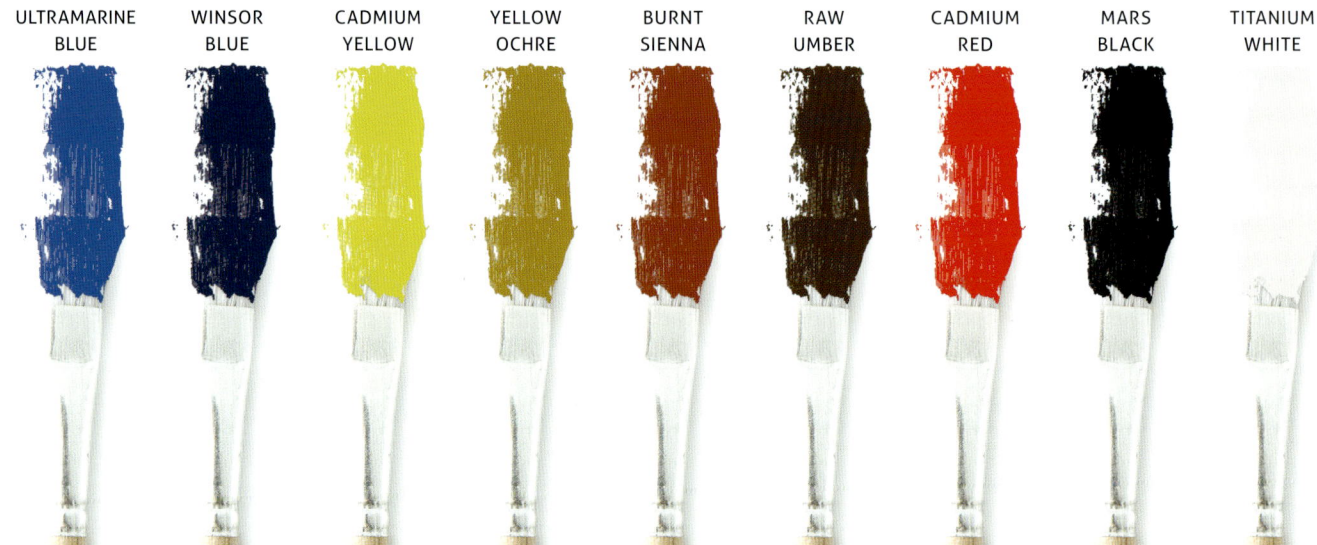

ULTRAMARINE BLUE   WINSOR BLUE   CADMIUM YELLOW   YELLOW OCHRE   BURNT SIENNA   RAW UMBER   CADMIUM RED   MARS BLACK   TITANIUM WHITE

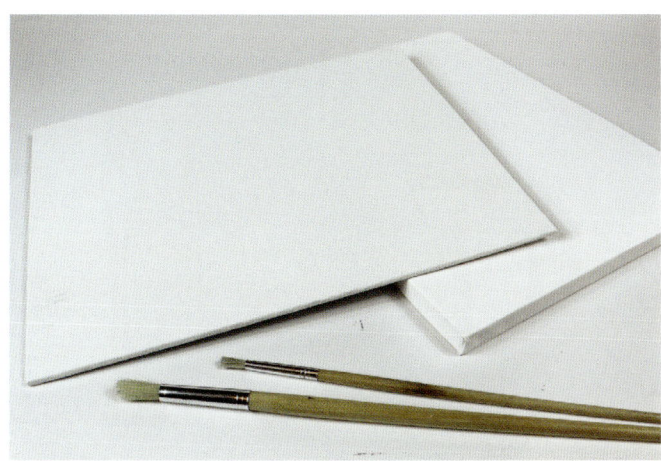

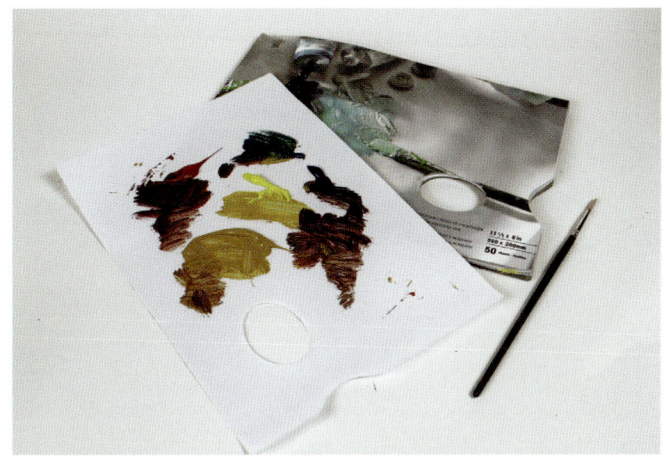

CARDBOARD

This sounds an unlikely material but the French artist Henri de Toulouse-Lautrec occasionally painted on cardboard. It is slightly absorbent but quite stable. The natural colour of cardboard makes a good 'ground' on which to start an acrylic painting.

WOOD

You can paint on all kinds of wood, from a piece of hardboard to a discarded cupboard door. There are also ready-prepared wooden panels available to buy, usually made from close-grained wood or fibreboard, primed with gesso. Softwoods such as pine aren't suitable because they tend to crack.

Painting mediums

Sometimes you may find your paint is drying too quickly and you need to keep it workable, or it may be that water alone is not allowing you to blend your colours effectively. In these instances an acrylic 'retarder' and an acrylic 'medium' will help.

An acrylic retarder works by slowing the drying time of your paint so it becomes more like oil paint. However, there is a danger that it may make the finished colour less opaque. An acrylic medium diluted the paint without diminishing its pigment intensity and allows paint to spread over the surface more effectively, creating good blends and glazes.

Mixing palettes

You can mix your paint on any smooth surface that has a light, neutral colour and is non-absorbent. Wooden palettes are not suitable because they tend to soak up water-based paint. Tear-off paper palettes are commonly used – these are disposable and create a minimum of mess. It is a good idea to moisten the surface a little before using them as this keeps the paint from drying too quickly.

Easels

Easels come in all shapes and sizes but they all do the same job of holding your work securely at a comfortable working height. Using an easel allows you to step back from your work to judge tones, colours and composition. The main types are: the studio easel, which is large and stable, the field easel, which is lighter and portable, and the desktop easel (right), which has no legs and sits on a work surface.

ABOVE *A tear-off palette makes a convenient, non-absorbent surface for mixing paint.*

ABOVE LEFT *Canvas board and stretched canvas.*

BELOW *Using an easel allows you to paint comfortably and to step back periodically to examine your work.*

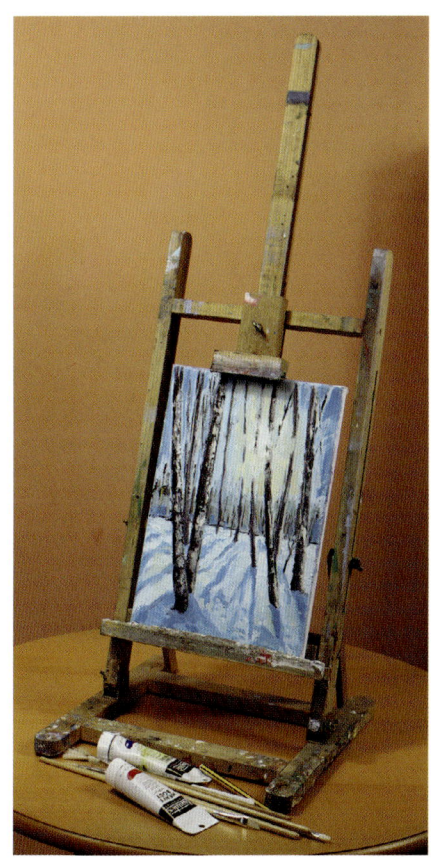

Something to paint with

For the projects in this chapter you will
need two main painting tools: the brush
and the knife. You can also use an old
plastic credit card to achieve some
interesting effects!

BRUSHES

There are two main types of brush:
synthetic and bristle. A synthetic, or
nylon, brush is very good for smooth
transitions of paint, while a bristle, or
hog-hair brush, leaves a more robust
and expressive mark.

These brushes can be round-headed
or flat. The rigger brush (**A**) has a thin,
sharp head and was originally used to
represent rigging on sailing ships. It's
great for putting in detail such as grass
and fine branches. The filbert brush (**B**)
is a hybrid: it's flat but with a rounded
tip that helps give a smooth stroke.

Synthetic brushes make different
marks to bristle brushes because of the
texture of the hair used for each. They
tend to leave smoother marks than the
bristle brush, as the hair at the tip is
generally finer and denser.

The strokes made in **1A** are typical
of a round-headed synthetic brush as
they leave slightly cone-shaped marks
that tail off as you lift the brush. If you
make the same sort of stroke with a
round bristle brush (**1B**) it leaves a much
more broken mark as the hair is coarser
and it tends to scrape the paint.

The rigger brush (**2A**) is normally
a synthetic brush and makes long,
wispy strokes. This effect cannot be
successfully achieved with the bristle
brush (**2B**) even if the head is long and
round, because the paint is soon broken
up when pressure is applied.

The flat brush exhibits different
qualities depending on whether you
use a synthetic or bristle version.

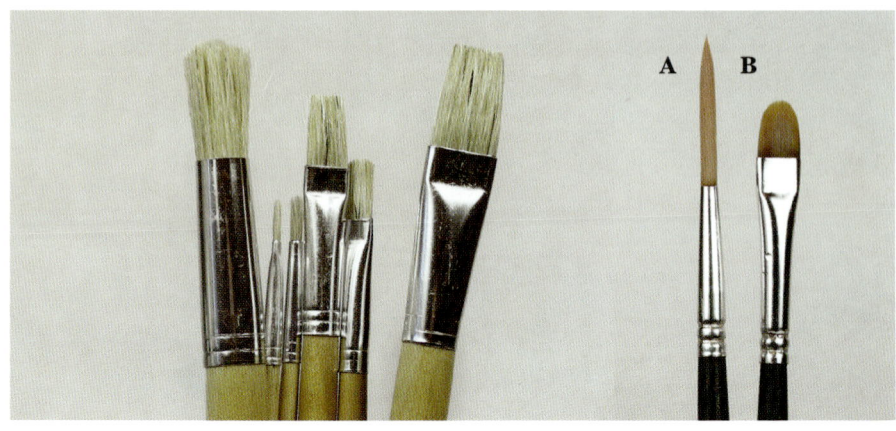

ABOVE *Bristle brushes and synthetic
brushes in different sizes.*

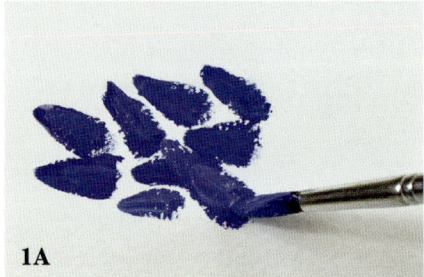

1A

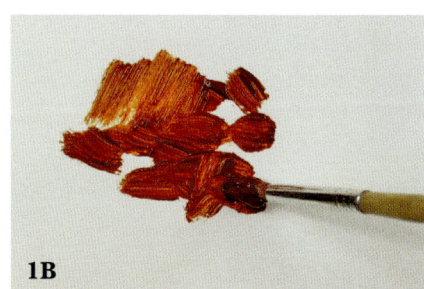

1B

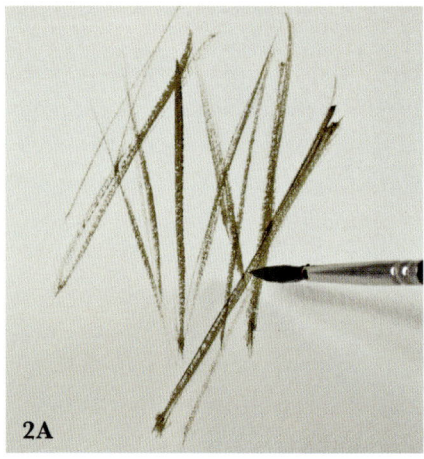

2A

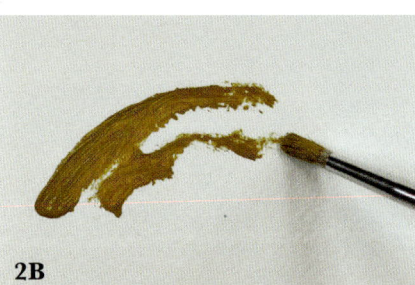

2B

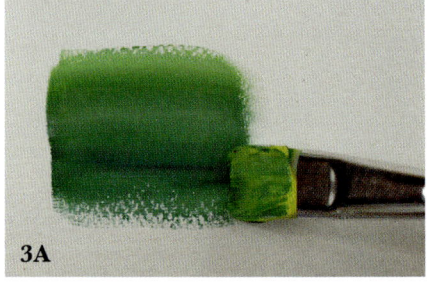

3A

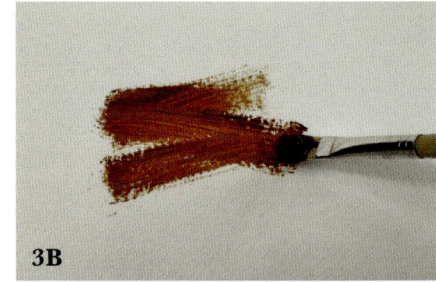

3B

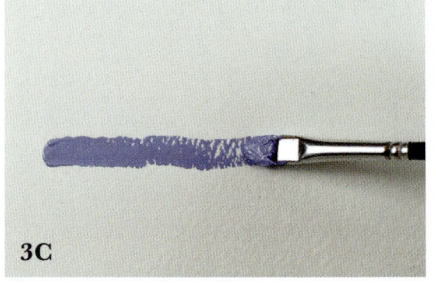

3C

If you make a mark with a flat synthetic brush (**3A**) the mark is smoother and more even than a bristle brush (**3B**). The flat bristle brush has lots of expressive qualities, but if you need smooth transitions the synthetic brush should be used. The filbert shape (**3C**) can be classed as a flat brush, but the curved head makes a more even stroke.

KNIVES

There are two types of knives used in painting: palette knives and painting knives. Strictly speaking, a palette knife is used only for mixing paint and a painting knife is used to apply paint instead of a brush. But depending on what type of mark you want to make, you can use either of these tools. The advantage of using a knife is that after you have applied paint, you can scrape it off and quickly reapply it to get the desired effect.

A painting knife has sharp angles, while a palette knife is more rounded. Both of these tools consist of a thin steel blade with a handle, or they can be made of plastic. Using a knife takes some getting used to, since it seems to have its own ideas about how much paint to put down! If you skid the knife flat on to a textured surface you get a bobbly, stippled effect. If you use the blade edge, you can create some very sharp lines.

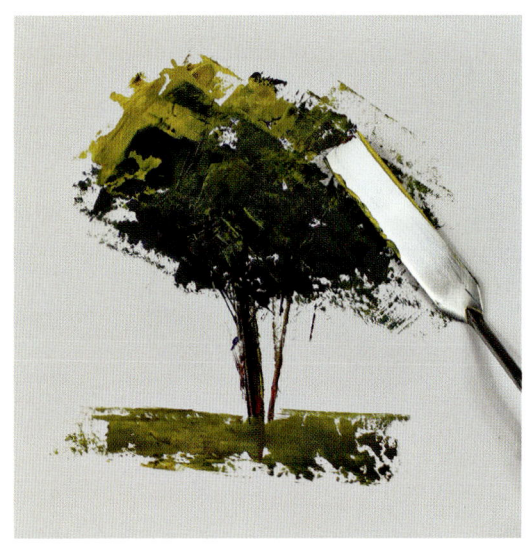

ABOVE *A painting knife is great for creating interesting layered effects.*

BELOW *Using a palette knife to mix paint.*

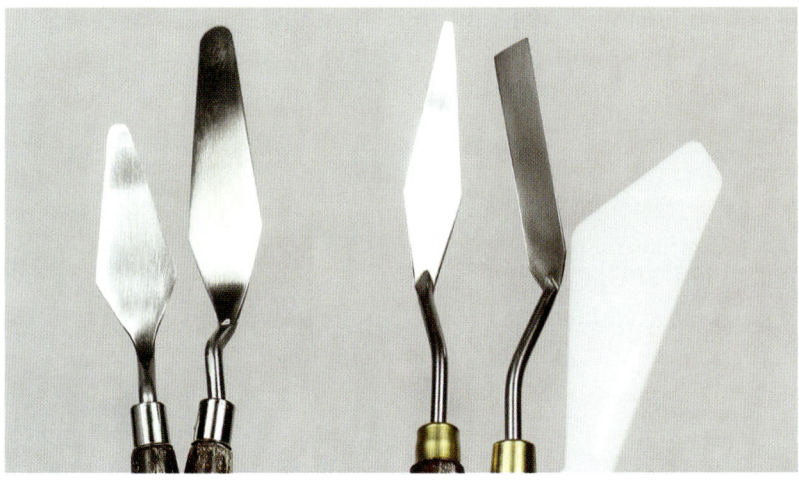

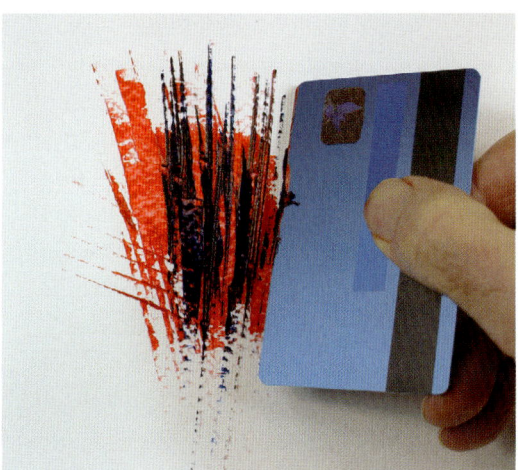

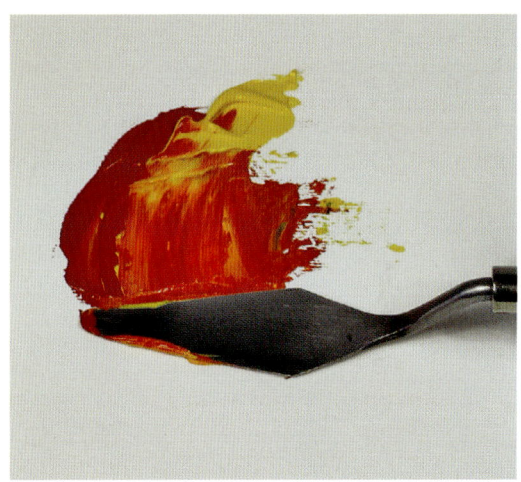

ABOVE *A selection of sharply angled steel painting knives, a steel palette knife and a plastic painting knife.*

RIGHT *Using a painting knife for textural effects.*

LEFT *Using a credit card to make lines.*

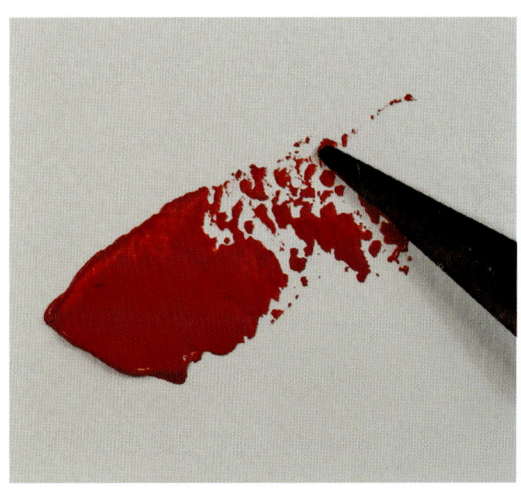

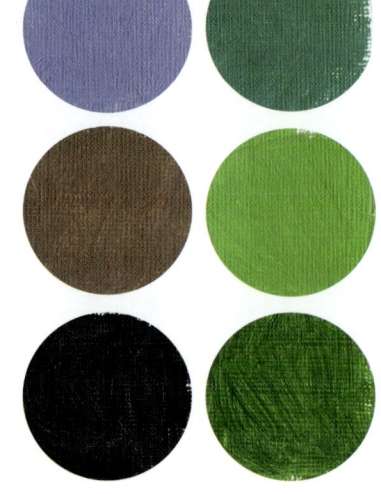

Colour Theory

Colour plays a vital role in the look and the mood of a painting, and if you know a little about colour theory it will help you to use your paint much more effectively. Here I describe how a colour wheel works, and how to harmonize colour so that you can make the most of your acrylics.

Most colours can be mixed by using a few crucial pigments. From just three primary colours – cyan, magenta and yellow – you can get a surprisingly large range of colours. The primaries are pure colours and are not made with any other pigment. The paints we buy usually have other colours mixed in with them; however, the colour-mixing charts shown here still work with most reds, greens and blues.

If you mix primaries together, they make secondary colours. Yellow and cyan mixed together make green, yellow and magenta make orange, and blue and magenta make purple.

If you mix a secondary with a primary you get a tertiary colour, but the primary and secondary colours must be beside each other on the colour wheel. For example, the tertiary colour orange is a mixture of 50% red and 50% magenta.

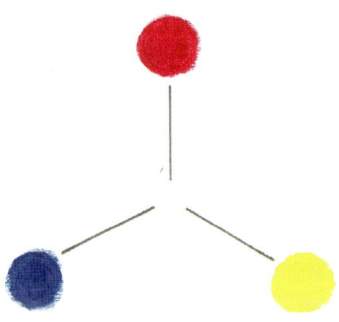

ABOVE *The primary colours: cyan, magenta and yellow.*

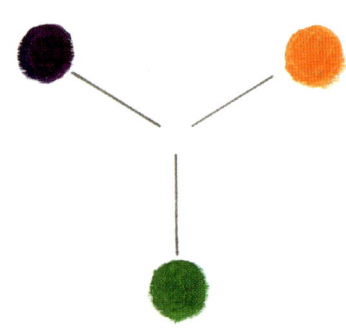

ABOVE *The secondary colours: purple, orange and green.*

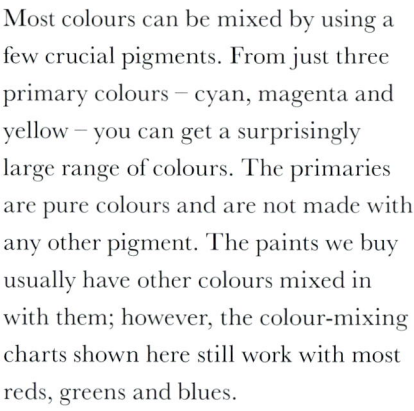

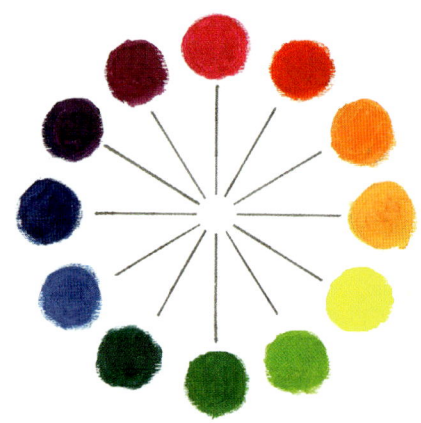

The illustration above shows what the whole range of primaries, secondaries and tertiaries looks like in the colour wheel. From this simple idea, you can expand the world of colour into contrasting colours, complementary colours, and warm and cool colours.

Complementary colours are two colours that, when combined, cancel each other out and produce a tone of grey. When placed next to each other, however, they create the strongest possible contrast for those two colours. Complementary colours can be found on opposite sides of the colour wheel.

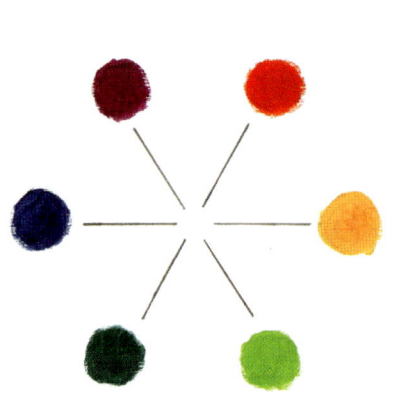

LEFT *The six tertiary colours are combinations of the primary and secondary colours.*

Harmonizing colour

A harmonious colour scheme is one that uses colours that are next to one another on the colour wheel. For example, yellow, yellow-green and green are harmonious colours, as are blue, blue-violet and violet. These colours look good together and are pleasing to the eye. However, adding a small amount of contrasting colour to the scheme can really enhance the final result.

In the charts below there are 40 colours that harmonize with one another, divided into cool and warm colours, made from just three colours and white. Here is the breakdown of the colours, should you wish to reproduce them in any of your paintings. The colours named as red, blue and yellow are Cadmium Red, Ultramarine Blue and Cadmium Yellow.

1. BLUE, RED, YELLOW AND WHITE
2. BLUE, YELLOW AND WHITE
3. BLUE AND WHITE
4. BLUE AND WHITE WITH A DASH OF YELLOW
5. BLUE, YELLOW AND WHITE WITH SOME RED
6. YELLOW, WHITE AND A LITTLE RED
7. BLUE, RED AND YELLOW WITH LESS WHITE THAN NO. 1
8. BLUE, RED, YELLOW AND WHITE, MIXED DARKER THAN NO. 7
9. BLUE, YELLOW AND WHITE
10. BLUE AND YELLOW, WITH LESS WHITE THAN NO. 9
11. BLUE AND WHITE WITH A SMALL AMOUNT OF RED
12. BLUE, YELLOW AND RED, AS NO. 11 BUT LESS WHITE
13. BLUE AND A LITTLE YELLOW
14. BLUE, A LITTLE YELLOW AND A TOUCH OF RED
15. AS NO. 14 BUT WITH MORE BLUE AND WHITE
16. BLUE AND WHITE, A TOUCH OF RED AND A HINT OF YELLOW
17. BLUE, YELLOW AND RED WITH A SMALL AMOUNT OF WHITE
18. BLUE AND RED BUT WITH MORE RED THAN BLUE
19. BLUE AND RED WITH AN EMPHASIS ON THE RED
20. BLUE AND RED WITH AN EMPHASIS ON THE BLUE

COOL COLOURS CHART

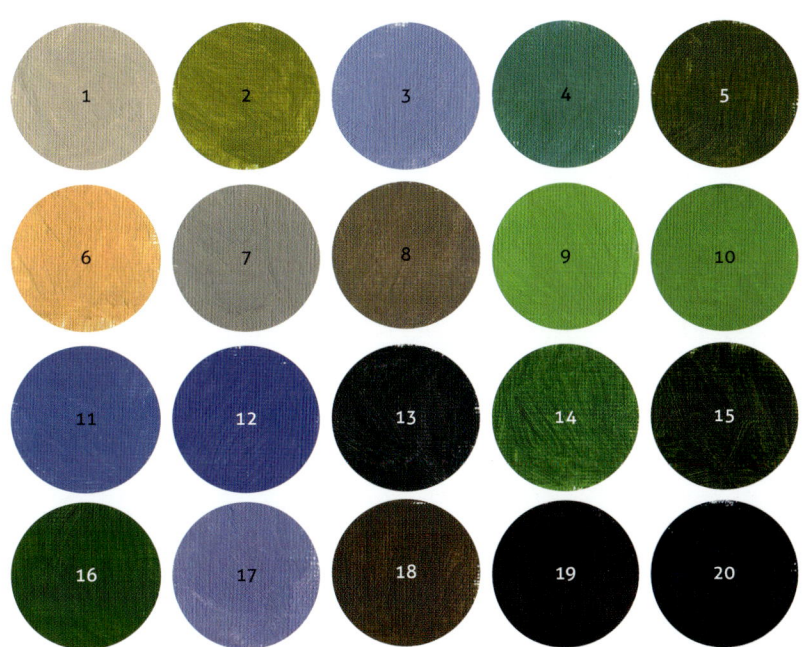

WARM COLOURS CHART

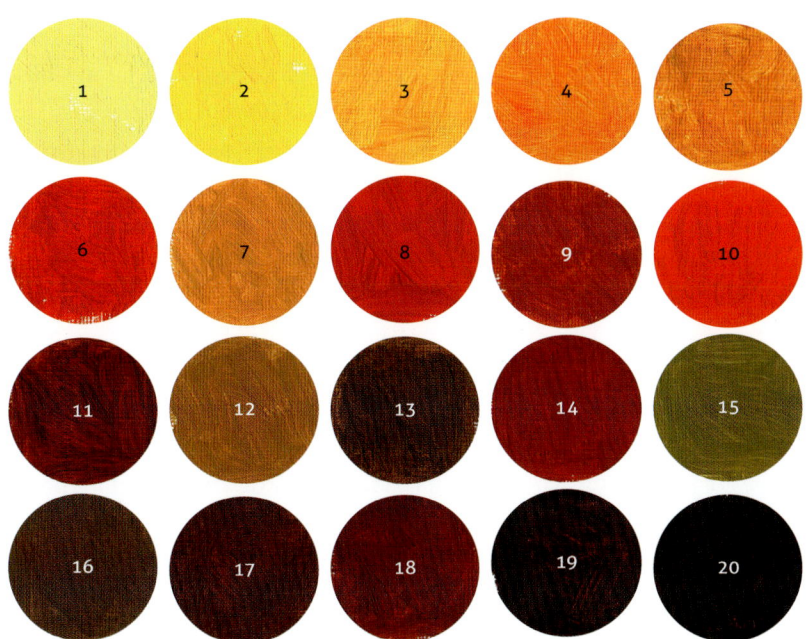

1. WHITE AND YELLOW
2. YELLOW AS IT COMES FROM THE TUBE
3. YELLOW AND A LITTLE RED
4. YELLOW AND A LITTLE MORE RED THAN NO. 3
5. YELLOW, RED AND A SMALL AMOUNT OF BLUE
6. YELLOW, A SMALL AMOUNT OF BLUE, AND RED
7. YELLOW, A DASH OF RED, BLUE AND WHITE
8. RED WITH A SMALL AMOUNT OF WHITE
9. YELLOW, RED, A LITTLE BLUE AND WHITE
10. RED AND YELLOW
11. RED, YELLOW AND BLUE
12. YELLOW, RED, BLUE AND SOME WHITE
13. YELLOW, A LITTLE BLUE AND MORE RED THAN NO. 12
14. YELLOW WITH MORE RED THAN NO. 6 AND A LITTLE BLUE
15. YELLOW, BLUE AND WHITE, WITH A LITTLE RED
16. MIX ALL THREE COLOURS TOGETHER IN EQUAL PARTS PLUS SOME WHITE
17. MIX ALL THREE COLOURS WITH MORE BLUE AND RED THEN ADD SOME WHITE
18. SAME AS NO. 17 BUT WITH MORE RED
19. MIX RED, BLUE AND YELLOW IN EQUAL PROPORTIONS AND ADD A SMALL AMOUNT OF WHITE
20. MIX ALL THREE COLOURS TOGETHER IN EQUAL PARTS

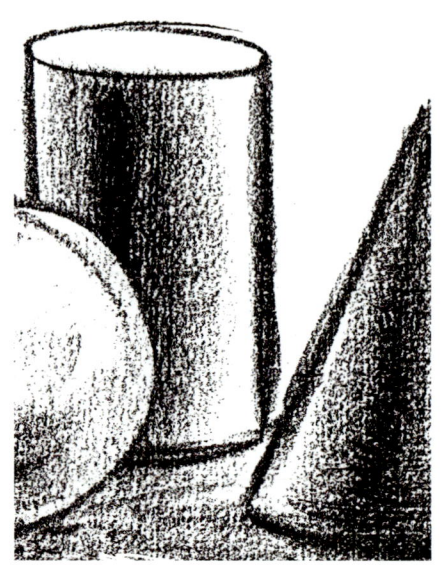

Drawing Techniques

Drawing is putting thoughts on to paper. It allows you time to think and it can resolve many problems before you start applying paint to the canvas. You do not need to be an expert at drawing, but it helps to familiarize yourself with some basic techniques and principles, and you'll find your drawing improves as your painting progresses. It is worth practising drawing with a brush as well as a pencil – underpainting, which is essentially drawing with a brush, will crop up several times.

Scribbling

Many people I have taught have been so concerned about making a mess that they miss the essential quality of drawing, and that is 'energy'. The energy in a drawing comes from your body, and the best way to channel it is to try to draw from your shoulder or, if that's not possible, use a loose forearm and wrist. Grab a sheet of paper and cover the whole area with lots of scribbles. To achieve expressive textures, charcoal, soft pencil and Conté crayon are all excellent media. Or why not try using a bristle brush with paint straight from the tube? You will find it is more like drawing than painting.

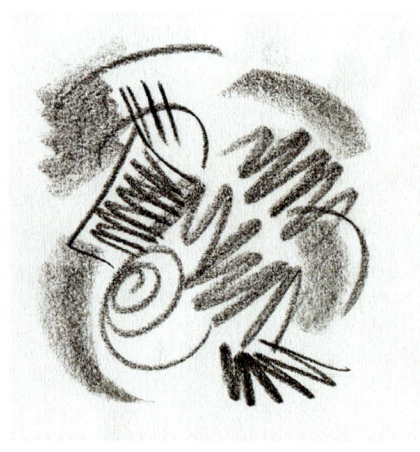

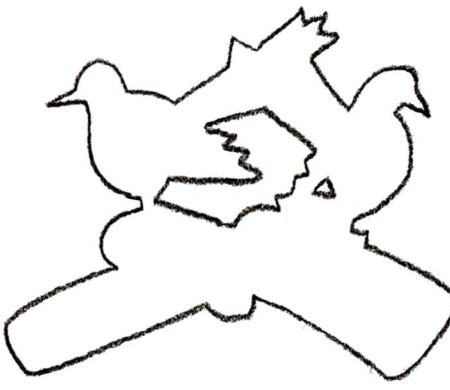

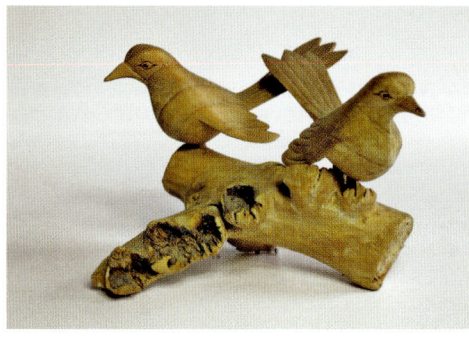

Contour drawing

This exercise will help train your eye and hand to work together. Start by looking at an object and specifically at its contours, such as the wooden birds above (right). Without taking your pencil off the paper or your eye off the object, begin to trace its outline on the paper, then pause. Have a look at your effort and continue the process until you have gone round the whole object in a single line (see above). No line should cross over another. After a number of attempts you will begin to see a marked improvement.

Perspective

In painting, perspective means how objects appear in relation to one another and is a device for how we depict reality. When talking about perspective you might come across the words 'eye level' and 'vanishing point'. Eye level is just another term for the horizon line, and vanishing point is the point at which the lines in linear perspective appear to converge at a single point (see diagrams, opposite, top). The magic of perspective is that all objects, from a skyscraper to a matchbox, obey the same rules. There is always an eye level and a vanishing point. More often than not, there are two!

Even a basic awareness of perspective is good enough to give your drawings and paintings a satisfying sense of space.

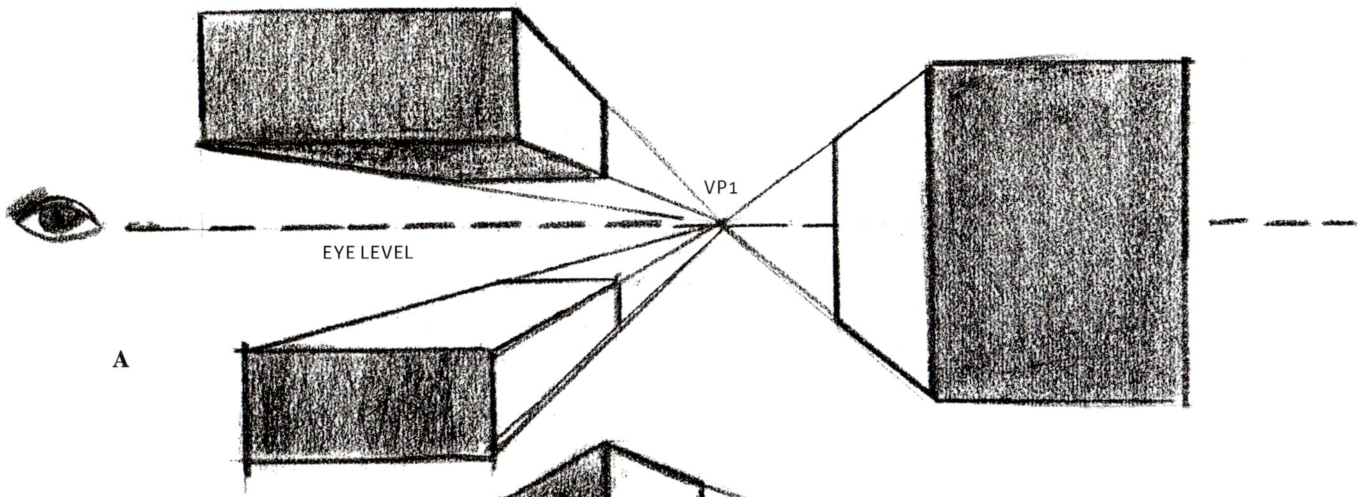

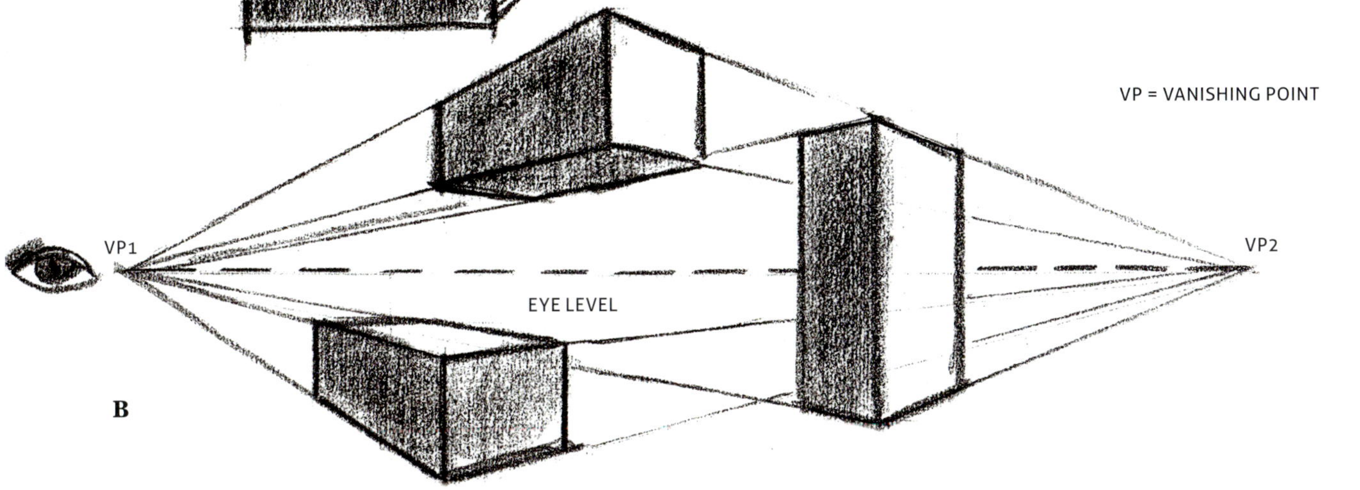

EYE LEVEL

A

VP1

VP = VANISHING POINT

VP1

EYE LEVEL

VP2

B

Shapes and shadows

It is probably true that most of the world can be described as a combination of four basic geometrical shapes: spheres, cylinders, cubes and cones. The shading on the objects illustrated here is based on light coming from the top right. There are different kinds of light and shade in the picture.

Light 'A' is called a highlight. This is where the brightness is at its maximum. Light 'B' is reflected light; it is where light from another object interrupts the shadow of a nearby object.

Shadow 'C' is the core shadow, the shadow that describes the form of an object. Shadow 'D' is a cast shadow, which means the shadow isn't part of the object but falls away from it on to another object.

When you are drawing it is a good idea to try to think in geometrical terms and to analyse the shape in front of you. Can you see a tree as a sphere on top of a cylinder, or a church as a cone on top of a cube?

ABOVE *In picture A, all lines disappear at the same vanishing point. In picture B, there are two vanishing points.*

BELOW *Light and shadows falling on different shapes.*

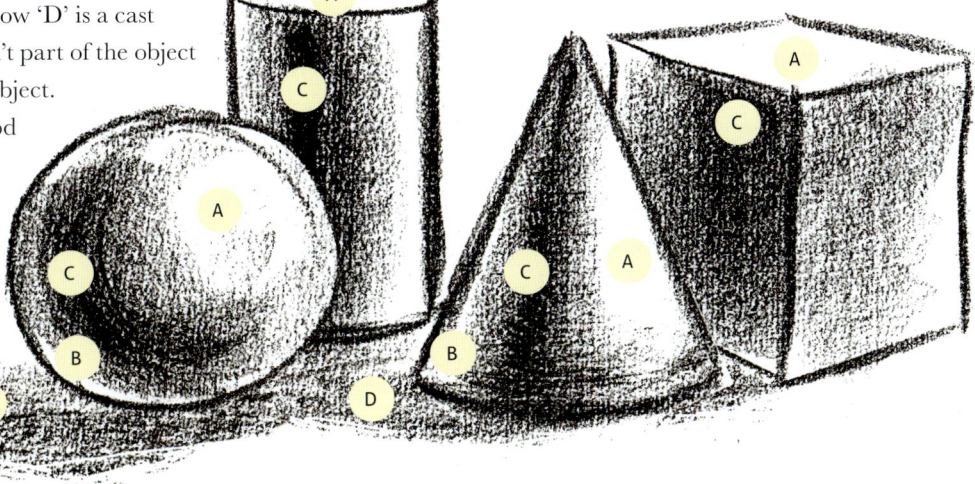

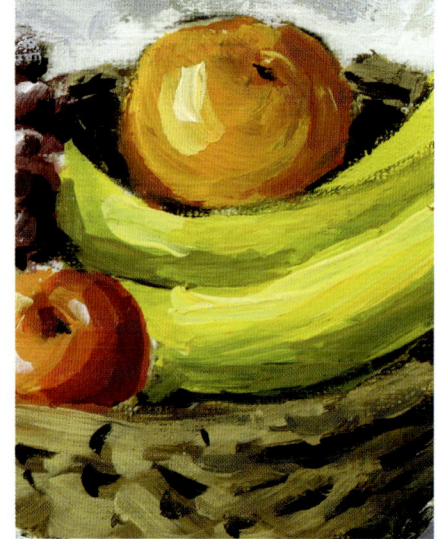

Painting Techniques

Acrylics are incredibly versatile and can be used straight from the tube like oil paints or diluted and used as a wash like watercolours. We are going to explore the basic methods of painting with acrylics using one simple picture throughout – a bowl of fruit – so you can see the distinct styles that can be achieved using the different techniques.

Classic

By the term 'classic' I mean a method of applying acrylic that is more akin to oil painting. Acrylic paint only differs from oil paint in the medium used to make it move across the canvas; otherwise, these two forms of painting are remarkably similar.

There are many ways to begin a classic acrylic painting, but one of the most tried and tested is the preliminary technique of underpainting. Using a purely tonal approach in the first stage helps you to put on your colours with more confidence later.

Try this short exercise to become familiar with this technique.

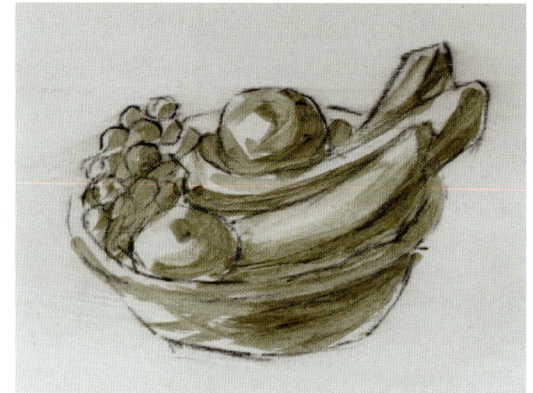

STAGE 1

Start by creating an underpainting of the subject. Raw Umber is one of the most commonly used colours for underpainting and it is applied slightly diluted, usually with a bristle brush. Start with the darker tones and add progressively lighter washes as you go (see page 81).

STAGE 2

Now for the overpainting. Start with the simpler shapes, such as the bananas, by painting the shadow side of the banana in green and put a yellow beside it. Then mix the yellow with a dash of the green to create a mid-tone. Paint the mid-tone between the light and dark tones. Do not 'merge' them to make a smooth transition. Try to make your strokes visible.

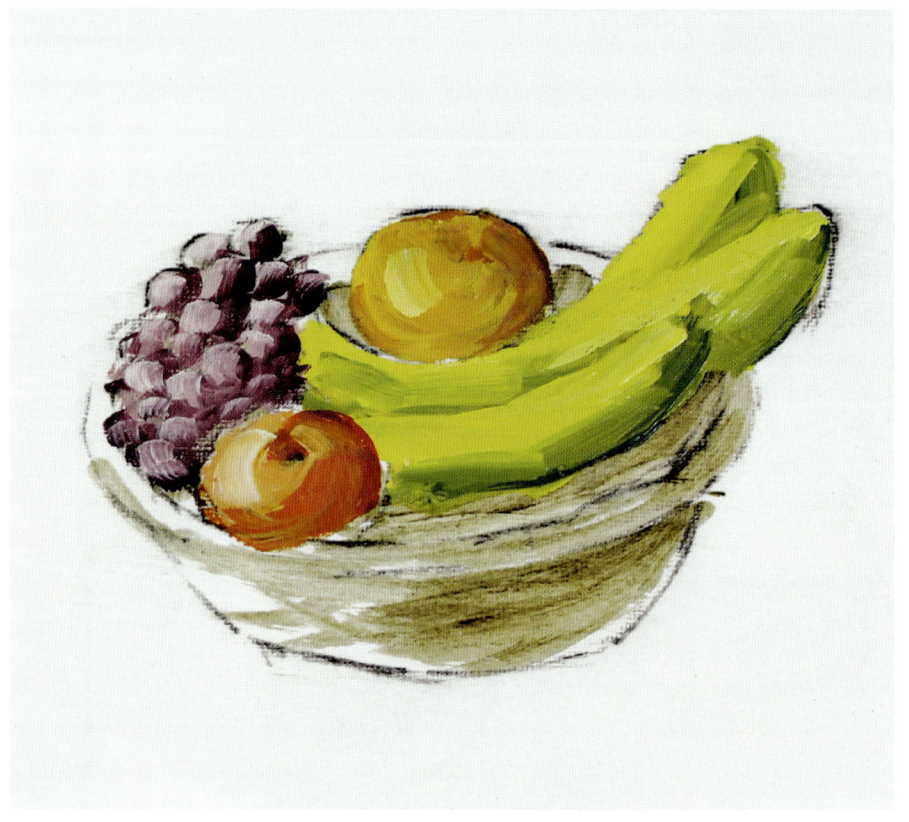

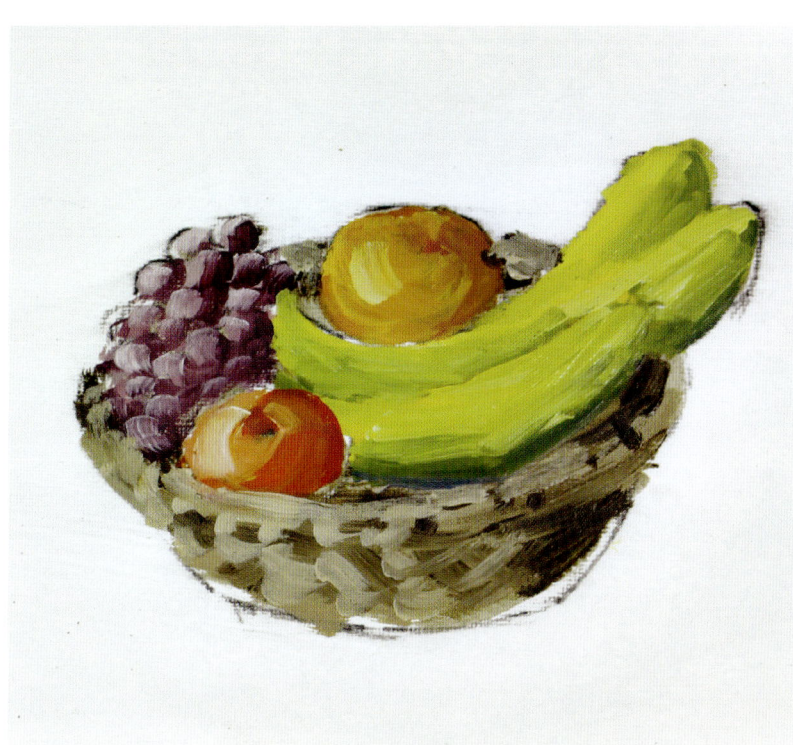

STAGE 3

For the apple, orange and grapes, begin with the shadow side and put a lighter tone beside it. Again, connect the two colours with a mid-tone, making sure the paint strokes follow the contours of the object. On your palette, add white to the lighter tone and mix a highlight colour. Put this on the lightest parts.

STAGE 4

You can further darken the shadows by adding a small amount of Ultramarine Blue to the original shadow colour on your palette. Finally, add some black in the very darkest places and, if you like, scumble in a background to make the colours come to life (see page 83).

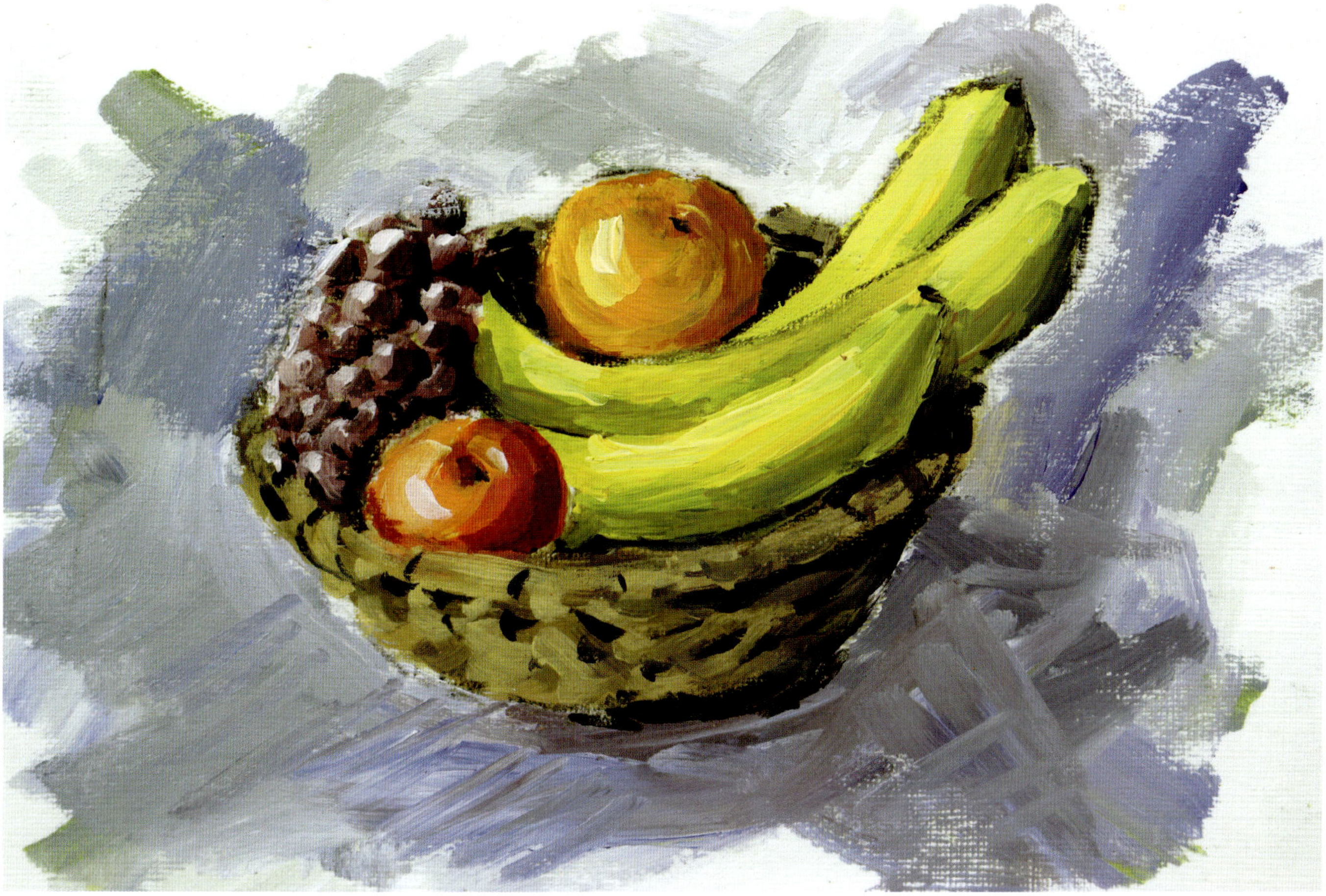

Grisaille

Pronounced 'gris-ale', this technique was traditionally used to imitate sculpture and was mostly executed in shades of grey paint. Painting in monochrome can help you understand tonal relationships more fully, so it is a good exercise to practise regularly.

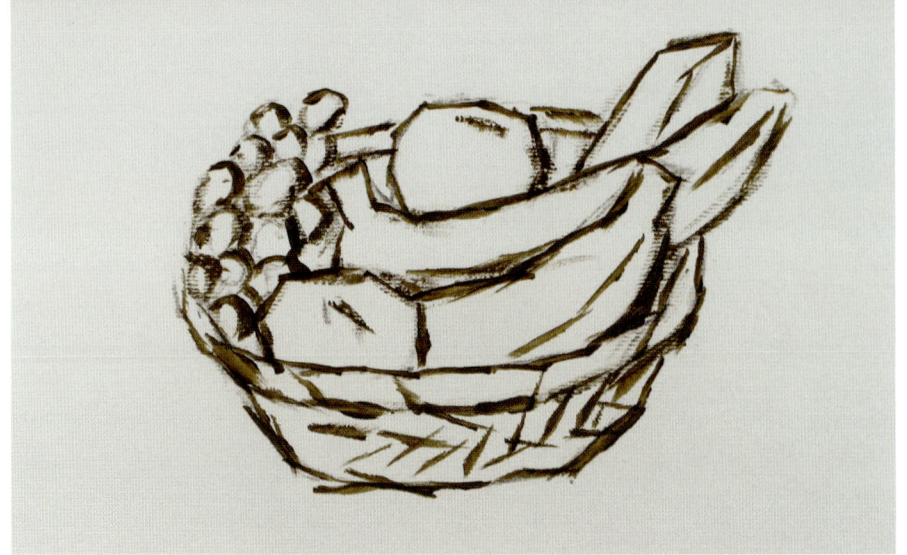

STAGE 1
Begin with an outline drawing (see page 83) in Raw Umber, preferably with a brush. It is always best to get a firm drawing down on canvas so you are confident about where to put in the tonal areas.

STAGE 2
For this exercise we will use five tones. Going from darkest to light they are: dark shadow, shadow, mid-tone, high tone and highlight. Once the drawing stage has dried, put in the main shadows using slightly diluted Raw Umber. These shadows describe 'mass' and are very important in establishing the solidity of the objects.

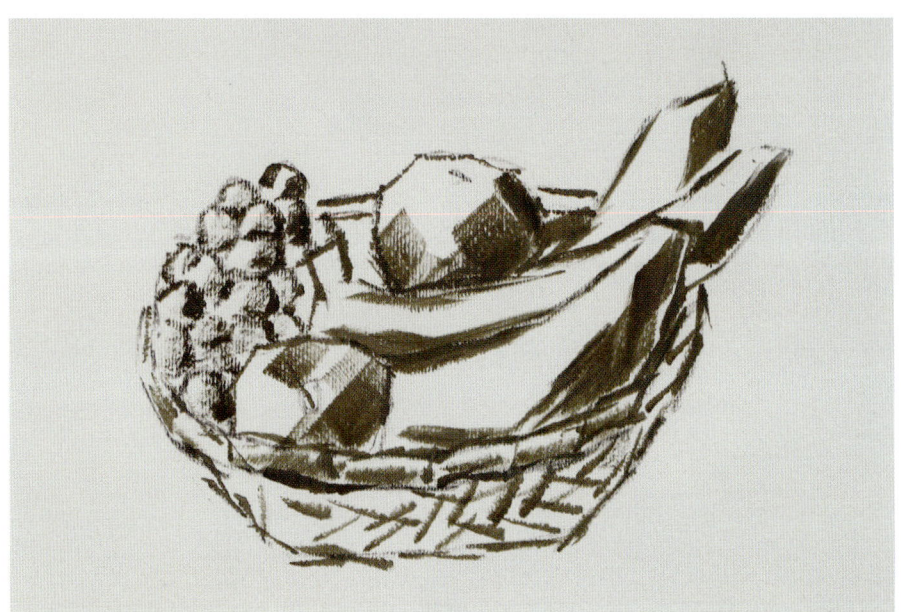

STAGE 3
Add a little Titanium White to the mix you used for the shadows and put that alongside the shadow shapes; these are your mid-tones. Next, add a little Titanium White to the mix you used for the mid-tones and put that in as the high-tone areas. Finally, add highlights to the very brightest areas by using Titanium White. Add a little Mars Black to Raw Umber and add some darker parts to the first Raw Umber shadows you put in. Be careful with these last two tones because it is easy to upset the balance of the piece with too much contrast. Highlights are just small spots of colour. The very darkest tone is reserved for the deepest shadows.

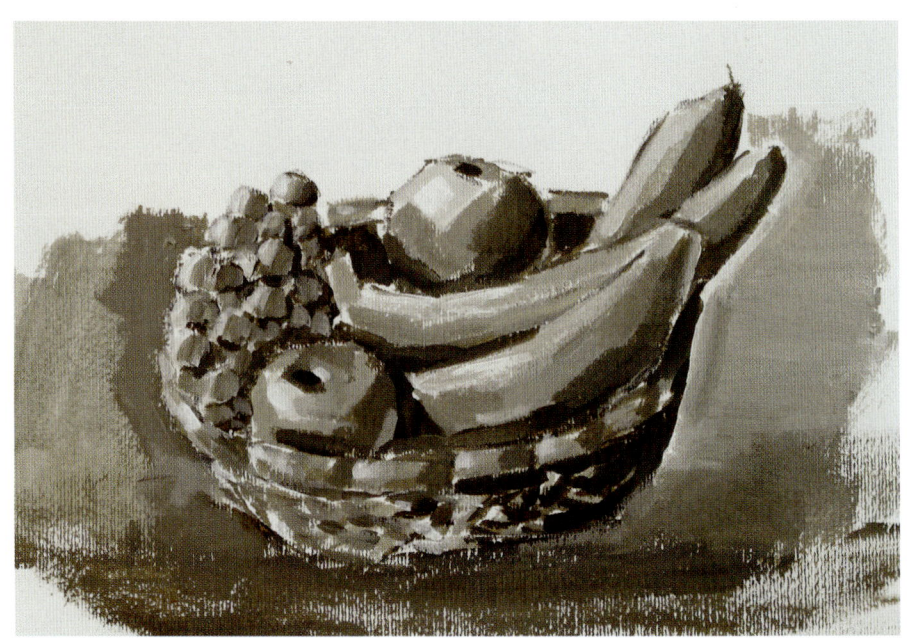

Impasto

This word derives from the Italian for 'paste', and a paste effect is just what you are trying to achieve. There is no underpainting required with this technique. Instead, you start with a faint pencil drawing, then, with a small painting or palette knife, apply paint thickly. The paint should be undiluted and applying it should feel like spreading bread with a thick layer of butter. Continue to add colours to the drawing using gentle dabbing strokes with the palette knife. Note that with this technique, much of the colour mixing is done on the painting itself. Because the paint is so thick, you will find that it will remain quite pliant throughout the painting time.

Make sure you always have a good amount of paint on your knife. If you apply too much pressure to the canvas or paper, the surface will show and you will lose the impasto effect.

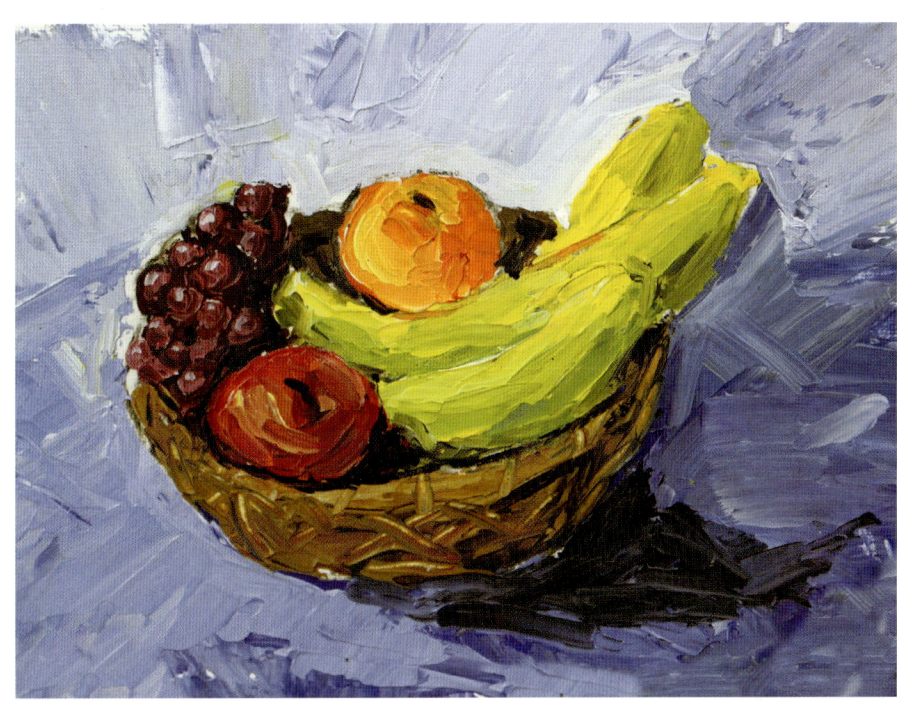

Watercolour washes

When mixed with a good amount of water, acrylic paint becomes fluid and can be used in the way watercolourists use watercolour: layers of paint can be laid over one another to create other colours or as wet-in-wet washes that flow into one another. These particular washes are known as wet-in-wet because you create them by applying fresh paint to the surface when it is still damp from the previous wash.

When working with washes, you need to apply your paint with fluid strokes. Let the paint soak into the canvas or paper. If the paint appears slightly stronger in some areas and starts drying unevenly, don't worry – that is an attractive watercolour effect.

Once the wash has dried a little, you can apply the next colours. Some parts may still be slightly wet, but this can create some nice running colour effects. At the very end, when the painting is completely dry, you can add some strong, undiluted colour to the edges of objects and deep shadows.

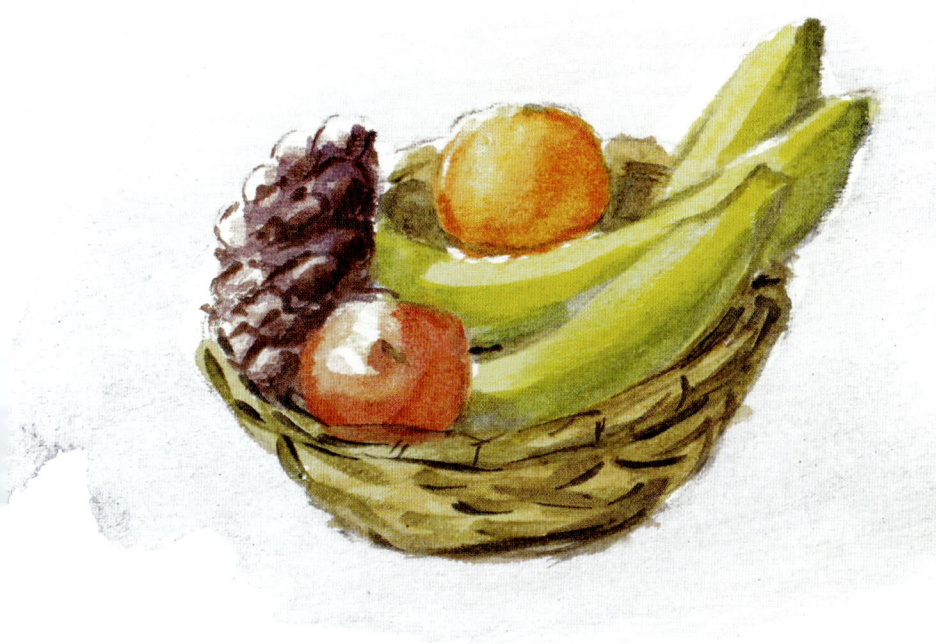

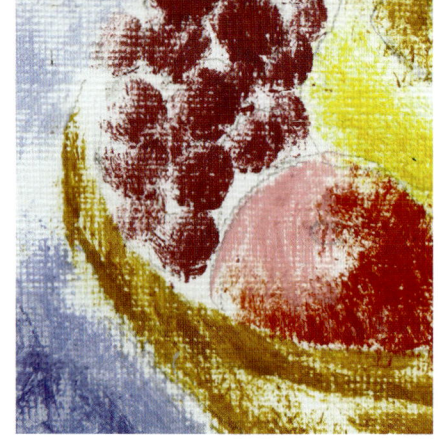

Simple Effects

It is worth practising a few simple effects to use alongside the basic methods of painting discussed on pages 78–81. Effects such as stippling, scumbling and outlining can add visual interest and really bring your paintings to life.

Stippling using masking

Stippling is a technique using the bristles of a paintbrush to make hundreds of tiny dots on your canvas or paper. The effect can give a painting a calm, diffused look, ideal for mists or smoke. The brush is held vertically and quick stabbing movements are made to build up a fine mesh of colours and tones. The stiffer and older the brush, the better the stipple. A hog-hair brush is the best candidate for this type of work.

Colouring with the stippling method is relatively straightforward: put the lighter colour on first and the darker stipple over the top. I suggest you do three shades of any one colour for each object, starting with the lightest shade, moving on to a mid-tone and finally adding the darkest shade.

A masking technique is a good way to control the edges of the forms. Simply tear a piece of ordinary paper roughly to the shape you want to follow and place it along the edge of the form. Stipple both the object and the scrap paper at the same time with the brush, and move along the edge. The middle of the form is easier to judge and doesn't require the masking paper.

For the grapes in this example, I made a tiny hole in my masking paper and stippled through it, moving from grape to grape. I used the same

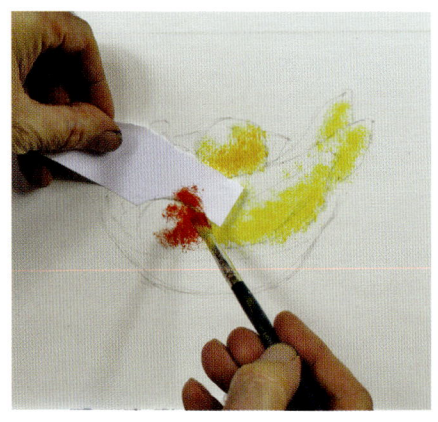 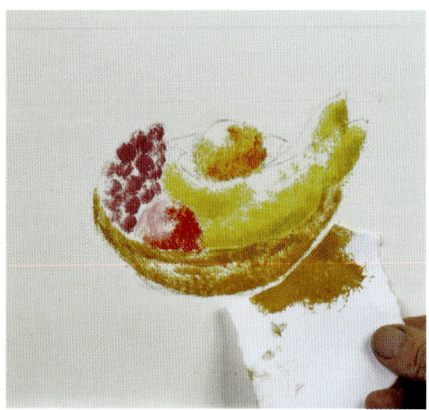

small hole for each grape but stippled more heavily on one side of the hole, which gave each grape a round shape with a shadow side. When I moved on to a different shape I wanted to describe (the basket in this case), I just

tore another piece of paper roughly in the same shape and placed it along the edge of the form. If you like, you can use a straight piece of paper for masking but you will have to move and turn it more times to follow the shape.

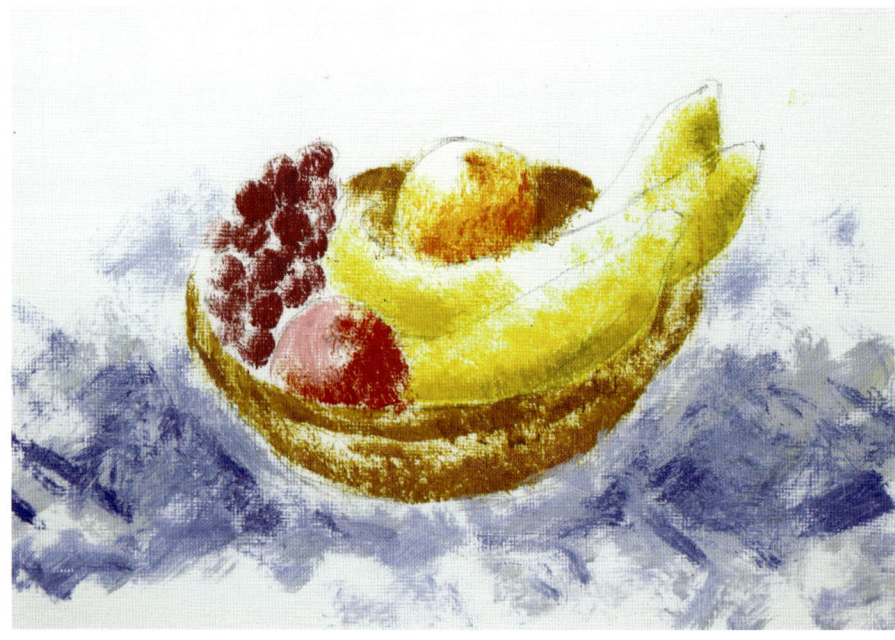

Scumbling

This is a dry-brush technique that involves a layer of paint being pushed and rubbed over another layer so that patches of the underneath layer show through. It is best to let the paint dry before you 'scumble' the next layer. Scumbling is a great technique for painting skies or patches of dry vegetation.

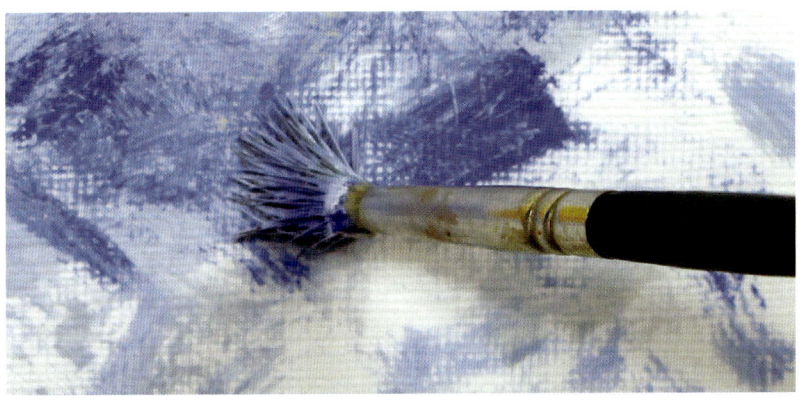

Outlining

This method, known as Cloisonnism, was used by various French Post-Impressionist painters, such as Émile Bernard and Paul Gauguin. The effect of a thick black outline around the objects in a painting allows the colours to stand out and become stronger and more forceful.

Begin with a black outline drawing, made using the side of a flat nylon brush. When this outline is completely dry, you can fill the shapes with colours. Don't worry too much about staying within the lines, as they can be reinforced later, and if the paint isn't mixed too thickly then the lines should still show through.

Once you have put in the first colours, allow the paint to dry; this won't take long. Then you can apply the second colours. Once these are dry, coat your flat brush with black paint and brush along the shapes, using a slight pressure. Try not to stroke the outlines with the brush because this will break up the solid line.

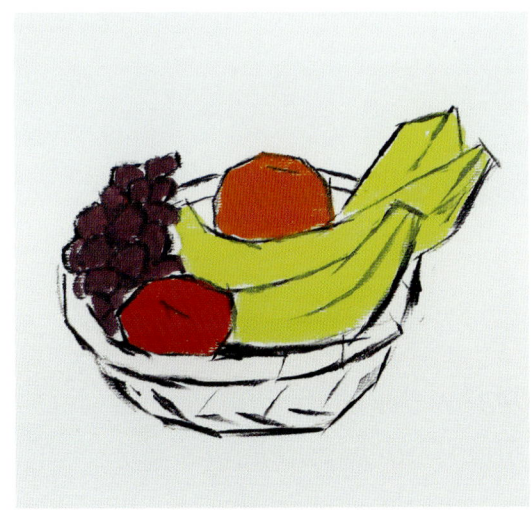

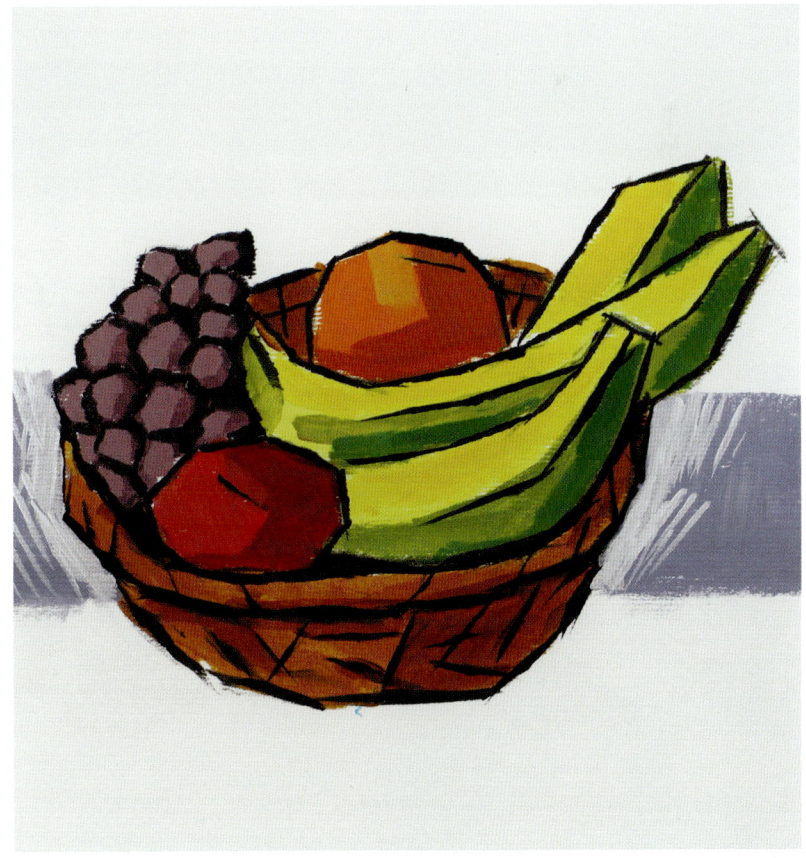

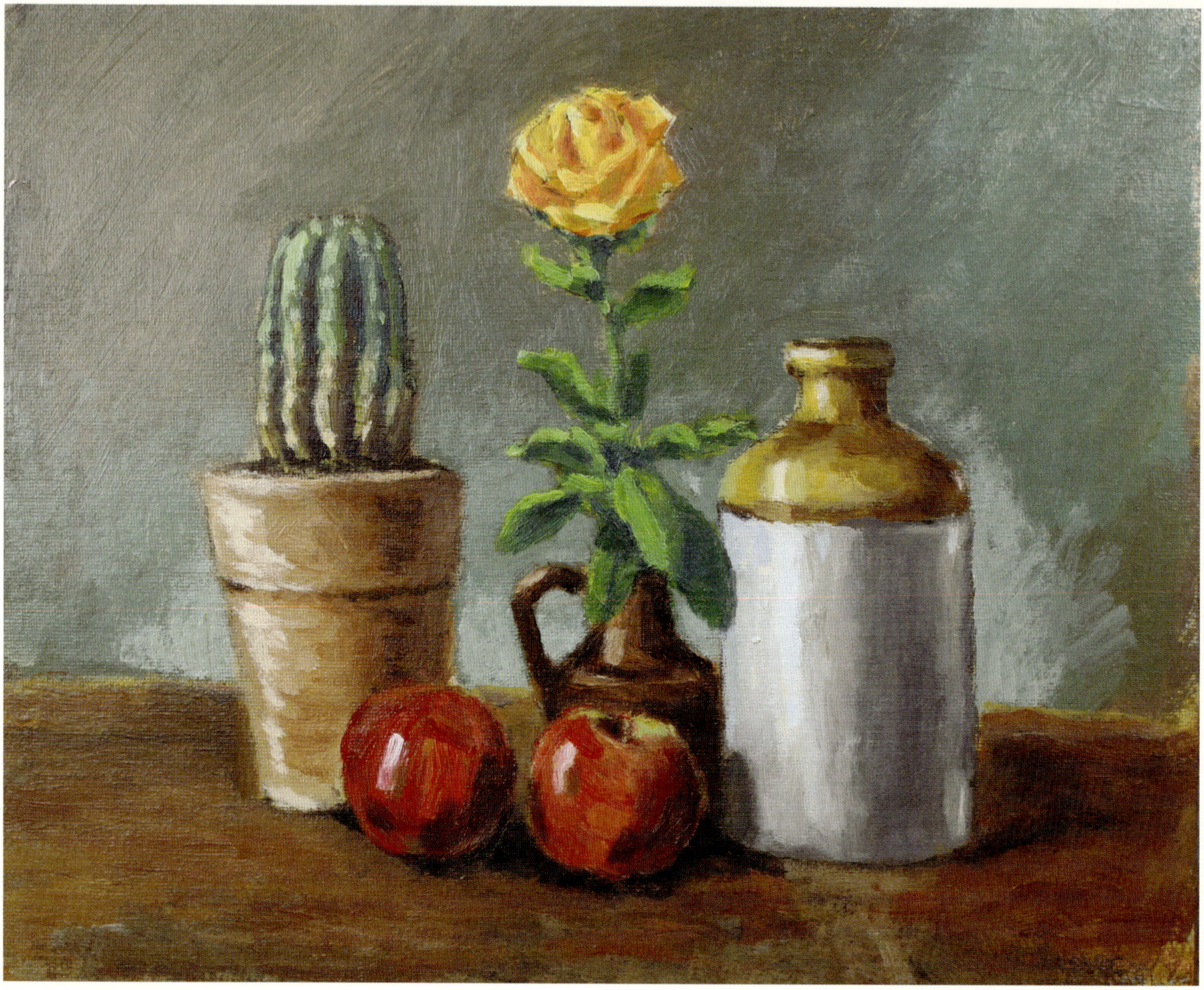

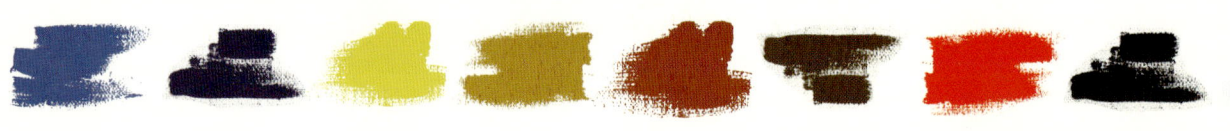

Still Life

This project explores the qualities of different textures within one painting. You will learn how to achieve a balanced composition both in colour and form by using the technique of underpainting.

COLOURS NEEDED

| Ultramarine Blue | Winsor Blue | Cadmium Yellow | Yellow Ochre | Burnt Sienna | Raw Umber | Cadmium Red | Mars Black | Titanium White |

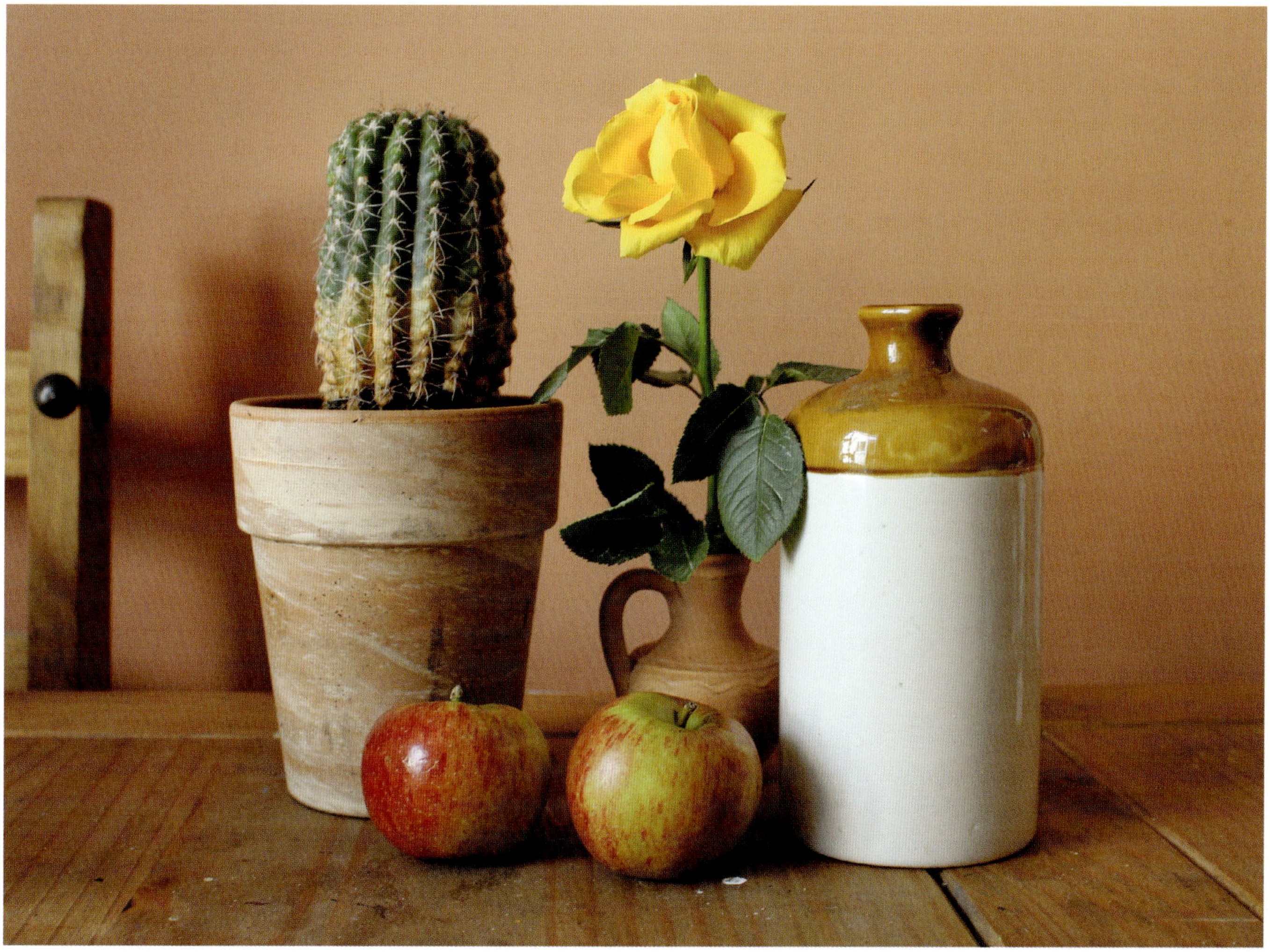

Still-life painting has a long history; it was often a means for an artist to show off his or her ability to tackle varied textures and lighting effects. This kind of painting sometimes had an allegorical meaning as well as showing a mastery of technique; it reached its peak with the Dutch Golden Age of painting in the 17th century.

When arranging a still life, lighting is quite important since it affects the mood of the picture. A still life that is bathed in an even light will have a very different mood to one that has a lot of dark areas with a few highlights. There is an Italian word from the 17th century that sums up the dramatic effect of light and shadow: 'chiaroscuro'. This means 'bright and dark', and can be seen in the painting *Still Life with Ham, Silver Jug and Roemer* by the Dutch painter Willem Claeszoon Heda. Notice how the background is almost completely dark, which emphasizes the bright objects in the foreground.

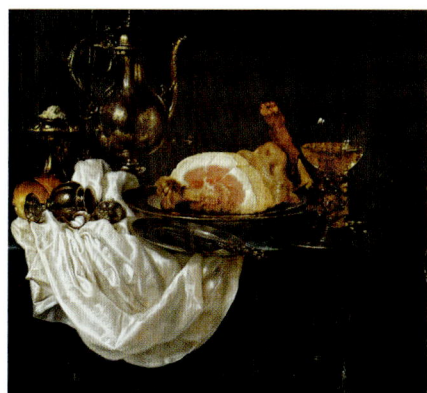

ABOVE Still Life with Ham, Silver Jug and Roemer, *by Willem Claeszoon Heda, 1656.*

REFERENCE PHOTO

I chose just five objects for this painting, but within those objects there is a range of textures. The prickly cactus is in an earth-coloured plant pot, the flower is in a slightly more glazed pot, the apples are shiny spheres and the jug is a highly glazed vessel of two colours. The background is a plain terracotta colour. I changed the background in my picture to a blue-green colour because I wanted the yellow rose, red apples and especially the plant pot to stand out. I also increased the height of the rose stem to improve the composition. All these things are possible when you are painting because you are the artist and therefore the one who decides what to put in and what to leave out.

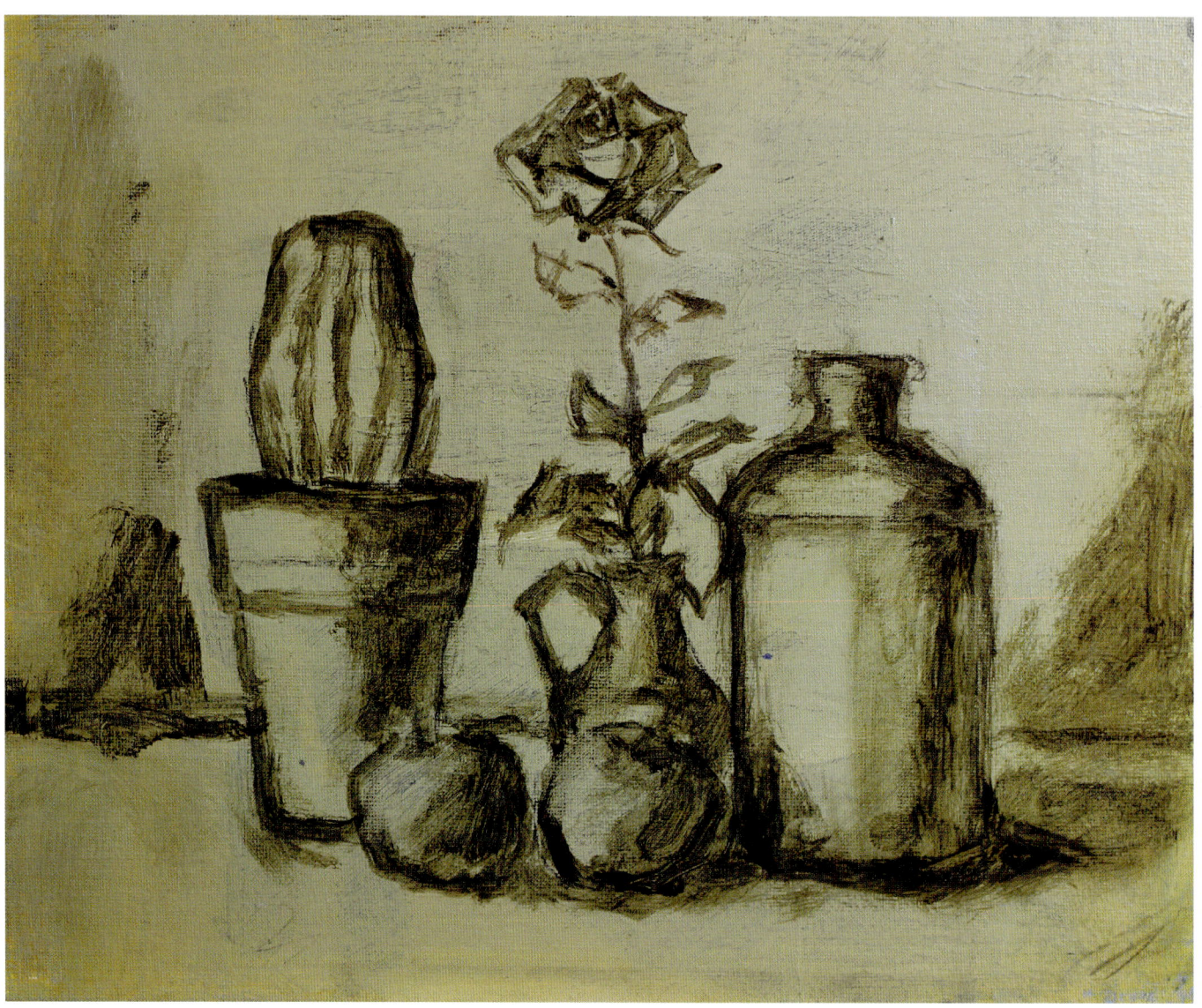

Tip

A still life can be just a few pieces of fruit on a table or an array of the most varied objects you can think of, from seashells to a vase or a toy aeroplane. Bear in mind that the more complex the composition, the harder it is to arrange without it looking like a jumble sale!

STAGE 1

For this stage, I have chosen to use a round hog-hair brush to sketch in the composition. This method of painting is called 'underpainting' (see page 78) and is a really effective way of starting out. The underpainting provides a wonderful tonal guide to follow throughout the painting process.

For the coloured ground, I used a mixture of Yellow Ochre, Titanium White and Raw Umber. For the underpainting I used Raw Umber with a little Mars Black, diluted with water, to draw the shapes and composition. Try to get as much tone in the first underpainting as possible without obliterating the background.

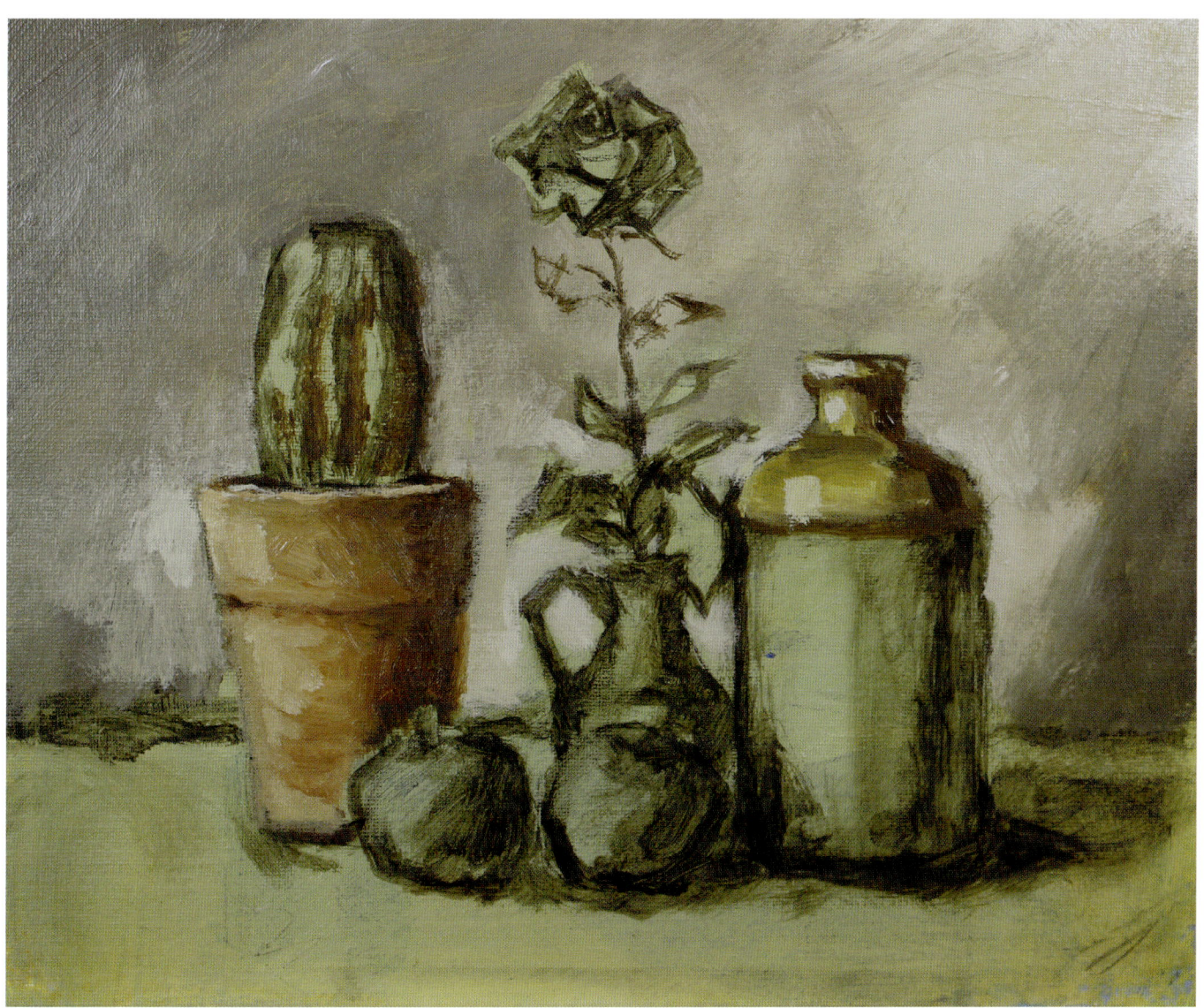

STAGE 2

Establish some colours on your objects. For the plant pot, I used Burnt Sienna and Titanium White, and tried to get as much texture in the painting as I could by loading my brush and painting in short, 'flaky' strokes to get the crusty feel of baked clay. I alternated between a round and a flat hog-hair brush for this stage. The plant pot is a dull texture, so the transition from light to dark is muted. The apples and the jug, on the other hand, have strong transitions and have highlights on them to give the impression of glossy surfaces.

The top of the jug is painted in Yellow Ochre and Raw Umber. The Raw Umber is cooler and darker than the ochre so is used on the shadow side. The highlight is Yellow Ochre and Titanium White.

Tip

Painting with an easel allows you to stand back from your work as you go along. This helps you to get an overall view of the composition, colours and tones and how they are working together. If you want a more radical view, look at your work in a hand mirror. It is startling how different it looks and how much easier it is to see unsatisfactory passages of paint.

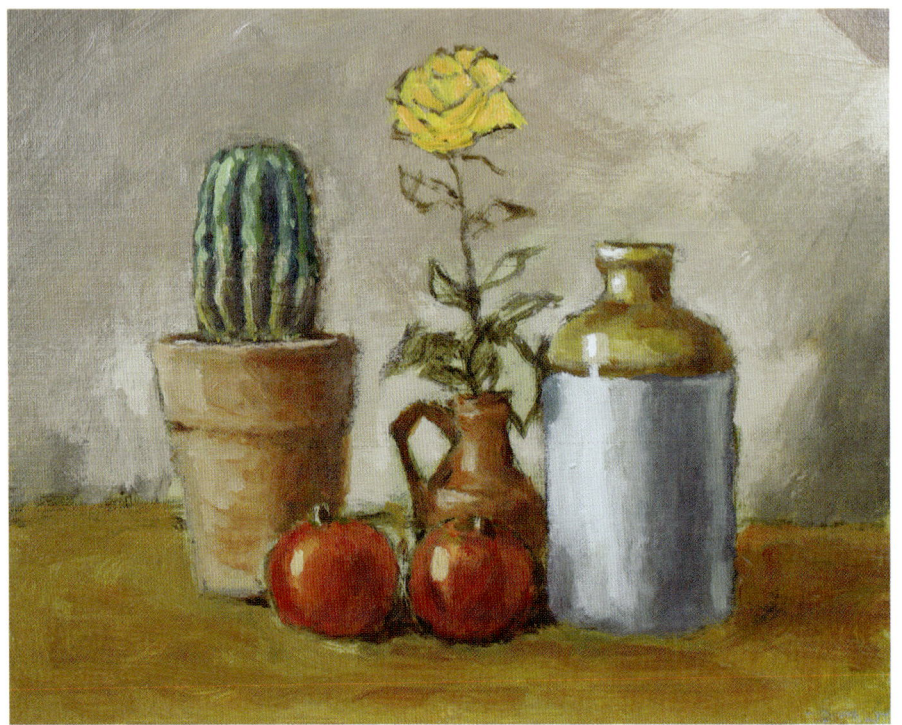

STAGE 3

The lower half of the jug is a different colour to the top but equally shiny. To give the impression of height, I have made my paint strokes go vertically instead of horizontally. The colour is a mix of Mars Black and Titanium White. Try to add lighter tones into the darker side to give the impression that light is being picked up by this reflective object from other sources in the room.

The cactus is painted as a series of vertical ridges. The green top part of the cactus is Ultramarine Blue plus yellow for the mid-tones; the same mix but with a little more Winsor Blue is used for the shadows. Add Titanium White to the colour you mixed for the mid-tones for the highlights. For the lower half of the cactus, use Raw Umber instead of Ultramarine Blue in your mix.

For the head of the rose I used Cadmium Yellow, followed by a mix of Cadmium Yellow and a little Cadmium Red to make a light orange for modelling the petals. For the apples, I used Cadmium Red and Cadmium Yellow for the main tones, mixing more yellow into the red for the brighter side of the apples.

This stage and the final one are best done while the paint is beginning to dry so you can blend the colours more effectively.

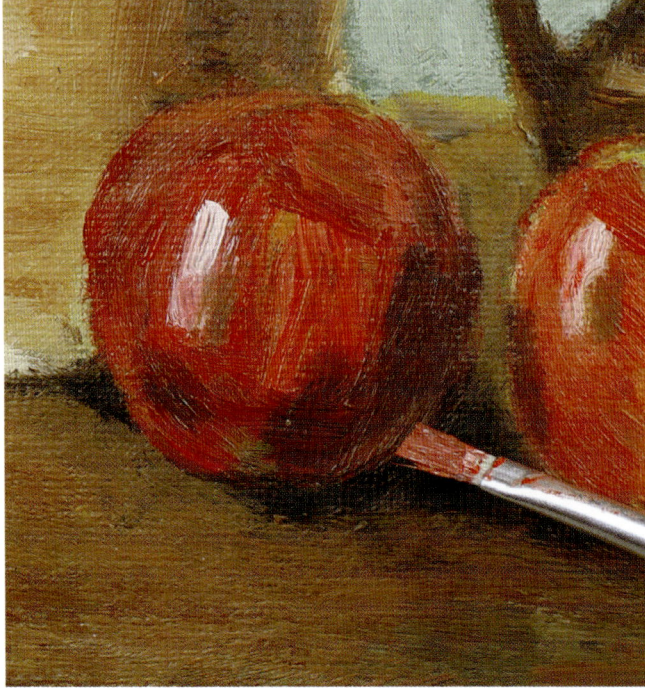

ABOVE *Not all shadows are dark! Light can be reflected from other objects onto the shadow. Add an area of lighter tone along the contour of an object to make the shape more convincing.*

STAGE 4

To deepen the colour of the flower,
add more Cadmium Red to the orange
you made in stage 3, and put it into
the darkest parts of the petals. Add
Titanium White to the Cadmium
Yellow on your palette and paint
highlights on tops of the petals.
Put tiny amounts of green into the
yellow parts of the petals to capture
the reflections off the green leaves.

The jug in which the flower stands is
treated much like the flowerpot but with
more of a shine in the treatment – that
is, with stronger contrasting highlights.

The background is made up of various
shades of green and blue; it is a good
idea to lighten this mixture towards
the table to make the objects stand out
against the table and the darker upper
half of the picture. The table itself is
made up of Burnt Sienna with Mars
Black and Raw Umber scumbled in
for the texture of the shadows.

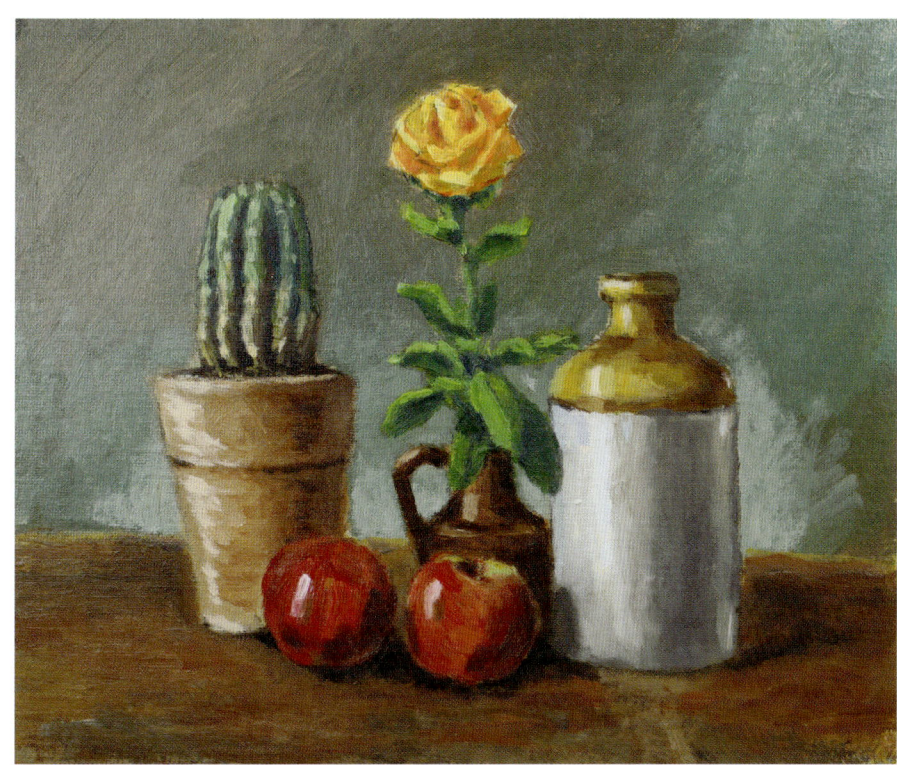

BELOW *Flowers are very complex structures, so it is best to simplify them as much as possible. A rose is a series of small folded sheets that become more closely confined towards the centre. Try to paint it as a concentric design and then add the modelling.*

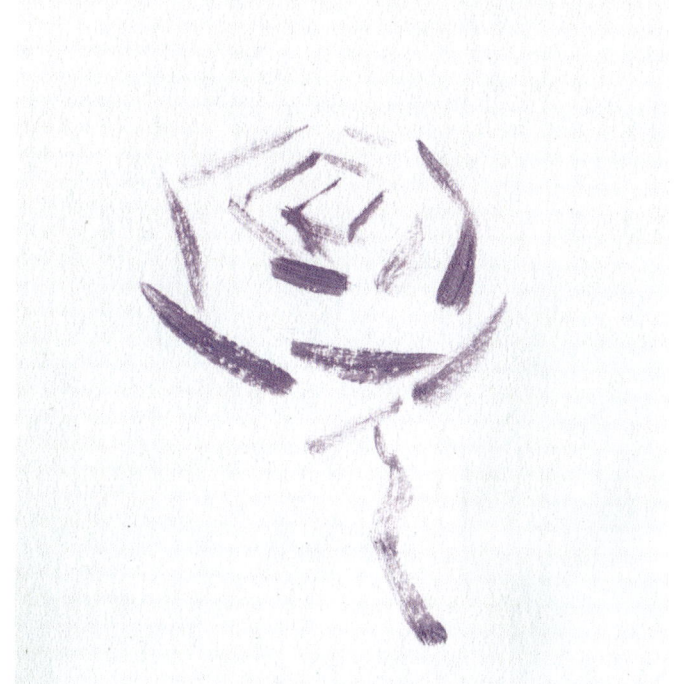

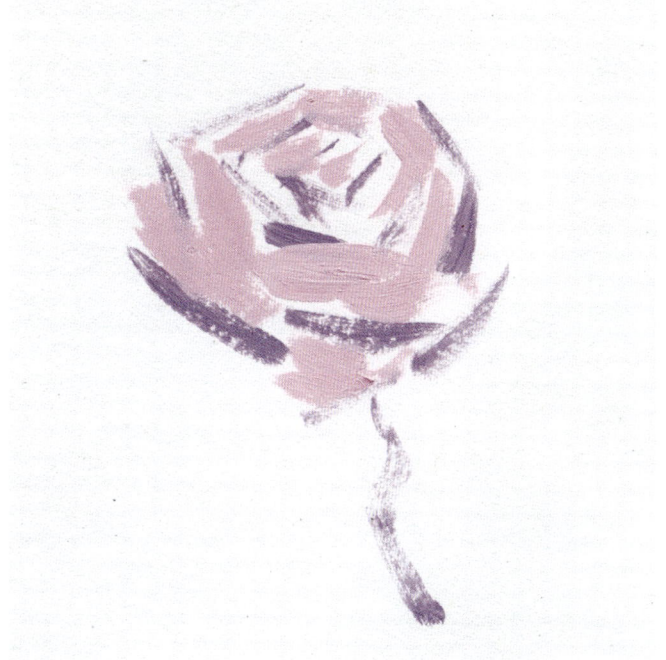

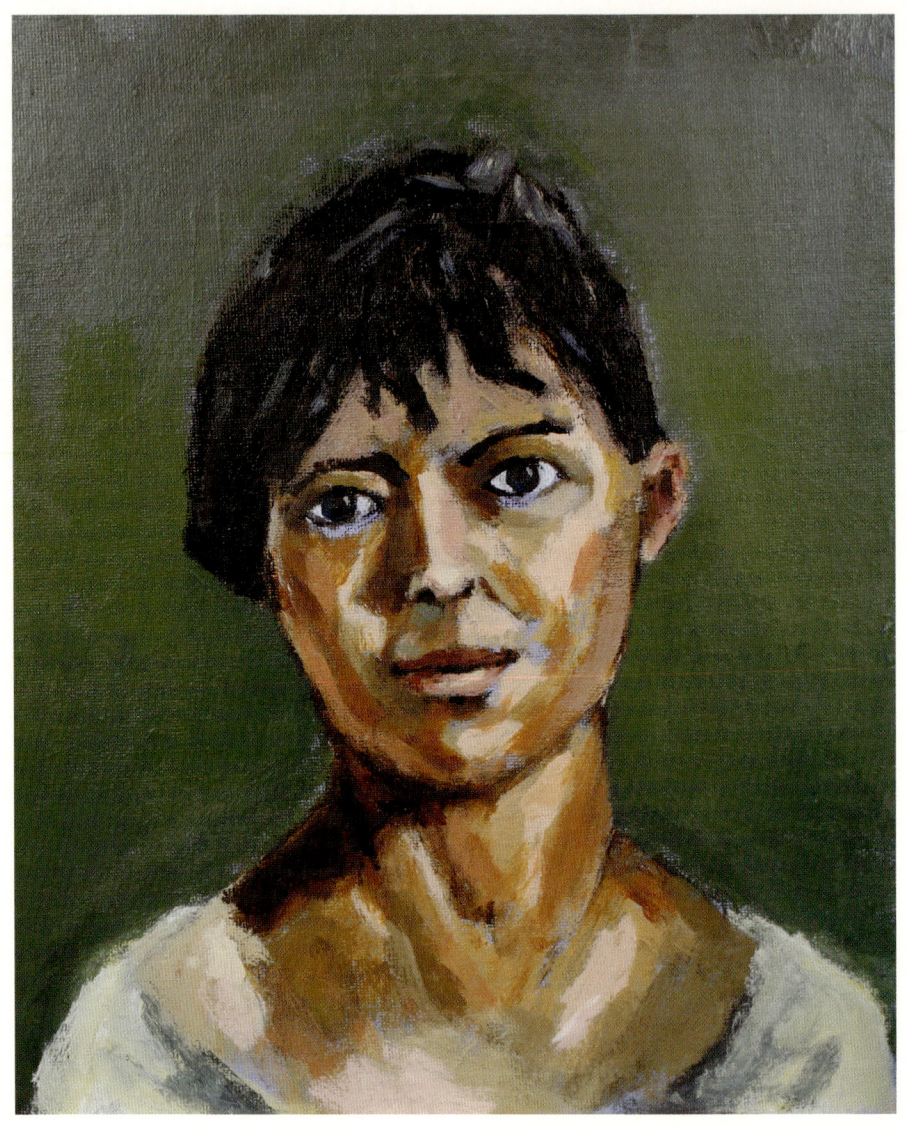

Portrait

*The aim of this study is to paint a convincing human face with just a few colours
and to make it look three-dimensional. You will learn how to build the shapes of the face,
the importance of a good background and how to tackle hair.*

COLOURS NEEDED

| Ultramarine Blue | Cadmium Yellow | Yellow Ochre | Burnt Sienna | Raw Umber | Cadmium Red | Mars Black | Titanium White |

If you look at portraits painted by a broad range of artists, there is a startling difference in styles and approaches. The main idea is to capture the 'essence' of the person rather than a photographic likeness. You can work from a photograph, from life or a sketch, or a combination of all three.

The human face is infinitely varied, but the underlying structure remains remarkably similar. The human skull is a collection of domes and plates that interconnect in the same way whoever you are.

REFERENCE PAINTING

Looking at the portrait of *Madame Cézanne in a Red Dress* by Paul Cézanne (right), we see that he has made the colours in the face quite distinct. Look across the face from the left to the right. You will notice the colours go from warm to cool in stages. If we start at the left we have a warm colour for the ear, then it goes into the cool of the cheekbone, then the warmth of the cheek itself. There is then a cool shadow cast by

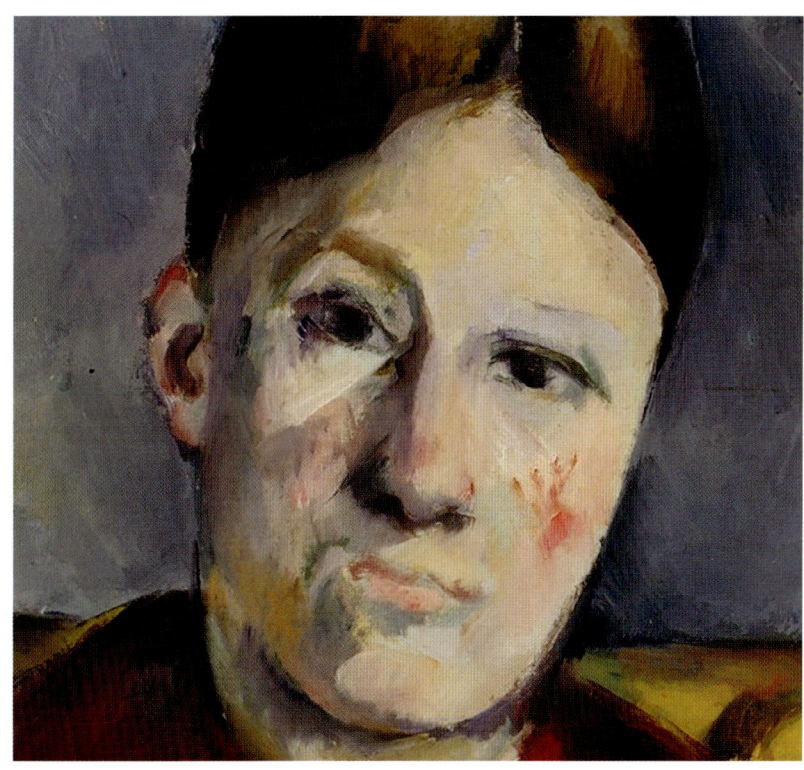

ABOVE Madame Cézanne in a Red Dress (detail), *by Paul Cézanne, c. 1888–90. The face is brought to life by subtle shifts of tone and colour.*

the nose, which is itself a warm colour. There is a small, cool shadow on the other side of the nose, which leads into the warmth of the subject's other cheek. Notice the reflected light from her collar on the left side of the painting and the cool shadows under the lips and nose. All these shifts of colour and tone help bring the face to life.

REFERENCE SKETCH

Knowledge of the structure of the face is very helpful in getting a convincing painting to emerge from your canvas. Looking at the sketch (left), you will notice that the eye sockets are halfway down the skull. The nose ends halfway between the eye sockets and the chin, and the mouth is roughly halfway between the nose and the chin. This is a great starting place for a full-face portrait like the one we are going to tackle.

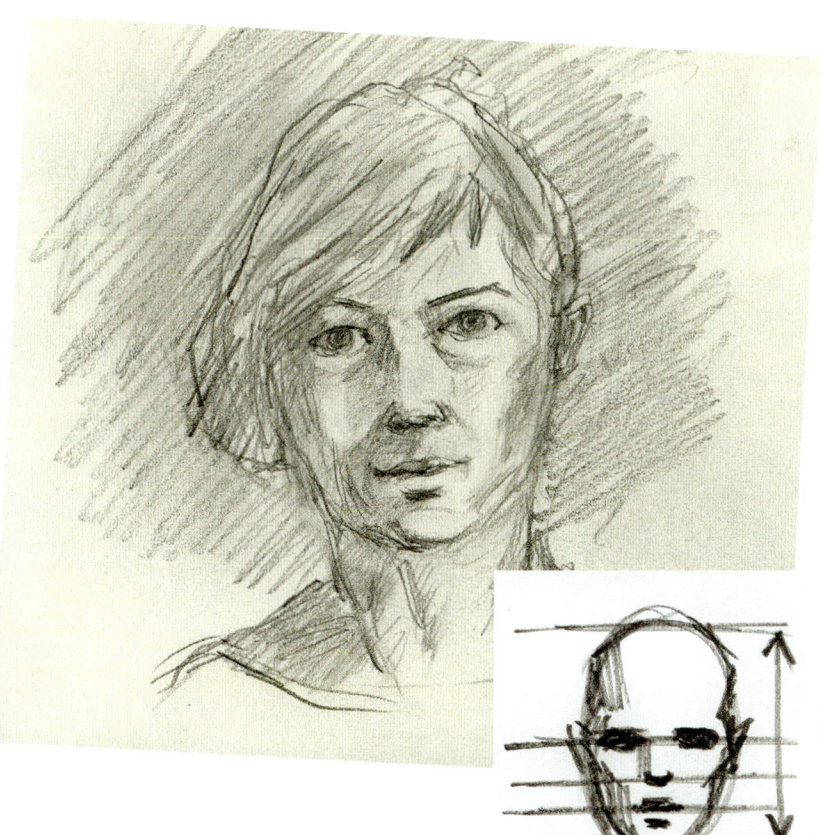

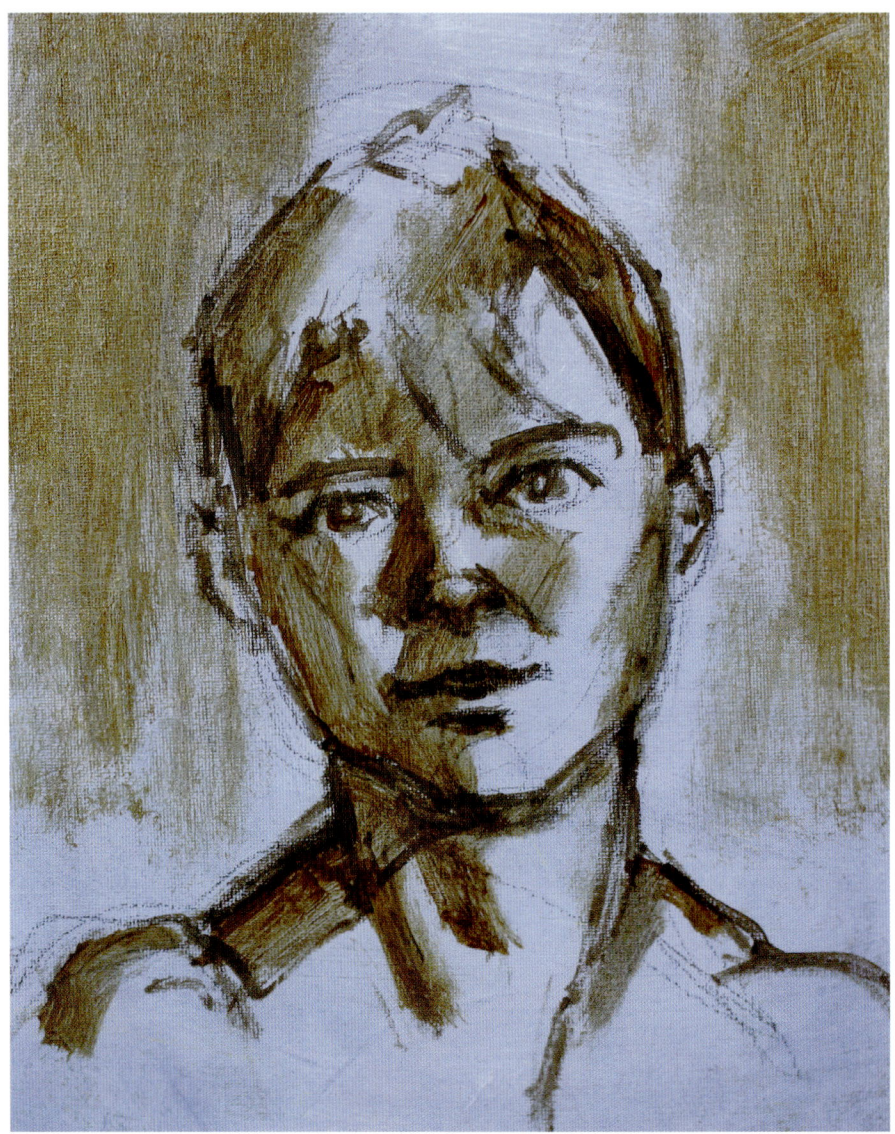

Tip

Although acrylic paint dries quickly, you don't want to be waiting around for your ground colour to dry before you start your painting. It is a good idea to prepare a few canvases beforehand with the colours you like best. There are no set rules for which colour you use for a ground, although it is usual to use a warm ground for a painting dominated by cool colours, and a cool ground for a painting dominated by warm colours.

STAGE 1

Cover a canvas with a light blue ground made up of Ultramarine Blue, Titanium White and a touch of Cadmium Red. Let the canvas dry for about two hours. Take a round or flat hog-hair brush and load it with Raw Umber. Using quick, jerky strokes, sketch in the shape of the face and then the features. Any lines that you use to 'construct' the face should be left in, since these are valuable marks that can act as guides for later stages in the painting.

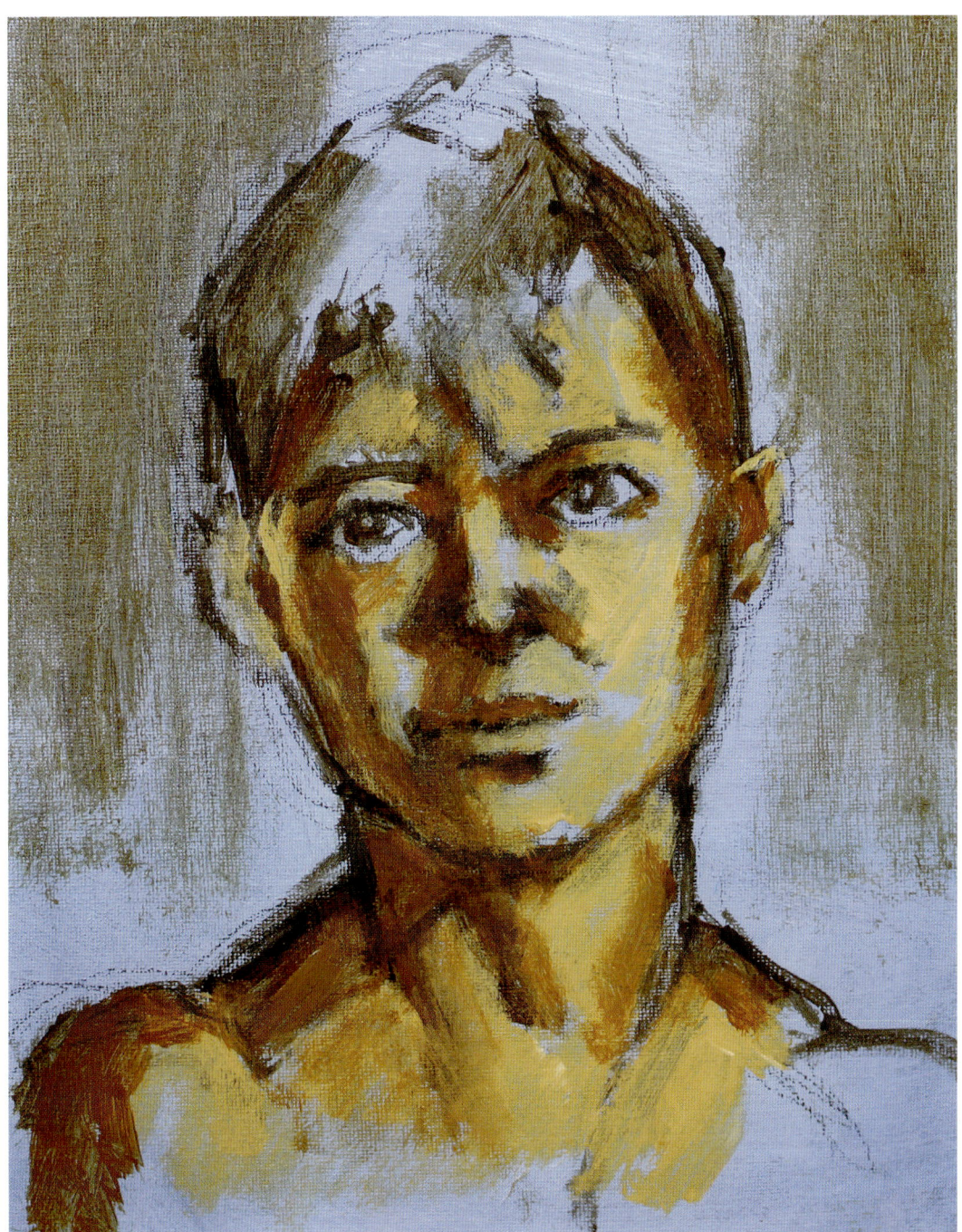

STAGE 2

Using Burnt Sienna, block in the shadows. These shadows are the most important thing in the painting as they 'fix' the structure of the face and describe the mass of the skull. Then mix Titanium White with the Burnt Sienna to create a mid-tone and place it alongside the Burnt Sienna and Raw Umber shadows. You can use the same brush throughout, as long as you clean it between colours. For this picture I used a hog-hair No. 4 brush.

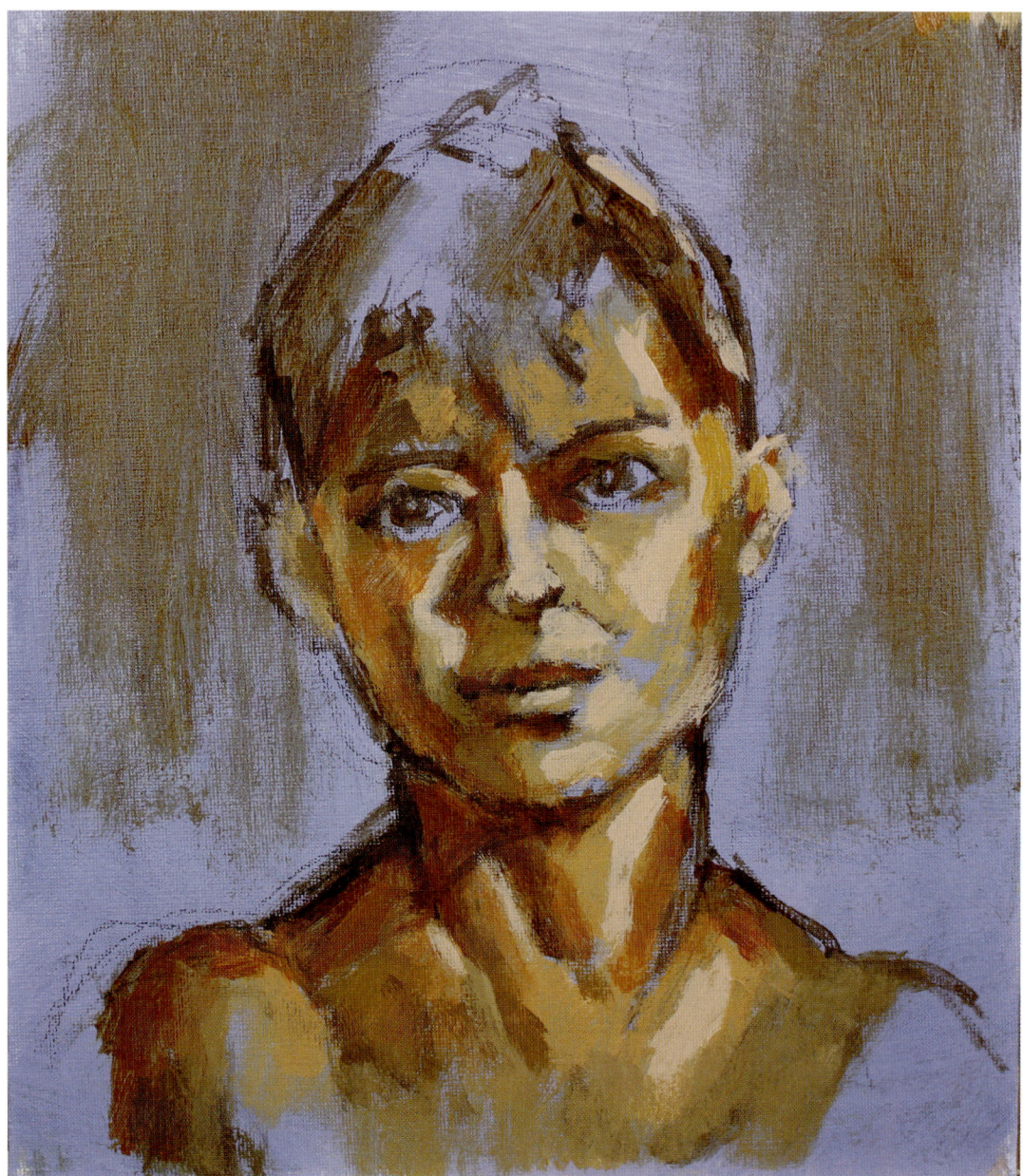

Tip

Throughout the painting, I have deliberately left the blue colour of the original background to add a cool sparkle to the face. To complement this, I added a small dash of Yellow Ochre in just one area to give another colour note to the painting.

STAGE 3

At this stage, we add the highlights. In this case, the highlights are a lighter version of the mid-tones, so mix a little more Titanium White to the Burnt Sienna and add a little Cadmium Red to warm it up slightly. The highlights are laid on the areas that are getting the most light; for instance, the nose, cheekbones and chin.

To introduce some cooler tones, I mixed Raw Umber with a little Titanium White and placed them alongside the highlights near the cheek and inside some of the dark shadows by the nose and chin.

STAGE 4

To introduce some warm tones, mix Burnt Sienna, Titanium White and Cadmium Red and apply this muted pink to warm up the lighter side of the face, which you can see on the side of the nose and along the jawline. Sometimes, warm tones are bounced up from other surfaces on the body.

Add in the mass of the hair. Do not try to paint every strand! You will find that a person's hair is a 'shape' more than anything else, and getting the right shape is the most important thing. For this, I used Mars Black with a lowlight of Raw Umber in places.

To make the head stand out from the picture plane, add a background that has some of the cool colours of the face in it. In this instance, I have put in a background mixture of Cadmium Yellow, Ultramarine Blue and a little Mars Black to contrast with and thus emphasize the lighter and warmer planes of the face. Add a mixture of Burnt Sienna and red for the lips. The upper lip is always a little darker, so only highlight the lower lip.

The hair is completed with some highlights of blue/grey made from Titanium White and Mars Black.

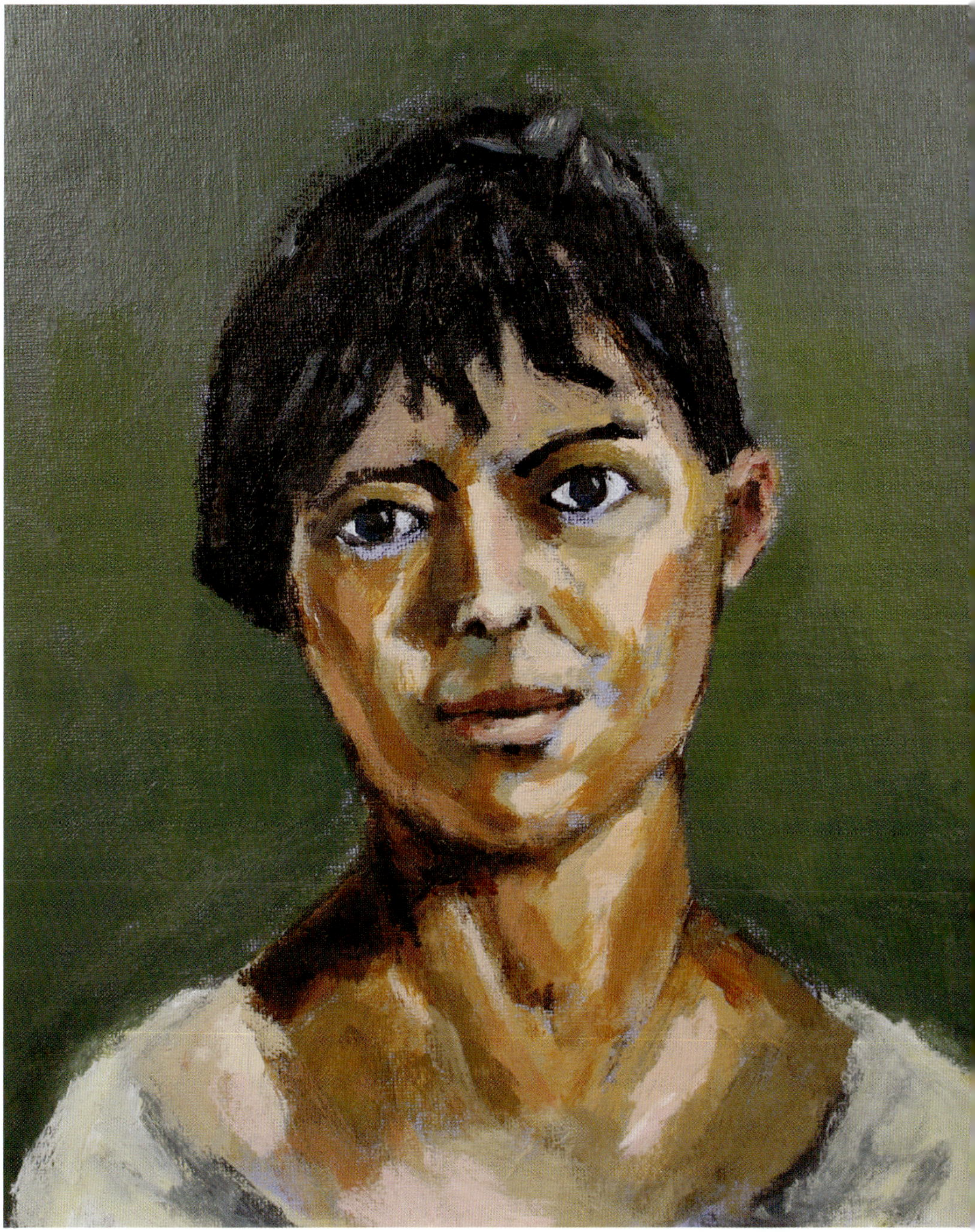

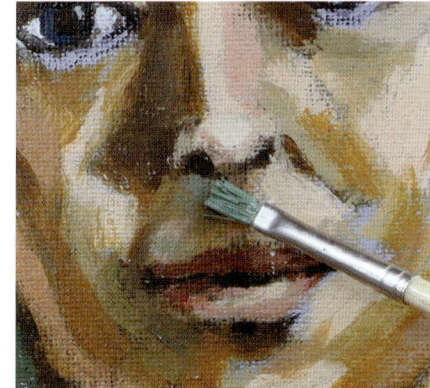

RIGHT *Artists sometimes follow a simple rule whereby warm colours come forward and cool colours recede. Here, a cool colour is used in the shadow area to make the warmer colour around it come forward. This is enhanced if you use the same colour in the shadows as you have in the background.*

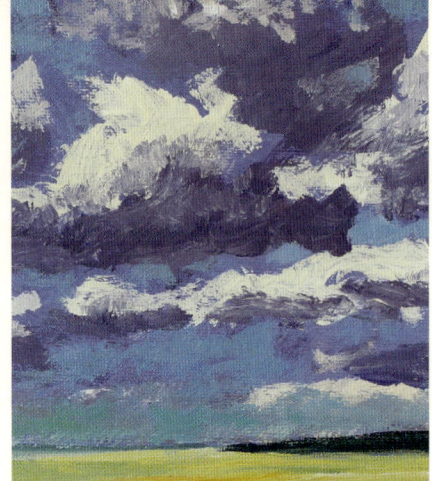

FOCUS ON
Skies

Very often, artists start their landscapes with the sky. This could be because the sky is the most fleeting of the natural elements. It has many moods and can have an enormous range of colours and forms within it. For this reason, the sky is a good place to start – it sets the scene.

How to paint clouds

Clouds are masses of water vapour named according to their shape and how high they float in the atmosphere. It helps to be aware of this when painting clouds because they vary so much in size and appearance. By holding your brush at an acute angle to the canvas and pushing the paint over the surface, you can achieve some remarkable clouds right from the start.

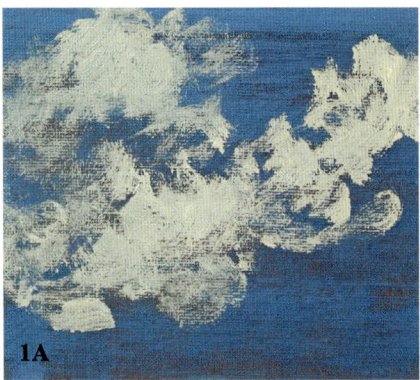

1A

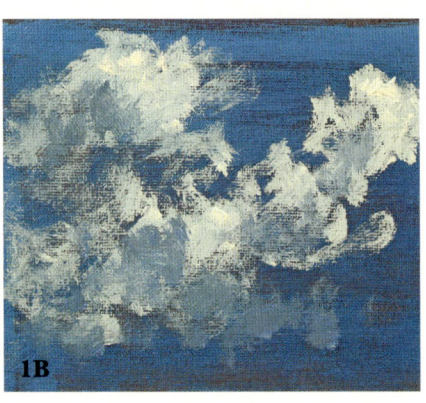

1B

1A Load a hog-hair brush with Titanium White and push it across the canvas, making the cloud shape as you go (see Scumbling, page 83).

1B While the first stage is still tacky, mix Ultramarine Blue and Titanium White and cool the colour down with a little Raw Umber. Using the same approach as in 1A, put in the shadow side of the clouds, applying light pressure to avoid obliterating the first cloud shape. Move the brush across the white cloud until you get a slight mixing of the two colours.

Palette-knife skies

Painting a sky with a painting knife or palette knife can be a surprisingly rapid method and yield some startling results. It is not a precise way of painting, so you must let the knife do the work to a large degree. All you can do is guide it and apply the right amount of pressure.

2A Load your knife with quite a generous amount of Titanium White and skid it across the surface with the flat side of the knife. Let it bobble and smear. Don't try and 'paint' with it like a brush. It is best to let this first layer semi-dry or dry, depending on how much you want the darker colour to merge with the white paint.

2B When you are ready, use exactly the same procedure but with Winsor Blue on your knife. Skid the paint across the white of the cloud but don't break the previous layer; it has to go on gently or you will expose the blue ground underneath. Keep this paint at the base of the cloud to make sure the top right of the cloud is receiving light from above. This is important since it gives the cloud the quality of an object in space.

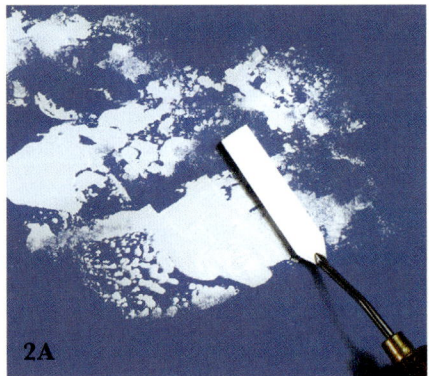

2A

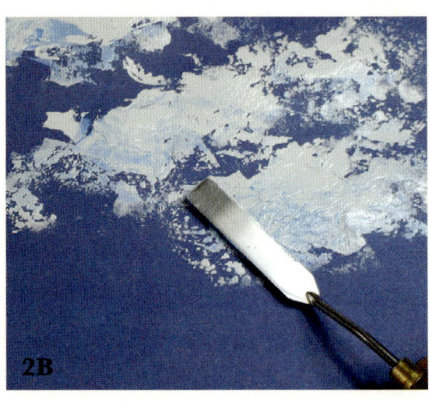

2B

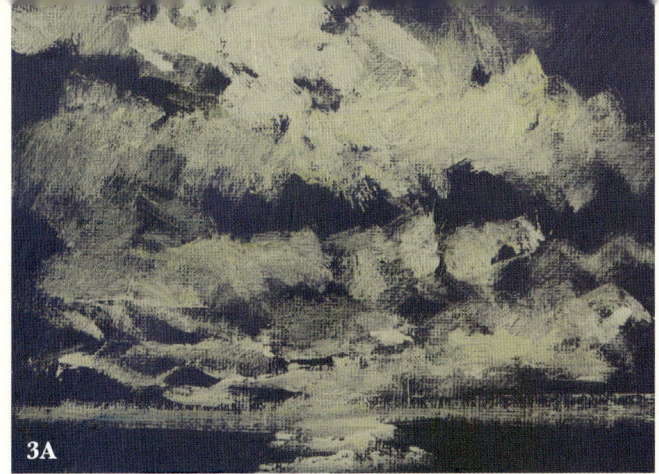

3A

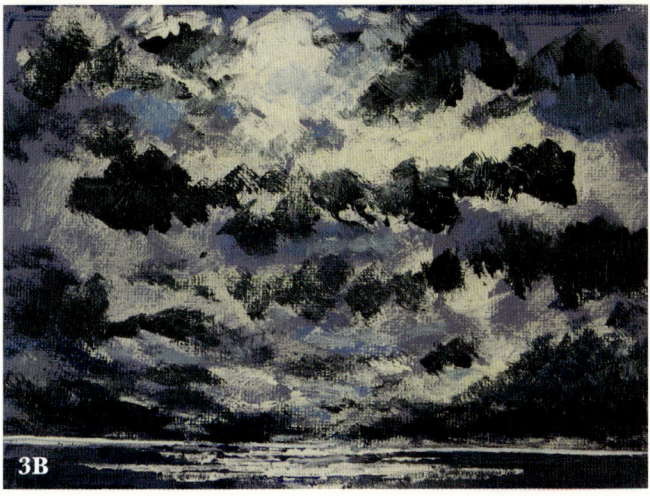

3B

Moonshine over the sea

Sometimes the sky is illuminated by the moon and not the sun. It is similar to day-time illumination, but the colours tend towards the grey end of the colour palette.

3A On a dry background of Ultramarine Blue, a little Titanium White and a hint of Cadmium Yellow, paint the white shapes of the clouds that go from large to small as they recede into the distance. Use a free, scumbling approach (see page 83) to give the clouds a wispy look where they are less dense.

3B Using a mixture of Winsor Blue and Mars Black, paint in the dark bases of the cloud along with the horizon and the reflections in the sea. Finally, add lighter patches of Winsor Blue mixed with Titanium White to the middle area of the picture to give the scene a central focus.

Large cumulus cloud

This is a wet-in-wet technique done with a flat nylon brush.

4 Put in a background wash of Winsor Blue mixed with some Titanium White. Leave it to dry, then paint the clouds with round, curving strokes in white. While the white paint is still wet, use the original blue to put in the shadow effects on the cloud. Use your brush delicately and you will get some very satisfying modulations of tone.

Perspective in cloudscapes

When clouds are drifting over the landscape, sometimes they appear to clump together in the distance. This is a foreshortening effect caused by one

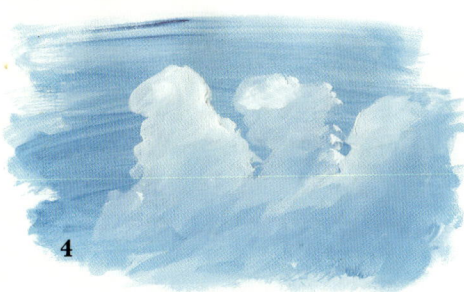

4

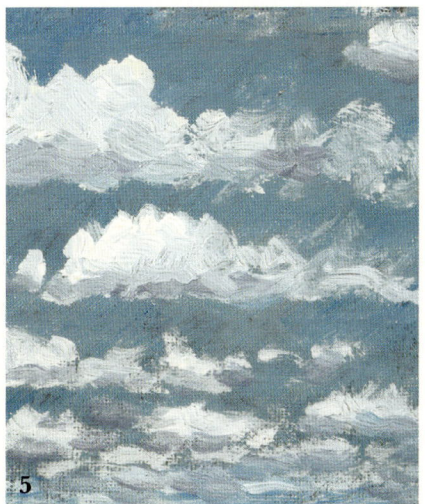

5

cloud being in front of the other all the way to the horizon. In this example, I have put in the clouds as progressively smaller shapes.

5 Using a hog-hair brush, paint the clouds in Titanium White on a background of Winsor Blue with a little Ultramarine Blue and white. While the white is still wet, add a mixture of Ultramarine Blue and a small amount of red to the bases of the clouds.

If you look at the kind of strokes I have used, you will see they are very simple. The darkest part of the cloud is at the bottom; by combining the white of the cloud with this darker colour, the mid-tone is mixed for you as you paint. As the clouds get closer to the horizon, they become smaller and less distinct, adding to the overall sense of perspective in the scene.

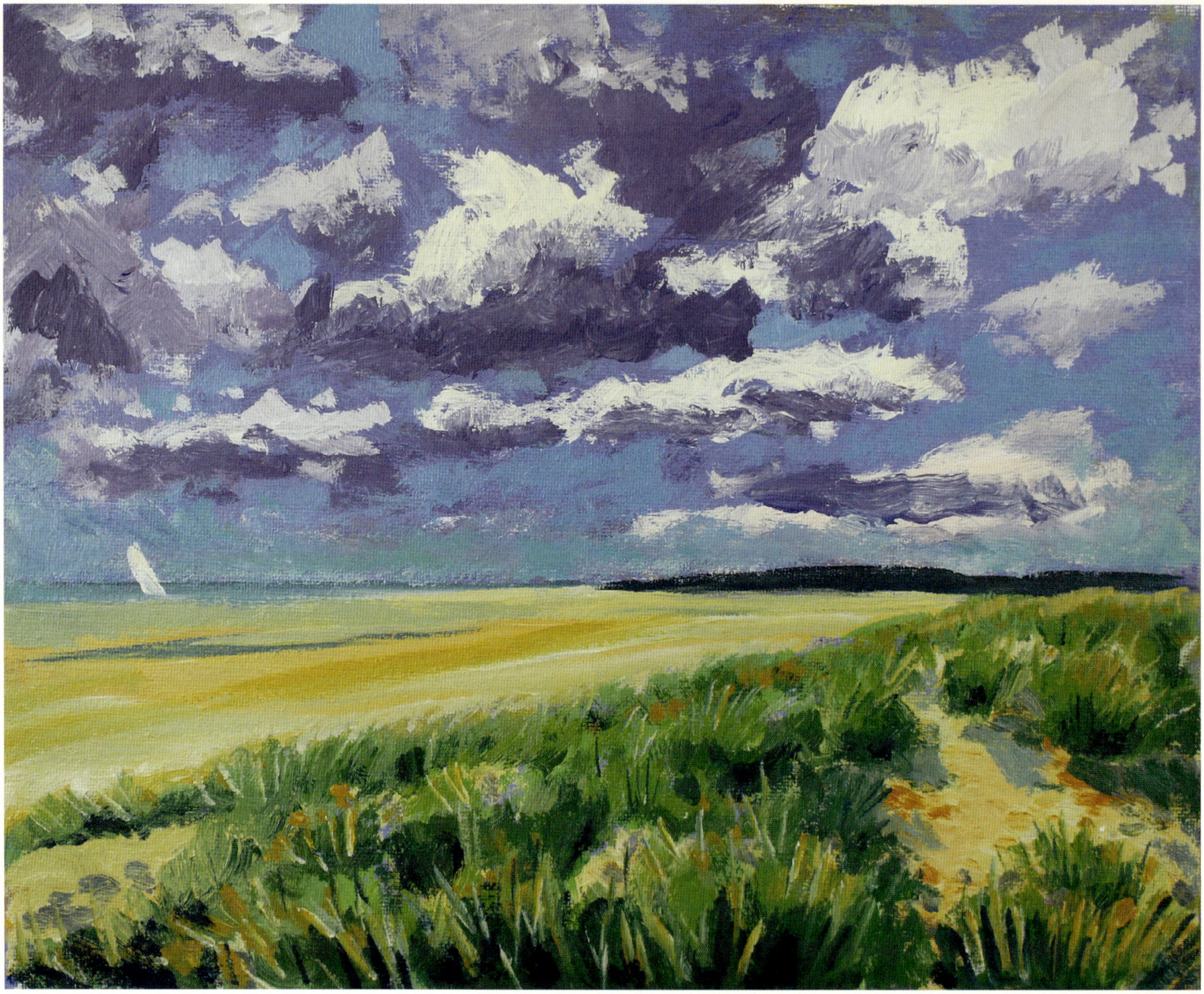

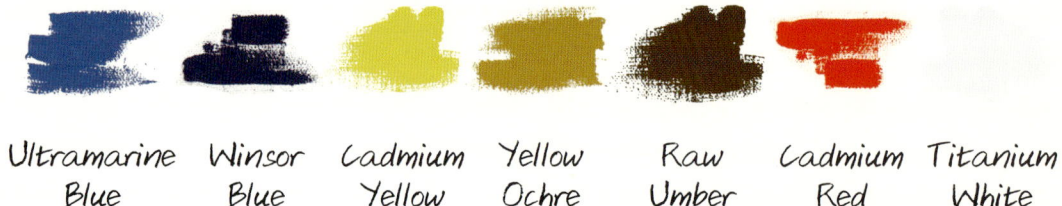

Seascape

Here you will produce a light and airy picture that evokes the breezy characteristics of a seascape. You will learn how to describe distance when there are no verticals, such as buildings, in the scene.

COLOURS NEEDED

Ultramarine Blue   Winsor Blue   Cadmium Yellow   Yellow Ochre   Raw Umber   Cadmium Red   Titanium White

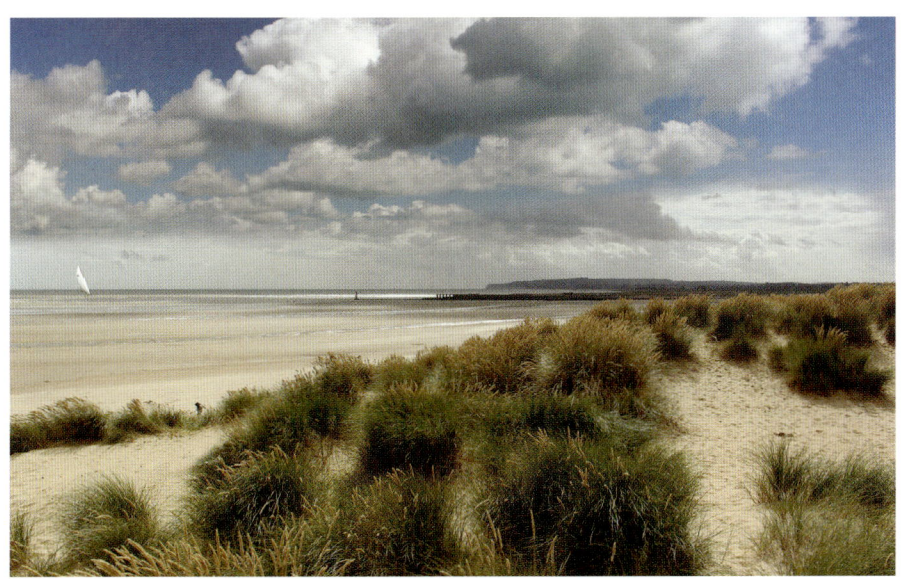

REFERENCE PHOTO

Artists have long been captivated by the drama of the sky and sea and the endless ways these elements can be combined. The sea can be calm or choppy, near or far away. The sky can be a dazzling blue or a dark, roiling mass. Seascapes are closely associated with cloudscapes (the sea is rarely seen without a sky), so look also at the Focus on Skies feature on pages 96–7.

In a picture where there are no verticals to give clues to the depth of the scene, it is important to use any visual pointers we have to hand. Those indications lie in the way the clouds behave and a phenomenon called 'aerial perspective'. The former is explained in stage 1 (see page 100). The latter involves using fewer strong colours towards the horizon. This is because the more atmosphere there is between you and distant objects, the less distinct those objects become. In the photograph above, you can see the boundary between sea and sky is indistinct and hazy, and the grasses lose their individual shapes and appear lighter. The hills on the horizon have a blue tint and their tops are broken and rough as they are lost in the light.

Another important element is the proportion of sky in relation to the rest of the picture. It is a common tradition in landscapes to put the horizon approximately two-thirds of the way down the picture. This is called the 'rule of thirds', where the picture plane is divided into nine equal parts and has the function of avoiding cutting compositions in half or putting objects bang in the centre of a picture. There is something about certain proportions that is satisfying, but in my opinion they are usually instinctive where art is concerned. The best way forward is to look at lots of good pictures and see how they are composed.

BELOW Study for Eagle Head, *by Winslow Homer, 1869.*
Notice the quality of light and the simple composition.

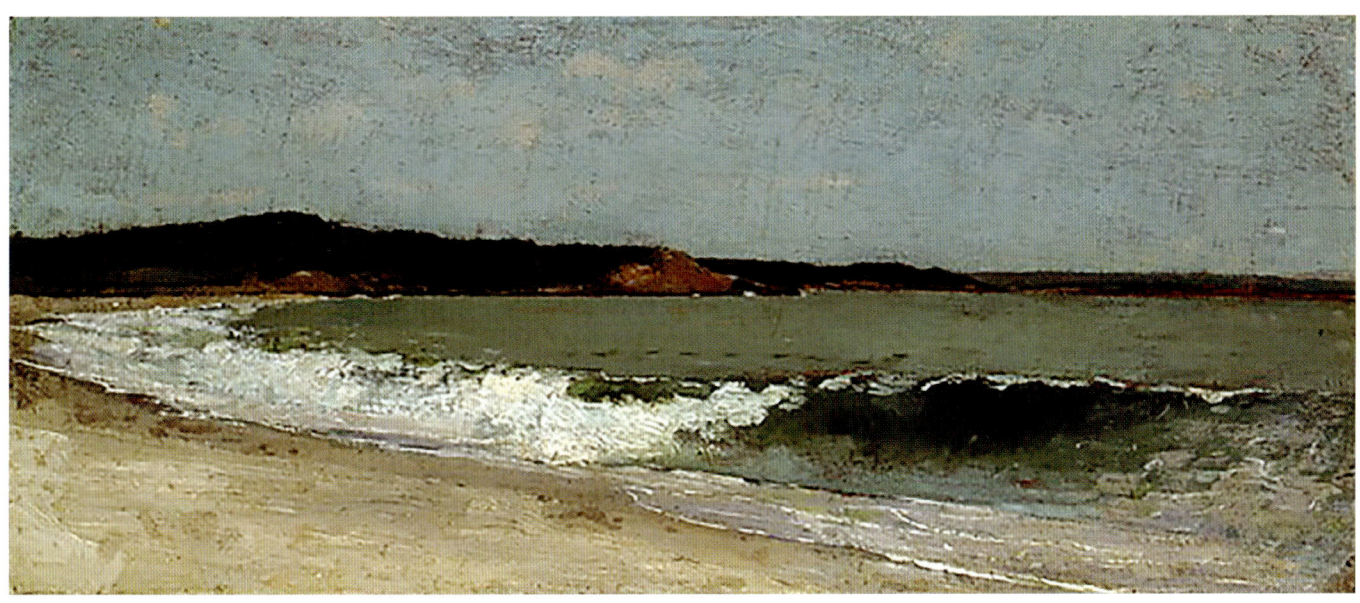

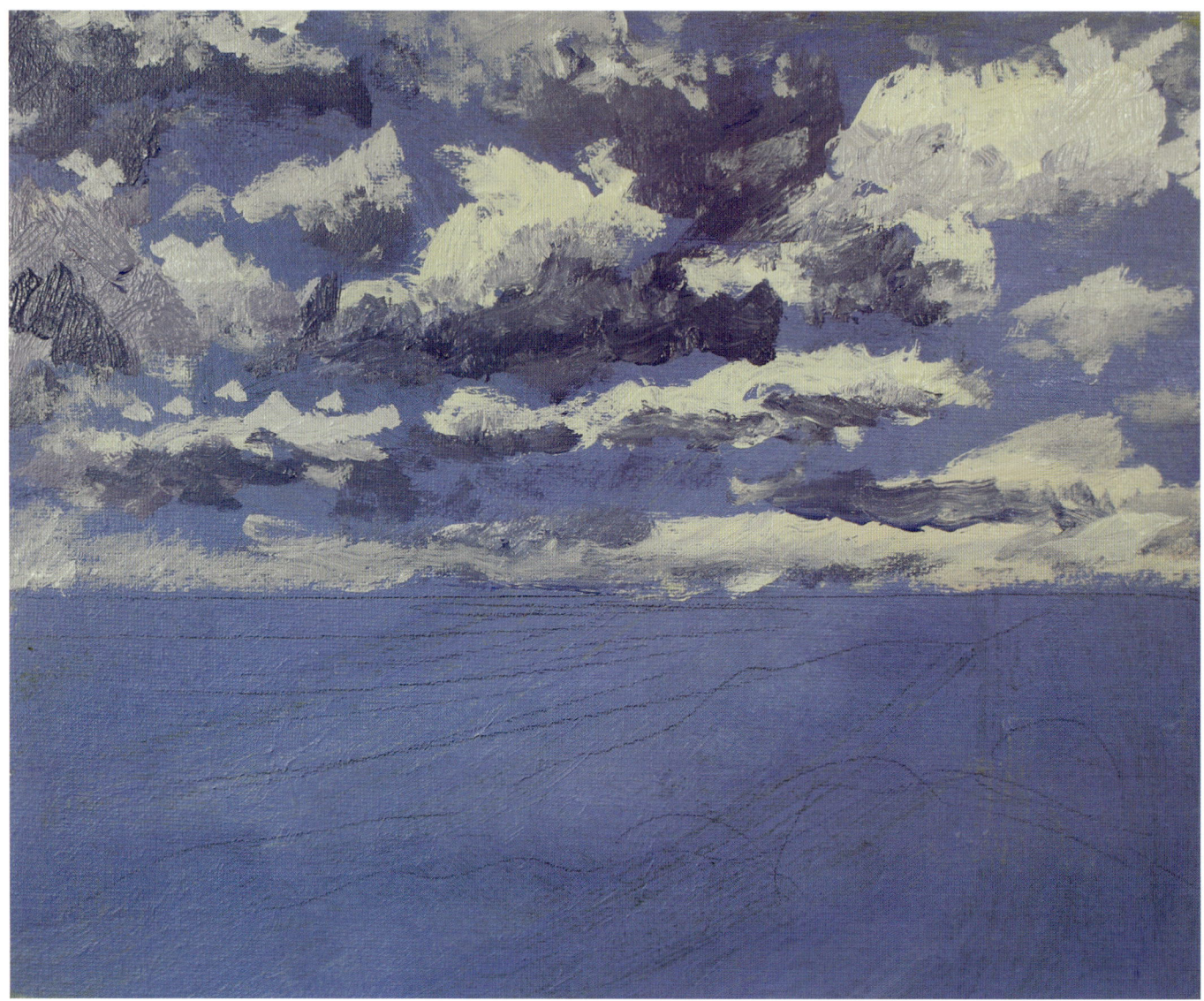

STAGE 1

Prepare a coloured ground of blue made up of Ultramarine Blue and a little Titanium White. Let this dry completely. Make a light sketch in pencil of the main areas of the picture. Add the clouds, making sure that they are larger and more separated the nearer they are to you. This is important when there are no visual references for perspective such as telegraph poles. The nearer to the horizon the clouds are, the smaller and more massed together they are.

Using a hog-hair brush, paint your clouds with Titanium White on the dry blue background. Be sure not to use the tip of your brush at this stage, but use the scumbling method (see page 83) to move your paint across the sky with the brush held nearly flat to the canvas (see Focus on Skies, pages 96–7). As the white paint starts to dry, mix Ultramarine Blue and a little Cadmium Red together, and, with the same kind of scumbling strokes, add the base of the clouds. Try to let the brush do the work of combining the blue and white.

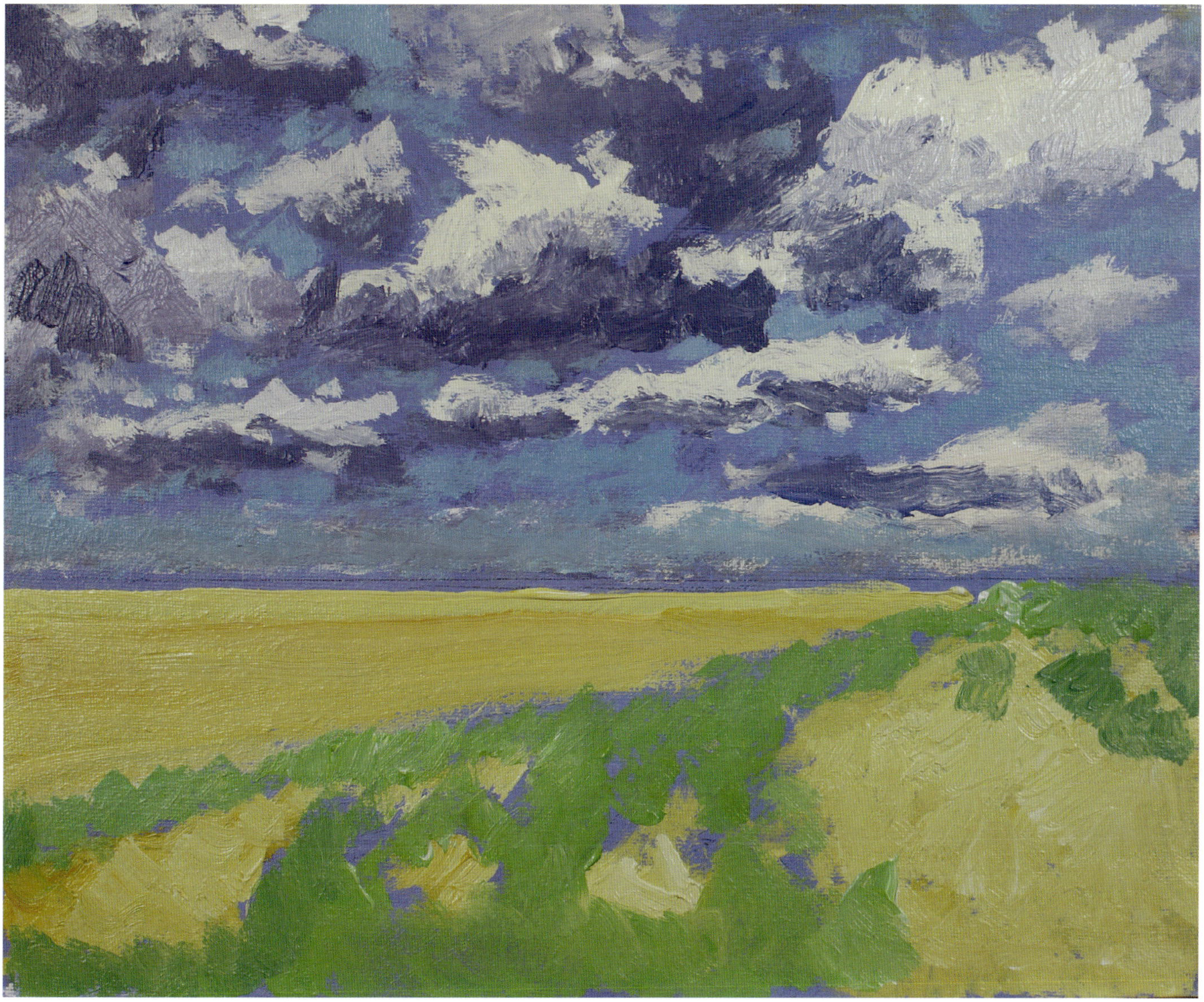

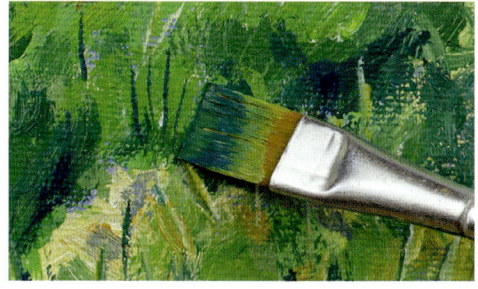

ABOVE *If painting on a light tone, load a flat synthetic brush with a darker colour, or a light colour if painting on a dark tone, and just place the brush on the canvas to make a straight mark. Spiny shrubs, grasses and reeds lend themselves very nicely to this technique.*

STAGE 2

To finish the sky, mix a little Winsor Blue with Titanium White so it is just a shade lighter than the blue ground. Add this colour in patches in between the clouds. Introducing another colour adds liveliness to the sky.

Mix Yellow Ochre with a small amount of Cadmium Red for the sand and Winsor Blue, Cadmium Yellow and Titanium White for the grasses. Make sure to leave patches of the original blue ground around the picture for added sparkle and interest.

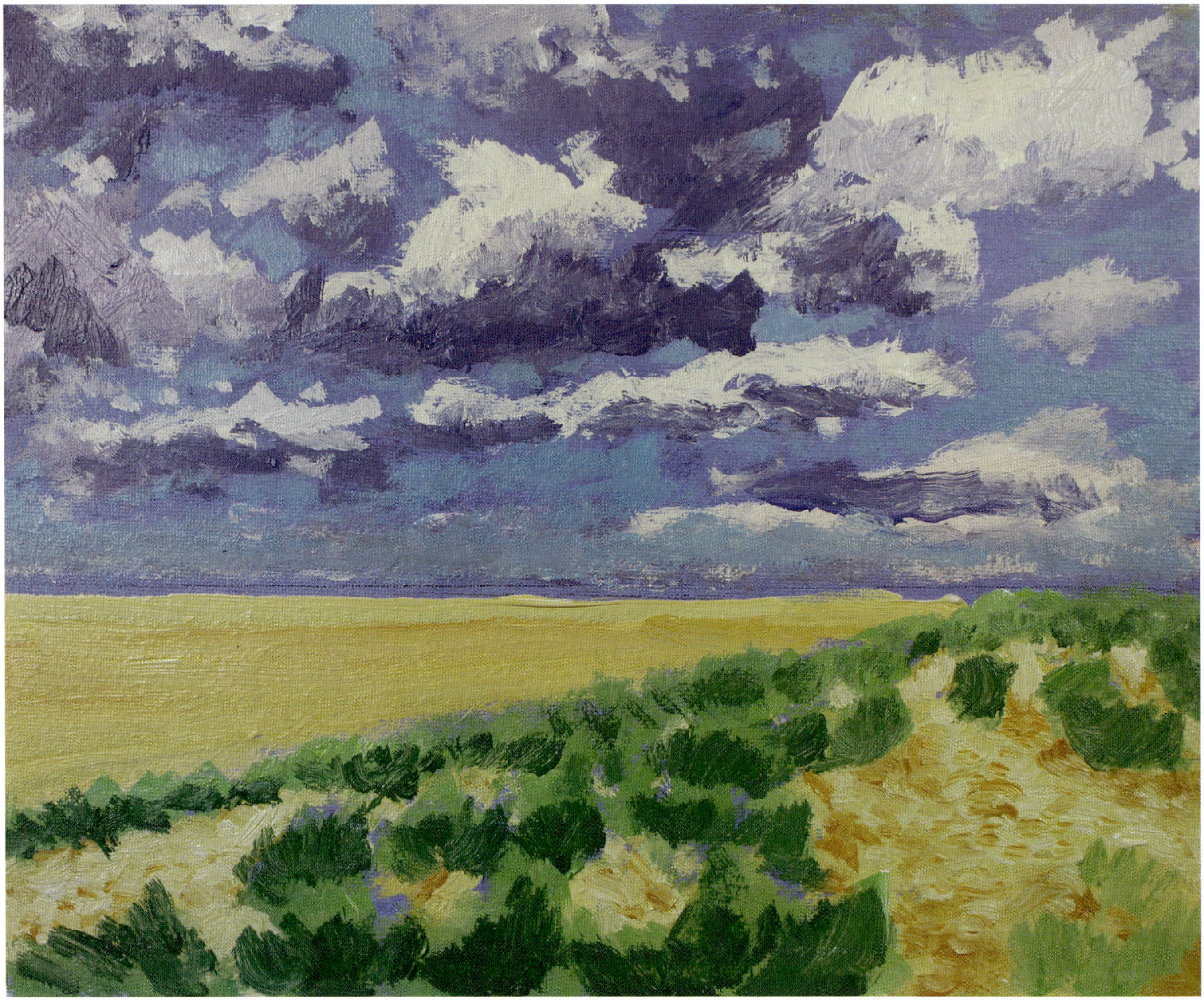

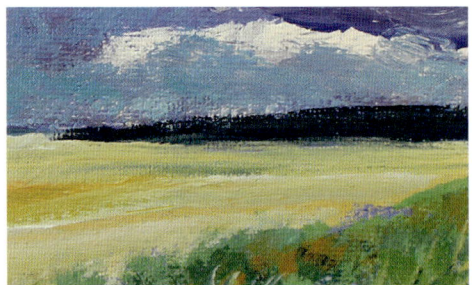

ABOVE *When something is far away, it loses definition, so it helps to roughen your distances. Load a bristle brush with some sky colour and drag it along the horizon. This will give an instant impression of mist and haze.*

STAGE 3

Add 'body' to the grasses by applying a darker shade of green made up of Winsor Blue, Cadmium Yellow and a little Ultramarine Blue. The small indentations in the sand are just a darker version of the Yellow Ochre, made by adding a small amount of Cadmium Red.

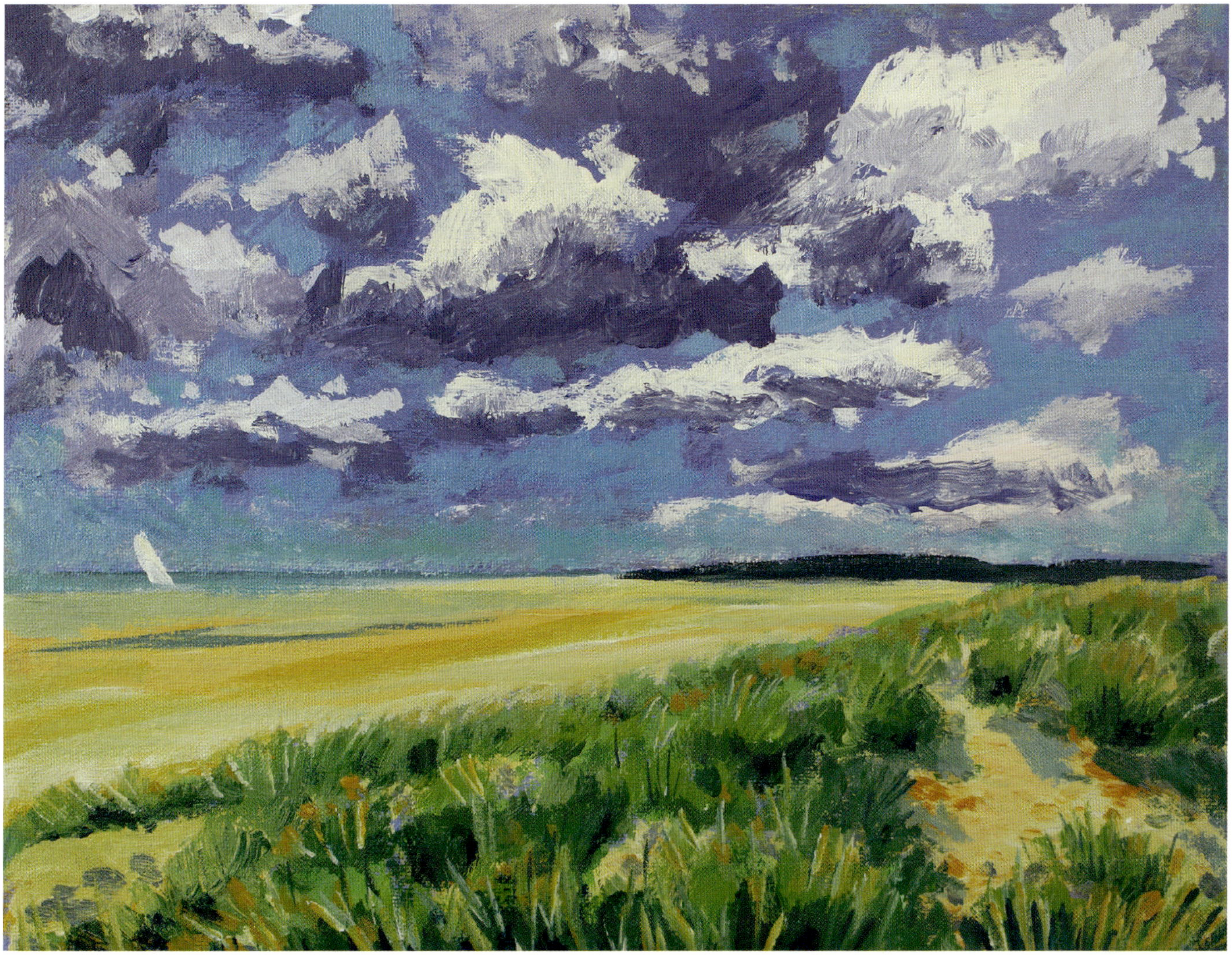

STAGE 4

At this stage, the grass in the foreground needs to be made more definite, but there should be less definition in the more distant grasses. This is called 'aerial perspective', meaning the atmosphere softens objects in the distance.

The grasses have different kinds of green in them. Make a green out of a mixture of Cadmium Yellow and Ultramarine Blue, plus a little Titanium White, and apply it to the tufts of grass with a flat nylon brush. Put in some Yellow Ochre using the same method and deepen the shadows with Winsor Blue, cooled down with a little Raw Umber.

Adding a mid-blue made from Ultramarine Blue and white to parts of the nearby sand gives good shadows. The distant hills are Winsor Blue and a little Cadmium Yellow, muted with Raw Umber.

Finally, use some of the colours you've used already as detail in the sand, with the final touch of a white sail in the distance.

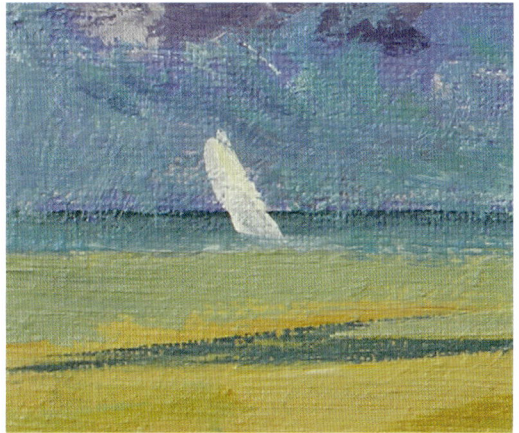

ABOVE *When a scene is mostly composed of planes such as sea, sky, water or grass, placing one small object in the composition such as this white sail can add a new and satisfying dimension to the final picture.*

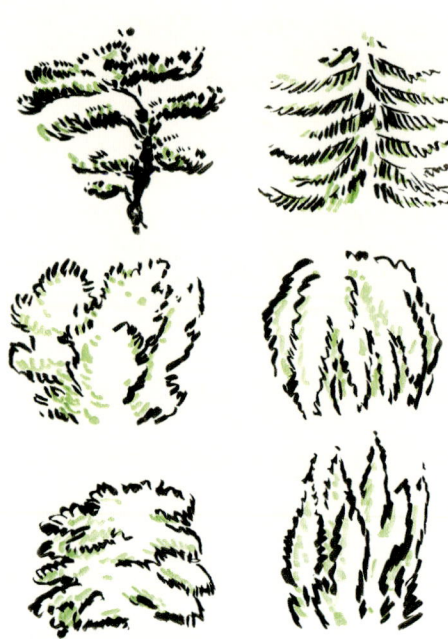

ABOVE *Here are some common tree shapes. As an exercise, when you go out sketching, simply record the overall shape of a tree and how the leaf canopies make a series of overlapping shapes.*

With the growing popularity of landscape painting in the 18th and 19th centuries, trees became centre stage in many works of art and were no longer consigned to the role of just being a backdrop to an allegorical painting. For example, take a look at John Constable's landscape paintings and notice how the trees are major players in his compositions.

Trees have a particular structure and you could say that trunks, branches and twigs are the 'skeleton' of the tree. Getting to know this skeleton helps you paint all kinds of trees, whether in summer or winter. When a tree is in leaf, the structure of the branches, twigs and leaves give the canopy its shape.

It is best to keep to three tones when attempting to paint trees. Try to find the overlapping shapes that describe the whole shape of the canopy.

FOCUS ON
Trees

Trees come in many shapes and sizes. In some ways, trees have the same painterly qualities as clouds. The same rules of light and shade (see page 77) apply to all trees.

Painting a simple pine tree

Here is an example of how you might approach a simple tree. First, work on the structure. Even though the branches may be hidden, try to imagine how the tree is made. What shape is it? Is it tall and narrow or squat and bushy? Then work on the canopy.

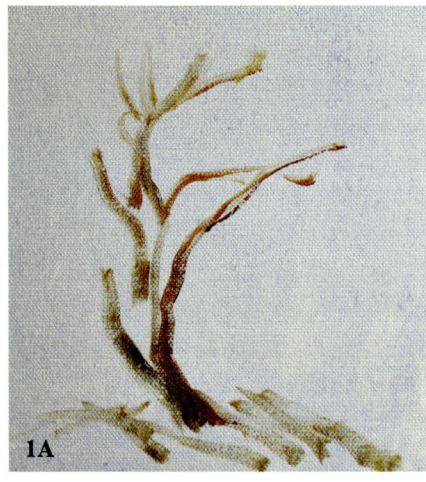

1A

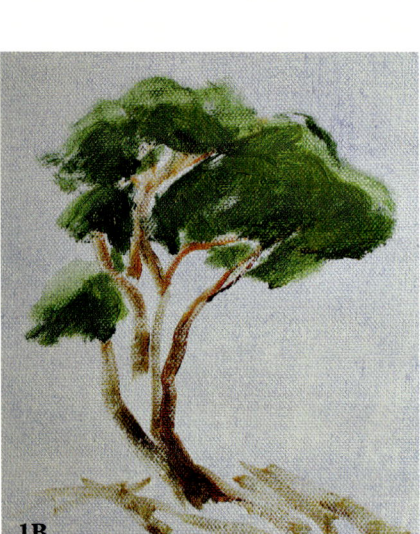

1B

1A Use a hog-hair brush to make the shape of the trunk and branches.

1B Find the shape of the canopy. Here, it is a single dome shape. Paint the canopy in a slightly dilute dark green made up of Winsor Blue and a little Cadmium Yellow, similar to a watercolour approach. It is best to keep the paint moist in this exercise as this will help combine the different tones of green.

1C Mix a thicker mid-green made up of Cadmium Yellow and some Winsor Blue and paint the lighter parts of the canopy. Finally, use a light green, made up of the previous mixture but with some Titanium White, to paint the very brightest leaves. Use this last colour to create smudged boundaries between the mid-tones and high tones. You can even put a dash of it straight into the darkest parts to help bring the canopy forward.

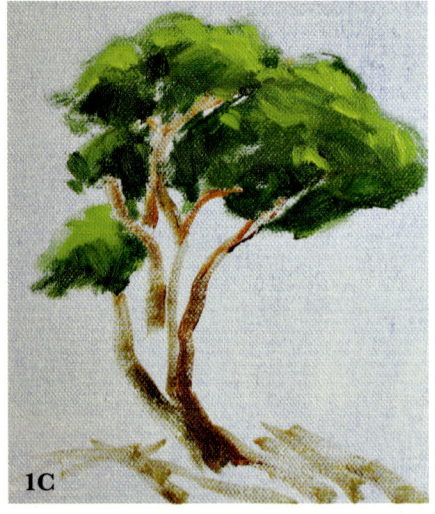

1C

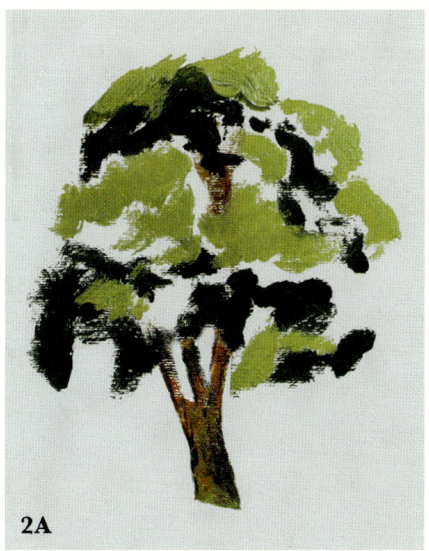

2A

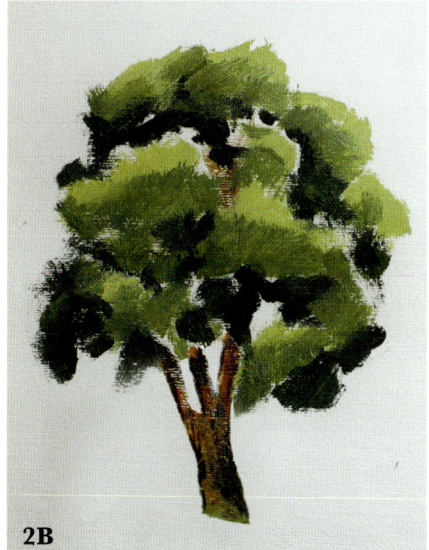

2B

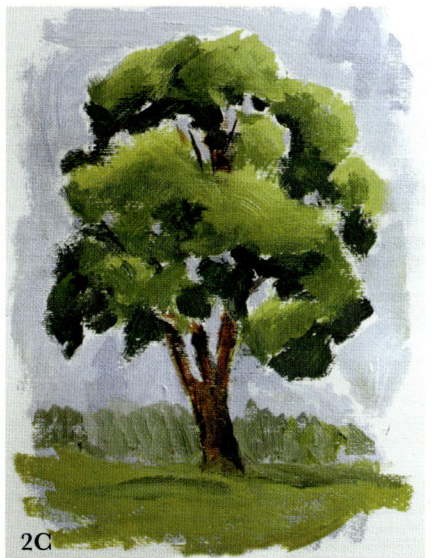

2C

Painting a forest tree

This study is of a more complex tree. Notice that the trunk divides into three boughs; each bough has branches that support more canopies of leaves.

2A Starting a tree like this allows you to get the whole shape in just a few brush marks. I have put the darkest shadows of the canopies in first and then the high tones. The darkest tone is made up of Winsor Blue and a dash of Mars Black. The high tone is Cadmium Yellow with Ultramarine Blue.

2B Paint in the mid-tones using Ultramarine Blue and Cadmium Yellow. These mid-tones lie between the dark and light areas of the canopy.

2C At this stage, I combined the three tonal transitions in the foliage. For this, I used some of the lighter green from the first stage and gently blended the darker and lighter tones together, all the while trying to keep the original shape of the canopy. Finally, I added a sketchy sky made from Ultramarine Blue and Titanium White and, where the sky is visible through the branches, put in small amounts of the blue there too.

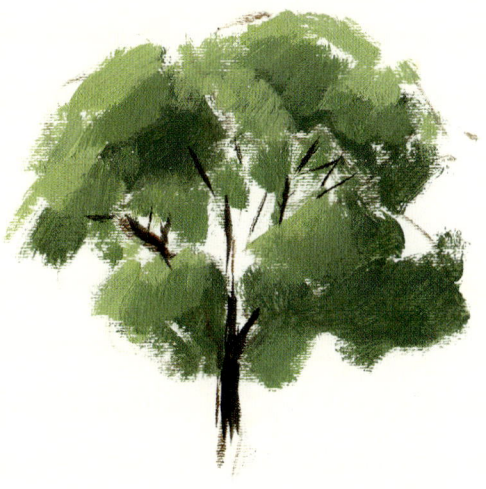

ABOVE *The maple tree has thin branches and a slender trunk. It has a large, spreading canopy, but the branches are slender and well spaced, allowing the light through the canopy onto the ground.*

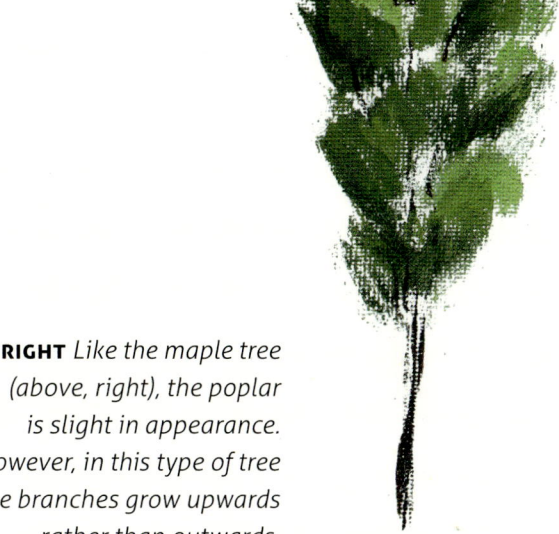

RIGHT *Like the maple tree (above, right), the poplar is slight in appearance. However, in this type of tree the branches grow upwards rather than outwards.*

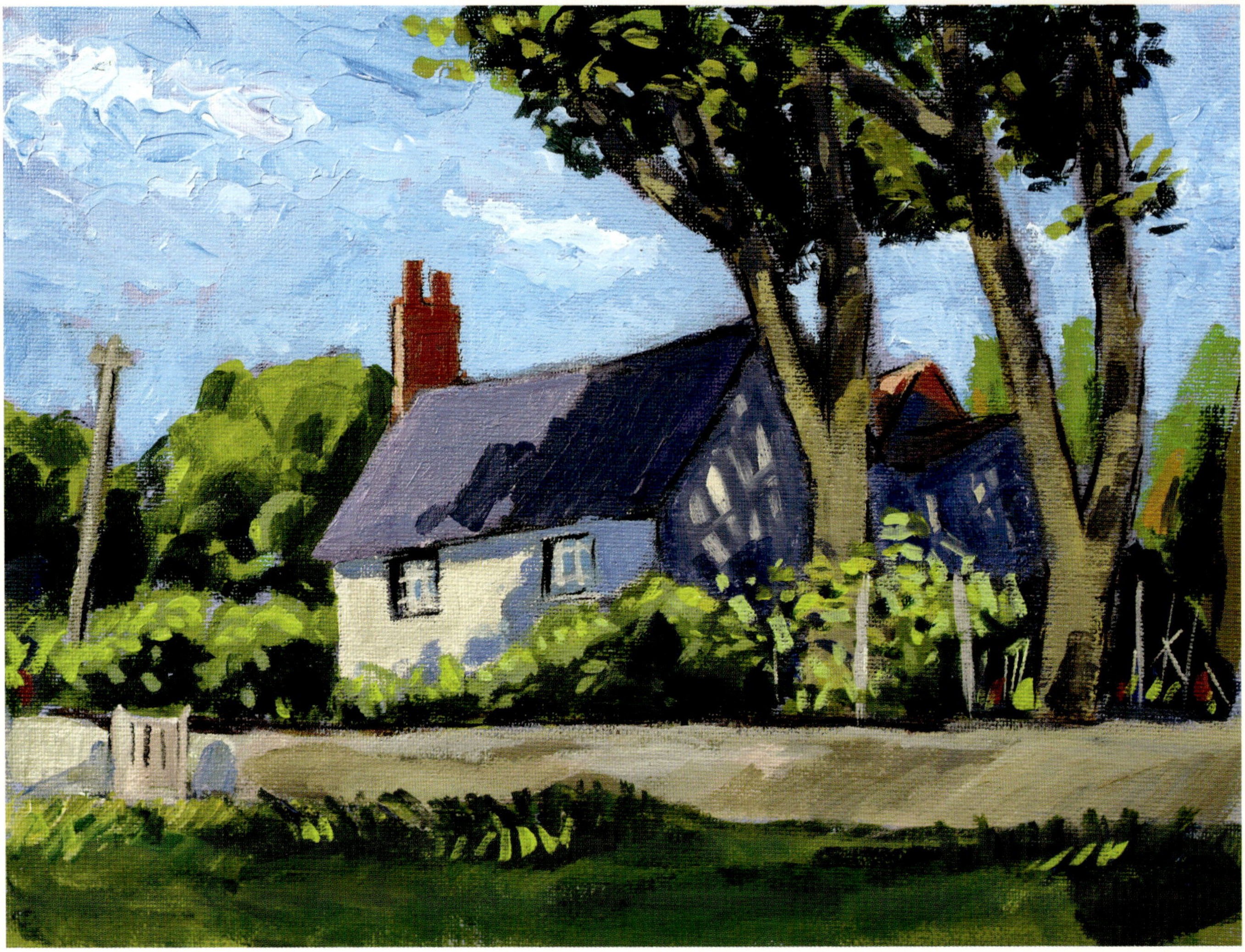

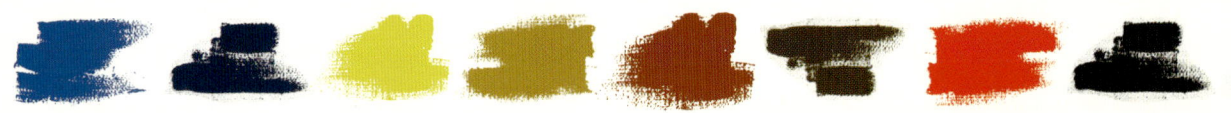

Summer Cottage

This project will show you how to paint a view of a cottage from a low angle with the effects of sunlight on walls and foliage. You will learn how to mix colours so they stay bright and how to build up shapes that represent foliage and architecture.

COLOURS NEEDED

Ultramarine Blue   Winsor Blue   Cadmium Yellow   Yellow Ochre   Burnt Sienna   Raw Umber   Cadmium Red   Mars Black   Titanium White

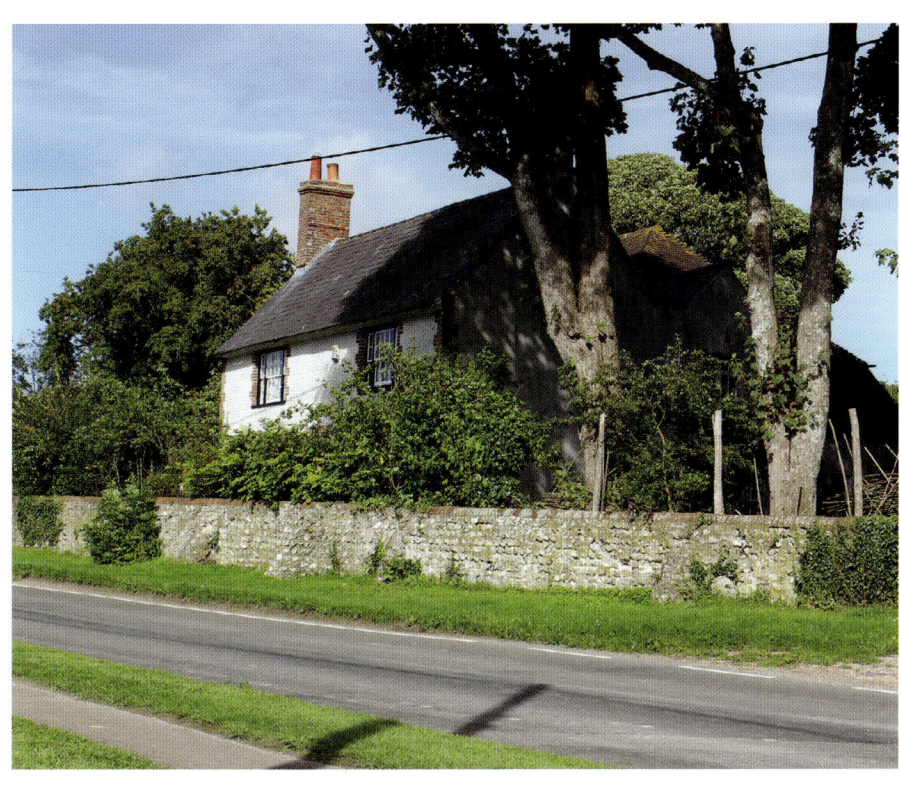

REFERENCE PHOTO

This painting is from a photograph I took one summer's day in Sussex, England. As you can see, the finished painting differs from the photograph in many ways. That is not a bad thing. In fact I think it's the reverse! If you can use your imagination to build on your reference photograph, all the better.

In the later stages, don't be afraid to add detail or re-paint areas as you see fit. The danger comes when you start 'fiddling'. There is a big difference between editing and fiddling. I think you instinctively know when you have gone too far in trying to change what you have. Very often the first strokes are the best.

PHOTOGRAPHY AND SKETCHING

You know, of course, that the camera lies. There is no such thing as 'reality' in a photo. A camera has one 'eye' and, depending on the focal length of the lens, you can get wildly different results of the same view. A 28mm lens will give a totally different view from a 55mm lens. It's the same with your eyes. Close one eye and look at a scene and do the same with the other – the scene shifts.

Tip

Doing a sketch on the spot, no matter how quickly, can give you an alternative perspective that can be very helpful when you paint from the photograph at home. This drawing was done in a small sketchbook in a few minutes while I was sitting by the side of the road. It doesn't have a great deal of information in it, but what it does record are my responses to the scene. You automatically draw what interests you most.

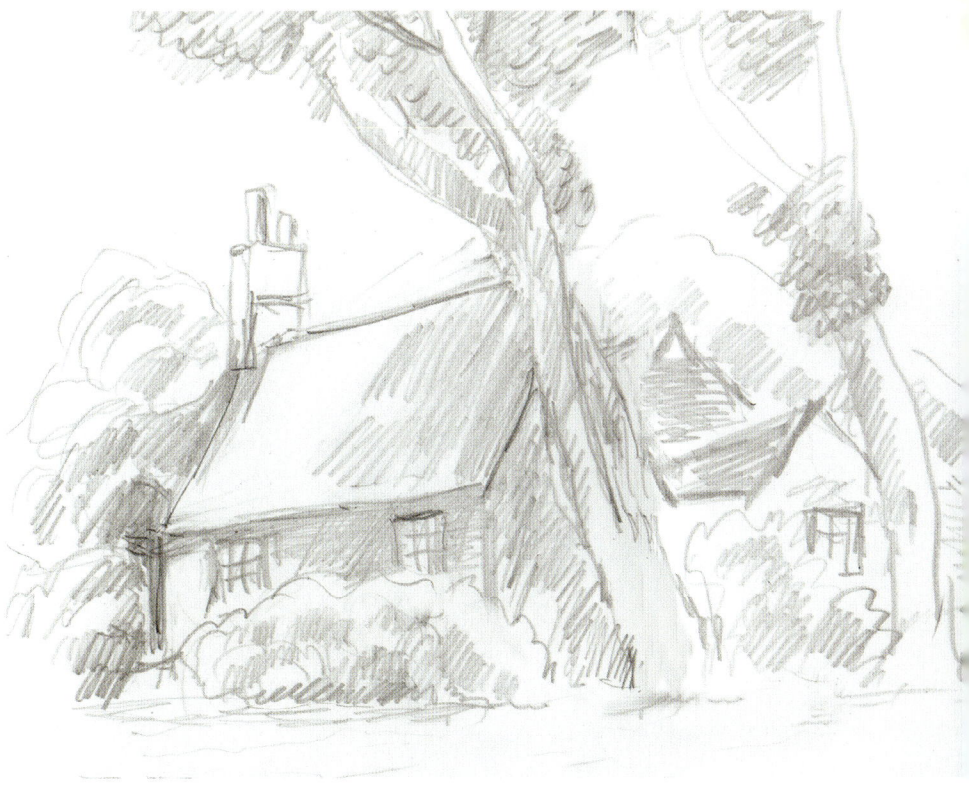

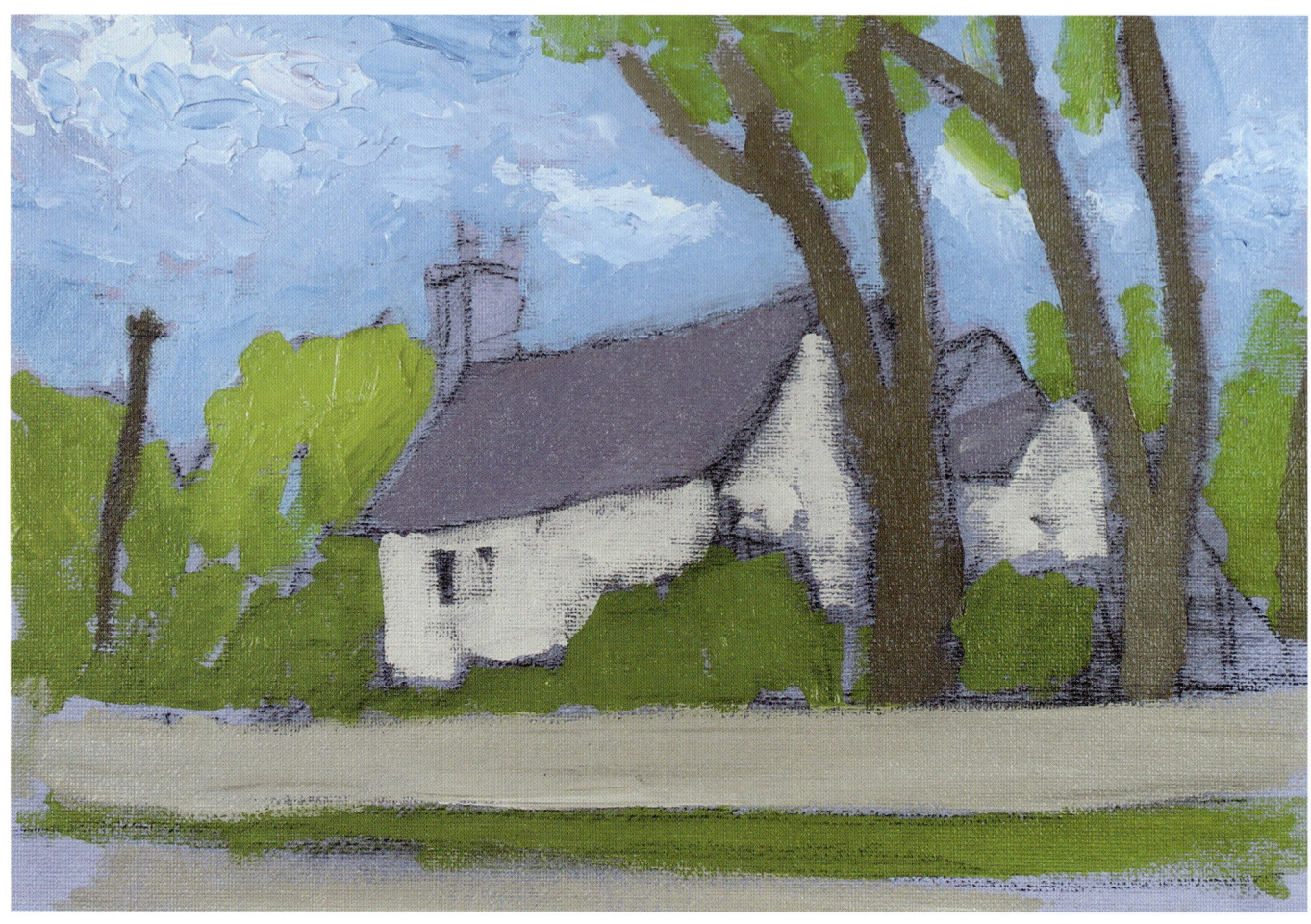

Tip

If you compare the line of the roof in the photograph with the same area in my painting, you can see that the line of the roof dips in the middle. Making straight lines a little crooked can add charm to older houses.

STAGE 1

Start by making a sketch on your canvas. In this case I sketched lightly with a soft pencil on to a ground colour of Ultramarine Blue mixed with a little Titanium White. Don't worry about smudging this drawing when you are painting; the paint will cover up any initial marks if it is applied thickly enough.

Now block in the main colour elements of the picture. Mix Winsor Blue and Titanium White and use a bristle brush to thickly apply the paint to the whole sky area. Warm up parts of the sky by adding a small amount of Cadmium Red into your blue. Add some clouds by applying Titanium White with your palette knife, using dabbing and skidding motions. Let the white paint mix freely with the blue of the sky but try and leave the tops of the clouds as white as possible.

Using a mixture of Ultramarine Blue, Cadmium Yellow and a touch of Winsor Blue, block in all of what you see as green in the picture. Next, paint in the trunks of the trees and the telegraph pole with a mixture of Raw Umber and Titanium White. The wall in front of the cottage is the same mix but with much less Raw Umber. The roof is a mixture of Ultramarine Blue, a little Cadmium Red and Titanium White. Finally, paint in the walls of the cottage with Titanium White and a tiny amount of Raw Umber to cool it down a little.

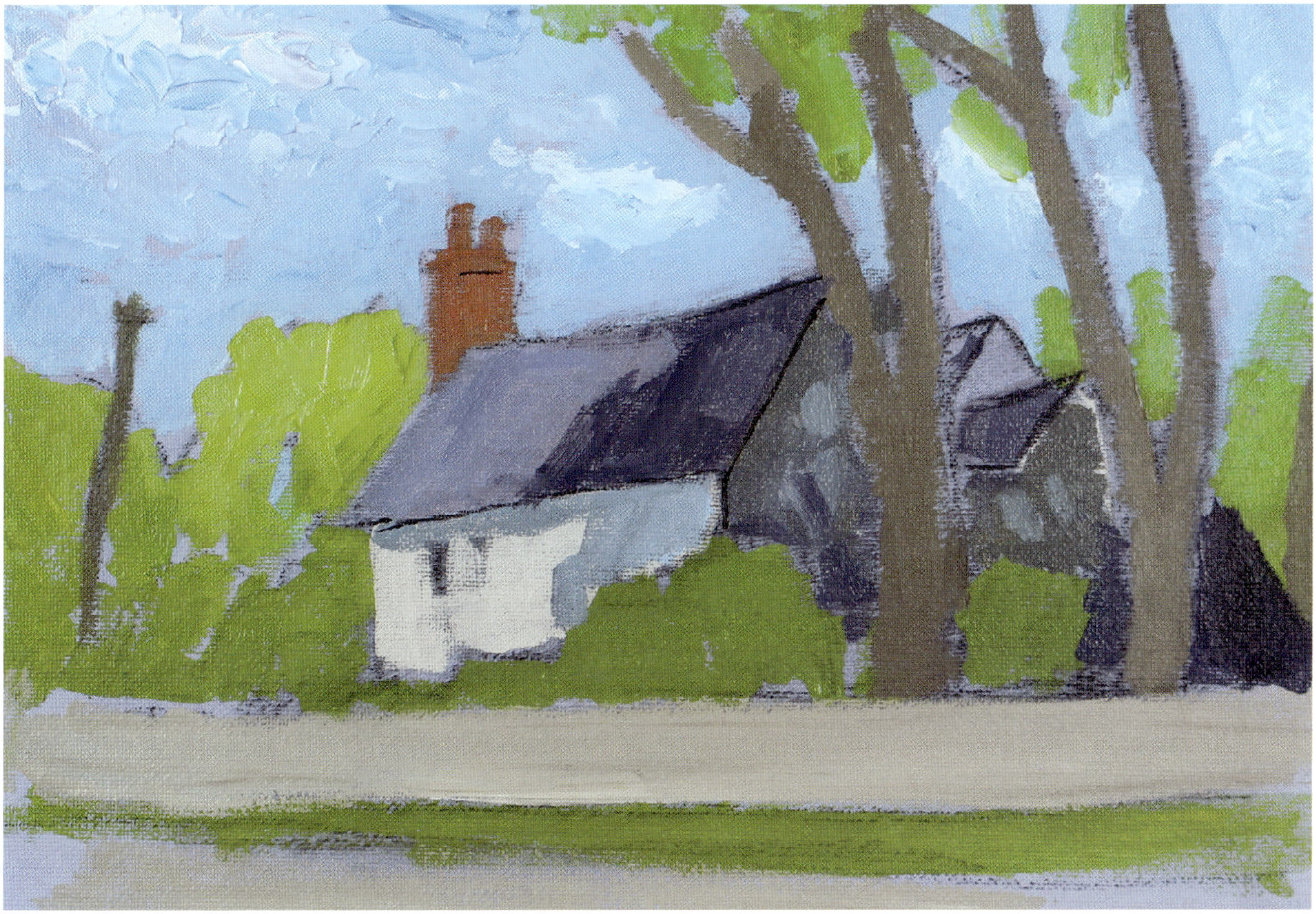

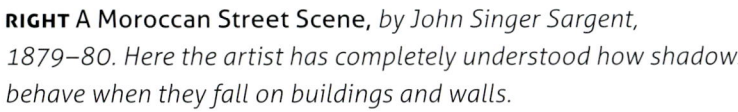

STAGE 2

Here we are going to think about shadows. There is a strong shadow cast by the tree on the cottage roof and behind the tree trunks. These shadows are made by mixing Winsor Blue with a little Cadmium Red cooled down with a dash of Raw Umber.

Some parts of this dense shadow have reflections of other colours in them. Mix Ultramarine Blue with some Titanium White and add Raw Umber until you get a warm grey colour and patch it in to the darker shadow. Add lighter areas of Titanium White mixed with Ultramarine Blue and a little Raw Umber for the dappled look in the shadows and on the sunlit side of the cottage. The chimney pot is Burnt Sienna.

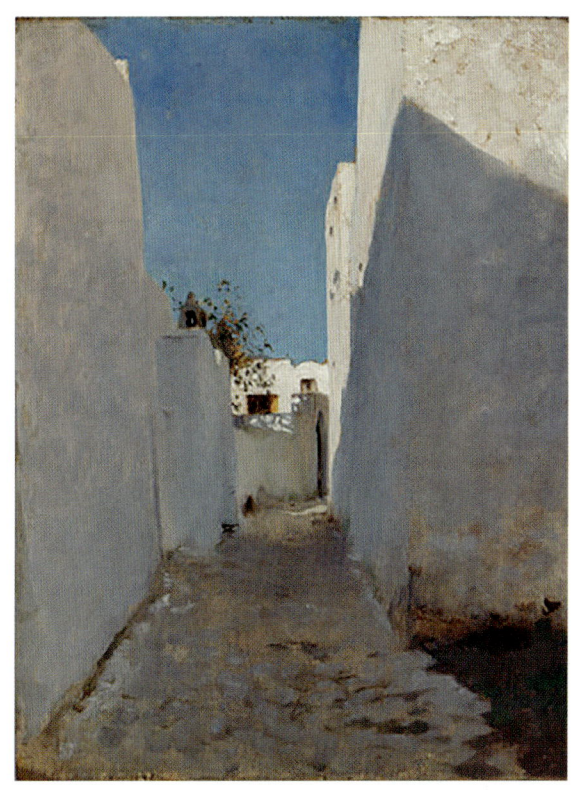

RIGHT A Moroccan Street Scene, *by John Singer Sargent, 1879–80. Here the artist has completely understood how shadows behave when they fall on buildings and walls.*

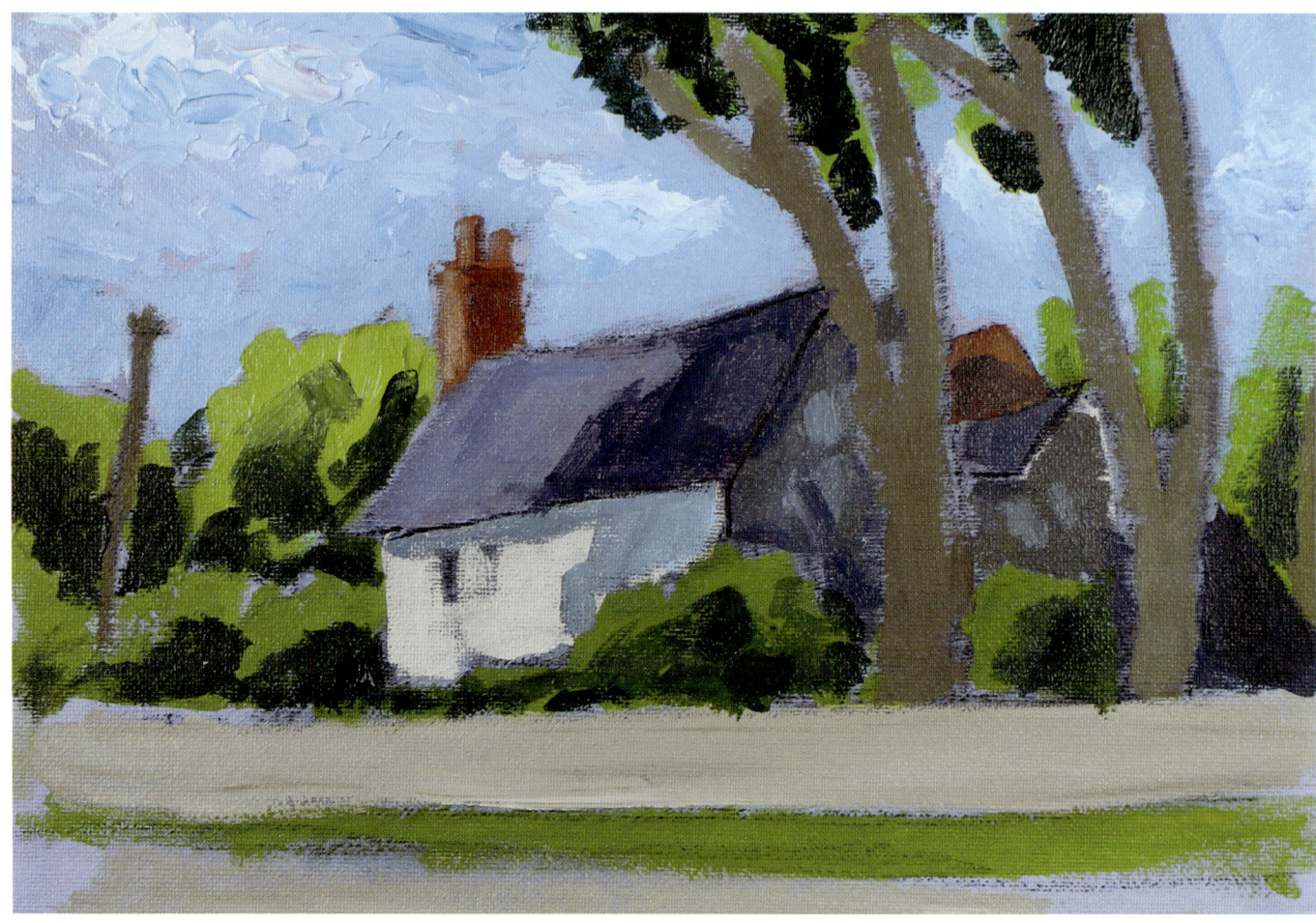

STAGE 3

In this stage we begin to give some form to the foliage in the picture, so mix some Winsor Blue with a little Cadmium Yellow and put in the shadow sides of the bushes and far trees. Use strokes that echo the general shape of the objects that you are describing. Push the brush over the underlying green colour so you get a varying thickness of paint. This process helps you get the feel of objects that are alive and growing. The undersides of the canopies of the foreground trees are almost completely in shadow so appear quite dark.

Tip

Keep an eye on your tones by standing back from your easel occasionally. Be careful not to overwork your piece during the final stages.

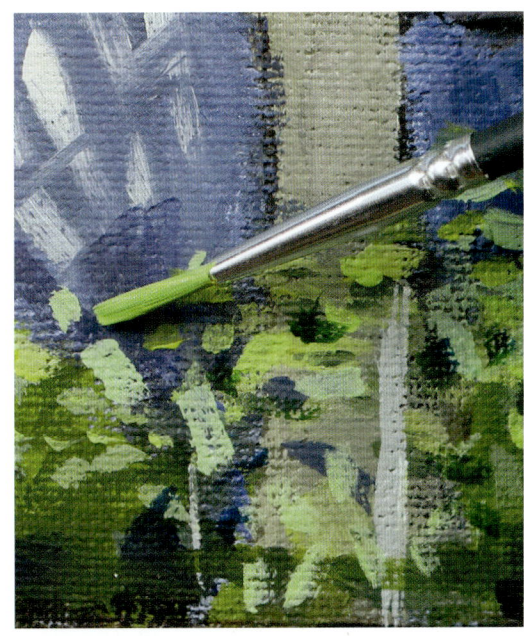

RIGHT *When painting foliage, sometimes it is good practice to paint a highlight directly on to a dark patch. This gives the effect of individual leaves catching the light and lends a sparkle to your picture.*

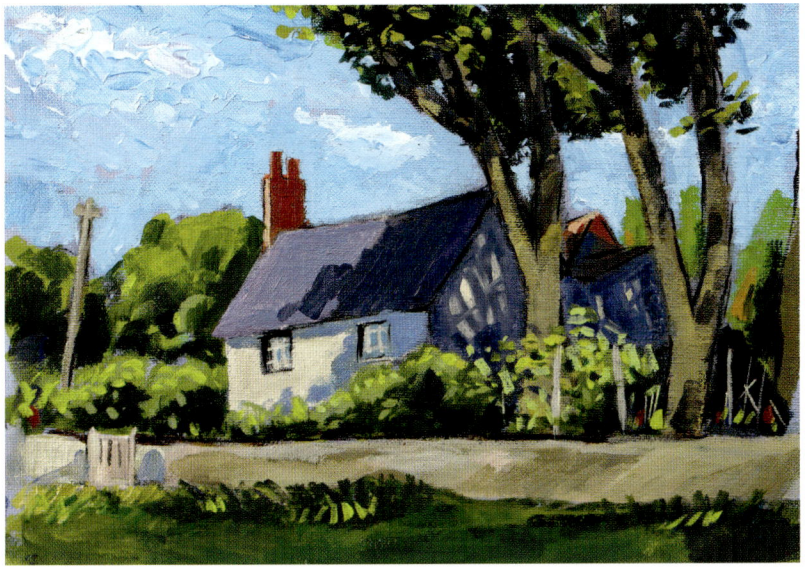

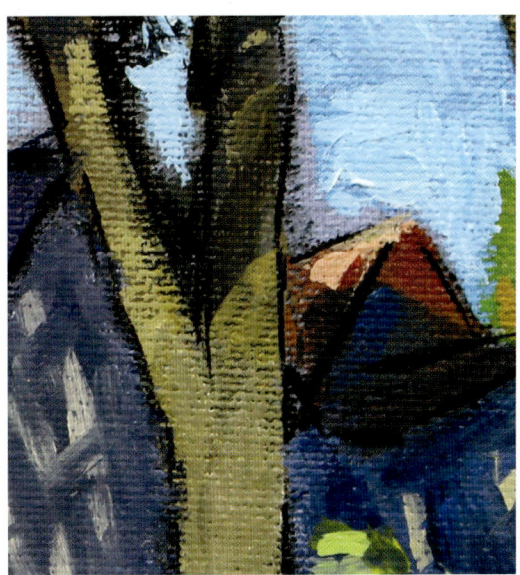

STAGE 4

To give the trees and bushes more shape we need to add a mid-tone green. Mix Cadmium Yellow with Ultramarine Blue, adding a little Titanium White to get a tone that lies between the light and dark tones of the foliage. Paint in this colour next to the darker tone. Try to get this green to join the other two greens without making the transition too smooth.

To create the sunlight on the bushes in front of the cottage and in the canopies of the two big trees I have added lively brushstrokes on top of the three tones already there. This is the lightest green in the picture made by adding small quantities of Winsor Blue and Cadmium Yellow to Titanium White. For these strokes I used a synthetic, round-headed No. 6 brush.

The darker shadows on the tree trunks are Raw Umber mixed with a little Titanium White. I further developed the shadows on the cottage wall under the trees by adding flashes of a light tone of Raw Umber and Titanium White. The light on the chimney stack is the same as your original Burnt Sienna but with the addition of Titanium White.

ABOVE *A 'cast shadow' occurs when a shadow from one object falls onto another. When you are painting a cast shadow, as on the trunk of the tree, make it follow the shape of the object it falls on. If a shadow cuts across a form it can destroy the shape of it.*

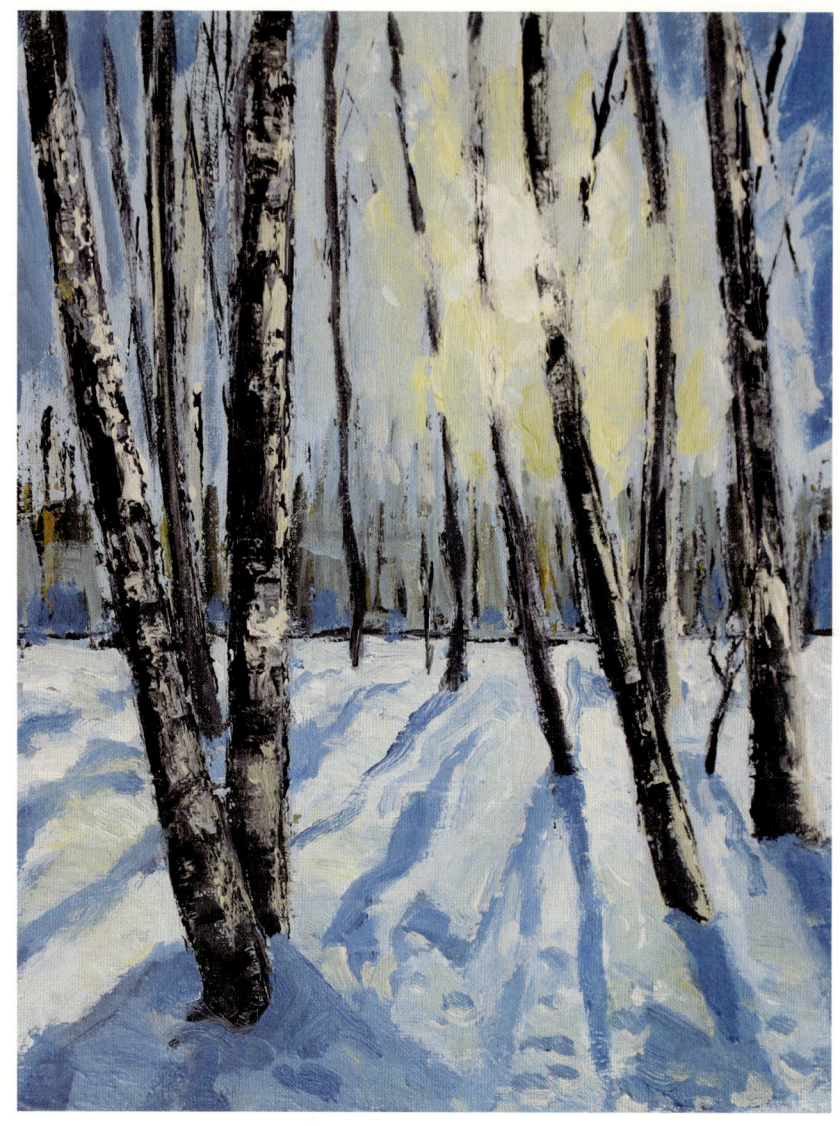

Winter Landscape

This exercise requires you to paint a snowy landscape where the light source is directly in front of you. Here you will learn about a limited palette and how to use knives and plastic credit cards as tools to achieve certain effects.

COLOURS NEEDED

Ultramarine
Blue

Winsor
Blue

Cadmium
Yellow

Yellow
Ochre

Mars
Black

Titanium
White

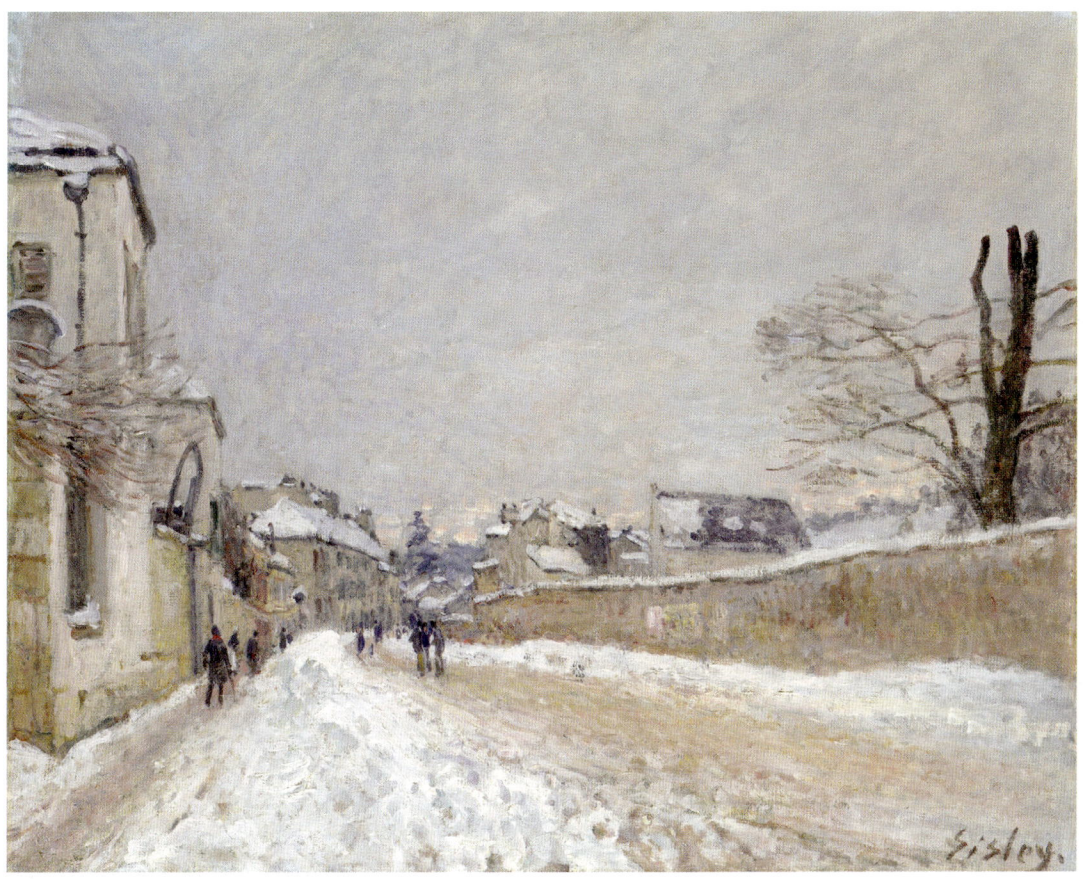

LEFT Rue Eugène Moussoir at Moret, *by Alfred Sisley, 1891. A subtle palette of warm and cool colours creates this snowy landscape.*

Tip

Make sure that all the shadows that are cast by the sun obey the rules of perspective. If the light source is directly in front of you, every object will cast a shadow that points directly at the sun.

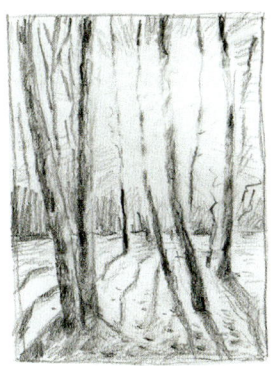

The snow scene is a common theme in art from northern latitudes. Snow is full of reflected light and transforms a landscape by creating startling new forms and contrasts. Many of the Impressionist painters were captivated by snow scenes because of the opportunity they presented of painting light inside shadows. The Impressionists can be rightly credited with discovering that shadows weren't just neutral dark patches but that they had colours within them. Painting snow scenes offered an exciting colour palette in which to express their observations and feelings about light itself. Claude Monet and Alfred Sisley were excellent snow painters.

When you attempt to create a winter scene, bear in mind that the landscape is very much altered by what is really a blanketing effect. This creates many interesting shapes and reduces the number of colours dramatically.

For painting snow we are going to use a lot of white! The shadows cast by snow are predominantly blue, but there are other colours in there too.

Please have a look at the section on skies on pages 96–7, as painting clouds is very similar to painting snow. Like clouds, snow is best tackled by laying down a thick covering of white paint followed quite quickly with either Ultramarine Blue or Winsor Blue for the shadows, depending on the effect you want to create. Ultramarine Blue has a slightly warm tinge, whereas the Winsor Blue looks much colder.

I think a hog-hair brush is the best for this type of work as it can move the paint around with greater expression than a synthetic brush. However, you may find a synthetic brush suits you better. Do some trial runs on a separate canvas or card before you start your painting.

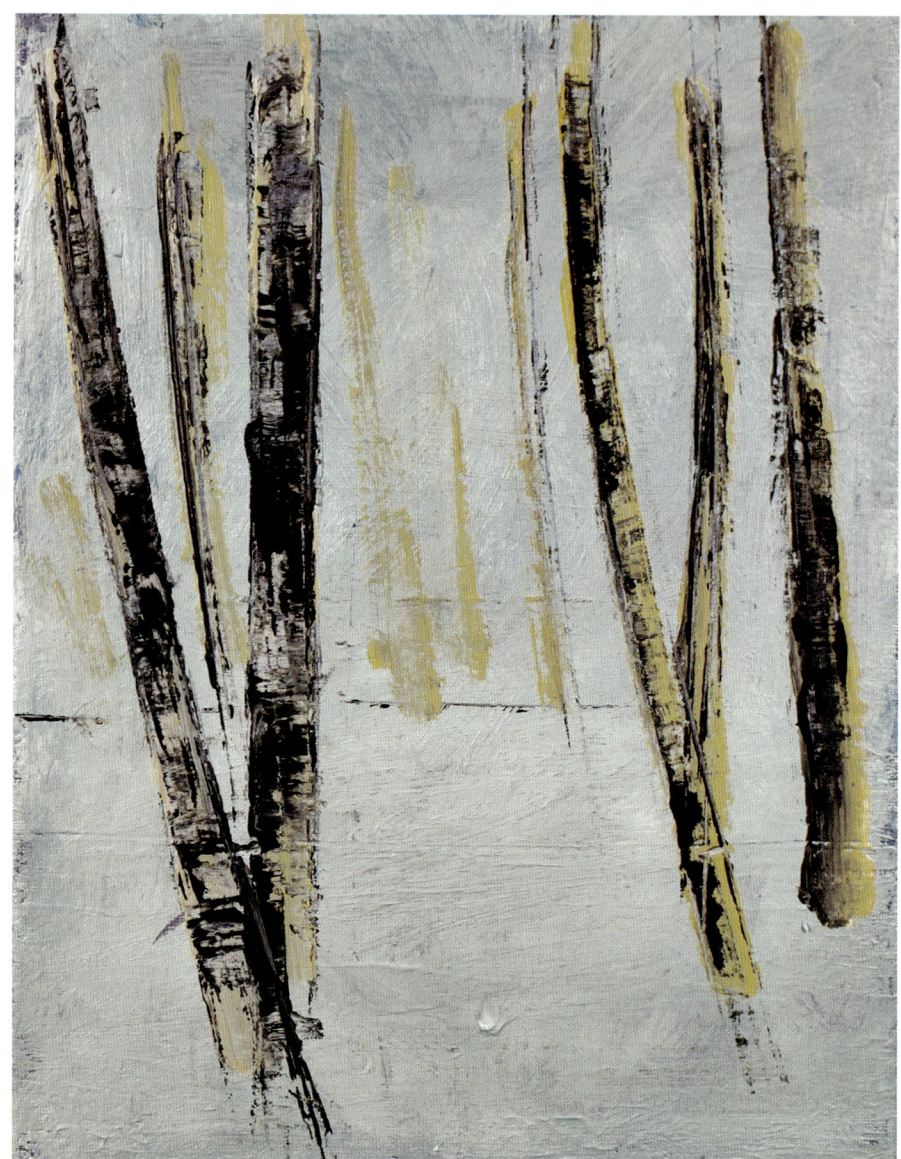

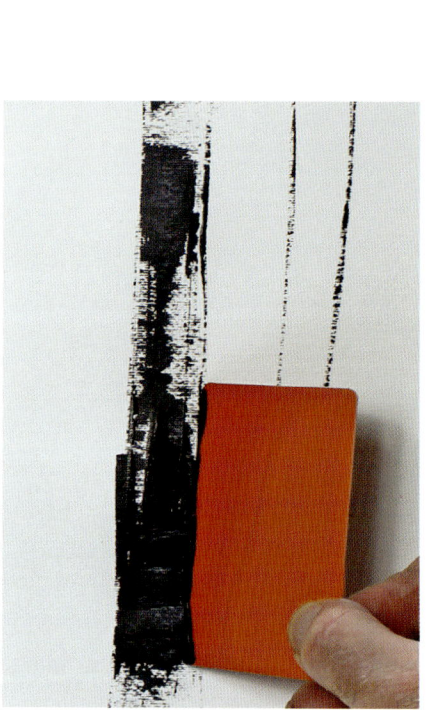

ABOVE *Use the edge of a credit card coated in paint to achieve a scraped, flaky effect.*

STAGE 1

In this painting, there is the strong presence of the sun. It is directly in your eyes and its golden colour is reflected in the snow and the bark of the trees. The ground colour is a neutral grey made up of Titanium White with a little Ultramarine Blue and Mars Black.

For the first colour, mix Yellow Ochre and Titanium White with a tiny hint of Ultramarine Blue for the base colour of the trunks of the trees. Lay this colour down quite thickly with a hog-hair brush. Let this light ochre colour become nearly dry. Coat the edge of a credit card or palette knife with Mars Black and lay the card edge on but at a slight angle at the side of one of the trees. Move the card horizontally across the width of the trunks to get a scraped, papery effect for the bark. Don't scrape too hard.

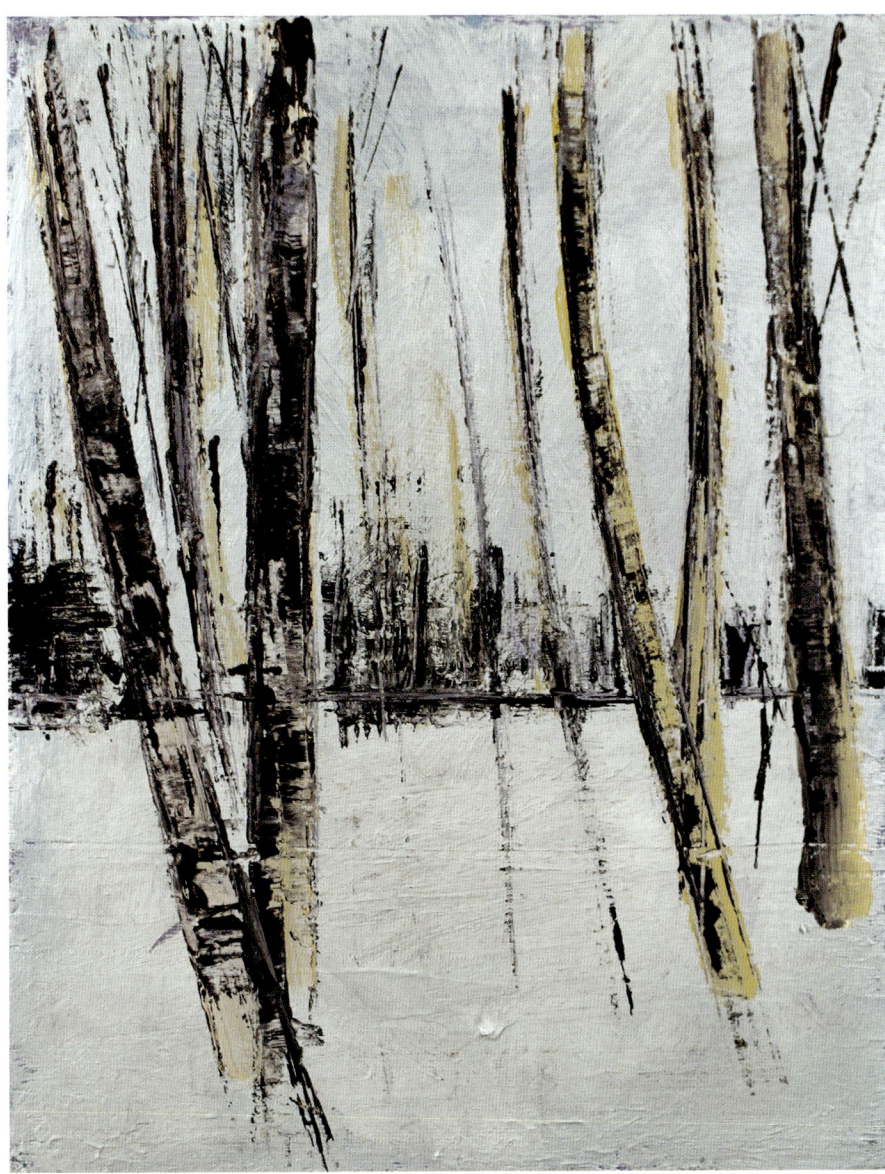

Tip
Paintings that contain smooth masses such as clouds, water or snow benefit greatly if you keep the paint moist and workable so that when you come to add another colour into a previous passage of paint, it will automatically blend in. See the Focus on Skies section on pages 96–7.

STAGE 2

Continue to use your credit card or palette knife to multiply the number of twigs and branches. Make the horizon line more prominent and add smaller 'chopping' lines for the background trees, scraping a little to the left and right to give the impression that you are looking into a mass of distant trees. Do not be afraid to add your own pattern for the branches and twigs. This landscape is intended to look semi-abstract and magical.

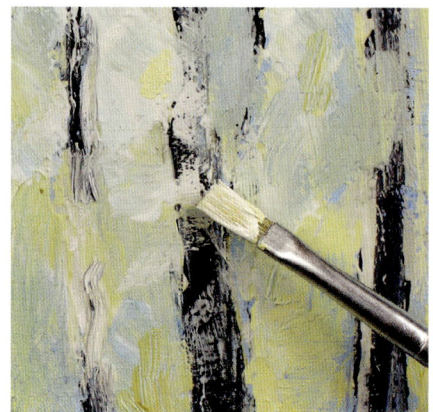

ABOVE *If you look directly into the sun, the objects that are between you and the light are lost in the glare. If you let the light source 'bite' into the darker shapes, it gives the impression of a blinding light, rather than just a silhouette. Let your brush encrust and surround the object, using the scumbling technique (see page 83).*

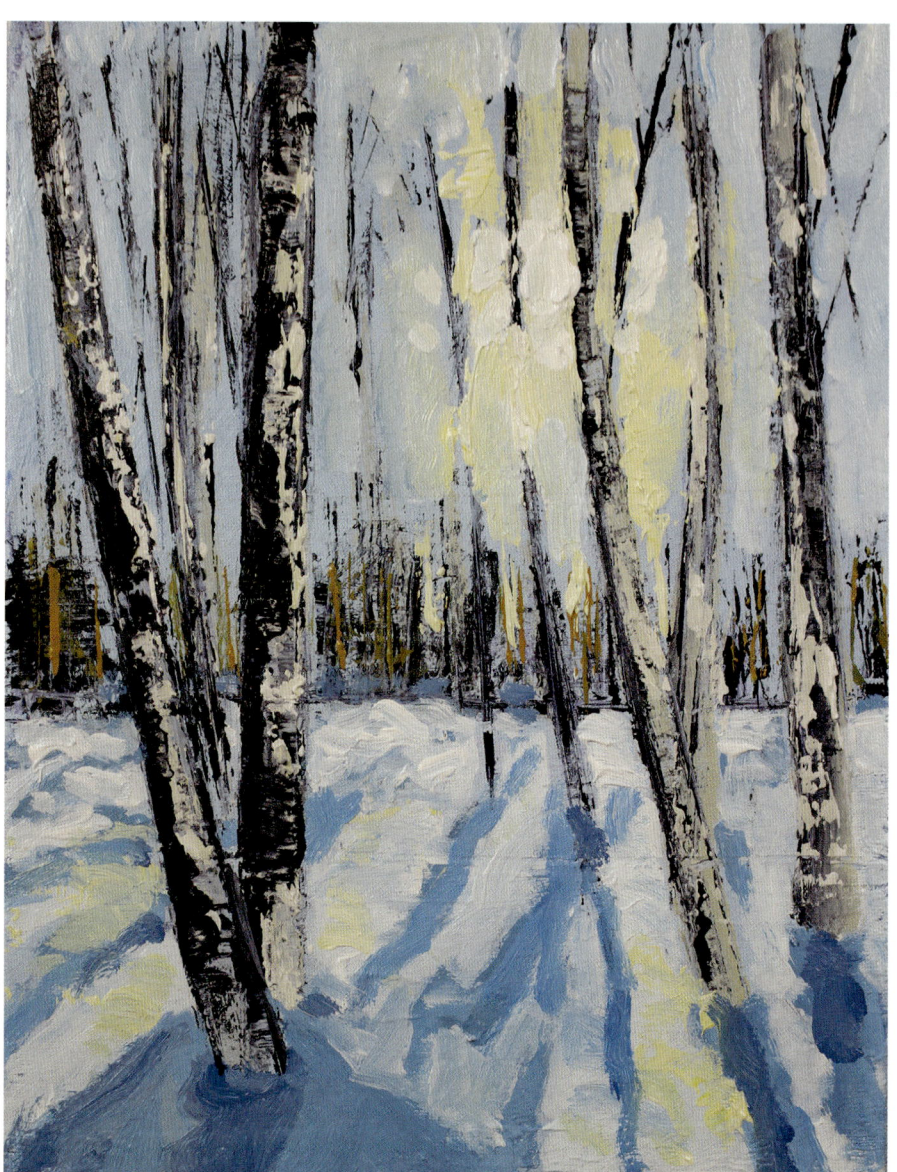

STAGE 3

When you are looking directly into the sun, some of the forms that are between you and the light become dissolved. Using just a palette knife, 'dab in' the Cadmium Yellow with Titanium White to represent the sun filtering through the branches and onto the snow and bark of the trees. Make sure that the sun colour 'bites' into the trunks of the trees. Begin to introduce some light blue into the sky by using Winsor Blue and Titanium White, then put some Yellow Ochre on to the background trees. To get the translucent look that snow sometimes has, add a little Cadmium Yellow to Titanium White and paint it into a few areas of snow. Don't overdo it; these are colour 'notes' and are only intended to echo the dominant colour of the sun coming through the trees.

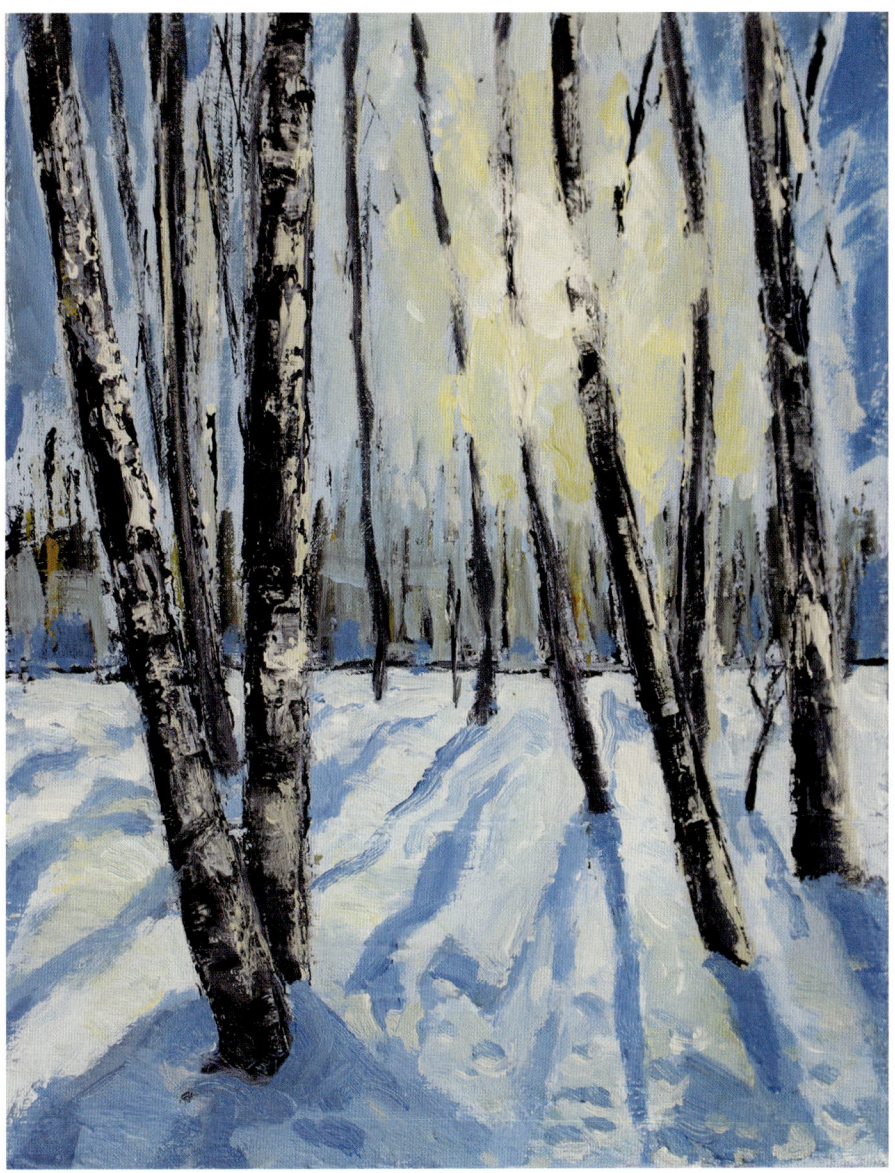

STAGE 4

At this stage, it is a good idea to stand back from your work. Ask yourself: is the balance of colour right and do you need to emphasize the darker elements of the trees? With this in mind, I added lighter and darker shades of blue to the snow by mixing slightly different proportions of Ultramarine Blue with Titanium White, and Winsor Blue with Titanium White. To improve the hints of yellow on the snow in stage 3, I mixed Cadmium Yellow with Titanium White but this time added a little Winsor Blue and blended it into the yellow areas to give it a more translucent look.

Tip

Remember that snow is not really white! White light is made up of all the colours in the spectrum. Ice crystals are excellent at reflecting all those colours but not completely, and sometimes hints of other colours come through, especially blue.

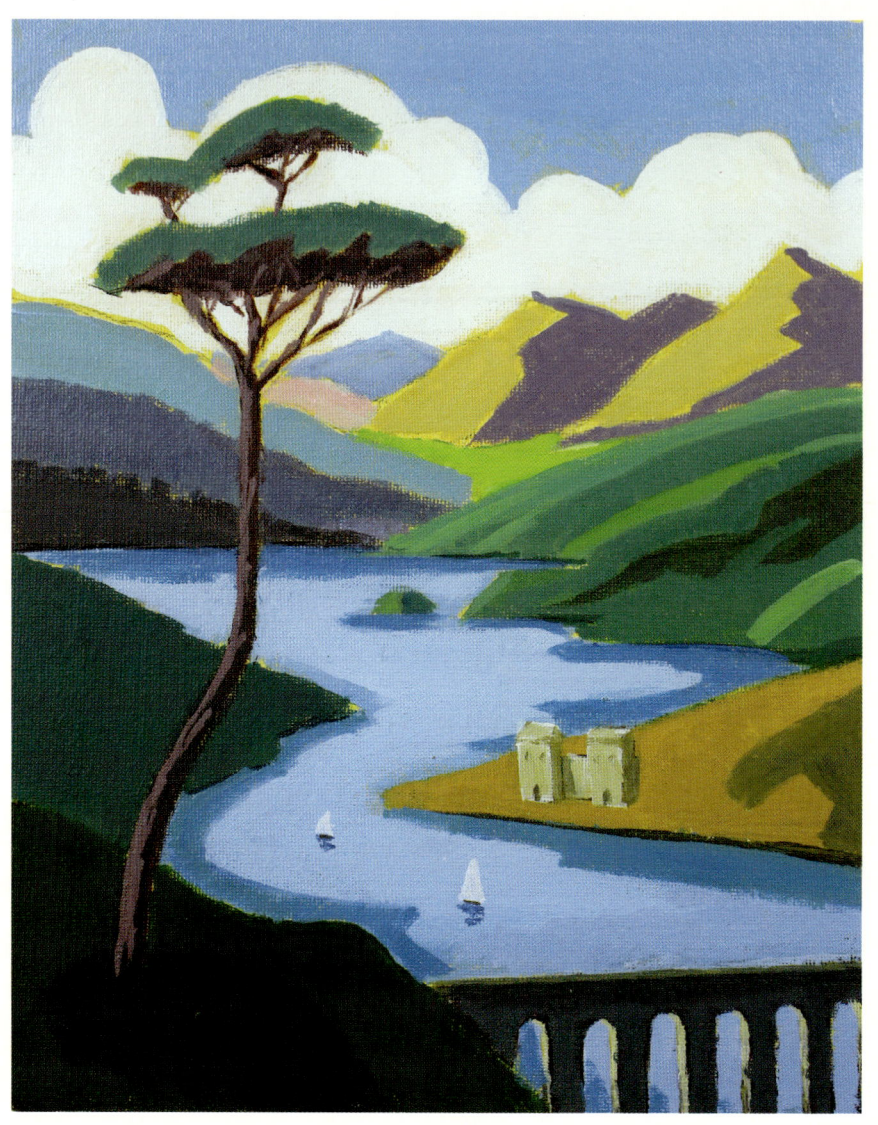

Travel Poster

Here you will learn how to create a composition from your own mind and how to keep colours flat and unblended, with bright, clean colour combinations.

COLOURS NEEDED

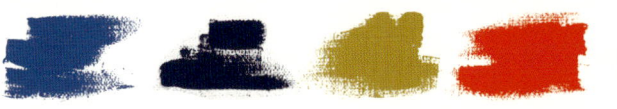

Ultramarine
Blue

Winsor
Blue

Yellow
Ochre

Cadmium
Red

Titanium
White

Travel posters have been around for a long time, but there was an age when they reached a peak of perfection. Using flat colours, dynamic perspectives and surprising compositions, the travel poster was at its most inventive in the 1920s, 30s and 40s.

Acrylic paint is a water-based medium and is well suited to flat colour. It dries quickly so colours can be added alongside and on top of existing colours, allowing the artist to move speedily across the composition. Bearing in mind the qualities of acrylic paint, designing your own travel poster becomes more straightforward than you might think. The main concern is getting the design right. Usually, when painting a landscape, you paint what you see in front of you, but in this case you have to combine several views into one.

In this example, I chose a Scottish landscape for my poster. It is not a specific place, but it has elements of several aspects of Scotland. I found some relevant pictures of the region and designed a scene around them. You can sketch straight from the Internet or use old postcards for source material. It's a good idea to sketch out some thumbnail designs, combining elements of several different views into a new composition.

Tip

Try to use colours that are next to one another on the colour wheel (see page 74), but add one or two colours from the opposite side of the chart to add a surprising colour contrast. Instead of blending tones, aim to achieve a 'stained-glass' approach, where each colour is separate and distinct.

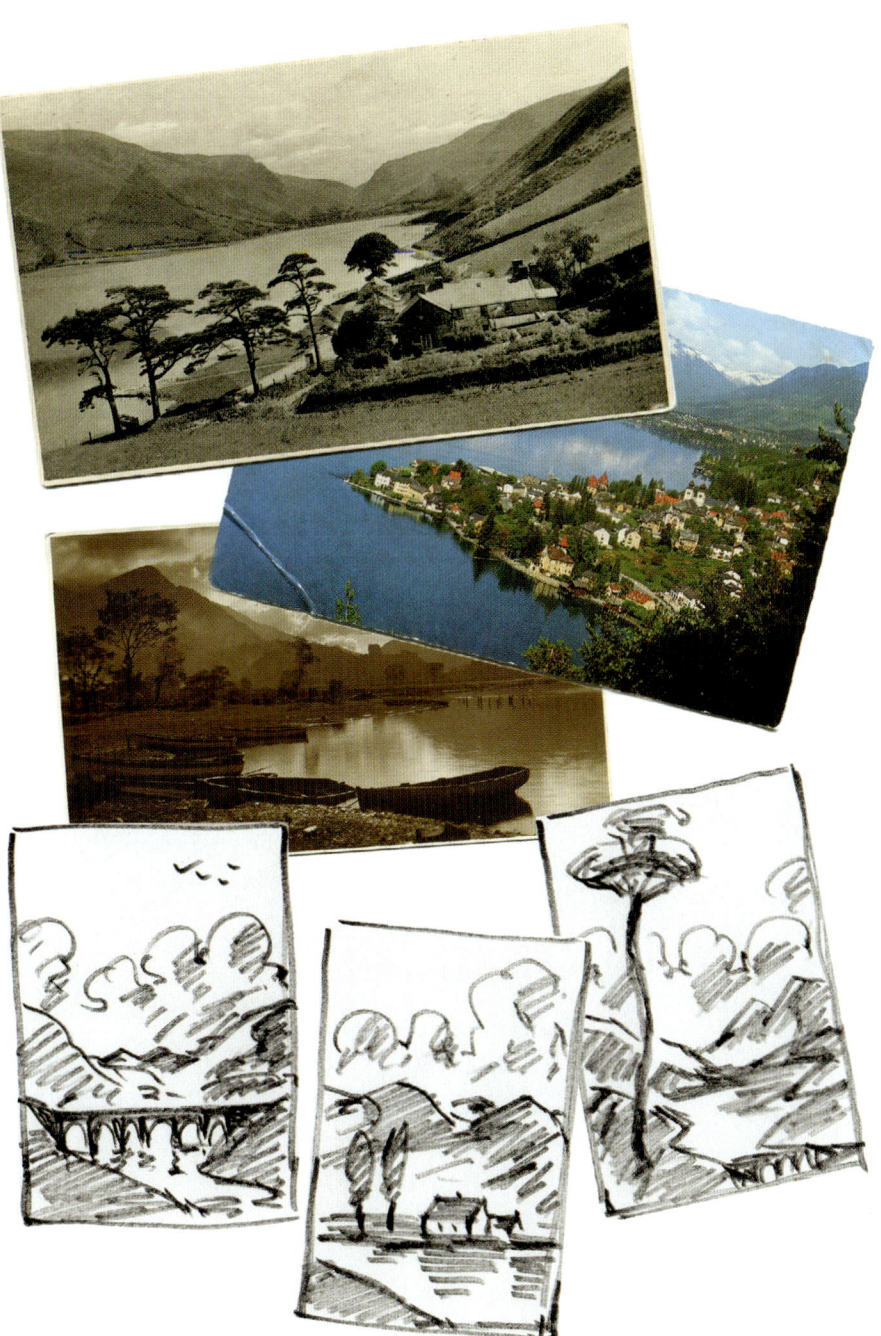

RIGHT *Sketch different elements on separate pieces of paper first so you can move them around to see what works best for your composition.*

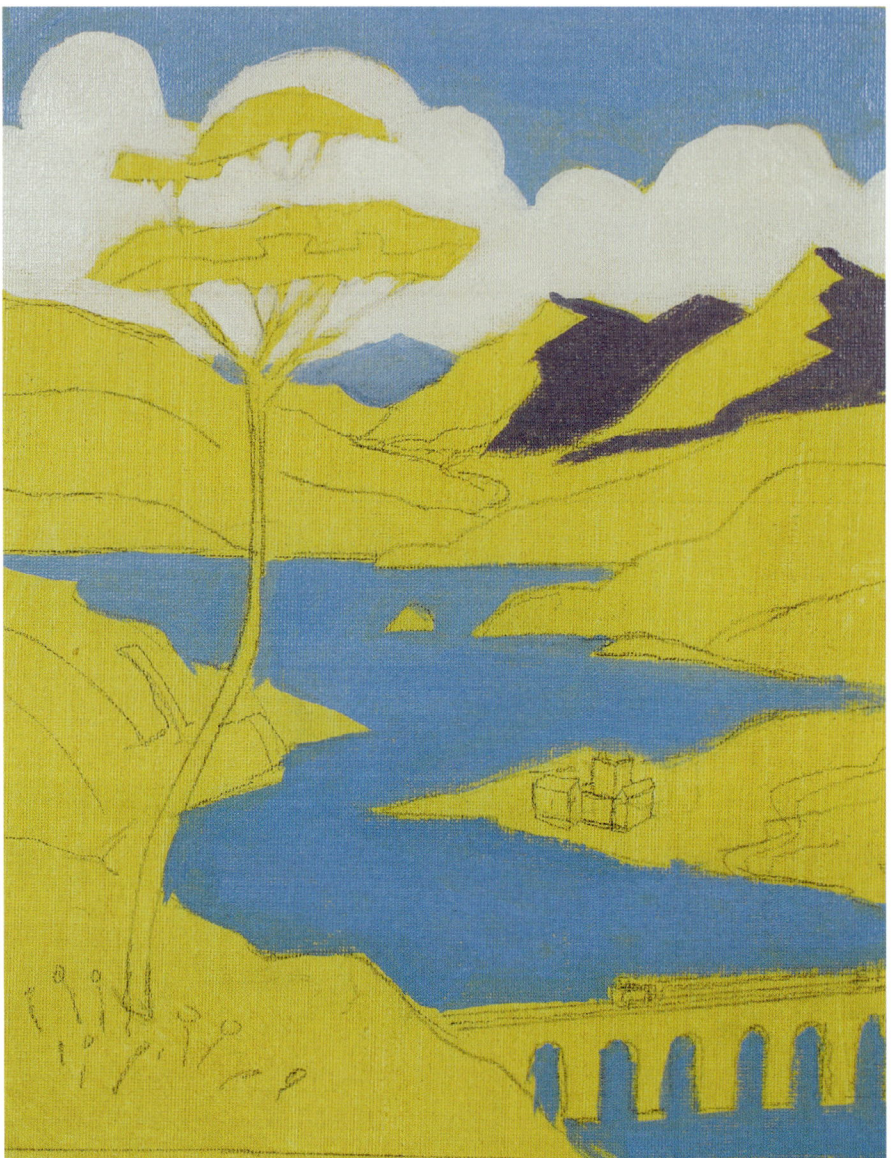

STAGE 1

Prepare your canvas, canvas board or acrylic paper with an even tone of Yellow
Ochre. When it is completely dry, sketch your design using an HB pencil. Try to
make the design as 'graphic' as possible and avoid putting in too much detail.

Mix a bright blue from Cobalt Blue and Titanium White with a little Cadmium Red
and lay it as flat as possible on the canvas. Use a synthetic filbert brush: this type is
good for close control of edges but is also ideal for flat areas of colour. Keep within
the pencil lines but try to butt the colours up against one another. The clouds are
Titanium White, with a hint of Yellow Ochre to give them a slightly warmer look.
The other major blue area is the loch; it is a lighter colour made up of Winsor Blue
and a little more Titanium White than the sky. The purple of the mountains
is a mixture of Winsor Blue, Cadmium Red and Titanium White.

STAGE 2

The light-blue mountains in the background are much the same colour as the sky and the loch but with a tiny hint of Cadmium Yellow mixed in to make them more turquoise. The two hills below the light-blue mountains are made from Ultramarine Blue with varying amounts of Cadmium Red.

Lay down a bright green made up of Winsor Blue, Cadmium Yellow and Titanium White for the series of hills on the right. Use this mixture with varying amounts of Winsor Blue to get the different hues of green. Add a little Cadmium Red to darken it. The hill on the left jutting into the loch is a variation on the yellow and blue theme but with more Winsor Blue in the mixture.

For the foreground hillock, paint a light green background for now (we will return to that in the next stage). The viaduct is blocked in as a grey, made up of Ultramarine Blue, Cadmium Red and some Titanium White.

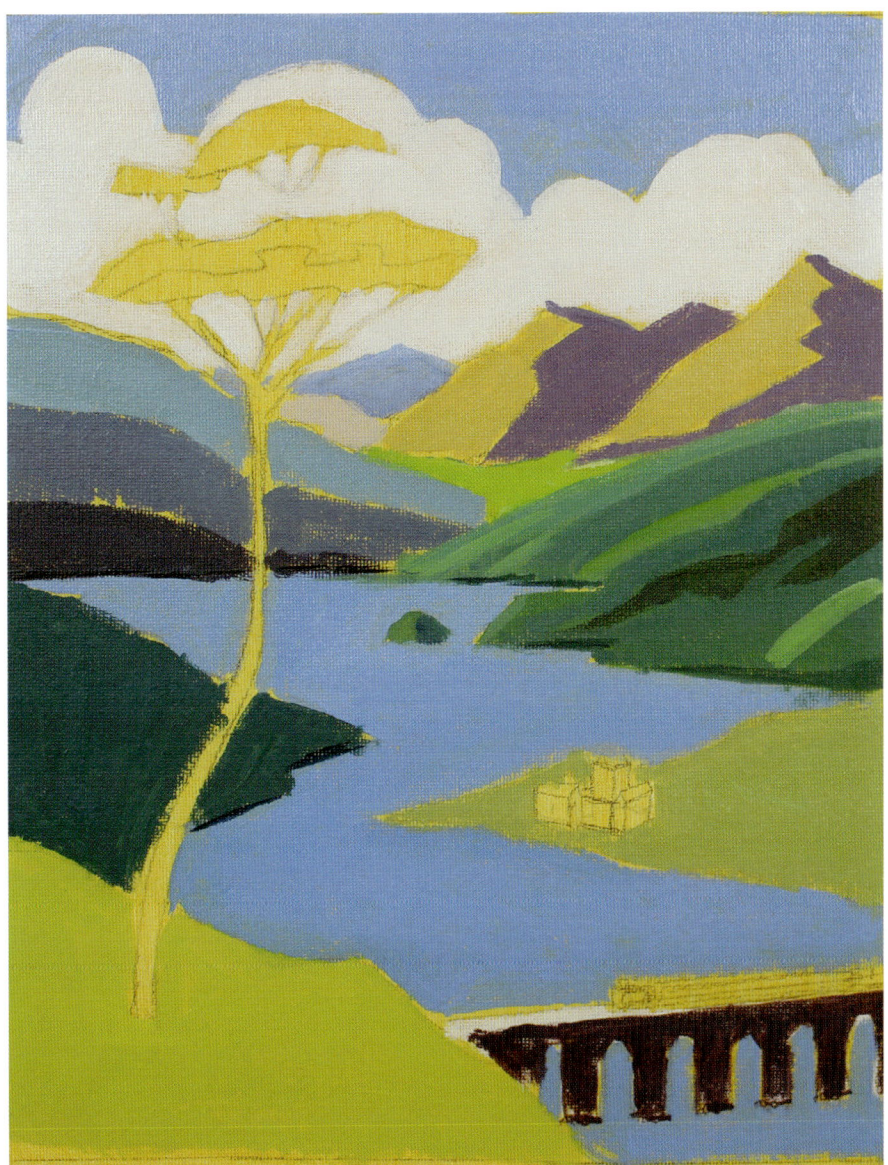

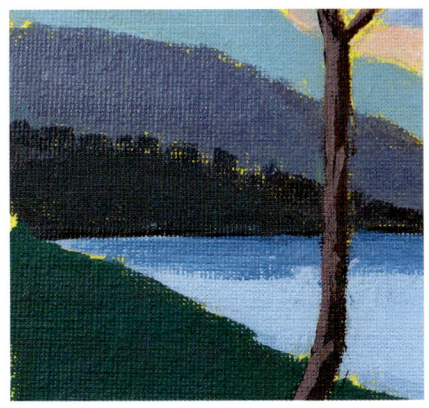

ABOVE *Due to the rough texture of canvas, occasionally the ground colour shows through. There is no need to correct this as it can look quite good. In this example, the broken edge looks like distant trees silhouetted against the light.*

RIGHT *Sometimes contrasting colours can give the composition a bit of a kick! Refer to the colour wheel on page 74 to see which colours have a contrasting but pleasing relationship.*

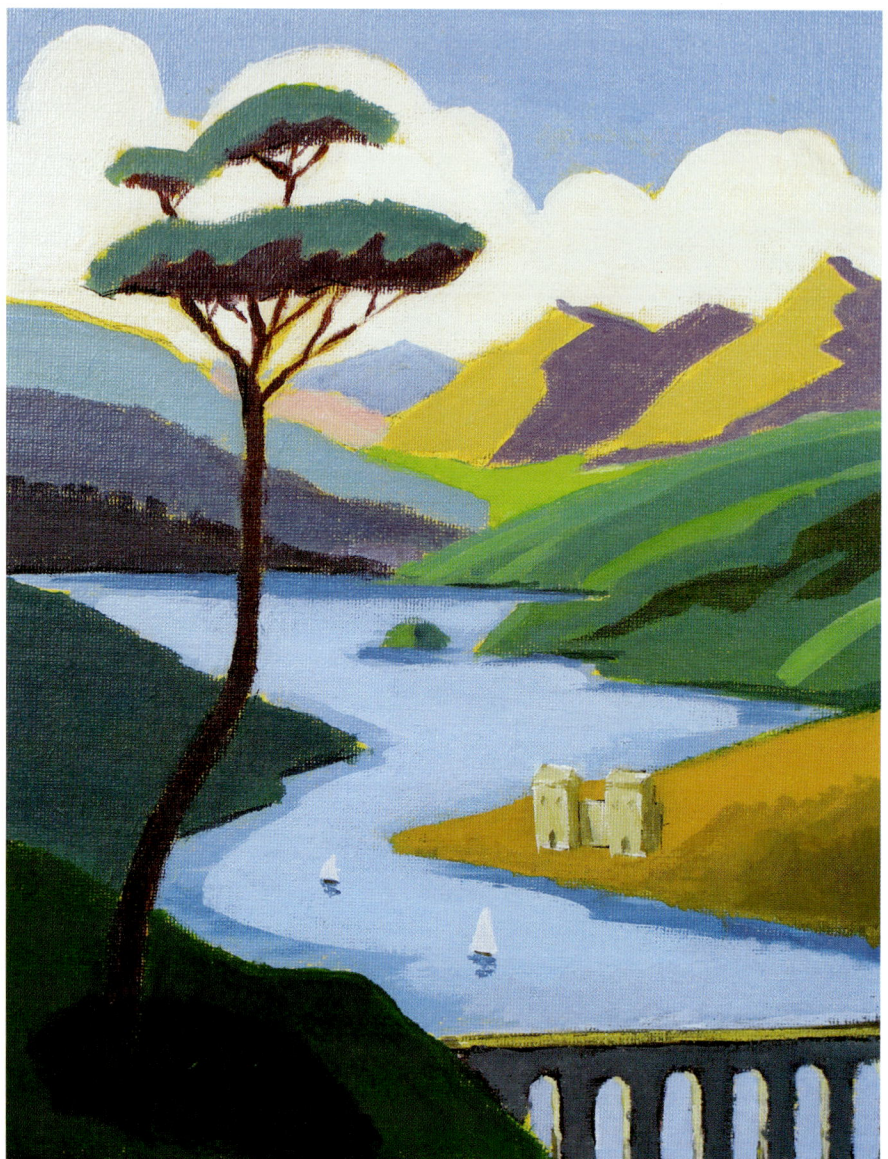

STAGE 3

Using Winsor Blue, Cadmium Yellow and a little Titanium White, paint in the canopy of the pine tree. The colour of the underneath of the canopy, the trunk and the branches are blocked in as a dark purple using Winsor Blue, Cadmium Red and a hint of Titanium White. The foreground on which the tree is growing is darkened with a mixture of Winsor Blue and Cadmium Yellow. Its shadow has a little Mars Black added to the mixture.

I have edited out the little train going over the viaduct as it made the foreground too fussy, and have extended the pillars of the viaduct down to the edge of the canvas using the grey, as before, but with less red and more blue and white. The baronial house and the spur it sits on are made up of Yellow Ochre and Titanium White. Note the patch of pink heather below the most distant mountain. This adds an interesting contrasting colour note at a central part of the composition.

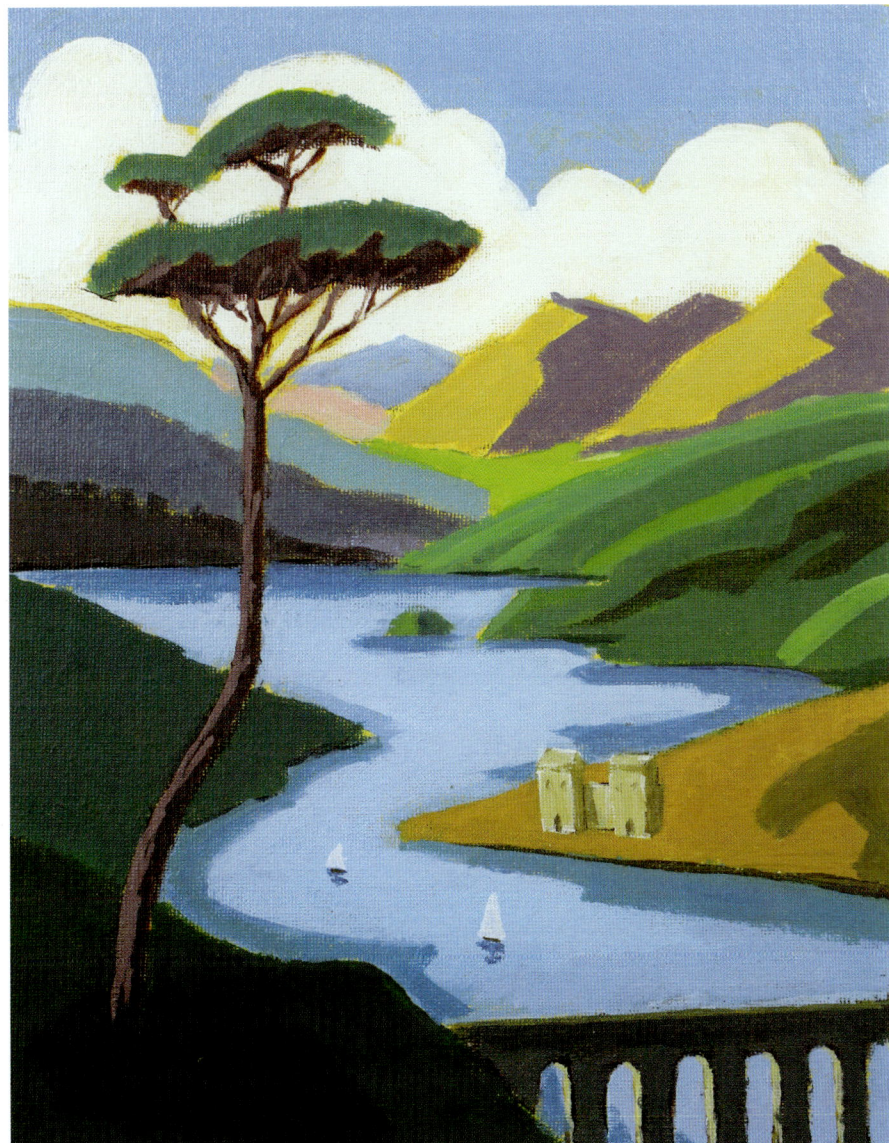

STAGE 4

Although this scene is conceived as a poster and is painted in flat, separate colours, it still has to work visually as a conventional painting. Following the rules of aerial perspective, the colours in the foreground generally have to be stronger than those towards the back of the picture. To this end I have strengthened the colour in the viaduct and added a graphic shape to the spur of land with the house on it.

I have also strengthened the contours of the loch by adding a darker blue to the water's edge.

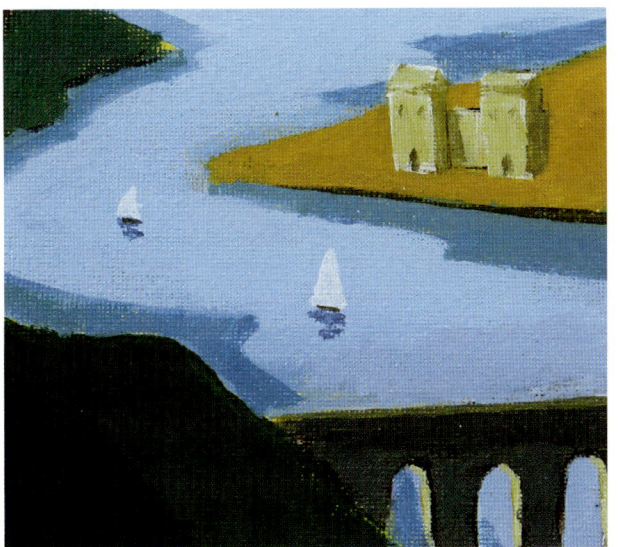

LEFT *Don't be afraid to leave some of the ground colour showing through in the final piece. This adds charm to the poster and shows it is handmade.*

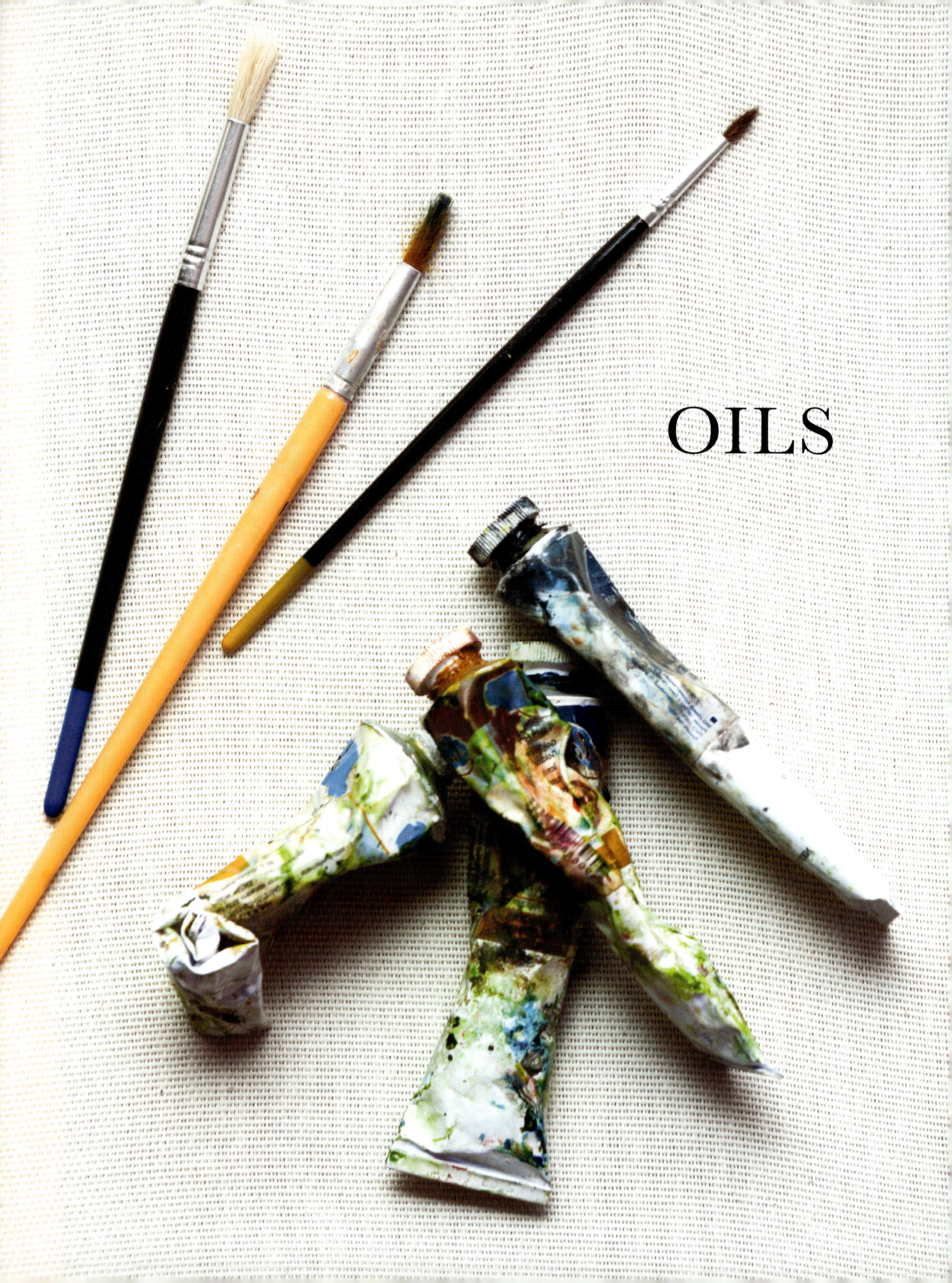

OILS

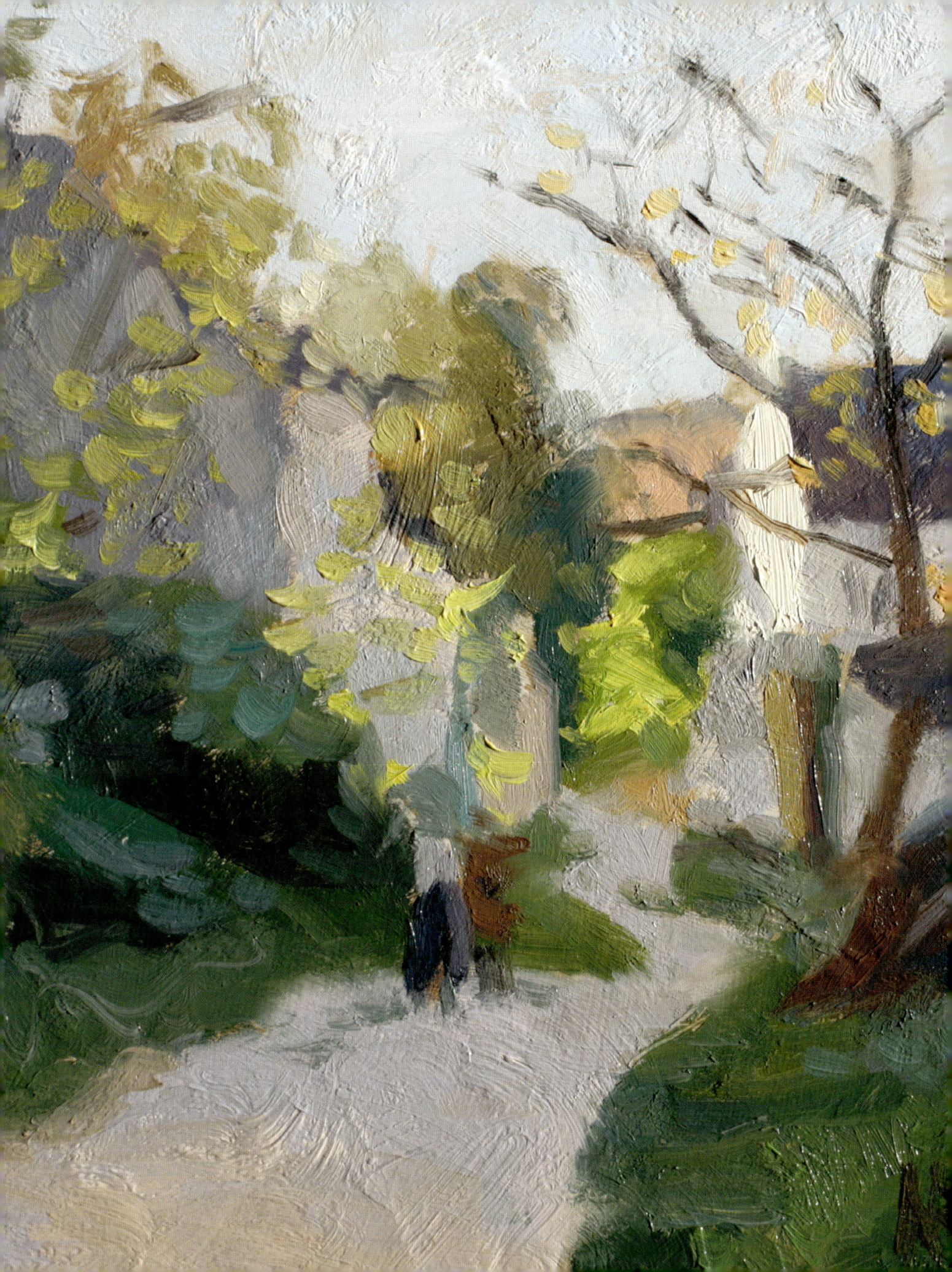

Introduction

Anyone who walks into my class or opens this book is already an artist. My job is not to make you paint like me, but to help you develop the skills to express your unique viewpoint.

I began oil painting at the age of ten and have loved it ever since. I have no doubt that you will too. It's no fluke that oil paint, which came into regular use in the 15th century, is still the most popular painting medium. Artists love the rich, gloopy nature of the paint, combined with the fact that it can be used in an infinite number of ways.

Famous for its slow drying time, oil paint is ideal for soft blending. Diluted as thin as watercolour, it makes rich, transparent glazes. Using a palette knife or hog-hair brush, we can create mountainous textures of paint up to an inch thick.

Unique to oil paint is the amazing ability to retain the three-dimensional shape of the artist's mark. Each brushstroke is like a little time capsule, showing us the exact touch and speed of the painter's hand.

Those who see oil painting as a difficult option, suitable only for the serious professional, have usually been put off by the mystery surrounding drying times, or confusing rules such as 'fat over lean'. In fact, the rules of oil painting are very simple. Once you know them, you are free to do almost anything while producing works that will last for generations.

For me, the best thing of all about oil paint is its forgiving nature. I'm one of those people who never get it right first time. With oil paint, you can scrape it off and repaint as many times as you like.

Starting out as a painter, you will learn more from doing several small paintings than labouring away on one huge canvas. In the step-by-step demonstrations, I give as clear instructions as I can, but remember that most artists are a touch rebellious. If you feel like tinkering with the techniques or substituting subjects, I won't tell.

The aim here is not to produce six gallery paintings in a uniform style. We will be tackling lots of different subjects and using a whole range of techniques. Give them all a try and discard the ones that don't feel natural. By the end of them, you won't be afraid of any subject and you'll have some really exciting approaches up your sleeve.

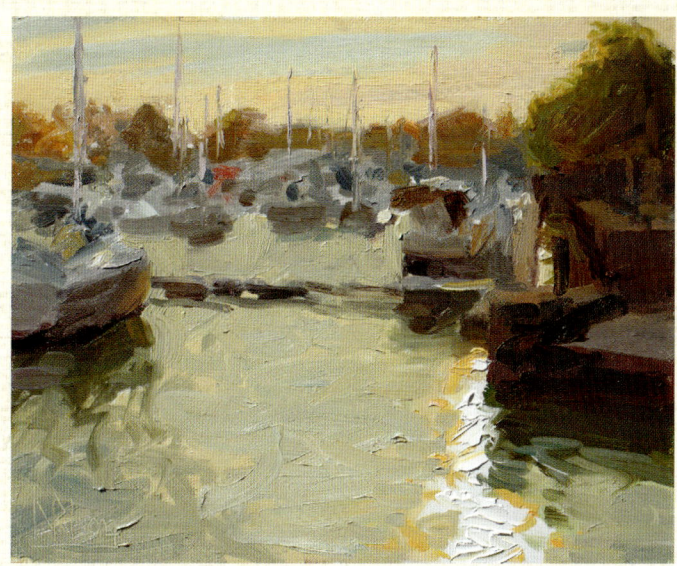

The approach to painting presented here is just one of many. It is my approach, developed through emulating great art of the past and based on my love of light, colour and paint texture. Take all you can from these pages, but borrow from other sources too. Don't be afraid of losing your artistic identity in learning from others. Your own personality will always shine through.

There are a couple of unexpected benefits to becoming an oil painter. One is the close and supportive community of artists you will discover in your local area and online. The other is the opening of your eyes to the beauty of the world around you. It comes with a warning. You might find yourself, driving around town, distracted by glorious reflected light from a brick wall.

Regardless of the stage in life you are taking up painting, there will be challenges and triumphs aplenty. It is not unusual for the absolute beginner to produce a scintillating, lively piece of art, while the veteran is still capable of something perfectly correct, but quite dull. I encourage you to embrace the unpredictable nature of art, have fun and take some risks. Your growth as an artist is guaranteed when you are willing to squeeze out some paint, put in some 'brush miles' and reach beyond your current skills.

Norman

Materials and Equipment

When you start oil painting, there are a number of essentials you need. The amount of choice in an art shop can be quite overwhelming, so this section lists the absolute basics required, from paints to palettes and other items. Oil paints are expensive, but fretting over the cost of oil paint and squeezing out meagre amounts will lead to stingy-looking paintings.

Oil paints

When buying oil paint, you will notice two grades – 'student' and 'artist's' – with a jump in cost between the two. To start with, I recommend buying student grade such as Winton by Winsor & Newton.

Some colours have the word 'hue' after their name. 'Cadmium Red Hue' looks like Cadmium Red but is actually made from cheaper, weaker pigments. For this reason, an affluent artist will prefer artist's quality paint for the cadmium colours, but the main thing is that you squeeze out plenty of paint and use it up without a second thought.

This is my recommended palette, with alternatives listed alongside:

- Titanium White – large tube (7fl oz/200ml)
- Cadmium Yellow Pale (Light)
- Cadmium Red (or Cadmium Scarlet/Cadmium Red Light)
- Permanent Alizarin Crimson (or Permanent Rose)
- Phthalo Blue (or Ultramarine, sometimes called French Ultramarine)
- Viridian Hue (or Winsor Green/ Phthalo Green, but not artist's quality Viridian)
- Yellow Ochre
- Burnt Sienna
- Ivory Black (or Lamp Black).

Supports and grounds

The 'support' is the material we paint on. The 'ground' is a layer of primer we apply to the support to stop the paint from sinking in. Wood or stretched canvas are traditional supports for oil painting. Though we will often refer to the painting surface as the 'canvas', we will actually be using hardboard (Masonite). This is available from your local wood merchant and is easily cut to size with a craft knife. Common sizes used in this chapter are 10 x 12in (25 x 30cm), and 10 x 10in (25 x 25cm).

Acrylic gesso is by far the handiest ground to apply to hardboard. Use a household paintbrush and give it two or three coats, brushing in random directions. If your hardboard has a rough side and a smooth side, try to avoid the rough side as it tends to overwhelm your brushmarks. These days, remarkably cheap canvases and canvas boards are widely available. As they are, many of them are too absorbent, but give them another coat of acrylic gesso and they will be fine.

BELOW *The tools used by an oil painter.*

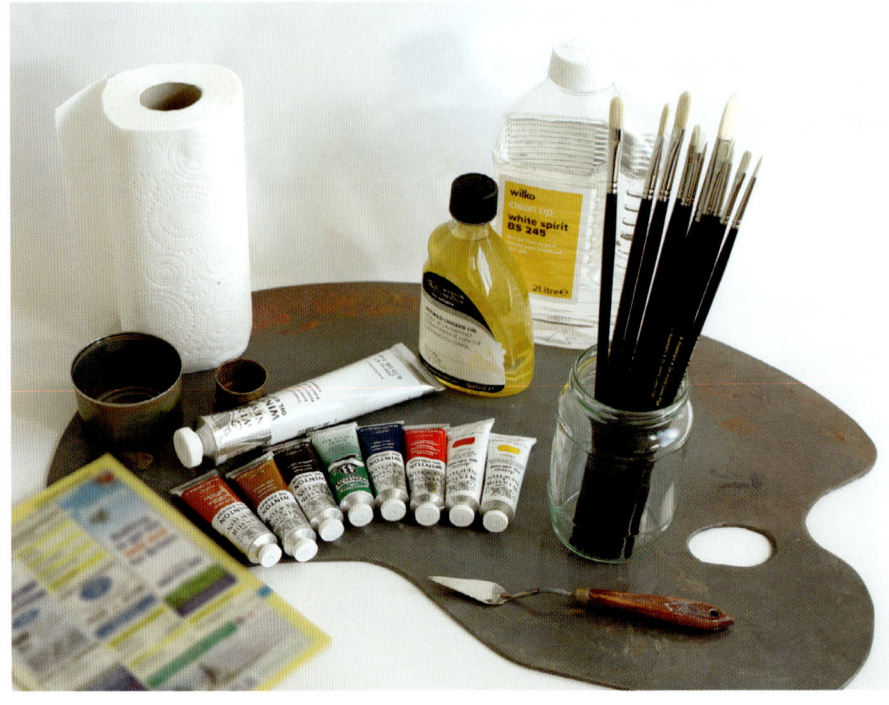

If you find yourself with lots of leftover oil paint, you can create an interesting surface by applying it to an already primed board. Use brushes and a palette knife to create the textures you like.

Working over old oil or acrylic paintings is an excellent idea and can create really interesting and unexpected effects. It is not advisable to use acrylic gesso over old oil paintings, as this layer will crack over time.

If the finished painting is likely to be stored somewhere damp, it's best to prime the back too, to prevent warping. You can bypass this step by buying white-faced hardboard. The white side is ideal for the back of the painting, meaning you just need to prime the brown side and you're ready to roll.

Once dried, paintings on hardboard can be stacked together. Tape bubble wrap to the back of each painting to prevent them sticking together or damaging the impasto (thick paint).

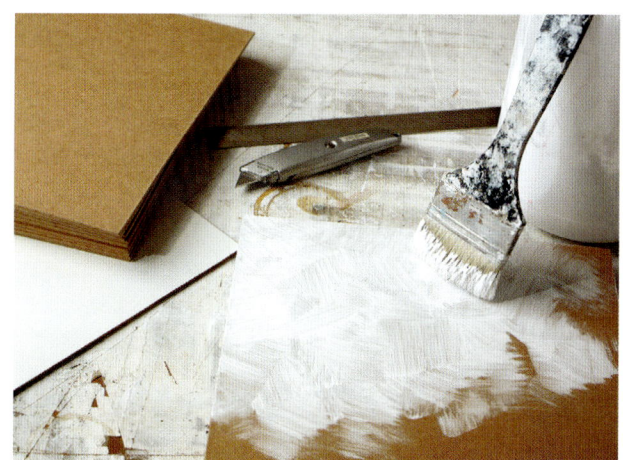

LEFT *Priming hardboard with acrylic gesso.*

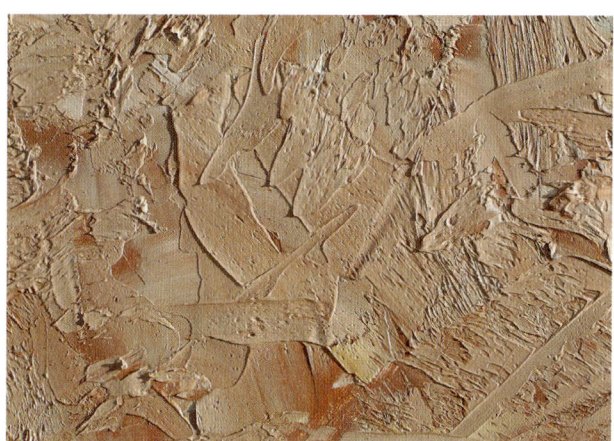

LEFT *Primed hardboard covered in a textured surface of oil paint.*

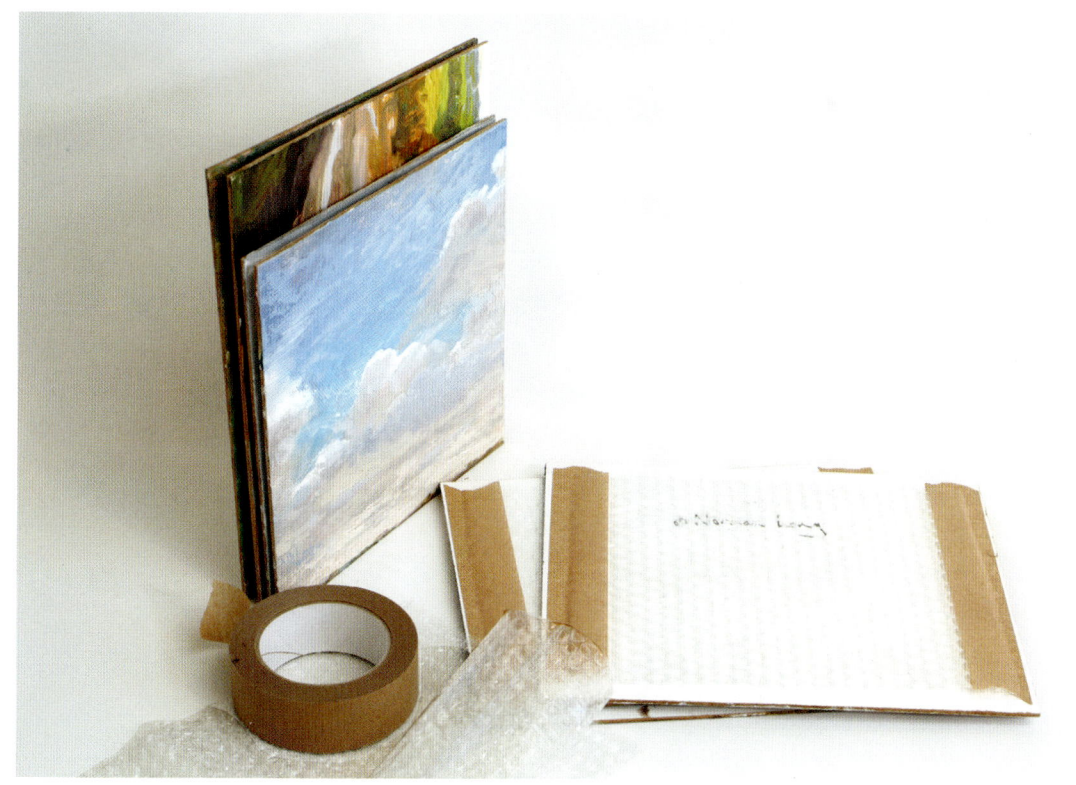

LEFT *Bubble wrap on the back of paintings prevents damage to the surfaces of other paintings.*

Brushes

There are three main shapes of brushes – rounds, flats and filberts. You will need at least 12 brushes of various sizes, preferably with long handles to keep you a comfortable distance from the canvas.

Hog hair is the traditional bristle for oil brushes. It gives distinctive brush-marks, ideal for big, bold strokes. I use hog-hair filberts for my larger brushes. Sizes 8, 6 and 4 were used for these paintings. When it comes to smaller details, a softer synthetic brush (such as the Ivory range from Rosemary & Co.) lays the paint on beautifully. No. 2 long flats and pointed rounds are a treat. The use of a No. 1 pointed round is permissible, but only in the last half hour of a painting!

Palette knife

A metal palette knife with a cranked handle is a great tool for mixing paint and cleaning off the palette. It is also used for various painting techniques. The most versatile are teardrop-shaped knives such as the Winsor & Newton No. 21 (or Liquitex small No. 15).

Palettes

Any surface that is large enough (at least 16 x 12in/40 x 30cm), flat and non-absorbent will serve as a palette. The traditional wooden hand-held palette is kidney-shaped with a thumb-hole, allowing the artist to stand back and mix colours as they contemplate the canvas from a distance. To keep wooden palettes in beautiful condition, rub a spot of linseed oil into the surface after cleaning. If you have a table it can rest on, a piece of safety glass (thick, with safe edges) makes the perfect studio palette. It is a dream to clean. The underside can be painted grey (or put a piece of coloured paper underneath) so that you can see both light and dark colours clearly. Disposable palettes are convenient, but tend to be on the small side.

Other essentials

Other items you will need are a small dipper for holding solvent or painting medium. Suitable solvents include white spirit, turpentine, Zest-it (Europe), mineral spirits or Gamsol (USA). Solvent can be mixed with refined linseed oil to make your own medium.

Laying brushes down on the palette is messy; they can easily roll off and they take up mixing space – so you'll need a wide-mouthed jar for holding wet brushes. You can use a washed-out tin can for cleaning brushes, but beware of sharp edges!

Keep a stock of cotton rags or good-quality kitchen paper, which does not crumble when wet, close to hand. An old telephone directory can be useful for wiping your palette knife or oily brushes on when you have finished painting.

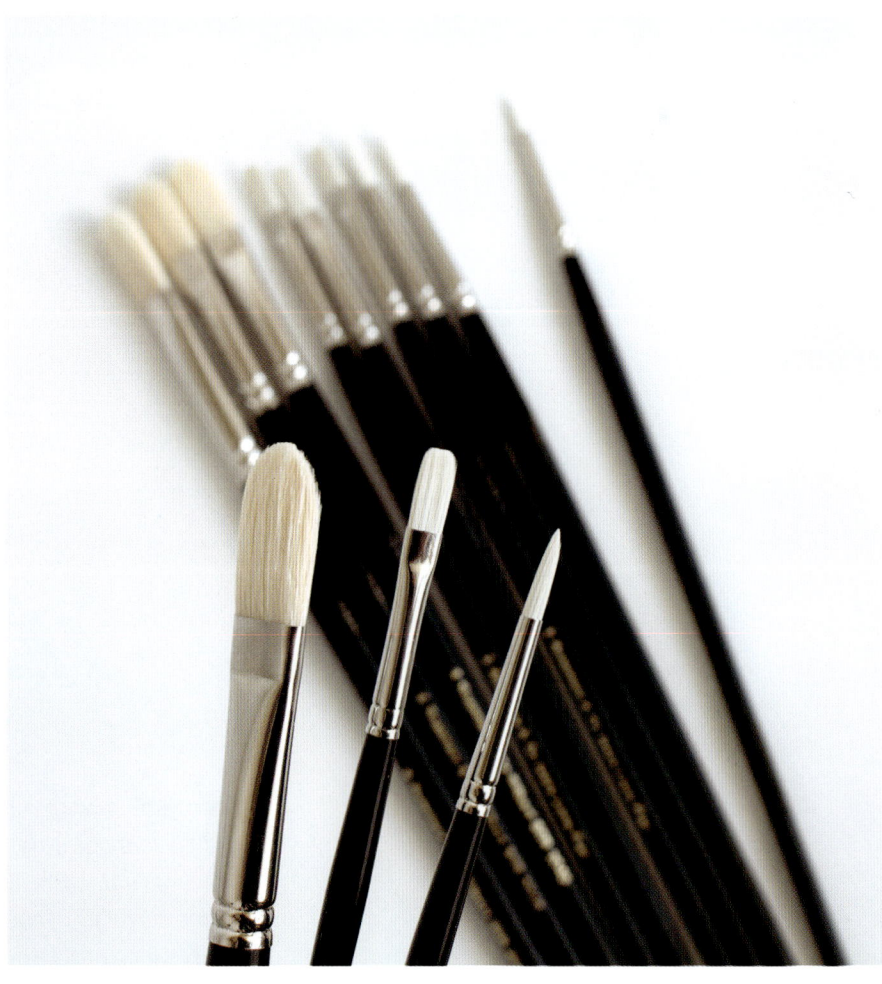

LEFT *Filbert, long flat and pointed round brushes.*

Easels

An easel is necessary to hold the painting vertically next to the subject so that you can make easy comparisons between the two. It also allows you to stand back to view the painting from a distance.

The metal sketching (or field) easel is designed for outdoors but can also be used inside and takes up very little space. Avoid wooden sketching easels (or the very cheap aluminium ones), as they are too flimsy. The French easel, suitable for indoors and out, allows you to carry a wet palette in a useful drawer. A studio easel such as the radial easel is a sturdy investment. It can handle even large canvases with ease. Specialist pochade boxes are handy when doing small outdoor paintings.

Cleaning

At the end of a painting session, use your palette knife to scrape the piles of paint off your palette and wipe the surface with a rag. The paint can be discarded or scraped into piles, stored in a biscuit tin and kept for up to a few weeks in the freezer. I call this my 'palette mud', and it can be used for the next painting.

The better you clean your brushes, the longer they will last. If you are painting the next day, you can store them temporarily in a plastic bag in the fridge. For a proper clean, wipe them first on a telephone directory, then swirl them in solvent and wipe with a rag. A final step of cleaning on your palm with hand soap will remove the last residue of colour.

Dirty solvent should not be put down the drain but can be recycled for use in cleaning brushes. Pour it into a jar and wait for the sediment to settle to the bottom.

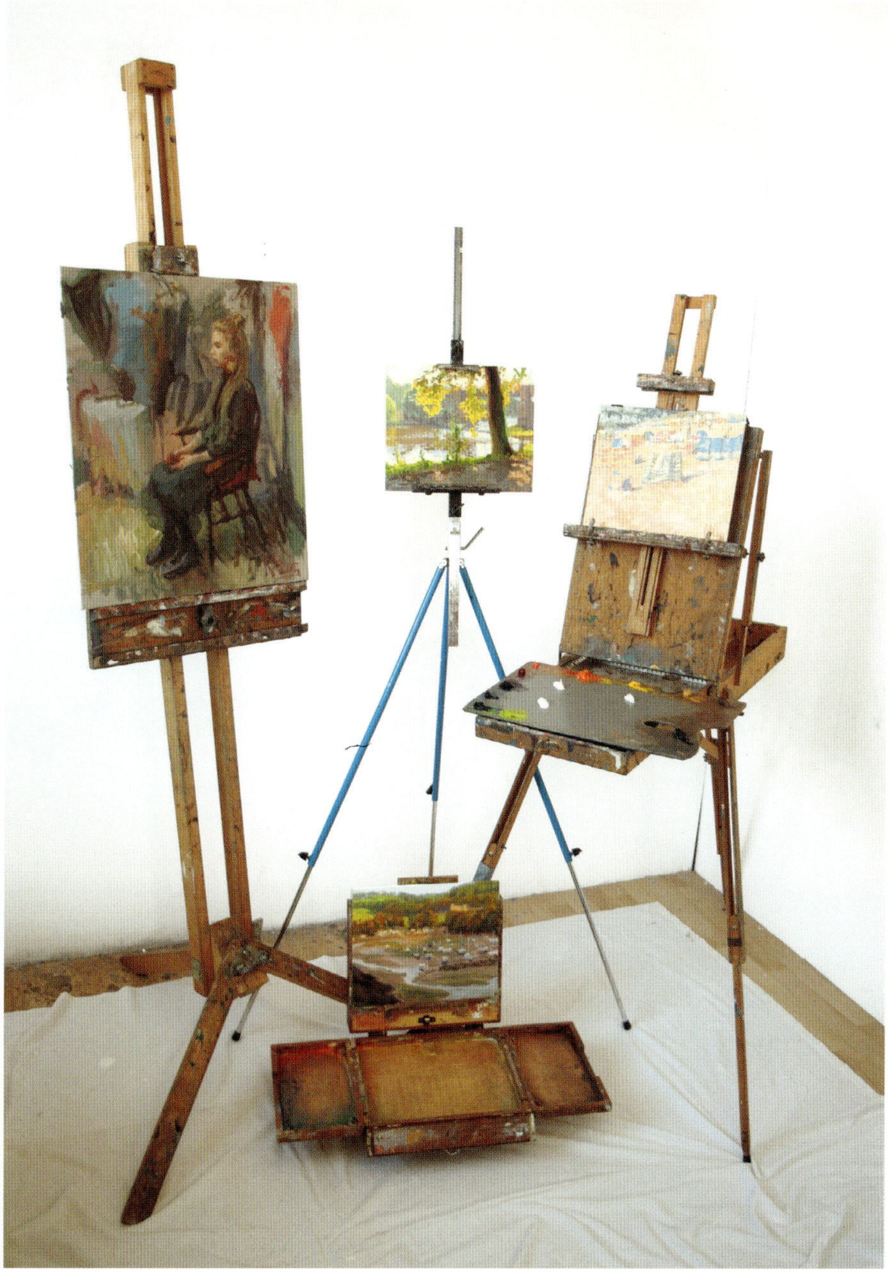

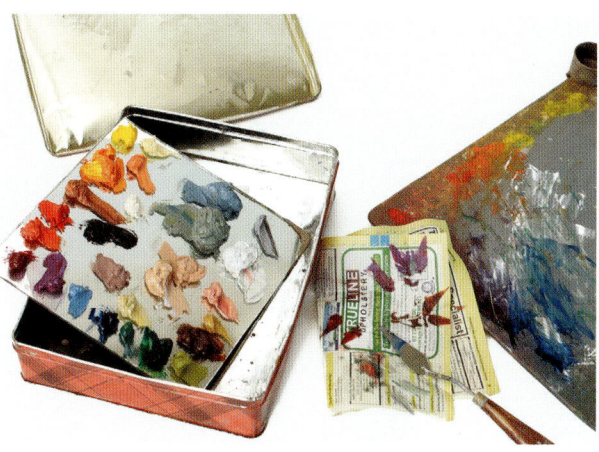

ABOVE *From left to right: radial, sketching and French easels. Front: pochade box.*

LEFT *Piles of paint stored in a tin for reuse.*

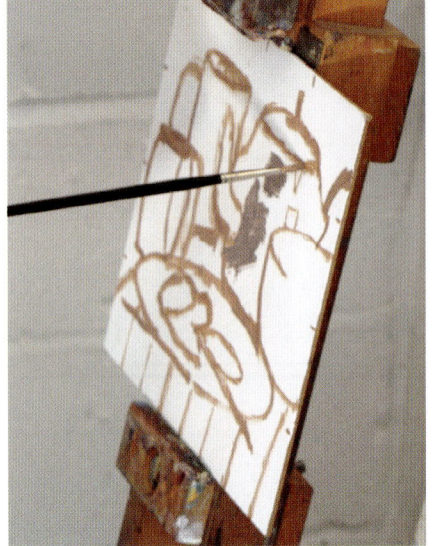

Drawing with Paint

My approach to oil painting is very direct – get the big things down first and add details later. A careful pencil drawing at the outset can take too long and, having invested time in a careful drawing, an artist may not wish to spend the time making necessary changes. It is better to use a brush and diluted paint to draw the big shapes.

To start drawing with paint, hold the brush at the far end and stand well back from the canvas so that you can see the proportions at a glance. For large strokes, hold the brush underhand (thumb on top) and use the movement of your arm. For finer drawing, hold the brush like a pencil and use your fingers.

The big trick in drawing is seeing everything as flat shapes, rather like jigsaw pieces. Start with the big shapes and keep moving around the whole drawing. The first aim is not a lovely drawing but to get things in the right place within the canvas. Resist the urge to finish any part of the drawing, but erase and redraw until you are happy with the size and positioning of the objects on the canvas.

The next step is to use the following techniques to check what you have – and continue to check and adjust your shapes until the last minute of the painting.

Measurements and alignment

If you can find two distances in the subject that are the same, you know that they will also match on your painting. Done properly, this simple matching measurement is extremely reliable.

1. Working from an actual subject, hold a paintbrush in your outstretched hand with your elbow locked and one eye closed. Try not to tilt the brush forward to match the angle of the subject but do keep it parallel to the lenses of your glasses (whether you wear them or not). You can only rotate the brush like the hands of a clock.

2. Look for two large measurements in the subject, one vertical and one horizontal, which are the same. Closing one eye, align the brush tip with the top of the mug and slide your thumb down until it meets the bottom of the plate.

3. Still holding your thumb in position, rotate the brush horizontally and look for a matching measurement.

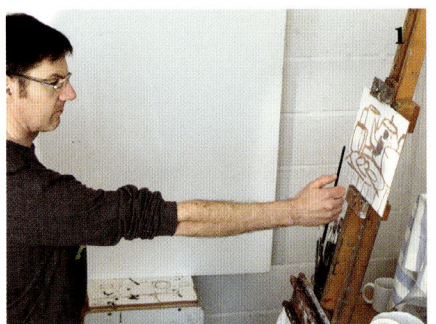

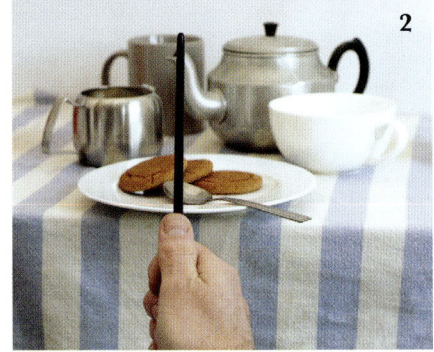

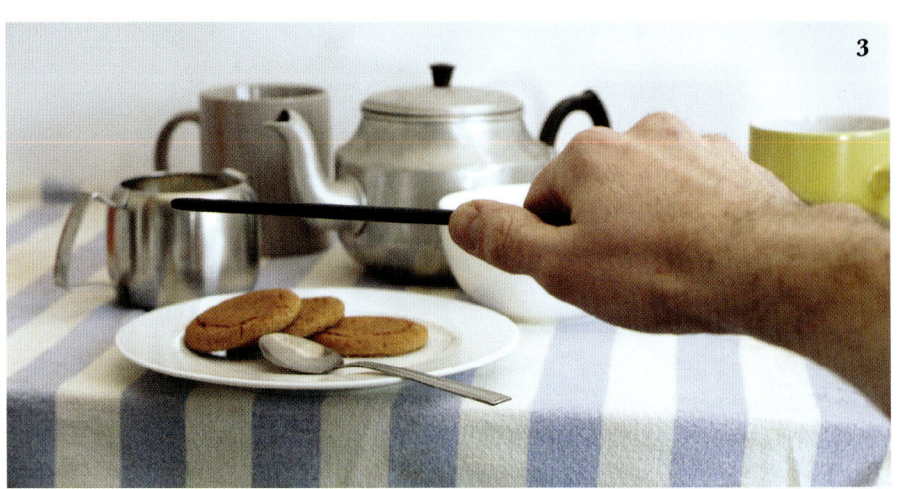

4. Don't take the measurement from the subject and transfer it directly onto the painting. Instead, remove your thumb and repeat the process on the painting. Placing the tip of the brush on the painting, use your thumb to measure the height.

5. Now compare this measurement to the width. If the vertical and horizontal measurements match, proceed with confidence. If not, adjust one or the other (or both) until they do.

6. You need things at the top of the drawing to line up with those at the bottom and things at the left to line up with those on the right. Use your paintbrush vertically or horizontally (or even at an angle) to find two things in the subject that line up. Then check that they also align in your painting.

Negative shapes

Any shape caught between or around objects is known as a negative shape. While drawing things can be hard, copying shapes is easy. Pay close attention to the kind of shapes outlined in orange (see bottom right) and you will find that the objects magically draw themselves.

Using a mirror

A mirror is the most useful tool of all for checking shapes and angles. Face away from your subject and hold a mirror roughly where your head was while you were painting, so that you can see the subject and the painting next to each other. Jump your eyes back and forth between the two, looking for the big differences in shapes or angles. Once you notice something, put the mirror down and correct your painting.

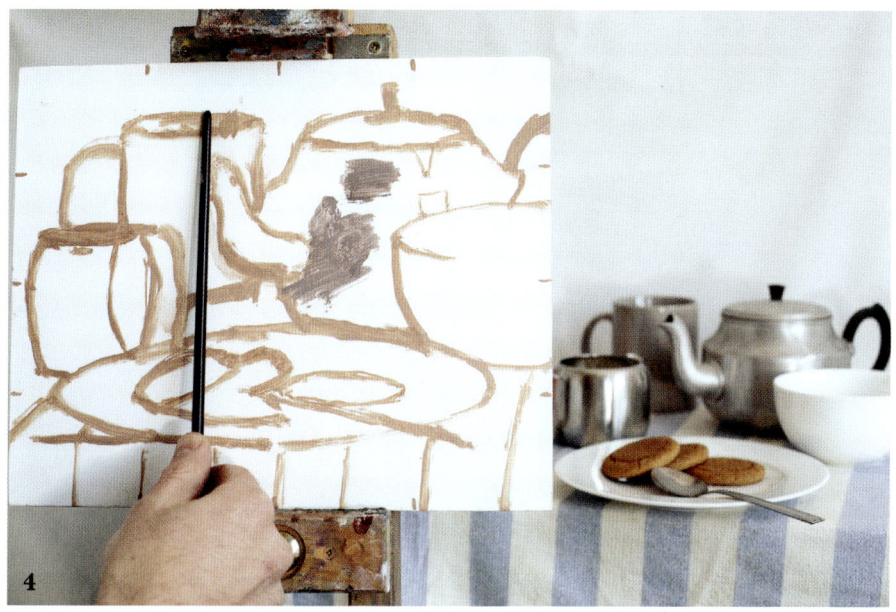

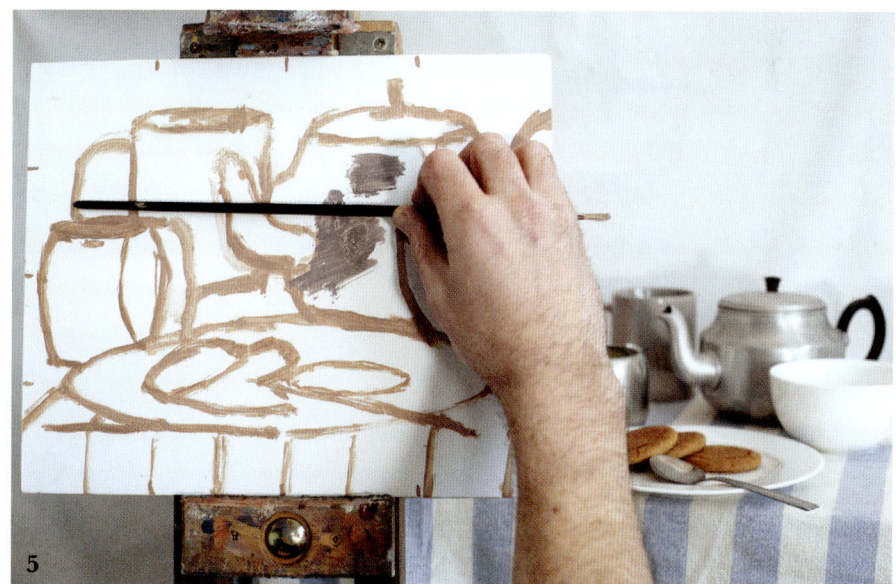

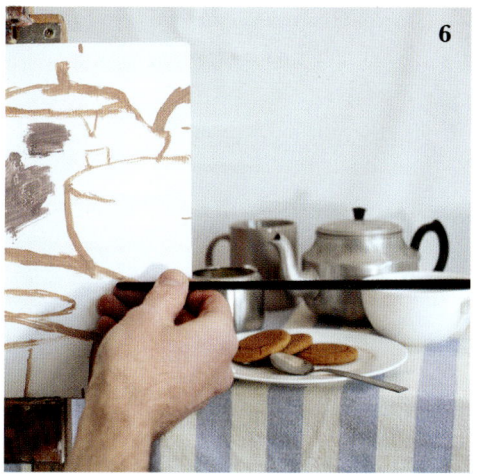

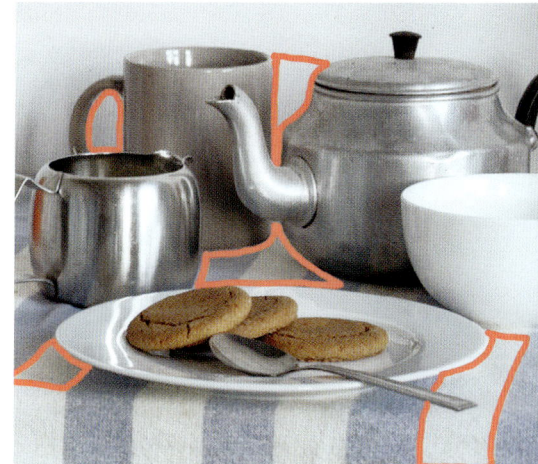

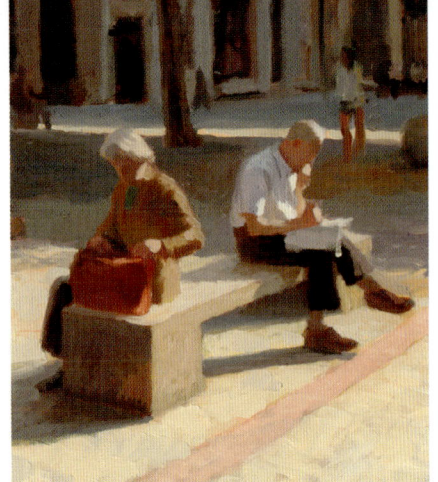

Light, Shade and Tone

Lines are magic. Since childhood, we have been able to create symbols using lines, which everyone recognizes. Yet those lines do not actually exist in nature. A line is the division between a light shape and a dark shape. To progress beyond drawing into painting, we need to move beyond lines into light and shade.

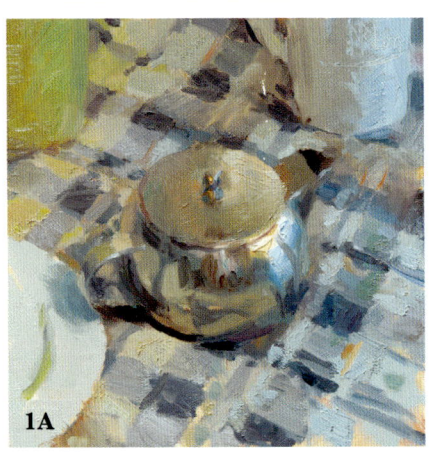

1A

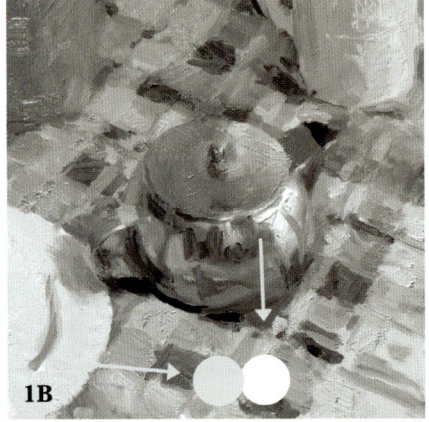

1B

in the egg is reflected light. Squint your eyes and compare it to the highlight. Which is lightest? The one rule of reflected light is that it can never be as light as the main light (**2B**).

Before you start painting a subject, whether from a photo or from life, ask yourself where the light is coming from (look for cast shadows to give you clues). Look through the projects in this chapter and try to guess the direction of the light in each painting.

Whiter than white

As painters, we hope to create the illusion of light, yet if the brightest thing we have is white paint, how can we make the highlight on a teapot glow? (**1A**). While colour can certainly enhance the illusion, the real secret lies in the tonal values.

The only way to make one thing look light is by making everything else a little bit darker. The highlight on the teapot looks shiny because it is the only area of white paint in the whole painting. Compare the swatches at the bottom of **1B** and you will see that the highlight is the only patch of white paint in the whole painting. Even the white plate is darker.

Light and shade

Light is logical. It can't bend around corners; it can only go in straight lines. This means that every object lit by a single light source will have a light side and a dark side. Draw as badly as you like; if you can keep the light side light and the shadow side dark, you will have a three-dimensional object.

Let's have a look and see what light does when it meets an egg. Place an egg on a flat surface with the light coming from one side. Where it first strikes the egg is the lightest part – the highlight. As the surface curves away from the light, it turns into a halftone. The shadow side is the darkest and the surface on which the egg sits will have a cast shadow (**2A**).

Now take a piece of brightly coloured paper and hold it next to the shadow side of the egg. The wonderful colour you see

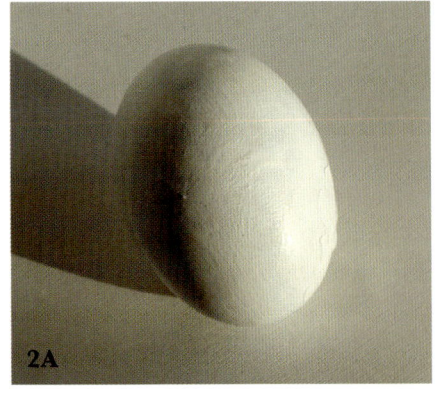

2A

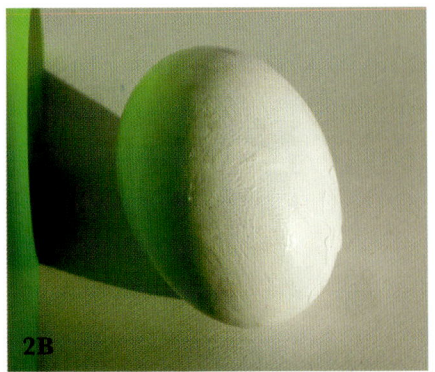

2B

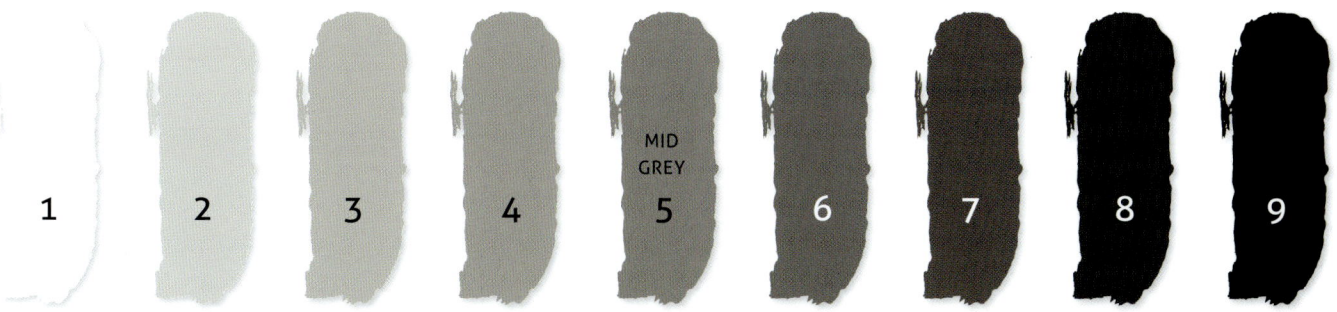

| 1 | 2 | 3 | 4 | MID GREY 5 | 6 | 7 | 8 | 9 |

ABOVE *The tonal scale from white to black.*

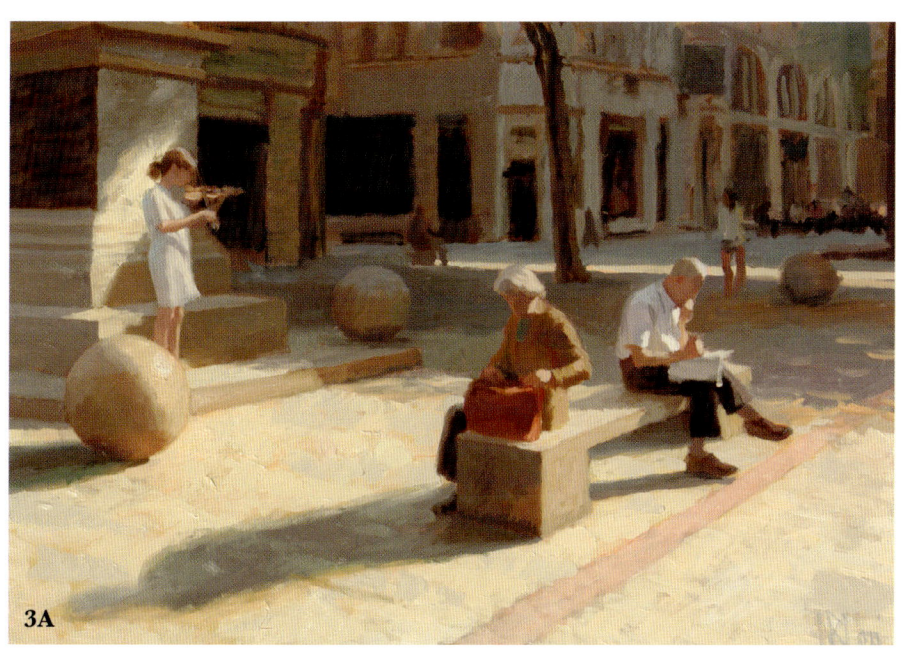

3A

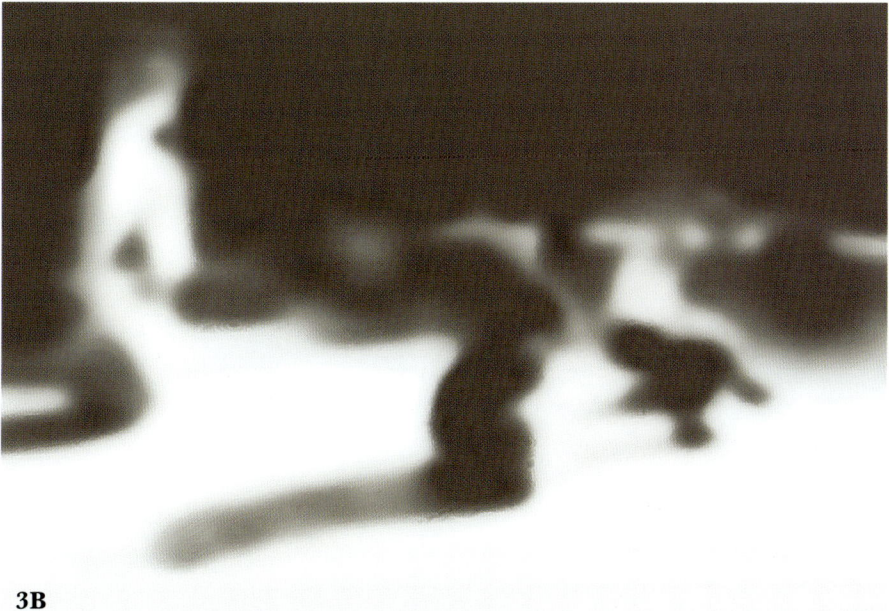

3B

Tonal scale

Judging the steps between black and white is so important that we sometimes use a tonal scale to help us. The scale has an odd number of steps so that we have a middle-value grey. In the first project we will be mixing values 1 to 5 of the 9-value scale. You may wish to create the full scale as an exercise in mixing accurate tonal values.

Tonal pattern

The success of a painting lies not only in achieving an accurate depiction of the subject. Most successful compositions (apart from the work of pure colourists) are based on a simple arrangement of light and dark shapes. This doesn't happen by chance. Artists deliberately select and adjust their subjects to achieve a simple pattern of tonal values.

Squinting at your subject (or a painting) reduces the amount of distracting detail and enables you to identify the pattern of lights and darks. Squinting at this finished painting (**3A**) will reveal a tonal pattern like the image below (**3B**). Note how, even in a complex subject, the light and dark shapes are grouped together into a relatively simple pattern.

Colour Theory

Colour is the most mysterious and wonderful aspect of painting. People respond to colours in an emotional way, but as painters we are privileged to observe and work with them on a deeper level. Basic colour theory is the ideal place to start our journey into the absorbing world of colour.

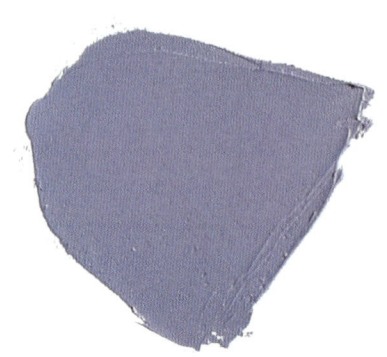

Single colour swatch

It's possible to think that learning colour theory will hinder your ability to use colour instinctively. My suggestion is that you absorb every theory you can in order to learn how colours behave, yet reserve the right to use any colour you like just because you feel like it.

In a painting, no colour is seen in isolation. Dark surroundings make colours appear lighter, while dull neighbours make some more vibrant.

Colour qualities

Any colour can be accurately described using just three attributes: colour, tonal value and intensity. Let's describe the swatch shown above by these qualities.

1. Starting with the most obvious quality, the colour, we can say it's a blue. Now look at the colour wheel (see opposite page, top right) and ask yourself, which way does the blue lean? Is it a greeny blue or a purple blue?

2. Now look at the tonal value. This is lightness or darkness, sometimes referred to as tone or simply value. If you were to take a black-and-white photo of a colour, you would see its tonal value. Choose a number from 1 to 9 on the value scale (see page 135) to match the tonal value.

3. Now consider the intensity. This is the quality of colour described by many different names (including chroma, power, saturation and depth), but they all mean the strength or purity of the colour. Is the colour intense or dull?

Normally, colours straight from the tube are at their most intense. As they get mixed with white, black or other (especially complementary) colours, they become duller. I would say it's a purply blue, with a tonal value around 5 and its intensity is dull.

Primary and secondary colours

In theory, we can mix all the colours in the rainbow from the three primaries: red, yellow and blue. In practice, I would say we could mix 85% of colours. By adding a red, so that we have a warm and a cool variety, I would say that jumps to 95%.

Secondary colours (green, purple and orange) can be mixed from primary colours. I couldn't resist adding a tube of a secondary colour (viridian) to our list because it makes mixing greens easier and without it we couldn't get my favourite colour – turquoise.

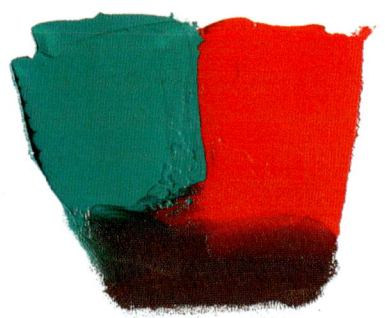
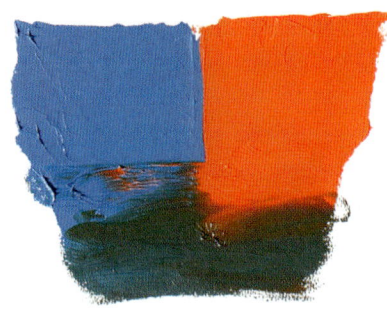
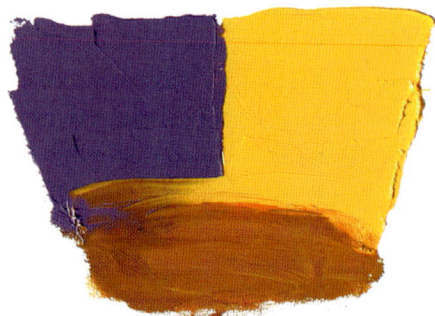

Complementary colours

Exploring colour

COLOUR WHEEL MIXES

If you've never done one before, it's a good idea to make a colour wheel from your actual colours so that you understand how they relate to each other. Start by laying out your tubes in a circle so that you can visualize where they sit. Make sure your cool red (Alizarin Crimson) sits next to blue and your warm red (Cadmium) sits next to yellow. A 12-segment wheel is easy to draw, starting with a cross through the circle. Begin with the primary colours, placed three spaces apart. We have yellow and blue, but no primary red, so mix your two reds to fill the primary red slot.

Some colours (Phthalo Blue/Viridian) appear almost black from the tube. Add a little white to these so that you can see their character clearly.

HARMONIOUS COLOURS

Harmonious colours get on really well together. They sit close to each other on the colour wheel and when combined in a painting, there's never any fighting.

WARM AND COOL COLOURS

On the colour wheel, there is a warm, orange side (like the colours of fire) and a cool, blue side (like ice). Then there are the in-between colours which can be either warm or cool. Any colour that seems orangey is warm, while one which leans towards blue is cool.

COMPLEMENTARY COLOURS

Complementary colours are the odd couples of the colour wheel – direct opposites, such as red and green, blue and orange, yellow and purple. Like strong personalities, put them side by side and by their difference they make each other shine. Mix them together and they kill each other.

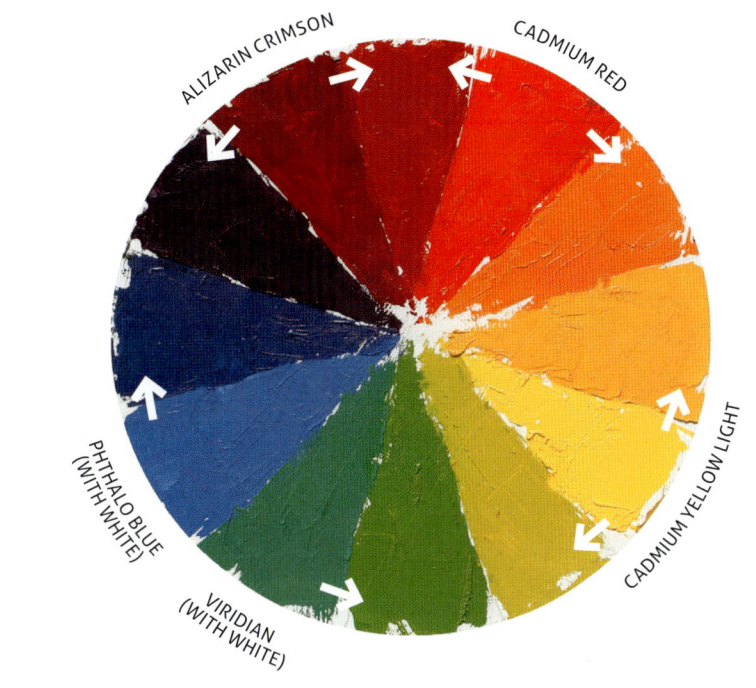

Colour wheel mixes

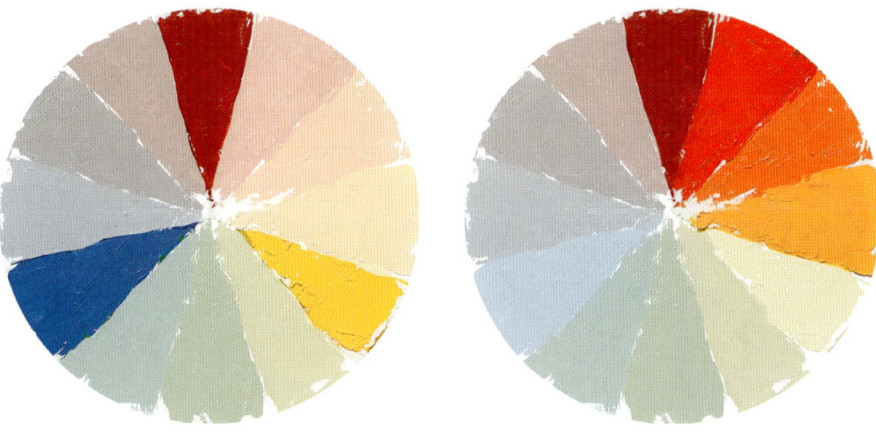

A primary colour wheel

Harmonious colours

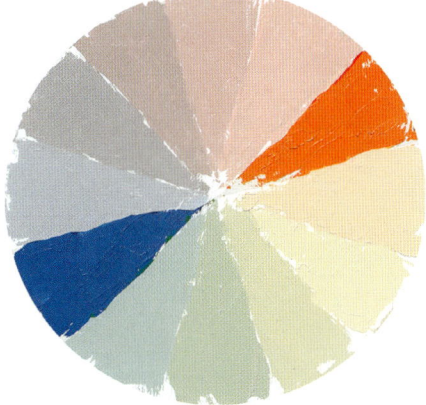

Complementary colour wheel

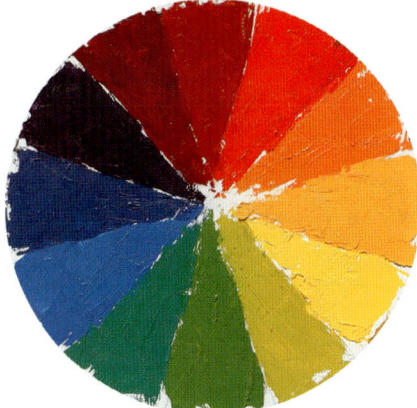

Warm and cool colours

THREE COLOUR SCHEMES

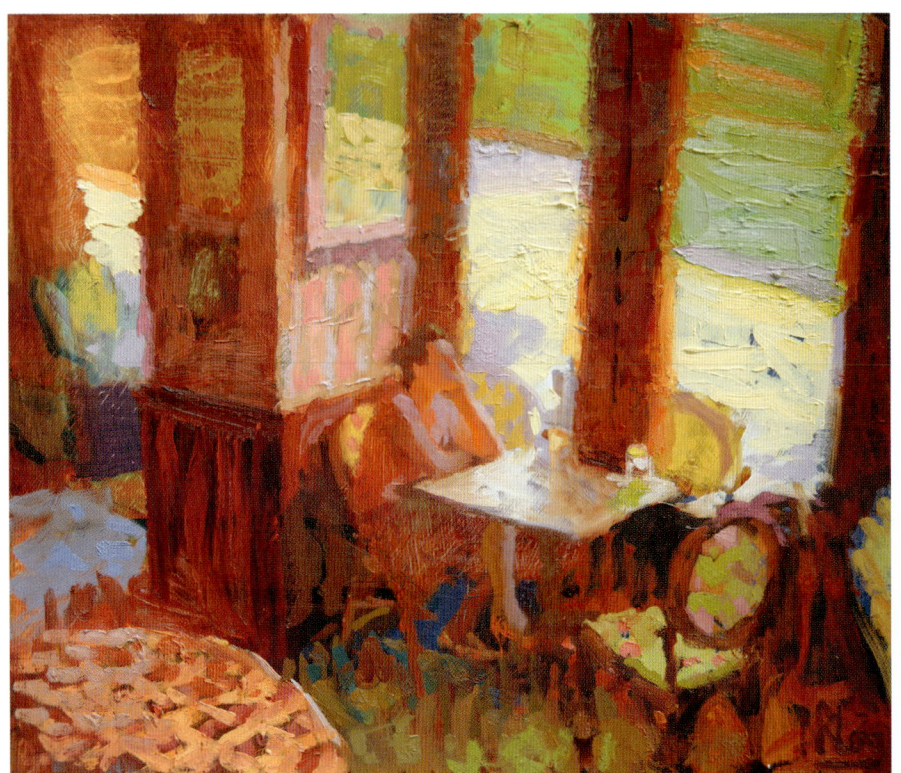

LEFT *This is a riot of colour for me. I was helped by working over a previous painting that had been abandoned by my wife. Allowing some of the original colours to show through broke me out of my own habitual colours.*

BELOW *A scheme based on orange/ blue complementary colours. Everything is suffused in a dim blue light in order for the furnace to appear stronger.*

RIGHT *The challenge here was to do an entire painting using leftover piles of 'palette mud'. Despite having no strong colours, the reddest colours appear stronger because they are surrounded by dull greenish ones.*

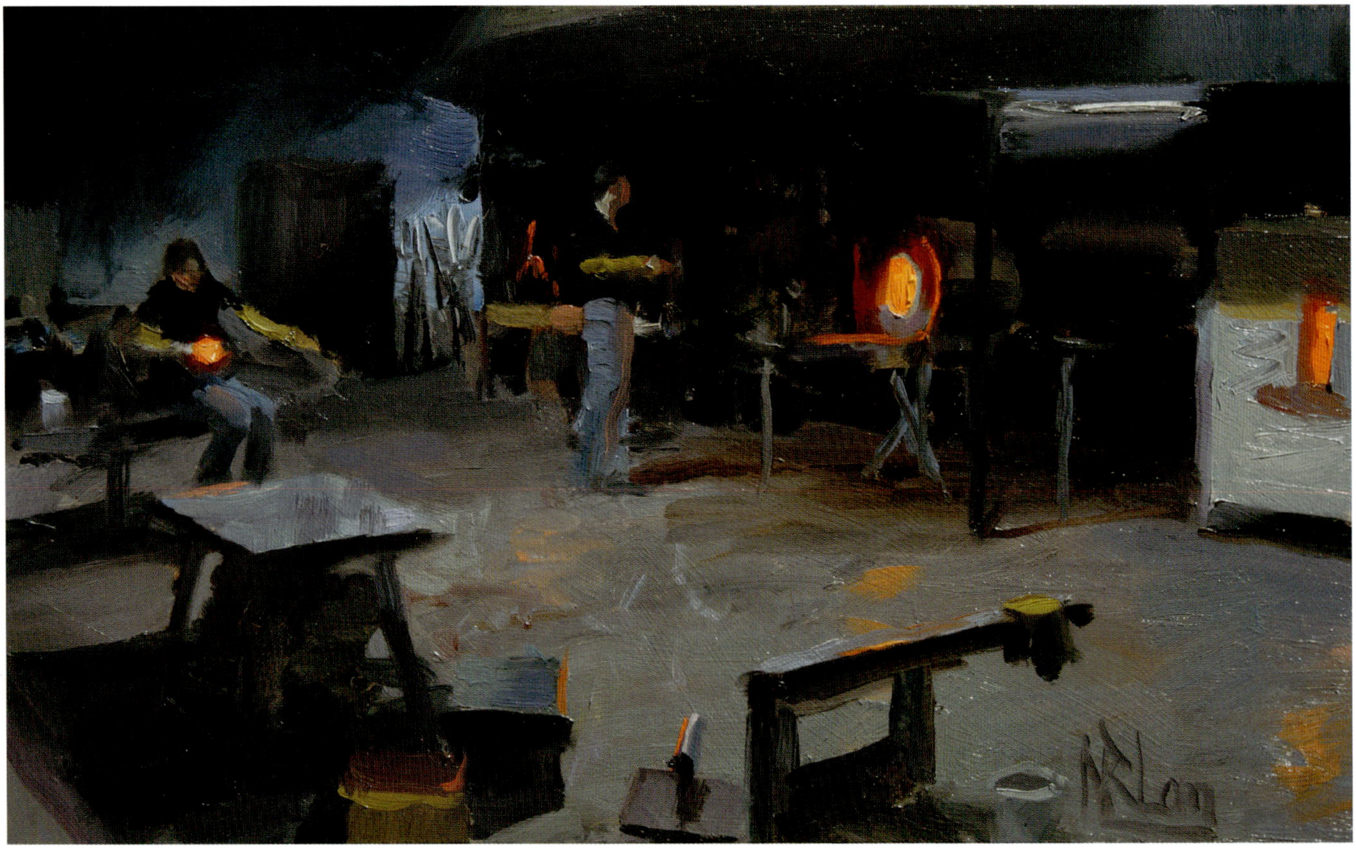

LAYOUT OF THE PALETTE

Squeeze paints out around the edge of your palette, leaving the maximum area for mixing in the centre. Set them out in a logical order, and use the same order each time you paint. You don't want to have to search for the right colour.

My palette (see right) is divided into two colour wheels. On the left is the chromatic colour wheel of five colours. These are the fun, children's paintbox type colours. On the right is the earth colour wheel, consisting of just three colours. Think of them as duller versions of the chromatic colours. Black is earth blue, burnt sienna is earth orange and yellow ochre is, you guessed it, earth yellow. They are not entirely necessary as they could be created from the chromatic colours, but they do save us time when mixing.

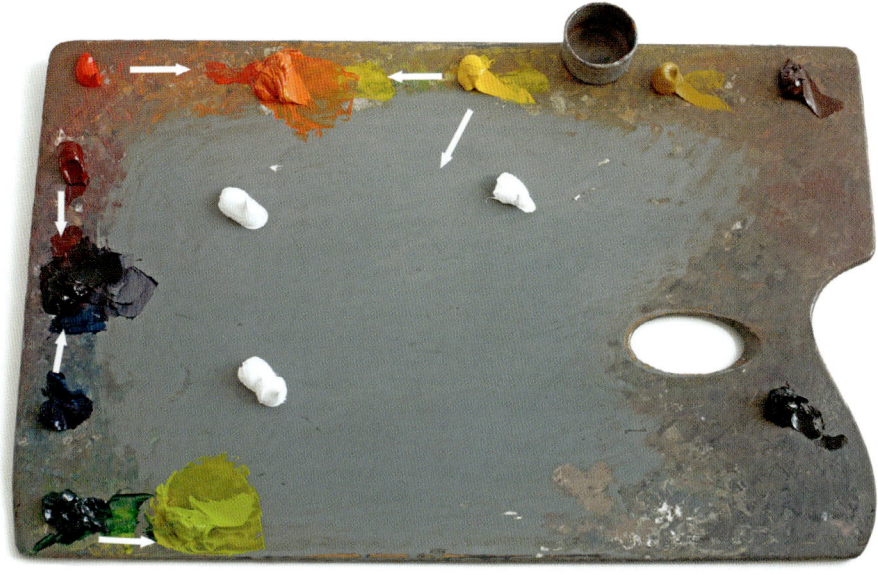

The layout of my palette.

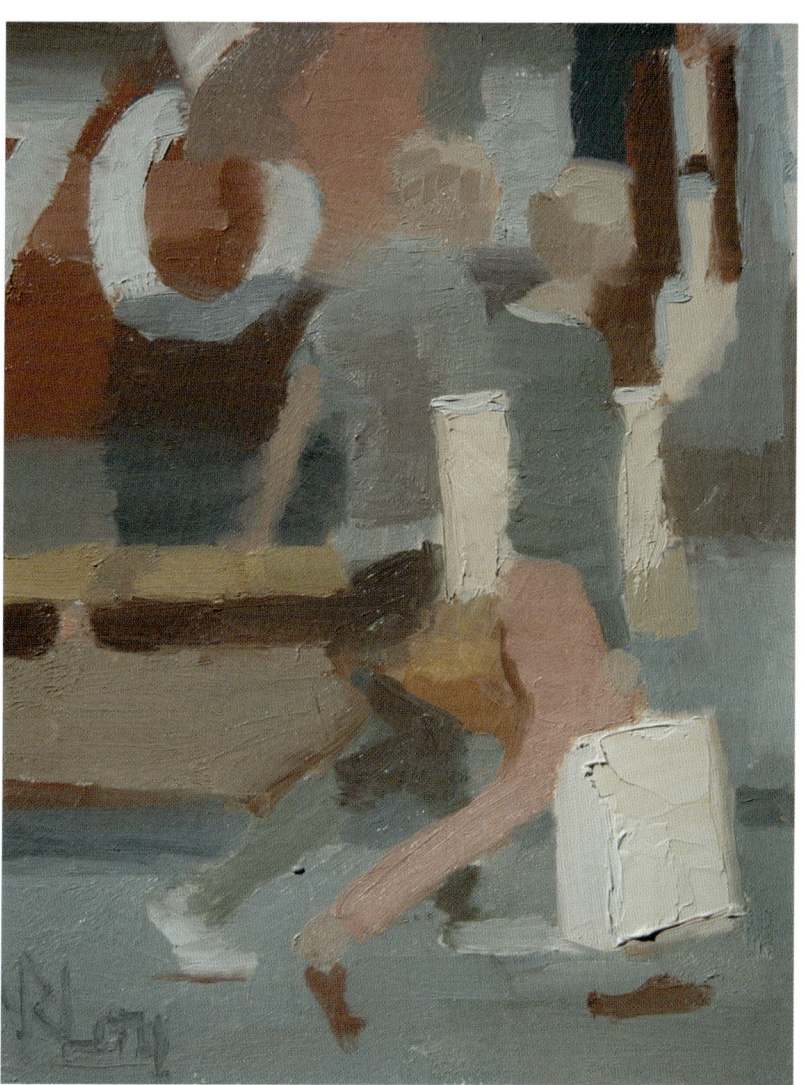

Always put out at least three blobs of white in the central mixing area. We use more white than anything else and we need separate blobs to mix with different colours. To give yourself a full range of colours, mix some nice clean secondary colours before you start. Use the palette knife to mix a purple from blue and crimson and an orange from cadmium red and yellow. If you are painting a landscape with bright greens, you may also want a yellow-green. If you wait till you are in the middle of the painting before mixing these colours, they are likely to get muddied.

WHEN PAINTING WITH COLOUR

Daylight is the best light for painting in as it contains all the wavelengths of light and gives full colour. Rarely can you get perfect light on the subject, the canvas and your palette, but aim for it anyway. You should almost never use colour straight from the tube without modifying it. When you need to mix colour, bear in mind that the strongest mixes come from colours which are close together on the colour wheel. For your best purple, use cool red (crimson) and blue.

Pure white and pure black are colourless. Always add something to keep them interesting. Blacks can be varied by adding crimson, blue or burnt sienna. Or make your own blacks from brown and blue or crimson and viridian.

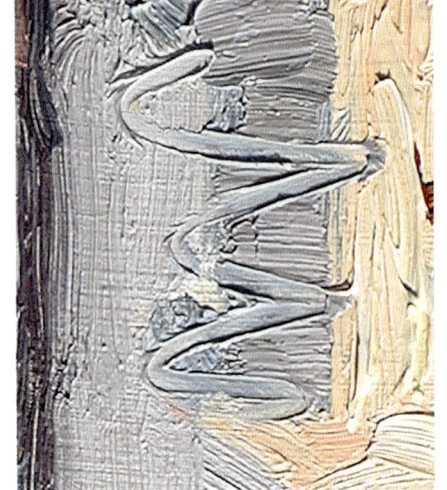

Painting Techniques

Every artist builds a personal repertoire of marks which they naturally use as they work. Here are some of mine. Experiment to see which suit you and which don't. Look at the techniques and tools used by other artists, invent your own and you will develop an armoury of marks to tackle any subject.

When using oils, there are no right or wrong brushmarks. A technique may be used to imitate the texture of the subject, but it doesn't have to. We are not painting a door; your strokes don't need to be neat or parallel. Remember, you can't mix colour accurately or make luscious marks with a meagre amount of paint. Squeeze out twice as much as you think you need – and use it all!

Diluting paint

For most of the painting, the consistency of paint that comes out of the tube is perfect. Don't leave your brushes bristles-down in a jar of solvent (as you might do when working with acrylics) because your mixtures will be too sloppy. However, there are times when you will want the paint to flow more readily, for ease of drawing or to apply thin washes.

In your first session on a painting, just use solvent if you need to dilute the paint. For all except one of the projects in this chapter, that is all you will need.

THIN WASH (MESSY)
This can be used to tone the whole canvas before you start, or for 'blocking in' various colours. Dip the tip of your brush into solvent and make a pool on your palette. Now dip into some paint and mix this into the pool. Apply the wash in all directions (**1**).

THIN WASH (WIPED SMOOTH)
Use a rag to gently wipe the thin wash for a more even coverage (**2**).

Painting wet-in-wet

Most of the paintings in this chapter are done 'alla prima', which means in one go. They are completed in anything between one and a half to four hours. To complete a painting in this way, we need to be able to paint 'wet-in-wet', laying wet paint on top of an already wet surface (**3**). Whether you are using

the brush or the knife, to make a mark that does not get mixed in with underlying paint, you will need: a well-loaded brush (or knife) of non-diluted paint, a light touch and a single, decisive stroke.

Decide where you're going to put the stroke, do it in one go and leave it. The mark will never be perfect, but it will look confident and exciting. Repeated corrections will muddy the effect. If it's really not an acceptable mark, wipe it off and re-do it. Before doing the next stroke, wipe off the brush on a rag and re-insert it in a clean pile of paint. One

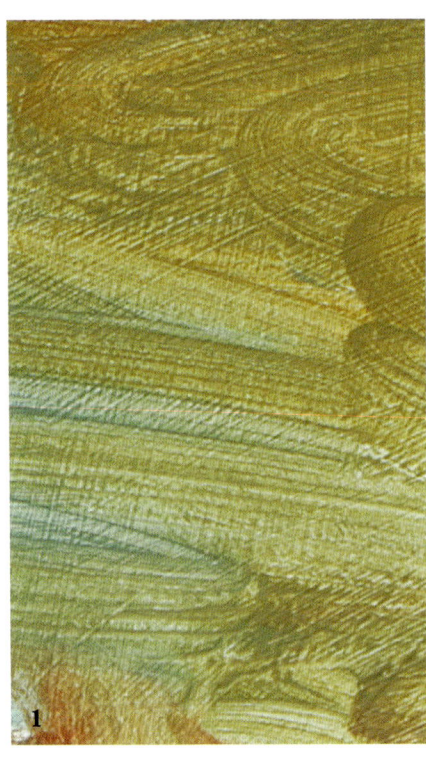

1

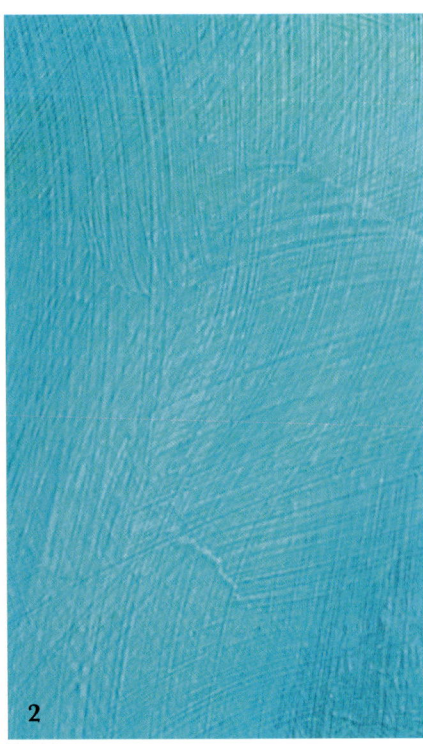

2

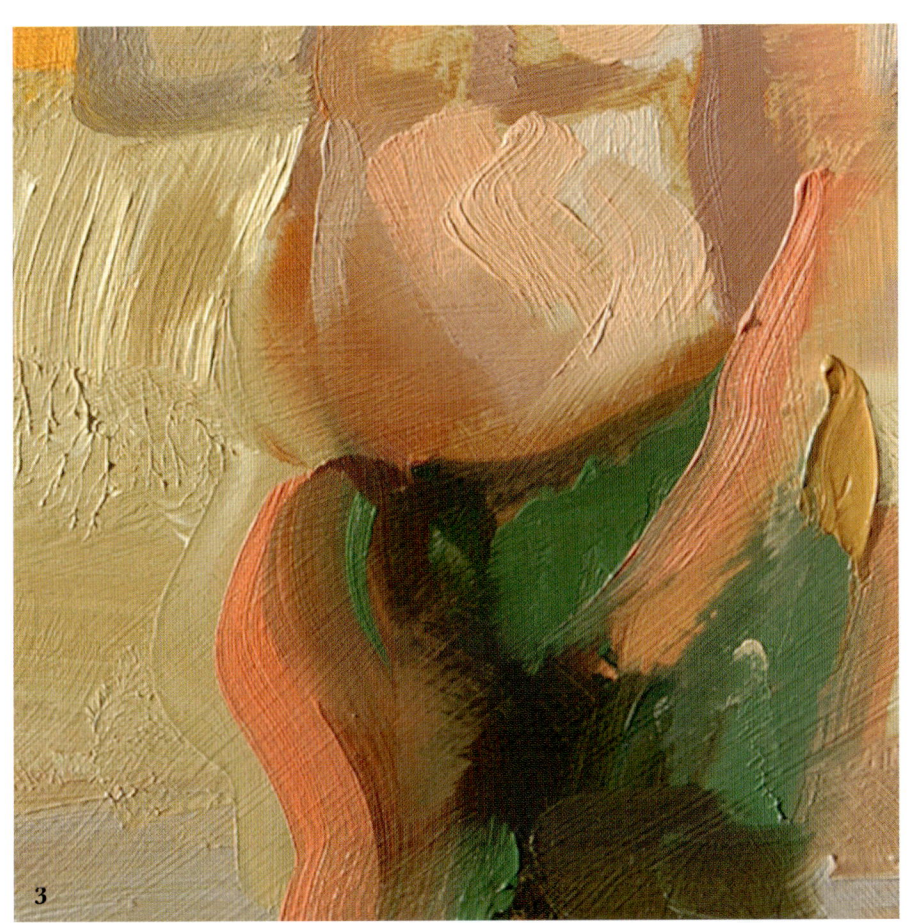

teacher told me that a paintbrush is a rifle that needs to be reloaded each time you fire, not a machine gun to be fired repeatedly.

IMPASTO WET-IN-WET

Undiluted thick paint is known as 'impasto' (Italian for 'paste'). The thicker it gets, the more messy and exciting it is to paint into! (**4**).

LIFT-OFF TECHNIQUE

Dip a brush into a large pile of paint. When you lift the brush out, a peak of paint will appear at the tip. Placed gently on your painting, this makes a deliciously sharp highlight (**5**).

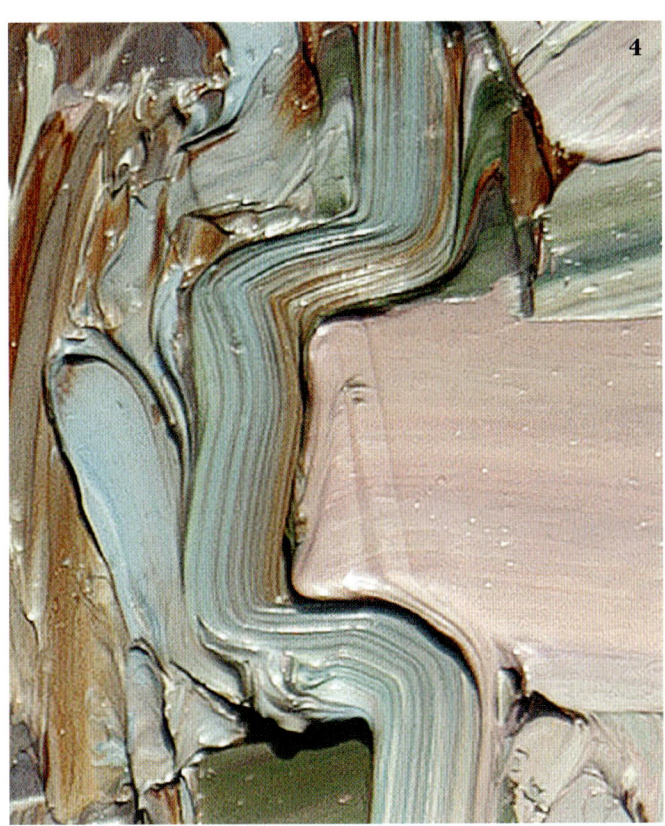

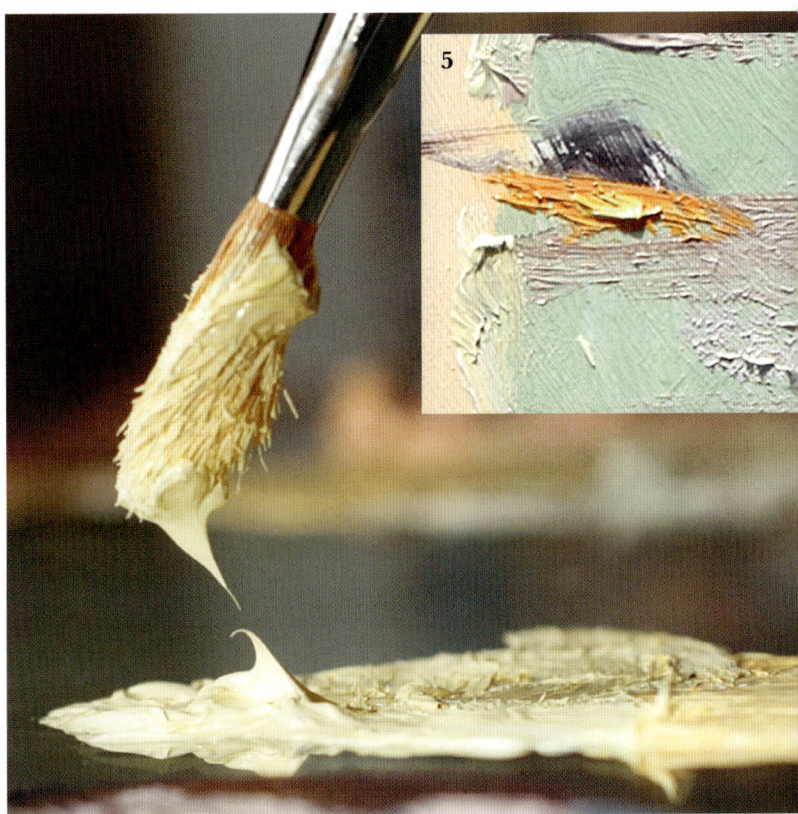

Starting to paint

You will always need more time at the end, so don't aim for perfection at the start. Get the canvas covered as soon as you can, leaving time to correct later. As you start painting, pick up a clean brush for each new mixture. Using lots of brushes (I used at least 12) keeps your colours separate and clean.

Remember, it's impossible to mix clean colours on a dirty palette. As soon as you are struggling to find a clean patch, wipe it off and refresh any depleted piles of paint.

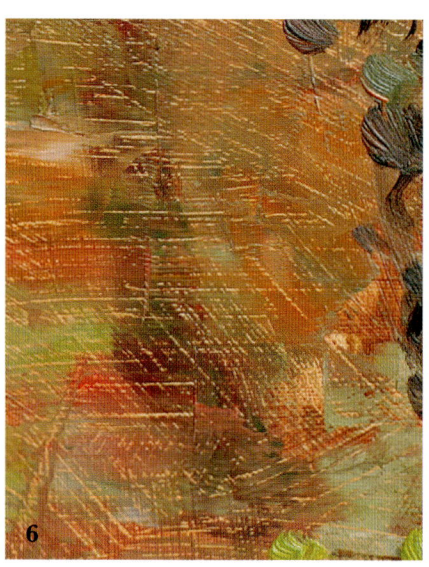

6

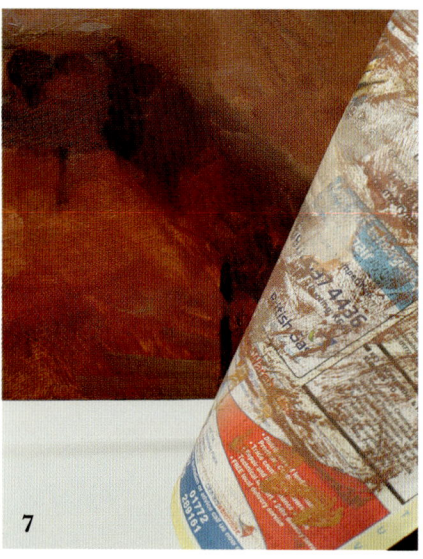

7

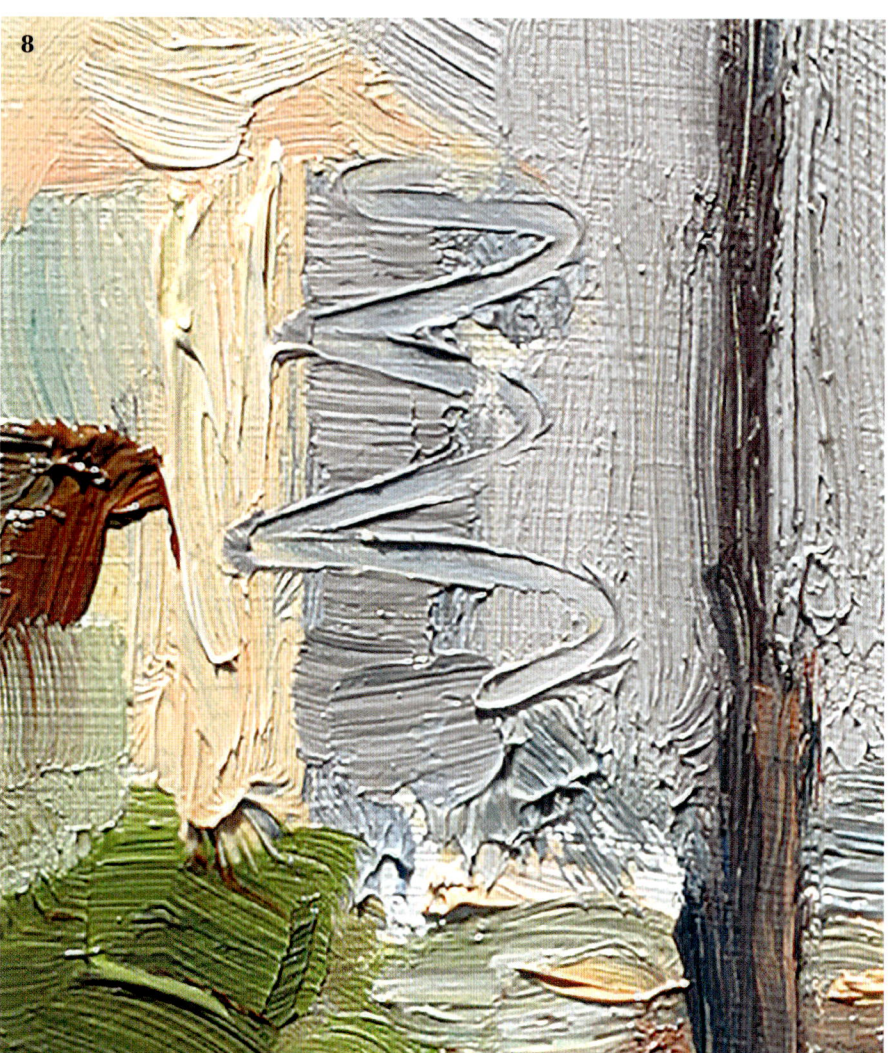

8

Removing paint

When painting wet-in-wet, most corrections can be made by applying the new colour directly on top. However, drastic changes (such as from a very light colour to a dark one) work best if you remove some paint first. The palette knife, rag and telephone directory are all ideal for removing paint, sometimes resulting in exciting textures, which can be left in the final painting.

PALETTE KNIFE

Use a palette knife for controlled removal of excess paint. It often reveals more exciting textures than you could create deliberately (**6**).

TONKING

Named after the British painter Henry Tonks, this technique aims to reduce the amount of paint on the surface without smudging the image. You just need to place a piece of absorbent paper onto the surface and peel it off. Just think, some day they could name a painting technique after you (**7**)!

SGRAFFITO

The Italian word for 'scratched' is used for the technique of removing paint with the wrong end of the brush or the tip of a palette knife. Lines scratched through wet paint sometimes reveal underlying colours. This technique can also be used to sign your painting (**8**).

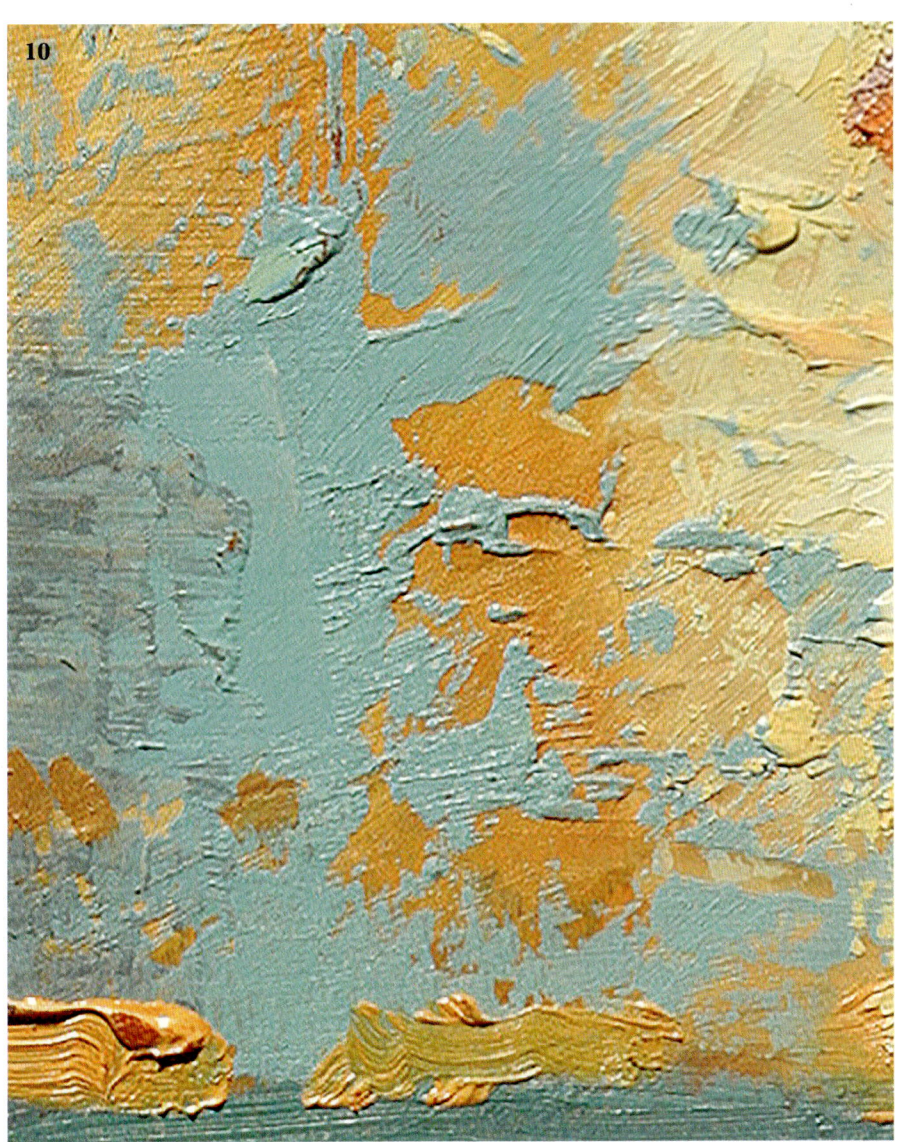

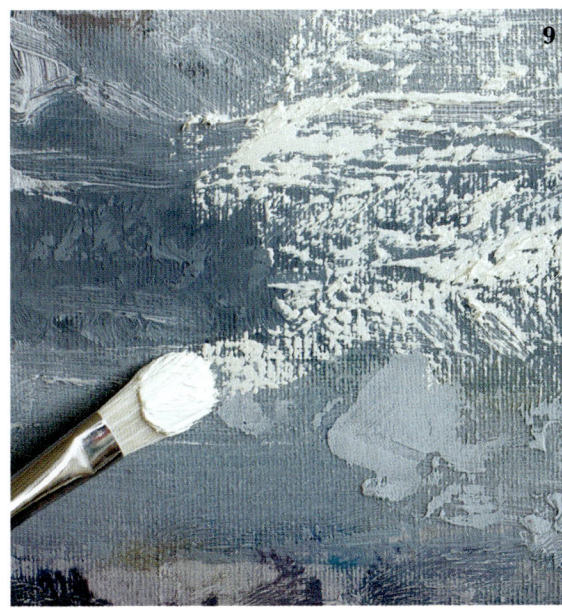

Textures with brush and knife

With hog-hair brushes and a palette knife, you can create hundreds of paint textures. While some work best wet-in-wet, others make use of dried paint layers.

SCUMBLE
Undiluted paint dragged over a rough, dry surface is called a scumble. Hold the brush gently at the angle shown so that the paint only catches on the top ridges of the underlying layer (**9**).

SCUMBLE EFFECT USING KNIFE
Undiluted paint on the back of the knife can be rubbed over a rough surface for a similar effect to the scumble (**10**).

KNIFE STAMP
To create straight lines, stamp the edge of the painting knife in paint and place it on the canvas (**11**).

KNIFE STRIATIONS
Put various colours into a pile of paint but don't mix them. When applied to the canvas with the knife, the striations of colour give a spectacular effect (**12**).

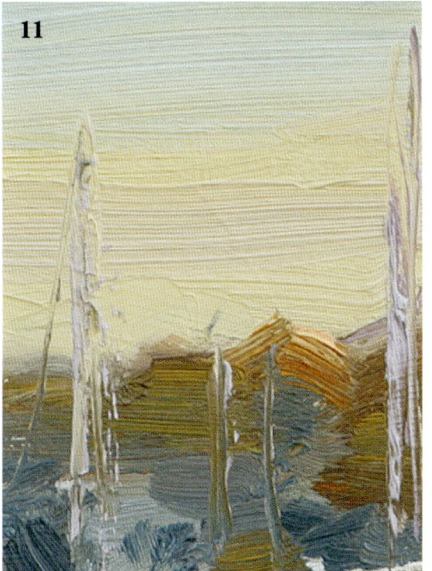

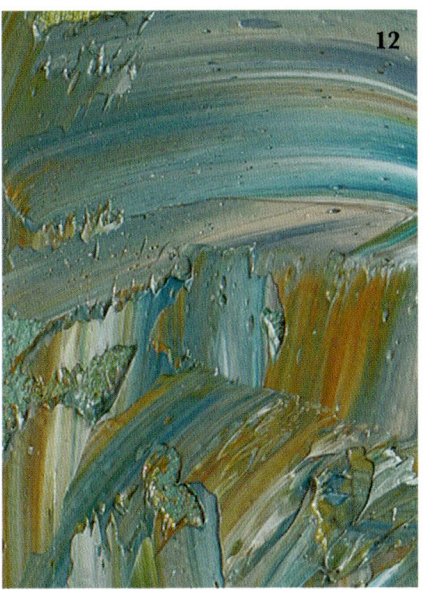

Softening paint

Most of the brushmarks we make have hard edges. Here are three of my favourite ways of softening things down to make subtle colour transitions.

TORN TOWEL

Use a torn piece of kitchen paper. Dragged gently through thick paint, the edges are softened in a lively way (**13**).

FINGER PAINTING

You can, of course, paint with your fingers, but more frequently I use them to create really soft or 'lost' edges (**14**).

SQUEEGEE SMUDGING

A piece of card, a plank of wood, almost anything with a flat edge can be dragged across the entire painting to smudge and remove paint. It's surprising how good the painting can look after this drastic move (**15**)!

Adding linseed oil

If you return to a painting after the first layer has dried, just add a little linseed oil to your solvent for whenever you wish to dilute the paint. This mixture of solvent and linseed oil is called a medium. (Two parts solvent to one part linseed oil is a reliable recipe.) In doing this, you are following the 'fat over lean' rule. The top layers of your painting will contain more oil (fat) and dry more slowly, meaning there is no danger of it cracking as it dries. (The same principle applies when painting oils over acrylics, which is all right because the oils dry more slowly. However, painting acrylics over oils is not recommended.)

Glazing

We use the same medium (solvent and linseed oil) to make a glaze. Check that the first layer of paint is completely dry,

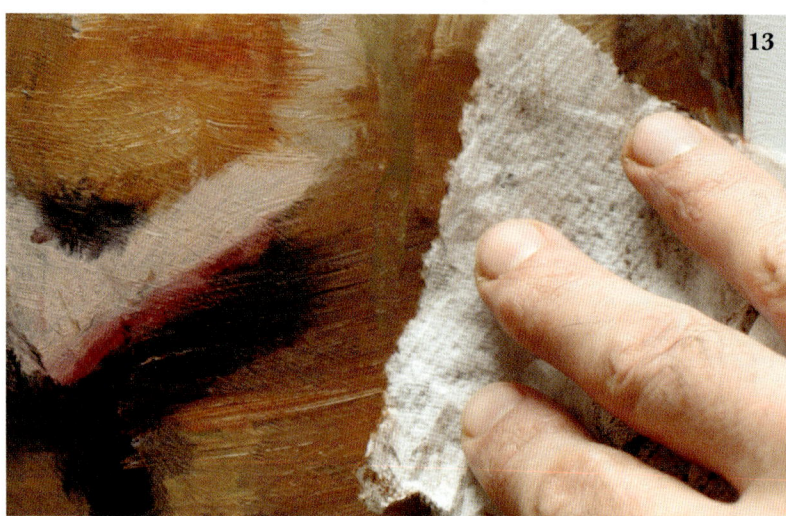

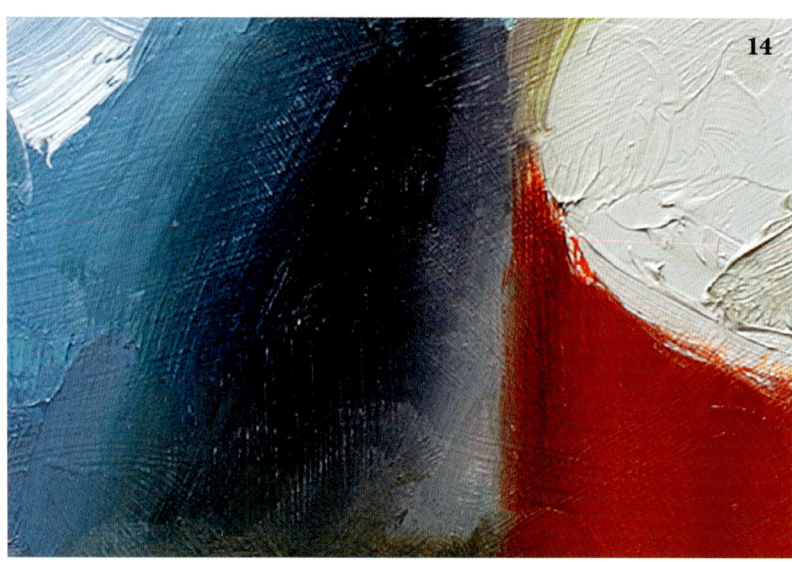

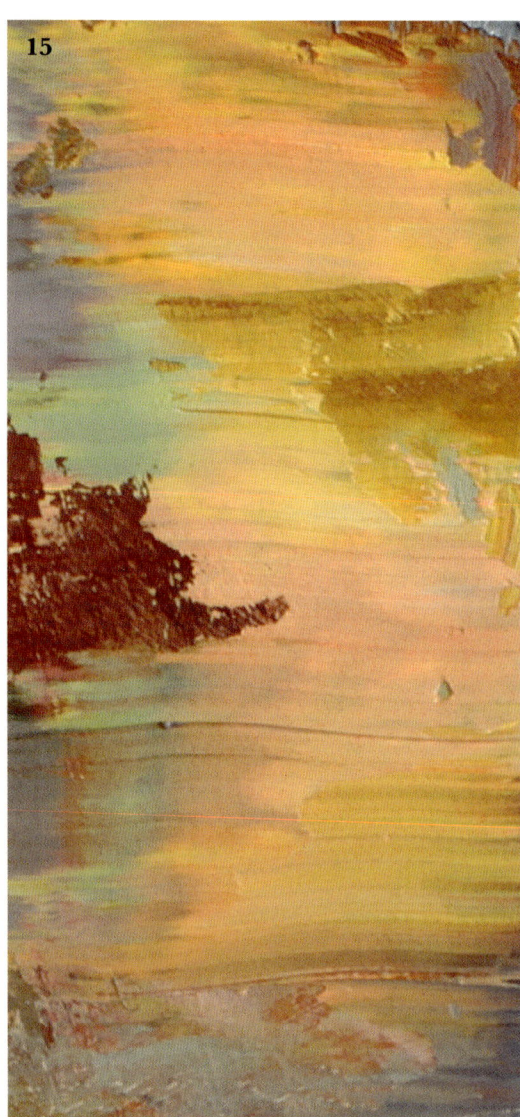

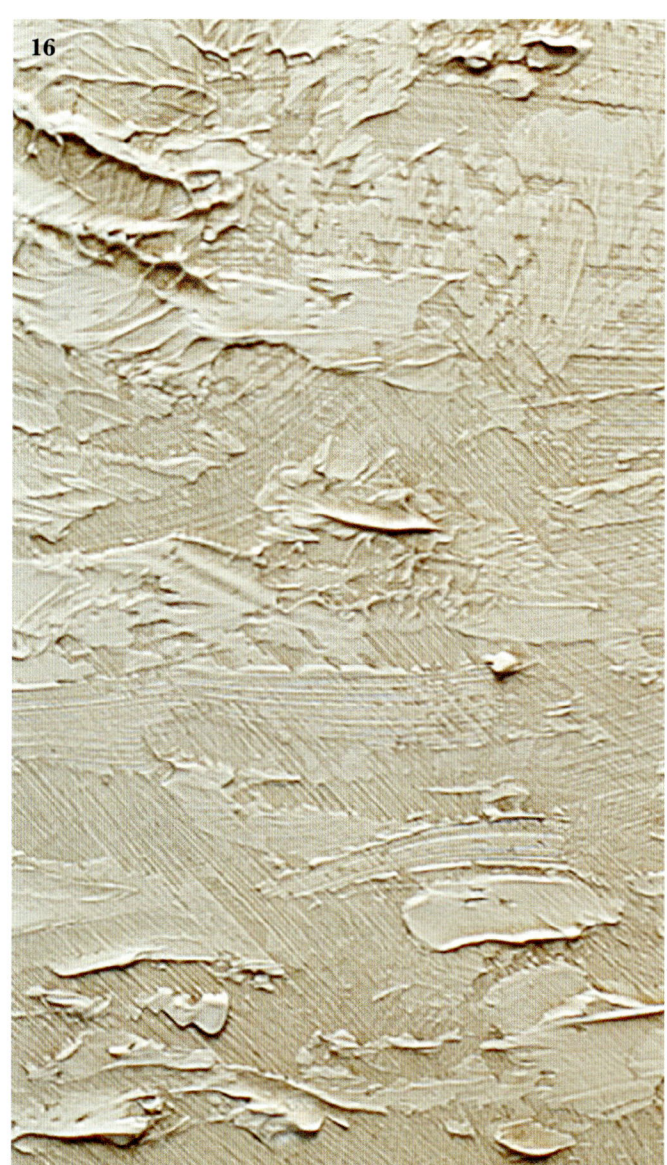

16

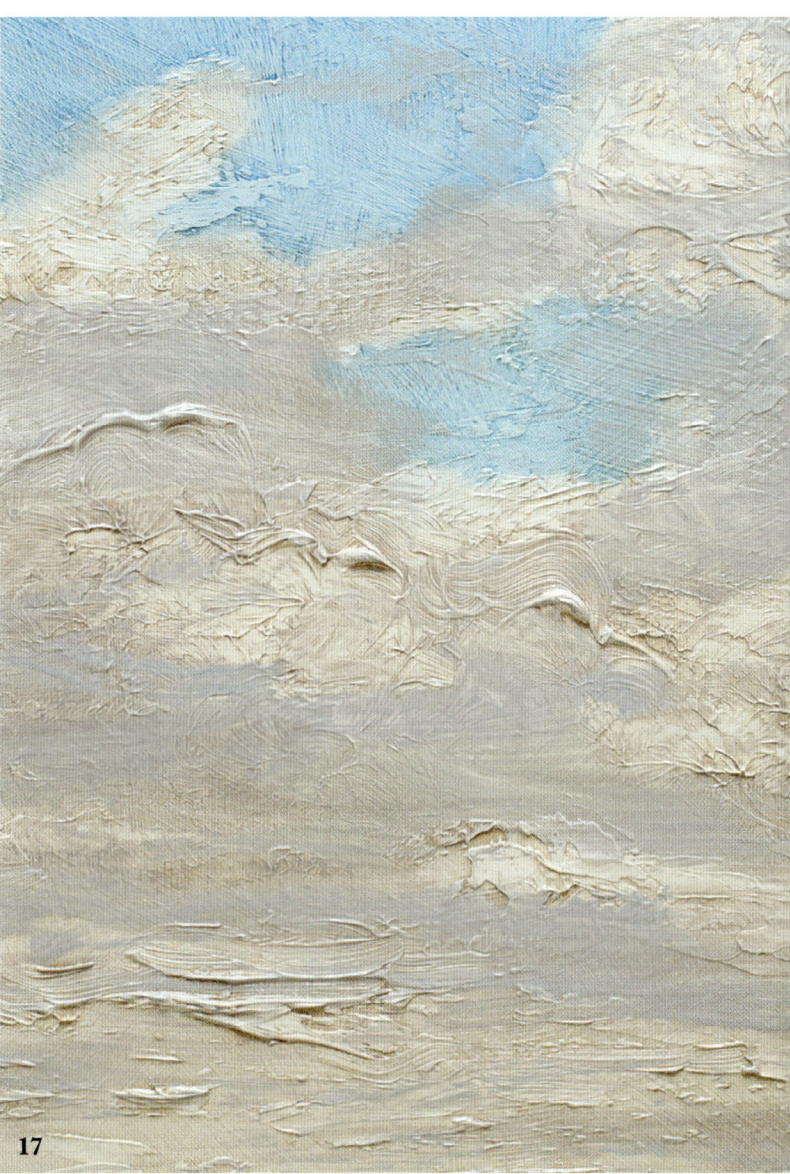

17

then mix your painting medium with any combination of transparent paints and you have a glaze. When applied, the effect is to change the colour of the underlying layer without losing detail.

Glazing is a technique you can easily do without – and many artists do. I'm including it here because it creates effects of transparent colour, which aren't possible through direct painting.

When selecting colours for glazing, it's important to check that they are transparent rather than opaque. Most (not all) paint tubes will tell you. Winsor & Newton use symbols on their tubes to indicate transparency. If in doubt, check the manufacturer's paint charts. Colours that are good for glazing are permanent Alizarin Crimson, Phthalo Blue, Viridian Hue and Burnt Sienna.

The technique of mixing a glaze is exactly the same as that used for making a thin wash (see page 140). The only difference is that medium is used instead of pure solvent and only transparent paints are used. Once applied, you may leave the glaze as it is or wipe it with a rag to adjust the darkness (more wiping leads to a lighter colour). Glazing will rarely be the final step in a painting. You can paint on top of a glaze immediately with any technique you like.

A glaze can be used to emphasize the texture of impasto brushmarks. After applying the glaze, gently wipe the top ridges with a rag, leaving paint in the hollows. This is a classic Rembrandt technique (**16**).

A velatura (meaning 'veil') is a glaze that incorporates white or opaque colours, resulting in a milky appearance. It is often used over distant mountains to help make them recede or to create realistic clouds (**17**).

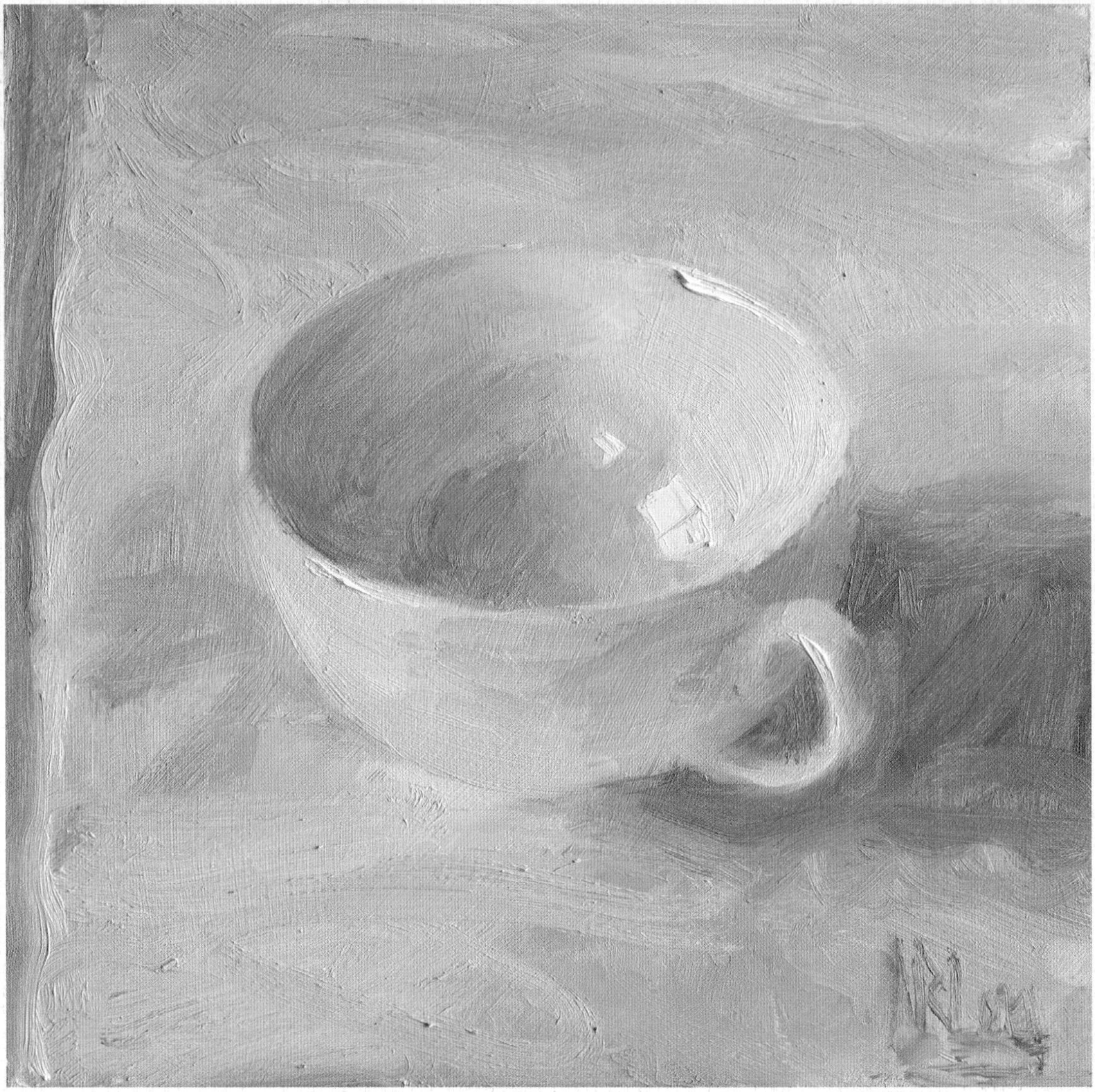

Teacup

In this project you will learn to mix a range of tonal values and use them to convey light and shade on a white object. Working in black and white helps you to master tone without being distracted by colour.

COLOURS NEEDED

Ivory
Black

Titanium
White

When you love colour as much as I do, it's tempting to skip over tonal value and head for the exciting stuff. Only when you buckle down and start to look carefully at a white object do you see the true beauty and subtlety that is there. If you can nail the ability to see lights and darks, you can use the craziest colour in the world and get away with it.

You can copy my painting of a teacup or do your own painting of any simple white object. Place your object on a white surface and make sure it is lit by one main light source from the side, such as window or a lamp. Position your canvas level with the subject so that you can compare them at a glance.

PRE-MIXING COLOURS

To give yourself a head start, it's a good idea to mix a few tonal values (see page 135) ready to drop into the painting. To paint a white object, we will only need five values (white to middle grey) and we already have white, so it won't take long. For pre-mixing colours, I encourage you to use a palette knife to gain some practice in handling this tool. The knife is very easy to clean off between mixes, meaning that you don't get bits of one colour mixed into another by mistake.

Start by squeezing out white paint for tonal value 1 in the lower left of your palette, followed by black and at least three blobs of white for mixing the rest of the greys. Mix middle grey (tonal value 5) first, comparing your mixture with black and white until it sits equally between them (you will use more white paint than black). Next mix tonal value 3, to sit equally between values 1 and 5, and finally values 2 and 4.

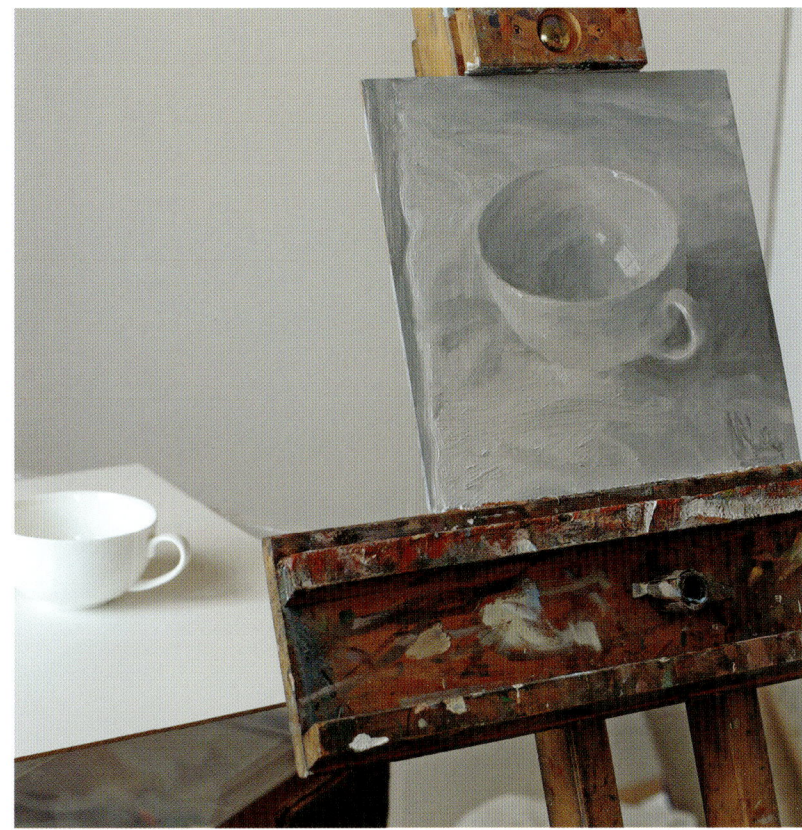

ABOVE *The setup for your work. If you are right-handed, it's preferable to have the easel to your right (so that you are not reaching across yourself) and your subject on the left.*

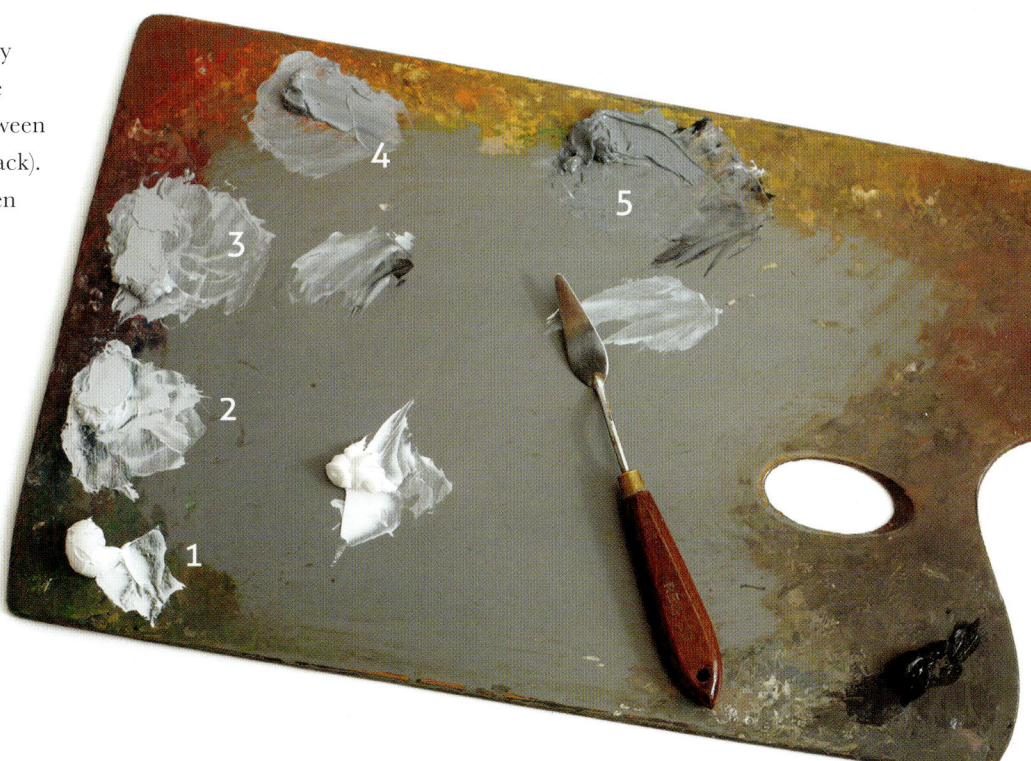

RIGHT *Mix tonal values 1–5. Check that you have fairly even steps between them and adjust if need be.*

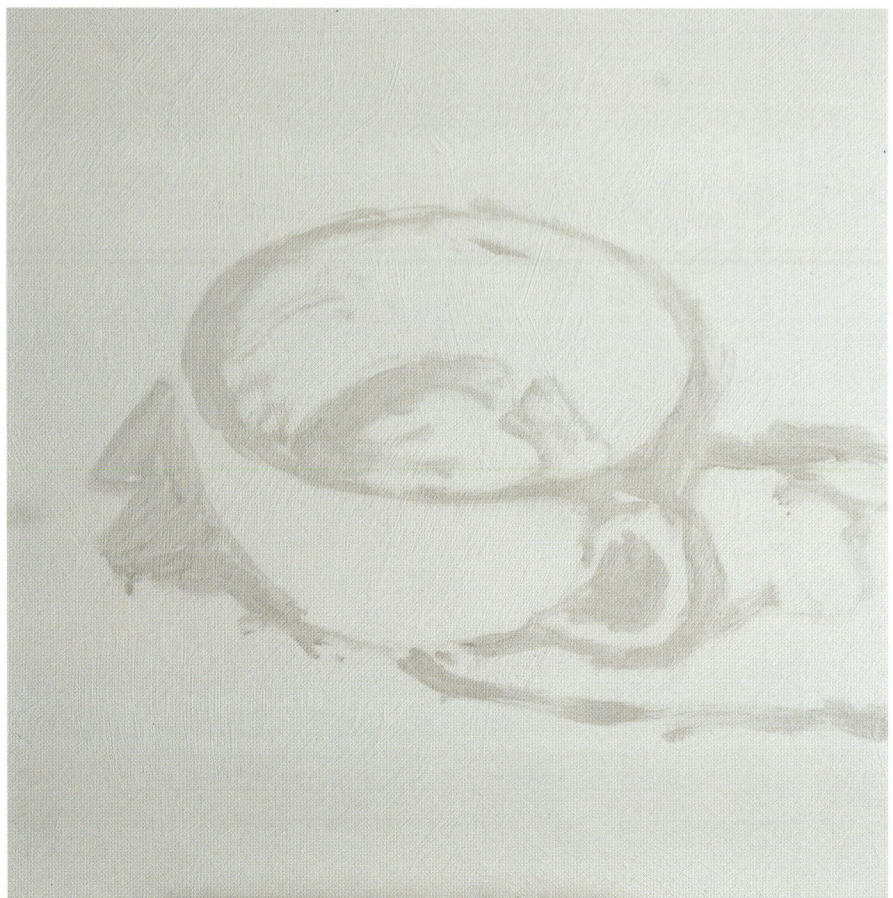

STAGE 1

There are two good reasons for using a light colour for the initial drawing. Firstly, it gives us chance to get it wrong. We can easily mix up a darker colour and redraw on top. Secondly, let's imagine we did our drawing in black. Every light colour we put on top will mix with the black and get muddy.

Dilute tonal value 2 to make the paint flow easily and use a No. 2 round brush to draw the shapes on your canvas. Make the shape of the object fill the square as much as possible. Outline the shape of the shadows too – they connect the object to the edges of the picture.

To make the inevitable corrections your drawing will need, use kitchen towel dipped in solvent as an eraser. If you feel like checking proportions, try to find something vertical that matches something horizontal in the picture. Here the height of the cup is equal to the distance from the left side of the cup to the middle of the handle. It's not critical at this stage, but if you want to check if your ellipse is symmetrical, look at it in the mirror.

Tip

Before you start, swing the brush around just above the surface of the canvas. Feel your confidence – you are in control of the whole painting. If you feel like it, splodge some paint anywhere on the canvas just to show who is in charge!

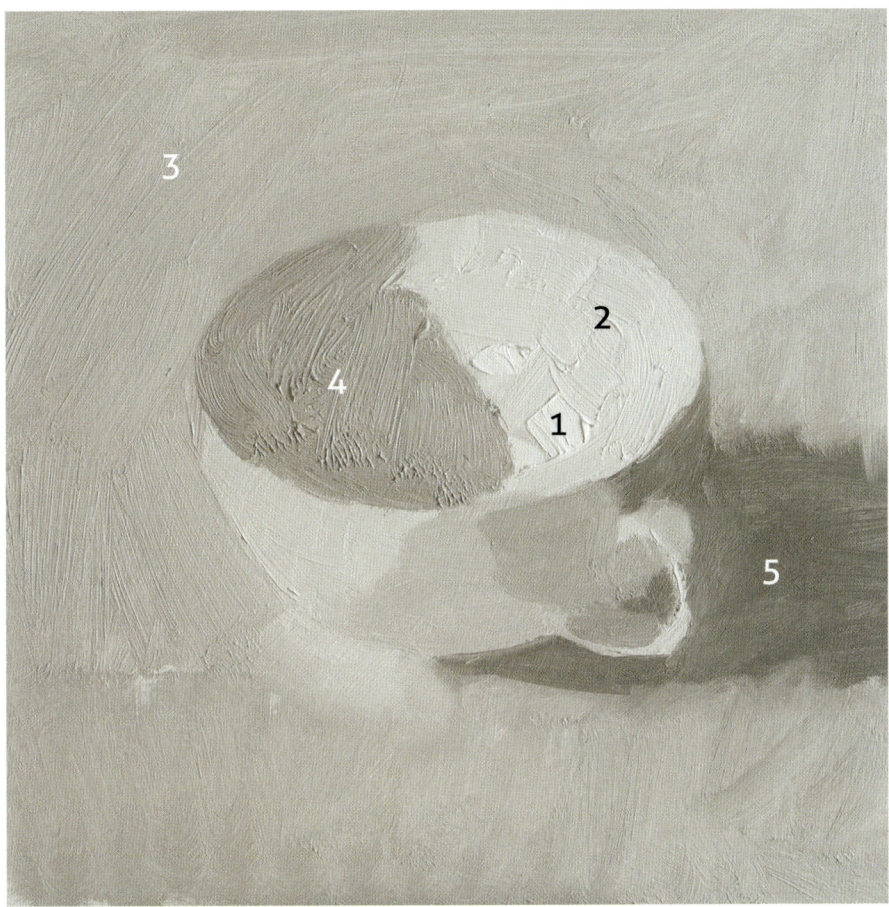

STAGE 2

The next step is to identify the very lightest thing in your subject. When looking for tonal values, try squinting. Almost close your eyes and notice how all the complexity of the subject is reduced to simple areas of light and dark. Here the lightest things are the highlights in the cup, reflecting the window. Blob in some thick white paint, just as a marker and reminder that everything in the whole canvas must be made darker than these notes in order for them to sing (**1**).

Now look for the very darkest parts of the subject, areas which are around value 5. Think only in terms of shapes, not objects. Note how I have painted across the edge of the cup, grouping the cast shadow and the dark side of the cup together into one shape.

Now that you have marked the lightest and darkest areas, you can work in any order, blocking in big shapes with one of your five tonal values. Many beginners ask what to do first. Is it darks before lights, or background before subject? The real answer is that you can do it in any order you please. In practice, I look at the painting, then at the subject and ask myself, what's one big thing I can do to make the painting more like the subject? That's what I do next.

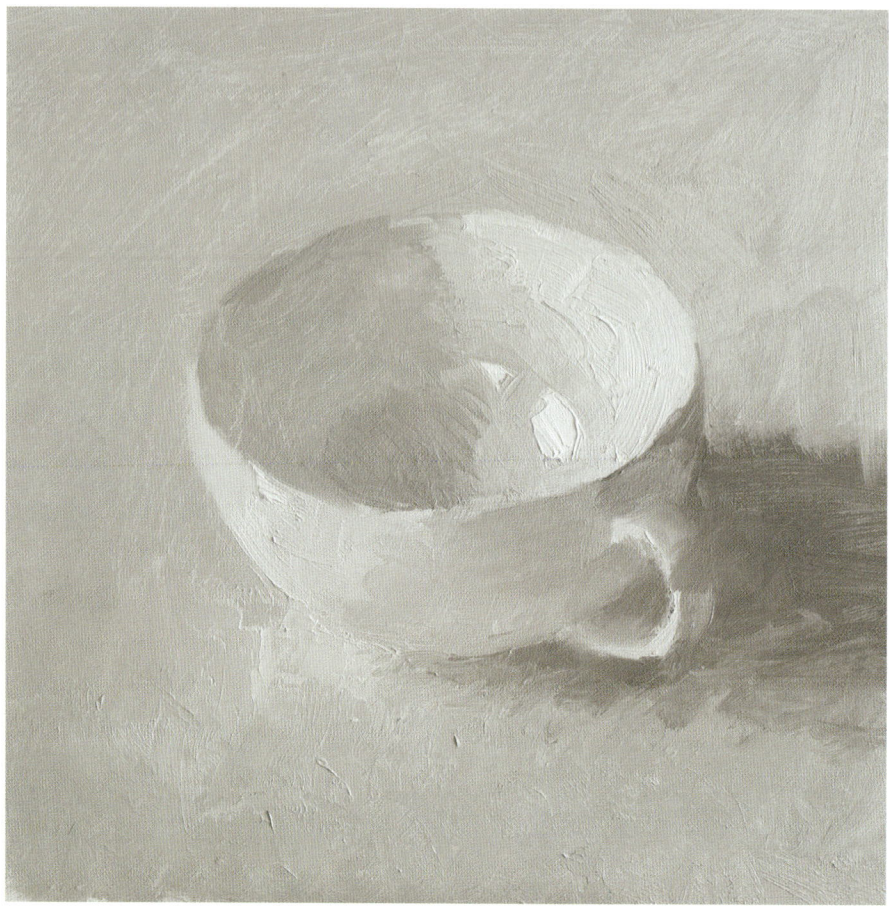

Tip

Use your finger to soften the hard edges of the block-in stage. I like to use the side of my little finger because it is smaller than my forefinger. It also seems appropriate to use your extended pinky for the delicate job of painting a teacup!

STAGE 3

To keep the viewer interested in a painting, aim for variety in many aspects of the painting. This includes the thickness of the paint. As a general rule, aim for thin darks and thick lights. This is because thick paint sticks out and catches the light, an advantage with light colours because it makes them appear lighter. In darker passages, we generally don't want too many ridges of paint because the light will catch on them and disrupt the effect of darkness. At this stage the thick paint in the shadowy interior of the cup was distracting, so I used the palette knife to scrape it off.

We noted earlier that every colour is affected by surrounding colours. While there is still some white unpainted board peeping through, we cannot truly judge all the tonal values. Now that the white is covered, we can see where we stand and make finer adjustments in tonal value. One such area is the shadow inside the cup, where one block of tone has been made into two.

STAGE 4

You could stop at the previous stage but for me, the cup just didn't feel very special, so I took a piece of torn kitchen towel and dragged it through the thick areas of paint, breaking the hard edges. I also used the palette knife, scraping paint off and moving it around to create more texture. If you are brave enough to soften all the edges in this way, each new brushmark will appear crisp and sharp.

I introduced the table edge because of the big empty space on the left and the sense that the cup was floating in mid-air. Swirly marks with the No. 4 bristle brush give a sense of cloth over the table. If you want your brushmarks in the final painting to have texture and swing, keep using large bristle brushes until the end. My smallest brush was reserved for the signature and the delicate cross in the highlight that indicates the window frame.

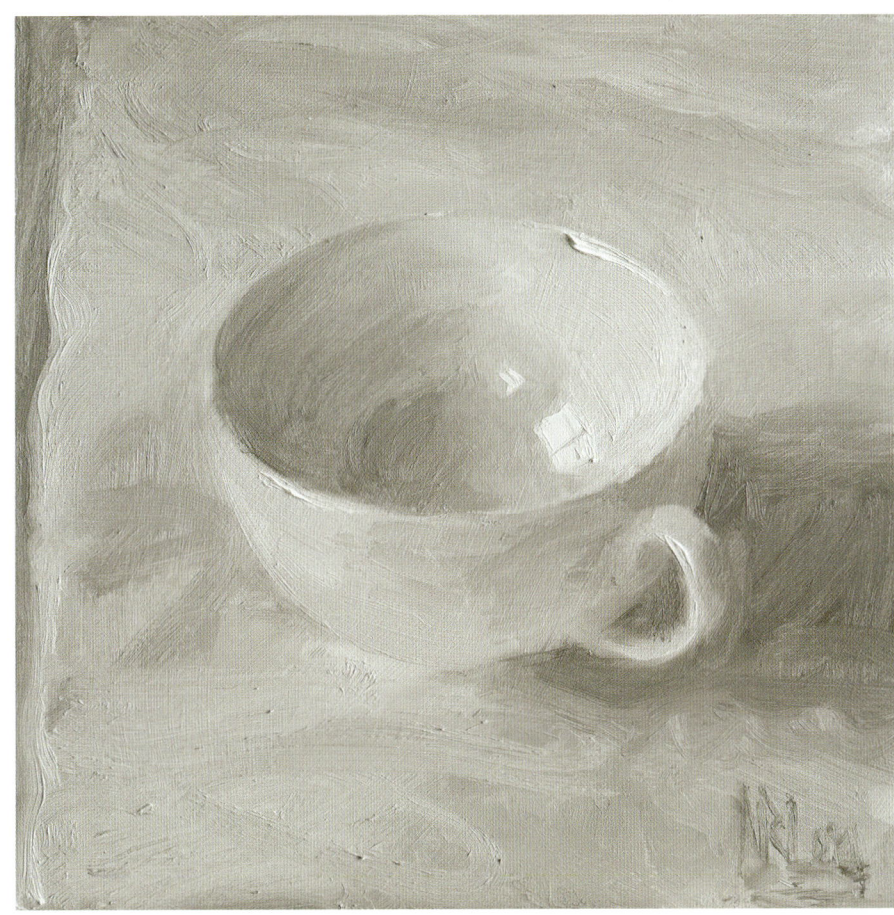

BELOW *Break up hard edges by dragging torn kitchen towel through the paint.*

BELOW *The lighter parts of the cup were painted with softer synthetic brushes and the highlights laid on gently after using the lift-off technique (see page 141) to get a nice glob of paint.*

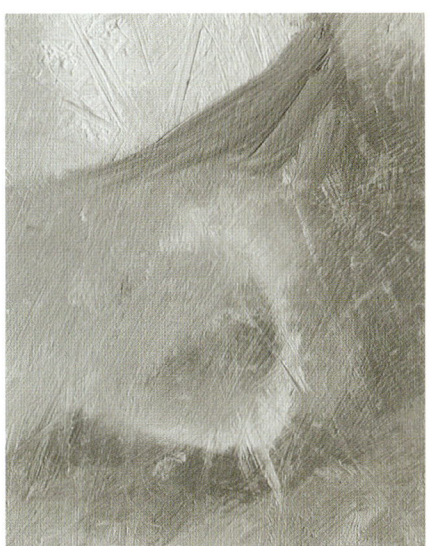

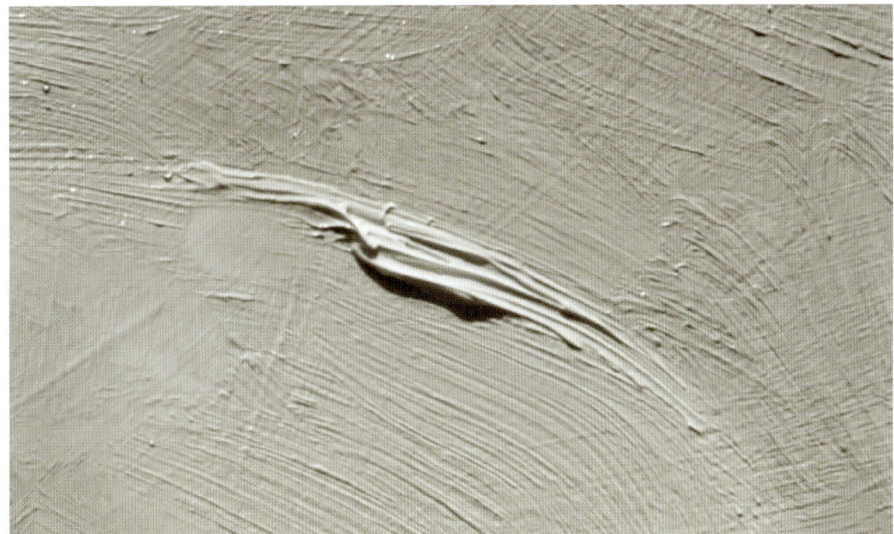

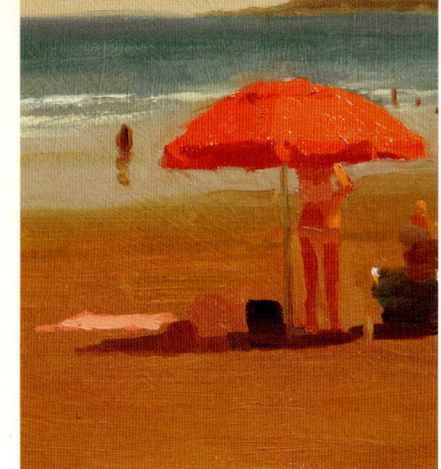

FOCUS ON
Composition

When you first start painting, it is enough to try to get some resemblance of the subject. Soon, however, you will feel the urge to move some element of the subject or omit it entirely. This is your natural sense of composition speaking and you should listen. Composition is simply the way things are arranged in a rectangle.

'Rules' of composition

Good compositions arise from a willingness to change things until they look right. Having said that, a few ideas about what to look for (or avoid) can help you if you get stuck. Like all rules in painting, they are there to be learned, understood and broken at will. Doing lots of small drawings of good paintings is the best education in how to put a painting together. Always include the borders of the rectangle (**1**).

FOCAL POINT

Just like a play, a painting needs lead characters and a supporting cast. If everyone has a lead role, there is chaos. Try to decide what you want the viewer to notice first in your painting and which elements you will keep subdued.

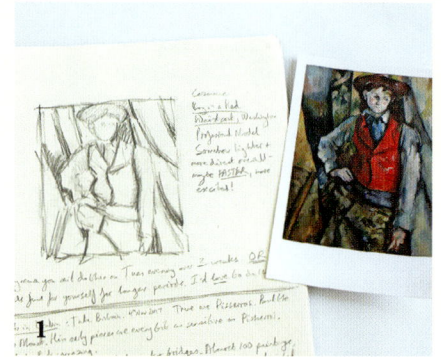

Things that catch the eye are detail and texture, contrasts of dark and light and contrasts of colour, hard edges, strong colours and people.

In this painting of Watermouth Harbour and Castle (**2**), the focal point is created by the contrast of the two strongest complementary colours, orange and blue, which have been put right next to each other.

DON'T WANDER OFF

Let's keep them interested. Unbroken horizontal lines can lead the viewer out of the painting. Well-placed verticals can stop them wandering off. The wine bottle and table leg perform this role in *Writer's Block* (compare the right-hand sides of **3A** and **3B**).

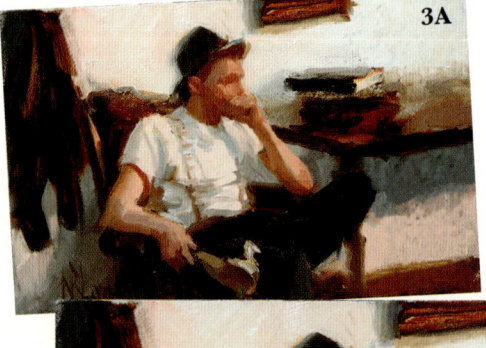

3A

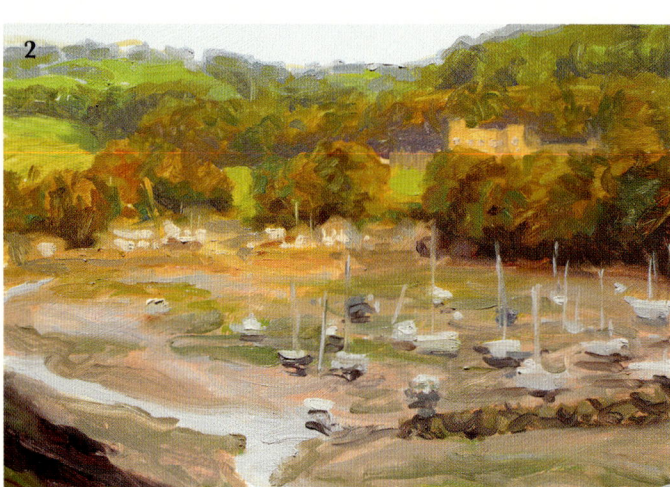

2

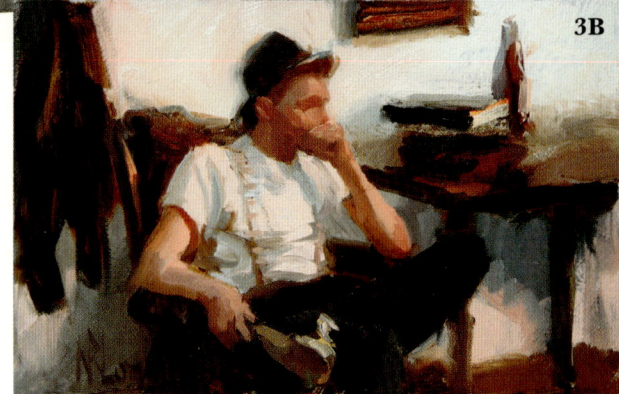

3B

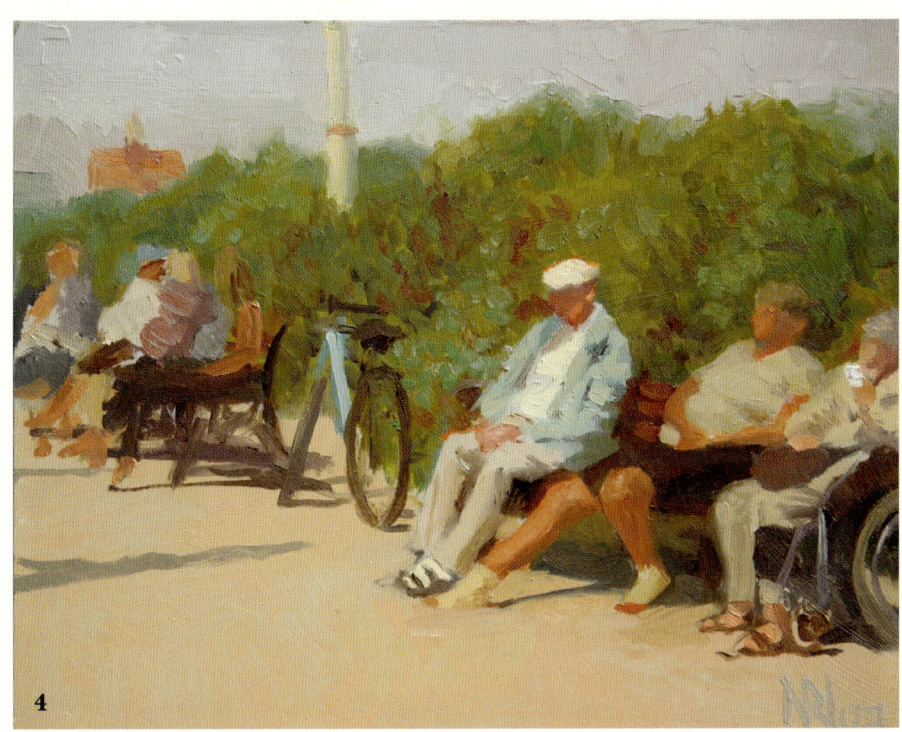

4

Viewfinder

One of the most useful tools to help you compose is the viewfinder. Especially when faced with an overwhelming subject, a simple piece of card with a hole in it can help you select a view and envision the arrangement of your finished picture. The proportions of the aperture (hole) should match your canvas. For a 10 x 12in (25 x 30cm) canvas, you should cut an aperture of 6 x 5in (12 x 10cm).

When you are happy with what you see through the viewfinder, you can translate that exact arrangement onto your canvas. Mark half and quarter ways on the inside edge of the viewfinder, as well as the outside edges of your canvas. Holding the viewfinder in position, note any part of the subject that coincides with (or comes close to) one of your edge marks. Now mark the position of that element on your canvas.

Use your first few marks as 'anchor points' to help you return the viewfinder to the same position. Once you have 8–10 marks on your canvas, you can connect up the drawing knowing that everything is in the right place (**6**).

DIAGONALS

Diagonals indicate movement and I love to incorporate them whenever possible. Like everything else, they need to be balanced. Lots of diagonals going one way will make the viewer feel like they are tilting. In the picture above, the upward sloping shadow in the lower left was introduced to balance a generally downward sloping composition (**4**).

RULE OF THIRDS

Lines which divide the rectangle equally down the middle (vertically or horizontally) leave the viewer not sure which half to look at. We are much more at ease with paintings divided into thirds (see bottom left). A focal point can also look better on a junction of thirds than bang in the centre (**5**).

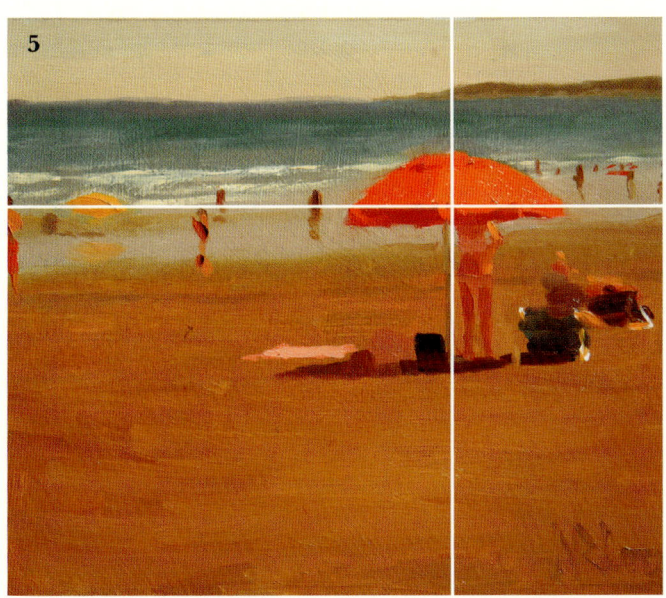

5

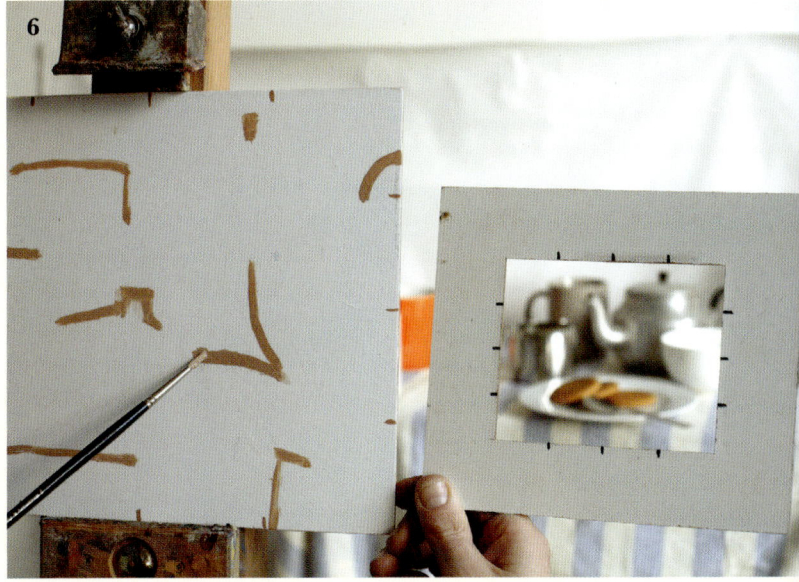

6

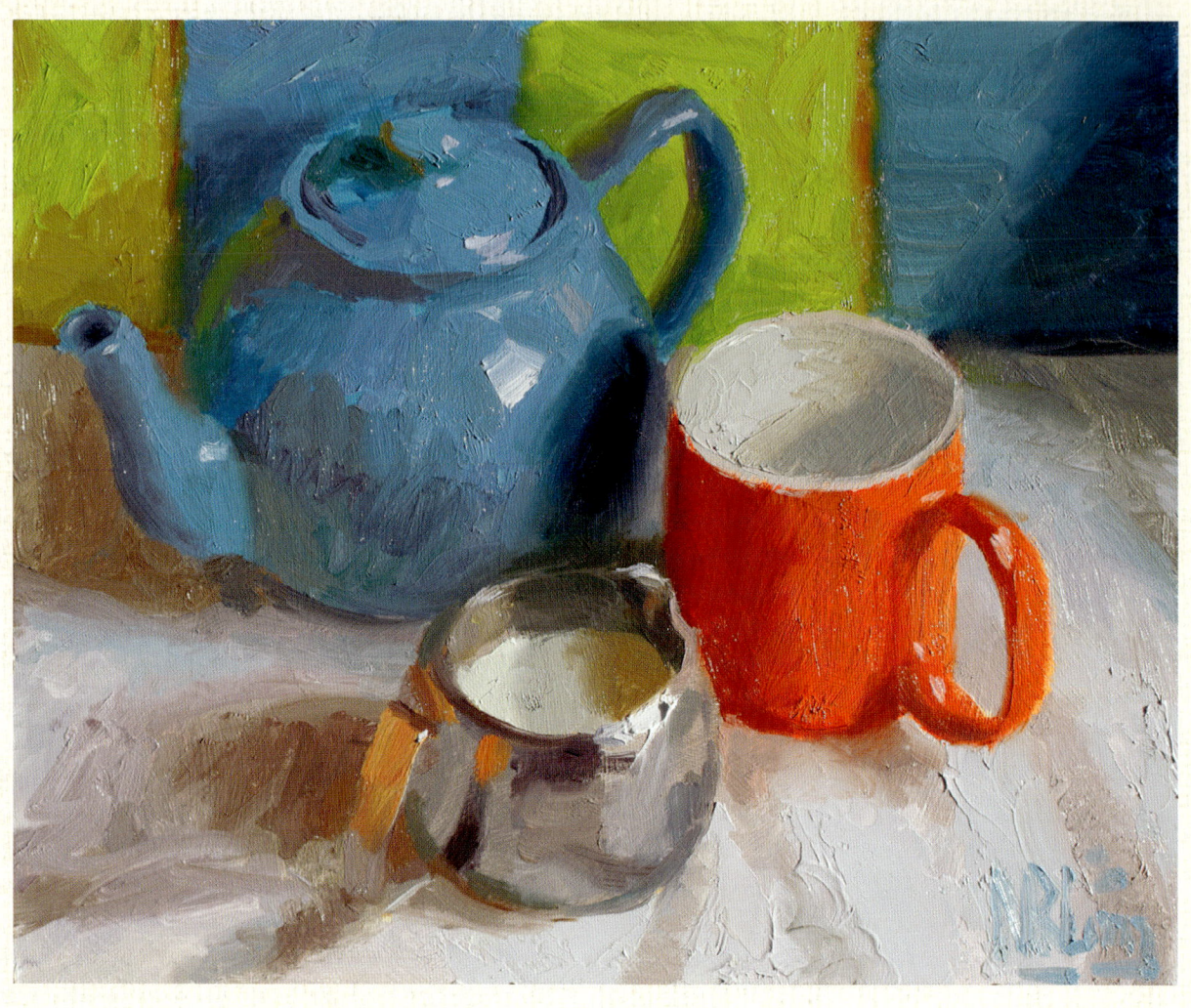

Kitchen Still Life

Still life is a great subject in its own right, but it is also ideal training ground for more challenging subjects. The skills you learn in this project (composing your shapes, creating light and shade, and mixing colours) will all be essential when you are faced with more fleeting subjects later on.

COLOURS NEEDED

Phthalo Blue	Viridian Hue	Cadmium Yellow Pale	Yellow Ochre	Burnt Sienna	Permanent Alizarin Crimson	Cadmium Red	Ivory Black	Titanium White

COMPOSING YOUR STILL LIFE

There are two things to consider when choosing objects to paint in a still life. Firstly, their shapes and colours should look good together. Look for simple, undecorated objects, not all the same size. The second thing is the theme: the story the objects will tell in the finished painting.

You may copy my painting if you wish, or compose your own still life of any three objects. The simple act of playing around with objects, swapping them around, moving them back and forth, develops your ability to compose.

As you arrange your objects, try varying the angles of the handles and overlapping your objects slightly to connect them together. Notice how different your subject looks from different viewpoints – seated or standing. As in the previous project, use a single light source from one side to give the objects a light side and a dark side. You may use a viewfinder (see page 153) to view the set-up, moving the objects around until you are happy with the arrangement.

Looking through the viewfinder at my subject helped me to see that the area in the top right was empty and that the horizontal edge of the table led straight out of the picture. I used a piece of card to cast an arrow-shaped shadow into this area, directing our attention back into the picture where it belongs.

Everything contributes to the composition, including the arrangement of colours. I have chosen objects in complementary colours – orange and blue. For variety, I introduced some lime green into the background. The orange mug looked a bit isolated, so I placed an orange shopping bag to the left of the objects. This reflects some orange into the teapot and milk jug.

Tip

Painting objects under a constant light source gives you time to work towards a realistic result in three easy stages. Start by blocking in the local (basic) colour of each object. Then develop the effect of light and shade (one side lighter, the other darker) and finally note the way colours reflect from one surface to another.

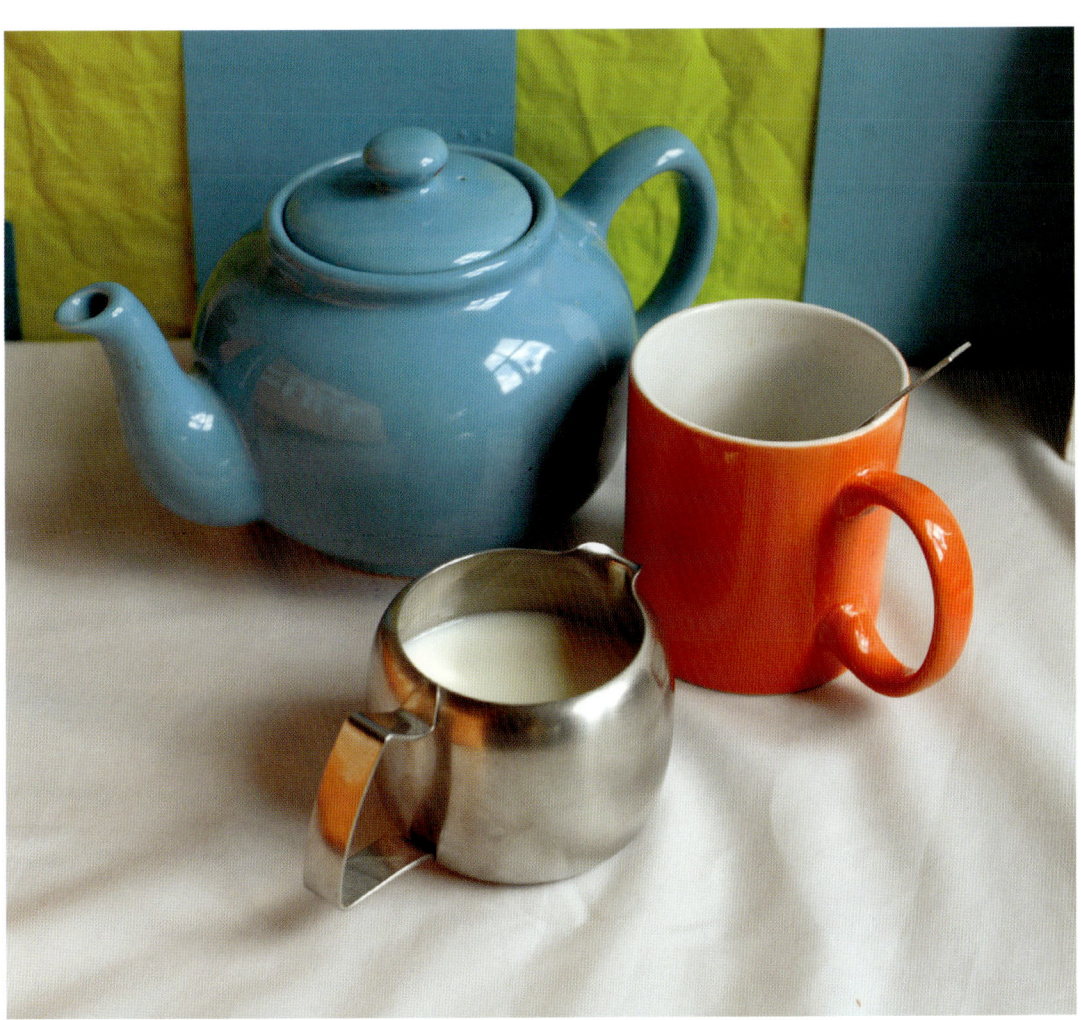

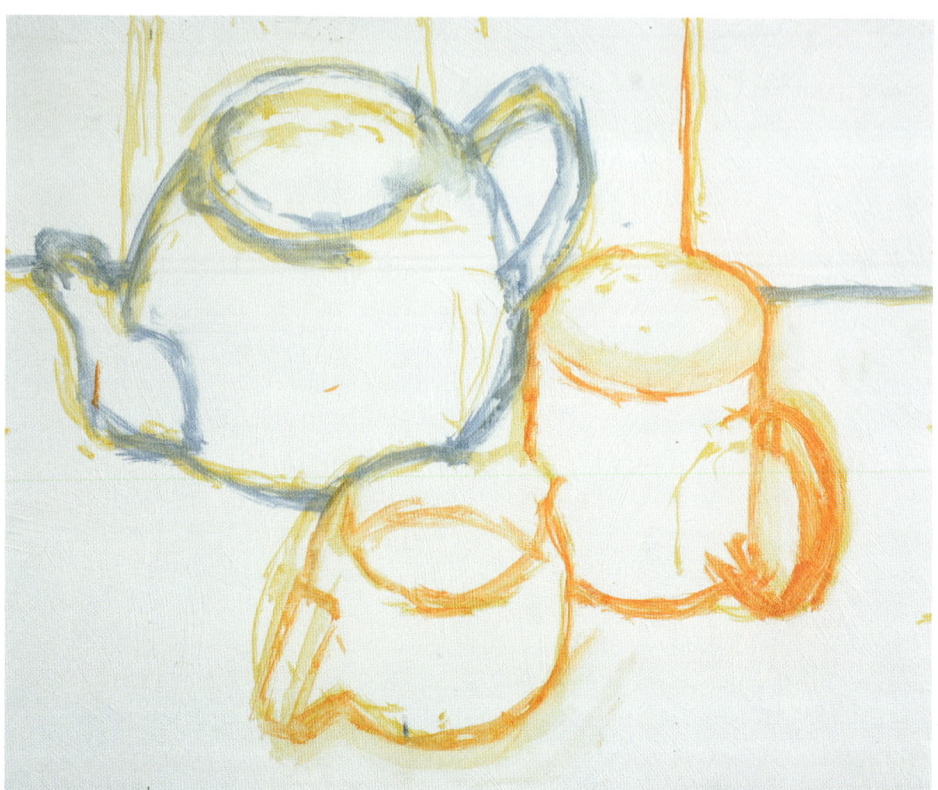

STAGE 1

The first job is drawing the position of the objects on the canvas. This is done with diluted yellow, which is easy to correct or paint over. Once you have the rough positions outlined, do a more accurate drawing on top, using different colours to distinguish it from the first drawing. You don't want these lines to muddy what you put on top, so use diluted blue for the teapot and orange for everything else.

STAGE 2

Now you need to block in the local (basic) colours of the objects. As colours mix together in the process of painting, they naturally get duller, so it makes sense to start slightly stronger than you eventually need. It's also much easier to subdue a colour than to make it more intense.

Yellow is one of the most easily contaminated colours, so let's start with the background yellow-greens. In the final painting we can make them darker and greener, but at this stage use pure yellow with a touch of viridian. Work around all the blocks of colour, diluting the paint slightly to make it cover more quickly. Within minutes, you will have achieved a strong effect with flat shapes of colour.

Some artists are adept at designing complete pictures with flat shapes. If this comes naturally to you, you may have found your style already!

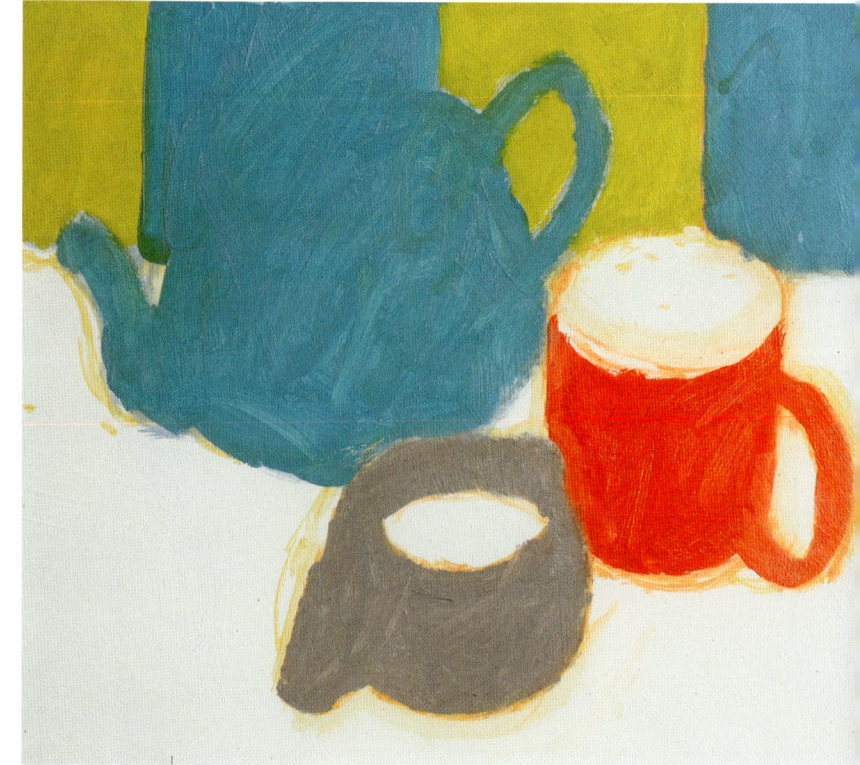

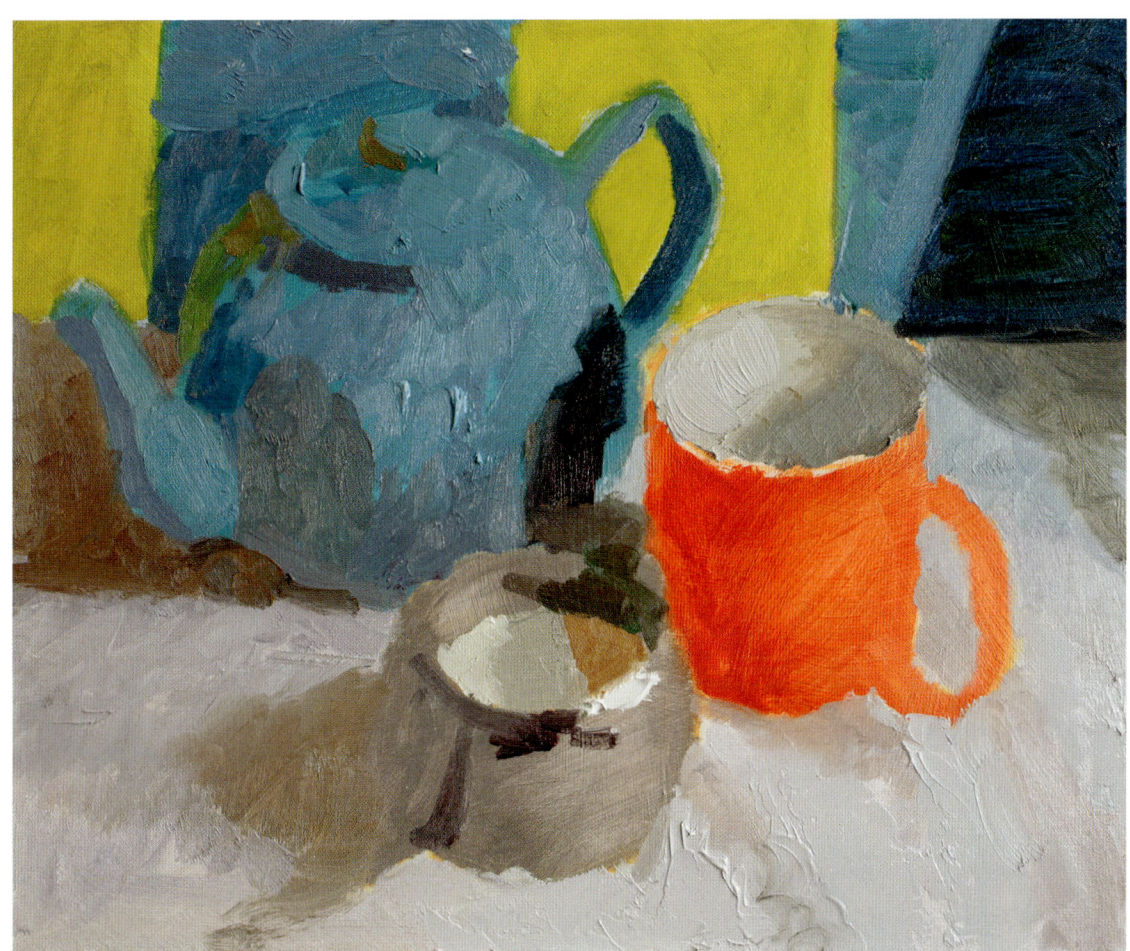

STAGE 3

Just because we are working in colour does not mean that the lessons of tonal value go out the window. Here we do exactly the same thing we did with the previous painting. Identify the lightest part of the scene (the rim of the milk jug) by squinting. Mark that with pure white, put on with the palette knife, and tell yourself that nothing must compete with that for whiteness. Even things we know to be white, such as the inside of the orange mug, cannot be pure white.

It can be more difficult to see differences in tonal value when we are looking at brightly coloured objects. One trick is to look at the subject reflected in the black screen of your smartphone or tablet. Like squinting, this makes everything darker, but it also reduces the confusing effect of strong colours.

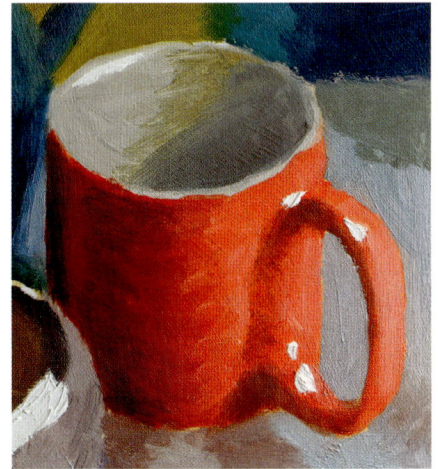

ABOVE *Here, I tried to create light and shade by adding white to the light side and black to the shadow side. It's not bad, but neither white nor black have any colour in them, so the mug loses some of its intensity.*

To make objects look three-dimensional, you need to create a light side and a dark side. The challenge is to do this without entirely losing the strong local colours we established in the previous stage. A simple approach to creating a light side can be seen in the orange mug and milk jug. Use a rag to gently wipe the light side of the objects. Where the paint is thinner, it appears lighter. The blue teapot has been developed further. Rather than just using black and white, use varied patches of colour to create lights and darks while maintaining colour interest.

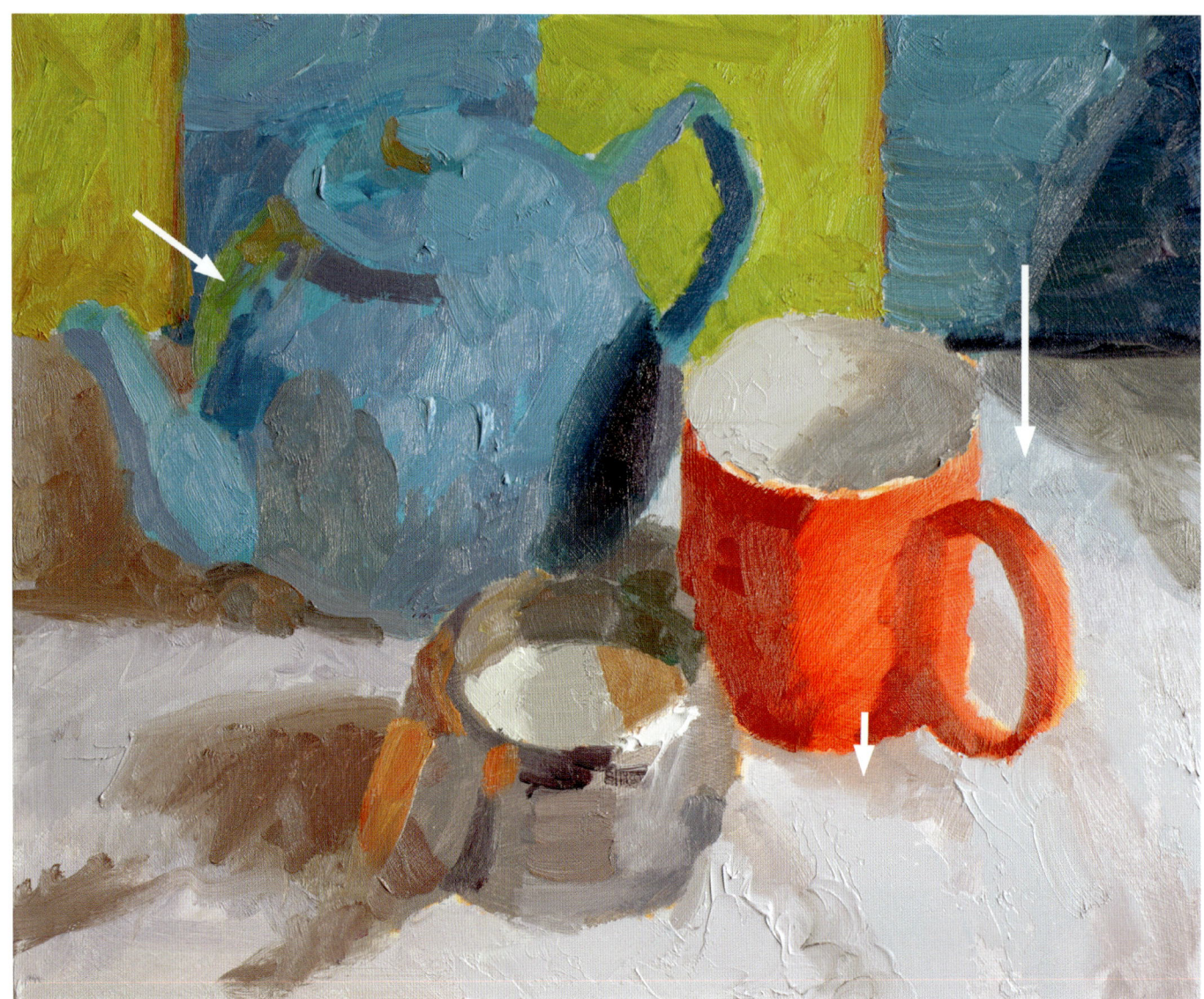

STAGE 4

For the shadow side of the mug, you need dark colours, which are also intensely orange. A mixture of crimson and burnt sienna does the trick.

Combining local colour with the effects of light and shade certainly gives a realistic look but there is another level of observation you could add to the visual excitement. The arrows indicate where the colour of one thing is reflected in another. The lime green wall reflects into the teapot and the white groundsheet takes on some of the colour of the mug and wall. Most people never even notice these subtle, beautiful effects, but you are an artist, so you will start to see them everywhere.

Tip
As well as creating more interesting colour, reflected colours tie all the objects together and make them look like they are sitting in the same space.

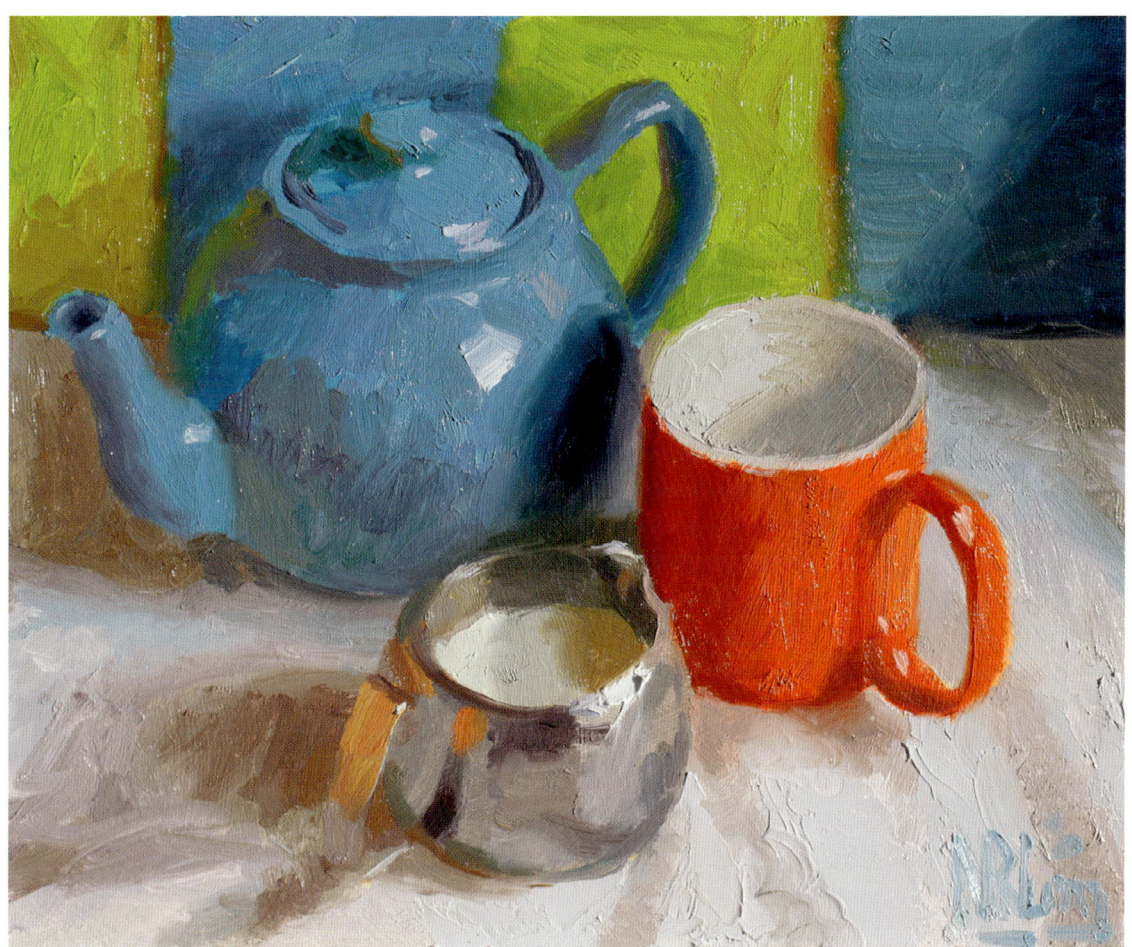

STAGE 5

This final stage involves softening some edges with the finger and adding the highlights. Like cherries on a cake, one or two highlights are a treat, but don't get carried away. Put them on confidently and don't fiddle. If a highlight really doesn't work out, it's better to wipe it off entirely and redo it.

Highlights should be distinct enough to sing, but also need to remain connected to the surface they are sitting on. The highlights on the blue teapot contain a touch of purple, while those on the orange mug contain a hint of crimson to keep them connected to the object. Softening some edges of the larger highlights is another way to prevent them looking stuck on. The example of the mug on page 157 shows some over-enthusiastic highlighting.

And now for the final flourish. Your signature is an important part of the painting. Sign with the materials you are using in the painting – that way it is much more difficult to forge! An ostentatious signature can distract from the artwork itself. You should be able to see it if you're looking for it, but it shouldn't scream at you. Artists tend to sign their work in the lower right or left corners. I look for a corner that looks a bit empty or badly painted. That way, the viewer will see the signature and not the poor work underneath! Your signature can also be a last chance to balance your painting. Here I felt that there was blue in most areas of the painting, but not in the lower right, so that is where it landed.

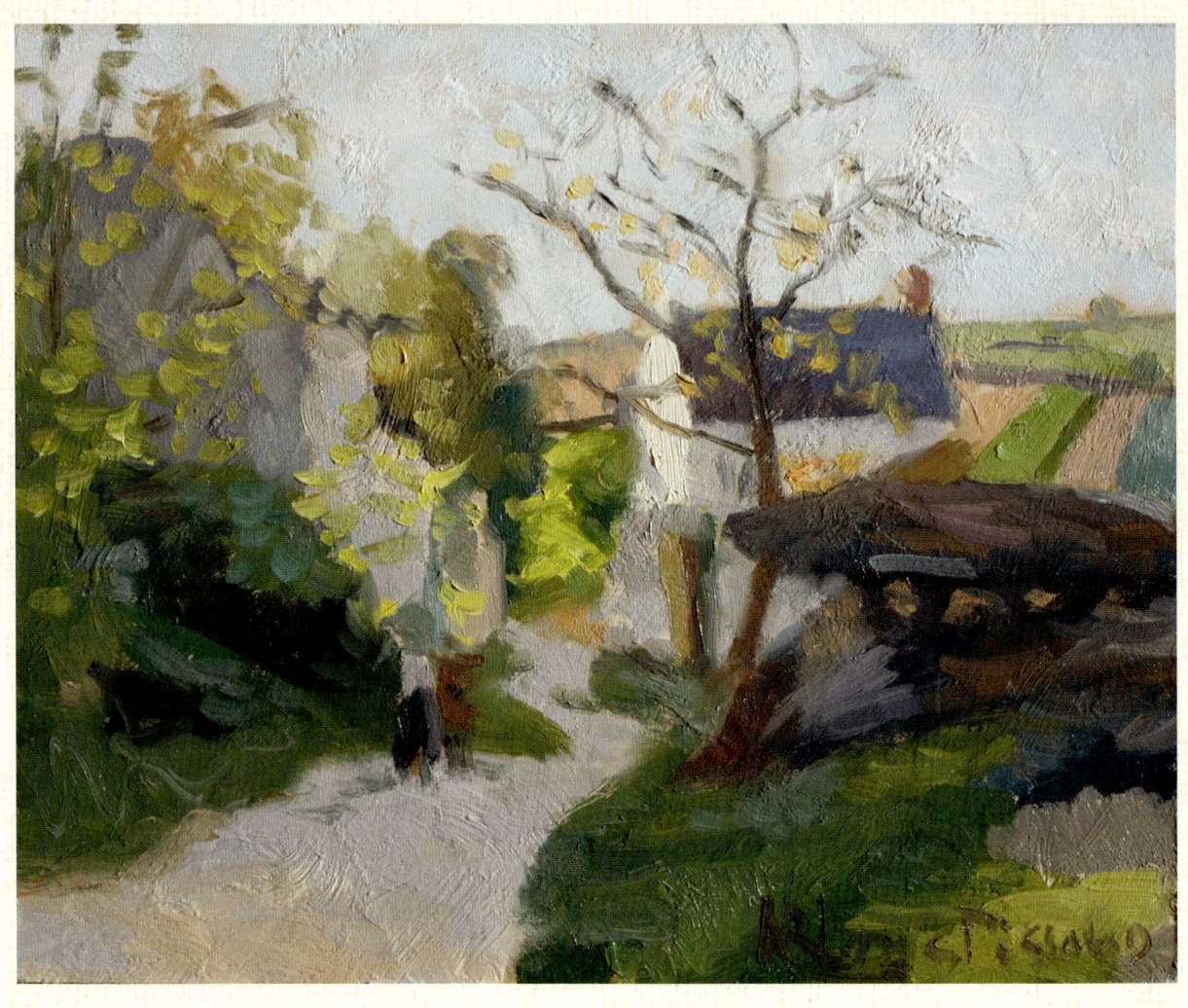

Master Copy

All great artists of the past learned by copying the work of those they admired. To learn about composition, copy the whole painting. If it is the brushmarks or the way the artist has painted particular objects that inspires you, copy a 'detail' (small section) of the original.

COLOURS NEEDED

| Phthalo Blue | Viridian Hue | Cadmium Yellow Pale | Yellow Ochre | Burnt Sienna | Permanent Alizarin Crimson | Cadmium Red | Ivory Black | Titanium White |

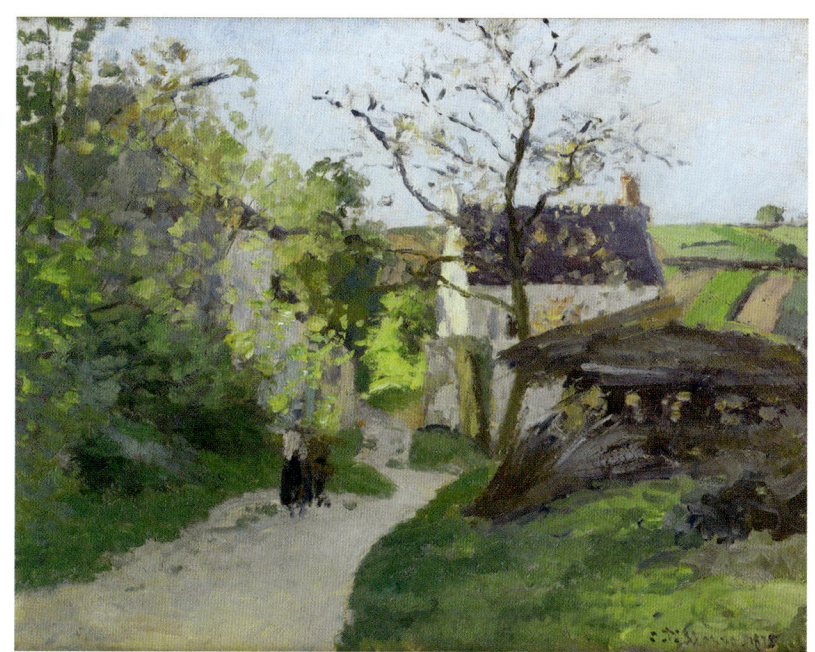

edges of the paper with one corner of the image. Make a dot where the opposite corner of the image is (**2**). The paper can then be placed in the corner of your board and a ruler located diagonally from the corner, through the dot, until it meets the edge of the board, marking where it needs to be cropped. Use a craft knife to crop the board and watch your fingers (**3**).

Now that the proportions are the same, you have the option of gridding up the original to make the drawing easier. Simply divide the image into halves and quarters. The same divisions drawn on your canvas (or even just corresponding marks around the edges) make the placing of the major lines much easier.

The Great Walnut Tree, *Pontoise, 1875,* *Camille Pissarro (1830–1903)*

It's fun to become your chosen artist for an hour or two and imagine what it was like to paint the original masterpiece. I love Pissarro for his honesty in front of nature. His colours are true, his brushwork unfussy. You don't need to know what it is you like about your chosen painting before you start – you will discover that as you go along. You may wish to copy the Pissarro I have chosen, but I think you will learn more by copying a painting that excites you personally, particularly if you can see the original masterwork with the actual colours and brushstrokes used.

CROPPING AND GRIDDING THE BOARD

It's important to crop your painting board to match the proportions of the original painting. If you are working from a photo without borders, just place it in the corner of your board and lay a ruler through the corners. Where this line intersects the edge of the board is where it needs to be cropped to match the proportions of the original painting (**1**).

If your photo has white borders, is in a book or on a screen, place a thin piece of paper (or tracing paper) over the image, aligning two

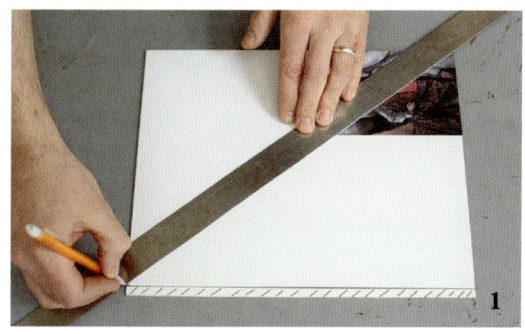

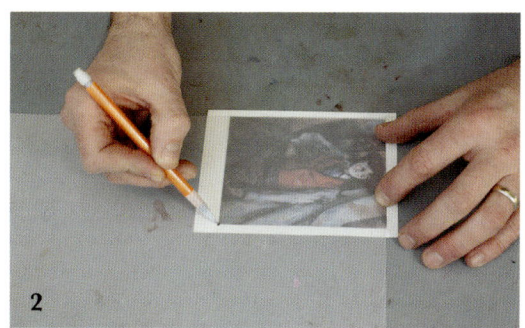

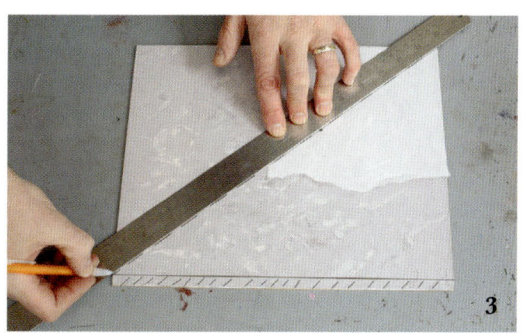

Tip

Try to find out the dimensions of the original painting, otherwise you could find yourself trying to copy a huge painting onto a tiny canvas, wondering why you can't get the same level of detail as the original. Of course, there is no reason why you can't make a small copy of a large painting, but yours will be a simplified version.

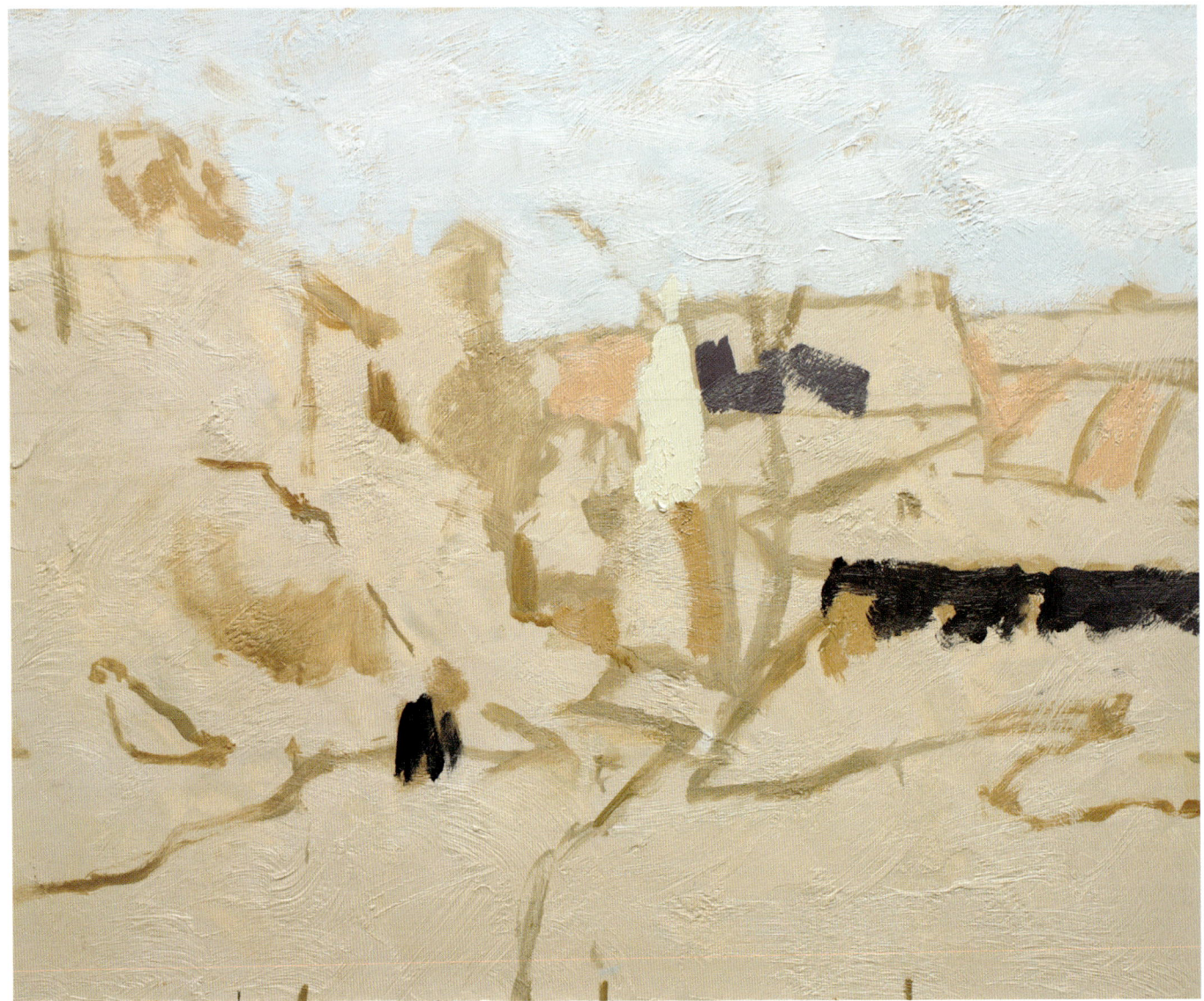

STAGE 1

Look carefully at your chosen original and see if you can identify any of the ground colour peeping through (this is much easier from actual paintings). For this piece, Pissarro worked over a textured ground, possibly even a previous painting. The few underlayers that peep through, around the branches of the trees, appear to be beige, so I chose a board primed with leftover oil paint to something like this colour. The oil priming gives the surface a little more roughness.

Using a grid over the original and related marks around the edges of your canvas to guide you, do a reasonably careful drawing with a No. 2 round brush and diluted paint. Then, starting with the lightest colour, paint the building with white and a touch of orange. To another pile of white, add a touch of blue and apply this roughly to the sky. The scattered clouds are made with white and a touch of cadmium red, to almost the same tonal value as the sky itself. Having noted the lightest colours, look for the darkest to give the full tonal range. These darks are not pure black but have blue, crimson and white mixed in.

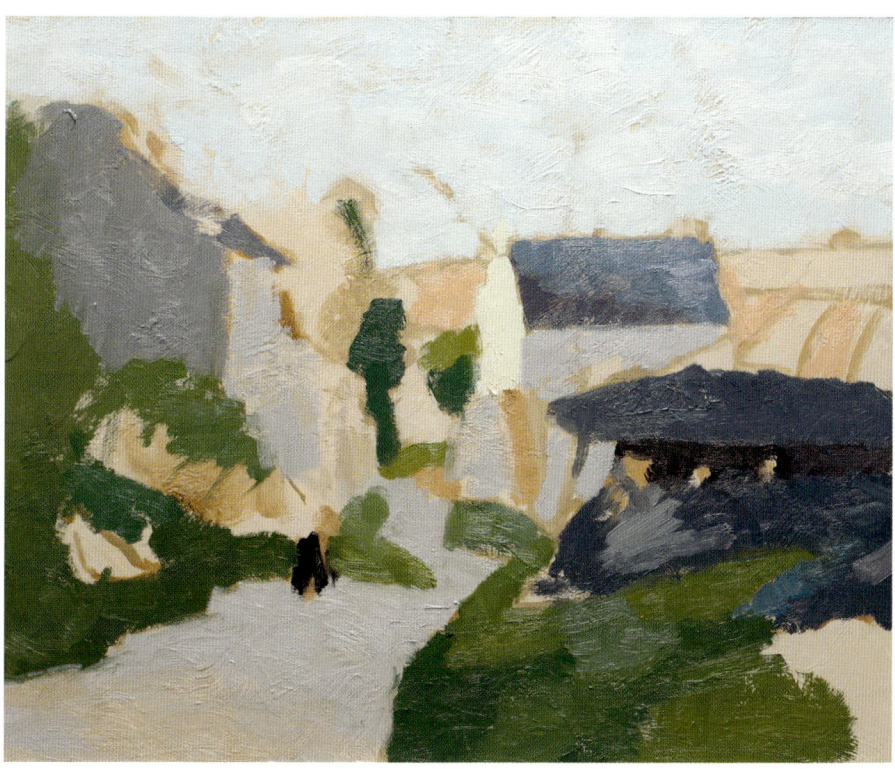

STAGE 2

In copying a painting, the problems of drawing and composition are all solved. The challenge lies in matching the artist's colours. You don't need any special training to achieve an exact colour match and there is never just one way to arrive at the right colour. I will take you through my process in matching the colour of the path in Pissarro's painting. It may seem slow at first, but you will get much quicker with practice.

Start with white and add some blue (**1**). Add more blue until the tonal value is about right (**2**). Now it is too intense (too blue). Add some orange (complementary of blue) to kill the colour (**3**). Now it is too dark and too green.

Add lots of white to lighten the colour (**4**).

Red is the complement of green, so add touches of both red and crimson to kill the green. Because these make the colour darker, also add white to bring it back to the correct tonal value (**5**).

Now for the final step. The colour needs to be slightly darker and warmer, so we use burnt sienna. Picking up a blob of paint on the knife risks taking it too far, so use the knife to drag a stain of paint towards the centre of the palette. Add this gradually until you arrive at the perfect match (**6**).

Tip
You will arrive at the right colour by asking yourself three questions: should it be lighter or darker, what colour does it need more of and should it be duller or more intense? Complementary colours are useful for quickly dulling each other.

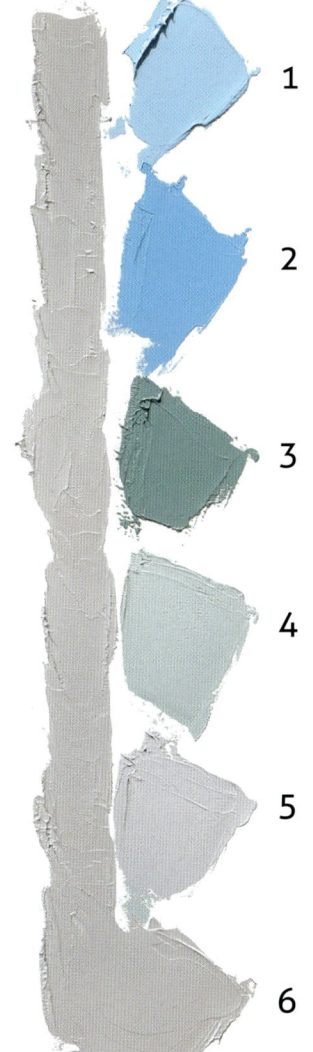

ABOVE *Creating the colour for the path.*

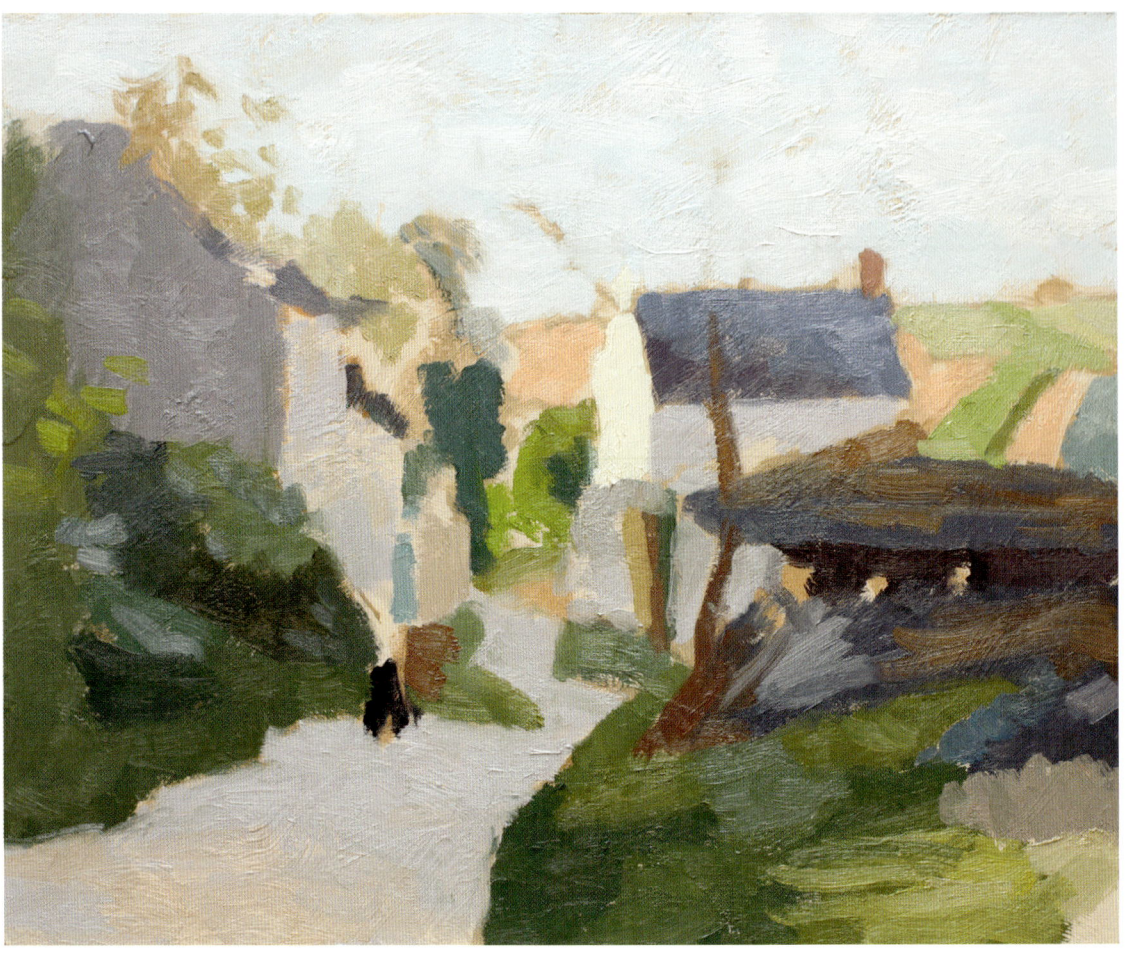

STAGE 3

Pissarro's painting is a lesson in creating a variety of greens. If we were to match each one individually, you can imagine how long it would take. A quicker approach is to mix generous piles of the most common greens with the palette knife and block these in to cover as much ground as possible. Then adjust the colours as necessary to match the variety in the painting.

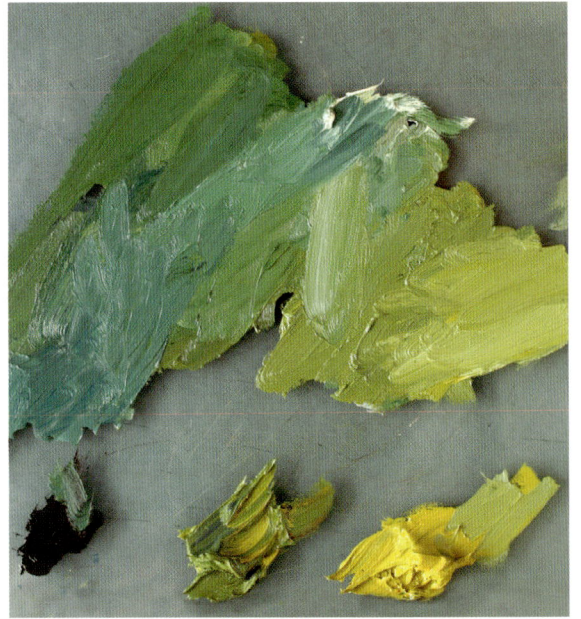

RIGHT *Large piles of dark blue-green, medium green and light yellow-green used as the starting point for all the greens in the painting.*

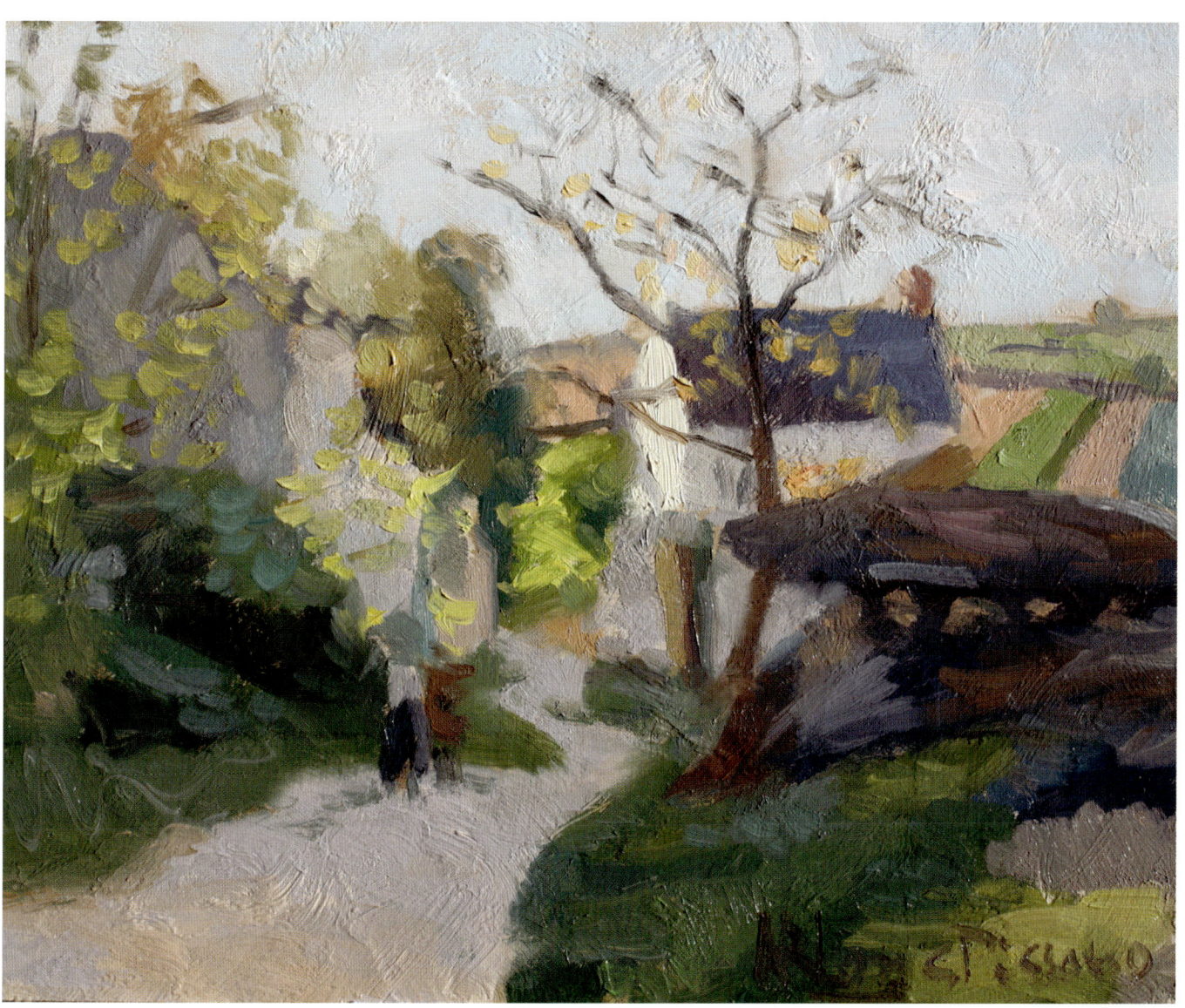

STAGE 4

The process of this painting involves mixing and applying large blocks of clean colour. It is only at this final stage that the finer lines, such as the branches and little commas of paint for the leaves, are applied. The original painting, at 16in (40cm) wide, is not significantly larger than my 12in (30cm) canvas. This means my brushstrokes can be fairly close to the size of those in the original.

Don't try to copy the exact shape of every brushmark, especially on an Impressionist painting. It is much quicker and simpler to emulate the spirit in which the marks were made. Imagine Pissarro on that dusty Pontoise road, jabbing his canvas excitedly to capture the last remnants of light.

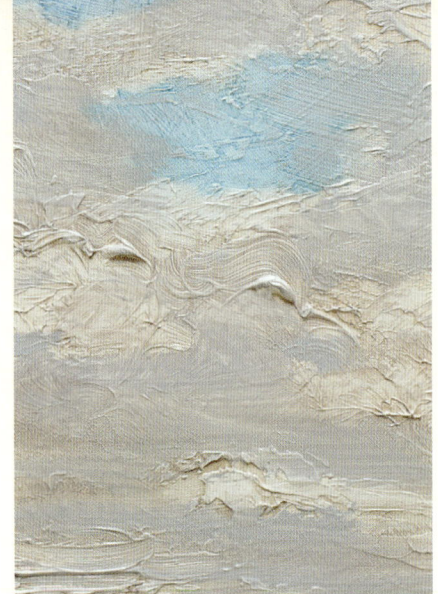

FOCUS ON
Painting Outdoors

How often have you photographed a breathtaking scene, only to find on looking at the photo afterwards that it captured nothing of what you saw and felt in the moment? That's why, in spite of the myriad challenges involved, painters happily pack up their paints and go outdoors. They also know that there is an authenticity and liveliness to painting done on the spot that is very difficult to replicate in the studio.

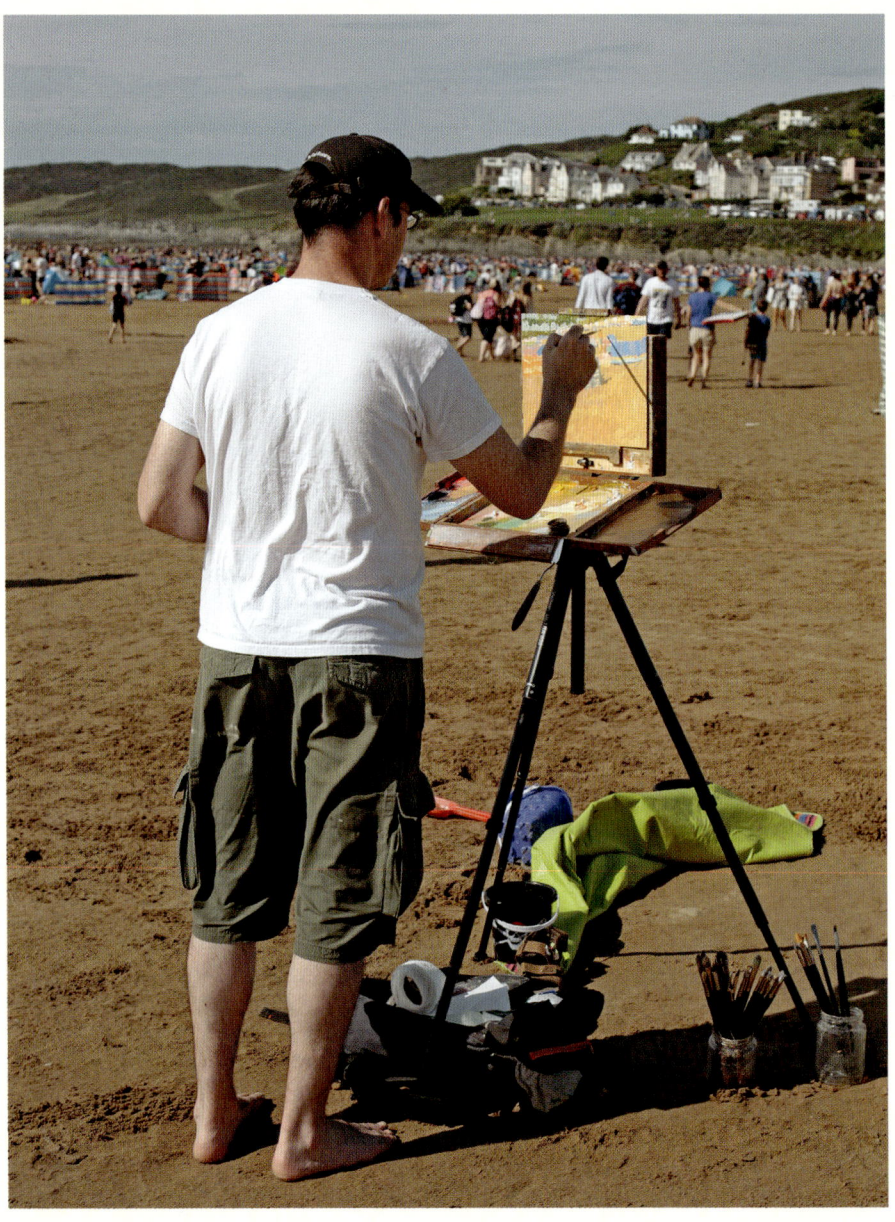

Outdoor painting became popular in France in the 19th century, helped by the availability of paint in tubes and the railway to take people to interesting locations. Hence we use a French term, *en plein air*, to describe the practice of painting outside.

Painting outdoors is the key to doing better paintings in half the time. The simple switch from cosy studio and static subject to the great outdoors, with its constantly changing sights and sounds, forces you to work quickly and simplify. Besides which, it's much more fun!

I'm not suggesting that you take your shiny new oil paints out into a field to do your very first oil painting. Play around first in the comfort of your home or studio. Get a few half-decent paintings under your belt to build your confidence, then get outdoors.

The first step is the hardest. It helps if you can find like-minded artists to go with when you first venture outdoors. Or you may ease into it by taking a few excursions with a sketchbook. That way, you won't be conspicuous, but you will begin investigating a subject face-to-face and you'll soon be hooked.

There are obvious challenges to painting outdoors. Here are some practical tips to keep you on track.

Outdoor Painting Materials

1. Primed boards of various colours
2. Backpack
3. Plastic bags for dirty rags
4. Tripod for pochade box
5. Kitchen towel
6. Pochade box (contains palette)
7. Baseball cap
8. Paints (obviously)
9. Dipper with lid
10. Low-odour solvent
11. Medium (2 parts solvent, 1 part linseed oil)
12. Palette knife
13. Old telephone directory
14. Mirror
15. Brushes and jar

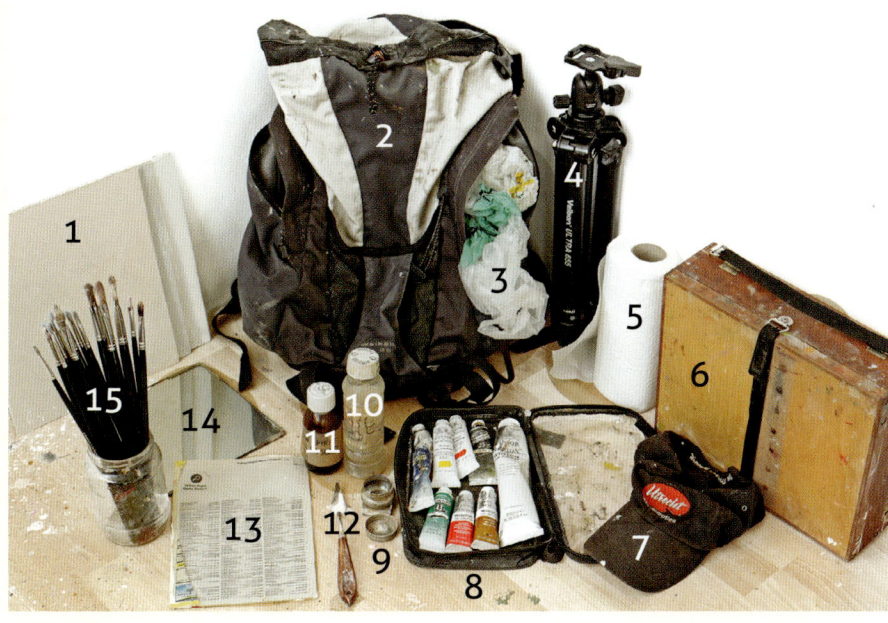

Practical tips

Learn to pack just what you need. This takes trial and error, so don't expect to get it right first time.

At the risk of sounding like your mother, wrap up warm and wear sensible shoes or a hat and sunscreen, whatever is applicable. You are going to be in one spot for some time. You may need a baseball cap to keep the sun out of your eyes. Don't spend too long when choosing a subject – the perfect one is not just around the corner. When faced with an overwhelming subjcct, the viewfinder (see page 153) can be helpful in isolating a view.

You can paint in any weather, but if possible keep yourself and your painting out of the wind, rain and direct sunshine – in that order. Wind is the worst. Flying materials are not easy to paint with. Rain is OK. It won't dissolve oil paint, but if you can find a sheltered spot, why not? Direct sunshine is lovely, but when it shines on your palette and painting, it makes it hard to judge colours. In compensating for the bright light, you may end up with a painting that is too dark.

Intrigued onlookers may wish to engage you in deep conversation about their aunt who paints. I find that polite but boring answers encourage them to move on to more interesting targets.

Expect the unexpected. Yes, a van may park right in front of you. Cows may appear from nowhere. Keep your sense of humour – it's only a painting.

Plein-air paintings can be an end in themselves or used as studies for larger works in the studio. The quality of the work does not depend on sticking to one method, indoors or out, but it's good to experience the benefits of both.

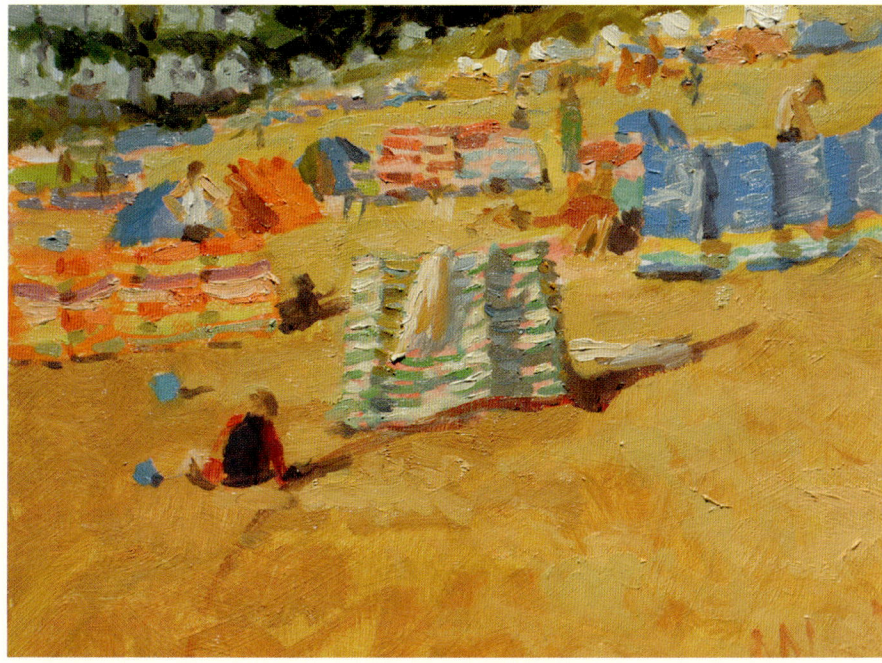

Woolacombe Beach, Devon, England.

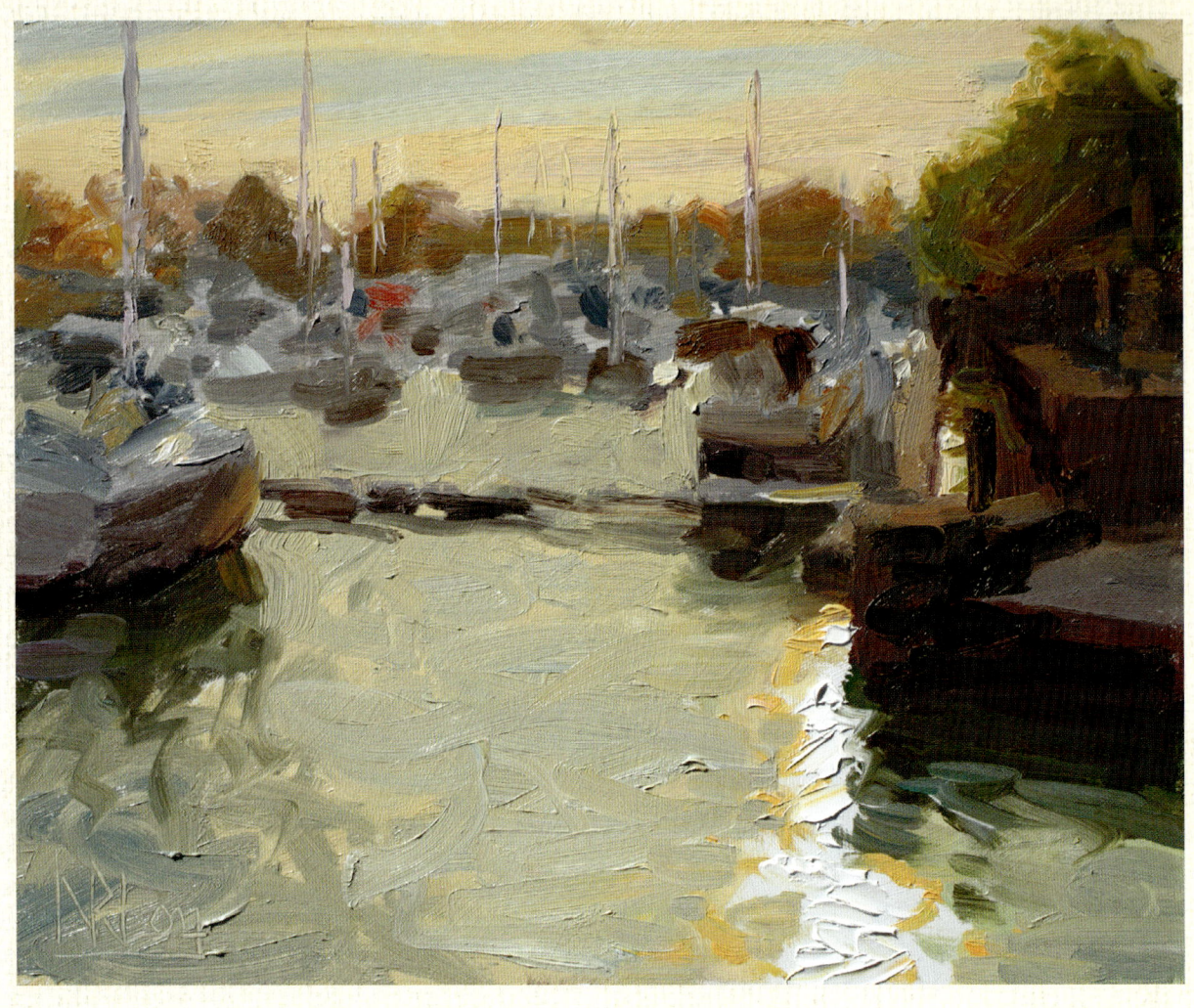

Boats at Sundown

This project introduces you to a quick technique suitable for painting fleeting subjects outdoors. You will devise a simple tonal plan, then proceed directly from a cursory drawing into applying thick, luscious paint. You will learn to use the effects of aerial perspective to create depth in your painting.

COLOURS NEEDED

| Phthalo Blue | Viridian Hue | Cadmium Yellow Pale | Yellow Ochre | Burnt Sienna | Permanent Alizarin Crimson | Cadmium Red | Ivory Black | Titanium White |

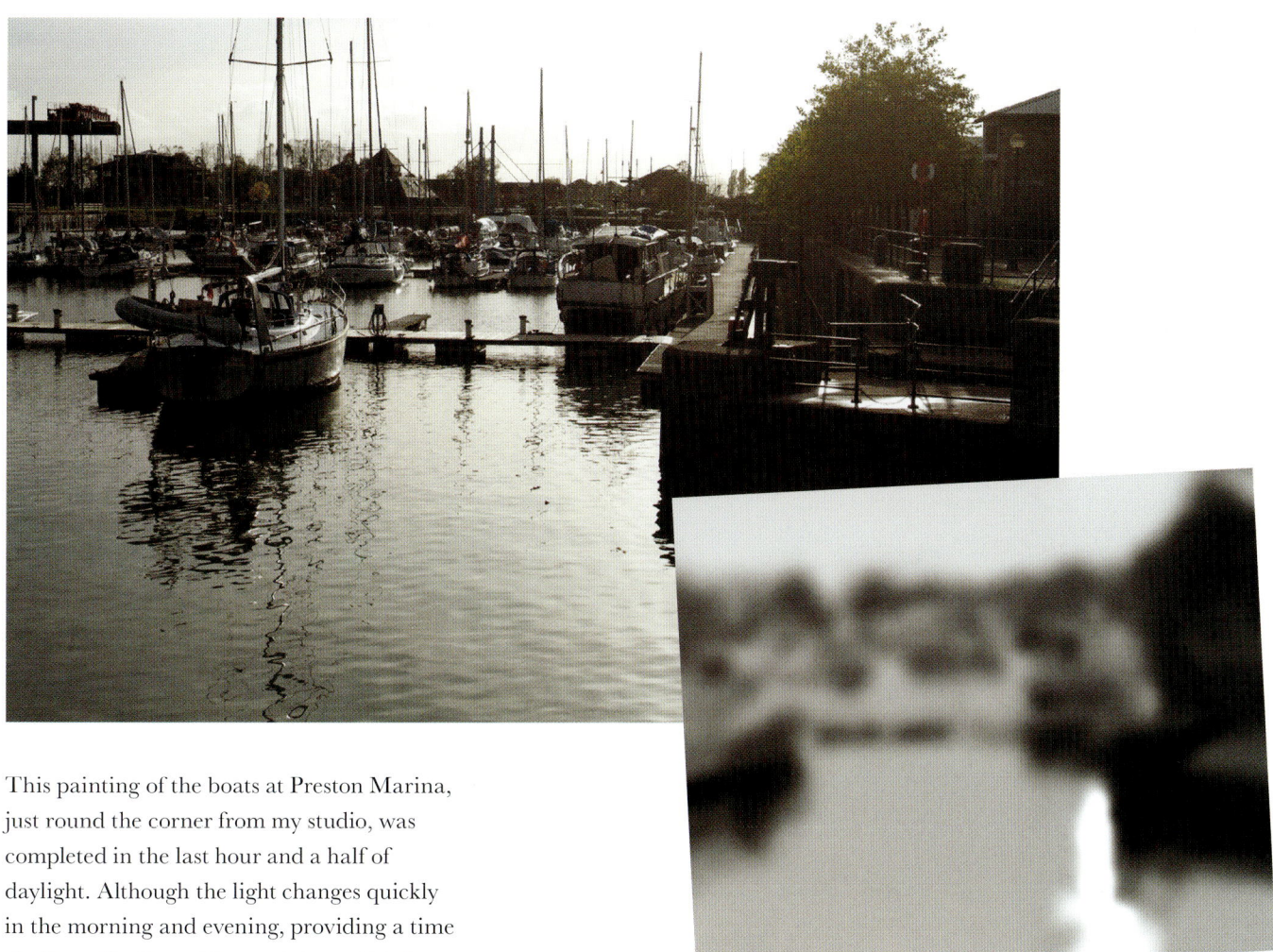

This painting of the boats at Preston Marina, just round the corner from my studio, was completed in the last hour and a half of daylight. Although the light changes quickly in the morning and evening, providing a time challenge for the outdoor painter, artists love these 'golden hours'. The low sun casts dramatic shadows and the light has a much warmer glow than in the middle of the day. You can see by comparing the finished painting to the photo how the camera struggles to capture the subtle beauty of such dramatic lighting situations.

This piece is painted 'contre-jour', a French term meaning 'into the light'. The sun is in front of you and most of the subject is in shadow, with just touches of light at the edges. You can copy my painting as an introduction to working in this direct manner or work from your own photo of a similar subject.

TONAL PLAN

When working outdoors in changing light, it is easy to start changing the painting over and over as the light moves. This chasing game is fun but unlikely to produce a good composition. To feel in control, it is best to devise a tonal plan before starting. Some artists do thumbnail sketches to organize their tonal values. I find it quicker to eye up the subject through a viewfinder (see page 153), squinting to reduce it to a pattern of light and dark shapes similar to this blurred photo (see above, right). Zoom the viewfinder in and out and try it both vertically and horizontally. The view you settle on is your tonal plan. Try to stick to this arrangement of lights and darks.

Trust your instincts. Go with what looks best to you at the time and you will often happen upon one of the compositional 'rules'. Here the lightest part of the scene, the reflection of the sun on the water, is bound to draw the eye, especially as it is right next to the darkest area of the harbour wall. I avoided putting this focal point in the middle of the painting, but found that it looked better around the lower-right third.

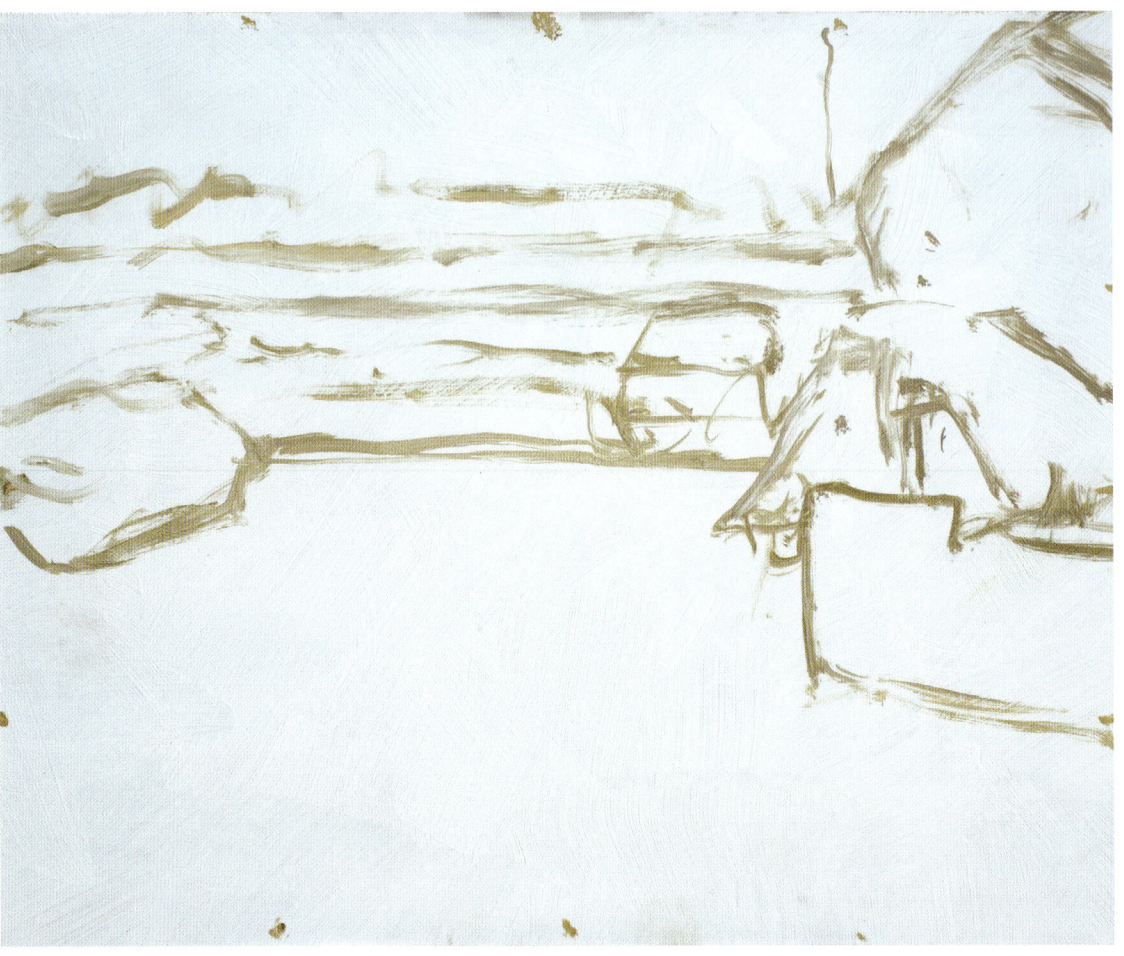

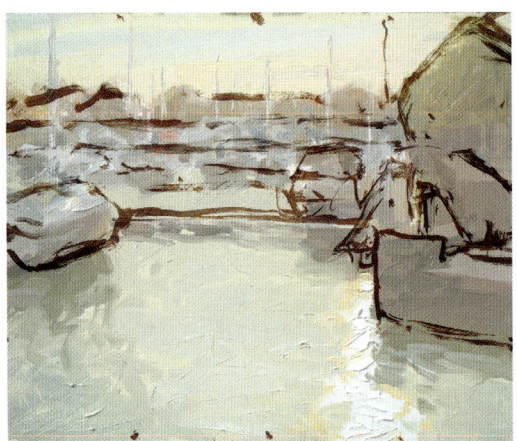

ABOVE *The overlay image.*

STAGE 1

The excitement (or sometimes panic) of trying to capture a subject outdoors leads to changes in technique. Rather than a careful drawing followed by the blocking in of local colours, here you will execute a rapid drawing using a mixture of brown, black and white, very diluted to make the paint flow.

The important thing, and the reason I went to the trouble of marking half and quarter ways around the edges of the canvas, is that the large shapes are where I want them, relating to the view through the viewfinder.

It takes courage to proceed from such a cursory drawing directly into thick paint, but remember you can always correct things later. To prove it, I have overlaid my initial outlines onto an image of the finished painting. You can see the places where I haven't quite got the drawing right to start with.

The marks in a painting tell the whole story of how it is made. Armchair painting will not result in lively, energetic marks. In this project, I challenge you to start piling on the paint right from the start. The edgy feeling of correcting as you go lends an urgency to your marks that you can't achieve in any other way.

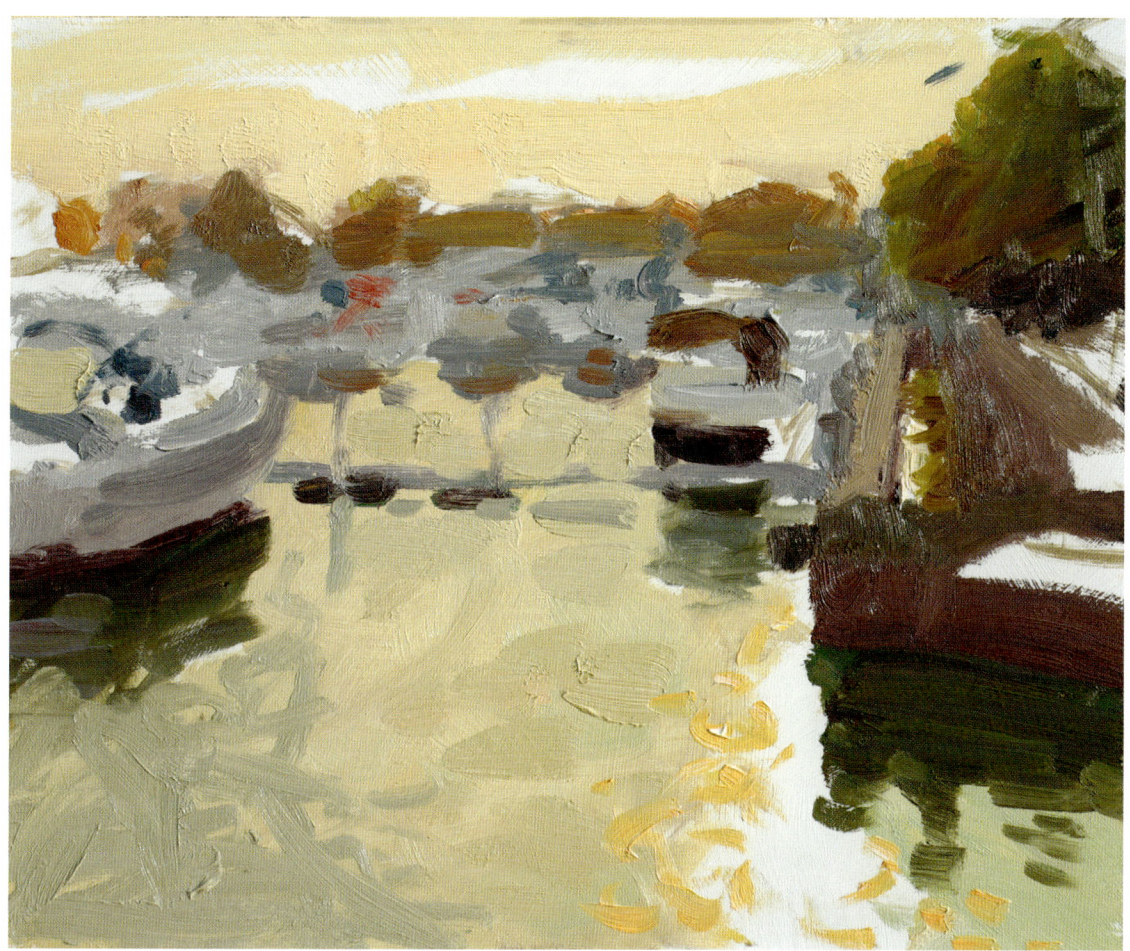

STAGE 2

To cover the canvas as soon as possible, use your largest brushes (Nos. 6 and 8) and start with the largest blocks of colour. The warm, delicate colours of the sky and water should be put down early so that they don't get muddied. The sky is a simple mix of yellow, red and white. Any colour reflected in water appears darker and duller, so add some viridian and crimson to this mix for the colour of the water.

Leave a slice of clean canvas in the sky (to be filled in later) and for the brightest reflection in the water. Notice how these areas glow once everything else is made a little darker. You can add to this impression of luminosity by creating a 'halo' of warm colours around the brightest areas. Have fun with the swirly strokes of orange around the sunlight on the water. Wherever the trees meet the sky, introduce more touches of orange and yellow.

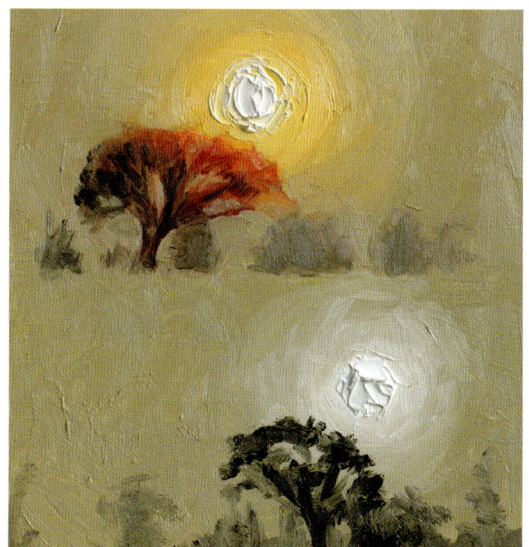

ABOVE *A halo of warm colour conveys the power of the light to dissolve the edges of whatever it comes in contact with. The painting shows glowing light with a warm halo (above) and without (below). Which do you prefer?*

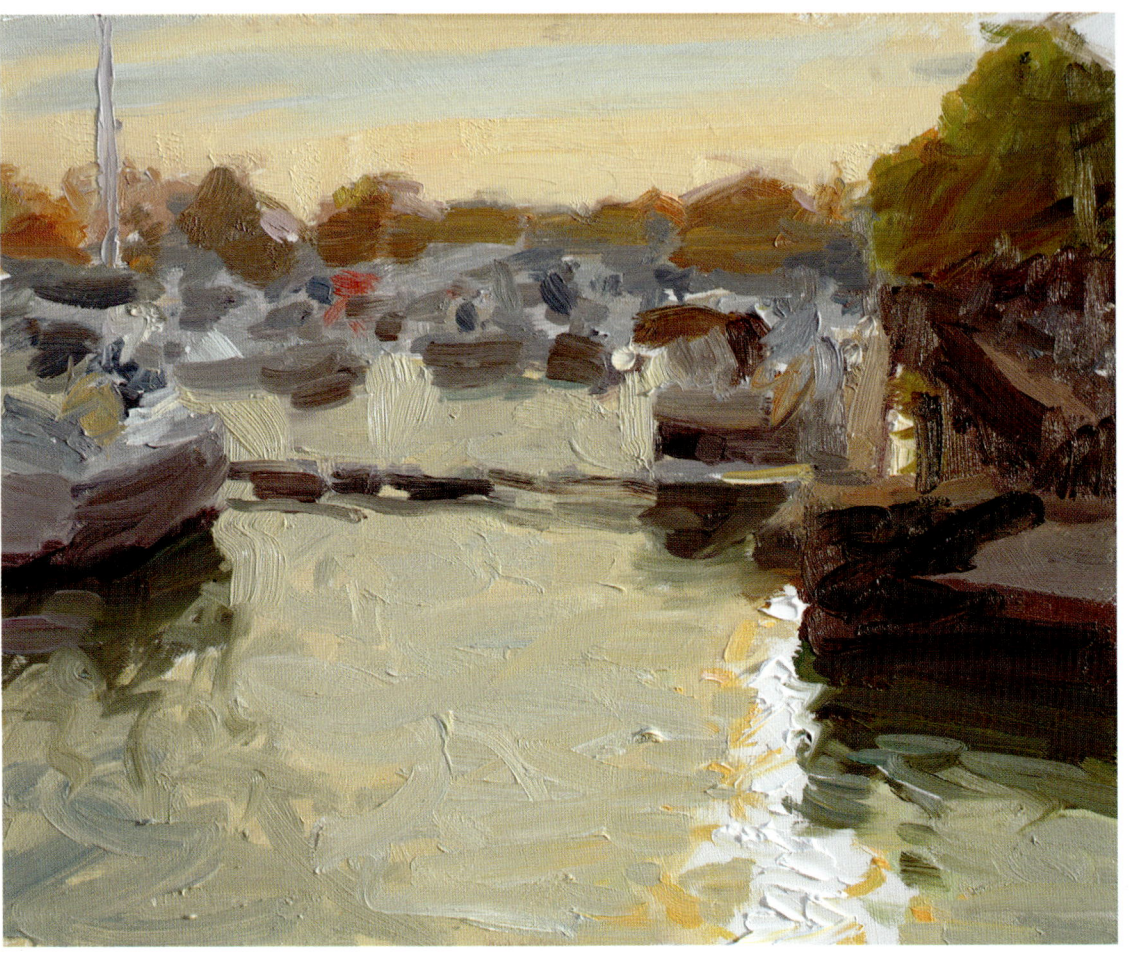

STAGE 3

To make the reflection of the sun on the water catch as much light as possible, use the tip of the palette knife to deposit pure white paint into that area.

Returning to the sky, mix up a generous pile of light blue and fill in the white gap with a few bold strokes, resisting the urge to correct or blend. If you had painted the whole of the sky with orange-yellow and then brushed the blue section into it, the resulting mix would have been a dull green – not great for a glowing sky. As it is, the orange and blue sit side by side, complementing each other.

Even though you haven't been too meticulous with the perspective lines, you can still create a sense of depth in this scene through a wonderful effect called aerial perspective. Paint your darkest tonal values in the foreground, gradually getting lighter as you move into the distance. This mimics the layers of atmosphere, containing moisture and dust, which make distant things more hazy.

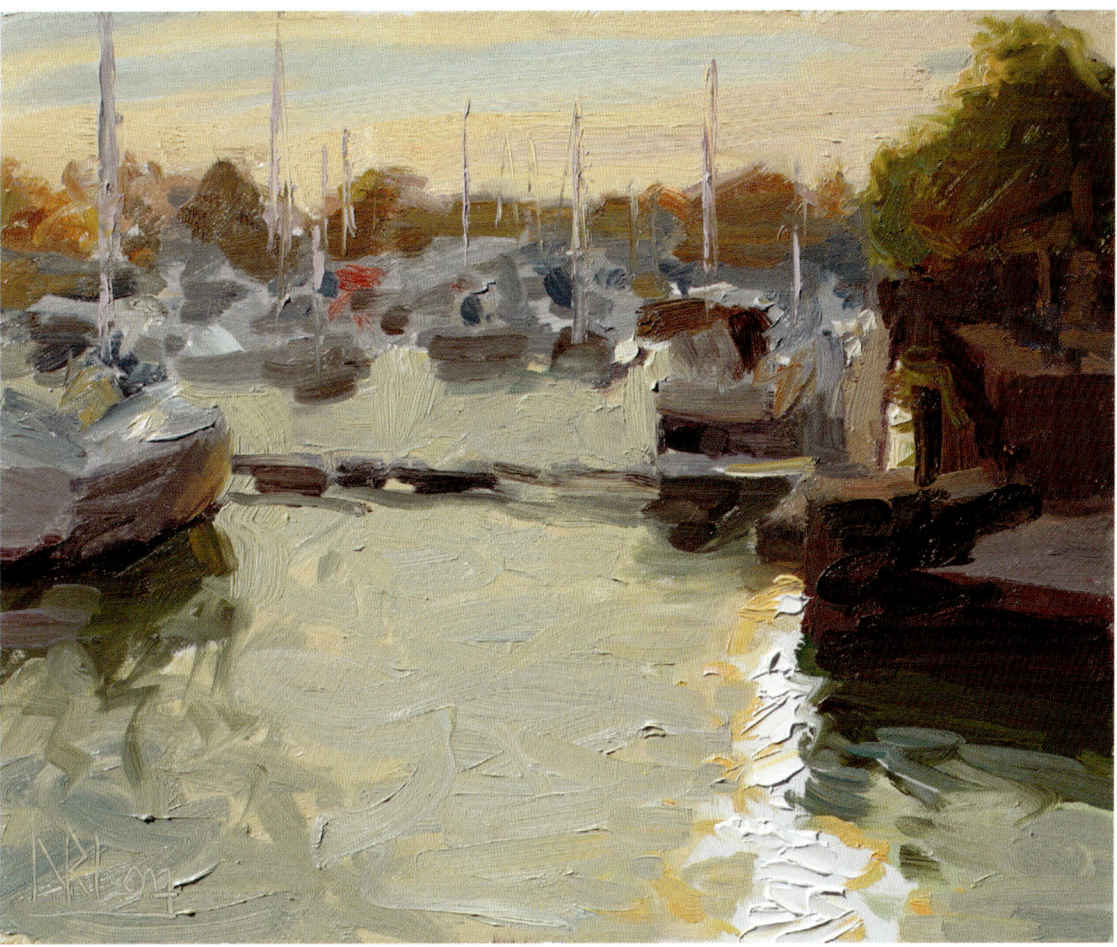

STAGE 4

You won't have time to paint every boat mast, but if you note the way they get thinner and their tops appear to get lower as they go into the distance, you can use them to add to the impression of distance. To make a mast, place the edge of the palette knife into a pile of pink/purple paint and stamp this onto the painting, sometimes dragging downwards. In accordance with perspective, the closest mast is darker and wider than the more distant ones.

As you can see, I'm no expert at painting boats, but I do love to paint light. Treat yourself to the highlight on the left-hand boat, but start with a large blob of orange-yellow to create a halo, followed by a smaller blob of white in the centre. There is just time for the warm (orange) reflected light on the underside of the hull and its reflection in the water.

Be careful if you find yourself having too much fun adding details – you must know when to stop. If your painting has captured your impression of the scene, the viewer can fill in the details. When it comes to your signature, if there is no obvious area that needs covering up, nor any colour that needs balancing, go for the unobtrusive option and scratch your name into the wet paint with the handle of your brush.

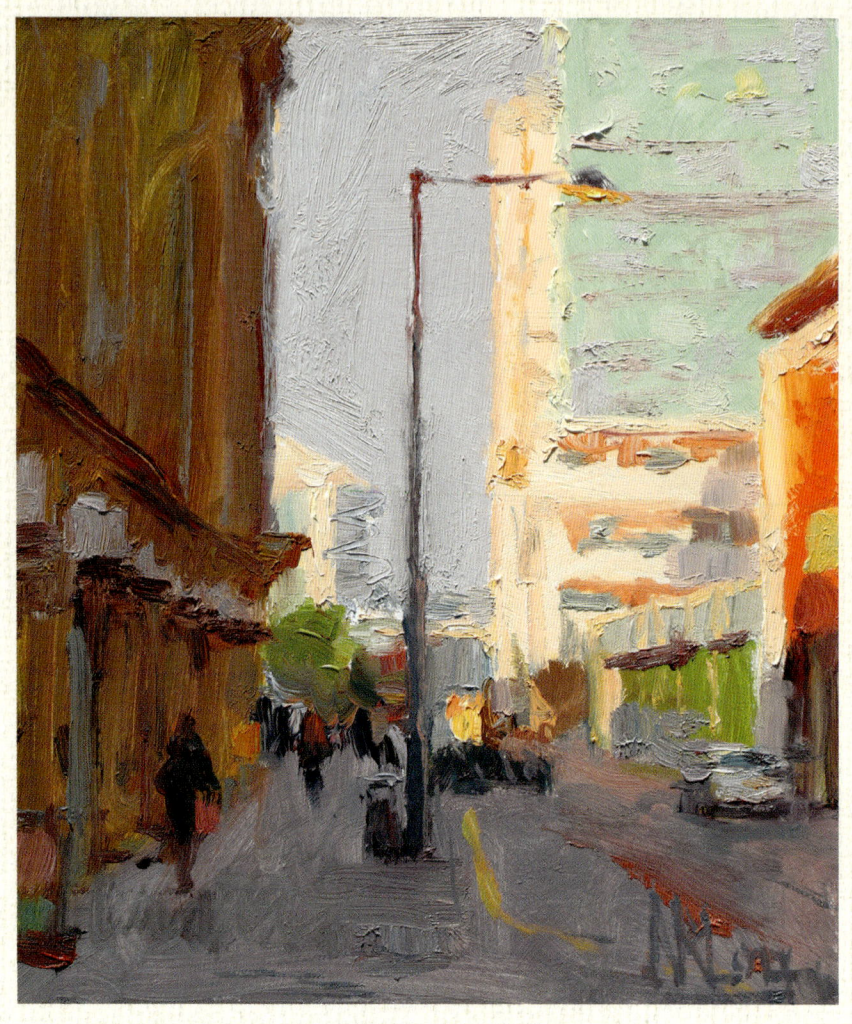

Cityscape

To paint the effect of morning light in the city, you will learn to mix warm light colours and cool darks. You will also create the illusion of receding space by learning the simple rules of perspective and applying them in your painting of buildings and figures.

COLOURS NEEDED

| Phthalo Blue | Viridian Hue | Cadmium Yellow Pale | Yellow Ochre | Burnt Sienna | Permanent Alizarin Crimson | Cadmium Red | Ivory Black | Titanium White |

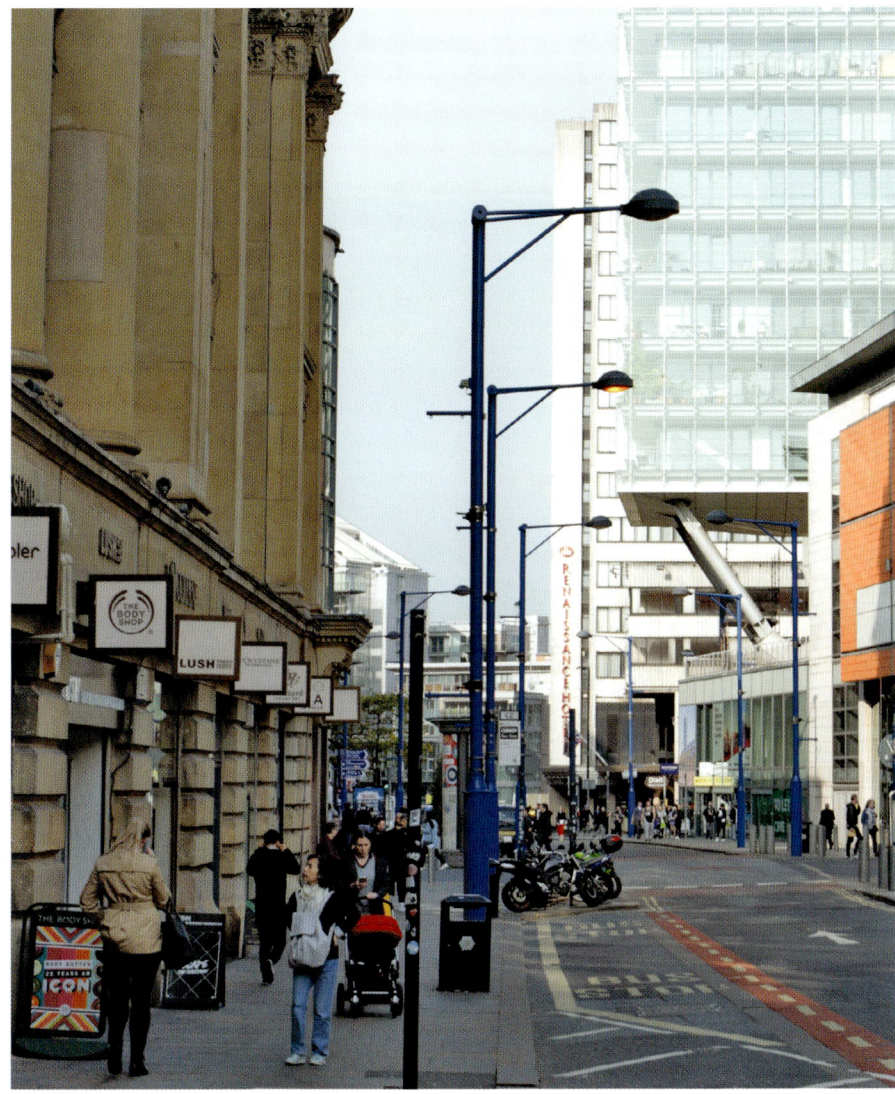

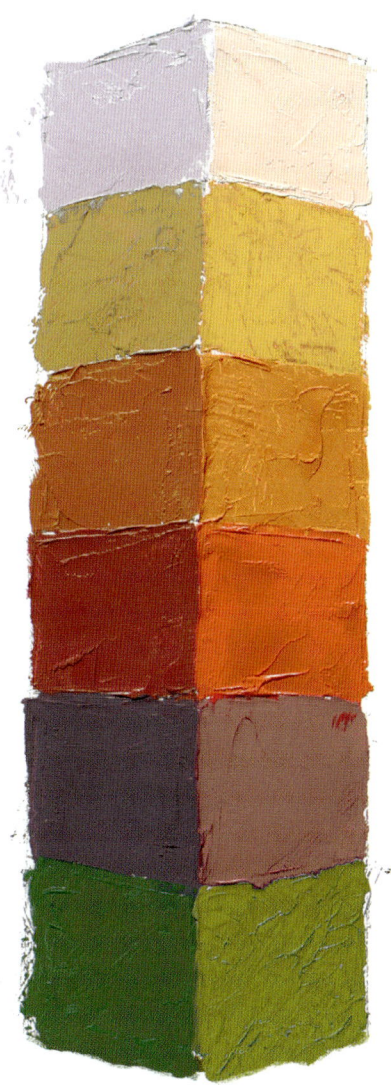

This cityscape was painted on a sunny September morning in Manchester, England. It was completed in about two hours, by which time the 'golden hour' of light had faded and the shadows were in different positions.

The thing that grabs me and makes me paint is often not the subject itself, but an effect of light or simple blocks of colour. Here the exciting thing was the colour of the buildings against the dull blue sky. I wanted to include some of that fabulous orange on the right but realized that it could easily take all the attention if it was too large a chunk of colour. I decided to crop all but a small slice of it on the right-hand side.

For this project, you may copy my painting but if you prefer to work from your own photo, try to find an image that has clearly distinguished areas of light and shade.

WARM LIGHTS AND COOL SHADOWS

This 'colour tower' (right) is made from swatches of colour taken from the finished painting. On the right-hand side the blocks are bathed in warm morning sunlight, which has an orange tinge. On the left are colours from the shadow area of the painting. These are all darker and cooler, tending towards purple-blue.

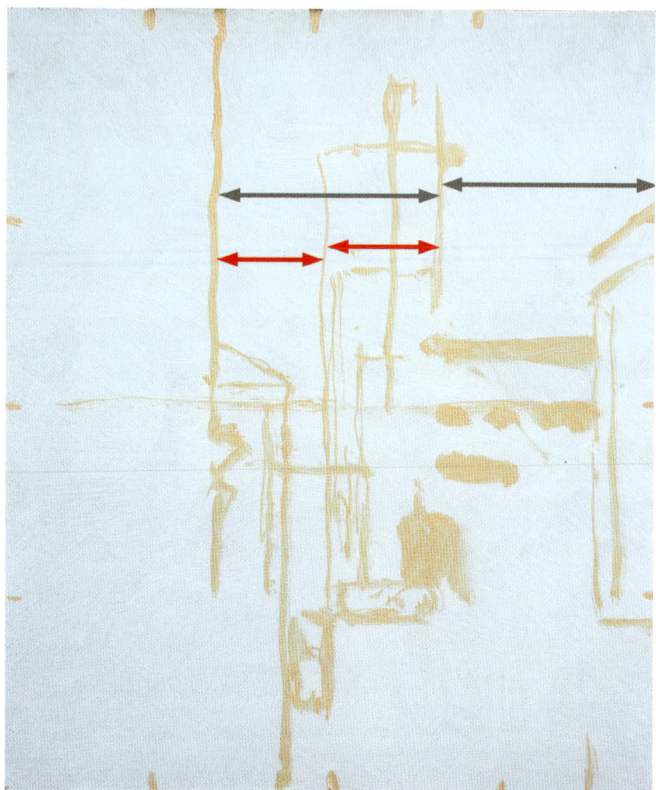

STAGE 1

This project is similar to the previous one in requiring a direct approach within a limited timescale. Do only as much drawing as is required to place the large colour shapes. Remember to look for matching measurements in the subject and make them match in your painting too.

By the time I had got even this much drawing done, the shadows had moved significantly. It is usually best to stick to the initial impression a scene makes upon you; a clear tonal plan (see page 169) at the outset can really help with this.

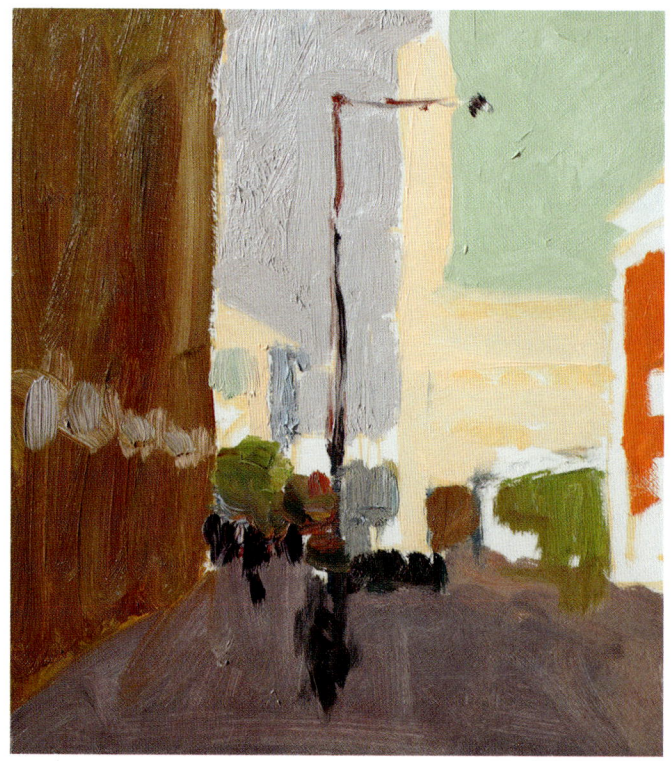

STAGE 2

This is go-for-the-jugular painting. Use your large brushes to pile on the thick paint right from the start. Too many times I have finished a painting only to wish I had used more paint.

In colour mixes, include your warmest colours (yellows and cadmium red) in the areas of warm sunlight and your coolest (blue and crimson) in the shadows. The glass building in the upper right is a mix of viridian and white with some yellow ochre to keep it warm. The sky colour, being a neutral (neither cool nor warm), is a mixture of a cool colour (blue) and a warm colour (cadmium red) plus white.

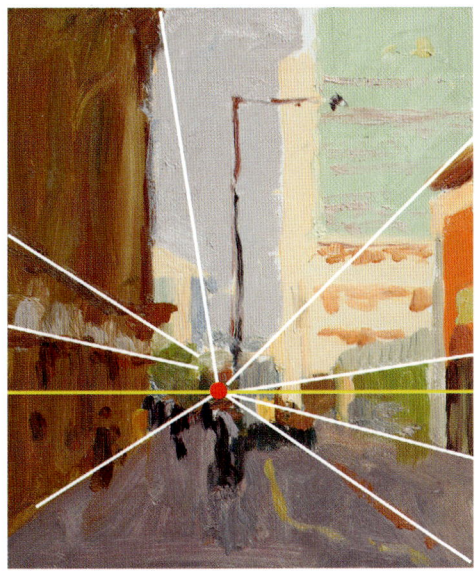

ABOVE *Hold a paintbrush up to your perspective lines (shown in white) to check that they all converge on the vanishing point (the red dot). The signs and ledge on the left-hand building did not line up, so in the next stage I will have to make those angles steeper.*

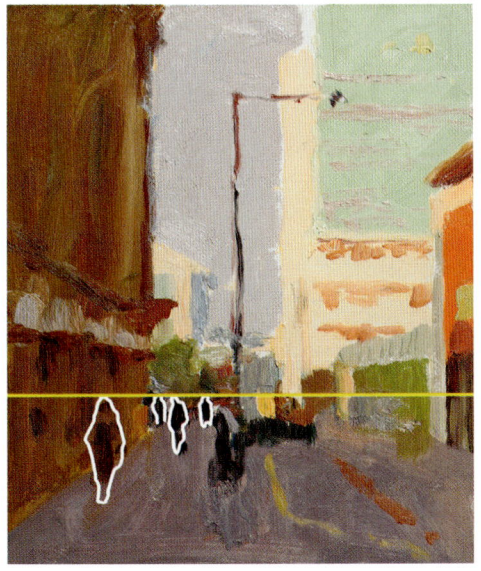

ABOVE *Perspective also affects people. Of course, people further away appear smaller, but in general their heads are on a similar level – close to our own eye level. Their feet, however, will be at varying heights.*

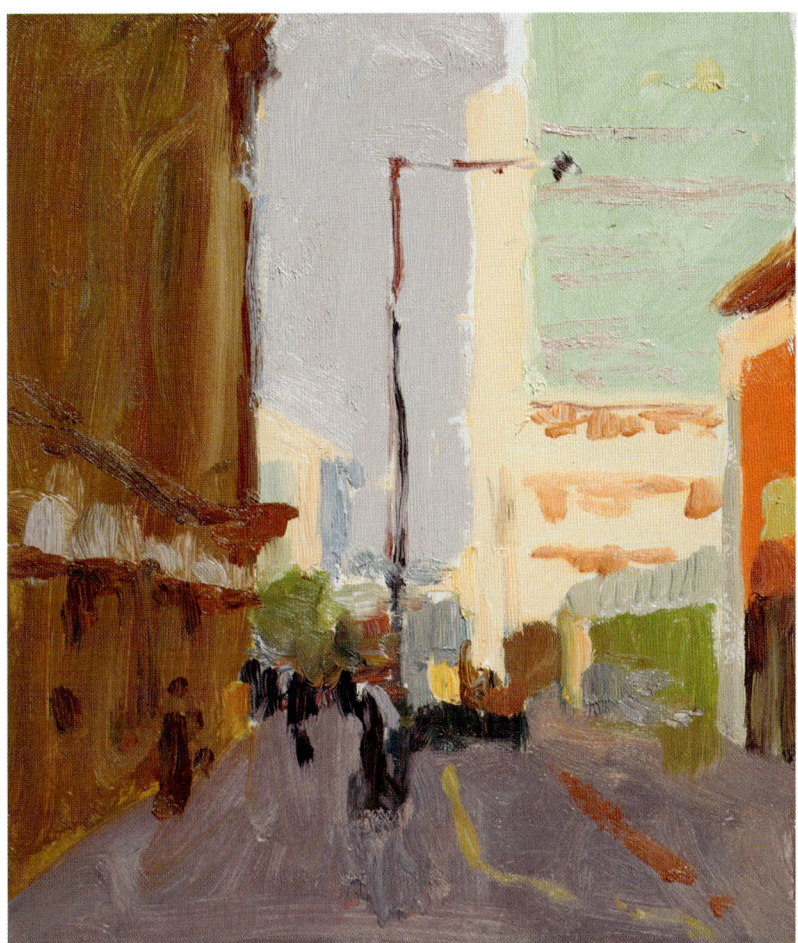

STAGE 3

At this stage you may begin to introduce lines and details using smaller brushes. As you do so, don't forget to keep the warm light areas distinct from the cool shadows. To simplify the effect, you can even paint details of the right-hand buildings lighter and warmer than they actually appear. Leave a gap of canvas to prevent the dull sky colour from muddying the delicate orange of the building. This will be filled in later with a small brush and orange paint.

Now is a good time to check your perspective. The essential effect of perspective is that things get smaller and closer together as they go into the distance. This includes the parallel lines of buildings, which all get closer together (converge) until they disappear at a vanishing point. This point always sits on our eye level (yellow line). Imagine standing in a flood up to your eyes. The level of the water would be your eye level. If you were to sit down, the flood would drain to give you a new eye level.

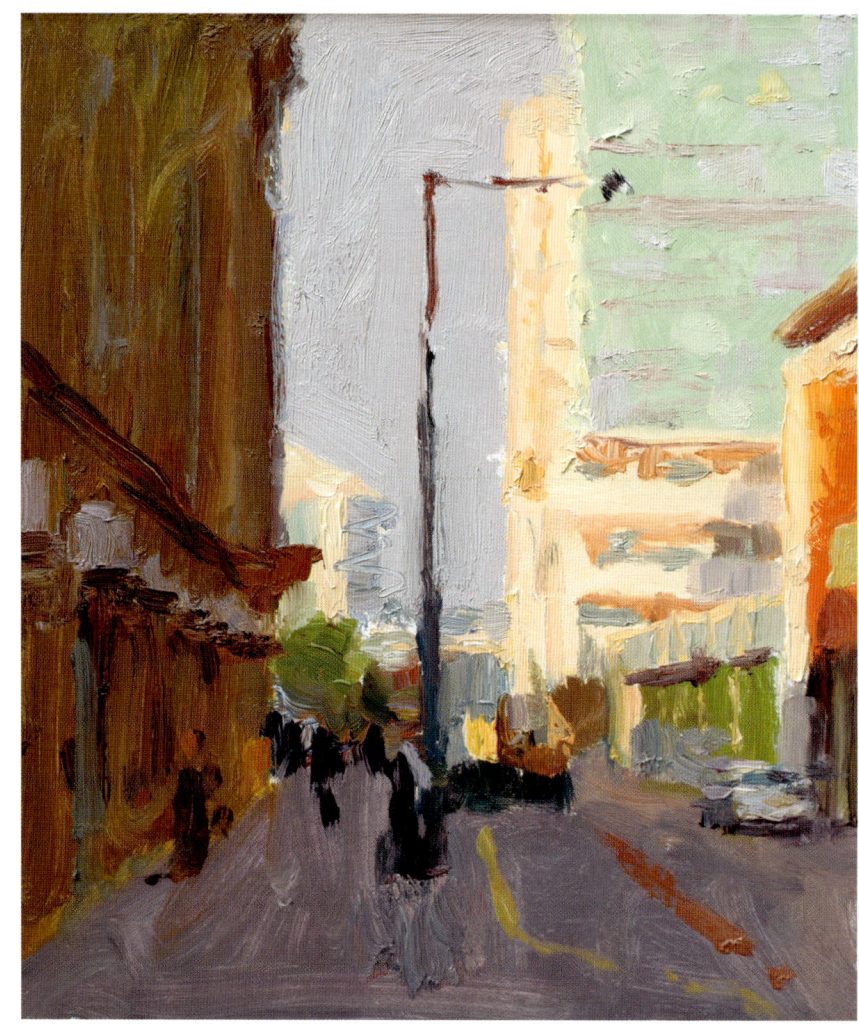

STAGE 4

We are about three-quarters of the way through the painting and there are hardly any details. It's easy to panic and start adding things to make it look more finished. In my opinion, this is the time when a mirror is at its most useful. You may think that stopping to look in the mirror will slow you down. On the contrary, it will tell you what is essential and you can leave out the rest.

Any details we add at this stage will make the subject a bit clearer, but can also be used to balance the colours in the painting. This balancing of colours is not an exact science and you shouldn't worry about getting it right or wrong, but it is true that echoing colours throughout the painting helps to tie it all together.

The strongest colours in this painting are the orange building on the right and the yellow square in the centre. If these were the only notes of those colours, they would feel isolated from the rest of the picture. The lines on the road, painted in duller versions of those colours, help to connect them to the rest of the painting.

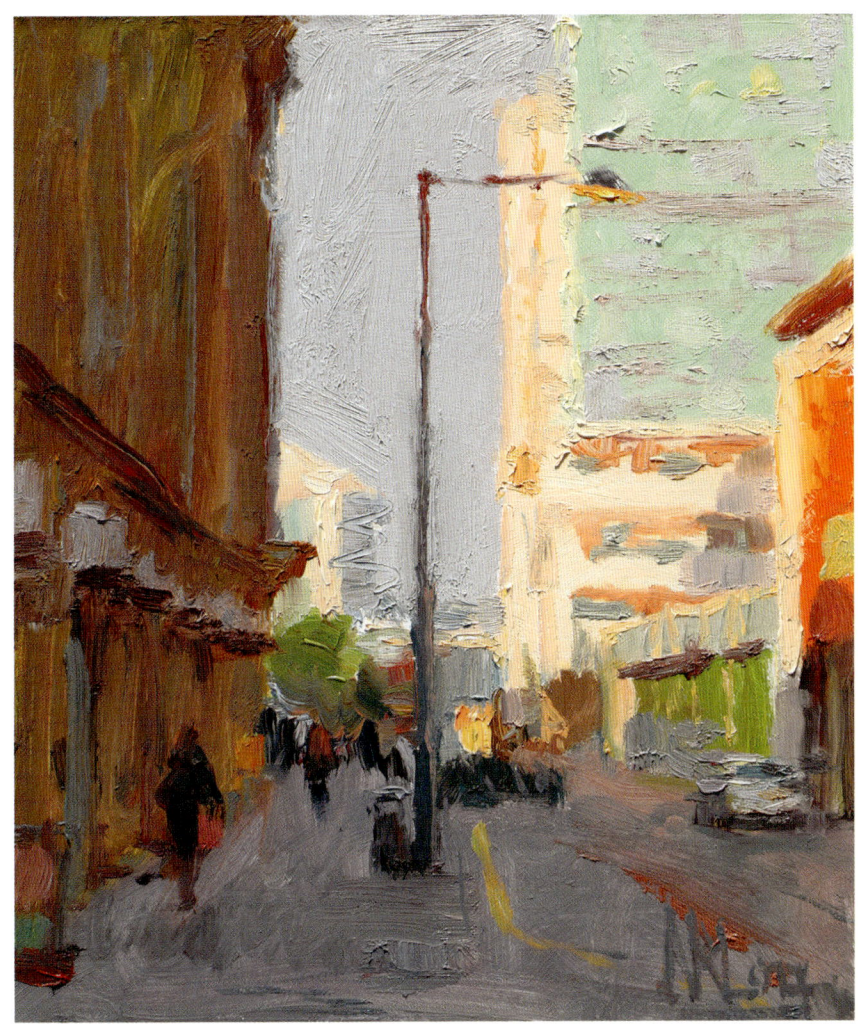

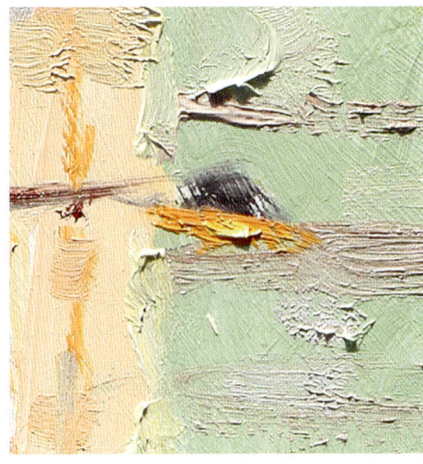

ABOVE *Use a lift-off highlight to create the glow of the street light.*

STAGE 5

A city isn't a city without people, but you only need one or two to give a sense of life. I encourage you to suggest the overall shape of people with as few brushmarks as possible. If you are painting on the street, glance at a walking figure for less than a second to fix the shape in your mind. You can combine parts from different glimpsed figures into one person. Keep the legs soft and don't paint the feet distinctly or the person will look static.

Remember that you can omit people or move them around to improve your painting. You can see in stage 2 that I thought of having a large central figure. This person commanded too much attention, stopping us in the middle of the painting, so was made into a dustbin!

The shadow side of the distant building was too defined, so the handle of the brush was used to scratch a quick squiggle through it. With the edges broken, it is no longer coming forward in space and the scratches might even suggest windows.

The lit street light is painted using the halo effect (see page 171). Start with a large dash of orange, then mix a large pile of yellow and use the lift-off technique (see page 141) to get a nice blob of paint on your brush. This is laid in the middle of the orange dash for that glowing effect.

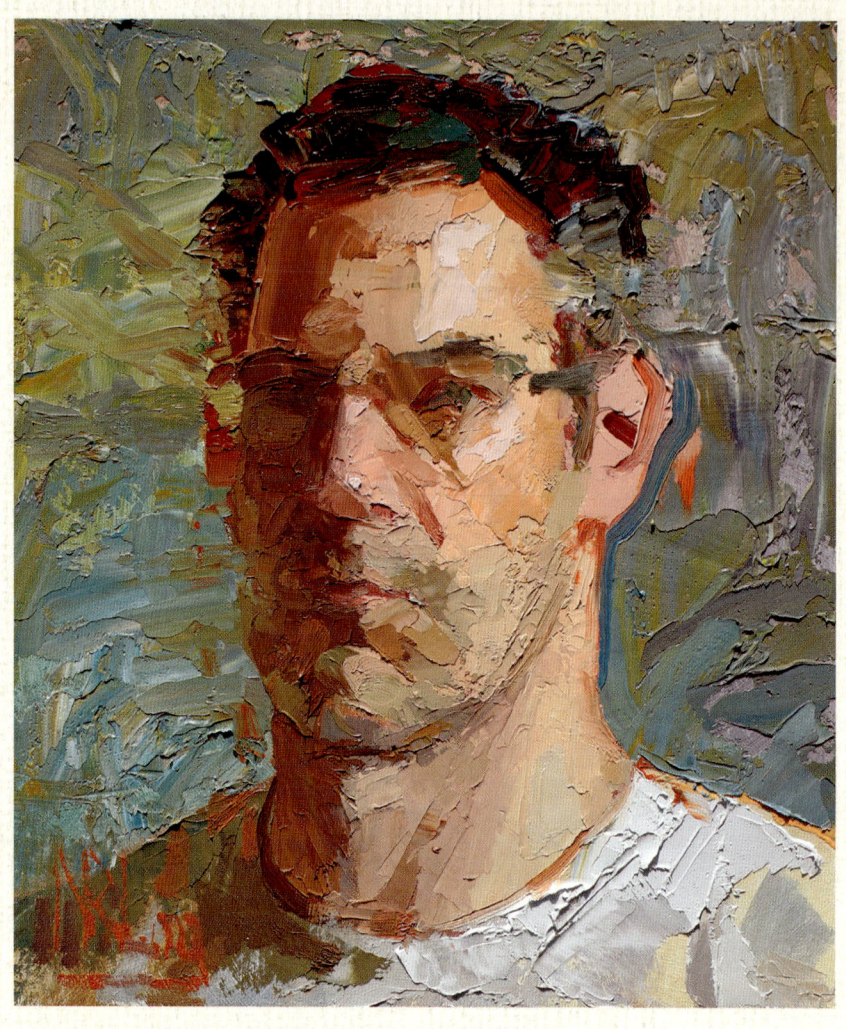

Self-portrait

*For practising portraiture there is no better model than the one in the mirror.
Not only does he or she only take breaks when you do, they won't be offended if
you don't achieve a perfect likeness. In fact, you will be painting with a palette knife,
so the aim is a well-painted head as opposed to a detailed portrait.*

COLOURS NEEDED

| Phthalo Blue | Viridian Hue | Cadmium Yellow Pale | Yellow Ochre | Burnt Sienna | Permanent Alizarin Crimson | Cadmium Red | Ivory Black | Titanium White |

For this exercise, you will use a lot of paint. If you are concerned about cost, you may consider using student-grade paints even for the cadmium colours.

I'm sure you will find painting your own image in a mirror both more bearable and more useful than copying my self-portrait. Tell yourself before you start that this one is a learning experience for yourself, not to show to your friends. It's unlikely you will be maintaining an elegant smile for the hours it takes to complete the painting.

SETTING UP

Before you start, experiment with your position in relation to the mirror and the light source. As you do this, half close your eyes to see the changing pattern of light and shade on your face. I positioned myself to have the light of a window coming from one side. If possible, have your canvas angled to receive good light. Keep the background simple on a small painting such as this.

Position the mirror and the canvas (on the easel) next to each other, then look directly at the canvas. Keeping your head locked, just swivel your eyes to look in the mirror and then back towards your canvas. Maintaining your head in one position and just moving your eyes makes it much easier to compare your beautiful subject to your masterpiece in progress.

You will still need to move your head to look down at your palette. Returning to the correct position is easier if you take note of an aspect of your face such as how much of your far ear you can see. I used the little triangle of wall colour caught in my glasses as my anchor.

Measuring with the brush is a little confusing when looking in a mirror as you see two hands and two brushes – one real and one reflected. The trick is to decide which one you are going to measure with and ignore the other. We know that the eyes are generally positioned about halfway between the chin and the top of the head. If we can find two such matching measurements, we can avoid the most common error in portrait painting, placing the eyes too high in the head.

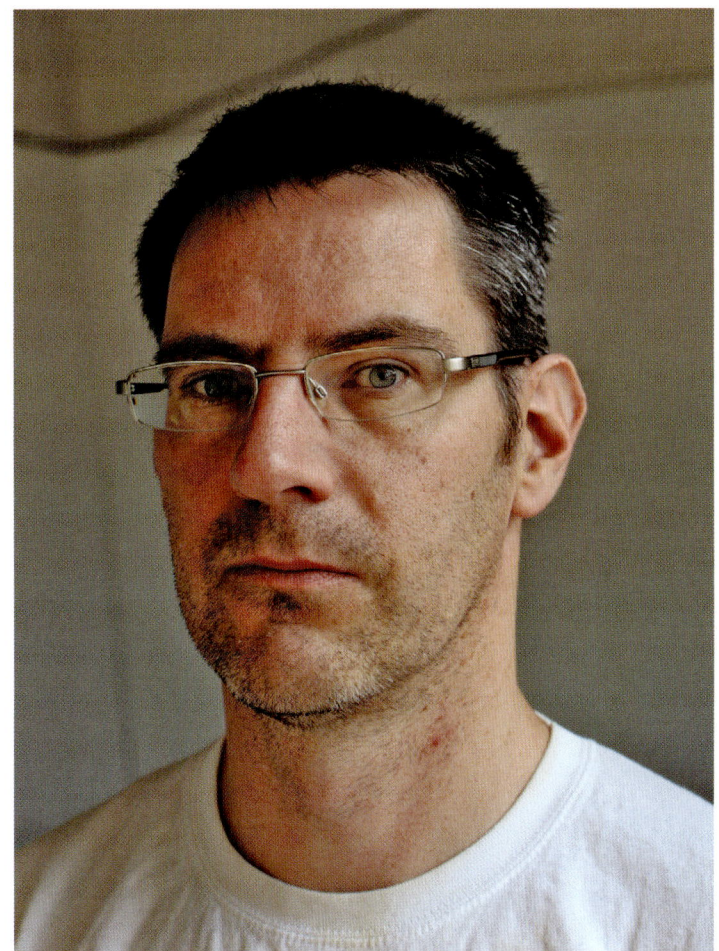

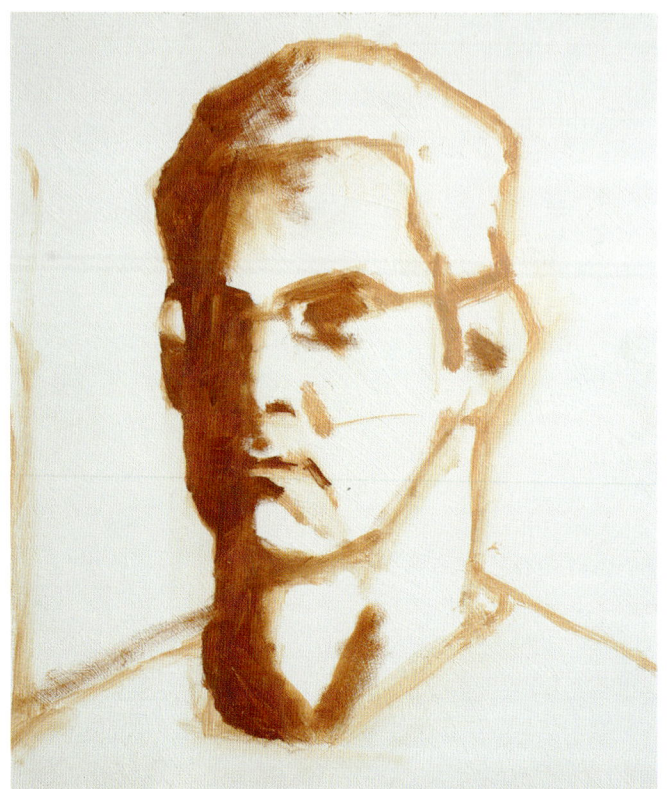

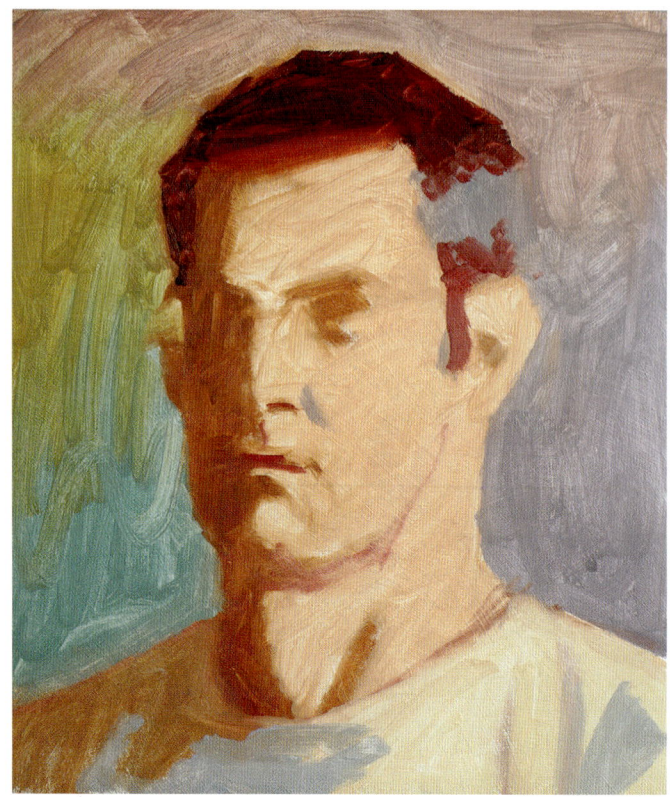

STAGE 1

Try to see your head as a series of flat shapes. Imagine your face, hair and neck as three adjoining countries, each with a distinctive outline. With a No. 2 round brush, begin drawing these three flat shapes, aiming to capture their relative sizes and the way they interlock. Use diluted paint and a delicate colour (I used yellow ochre with a touch of red and white) which will not muddy subsequent layers. Erase mistakes with a rag dipped in solvent and redraw as many times as you like.

Include the shapes of your shoulders, going right to the edges of the canvas. Hold your brush to match the angle of a shoulder, then transfer this angle to your painting.

With a slightly diluted mix of burnt sienna, black and yellow ochre, indicate the pattern of shadow shapes which appear on your face. Don't be alarmed by how dark this colour looks. You are seeing it in relation to the white canvas.

STAGE 2

Using diluted paint, wash in the colour for the light side of your face (for me it is yellow ochre, red and white). For the remaining areas of hair, clothing and background, aim for a similar tonal value to what you see, but take some liberties with the colour. Anything peeping through the thicker layers on top will look better than the glaring white canvas.

Tip
Mark the positions of your features, but don't get enticed into details. There is no point painting a perfect eye until you know that it's in the right place.

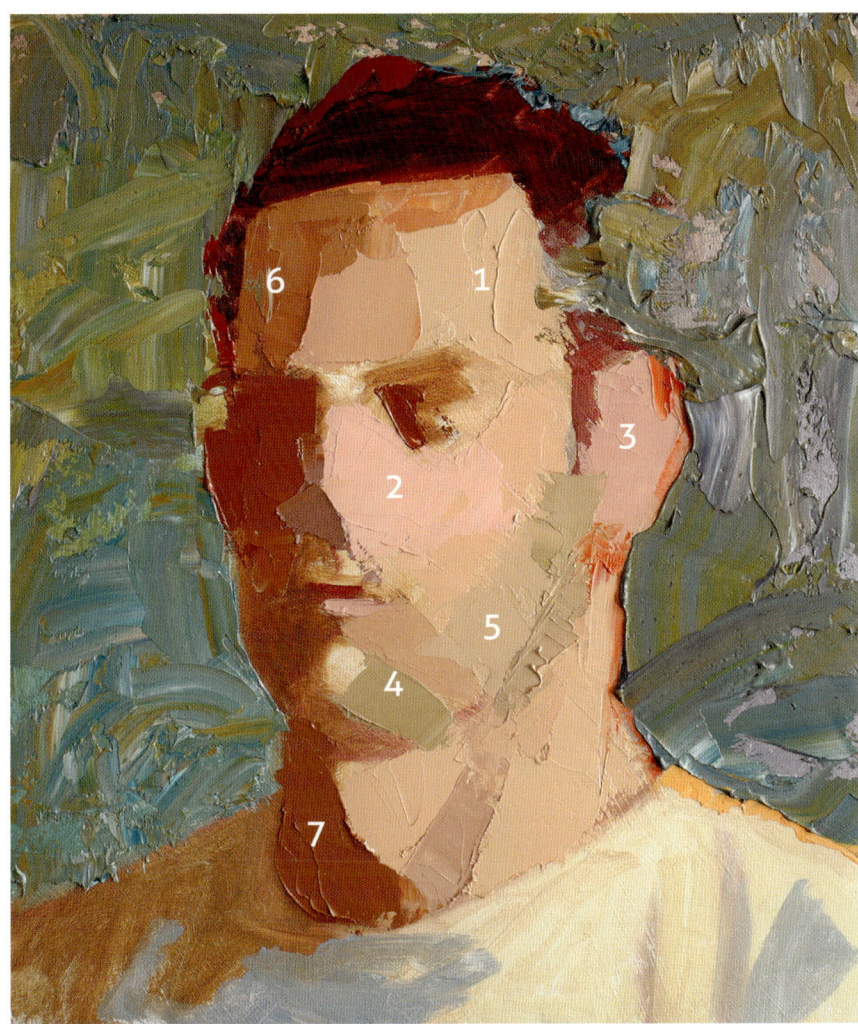

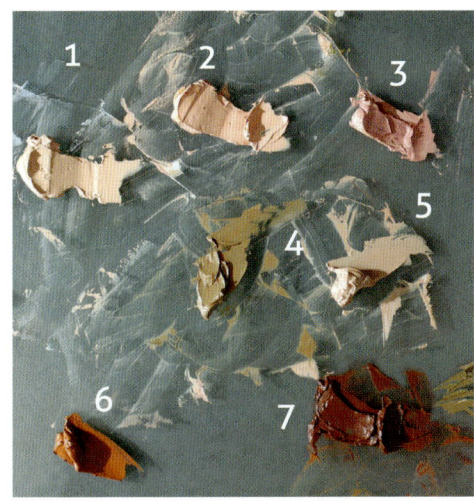

ABOVE *Mix generous quantities of flesh colours with the knife.*

Tip

Apart from the obvious area of the lips, the parts of the face which appear redder are usually those which feel cold in winter – ears, nose and cheeks.

STAGE 3

Flesh colours vary drastically according to the complexion of the individual and the lighting conditions. Here I show you eight mixtures and where I use them on the face.

For basic Caucasian flesh colour, use white, yellow ochre and red (**1**). This is the starting point for lots of the other mixtures. Add more red and orange for warmer areas of flesh such as the nose and cheek (**2**). The reddest flesh colour, found in the ear, is the previous mix with crimson and blue added (**3**).

Duller colours (known as neutrals) occur in the beard area. My dark neutral is made of basic flesh colour plus viridian and orange (**4**). The light neutral (**5**) is once again based on the basic flesh colour this time has some dark neutral, burnt sienna and white added.

The flesh colours are mixed thoroughly to a unified colour. When it comes to the background mixtures, feel free to dip the tip of the palette knife into lots of different colours and not mix them fully. As you apply this unmixed colour to the painting, it creates exciting 'broken colour' effects.

A warm shadow colour is made of burnt sienna with yellow ochre and white (**6**). Adding crimson and more burnt sienna gives the darkest shadow (**7**).

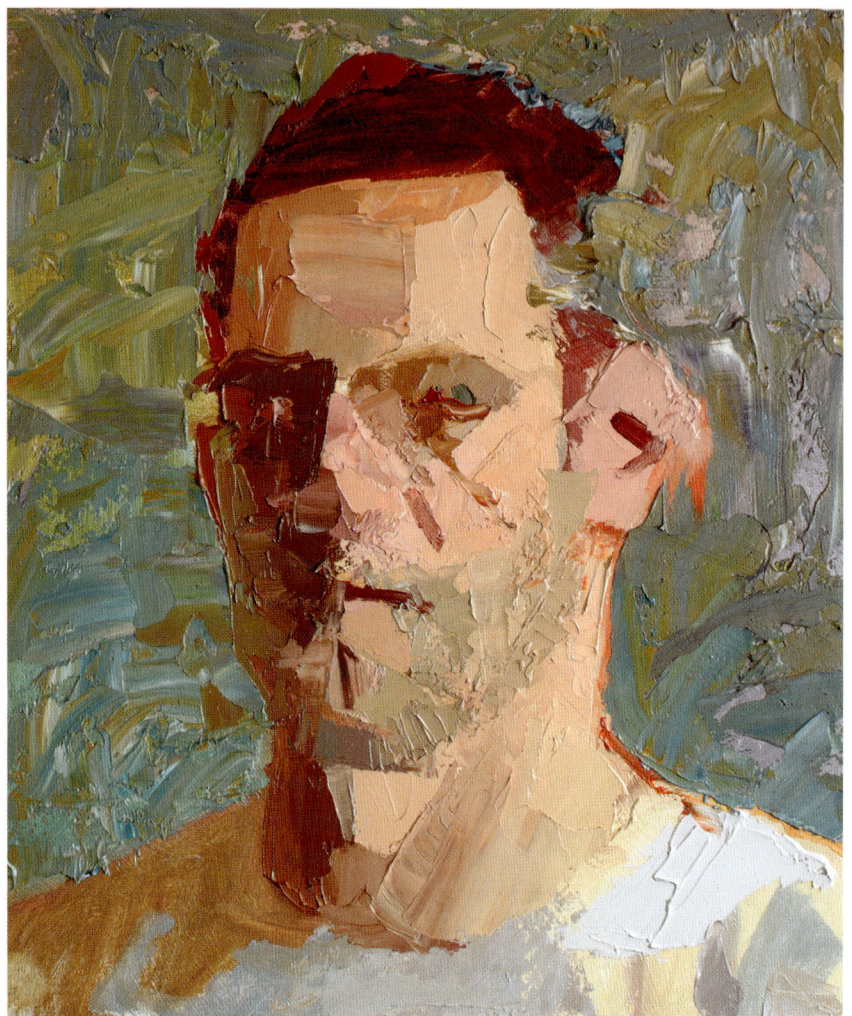

STAGE 4

Painting with the palette knife can feel awkward at first, but keep using it for as long as you can. It forces you to simplify and leads to freshness of marks. If you do need to measure and make a few correcting marks for the position of things, use a No. 2 round brush.

Here I measured the position of my eye using the paintbrush and found that I had it way too far to the left. I marked the new position using the brush and am in the process of moving the nose and mouth to the right to fit in with the new eye position. It's never too late for major corrections.

If the edge between the head and the background is kept too rigid, it can look like a cutout. To overcome this, colours from the background are dragged into the hair and some colour from the cheek is lightly dragged into the background.

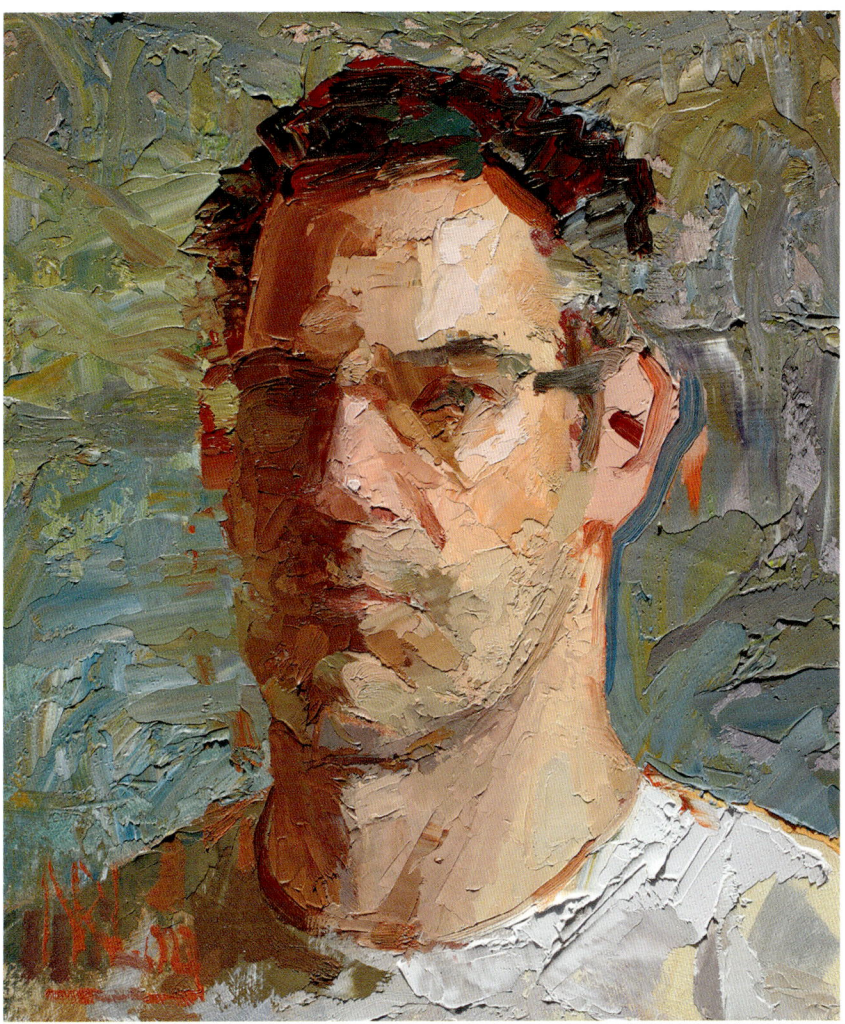

Tip
Rather than black, use dark red for the nostrils and ear cavities to keep the feeling of life in the portrait.

STAGE 5

Beware of using too much white in the flesh colours as you make your final corrections. Keep the colours rich and reserve your white for the highlights at the end. Even here, my highlights have a little purple mixed into them.

In painting the eyes, the key is to paint only what you see. Particularly avoid details and highlights in a shaded eye. Look how little information I have given about mine. To avoid a staring look, make sure the top section of the iris is covered by the eyelid. The 'whites' of the eyes are rarely white. In most circumstances, a greyish colour to the same tonal value as the flesh looks much better.

Oil paint dries on the surface first, forming a skin. Thickly applied paint such as this may be touch dry within a week, but will remain wet under the surface. Be careful not to squash the impasto by putting anything against the face of the painting for a month or so. You can test if the paint has dried solid by gently pushing it with your finger. If it moves, it is still wet underneath.

COLOUR PENCILS

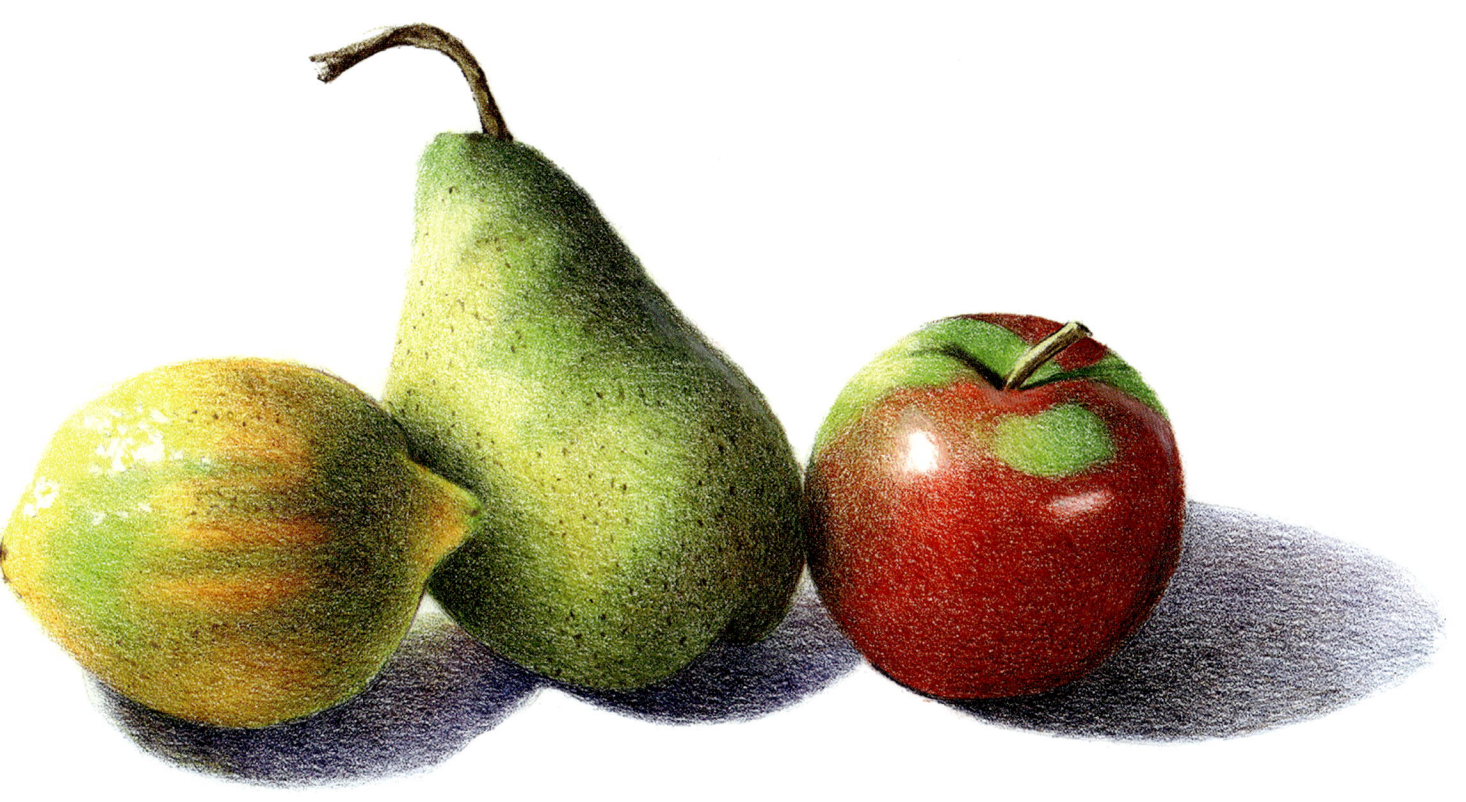

Introduction

For as long as I can remember, I have always enjoyed drawing and creating art. As a child, I was inspired by my cousin, who was a primary school art teacher. I decided to follow in her footsteps and also become an art teacher some day. My parents enrolled me in art lessons, but it was my secondary school art teacher who really encouraged me to practise and become proficient at drawing. For three years I studied line, shape, texture, value and composition while working only in graphite pencil and black ink.

I discovered coloured pencil in college, when I took a coloured-pencil illustration class. I learned to combine my drawing skills with colour theory and began to experiment and sketch a variety of subjects. College painting classes taught me that any colour could be created by mixing only the primary colours, and I found out how to create rich, dark values without ever using black. I love vibrant colour, and I prefer layering colours on the drawing surface to mixing paint on a palette. The translucency of coloured pencil allows each layer of colour to show through the preceding colours and thus achieves that hint of luminosity in my work.

There are many possibilities for using coloured pencil: it can be used as a preliminary sketching tool for colour studies, for beautiful illustrations or portraits; and it can be mixed with other art mediums for some interesting effects. Coloured pencil is also an easily transported medium and one that can be picked up or put down quickly without the hassles of set-up and clean-up.

I have been teaching art to students of all ages for almost 20 years through various art associations, in my studio or in private lessons. My greatest pleasure as a teacher has been to give students the creative tools and then encourage them to develop their own style. In this chapter I have put together all the information you need to be able to draw with coloured pencils. We will start by looking at materials and equipment, colour theory, techniques, composition and perspective. Then we will work through a series of step-by-step projects to help you become more proficient with coloured pencils.

You may be familiar with the saying 'The secret of life is in art.' To me, art is my life. Every day I feel an inner drive to create. My greatest satisfactions are inspiring viewers with my art and inspiring my students to see all the possibilities. If you are passionate

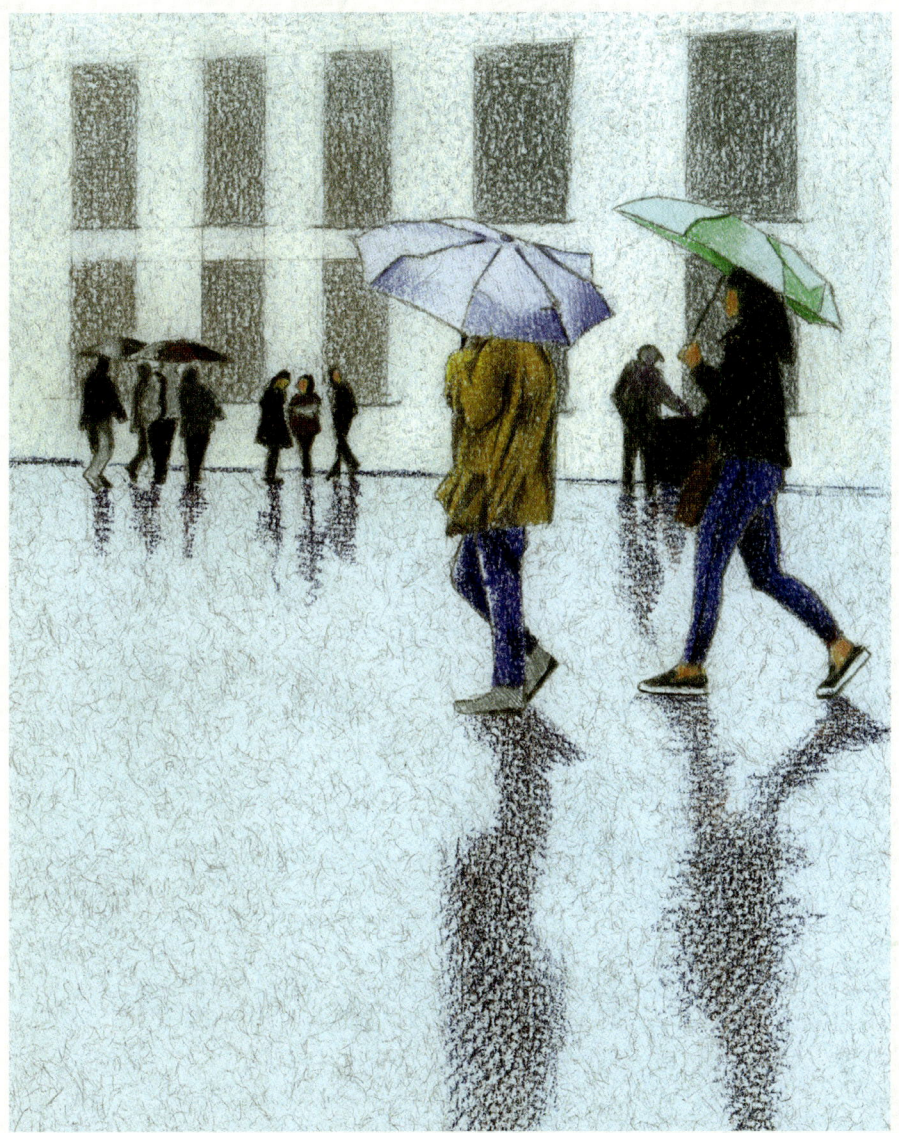

about your drawings, others will be too. Art calls for a lifetime of learning, not only from your own practice but also from looking at the artworks of other artists. I enjoy the process of looking, interpreting and teaching what I see.

So, find some paper, sharpen your pencils and let's start creating!

Kendra

Materials and Equipment

As an art form, drawing with coloured pencils has several benefits: it requires very few materials and equipment, and they are relatively inexpensive; the pencils are easily portable, making them ideal for sketching outdoors or taking away with you; and you can pick them up and put them down at a moment's notice and create some lovely art.

Coloured pencils

Two types of coloured pencils are available: wax-based and water-soluble. Wax-based pencils are composed of colour pigments, wax and other binder ingredients that help the pigment adhere to the paper. All dry pencils are made of wax, but certain brands are considered oil-based because they contain a greater concentration of oil than wax; they are less brittle and a bit harder than wax-based pencils. Both types of coloured pencils can be used together or separately within a drawing. Water-soluble pencils can be applied dry and then blended with water to dissolve the pigment, allowing it to flow like watercolour paint.

There are lots of different brands and qualities of coloured pencils to choose from. Professional-grade pencils have a higher percentage of pigment and a better quality of construction than student-grade pencils. Professional-grade and water-soluble pencils are softer and can be more easily blended and layered.

I try to select pencils that are lightfast, meaning colours won't fade over the years. Lightfast guides rate pigments according to their lightfast qualities and permanence.

Because coloured pencils are layered onto paper, not mixed on a palette, I always suggest that beginners purchase a set of at least 48 colours so they have a wide enough range of

BELOW *There are many different brands and qualities of coloured pencils to choose from.*

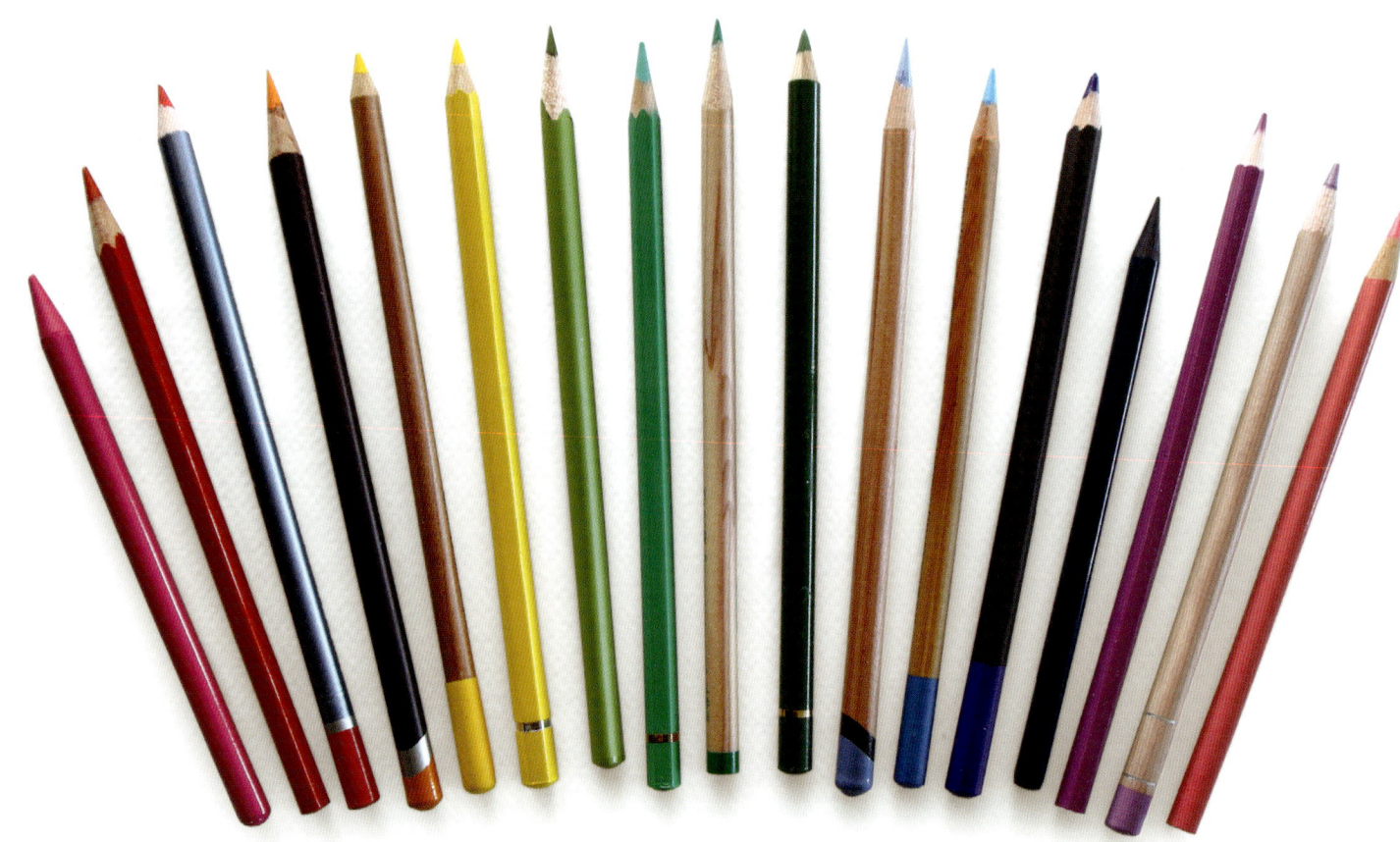

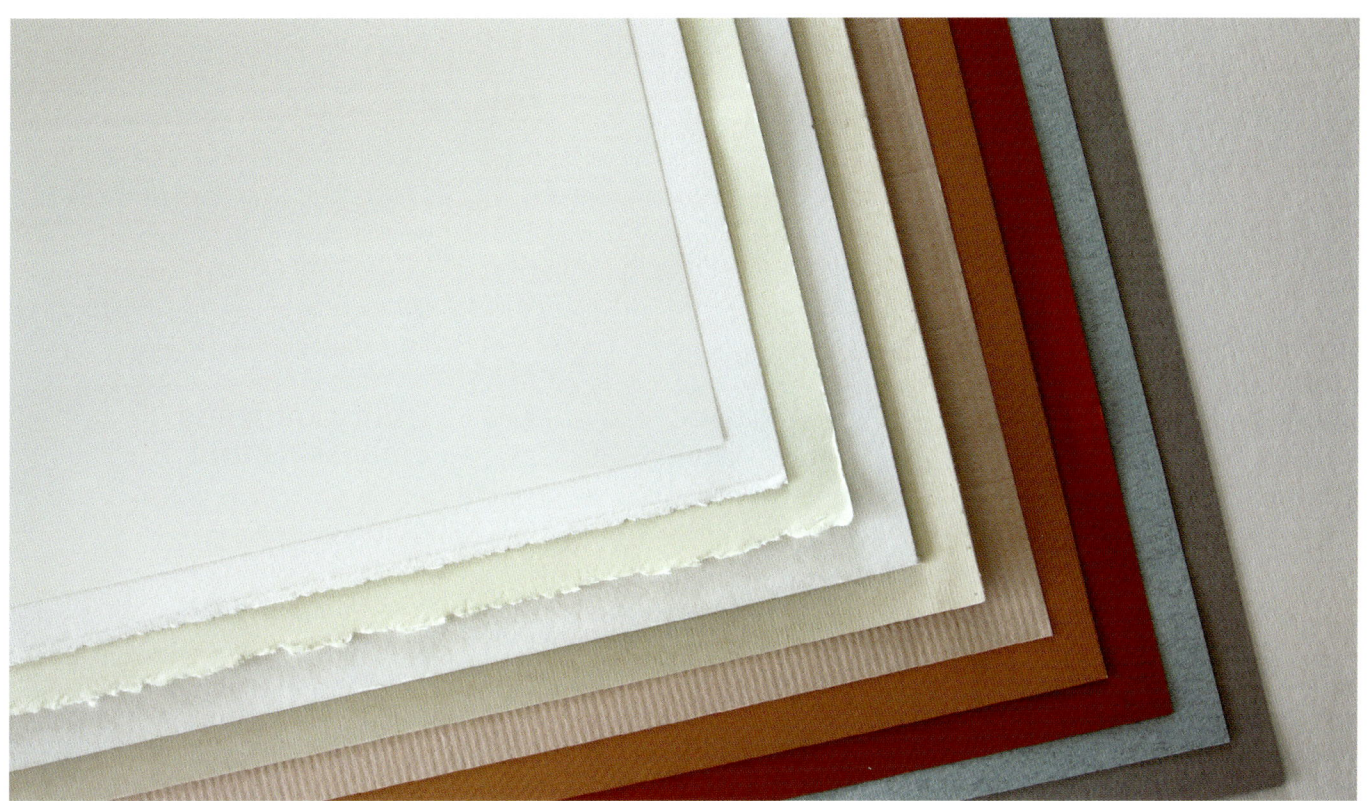

colours. Pencils can also be bought individually, making it cost-effective to add to the set a few at a time.

For the projects in this chapter, I chose specific colours and brands. However, these are just guidelines – there are many fine brands of pencils, and you are encouraged to use similar colours in any brand you prefer.

Surfaces

The surface grain of a paper is referred to as a finish. The amount of tooth, or texture, to a surface finish will determine how many layers of coloured pencil can be applied. A smooth surface has less tooth so will accept fewer layers of pencil. But rough-textured papers, such as sanded, velour or cold pressed, have more tooth and therefore more layers of pigment can be applied.

Softer pencils layer more easily to smoother surfaces, while harder pencils tend to work better on rough surfaces because they don't crumble as easily. Some textured papers have a patterned or lined surface that can complement a drawing; experiment to find what surface works the best for your artwork. It is also best to choose archival-quality or pH-neutral papers that won't turn yellow or fade over time. I will talk more about surfaces and the surface colours I've chosen when we come to the individual step-by-step projects.

Sharpeners

A sharp pencil point is easiest to work with when colouring the surface and layering colour. There are many types of pencil sharpeners, including electric, battery-operated and small handheld sharpeners. I most often use an electric sharpener to quickly obtain a nice sharp point. However, battery-operated and handheld sharpeners are also good for sharpening and portable for travel or sketching outside.

ABOVE *Smooth and rough surfaces include sanded papers and boards, drawing papers, watercolour papers, illustration board, velour papers and drafting vellum.*

Fixatives

Workable fixative can be used between layers of coloured pencil to hold the colours in place and prevent them from smudging. Fixative can also be used if the surface tooth is becoming saturated: spraying a layer of workable fixative on the drawing will add texture to the surface, thus allowing a few more layers of pencil to be applied.

A second type of fixative is called a final fixative. This comes in a gloss or matte finish and is used to spray the finished drawing and give it a protective coating. I chose a final fixative that contains UV filters, which will protect my drawings by filtering out harmful ultraviolet rays. Final fixatives will also help something called wax bloom, which is created by some types of coloured pencils. Wax bloom happens when wax rises to the surface and creates a hazy effect on the drawing. This is especially prevalent in heavier applications of pencil or dark-coloured tonal values. If wax bloom occurs, you can just wipe off the haze with a tissue and spray with a final fixative. Always spray fixatives in a well-ventilated area or outdoors.

BELOW *Block-style erasers (left), including the grey kneaded eraser, and pen-style erasers (centre), can be used to remove colour. The embossing tool (far right) will impress lines to resist colour and a utility knife will lift or scrape off colour.*

Erasers

Different types of erasers can be used to make corrections, lighten pencil marks and also as drawing tools to lift out highlights or small areas of colour.

The kneaded eraser (also called a kneaded rubber) is my favourite. It's pliable and can be moulded to any size and shape so you can erase larger areas as well as small details. It also removes pigment without damaging the paper or leaving eraser crumbs on the surface.

A battery-operated eraser that looks like a drawing tool is another favourite option for erasing coloured pencil. It will quickly lift fine lines and areas of colour, and you can also use it as a drawing tool – for example, when creating highlights. Other tools such as the eraser pencil and pen-style mechanical eraser will do the same type of erasing for small areas. Use an erasing shield if you have one, to keep adjacent colours intact.

White vinyl erasers, art gum erasers and other block erasers are good for removing larger areas of colour, but use these tools carefully to avoid smearing pencil or damaging the tooth of the paper. Masking tape and clear tape are also helpful for lifting colour. See page 201 for more information on techniques for erasing and lifting colour.

Utility knife and embossing tool

A utility knife can be used to gently scrape away small areas of pencil colour in order to add highlights, create texture or allow a layer underneath to show. An embossing tool is a pointed instrument that enables you to make an impression in the paper. When adding colour to the drawing, the pencil will skip over the impression, allowing the tone of the paper to remain. This is handy for areas such as strands of hair. See page 201 for more information about using these tools.

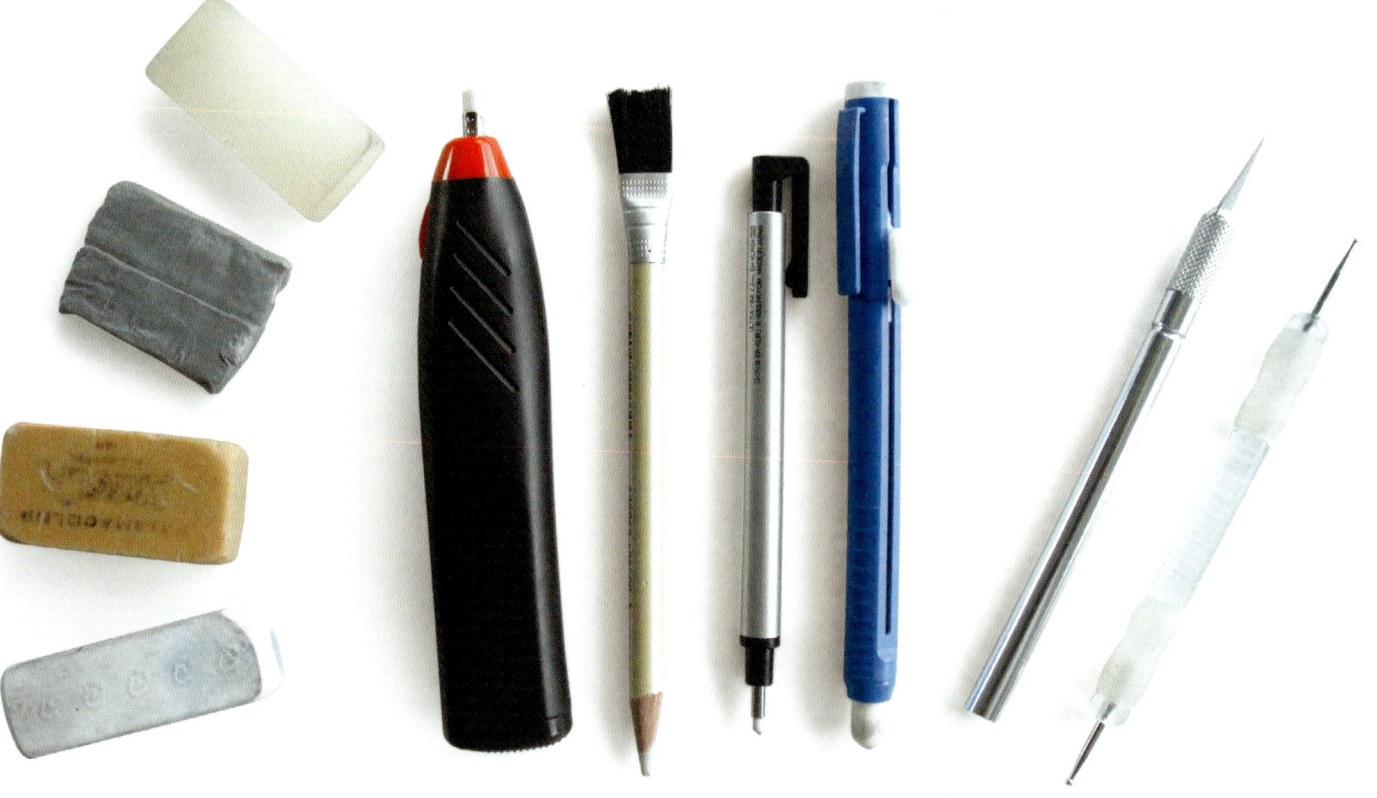

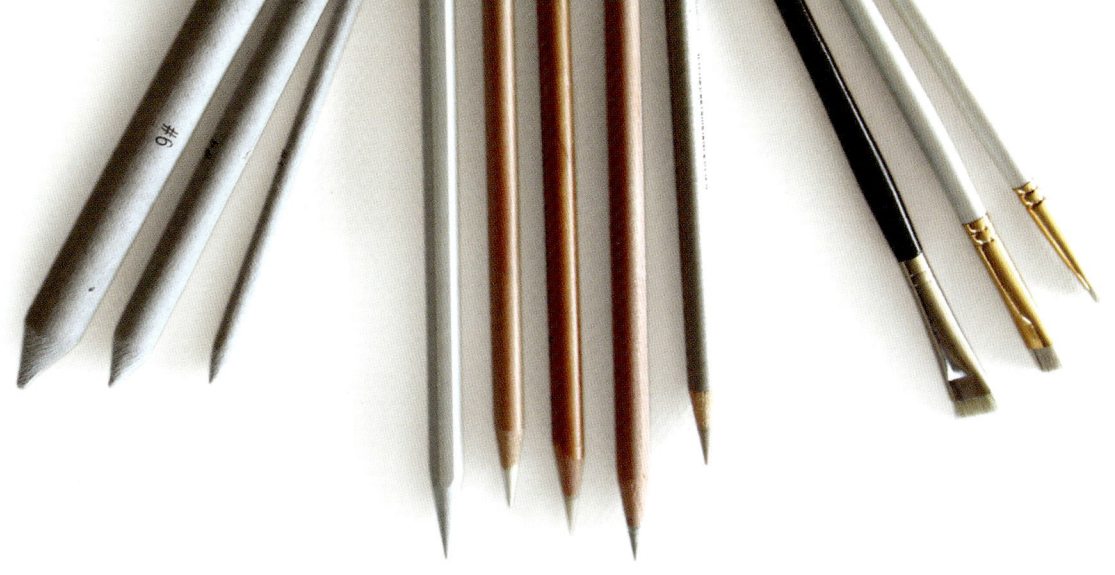

LEFT *Useful tools for blending and burnishing include (from left to right) paper stumps, colourless blender pencils and small, stiff bristle brushes.*

Blending and burnishing tools

Colourless blender pencils, stiff bristle brushes and paper stumps are helpful tools for burnishing coloured pencil. To burnish an area of colour means to press the pencil into the paper, creating a smooth, glossy surface in which no paper texture will show through. The resulting colour will be richer and brighter. To find out more about burnishing, see page 200.

Other useful items

You will need a good smooth drawing board or table on which to work. Some artists work on an easel, but I find it easier to work on an adjustable drawing board propped at an angle so that I don't lean too far forwards and hurt my neck or back. Good lighting is also essential in order to see details, tones and colours. I like to position a desk lamp on my drawing table so that it shines onto my surface.

It is important to keep the surface of the drawing clean. I use a drafting brush or other type of soft brush to sweep away pencil and eraser crumbs – an inexpensive make-up brush will do the trick. You will also need a ruler, and tracing paper to transfer a sketch onto drawing paper.

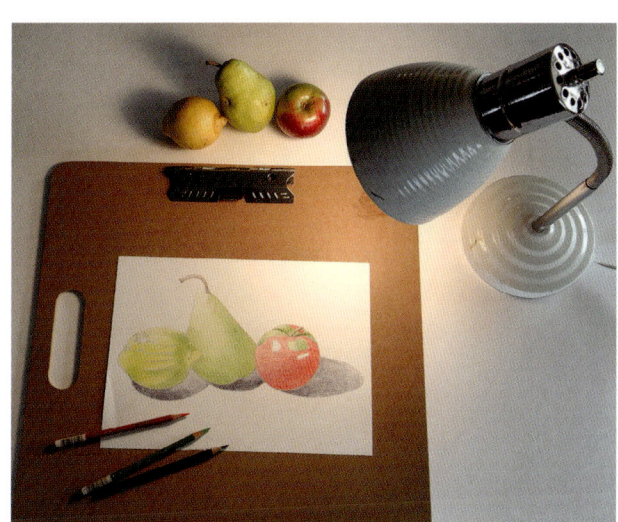

LEFT *I like to work on a firm drawing surface such as this hardboard, which can be tilted towards you as you draw. A desk lamp is handy to light the subject and the drawing.*

BELOW *Useful items include pencil sharpeners, fixatives, a soft brush, a ruler, and pencil extenders when pencils become too short to hold. Graphite, transfer and tracing papers help transfer a sketch onto good drawing paper.*

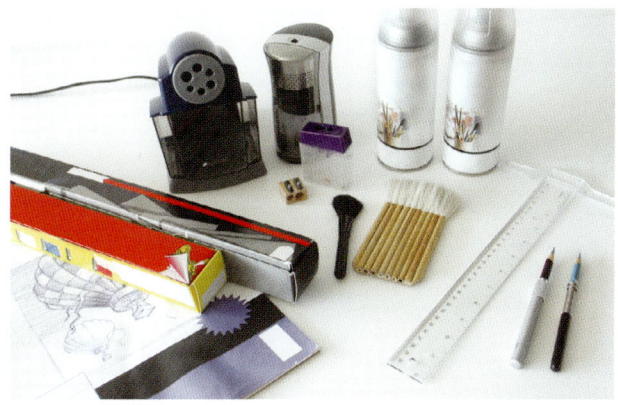

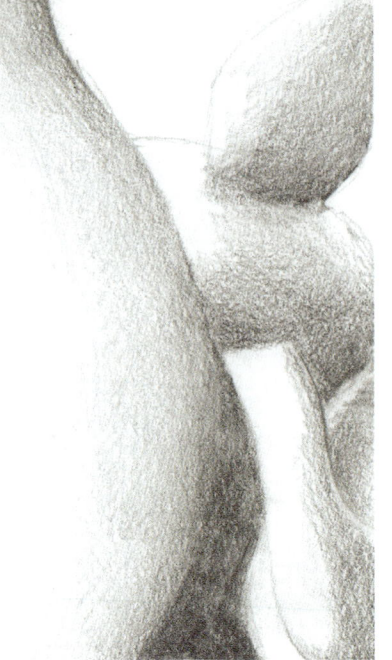

Colour Theory and Tonal Value

Colour theory is a collection of rules and guidelines for using colour in art. Tonal value is the degree of darkness or lightness of a colour or tone, and it is the most important element of a drawing as it provides good structure. Accurately combining colours and understanding how colours and tones relate to one another are essential skills for an artist.

The colour wheel

Every colour in the universe is made up of three primary colours: red, yellow and blue. You can mix every other colour from just these three colours.

Orange, green and violet are secondary colours, and are created by mixing two equal parts of the primary colours: for example, orange is made of red and yellow.

The next set of colours is called the tertiaries. The six tertiary colours are made up of equal parts of one primary and one secondary colour. For instance, blue (primary) plus green (secondary) make a blue-green tertiary.

Together, the three primary, three secondary and six tertiary colours create the colour wheel (see right), a basic tool for combining colours.

Other helpful properties of colour are hues, tints, shades and tones. A colour in its natural state is called local colour or a pure hue. The addition of white to a colour changes that colour to a tint. Adding black changes the colour to a shade and creates a darker value. If both black and white are added, then a tone is created; this creates a greyer version of the colour.

I created this colour wheel using the primary, secondary and tertiary colours. The outer ring is the pure hue, the next is the tint and the third is the shade. The inner circle is each colour combined with its complementary colour directly across the colour wheel. Notice how their dark tones are livelier than the shades.

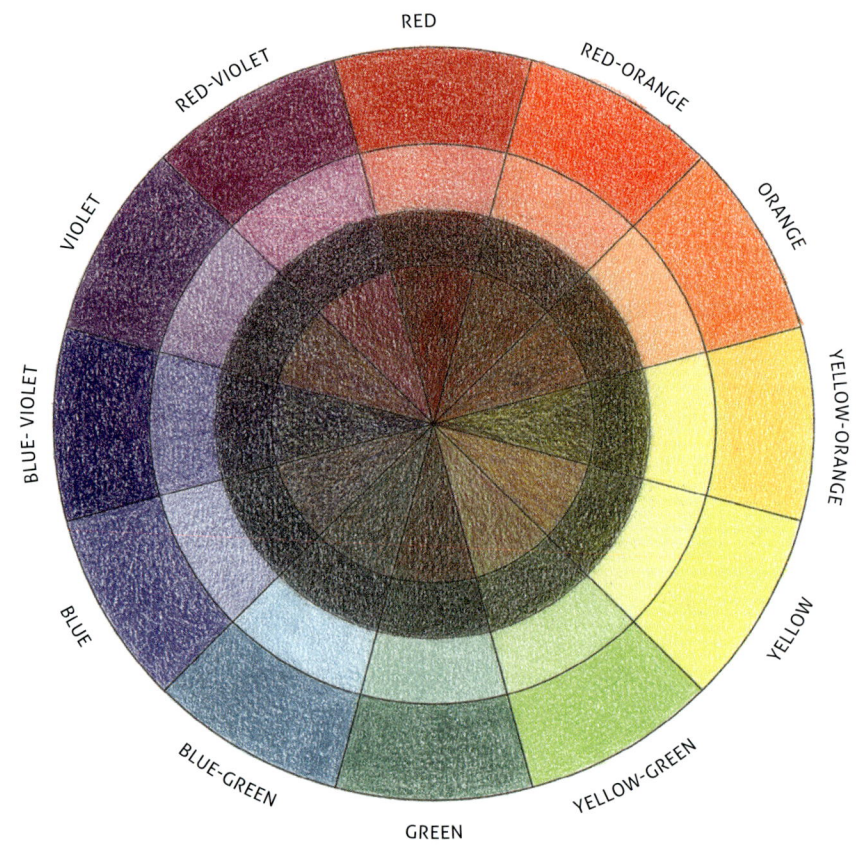

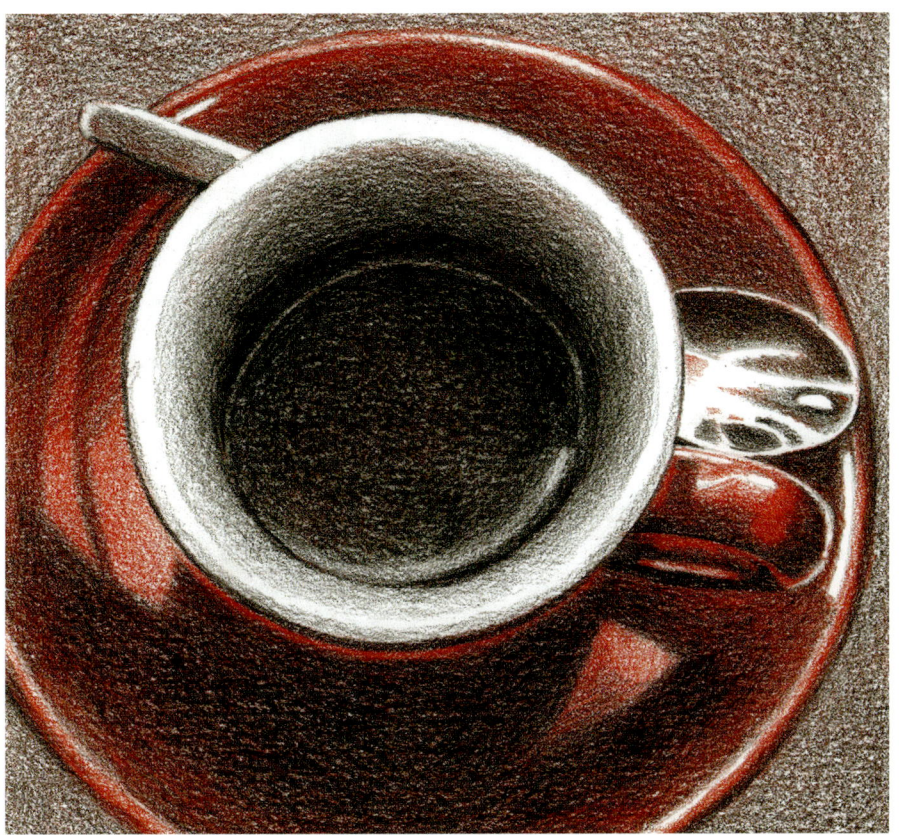

LEFT *Monochromatic drawing with one colour: red, with black and white.*

A

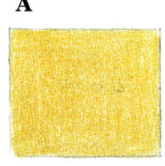
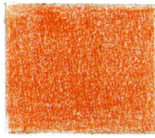

LEFT *Warm colour scheme with three analogous colours: yellow, orange and red.*

B

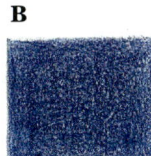
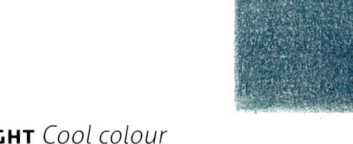

RIGHT *Cool colour scheme with three analogous colours in blue, blue green and green.*

Colour temperature

Another characteristic of colour is temperature. Colours can be considered warm (**A**) or cool (**B**). Warm colours have red, orange or yellow present and cool colours contain green, blue and violet. However, it is also possible to have a warm blue or a cool red. If a little of a warm colour is mixed with blue, it will become warmer; and the same principles apply if a bit of a cool colour is added to red.

Colour temperature can create a mood as well as depth: warm colours come forwards, while cool colours recede. This is especially helpful when painting objects in the distance. We will learn more about colour temperature in the Flower Burst project (see page 222), where the overall colour temperature is warm.

Colour schemes

Colour is all about relationships and creating an overall colour harmony in a drawing. Putting colours together can be exciting, but sometimes it's difficult to know where to begin. Different types of colour formulas can be created using colour, and here are a few to try. One type, the easiest to begin with, is a monochromatic colour scheme (see top, left). This means using variations of one colour only. The colour can be modified by adding black and/or white to create tints, shades and tones, and will vary the intensity of the colour. This type of colour scheme is rather subtle and unified, and is a good way to learn about tones and contrasts.

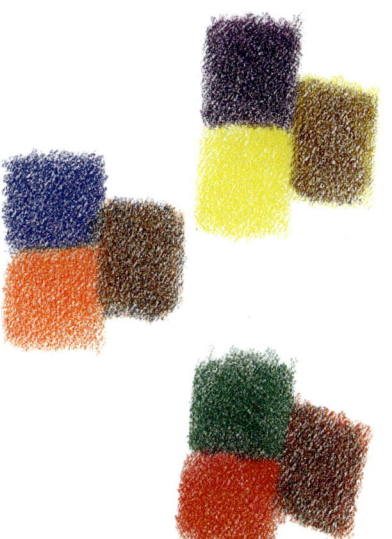

RIGHT *Complementary colours next to each other and then mixed together.*

Another type of colour scheme is the analogous colour scheme (see right), which involves using two or three colours that are adjacent to one another on the colour wheel. An example would be green, blue-green and blue, and the intensity of each colour can be varied with black and white. This type of colour scheme works well because the neighbouring colours create a colour harmony.

The strongest colour schemes use complementary colours. Complementary colours are directly across from each other on the colour wheel. For instance, red and green, blue and orange, and yellow and violet are complementary colours. When complementary colours are placed next to each other, they create energy and movement. When a colour is mixed or layered with its complements, the result is a greyer or neutral version of the colour.

Tonal values

One of the most important principles in art is learning and understanding the tonal values on the value scale. I always tell my students that value is more important than colour, as it forms the structure of the artwork. A good range of tonal values helps create space, illusion and atmosphere.

The value scale consists of a series of greys ranging from white to black (see far right) and is used to determine the relationships between light and dark in a scene or subject. We see light on a subject first, but as the subject turns away from the light, or falls into shadow, it becomes darker and creates a range of values. We see form through light and dark in values. Using a full range of values in a drawing will make it visually more exciting; using a limited range of value will create a unified drawing but can lack energy and vitality.

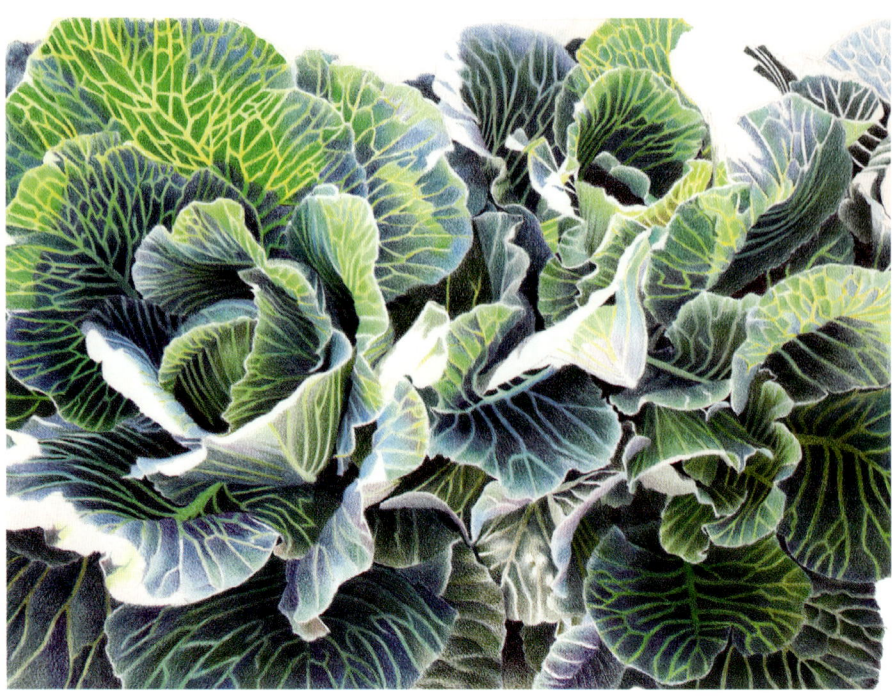

ABOVE *This drawing (above) of colourful cabbages was created by focusing on cool colours in an analogous colour palette.*

BELOW *I created a value scale of ten tonal values ranging from black to white (right). Using these, I then made a small drawing to show how tonal values produce form and structure (below).*

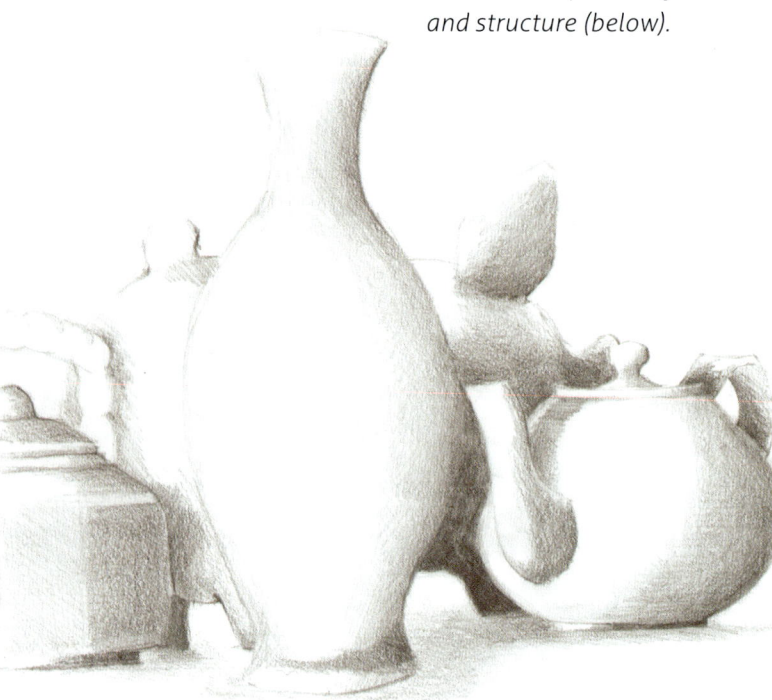

One way to better understand and train your eye to see value would be to shine a light on a white object and study how the light moves across the surface. The object will have the lightest value where the light is closest. Notice how the values darken as the object turns away from the light. The area of your object that is furthest from the light will have the darkest value.

Colour and mood

Not only is colour a way to describe what we see, it can also be manipulated by the artist and used to create a mood or emotional response. A brightly coloured drawing using light tonal values is considered high-key (see right) and will evoke a feeling of happiness or a light, airy feeling. A drawing using darker valued colours is considered low-key (see below) and will evoke feelings of quiet, mystery or drama.

As you work on the projects in this chapter, you will begin to understand more about colours and values. A colour's value, intensity and temperature are affected by everything around it. A coloured pencil drawing is affected by the colour or tint of the drawing surface, which will alter the value, intensity and temperature of each colour layered on that surface.

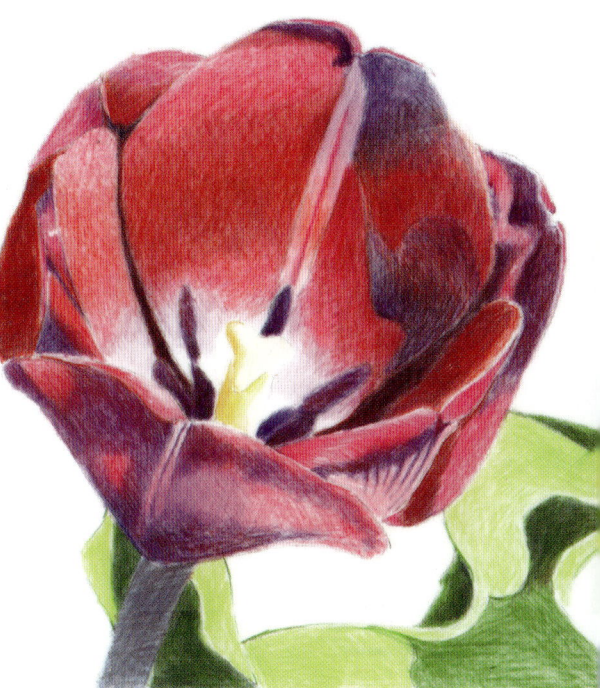

RIGHT *High-key drawing of a brightly coloured tulip: light, airy and consisting of vivid colour.*

BELOW *Low-key drawing of a dark, dramatic scene drawn on black paper with overall dark tones.*

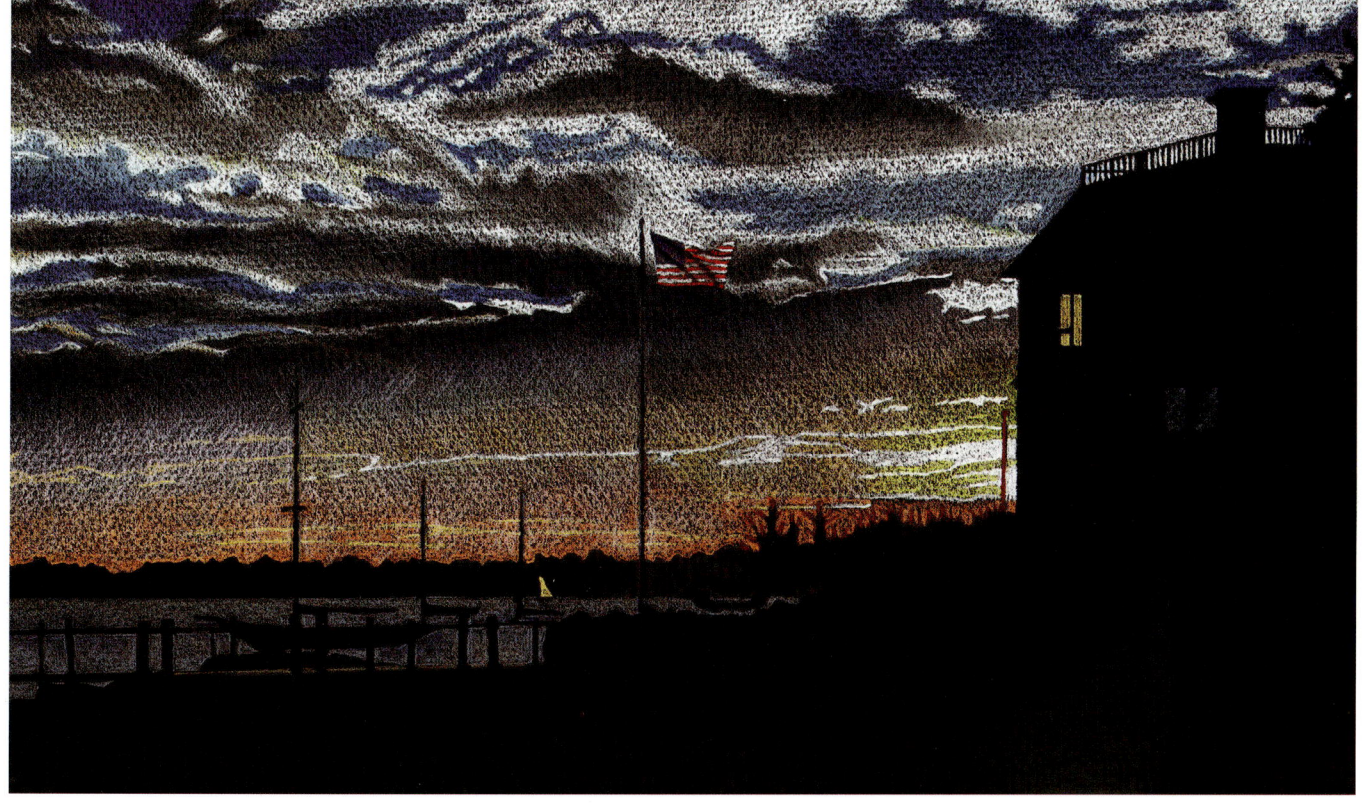

Basic Techniques

Varieties of colour and strokes are developed by making marks and layering with coloured pencil. These and other fundamental techniques will help you learn to create your own style of coloured pencil drawing.

Making marks

Pencil strokes can be made in any shape, direction, thickness and strength. With light pressure you can allow the texture of the paper to show through and heavier pressure will fill in the paper's fine indentations, creating a solid appearance.

To build up colour, begin with a sharp point on your coloured pencil and apply short, even strokes to the paper, placing them close together. Press lightly and build colour slowly – if you press too hard and saturate the tooth of the paper, it will be difficult to add more layers of coloured pencil.

Turn the paper and continue to apply more strokes in a cross-hatch form (**A**). Applying strokes in different directions will smooth out the surface and blend any visible directional lines. You can apply different colours in the same manner, working from light to dark and keeping each layer light and blended.

Layering colours

Unlike paints that are mixed on a palette, coloured pencils are mixed on the paper by adding layers of colour (**B**). One colour on the paper can look flat, but two or more colours layered together can create a third colour (**C**)

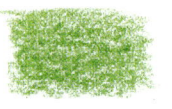

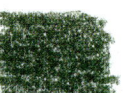
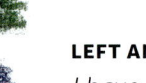

B

LEFT AND BELOW
I have layered the five colours on the left, and because the pencil is translucent, the bottom layers show though the top ones (see below).

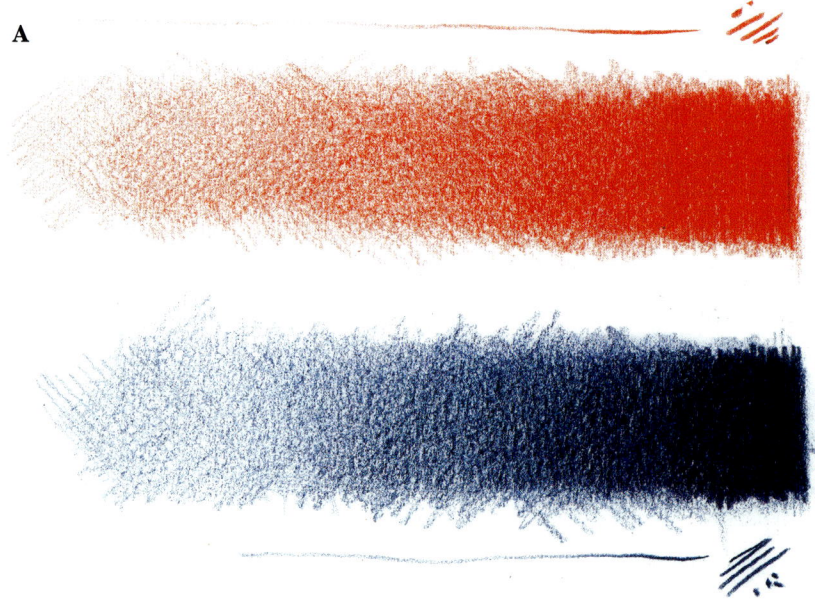

A

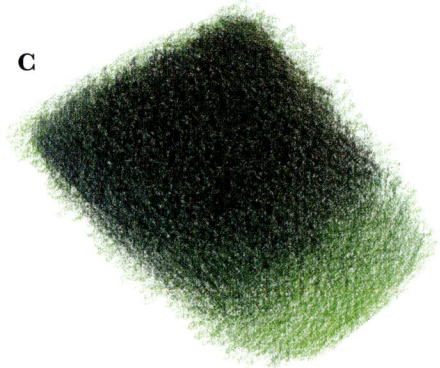

C

LEFT *The red and blue areas are examples of different types of pressure, ranging from light (left) to heavy (right). Keep your strokes small and close together.*

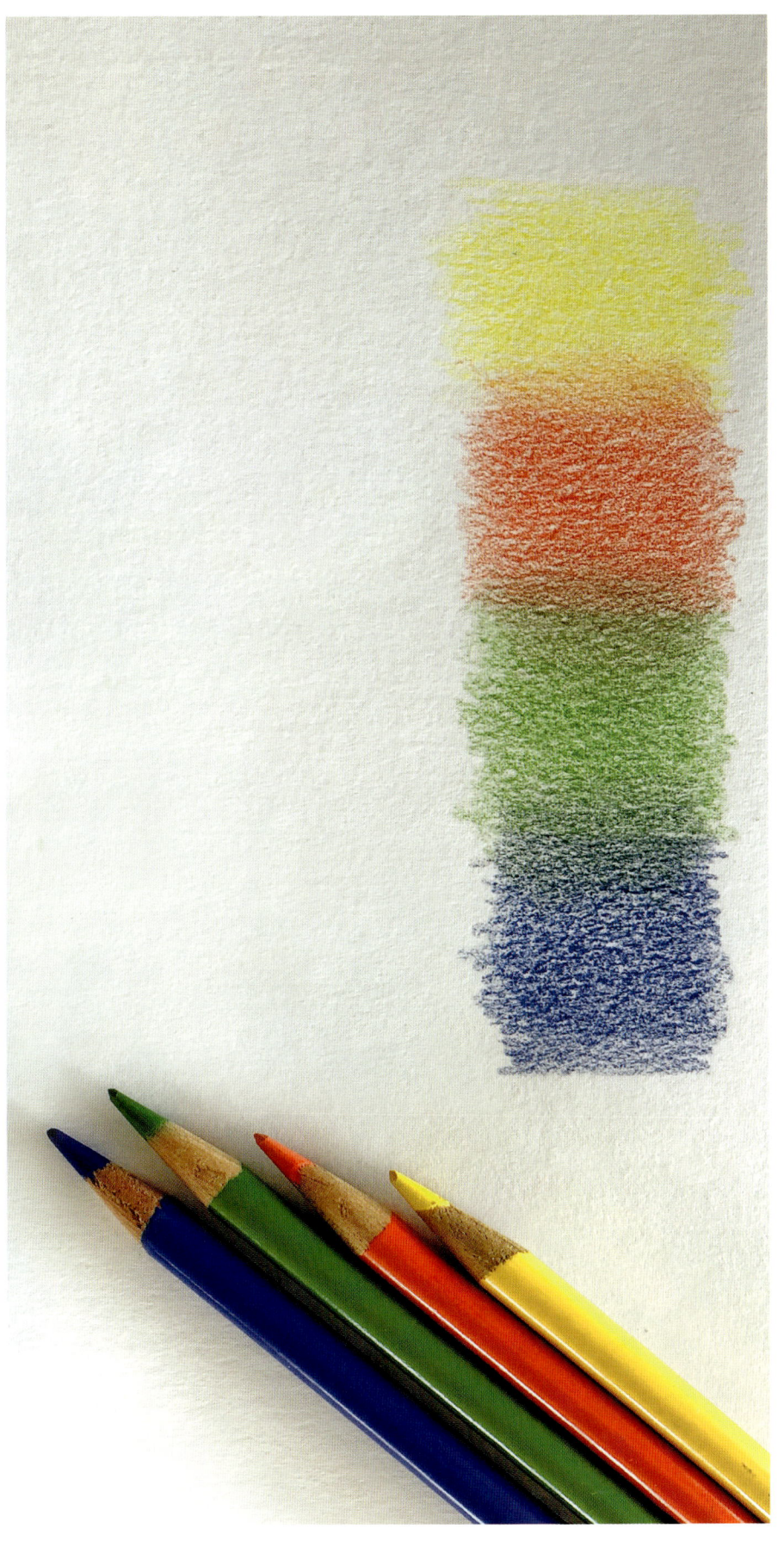

LEFT *Lay colours side by side and softly blend the edges together by using a light pressure.*

and show greater depth and vibrancy. Each layer of colour is influenced by the coloured layers beneath it, as well as the colour or tone of the paper surface you are working on.

Keeping layers light helps make erasing or changing colour easier. If too much pressure is applied in early layers, the tooth of the paper will be saturated, making it difficult to add additional layers. Experiment with different pencil pressures, layering colours and trying different paper surfaces.

As you progress with the layering, you can increase the pressure on the pencil. Continue to blend by cross-hatching and layering until you achieve the colours and tonal values you want to achieve (see page 196).

Optical mixing

Juxtaposing colour, known as optical mixing, means to put two colours side by side, instead of layering them, to allow the viewer's eyes to blend them optically. It's a much quicker method of creating colour and value than layering, and you'll find more information on this in the Flower Burst project on pages 222–7.

Tip
Coloured pencils are translucent so you will be able to see the surface of the paper through the layers.

Burnishing

The technique of burnishing involves applying heavy pressure with a tool in order to blend layers of coloured pencil. This ensures none of the paper texture shows through and creates a shiny, smooth appearance. The effect gives a rich lustre and results in a painterly look. Burnishing can be done with a colourless blender pencil (**A**), small stiff bristle brush (**B**), paper-blending stump (tortillon) or another coloured pencil (**C**). Be sure to use clean pencils, brush and paper stump for each colour burnished. Burnishing will be included in many of the projects in this chapter.

Painting with pencils

Water can be added to watercolour pencils, and solvent, such as odourless mineral spirits, can be added to wax-based coloured pencils to dissolve the wax. Both techniques allow the pigment to flow like paint and create a rich painterly effect. Adding water to watercolour pencils (**D**) will make the colours transparent and more vibrant. Adding solvent to wax-based coloured pencils will deepen colours and cause them to be more opaque (**E**).

A painterly technique can be helpful when creating an underpainting – a layer of colour or tone that serves as a base foundation for a drawing. It's also helpful for drawing backgrounds or for building colour quickly. Use a small soft brush for applying water or solvent to a layer of coloured pencil and work small areas. Additional layers of pencil can be added over the solvent when dry, or added to watercolour while it is still wet or after it has dried.

For more information about adding solvent to wax-based colour pencils, see the Toffee Apples project on page 242–7.

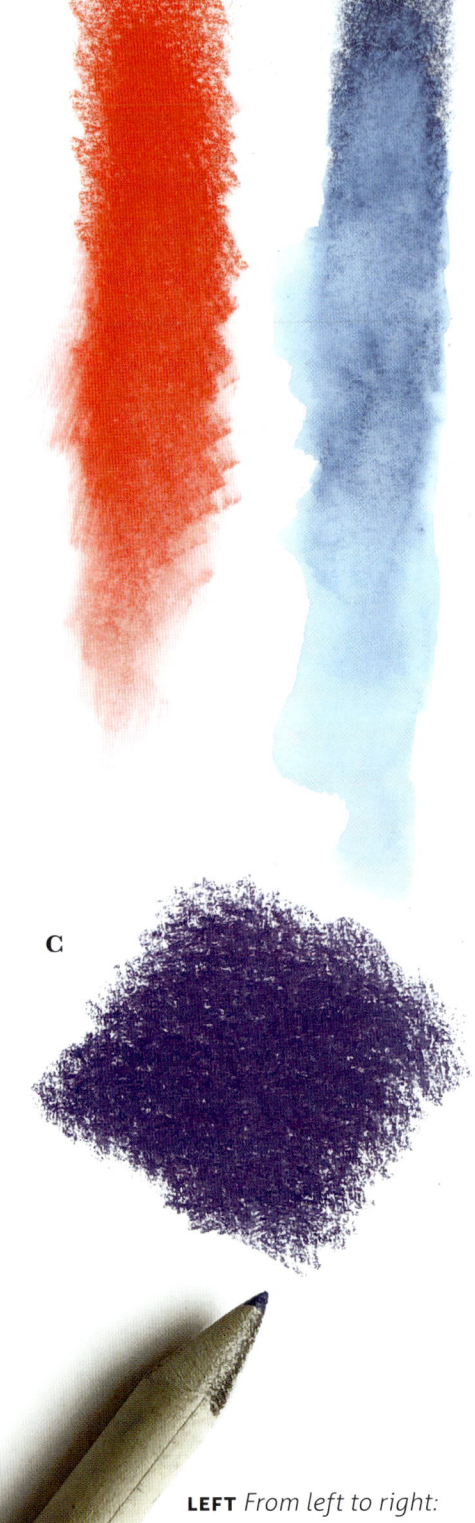

Tip
To avoid contamination of lighter colours, burnish light colours first.

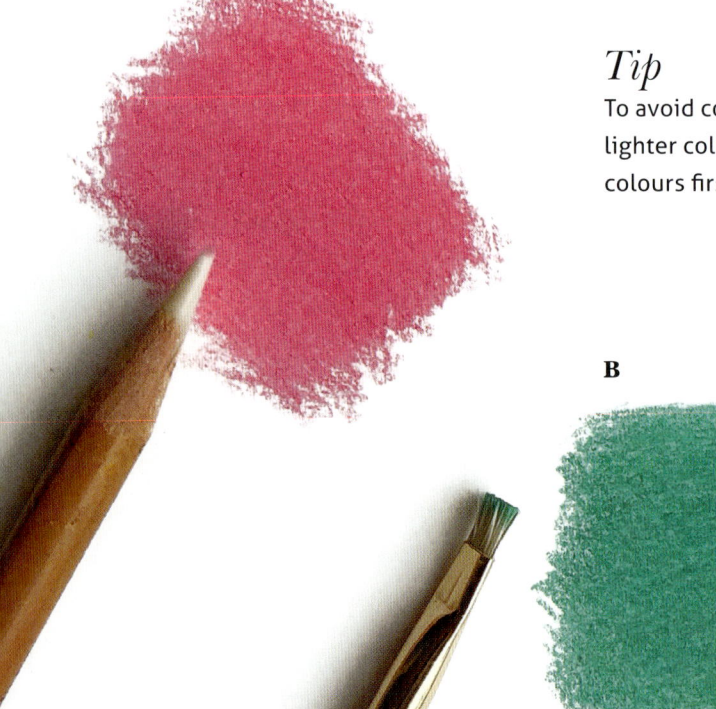

LEFT *From left to right: blender pencil, small bristle brush and paper-blending stump.*

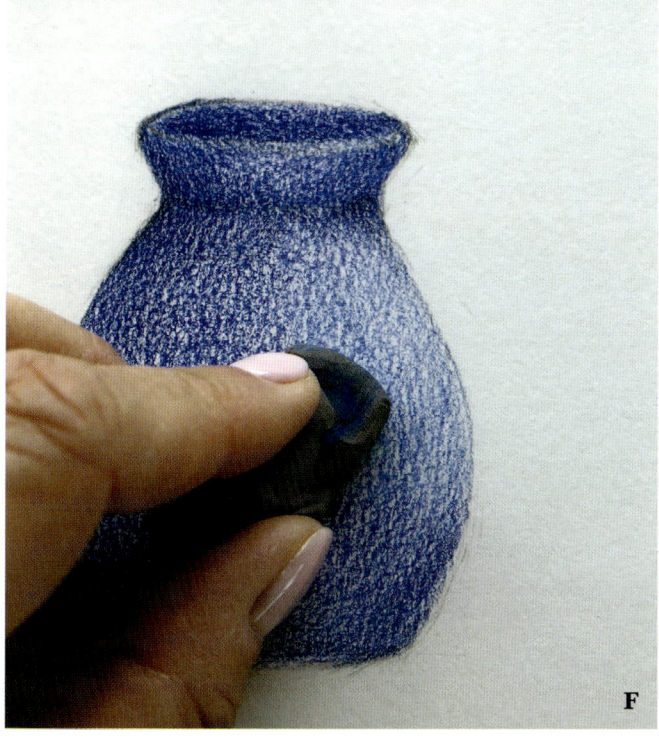

F

LEFT *Here I have lightened the right side of the vase and also highlighted the area around the rim.*

Erasing and lifting out colour

There are various erasing materials (see page 192) and different techniques for removing or lifting coloured pencil. With a kneaded eraser, you can lightly dab it on areas of colour to lift top layers and leave bottom layers intact (**F**). Note that when the colour particles adhere to the eraser, it will need to be re-kneaded in order to absorb the colour before moving to another area, otherwise they will transfer to the drawing surface.

With a battery-operated eraser, eraser pencil or mechanical pen-style eraser, you can lift fine lines and areas of colour. This is especially good for creating highlights and cleaning up edges.

Take care when erasing so as to avoid damaging the paper surface or texture. Test an eraser on a small area or scrap paper first to ensure it is the correct method for your drawing.

Sgraffito

The sgraffito technique involves scratching away the top layer of colour to expose a lower layer or the paper surface. You can use a small utility knife to do this (**G**). Keep the knife at an angle and scrape the surface lightly to avoid damaging the paper. An embossing tool will allow you to create an impressed line and leave areas of the paper visible. This technique is useful when creating animal whiskers, hairs or veins in a leaf. We'll learn more about this tool while working on the Portrait of a Pet project (see page 236–41).

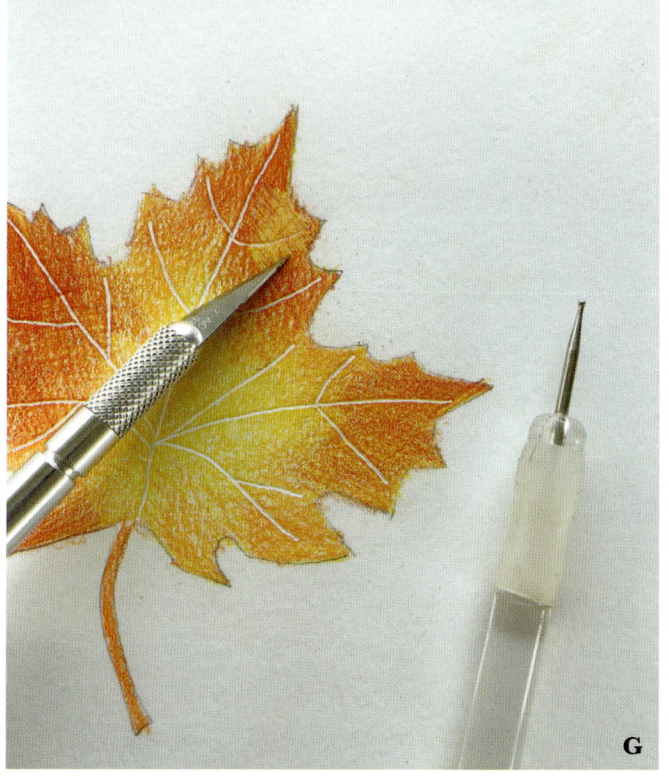

G

LEFT *Here I am using a utility knife to scrape off top layers of coloured pencil. I also used the embossing tool to impress lines into the paper where the leaf veins will remain white.*

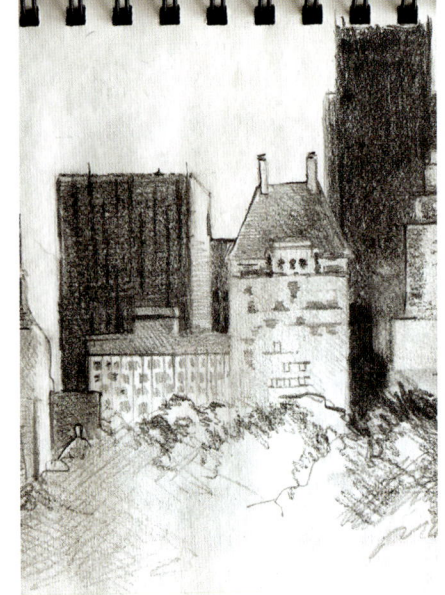

Sketching and Composition

Sketching on paper is good practice when putting ideas and subjects together for a drawing, while composition involves arranging visual elements so that everything works together as a whole and keeps viewers engaged. Both these techniques will be invaluable when composing your work of art.

My new students often say on their first day of class, 'I can't even draw a straight line!' And my answer is, 'Neither can I!' The shapes we draw consist of a series of curved, angled or straight lines that we evaluate, erase, redraw and sketch some more. I always begin my drawing with a graphite pencil unless I'm working on a dark surface, in which case I use an erasable white pencil in order to see my pencil marks.

BELOW *I use transfer paper to transfer my initial sketch onto good drawing paper. I'm using white transfer paper here so that I'll be able to see the lines on the dark red surface.*

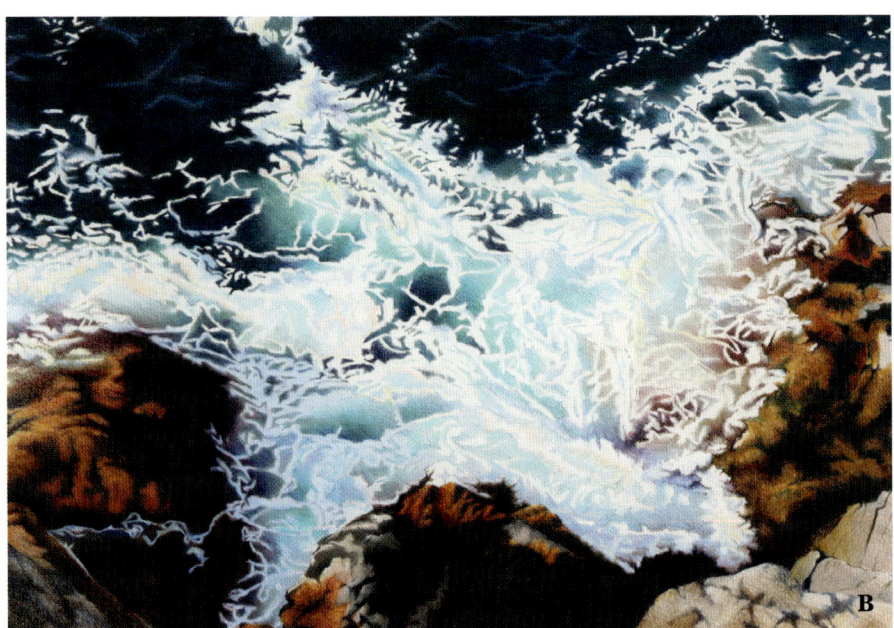

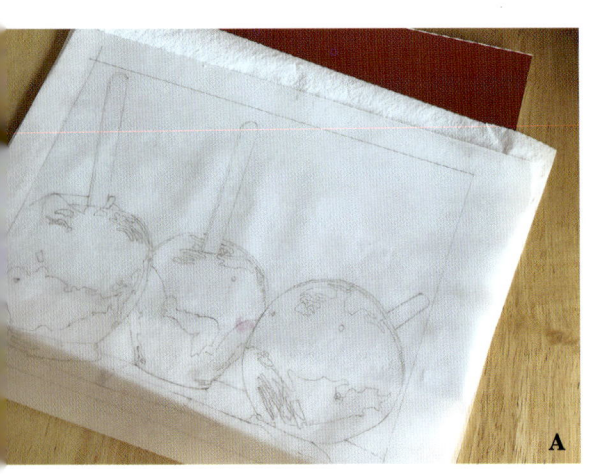

I often start on sketch paper by drawing lightly with graphite pencil to allow for alterations and erasing. I draw the shapes and outlines, then fill in the characteristics and details. As my composition is finalized and I am satisfied, I will transfer it to good drawing paper using tracing paper and/ or graphite transfer paper (**A**).

The most important first step before even making a mark on the paper is to really study the object(s) or scene you want to draw. Decide what interests you most about the subject and how

Here the use of line depicts the white foam of the surf. The texture of the surf contrasts with that of the rocks surrounding it.

you would like to portray it. Observe the shapes, their proportions, how the shapes relate to one another, their details and textures (**B**). Also look at positive space and negative space (**C**). Simplify your beginning sketch by developing and placing large shapes and forms where you want them on the page, then add the details later.

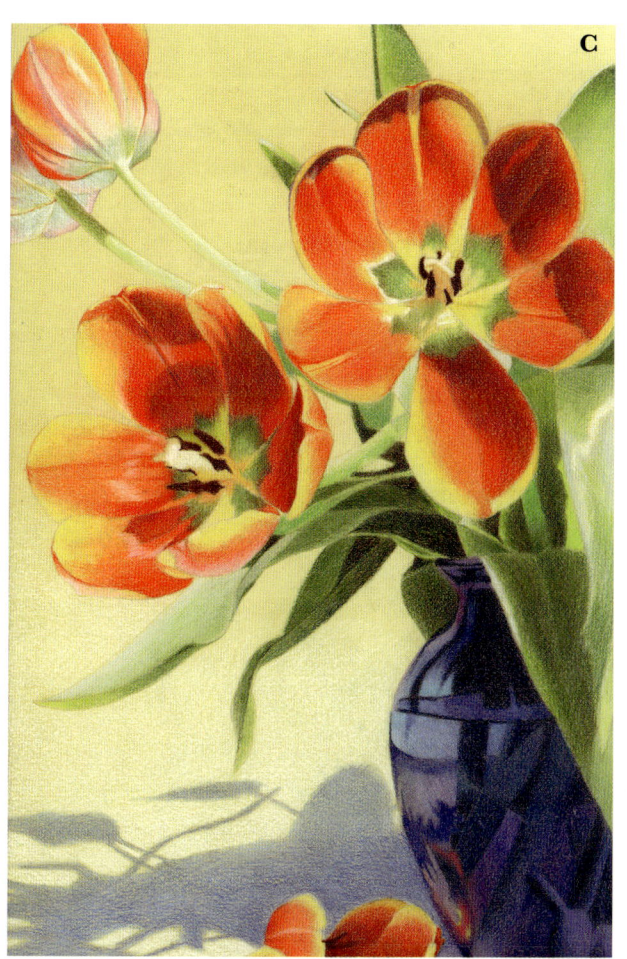

C

Small tonal value sketches can be very useful when beginning a drawing (**D**). I often create a quick sketch of my subject with graphite pencils, placing just three tonal values – light, medium and dark. This allows me to evaluate the design and make adjustments to light and dark areas, form and composition before adding colours.

LEFT *This drawing of tulips contains some interesting negative spaces and illustrates different textures between the tulips and the vase.*

BELOW *Compositional sketch drawn while in New York City that shows tonal value, space, line, shape and texture.*

Tip

I plan my drawing out in graphite pencil and then erase or lighten graphite lines, because once coloured pencil is added, you won't be able to erase the graphite.

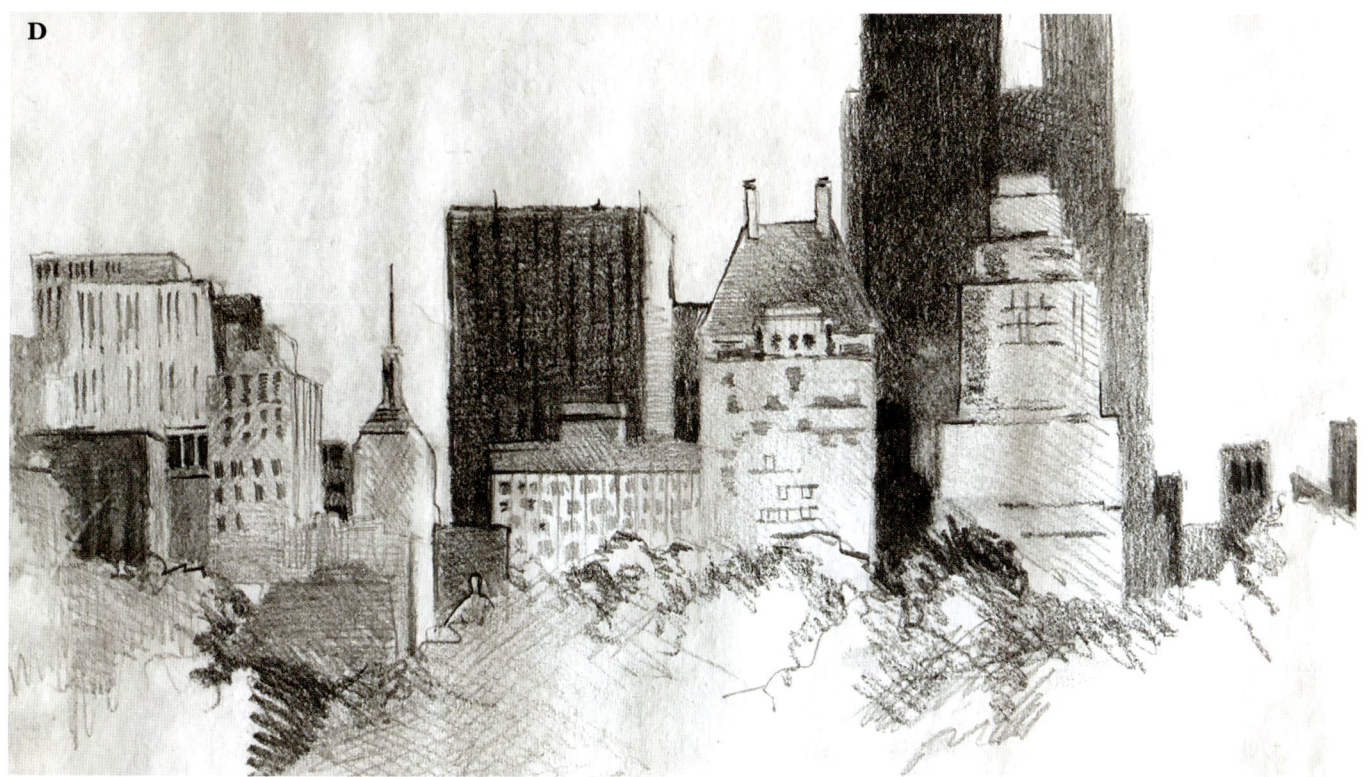

D

Elements of composition

If you want your picture to have a successful impact on viewers, you will need to create a strong composition. Several design elements are used to arrange the subject(s) in a pleasing way, and an artist will strive to make them all work harmoniously to give a sense of unity. The ability to see and understand these elements will help you produce a great drawing and composition, so let's look at each of them in turn.

BELOW *In this drawing, the use of line creates a circular motion and leads the viewer's eye around the page.*

SIZE

When beginning a drawing, the first choice is to decide on the size of the subject to determine its importance. Will it be life-sized, larger or smaller? Placement on the page is also important. If the subject is centred on the page, it will show stability and balance. Cropping the sides or moving the subject off-centre creates visual interest.

COLOUR

To create colour harmony in a drawing, see pages 194–5.

SPACE

Space is about the relationship between positive space and negative space. Positive space is the subject or subjects you are drawing. Negative space is the space within, between and around the subjects, and helps balance the composition: too much negative space can make a drawing feel empty, while too little may cause it to look crowded.

SHAPE

All subjects are made up of basic shapes or forms that relate to each other in the drawing. Variety in shapes will lead the viewer's eye around the drawing.

LINE

Line creates activity or motion in the composition and suggests the direction of movement. Lines that are angled or

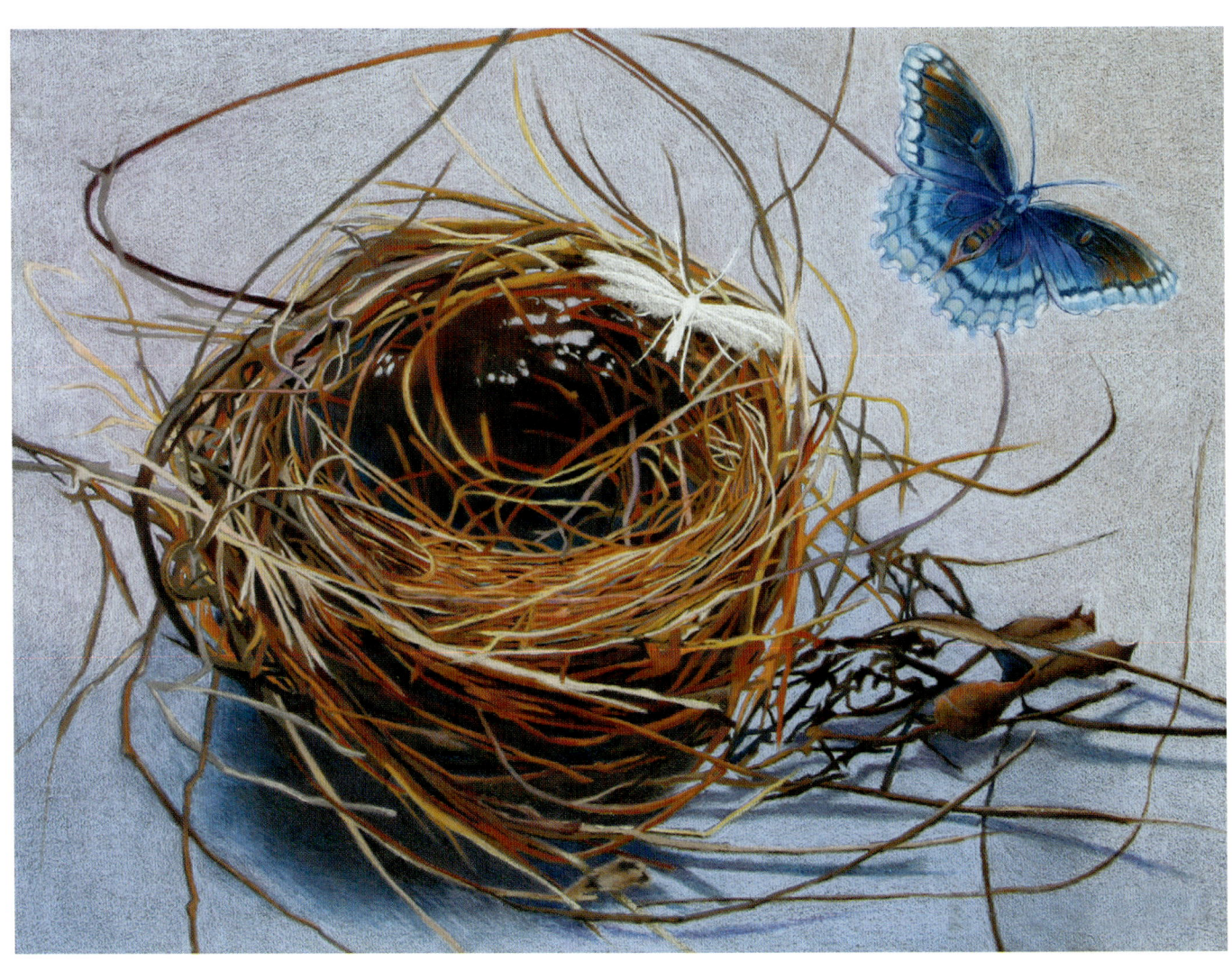

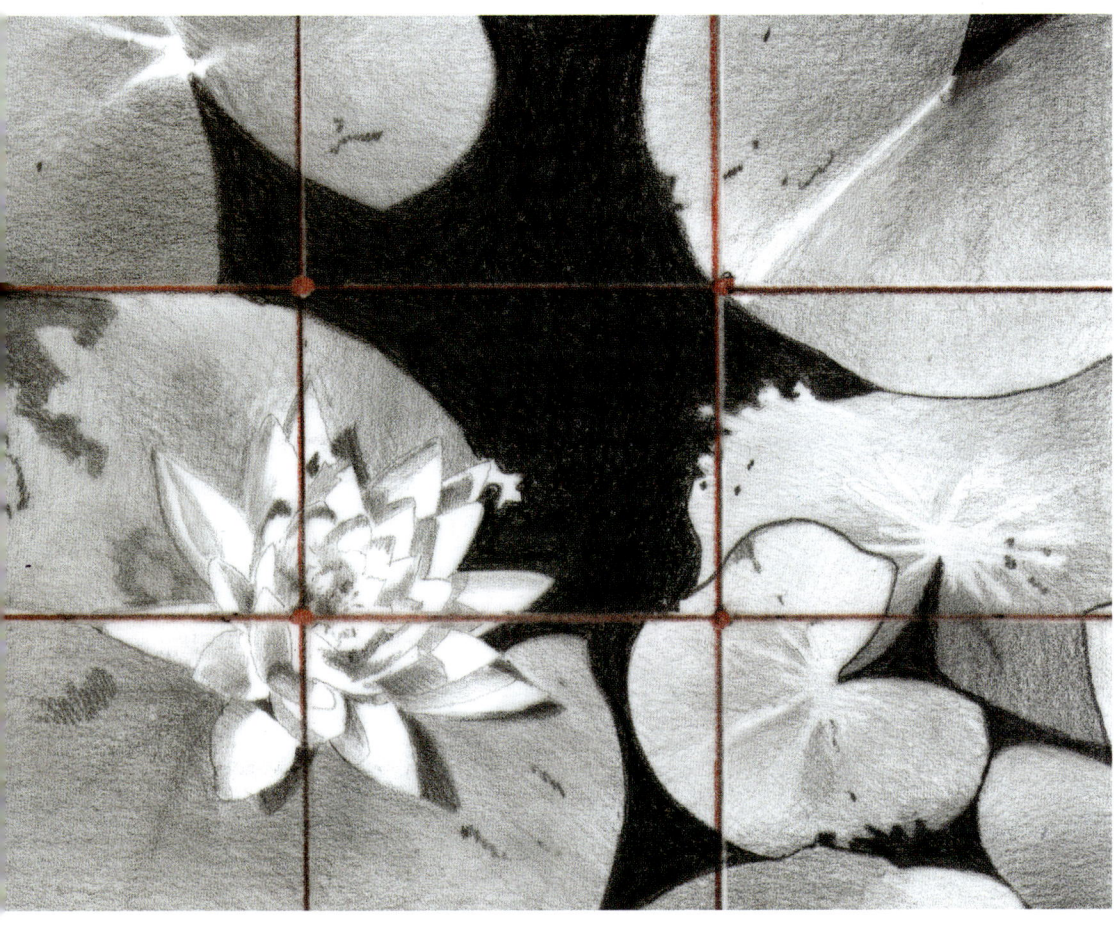

LEFT *In the rule of thirds, the picture plane is divided into a grid. Important subjects are positioned on the lines or where they meet.*

curved add visual interest and movement around the drawing. Horizontal lines imply tranquillity and rest, while vertical lines suggest power and strength. A contour line is the outline or silhouette of an object or figure. It helps build dimension and show changes within an object.

MOOD

Mood is when the artist elicits an emotional response from the viewer through elements such as lighting, colour or compositional design.

TEXTURE

Texture refers to the surface of objects – for example, they may be smooth, rough or shiny. We vary textures and patterns in subjects or elements to create visual interest.

TONAL VALUE

A drawing should have a full range of tonal values, from light to dark, in order to create good contrast. Light shapes will come forwards and dark shapes recede. A darker area next to a very light area will stand out and attract the viewer's eye. See page 196 for further information.

Together, these design elements create the focal point of a composition – the main subject or centre of interest that pulls the viewer's eye into the drawing and leads it around. The focal point can be an important feature, an area of high contrast, or a form or shape that stands out from the others. Without a focal point, your drawing may have no real direction or purpose.

A popular way to help place focal points and compose an interesting composition is the rule of thirds. This involves dividing an image into nine equal parts using two horizontal lines and two vertical lines, as shown in the image above. Focal points are then placed along the lines or at the intersections. In landscape or seascape drawings, positioning the horizon line above or below the centre of the picture plane will make it more interesting.

Tip
A good composition keeps the viewer's eye moving around the drawing. Colour, light, line and shape are all ways to achieve this.

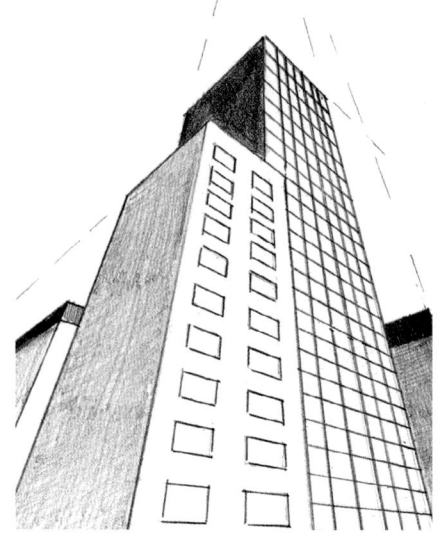

Perspective

Perspective is a technique used for creating the illusion of depth and distance. It gives a drawing form and conveys space. Perspective refers to the art of making two-dimensional objects appear three-dimensional. It is a fundamental concept that needs to be understood in order to create the illusion of space and realistic, believable scenes.

Artists use a variety of perspective techniques to create the illusion of depth and distance.

One-point perspective shows things converging towards a single vanishing point, becoming smaller as they recede into the distance. Two- and three-point perspectives are better for adding realism. Aerial or atmospheric perspective establishes a foreground, middle ground and background in a picture to create a sense of depth.

Basic or linear perspective is where parallel lines appear to meet as they get further towards the horizon, where they disappear. The point at which the lines meet is called the vanishing point.

One-point perspective

In one-point perspective (**A**), lines converge towards a single vanishing point on the horizon line. Objects appear smaller as they get further away, giving a sense of depth and distance. An example would be if you were to look directly down a long straight road. Practising one-point perspective is a good way to learn and become familiar with perspective.

RIGHT *One-point perspective shows how elements appear to get smaller as they move further away.*

Two-point perspective

Two-point perspective (**B**) has two vanishing points, which are usually outside your actual drawing and far away from the scene. Two-point perspective is helpful for drawing geometric objects and buildings that are somewhat far away when looking at them straight on.

Three-point perspective

Three-point perspective (**C**) is used for a more extreme view from a very low or very high vantage point. It uses two vanishing points on the horizon line and a third point either above or below the horizon. Three-point perspective can create the illusion of height or depth in a subject.

A

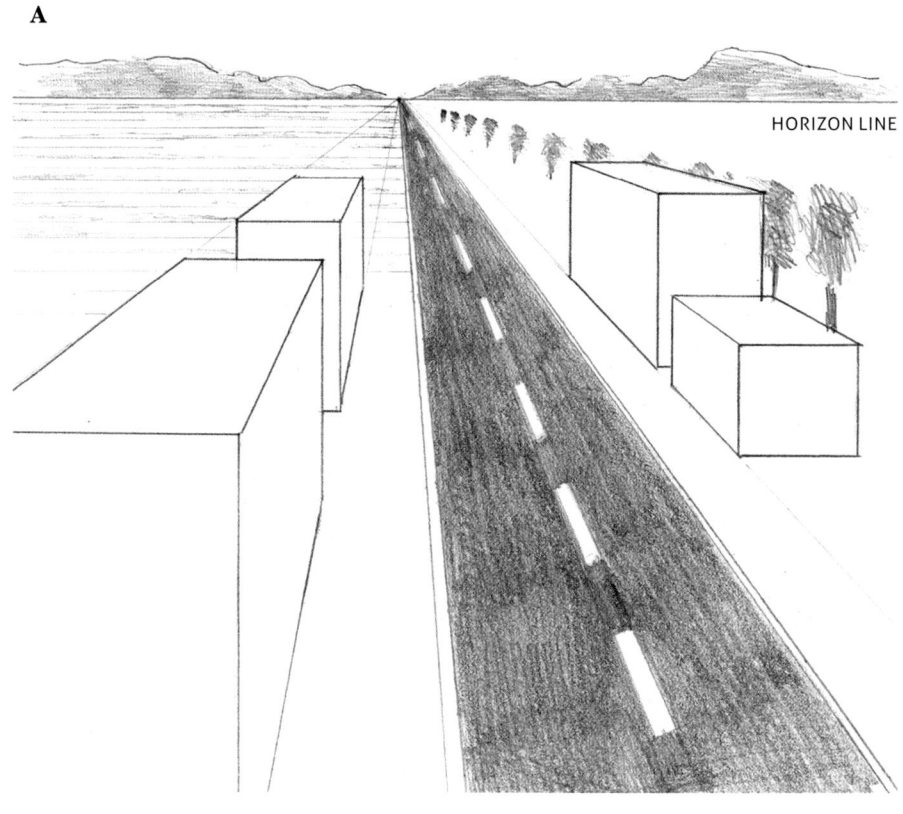

HORIZON LINE

B

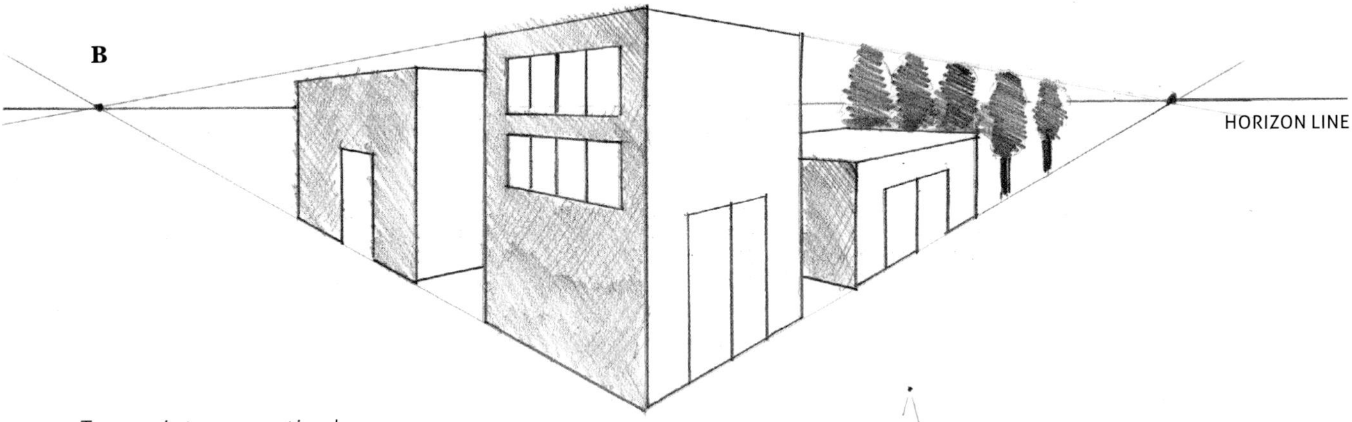

HORIZON LINE

ABOVE *Two-point perspective has two vanishing points from your point of view, and helps to create realistic geometric objects.*

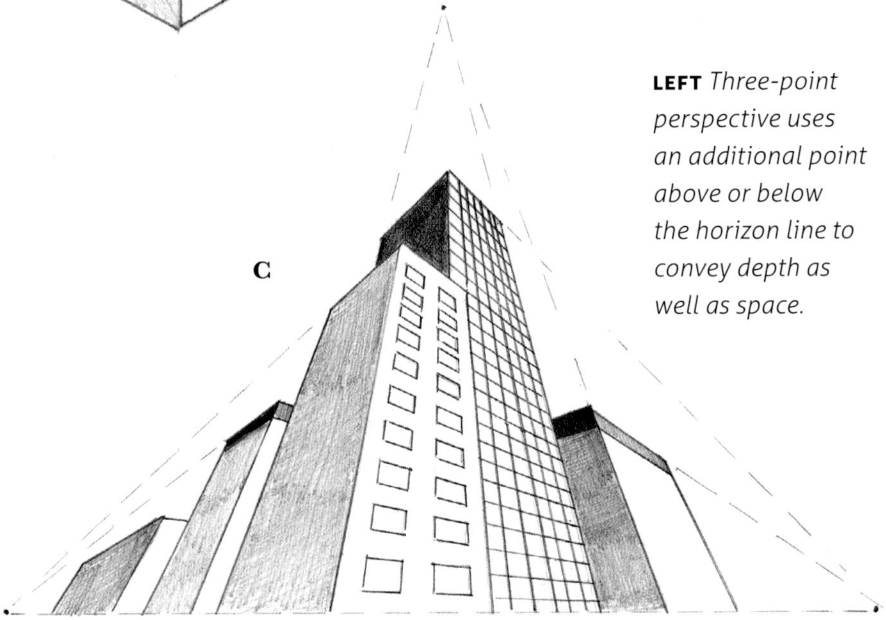

LEFT *Three-point perspective uses an additional point above or below the horizon line to convey depth as well as space.*

C

HORIZON LINE

Aerial or atmospheric perspective

Aerial or atmospheric perspective creates a sense of depth by establishing a foreground, middle ground and background in a picture (**D**). This is achieved by reducing the colour, clarity, tonal value and scale of objects in the distance. As they recede, they become smaller and less defined; colours become cooler and edges softer. Atmospheric perspective can add mood, beauty and drama to a scene such as a landscape, which you will learn more about in the Layering a Landscape project on pages 214–9.

Now we have learned about colour theory and fundamental drawing techniques, it's time to put this knowledge into practice and start working on the projects.

D

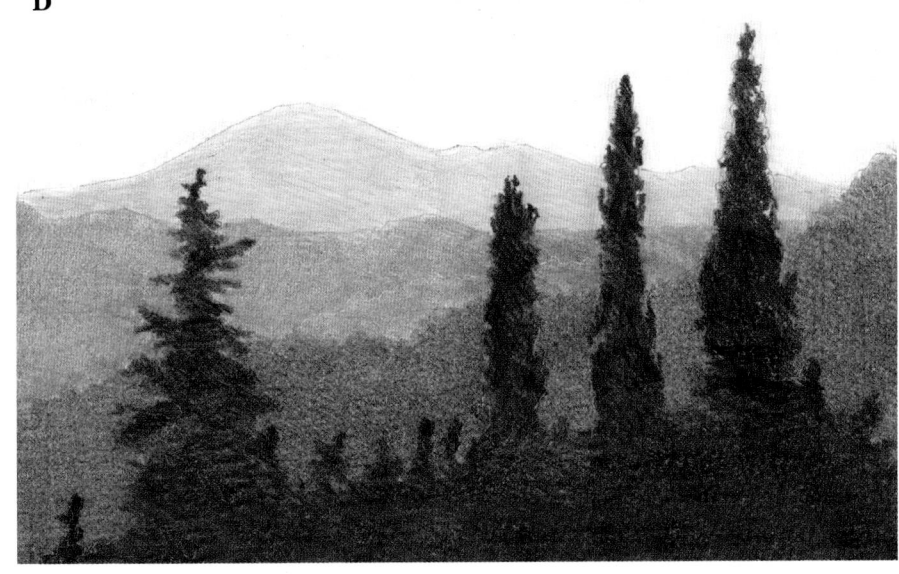

RIGHT *Atmospheric perspective conveys space or distance by modifying the colour, clarity and scale of objects so they appear to be further away.*

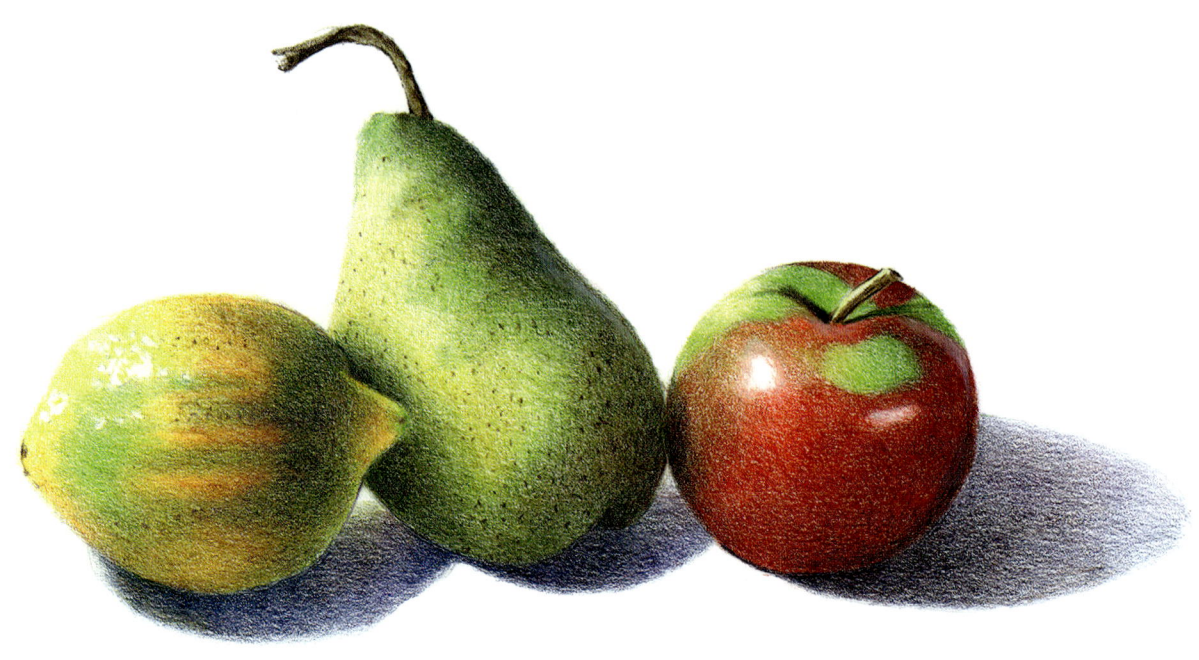

Fruit Still Life

This project will get you thinking about how best to arrange objects for a pleasing composition and will enable you to practise making realistic representations of simple three-dimensional shapes. It will also show you how to build up strength and harmony in colour tones as well as hint at highlights and reflections.

PENCILS USED: PRISMACOLOR

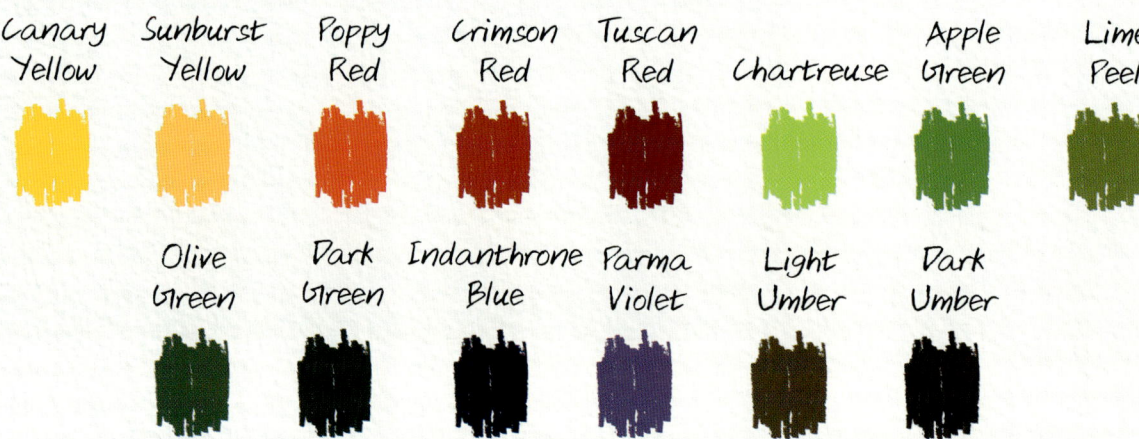

Canary Yellow	Sunburst Yellow	Poppy Red	Crimson Red	Tuscan Red	Chartreuse	Apple Green	Lime Peel
	Olive Green	Dark Green	Indanthrone Blue	Parma Violet	Light Umber	Dark Umber	

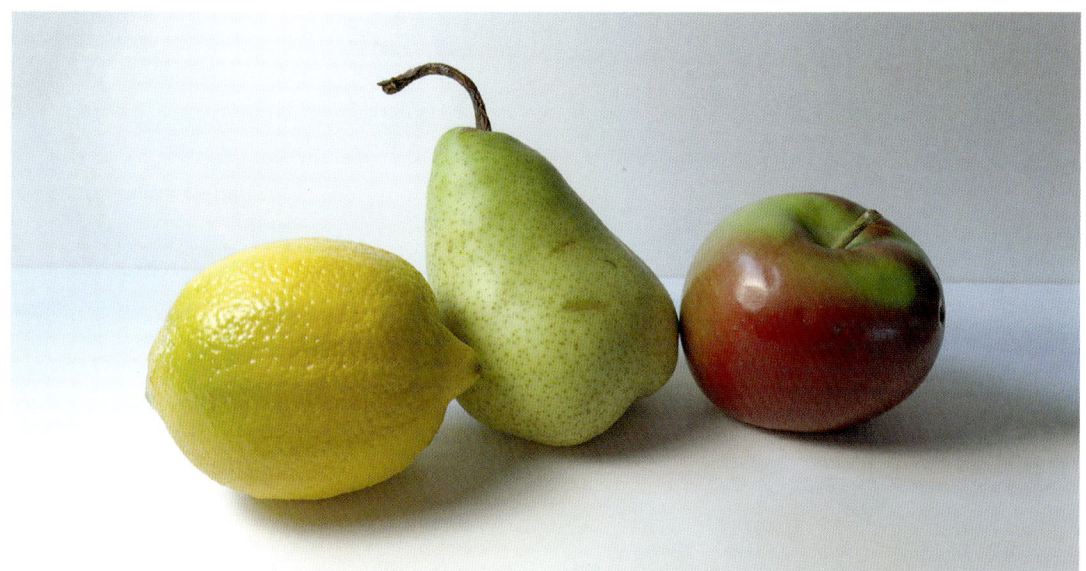

LEFT *Bring objects close together to unify the composition, with edges touching or overlapping.*

Working on a simple still life of a few objects is a good beginning for creating many other types of artwork. Still-life drawing will assist you in becoming more familiar with how to lay out a group of various objects on paper, and improve your ability to sketch the different shapes and add tone and colour so the objects have dimension and characteristics.

CHOOSING MATERIALS

I chose a traditional white drawing paper for this project. It is 100% cotton, which gives the paper a nice smooth texture to hold the colour. The paper is acid free and will retain its nice white colour for many years to come. I like to purchase a particular drawing paper by the sheet and then cut it to size.

I used Prismacolor pencils in this project because they work well with this particular type of paper. They are wax based and easily blended; I try to choose lightfast colours, but you can use similar colours in any brand you like.

PLANNING THE COMPOSITION

For this still life, I chose a grouping of three pieces of fruit. Odd numbers of subjects in a composition are more dynamic and create balance and visual harmony. This is because the eye and brain want to group objects in pairs, while an uneven number keeps the viewer's eye moving around the page.

I placed the fruit on a white surface with a white background to simplify the surroundings so that the fruit was the only point of focus. It also meant I could clearly see the colourful shadows they created. I positioned a light to shine on the left side of the still life so I could study the lights, darks and shadows cast, as well as the variety of colour, texture and pattern in the fruit.

ESTABLISHING TONAL VALUES

When you are grouping objects, it is good to be aware of the positive spaces they create, as well as the negative spaces within, between and around them. You might find it helpful to take a photo of the still life and convert it into a black-and-white image. This will make it easier to see the light, medium and dark tonal values without the colour interfering. A good range of tonal values will help to create dimension and depth in a drawing.

Tip
If using a photo for reference, convert it into black and white so you can see the range of tonal values in the composition.

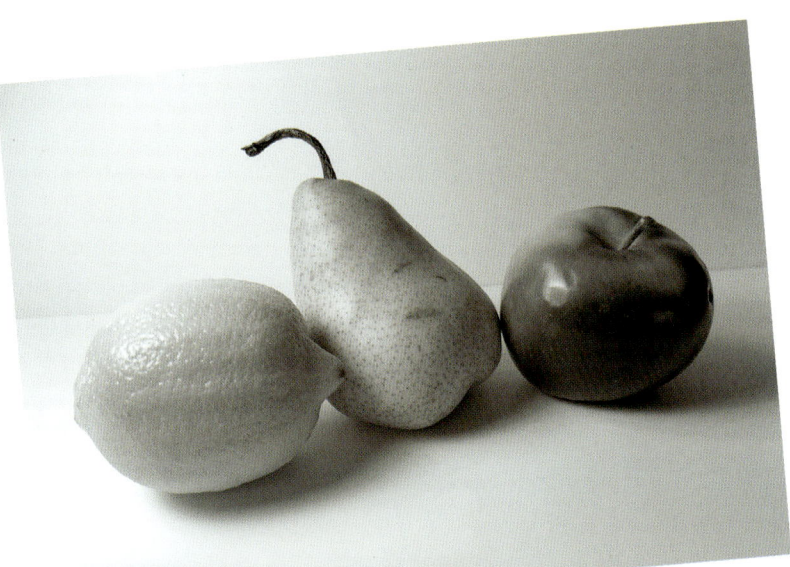

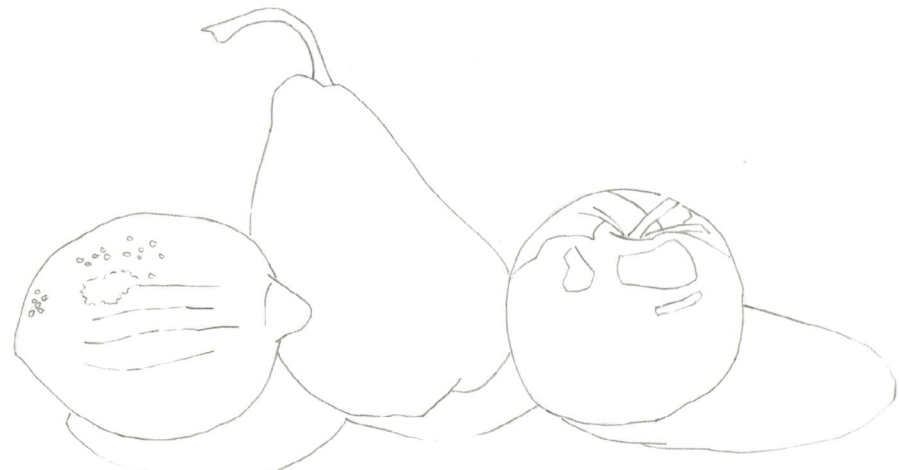

STAGE 1

Begin by drawing the shapes of the fruit and shadows, putting in details, markings, stems and white highlights for reference points. I have used darker graphite lines so they can be easily seen but I will lighten these with an eraser at a later stage.

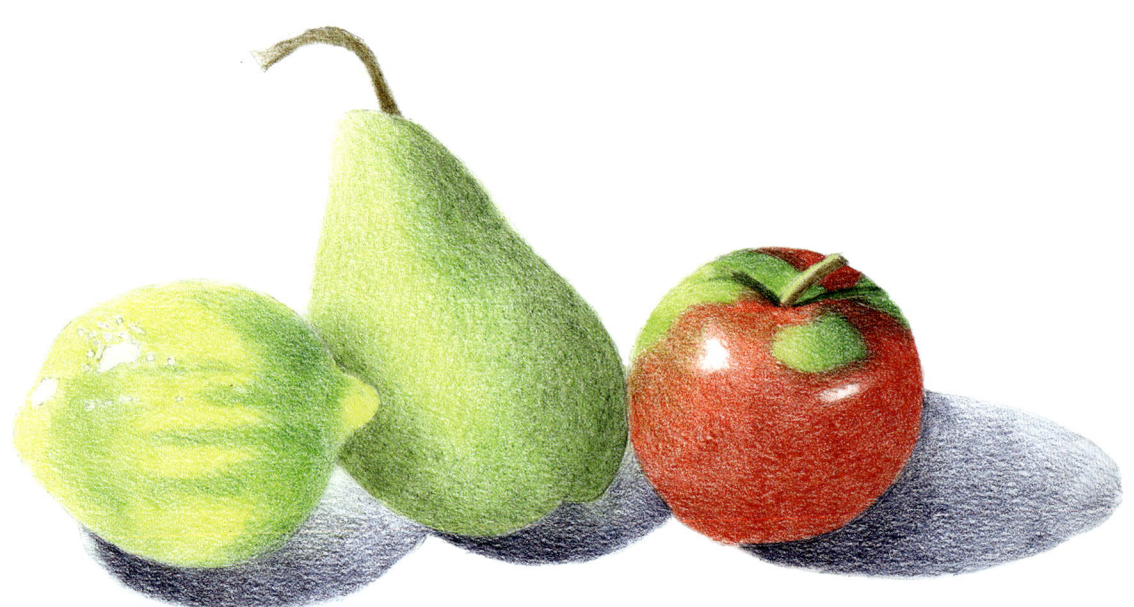

STAGE 2

Now you can block in base colours. Starting with the lemon, apply a light base of Canary Yellow, keeping your pencil strokes close together to create a smooth, even layer of colour. Add Chartreuse for the greenish tint that is on the left side and Apple Green on the right side of the lemon, near the point. Next, work on the pear, applying a light wash of colour using Chartreuse. Build tonal values with Apple Green and Lime Peel on the sides to show rounded form. Lightly colour the stem in Light Umber.

Moving on to the apple, apply Poppy Red, carefully working around the highlights you drew earlier. Add Crimson Red over Poppy Red on the right side of the apple and fade it out as it gets nearer to the light source. Apply Chartreuse and Apple Green to the areas near the top and base of the stem. Add Olive Green to the two areas where the stem is casting shadow on the apple. Lightly colour the stem in Lime Peel and Light Umber. Then create shadows with Indanthrone Blue, varying the lights and darks as shown.

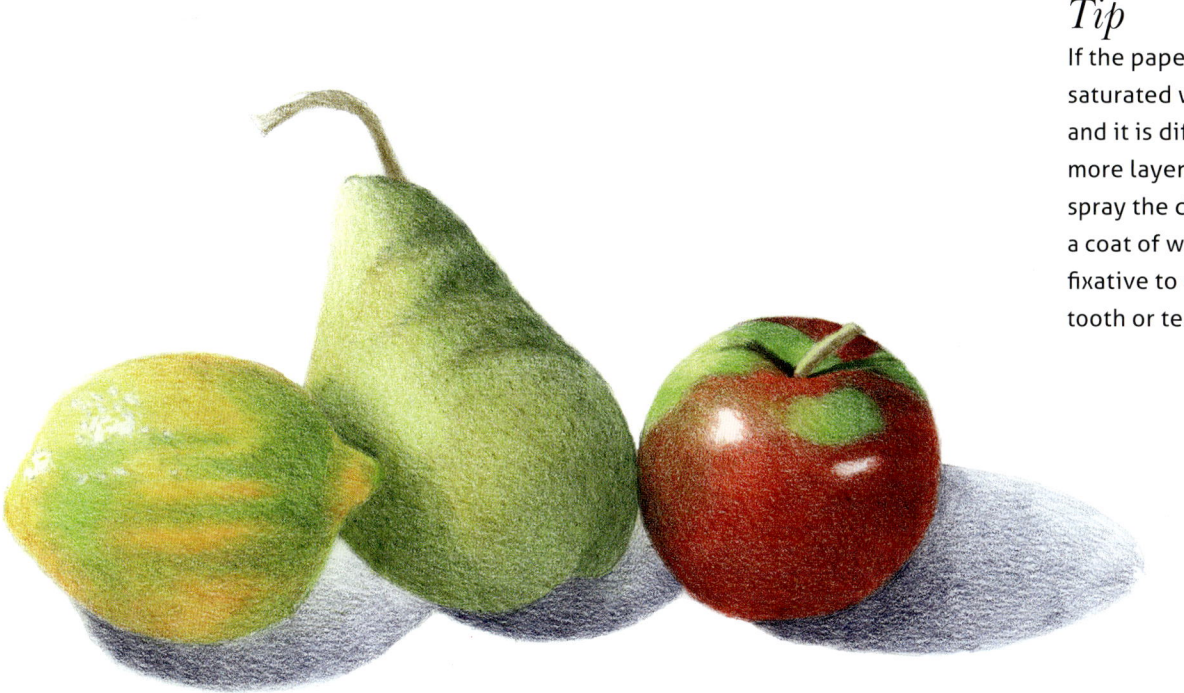

Tip
If the paper becomes saturated with colour and it is difficult to add more layers of pencil, spray the drawing with a coat of workable fixative to create more tooth or texture.

STAGE 3

This stage involves building up tonal values, form and colour, but do erase the graphite pencil lines before layering additional coloured pencil.

Lightly layer Poppy Red on the lemon, along the top, middle and bottom as shown above. Next, lightly add Light Umber to the pear, along the base, up towards the middle and to the right. Add Olive Green to show darker tones on the bottom and sides of the pear, where it touches the other fruit.

Working on the apple, add some Lime Peel on the left side, where there is a greenish tone under the red. I have lightly layered the red so I am able to add the green and let the two colours blend, creating the reflected light from the pear. Blend a layer of Olive Green onto the red, on the right side of the apple where the tonal value is darker. I often use the complement of a colour to darken or neutralize where the colour moves into shadow. And I like to emphasize an object by looking for other colours besides its natural colour to create visual interest.

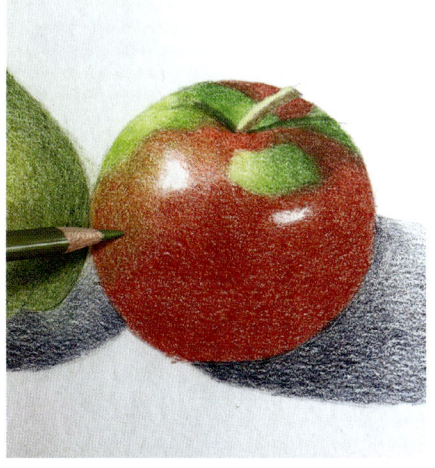

ABOVE *Coloured pencil is translucent, enabling layers to show through one another, so the green can be added over the red.*

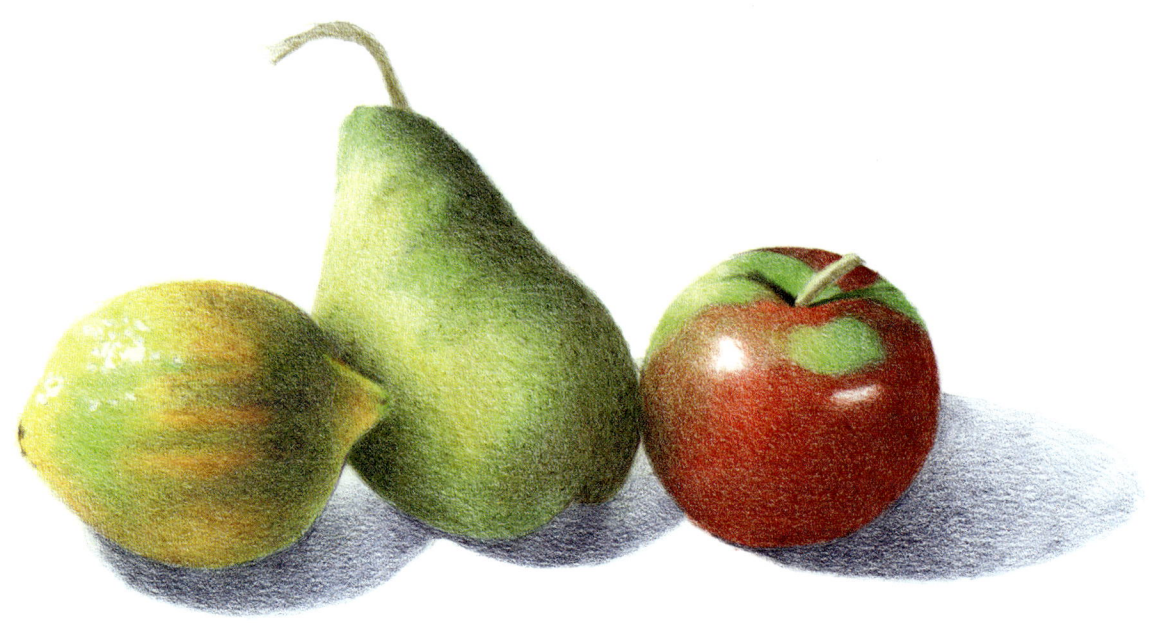

STAGE 4

Let's add more colour, deepen tonal values to create depth in darker sections, and find places where colour is reflected. The colours of objects grouped together will be reflected in one another. Here, yellow from the lemon is reflected in the pear, green from the pear is reflected in the lemon, and a little red from the apple is reflected in the lower right side of the pear.

Incorporate those subtle layers of colour, and continue to deepen the tonal values where the light turns to shadow. Add the complementary colour of yellow, which is Parma Violet, to the darker areas of the lemon to create rich, colourful darks. Apply Crimson Red to the pear and Tuscan Red to the darkest part of the apple to create a full range of tonal values in your still life. Now deepen the shadows at the base of the fruit to create the darker tones. Use more pencil pressure when adding layers of colour (see page 198) to deepen the colours.

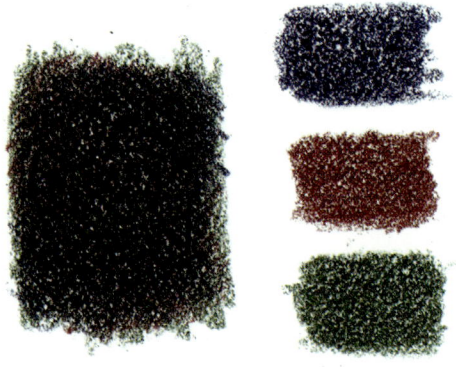

ABOVE *I rarely use black pencil. Instead I prefer to create my dark tones by mixing Dark Green, Tuscan Red and Indanthrone Blue. Experiment with layering the three in different orders for variations of colourful darks.*

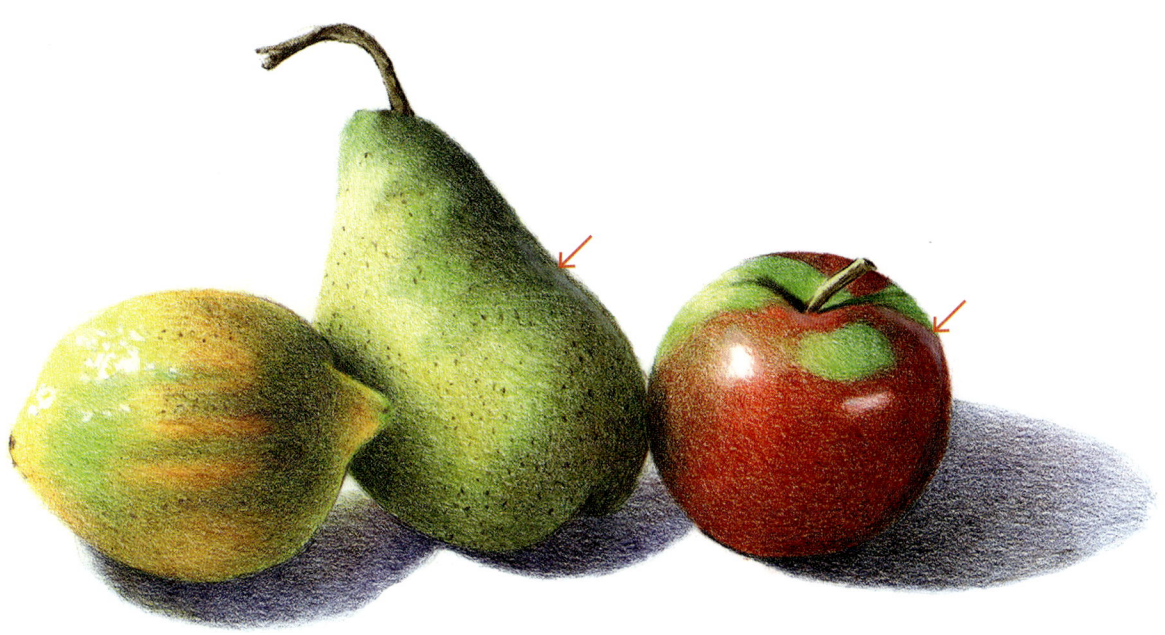

STAGE 5

Finally, it's time to define the details and create colourful shadows. Using the Dark Umber pencil, add detail and dimension to the pear and apple stems. The pear stem has more texture so add more lines and just give the apple stem a dark right edge.

Add some of the darker dimples to the lemon and add speckles to the pear, keeping them random and varying the distance between the speckles. Don't attempt to include every marking, because it will look unnatural: the viewer's eye will connect what isn't there.

The arrows indicate where light is bouncing back as reflected light on the right sides of both the apple and pear, making them appear shiny. You can show this by burnishing those areas using a white pencil with a hard pressure.

Now introduce colour to the shadows. Start by adding Parma Violet to the Indanthrone Blue base, then apply colours to show where the fruit is reflected in each shadow: Sunburst Yellow and Poppy Red from the lemon, Apple Green and Crimson Red from the pear, and Crimson Red and Tuscan Red from the apple.

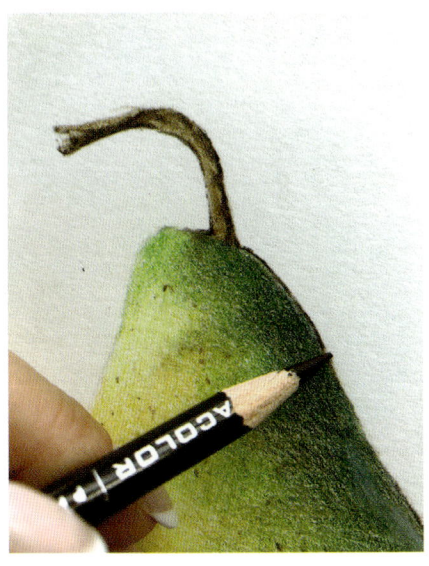

ABOVE *I sometimes use a contour line in small areas to define a form or an edge. Contour lines can give visual interest to an object and move the viewer's eye around the forms. Don't outline the whole object, just parts, and let the line fade at the edges.*

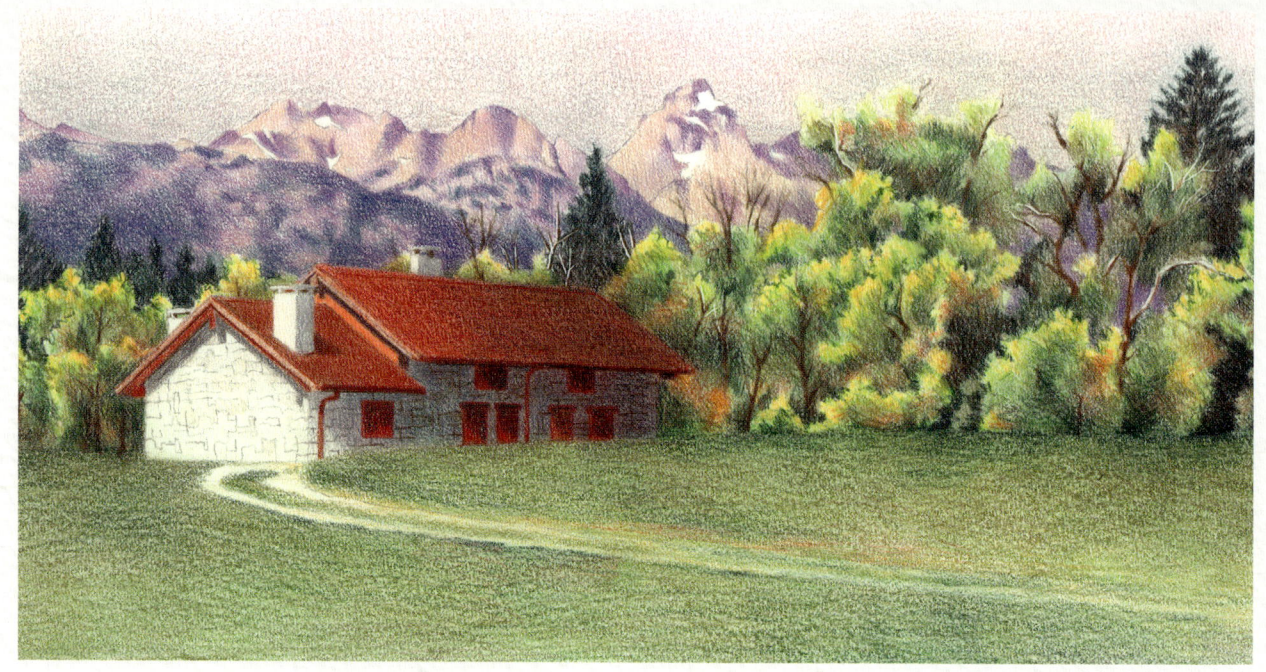

Layering a Landscape

In this project we will create a landscape with a foreground, middle ground and background to practise perspective. We'll also work with colour, line, shape and texture, and explore ways of adding visual interest to the scene.

PENCILS USED: CARAN D'ACHE PABLO AND LUMINANCE, AND PRISMACOLOR

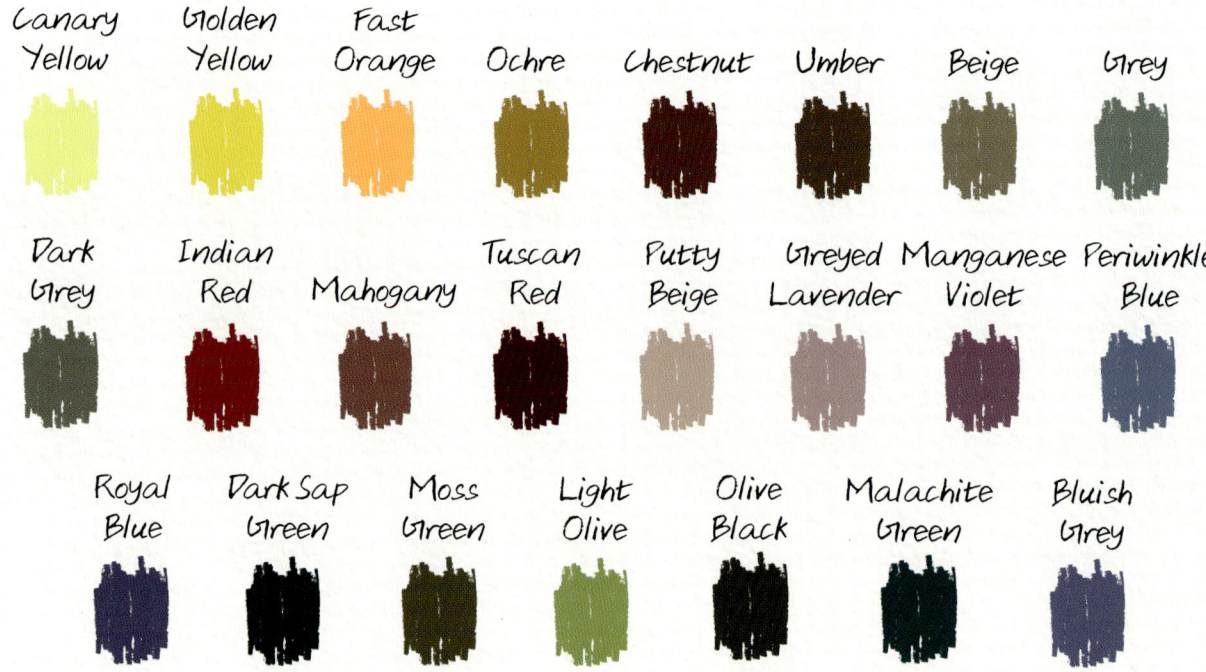

| Canary Yellow | Golden Yellow | Fast Orange | Ochre | Chestnut | Umber | Beige | Grey |

| Dark Grey | Indian Red | Mahogany | Tuscan Red | Putty Beige | Greyed Lavender | Manganese Violet | Periwinkle Blue |

| Royal Blue | Dark Sap Green | Moss Green | Light Olive | Olive Black | Malachite Green | Bluish Grey |

When creating a landscape drawing, you need to decide what you'd like to portray about a particular place and how you can best capture the essence of your surroundings. Colours, atmosphere, detail and tonal values will all work together to create an alluring landscape.

Working *en plein air* – a French phrase meaning 'in the open air' – will give you a good sense of moments in time, allowing you to soak up light and ambience. When choosing an area to sketch for a landscape, study colour, shape and texture in nature, and think about what intrigues you the most. Remember that there is no perfect composition, and you may change or remove unwanted objects you don't want in the scene.

Drawing en plein air has to be done quickly, as the light and atmosphere swiftly change throughout the day, and it can be challenging. I like to write notes and make colour jottings in a sketchbook along with my drawing. I also take several photos so I can recreate the scene when working in my studio.

USING PHOTOGRAPHIC REFERENCE

Drawing from a reference photo can make life easier than working outside, as you can work on your creation over a longer period of time. But bear in mind

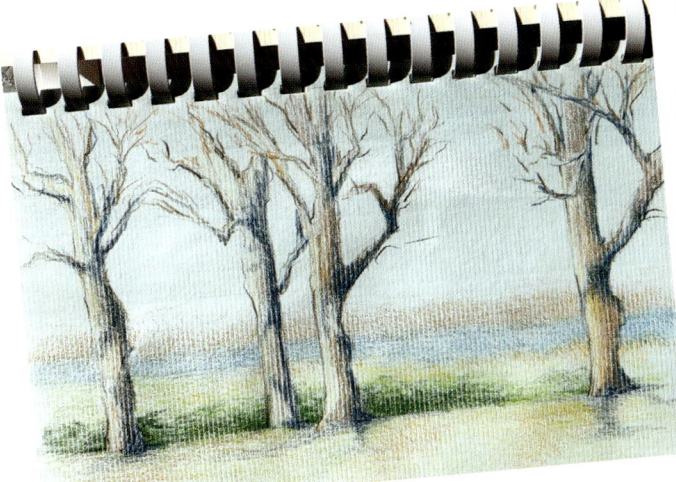

LEFT *Sketching outdoors can help you get a sense of the scene.*

that this will limit your vision to a flat, rectangular scene, so you must add your own insights into the drawing. Photos can also darken areas such as shadows.

For this project I chose a reference photo of a landscape with woodland, a house in the foreground and mountains in the distance. I like the road leading to the house, as it breaks up the foreground. I also like the warm red roof, yellow in the trees and purples in the mountains, so I emphasized these with colour. There's a great variety of textures, too. The foliage and grass are rough, the mountains are rocky and uneven, and the sky and roofs are smooth, with an illusion of smooth stone on the sides of the house.

PLANNING THE COMPOSITION

As I planned a composition for the drawing, I asked myself what I wanted viewers to see. To add visual interest, I made the horizon line high, so there would be less sky and more foreground, making the scene more interesting than if the horizon line had been placed directly in the centre. I also made the building slightly smaller, so it didn't appear so dominant, and moved it slightly to the left so it wasn't quite so centred.

CHOOSING MATERIALS

I chose to draw this scene on off-white paper and decided it would be mainly warm with a small percentage of cool in the mountains and sky – a suggested ratio of warm to cool in a composition is 70 per cent to 30 per cent.

I chose Caran d'Ache Pablo coloured pencils for this project as they are an oil-based pencil with a harder tip that works nicely for creating thin lines such as for the trees and foliage and have sharper edges for working on areas such as the house and rooflines. I added a few Prismacolor and Luminance pencils for colour choices that were not available in the Pablo range, but you can chose the ones you like – there are many brands of good pencils on the market.

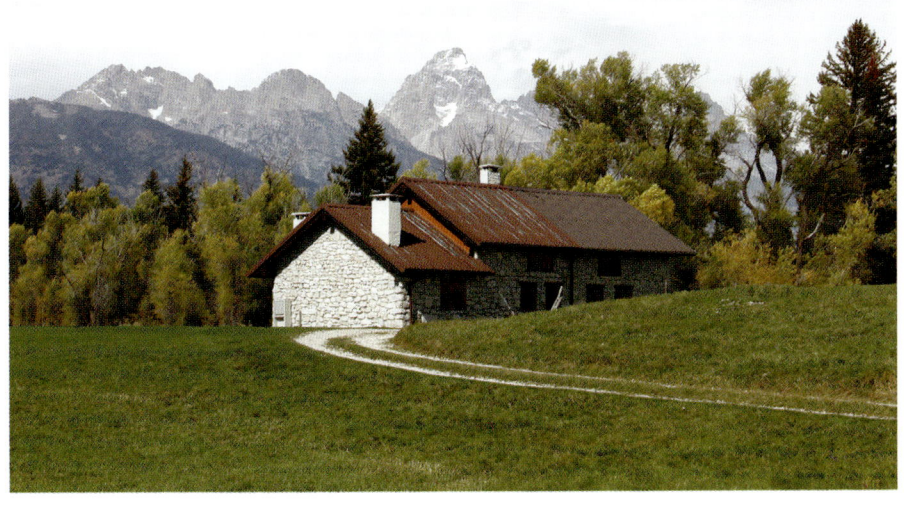

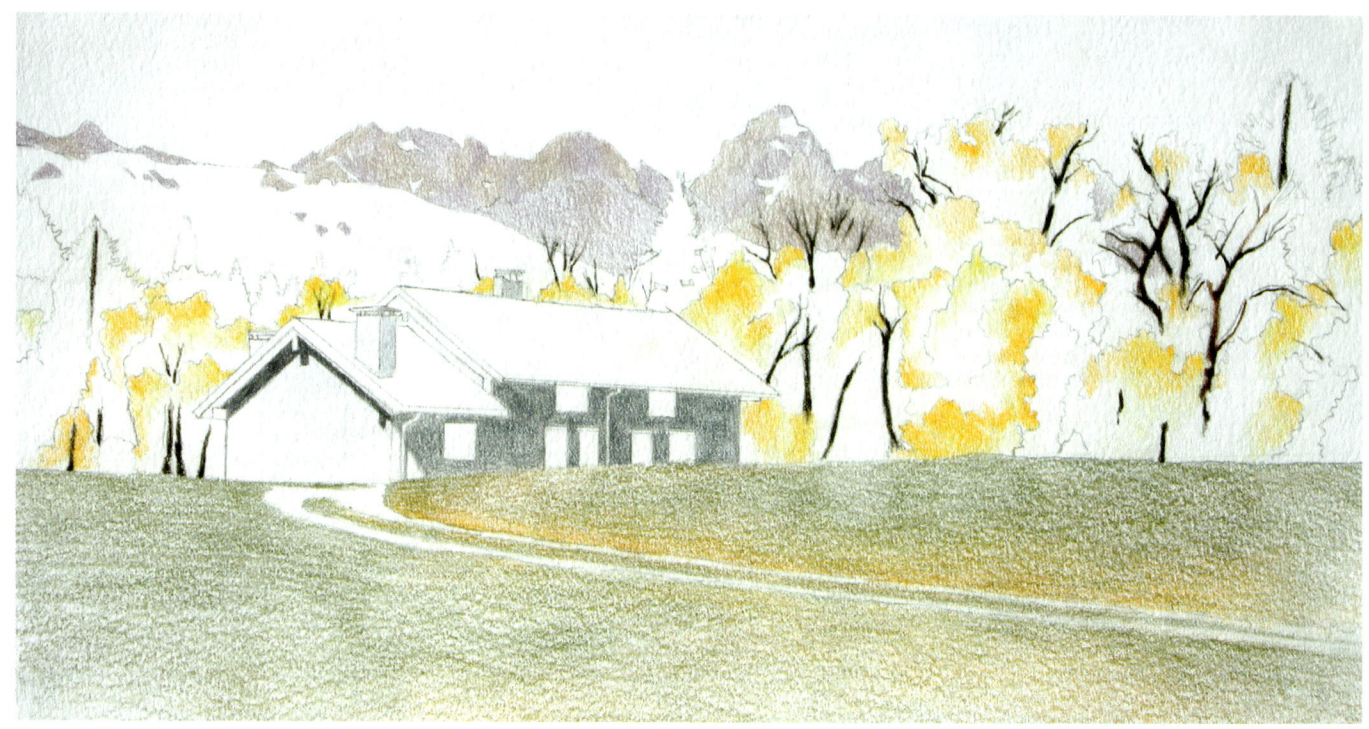

STAGE 1

There are many elements in this scene, especially with all the different trees and various mountains. So the first job is to simplify all these elements by selecting the main shapes and then sketching a quick outline of them.

Now you can start adding colour. Use an embossing tool to indent lines on the lightest parts of the branches so they will stay white. Then apply Umber and Chestnut to the tree trunks and branches, lightening your pressure at the ends of the branches so they blend softly into the scene.

Put Canary Yellow and Golden Yellow in the tops of the trees, where they will be the lightest colours. Roughly colour the grass with Golden Yellow, Ochre and Moss Green, then use Greyed Lavender and Putty Beige for the far mountains.

To draw the house, I suggest using a ruler for the straight lines and roof angles, and you may find it helpful to refer to the section on Perspective (see pages 206–7). Create shadows using Beige, Grey and Dark Grey. The chimneys are the lightest, so use Beige on these. Apply Grey to the side of the house facing away from the sun and use Dark Grey for the shadowed area under the roofline.

Tip

A landscape drawing is a placement of shapes. Start by finding the main shapes in your composition. Draw one main shape, then move on to the others. Block in the colour and tonal value of each shape, and add details later.

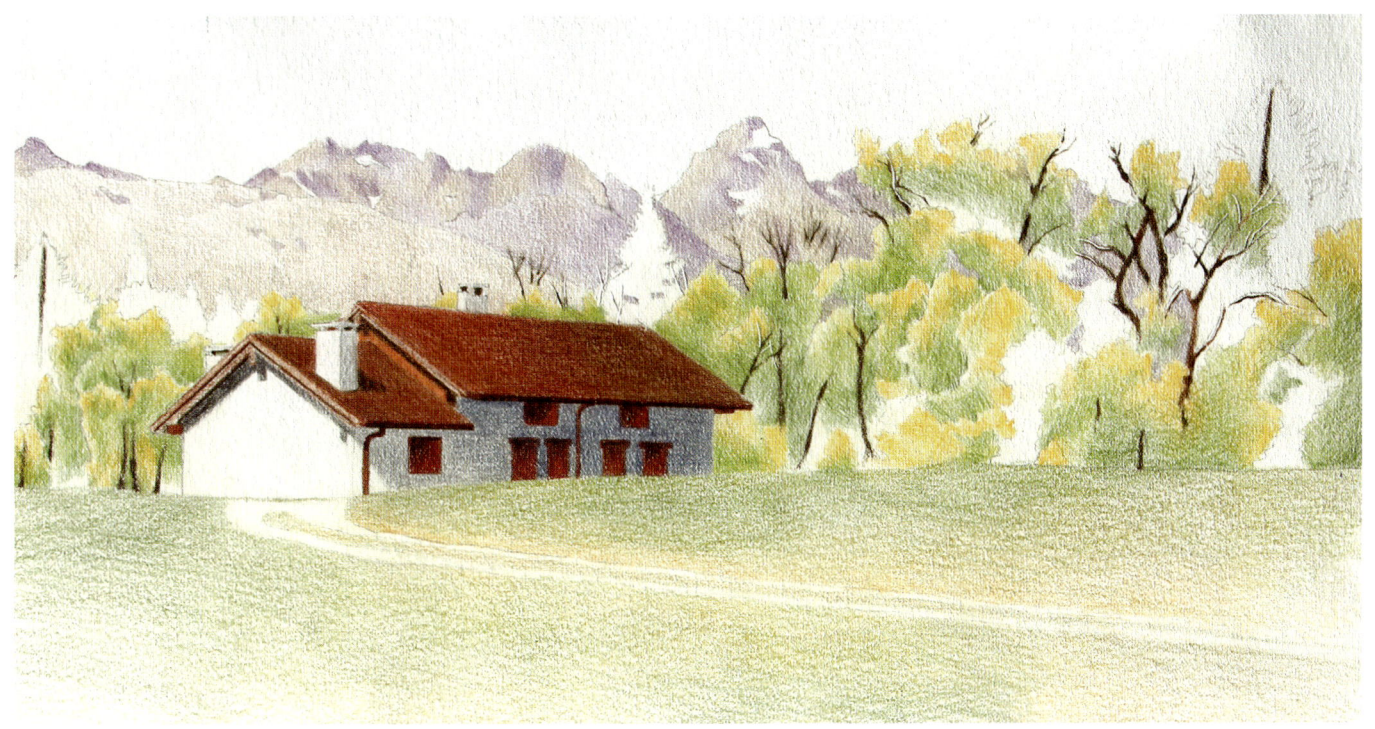

STAGE 2

Atmospheric perspective is the way in which colour, tonal value and detail diminish as objects move into the distance, creating a feeling of depth. In this scene, objects in the foreground have stronger colour and contrast; warm colours come forwards, while cool colours fall back. As objects recede, colours lose their brilliance, so in the reference photo you'll notice that foliage on the faraway mountain is blue rather than green.

At this stage we are still blocking in shapes and adding base colours, as we don't want to get caught up in too much detail early on.

Add Light Olive and Moss Green to the yellow colours on the trees. You can use Canary Yellow and Golden Yellow to blend the green into the yellow tones. It's also fine to colour over tree trunks with lighter colours – the dark browns will still show or can be reapplied later. Add Putty Beige to the nearest mountain and Manganese Violet to the darker areas of further mountains that fall into crevices or shadow.

Now work on the house. I've eliminated the lines of different-coloured tones in the roof and made them smooth. Colour the roof with a light even tone of Mahogany and add Umber to the right side, which is darker in tonal value. Blend Indian Red on the lighter area to the left and on the small roof. Mix Golden Yellow and Indian Red for the small, orange-toned part between the two roofs. Colour the windows with Mahogany and add Tuscan Red to the tops and right sides, where the windows move into shadow. Colour the dark rooflines in Tuscan Red, then use a very light pressure to apply Mahogany to the roof edges facing the light. Add a layer of Bluish Grey to the side of the house.

Apply Light Olive to the grass and more Ochre to build colour and texture.

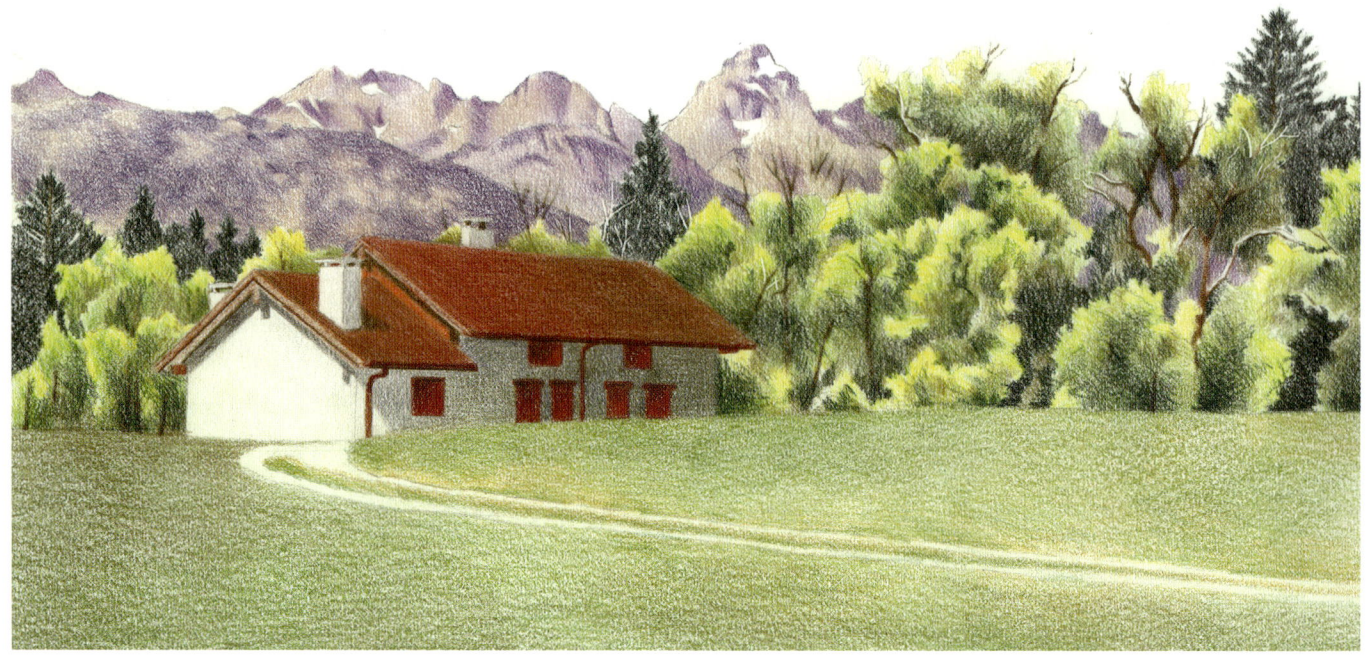

STAGE 3

Next, we'll start adding details and creating soft edges and hard edges. We will also use other compositional elements of design to bring this scene to life. We have already begun to use texture, and now we'll build shape and line in the different elements in the scene. Look at the relationships of space, particularly between the foreground house and foliage, then compare them with the mountains in the background.

Put Olive Black on the foliage followed by Dark Sap Green. Also colour the background evergreen trees with Dark Sap Green. Leave some areas of white paper between branches to show where they part. Continue adding Dark Sap Green to the darkest areas of the foliage to add depth.

Add Periwinkle Blue to the distant mountains to further define the crevices, then add Royal Blue to the nearest mountain to define the dark foliage areas. Note that although these colours are called blue, they actually appear to be more violet.

Add a layer of Olive Black to the side of the house to neutralize the blue-grey and blend it into the foliage and shadow. As you build colours on all the elements, you'll need to adjust the grass, so layer more of the same grass colours with a slightly heavier pressure.

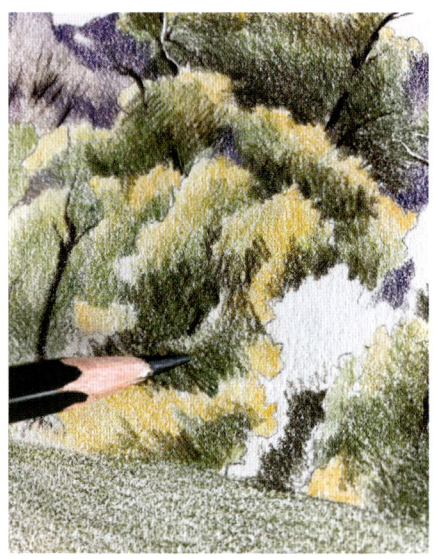

ABOVE *Colours in foliage are roughly layered next to or over parts of each other to show the texture of leaves.*

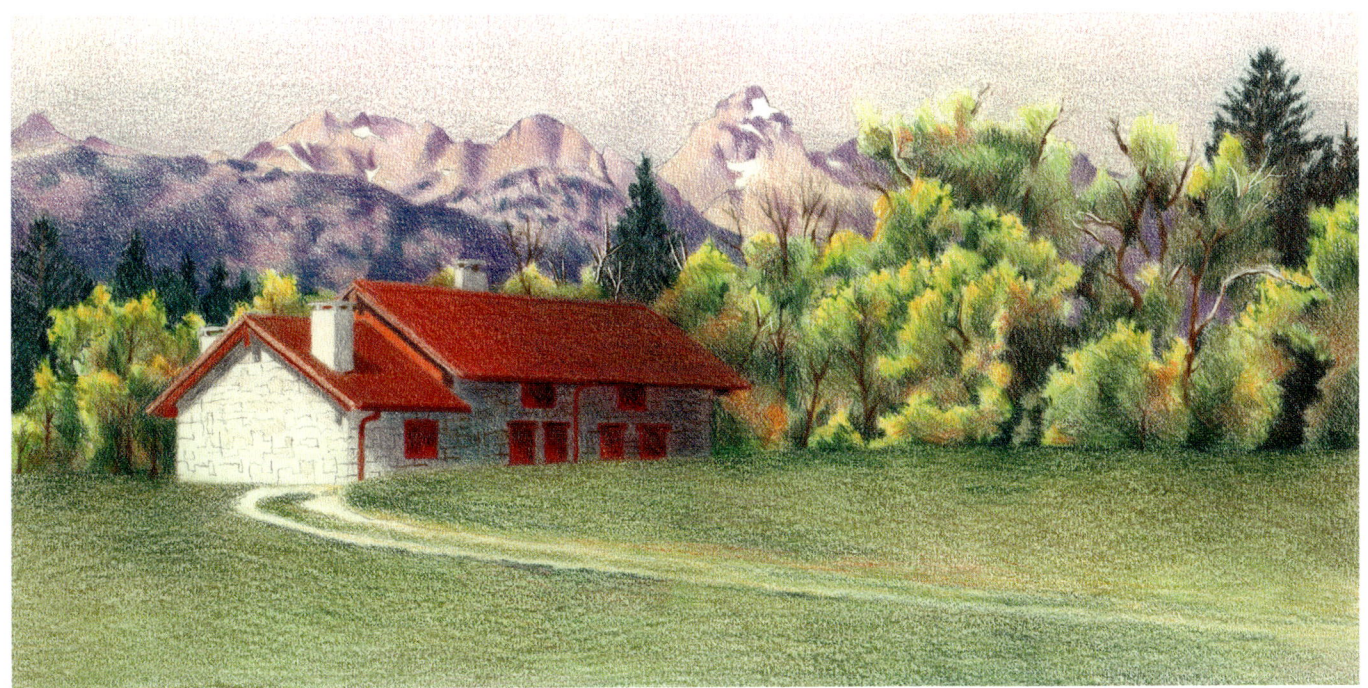

STAGE 4

Finally, we'll add more colour, but more importantly we need to unify the different elements so they form a whole. We'll do this by working on colours, tonal values, textures and by adding details. You may also make any additional changes you think necessary.

The only element we haven't yet coloured is the sky, so apply a layer of Greyed Lavender with a light, even pressure, and add Grey where the sky meets the mountains and foliage.

Using a stiff bristle brush, lightly burnish the grass and foliage – particularly the evergreen trees – to remove any paper showing through. Lightly add Fast Orange and Indian Red to the grass as well as some of the yellow areas in the foliage. I have also coloured over parts of the road so it blends in as it moves off the page, rather than leading the viewer's eye out of the scene.

Add Malachite Green to the dark areas of the nearest mountain just behind the house, then add Periwinkle Blue to the lighter areas to adjust tonal values. Add a layer of Bluish Grey to the mountains showing between the trees on the right.

Apply a light layer of Tuscan Red to the front of the house to darken the tonal value and blend it into the shadows. Then apply a light layer of Dark Sap Green to adjust the tonal value of the roof, darkening and blending it into the foliage. Dark Sap Green is the complement of Tuscan Red and will neutralize it into shadow.

Finally, using a sharp point on your pencil, add lines to pick out the stone texture on the house: on the side facing the sun, I used Grey with Putty Beige, and on the shadowed side I used Umber.

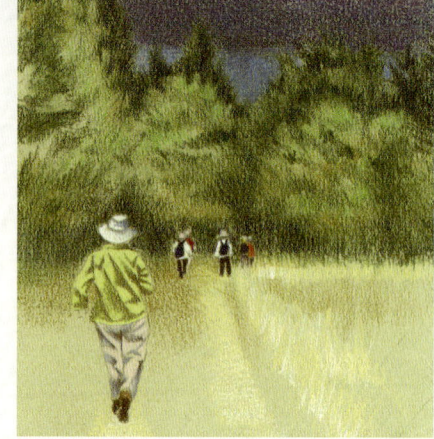

FOCUS ON
Figures in a Scene

Placing figures in a scene and sketching people or groups of people can help add a sense of movement and scale to your picture. You don't need figure-drawing or portrait skills in order to effectively place a few simple figures in your work.

Have you wanted to introduce figures to your drawing but were unsure how to do it? Figures can add interest and a touch of humanity to a scene as well as help tell a story or describe the setting. They can bring a picture to life by adding movement and balance for the composition. They can also help show scale and proportion. Figures are identified by their shapes. You should observe the gesture – motion or pose – of each figure and keep details to a minimum. Show perspective by decreasing the size of the figures to create a sense of depth and scale as they move into the distance (**A**). As figures recede, they become smaller and shorter. Just like any object in perspective, figures nearer to the viewer will show more detail and as they recede into the distance they become much less detailed (**B**).

You don't need figure-drawing or portrait skills to be able to add people to a scene: shape and gesture are the important parts, not all the details. Figures can be kept simple to support the drawing without becoming the centre of interest. Think of them as you would a subject – a group of shapes, colours, textures, light and shadow (**C**). You only need to add relatively little detail to facial features, fingers or feet.

Look for the largest elements first and keep your drawing basic (**D**). Observe where light falls and where the form turns into shadow. Build up dark or shadow tones by working across the solid form. Include lines, when needed, for extra definition. Folds in clothing can describe movement and the contours of the body (**E**).

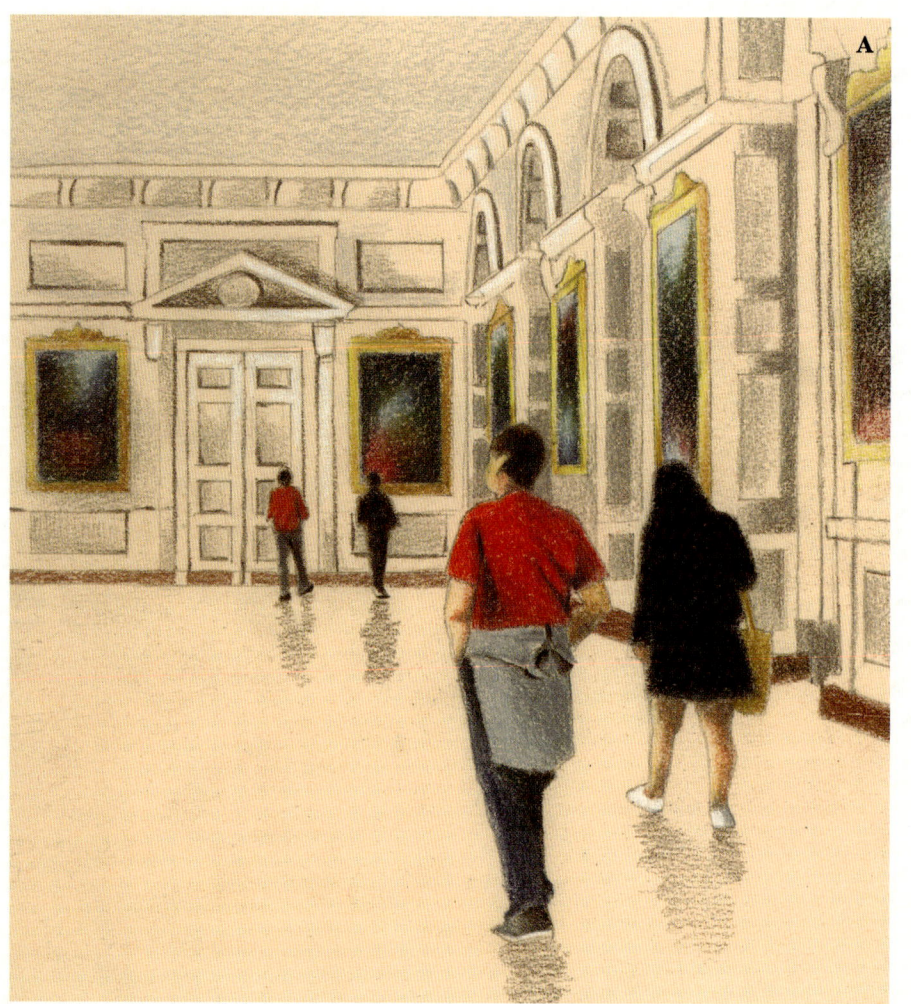

A

LEFT *Figures should complement a scene, not dominate it. They can serve as a way to lead the viewer's eye around the picture, so when beginning your drawing, decide figure placement early on. Notice how the position of the feet and tilt of the bodies makes it more interesting than if they were all standing still.*

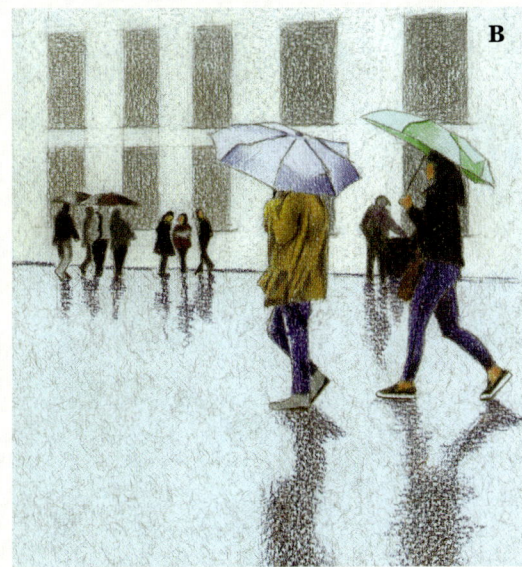

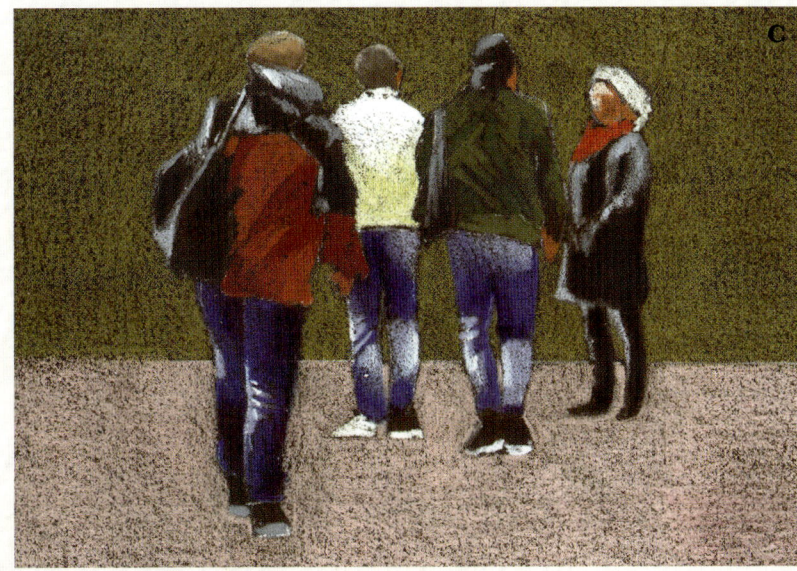

ABOVE *Grouping is important. Here I have superimposed the two foreground figures on the distant figure in between. The small groupings of figures in the background support the larger foreground figures. The shadows on the street help connect all the figures to the surface and create interesting foreground shapes.*

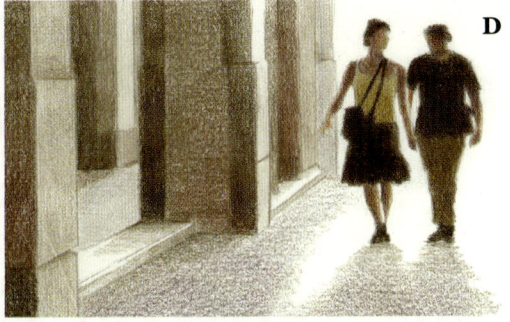

ABOVE *These figures are backlit as they walk into a corridor with light coming in from behind. I have omitted the facial features and kept shapes very simple and flat.*

ABOVE *I used black paper to draw this colourful group of figures and integrated the paper into my drawing. Notice the negative spaces created within the group and how they overlap to make the group more interesting. The trousers and jackets consist of shapes of colour and light that show both form and movement.*

Balance and shape

Balance in a figure is achieved by comparing the upper body with the hips. Begin by checking if the figure is standing upright or if their weight is shifted to one side or the other. Look for patterns of movement – how the body turns or changes in weight distribution and gestures. To add further interest to the picture, vary the shape and pose of the figures rather than giving them all the same regimented stance. Shape and gesture should be enough to describe the figures accurately, showing characteristics such as tilt of the hips and angle of the shoulders.

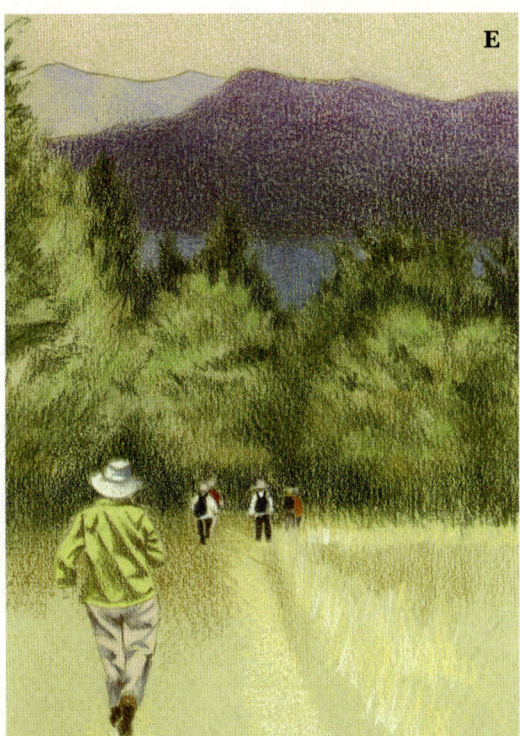

LEFT *This ordinary landscape becomes more interesting with the introduction of figures. They show a sense of movement and perspective. We can also see that we are looking down a hill.*

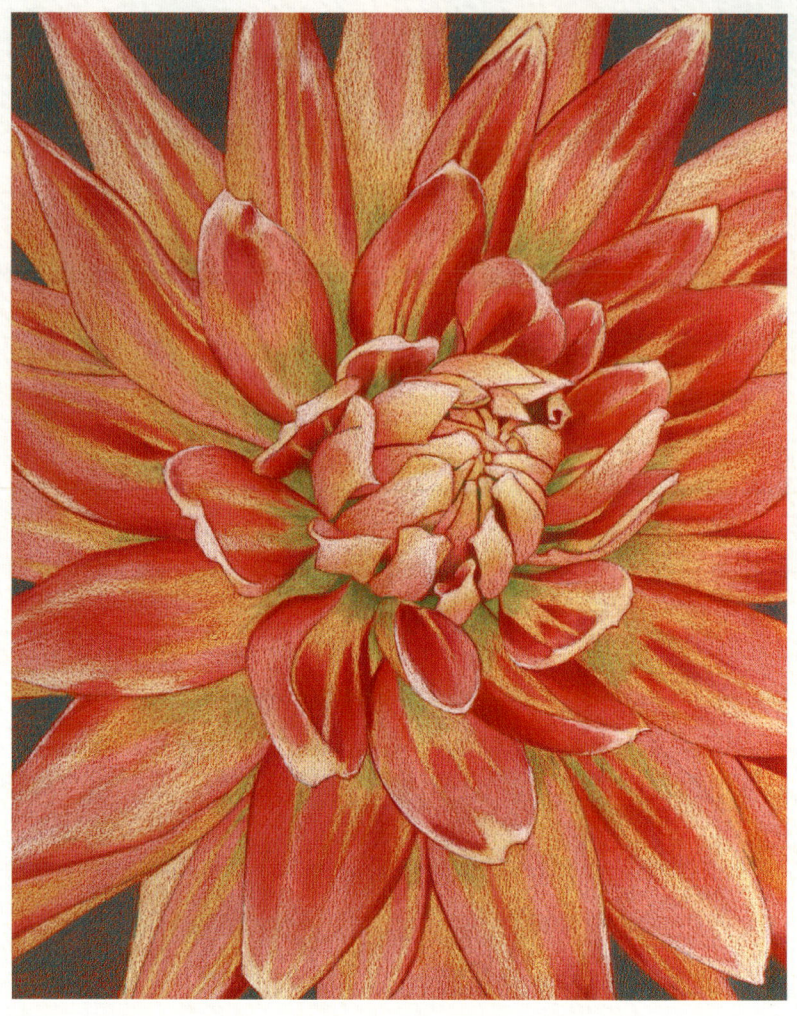

Flower Burst

In this project you will learn about juxtaposed colour and become more familiar with colour relationships. To create this vibrant dahlia, we will place colours next to one another, instead of layering them, and allow the viewer's eyes to mix them optically. We'll also explore composition, complementary colours and colour temperature.

PENCILS USED: PRISMACOLOR

White · Lemon Yellow · Blush Pink · Pink · Pomegranate · Crimson Red · Apple Green · Parrot Green

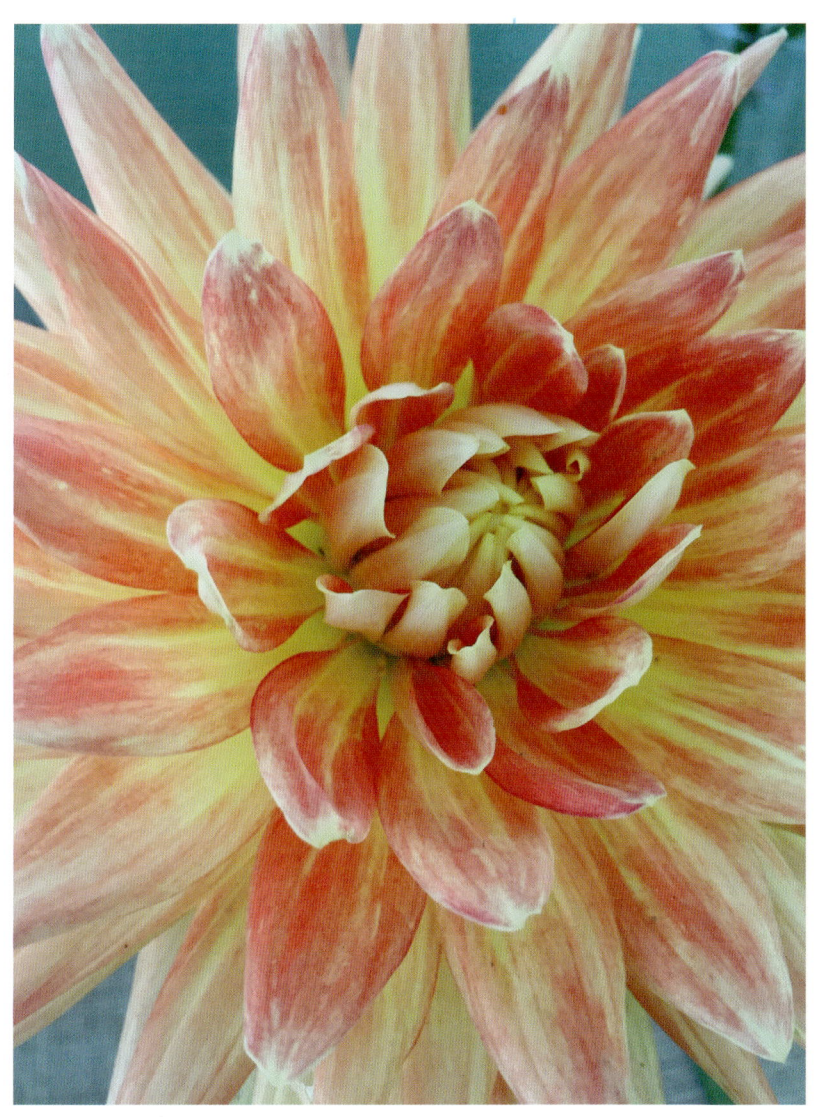

While the petals flowing outwards give the composition energy, the folded petals close to the centre of the flower create a focal point. There is variety and repetition in the shapes, sizes, tones and colours of the petals. The negative space between them works with the positive spaces to balance the composition and create harmony, and the different shapes lead the viewer around the page. There is so much movement in this composition.

This dahlia radiates warmth and energy, so I chose red drawing paper as a base for the drawing. The coloured paper complements the drawing, and layers of colour show through one another. This drawing has an overall warm colour temperature (see page 195).

COLOUR SCHEME AND COLOURS

The photograph contains tones of yellow in the petals, but I wanted to emphasize the pink and red so I changed the colour scheme slightly. As an artist, you don't have to draw exactly what you see. A subject can be much more interesting if you give it your own creative ideas.

The complementary colours – blue-green in the background and the green at the centre of the petals – balance the warm red tones and cause them to pop. Complementary colours show more contrast when placed next to one another; warm tones come forwards, while cooler negative spaces stay quietly in the background.

COMPOSITION

This photograph of a lively dahlia contains many interesting compositional elements and is composed of warm bright colours. Its vibrant, closely cropped composition is far more engaging than if it had been placed centrally with lots of negative space around it.

Notice how the petals flowing off the page create movement and push the boundaries of the page edges. The shapes of the petals are made up of a series of curved and angled lines that give the flower depth, texture and detail. These lines flow outwards, leading the viewer's eye from the centre of the flower in all directions towards the edges, almost like a starburst.

Tip

Feel free to make changes to the colour scheme to emphasize particular colours, add contrast and balance out tones.

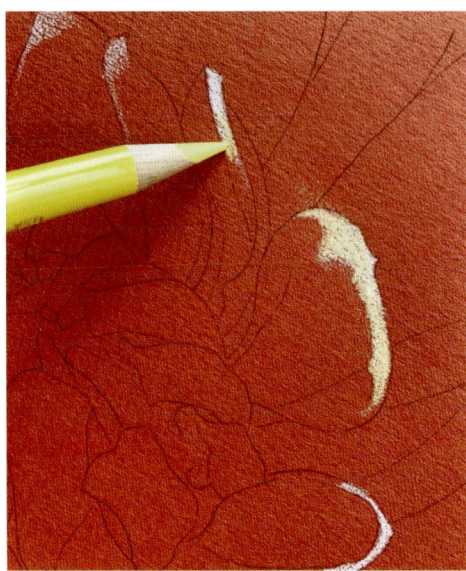

ABOVE *The first step after producing a line drawing is to add White and Lemon Yellow to the lightest areas of the petals.*

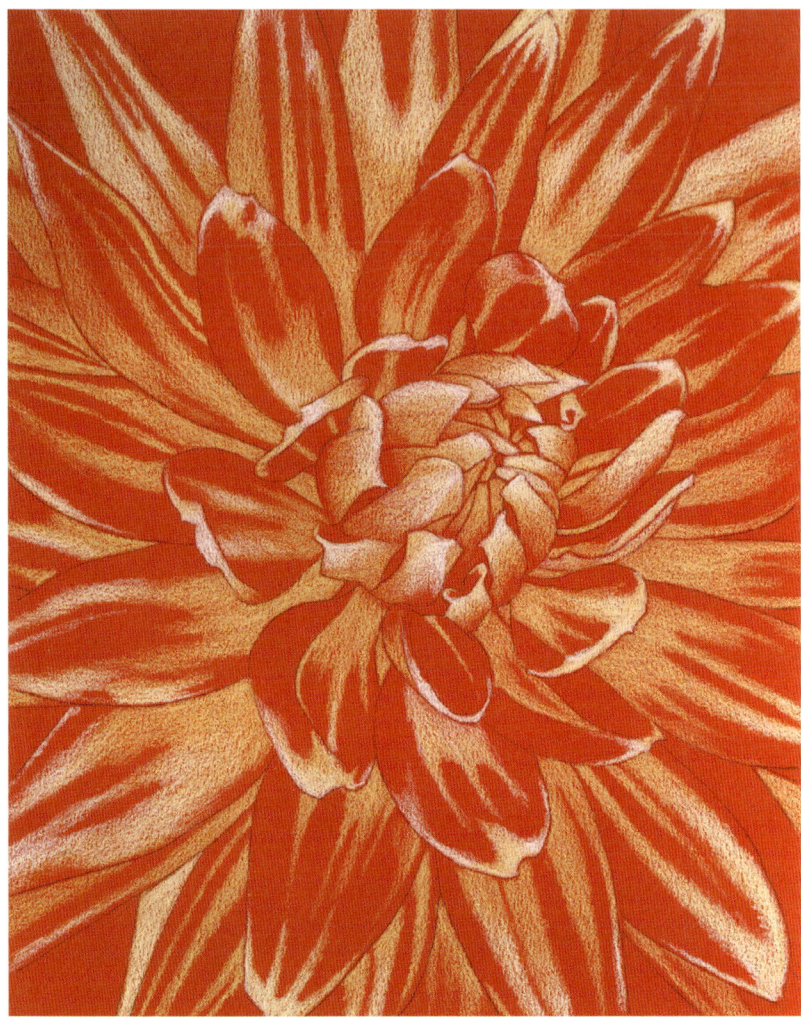

STAGE 1

Start with a graphite line drawing of the outline of each of the petals. With a complicated subject such as this one, it is sometimes easier to work out the drawing on sketch paper first, then transfer it to the final drawing paper when all the erasing is finished and the shapes are correctly drawn.

Once the outline drawing is complete, you can begin to add details with coloured pencils. The dahlia has many petals and may appear intimidating, but just work on one petal at a time. Begin with the lightest value – white – and, using a light pressure, apply White to the tips of each petal, moving towards the centre of some of the lighter petals as indicated. Add White to some of the lightest areas of the folded petals, especially the folded petals in the centre. Also add White to the lightest areas on the edges of a few of the petals curling forwards.

Now, using a light pressure, apply the second colour – Lemon Yellow – to parts of each petal to show the striations. It is important to set out the structure and markings of each petal with the yellow pencil. Look at the reference photo and add Lemon Yellow to one petal at a time, working around the flower from the centre outwards. You don't need to get caught up in exactly recreating each petal – you can be creative. Colours can always be adjusted later.

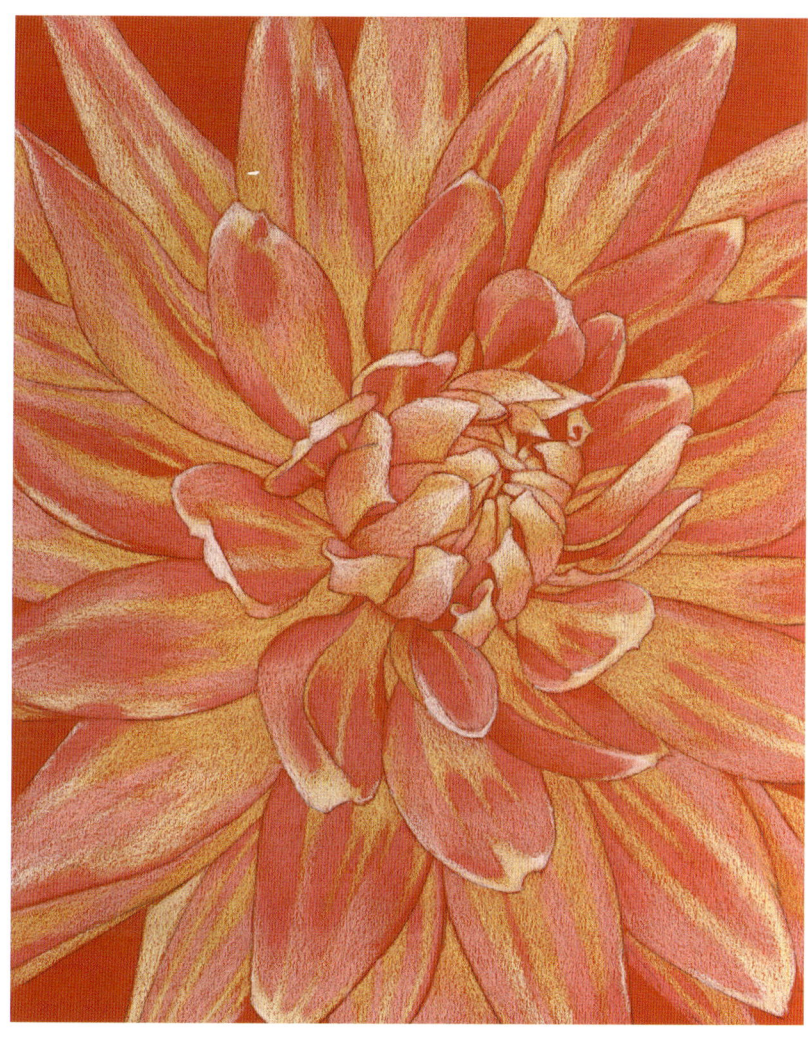

Tip
Using a light pressure makes it easy to change colours or lift or erase a colour.

STAGE 2

Lightly erase some of the graphite outlines before adding more coloured pencil. In this stage we will be using the two pinks – Blush Pink and Pink – to create the lightest tints of red within the petals. Begin by adding Blush Pink next to or around the Lemon Yellow areas on each petal where the colour changes from yellow to tints of red. Gently blend the edges together using a light pressure. Keep the tips of the petals the lightest values because they are flowing outwards into the light.

Next add Pink. This will start to add dimension because Pink is darker in tonal value than Blush Pink. Place the Pink next to the Blush Pink and some of the Lemon Yellow areas. Keep referring to the photo while you create the colours of each petal. Apply Pink with a medium pressure to add more tonal value towards the darker pink areas of the petal bases where petals overlap each other.

Now you have a good idea of how to juxtapose colours as opposed to layering. You are creating colour and depth but placing colours next to one another and gently blending the edges together.

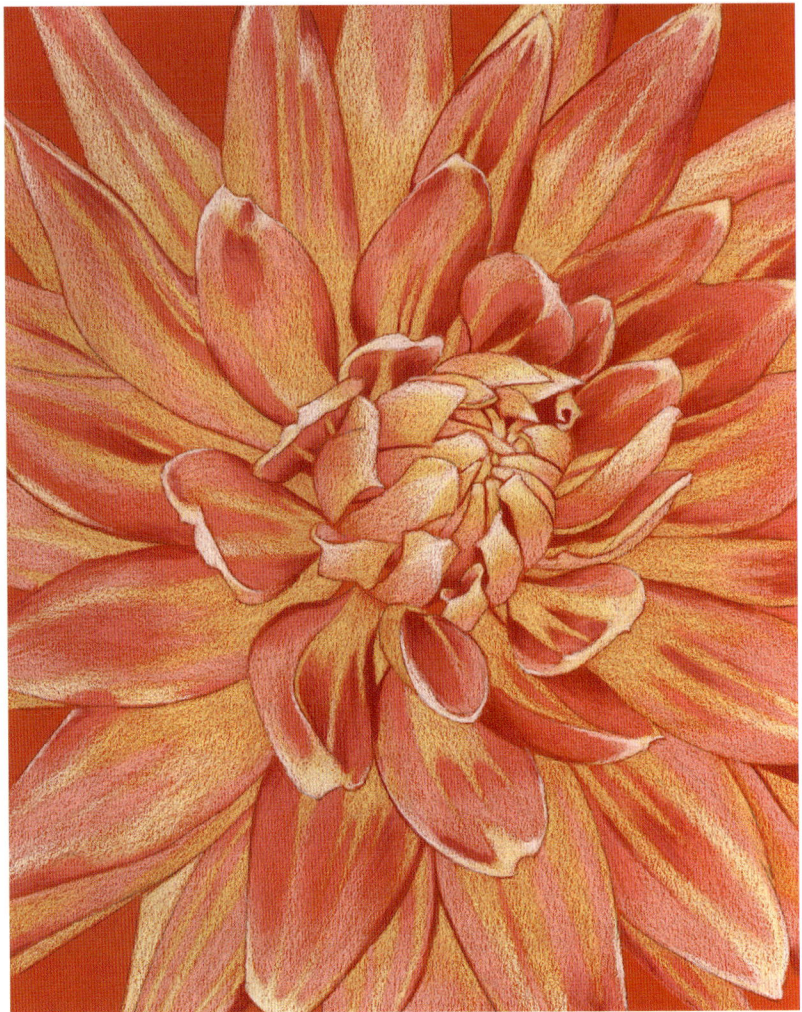

STAGE 3

At this point you have used four colours on the petals: White, Lemon Yellow, Blush Pink and Pink. Work a little more on building up the colours, using medium pressure in areas where the colours could be bolder, especially where they fold under one another. Continue blending the colours together until you are satisfied that you have captured the colours, tonal values and patterns of each petal.

Next you can begin to add a darker tonal value to provide variation in colour and tone. The colour Pomegranate will do this, and create depth and shadow on the petal edges. Apply Pomegranate to areas where the petals curl inwards, to the petals that tuck behind petals coming forwards, and also to some of the edges. Look at the reference photo to help you find these darker areas. I have also used Pomegranate to add contour lines on the edges of some petals to differentiate one from another.

Now we have used five colours, juxtaposed side by side. Notice how the dark Pomegranate placed next to the very lightest colours – White and Lemon Yellow – are making them pop forwards, and the drawing is interesting to look at because it has a good range of tonal values.

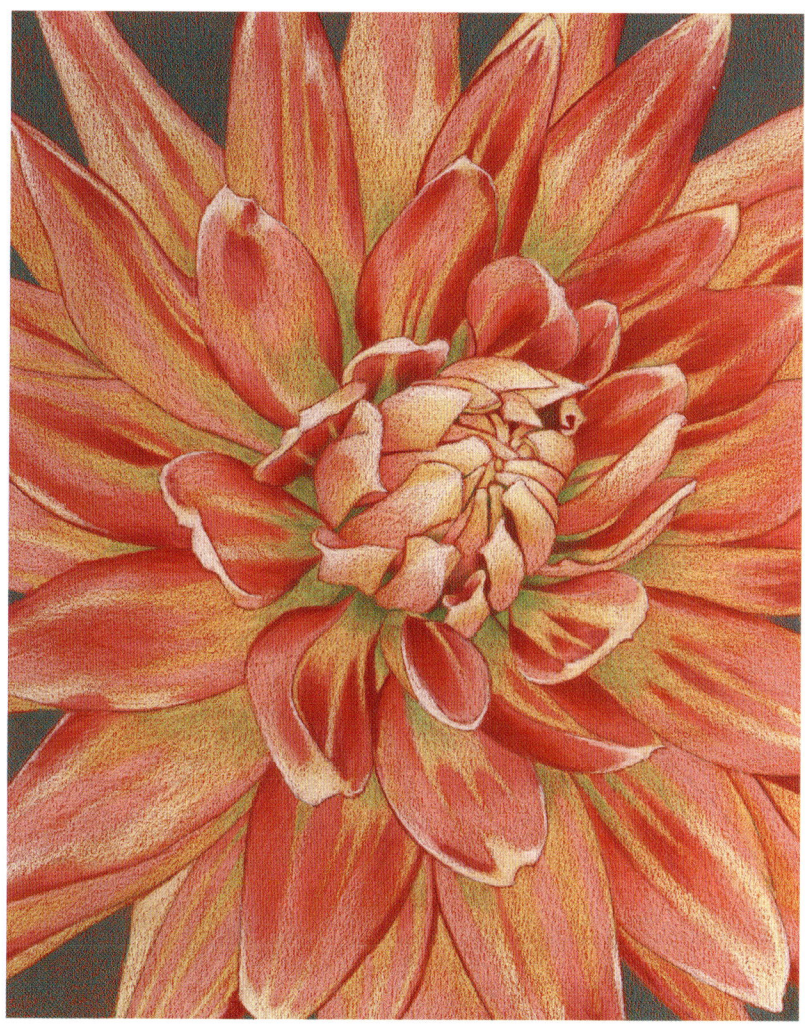

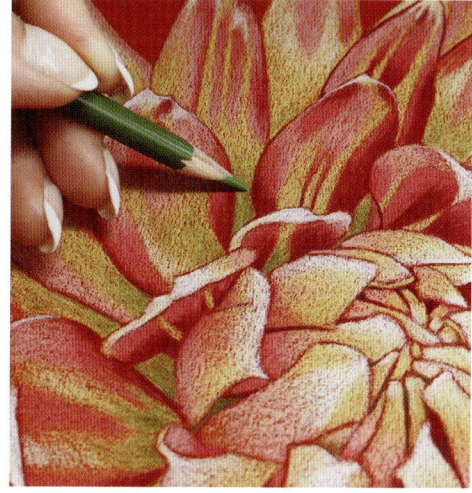

STAGE 4

Colours have been applied with medium pressure, allowing the texture of the red paper to show through all colours placed on the surface. This effect will create colour harmony throughout the drawing. Layer Crimson Red over some of the Pink and Pomegranate to give the flower warmer tones. Next, using light pressure, add Apple Green over Lemon Yellow just along the base of the petals where they meet in the centre of the dahlia and continue outwards (see inset).

I chose Parrot Green for the background because it is a blue-green, which is the complement of the pinkish-reds, and also because it is a duller green that won't overpower the dahlia. Add Parrot Green to the background between the petals with a medium to heavy pressure, allowing some of the red paper to show through.

Now the drawing is almost complete. Add a little more White to the tips of the centre petals to make them pop forwards and stand out. Finally, readjust any areas that need more colour or blending until you are satisfied with your finished piece.

ABOVE *Apply Apple Green over Lemon Yellow and lightly blend outwards on the petal.*

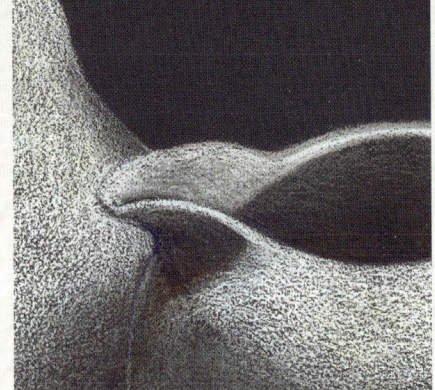

Colourful Greys

In this study we will learn how to create colourful grey tones by mixing various colours. Greys are used to complement bright colours and as restful places in the drawing.

Greys and neutral tones have many different purposes in art. They are essential for giving a drawing structure and depth, as without them our drawings would contain too many pure colours and appear overwhelming. Look around you and notice how many objects or areas contain greys or unsaturated colours. These neutrals are restful places in our environment and in our art, and a way of conveying both colour and tone.

Mixing neutrals and colours together

I like to create colourful greys by mixing neutrals and colours together. You might wonder why we can't just create a grey by mixing black and white. Well, this will produce grey but it will be a dull grey. And layering white coloured pencil over black coloured pencil will simply create a dull opaque grey. If you look at greys, you will see

LEFT *Each neutral in the top row was created using two complementary colours. In the bottom row, the left square is a neutral made by mixing the three primary colours. The middle square is blue layered over violet. The right square is a dark violet and a blue layered over a grey coloured pencil.*

they contain tints of red, blue or brown hues often mingled with purple, green or yellow, and they aren't dull at all. If you create greys by mixing colours, you will have more control over your neutrals and will be able to produce warm and cool greys in your drawings.

We also use grey tones and neutrals for creating shadows, backgrounds and to show distance. Shadows are actually blue combined with tints and shades of the local colour of the object or objects casting the shadow or creating reflections. The mixture of these tints, shades and blue will create colourful grey tones and neutrals. As shadows recede, the amount of contrast will be reduced and edges will become softer. Colour, tonal value and texture diminish as an object or scene moves towards the background and become more neutral (for more information, see Layering a Landscape, pages 214–9).

Creating greys with coloured pencils

There are various ways of creating greys with coloured pencils. One option, which we learned about in Colour Theory and Tonal Value (see pages 194–5), is to combine two complementary colours. We reduce the intensity of a particular colour by adding its complement and neutralizing or greying the colour. As the intensity of a colour drops, it is referred to as being greyed down. Creating greys by mixing

RIGHT *Grey can help brighter colours pop forwards. When grey tones are juxtaposed or placed next to pure colours such as red or blue, these already intense colours become even more vibrant.*

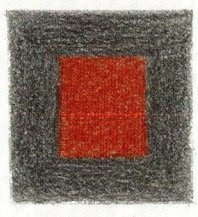 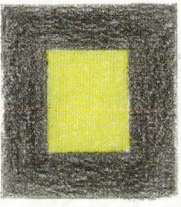 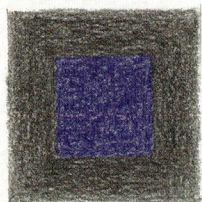

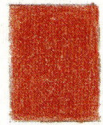  

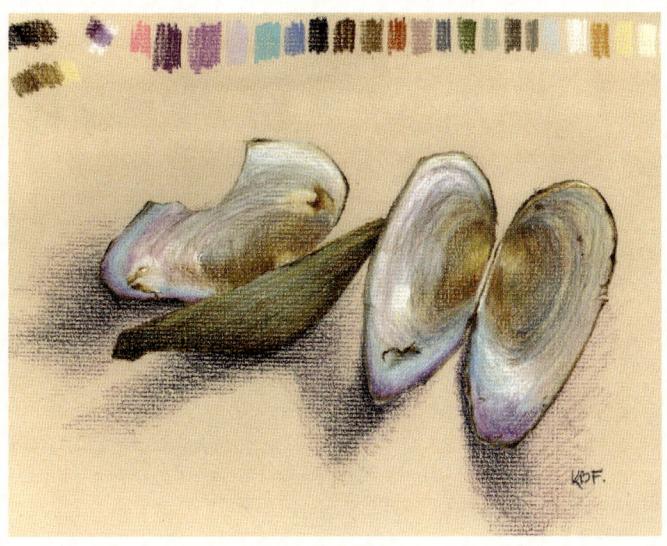

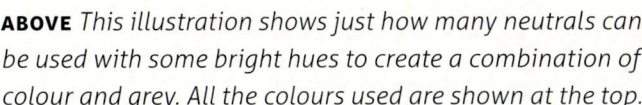

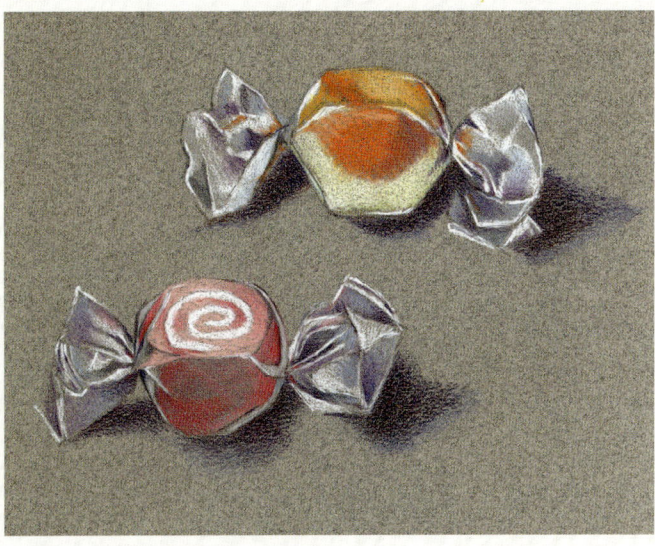

ABOVE *This illustration shows just how many neutrals can be used with some bright hues to create a combination of colour and grey. All the colours used are shown at the top.*

ABOVE *Here I worked on grey paper and created the cellophane sweet wrappers with blue, violet, white and grey. The white highlights add liveliness.*

complementaries of hues used within the drawing can add colour harmony. Another way is to layer the three primary colours, red, blue and yellow.

Alternatively, you can start with a grey coloured pencil and then layer other colours, such as blue or violet, over it to make it more interesting. Manufacturers of coloured pencils make a range of wonderful greys with various percentages of both cool and warm tones. The Glass Bottles project (see pages 230–5) uses a few warm greys in different percentages to create the illusion of clear glass.

In coloured-pencil drawing it can sometimes be tricky to create the right neutral or colourful grey with just colour. Pencil manufacturers produce greys in different percentages of tonal value that can help with finding the right mixture. You can dull a colour or colour combination with a grey pencil, or you can begin by drawing with a grey pencil and layering some colour on top. Adjust the colour temperature by using either warm or cool grey pencils.

Find the correct degree of lightness or darkness by using grey pencils in different percentages.

We rarely see landscapes and objects with high chroma, so by controlling colour intensity with greys, you will produce realistic, true-to-life images.

BELOW *I often ask my students to draw white objects, to see what colours and neutrals are contained within the shadows. Besides greys, the colours used are blue, violet, yellow and red.*

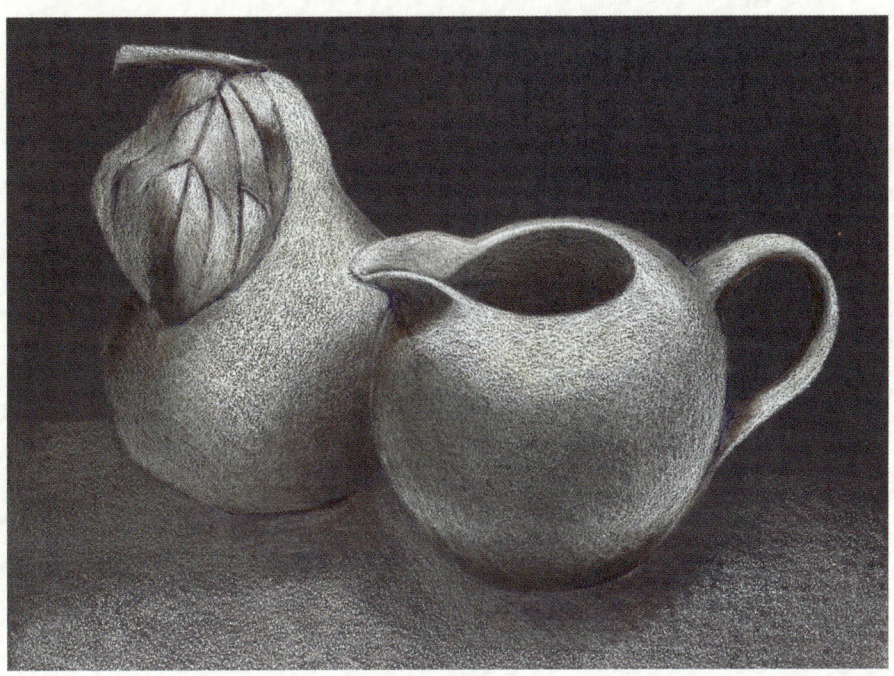

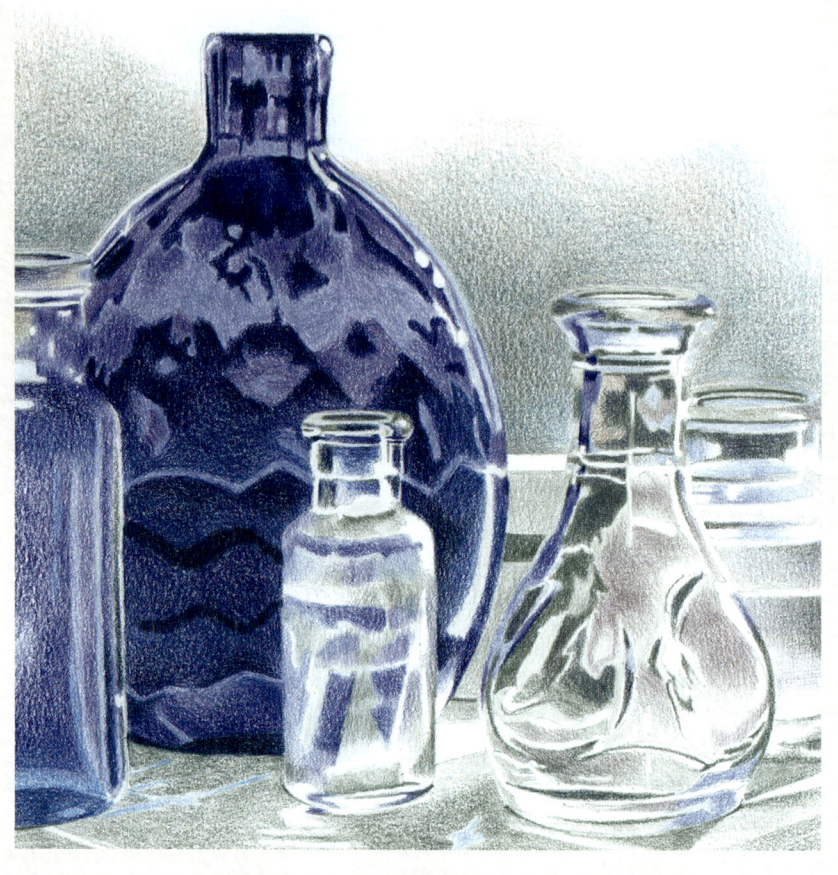

Glass Bottles

Here we learn how to draw transparent, opaque and coloured round glass objects. We will create the illusion of smooth glass by building line, shape, and light and dark patterns. This project will strengthen your ability to draw reflective surfaces and work with different ellipses to create rounded forms.

PENCILS USED: PRISMACOLOR AND CARAN D'ACHE LUMINANCE

Warm Grey 10%	Warm Grey 20%	Warm Grey 50%	Sky Blue Light	Caribbean Sea	Cobalt Blue Hue	Imperial Violet	Violet Blue

Indanthrone Blue	True Blue	Mediterranean Blue	Copenhagen Blue	Kelly Green	Genuine Cobalt Blue	Burnt Sienna 50%	Light Aubergine

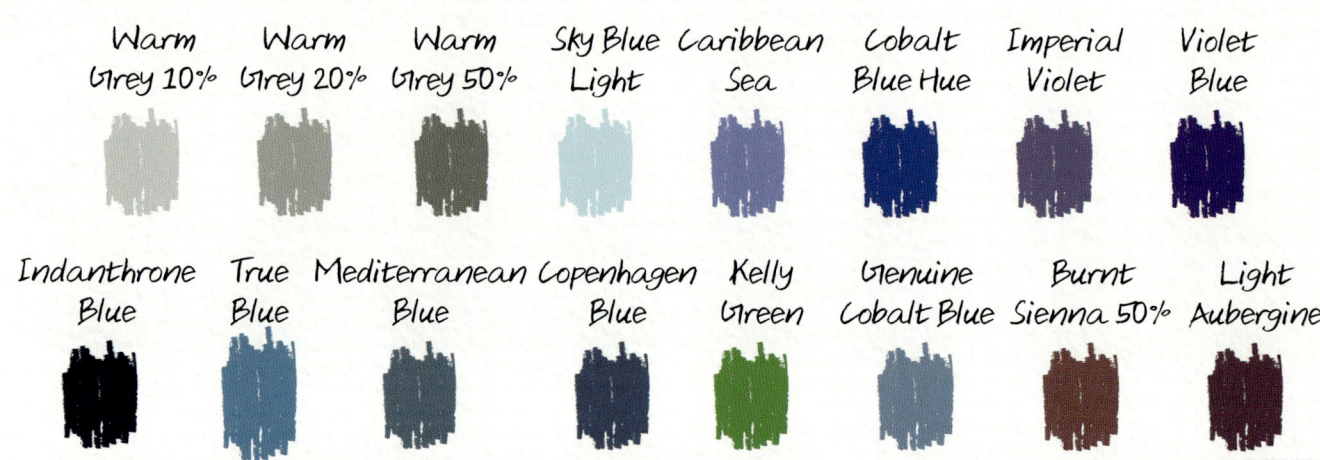

Glass is a transparent material, its contours and shapes being formed by light and the reflections of objects surrounding it. In the previous projects we learned to construct solid forms and to create lights and darks by looking only at the surface of an object. But glass is a transparent grouping of abstract curves, patterns and distortions that are broken down into shapes of light, medium and dark tones. We don't just look at the outside of the glass; we look through it. We see the inside, outside and what is behind the glass all at the same time, not the material of the glass itself.

HOW TO DRAW REFLECTIONS

In the photo, the light comes from the window as the sun shines in from the right-hand side. The sunlight bounces off the bottles and creates reflections on the windowsill where they sit. The movement of sunlight on the glass makes bright reflections, and pure white highlights cause the glass to sparkle. Notice also how the light is distorted as it flows through the glass, forming abstract and fragmented shapes.

Reflected shapes can appear intimidating, though they are actually fun to draw. My students are usually nervous about tackling glass, but they always end up really enjoying the lesson. Start by looking for light and dark patterns that can be broken down into shapes, as the contrast between bright highlights and strong darks gives the glass its character and dimension.

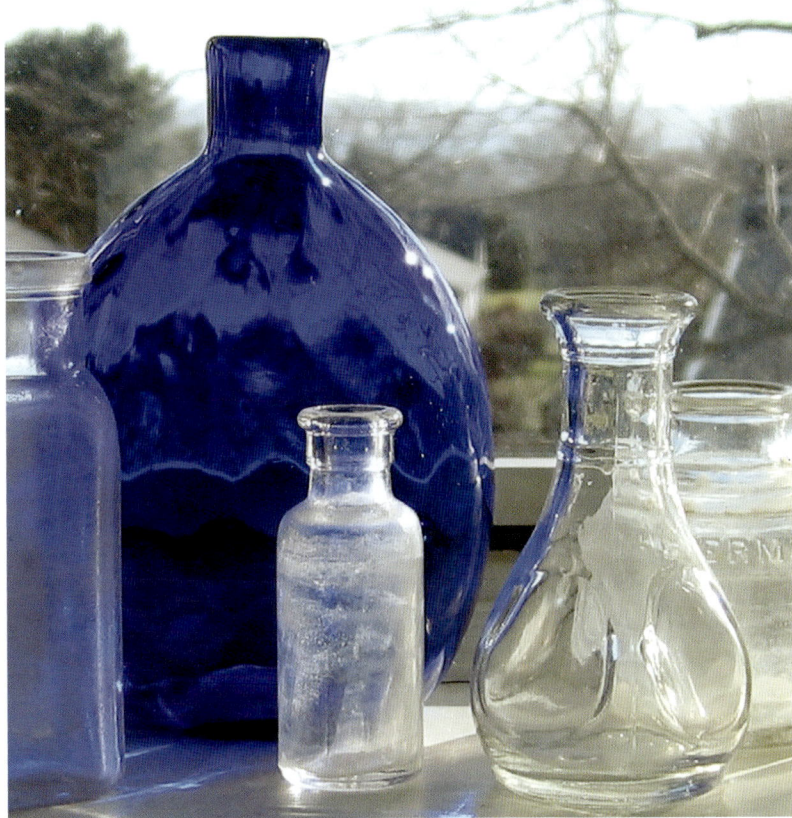

ABOVE *The clear bottles reflect the colours of the window frame and the outside scene, plus the blue tones of the blue bottle. The blue glass is also reflected in the shadow of the windowsill.*

RIGHT *Drawing a vertical line down the centre of the bottle will ensure the sides are even, while horizontal lines will ensure the ellipses aren't lopsided. The circles on the right illustrate how the ellipses flatten near eye level and begin to open below eye level.*

The round parts of the bottles and vases are made up of a series of ellipses that help each piece look three-dimensional. An ellipse is a circle that is viewed from a different perspective or vantage point so it appears flattened and foreshortened. The only time the ellipse at the top will be a complete circle is when you look straight down from above the bottle.

I selected a smooth white paper called Bristol vellum for this project. It's a good choice for drawing glass because it will accept layers of pencil and is excellent for detailed drawing. Before I began, I studied my reference photo and each bottle as a subject. I evaluated the reflections and picked out the shapes and highlights that were most important. Seeing so many little shapes of colour can get confusing to the eye, so I have left some out. I have also left out the letters imprinted in the glass on the right.

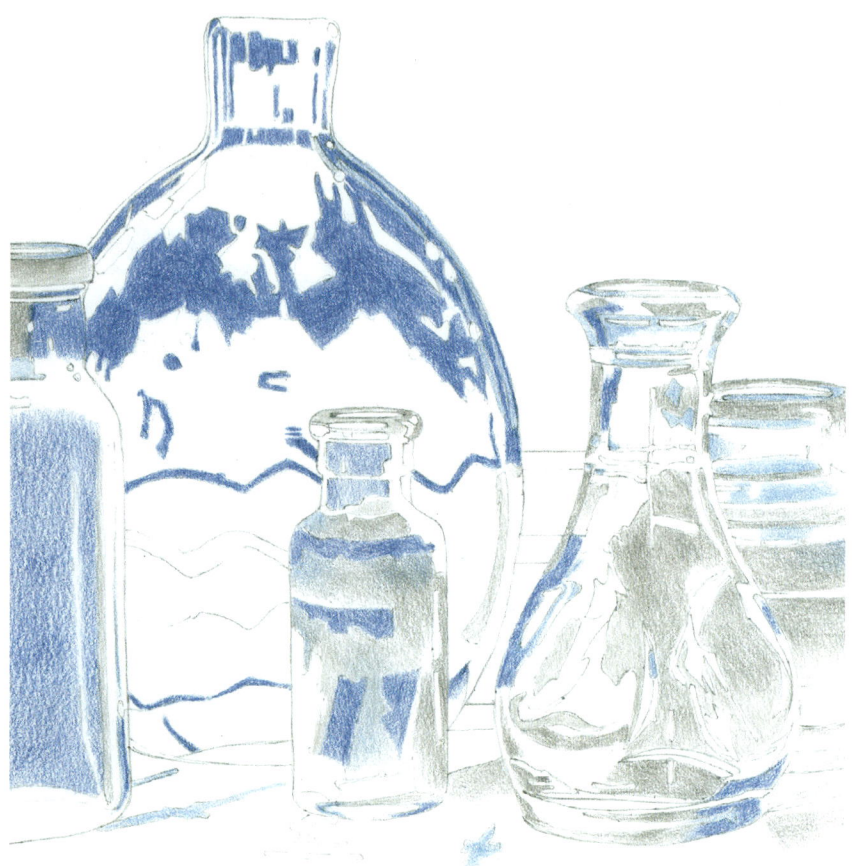

STAGE 1

Draw the outline of each bottle and, using horizontal or vertical guidelines,
check that your bottles are symmetrical and ellipses are correctly rounded.
If you look at my line drawing, you'll see that I have simplified and omitted
some of the reflected shapes, particularly in the rounded bottle to the front
right. Notice how the distorted shapes follow the contours of the bottles.
The clear bottles are reflecting the colours of the window frame and the outside
scene behind them. They are also reflecting the blue tones of the blue bottle.
The blue glass is reflected in the shadow of the windowsill. Notice the two left
bottles have areas that are somewhat cloudy and not completely clear.

The highlights will remain the white of the paper rather than being coloured
with pencil. Take Warm Grey 10% and Warm Grey 20%, then colour the
lighter tonal value areas of the clear bottles – use Warm Grey 10% in the
lightest areas and Warm Grey 20% where the glass begins to darken in tone.

Put Caribbean Sea in the lighter blue areas of the bottles and on the blue
reflections of the windowsill surface. Add Genuine Cobalt Blue to the darker
blue areas of the bottles.

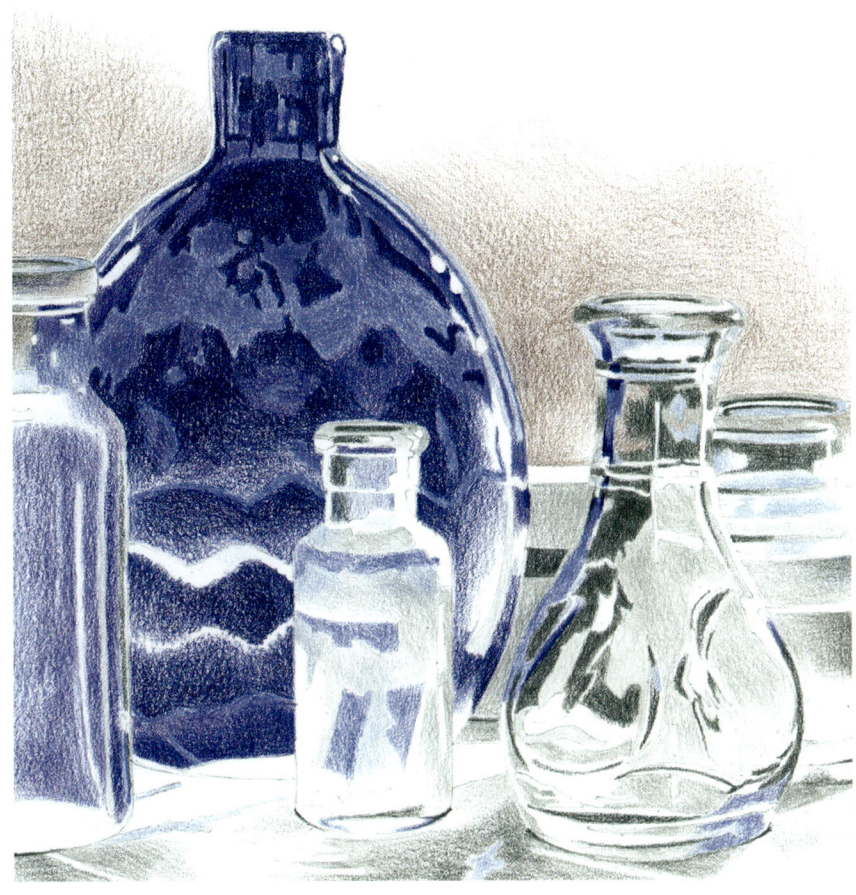

STAGE 2

Layer pencils with medium pressure to build areas of dark colours. Add Warm Grey 20% and Warm Grey 50% on the small area of window frame behind the bottles. Put Warm Grey 50% on the dark grey areas of the clear bottles and add Warm Grey 20% and 50% on the windowsill surface to create lighter and darker tones. Add Imperial Violet to the purple reflected areas on the blue bottle and on the clear bottle to the left. Colour the darkest areas of the blue bottle with Violet Blue. Vary the pressure and lightly apply some Violet Blue so it will fade into the other colours to be added later.

Notice that some areas of the bottles have distinct shapes with hard edges, and in other areas the colours have soft edges and are lightly blended together. Most of the lines and shapes are curved and contoured, following the shape of the bottles. Pay attention to changes in tone and form. Use your kneaded eraser to make sure lines on the edges and ellipses are crisp. You can also use the electric eraser to clean up sharp edges.

Using a light pressure, colour the background with Burnt Sienna 50%. We will layer colours to build up an illusion of the outdoors behind the bottles. The background will remain soft and out of focus as we don't want it to distract from the bottles, which are our main subjects.

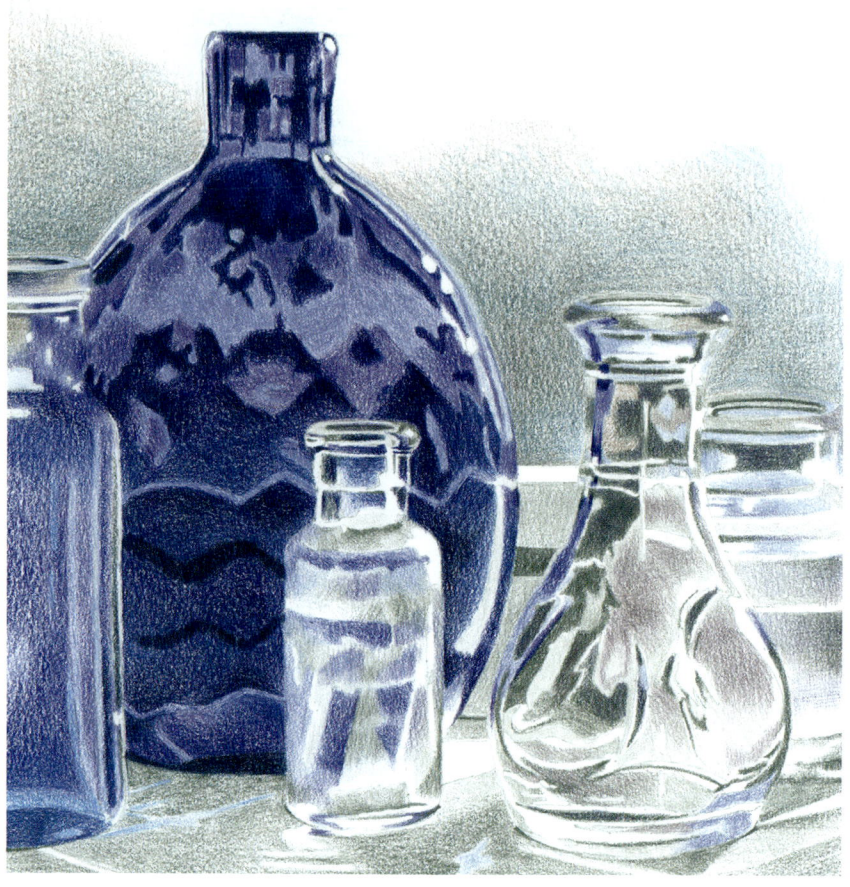

STAGE 3

Take the Indanthrone Blue pencil and work on the blue bottle. Add the colour to the darkest areas, working it into the Violet Blue. Also use it on the bottom edge, the stripes across it, the upper part and on the neck.

The blue bottle is mostly made up of warm blues (leaning towards violet on the colour wheel), but it also consists of cool blues (leaning towards green on the colour wheel). Lightly layer True Blue and Copenhagen Blue on the bottle to add warm blue tones. True Blue is the lighter of the two colours so add it to the lighter areas. Copenhagen Blue is darker and can be layered over the darker areas.

The clear bottles all contain reflected blue tones. Work on building these with the different pencils. The three bottles on the right have edges that are crisp and distinct. The bottle on the left is somewhat cloudy, so colours should be soft and

blended except for the edges. The left bottle also contains the warmer blues, True Blue and Copenhagen Blue, reflected from the blue bottle.

The blue areas in all the bottles link the subjects together and create a colour harmony within the drawing. I have also added another layer of Warm Grey 50% to the windowsill to add more tone to the surface in which the bottles sit.

Add Light Aubergine over some of the grey areas in the rounded bottle to the front right. Lightly add Imperial Violet to the other two clear bottles on either side. These colours will add subtle warmth and variety to the grey tones.

Layer Mediterranean Blue over the Burnt Sienna 50% in the background. Apply the pencil with cross-hatch strokes to achieve a soft blended appearance.

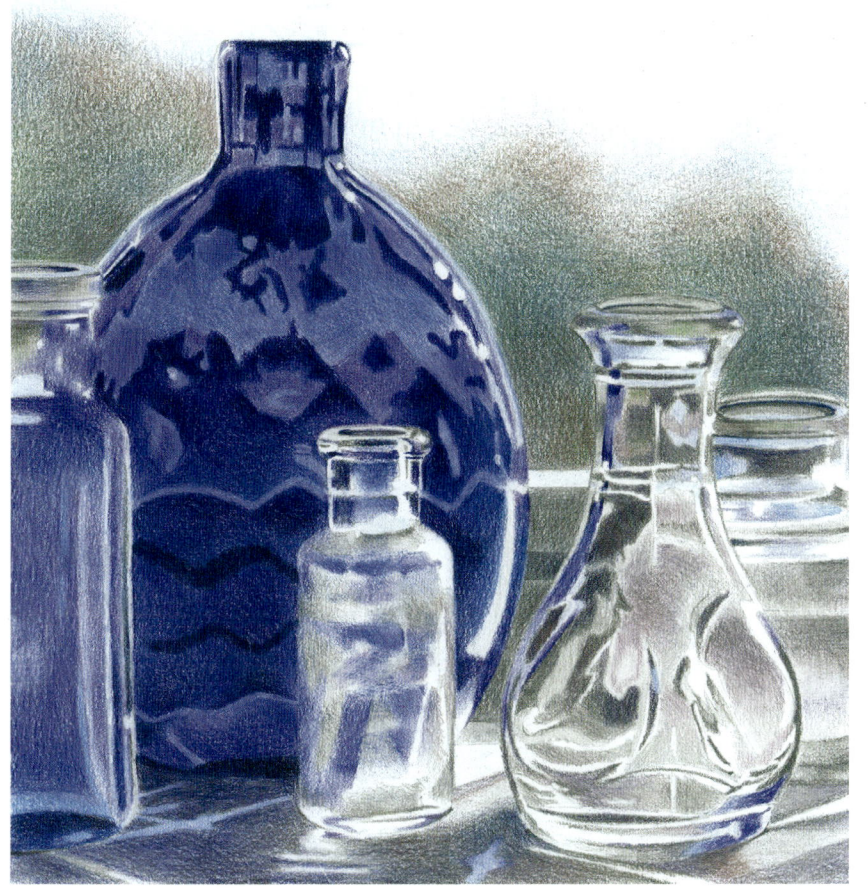

STAGE 4

To create the smooth appearance of the glass, take a stiff bristle brush or colourless blender pencil and burnish the blue bottle to remove the texture of the paper showing through (see page 200). Burnish carefully around the white areas so they don't become smudged with blue.

Now burnish the other bottles. Don't use the same brush on these areas – use different brushes for different colours, or sharpen colourless blender pencils to remove colour using the point. You can still make adjustments to the colours after you have burnished them.

I darkened the grey tones on the small area of window frame behind the bottles and made a few more adjustments to the shapes and highlights within the bottles. The contrast between the dark and light shapes and the smooth texture will help to give the illusion of glass.

Then I continued to build up shadows and reflections in the windowsill. I decided it needed to be darker in tone, so I added another layer of Warm Grey 50%, Light Aubergine and Violet Blue where colour and light are reflected through the bottles.

I also continued to work on the background by adding a layer of Kelly Green overall, then went back to areas of the foliage and, using medium pressure, applied more Burnt Sienna 50% and Mediterranean Blue. The upper part of the sky is coloured with a light layer of Sky Blue Light.

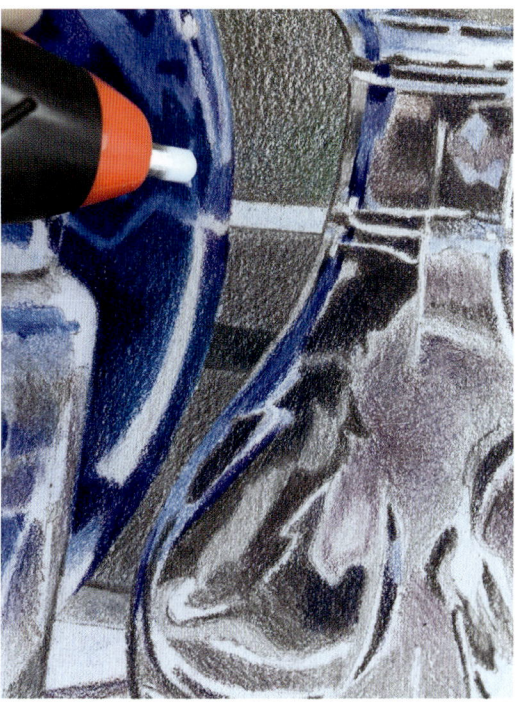

LEFT *A battery-operated eraser can be used as a tool to redraw areas of white highlights that were smudged or covered up.*

You can use the electric eraser to redraw white highlights that have been smudged or covered up. Check your edges and ellipses, then add contour lines on the edges to create depth and dimension.

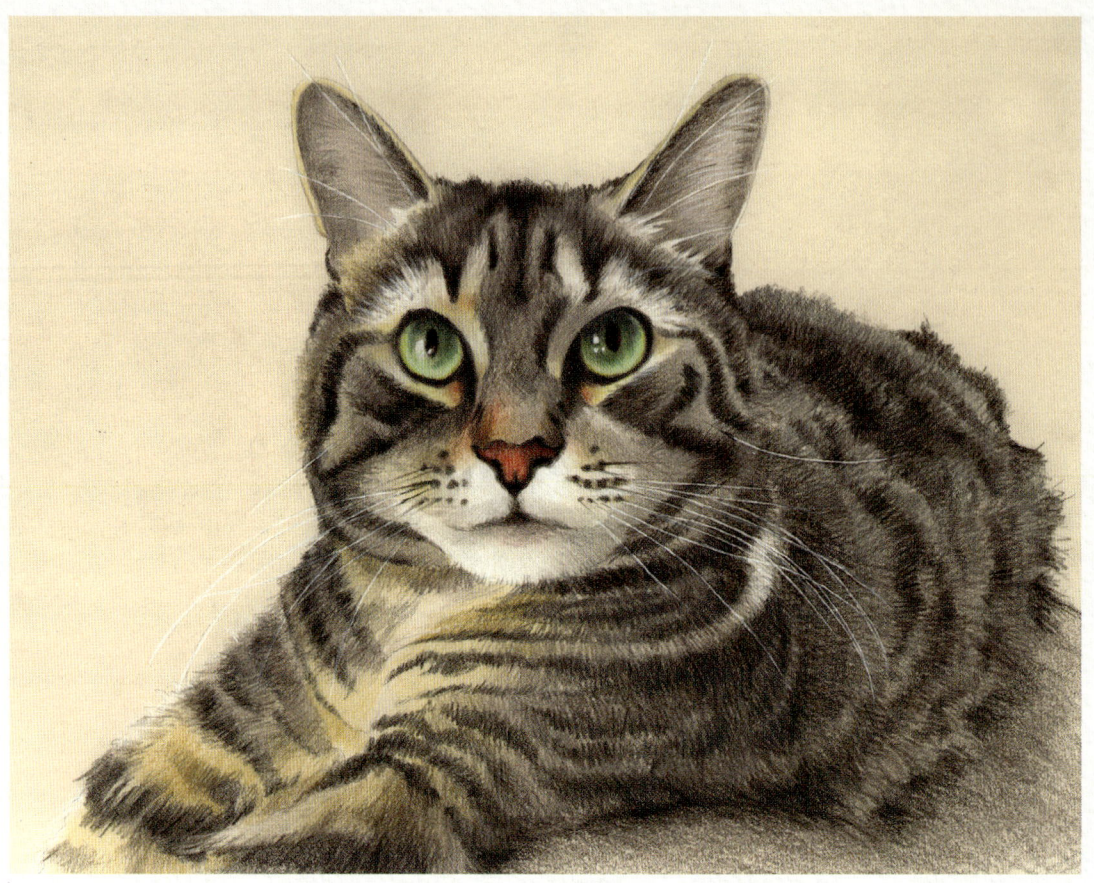

Portrait of a Pet

Coloured pencils are ideally suited to creating a beautiful, realistic drawing of a pet, as they can capture the texture and subtle details of fur. In this project you will learn how to simplify colours and patterns in fur, and use strokes to show its direction of growth. You will also discover how to draw three-dimensional eyes and use the sgraffito technique to depict whiskers.

PENCILS USED: CARAN D'ACHE PABLO

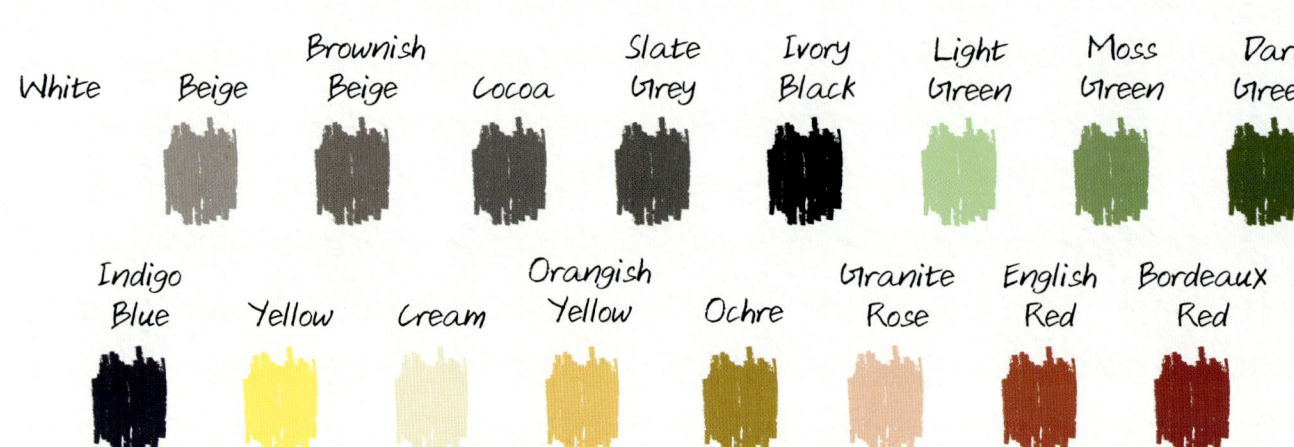

White | Beige | Brownish Beige | Cocoa | Slate Grey | Ivory Black | Light Green | Moss Green | Dark Green

Indigo Blue | Yellow | Cream | Orangish Yellow | Ochre | Granite Rose | English Red | Bordeaux Red

For many years I have been drawing coloured pencil pet portraits for clients. I always work from photographs, as it would be difficult to have the pet sit still for the period of time it takes to draw them. I like to have a few reference photos, and if possible I like to meet the pet to study their characteristics. It's very important to select a photo that has good lighting, captures the personality of the pet and possibly has an interesting angle or pose.

The pet model I chose for this project is a family member's cat named Cato. I am already familiar with Cato and his characteristics, so that made it easier for me to draw him. I liked this particular photo of him because it depicts a little of his personality. It also provides a good close-up view of his facial features and shows the variations of colour in his fur.

It's very helpful to have a little understanding of an animal's physical anatomy. Knowing the basics of how their bones and muscles connect will help when drawing their physical structure. Look at their body parts – the head, legs, ears and tail – and notice how and where each part connects to the body. You also need to be able to convey the illusion of skin and fur. Notice their different textures: skin can be smooth, sagging or contain wrinkles or rolls; fur can be short, long, curly or wiry. To draw fur requires patience, paying attention to detail and building strokes and layers. Strokes need to be random so that hairs appear to grow naturally.

FOCUSING ON THE EYES

In our drawing, we want to focus on Cato's facial features, in particular, his eyes. The eyes are an animal's most important feature, as they capture their personality and soul, and will captivate the viewer so they look further into the drawing. Cato has beautiful green eyes so we're going to accentuate the colours to make them appear bright and lively. Highlights in the eyes are reflections of the surrounding environment. Highlights and variations of colour will help the eyes appear three-dimensional and glassy.

CHOOSING MATERIALS

It is important to choose a paper that will complement the pet. I could have selected a white paper, but it would have taken much more time to cover with colour. Instead I opted for a beige 100% cotton smooth drawing/printmaking paper, which has a soft finish and isn't overly textured. The cotton finish holds the pencil nicely and beige is one of the colours in Cato's fur, so letting the paper show through did some of the work. It also serves as an attractive background colour to complement the drawing.

I chose Pablo coloured pencils for this project because they're made of a firm oil-based lead that doesn't crumble. They are perfect for drawing fine lines and details in fur and are also easy to erase or lighten with a kneaded rubber.

BELOW *When drawing a pet portrait, it's much easier to work from a good photograph that is well lit.*

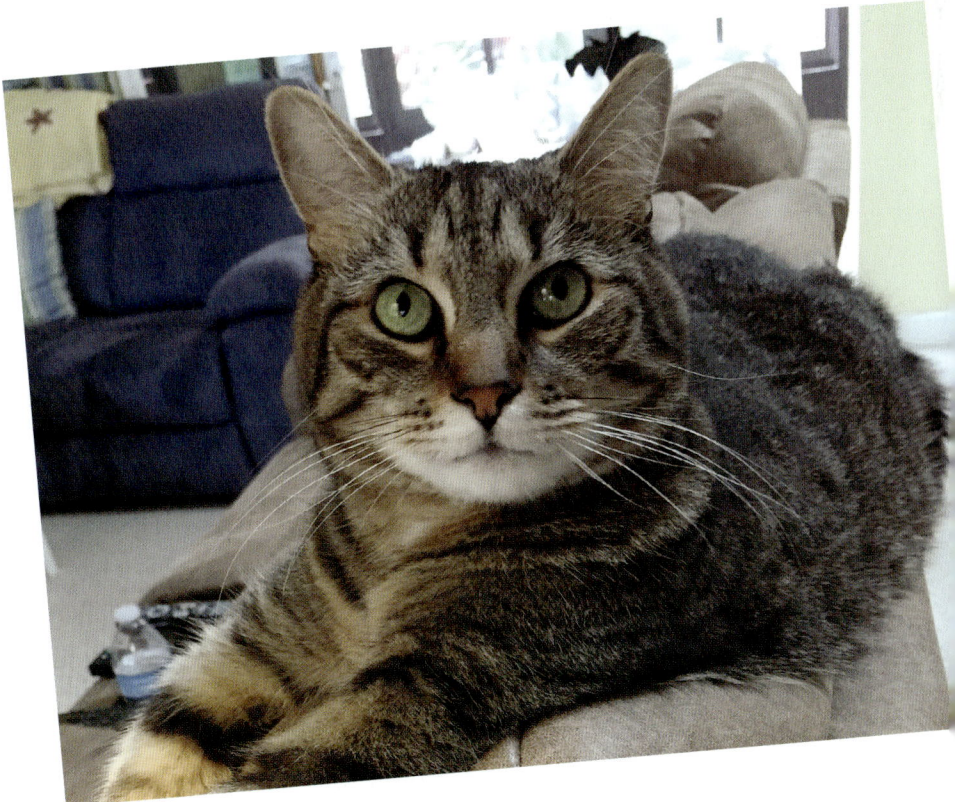

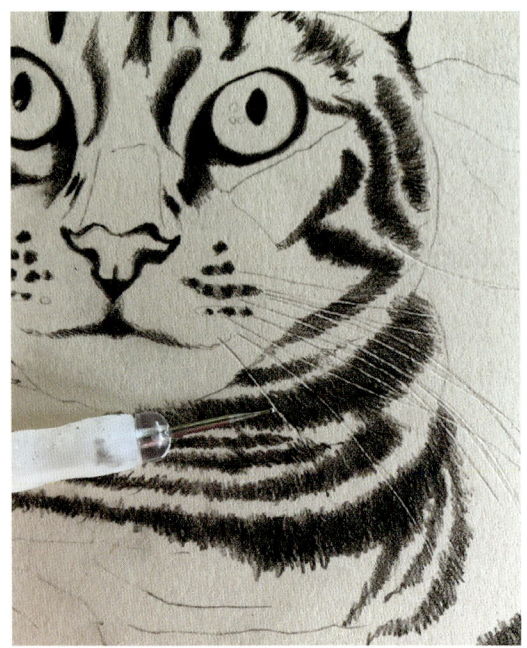

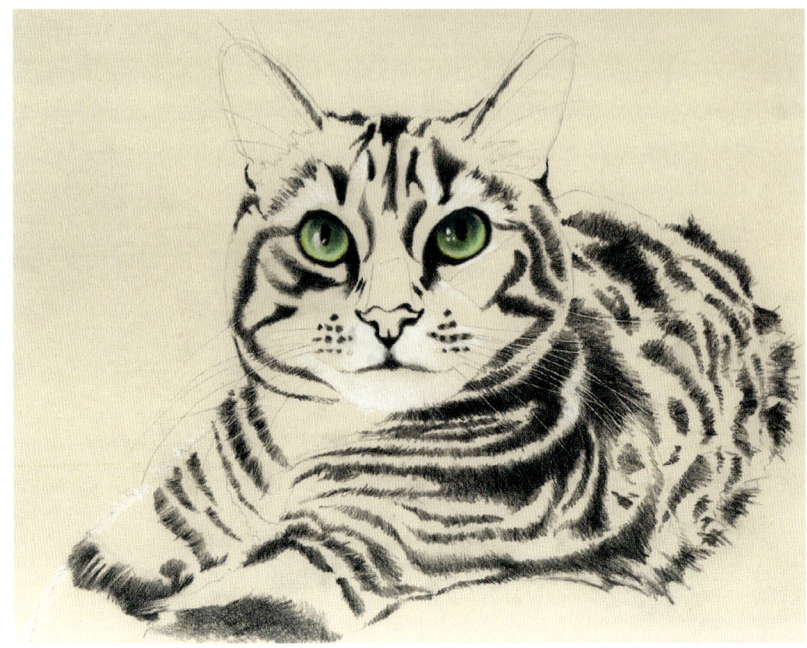

ABOVE *Use a medium to hard pressure to emboss lines for the whiskers so that they will remain the colour of the paper. I have added Ivory Black to demonstrate this. Notice I have also put highlights in his eyes so I will know their position when I draw them.*

STAGE 1

Begin with graphite pencil and draw Cato's outline, facial features including whiskers, and the striped patterns on his fur. Take time to observe the proportions, features and patterns in order to draw them correctly. Notice the direction in which the fur moves to form the body contours and look for changes in direction. Use a light pressure so you will be able to correct mistakes.

When the sketch is complete, use an embossing tool to indent lines in the paper for each of Cato's whiskers (see close-up, top left). If you don't have an embossing tool, you can use another bluntly pointed object such as a thin knitting needle.

Using Ivory Black, block in the black stripes of the fur and Cato's other facial features. This will serve as the foundation for the other colours to be added later. It requires patience to lay in all those dark stripes and areas, so be sure to take your time. Next, add White to Cato's mouth, the highlights in his eyes, above and under his eyes, and where the light hits his fur under the whiskers as well as on the edge of his right leg.

BELOW *Keep your pencil strokes smooth to make the eyes appear rounded and glassy.*

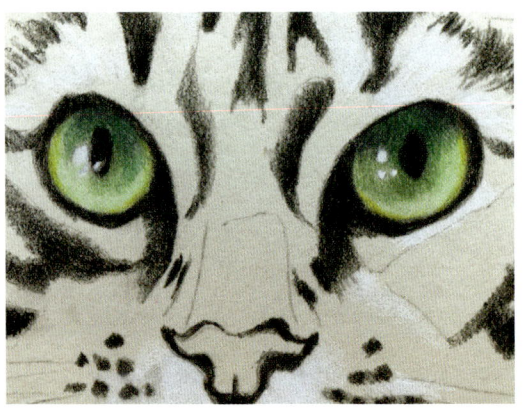

As I mentioned earlier, eyes depict an animal's personality so it's important to position the highlights correctly to ensure they look natural. Too many white highlights will look unnatural, which is why I chose only the largest. Draw these in White, then add the other colours. Start by lightly laying in Yellow along the bottom rounded edges and then continue with Light Green, working it into the Yellow. I used Moss Green to transition light colours to dark colours. The tops of the eyes will be darker because they are pushed back and shadowed by the lids. Use Dark Green and Indigo Blue for the darker areas in the upper part of the eyes.

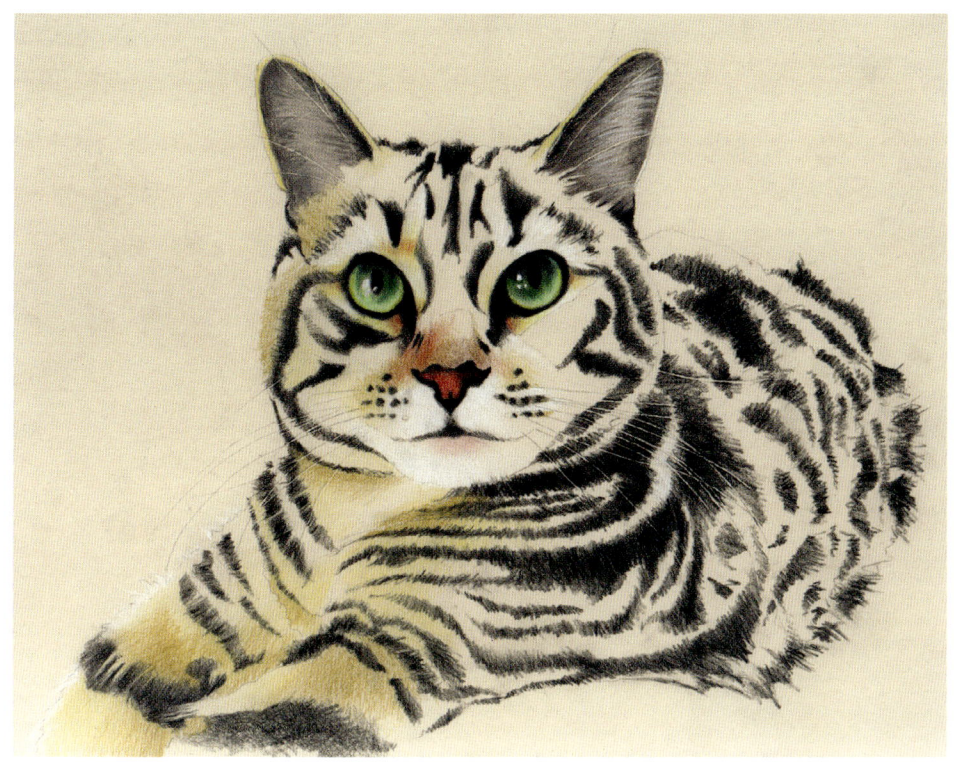

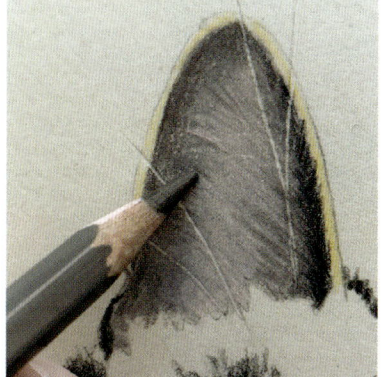

STAGE 2

Having blocked in the black stripes and white areas, and worked on the eyes, you have a good foundation for your drawing. Now you can start adding details.

Cato has beige and yellow tones under parts of his fur, on his face, chest and front legs. Use Cream, Orangish Yellow and Ochre on these areas to build the undertones. Blend the colours on his face where the hairs are short and smooth, and use directional strokes on his paws where the fur is longer.

For Cato's nose and nostrils, use a medium pressure to apply English Red and Bordeaux Red within the Ivory Black outline. Lightly layer the two colours around and above the tip of his nose, then very lightly apply Bordeaux Red under his mouth.

The colours we're using for Cato's ears are Granite Rose, Beige, Brownish Beige, Cocoa, Orangish Yellow, White and Ivory Black. Start by applying strokes of Granite Rose to the centres, using a light pressure to build up colour. Layer Beige and Brownish Beige next, paying attention to the outwards direction the fur is growing and allowing the base colours to show through.

Add Cocoa and Ivory Black to the dark edges of the fur on the inner ears, and combine lighter and darker colours by interlacing the hair strokes. All the pencils are lightly layered, so you can add a few strokes of White on top to show lighter hairs. Notice the edges of the ears curve inwards and the darkest areas are closest to the centre of the head. Place Orangish Yellow and White on the very edges around the dark area.

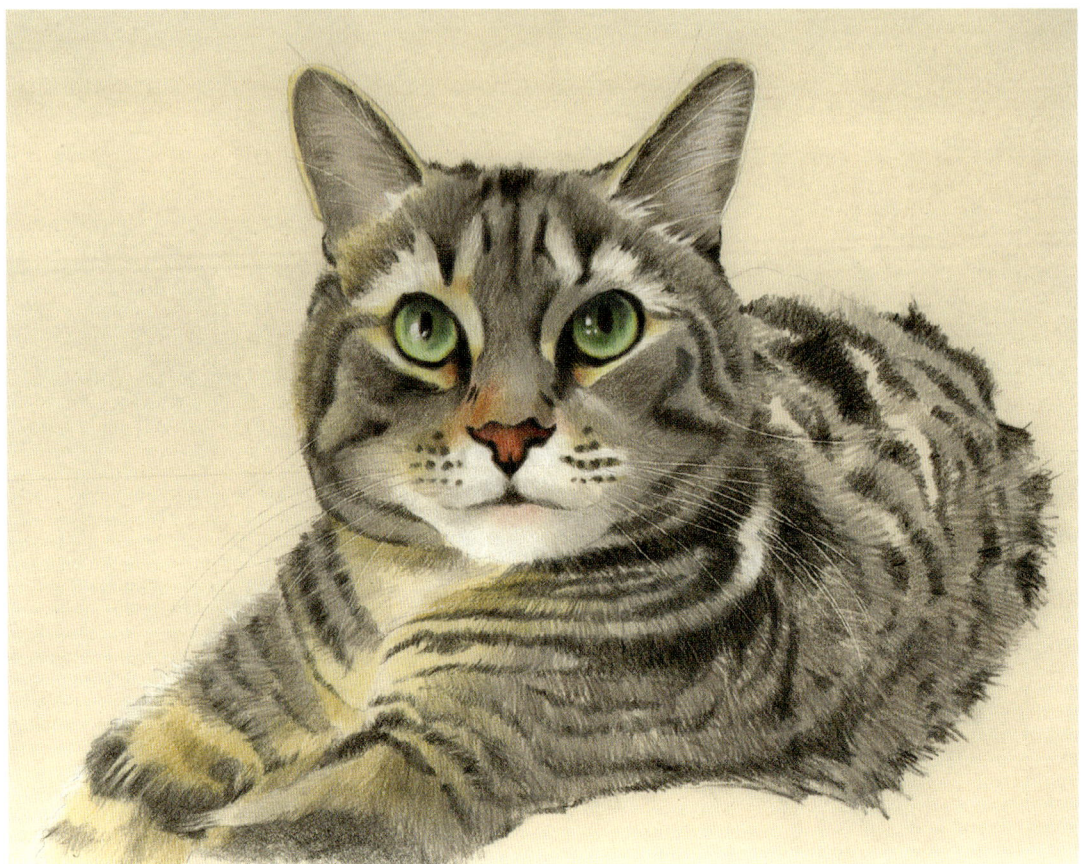

STAGE 3

The next step is to add Beige and Cocoa to the fur, giving depth and dimension to Cato's head and body. Begin with the lightest colour, Beige, on his face, and add a little to his chest, paws and body. Layer Cocoa over the Beige, allowing some of the Beige to show through in the lighter areas. It's almost impossible to draw every hair, so I like to work on small sections at a time. Use the black patterns as a guide when placing the different greys.

Keep your pencils sharp to create the look of hair strands and make sure your strokes follow the direction of the fur and the contours of his body. The hairs on Cato's face are shorter and smoother, while the hairs on his body and legs are longer. You'll see that I have added rough strokes of fur on his body, which I'll refine later. Also notice where the paper shows through, serving as a base layer of colour for the drawing.

The pencils are soft and can be smudged into lighter areas as you work with them, so I often put a sheet of clean paper under my drawing hand to avoid accidentally smudging them. But the pencils are easily cleaned up or lightened by dabbing areas with a kneaded eraser.

Tip
You don't have to draw every cat hair, just strokes that will be combined with other colours to give it a natural look.

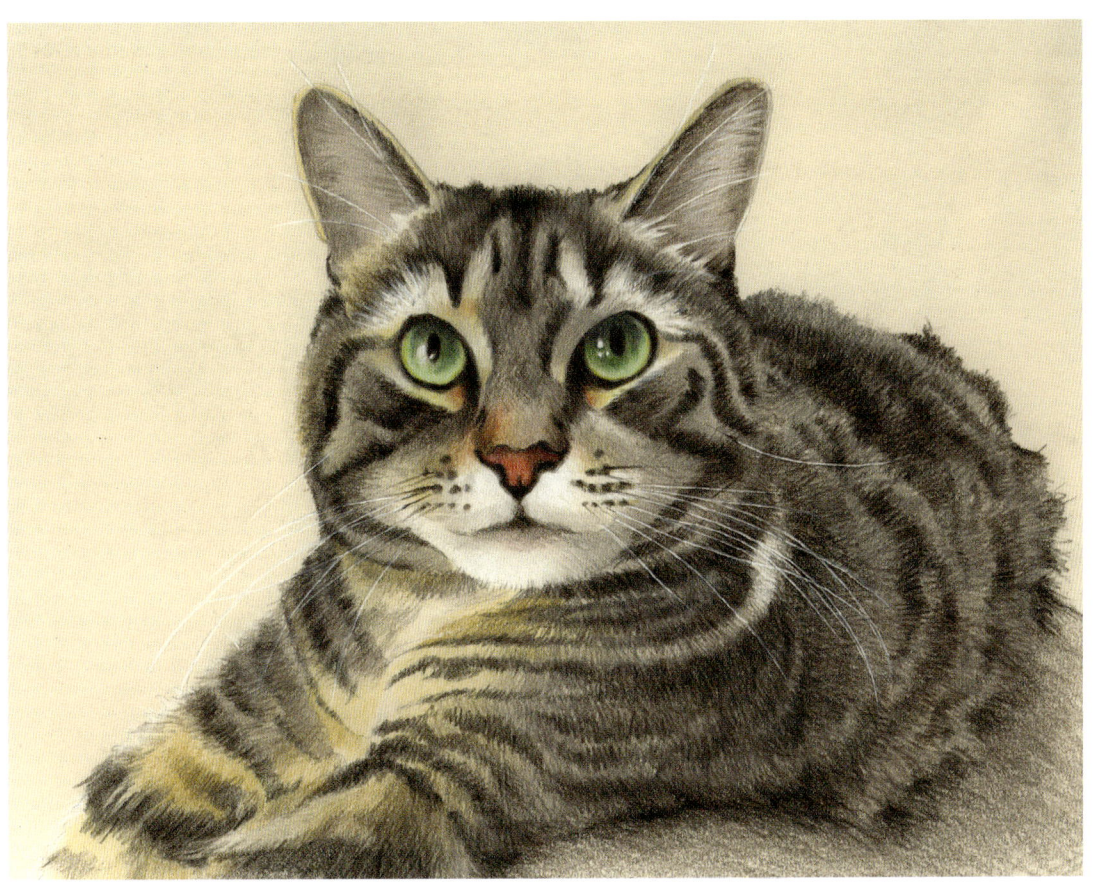

STAGE 4

Now take the last fur colour, Slate Grey, and layer in the darker areas to give Cato yet more dimension. Add short strokes of Slate Grey around the black areas above his eyes and on the sides of his cheeks. Then add it to the darker areas on his back and right side. The rough strokes will allow the other layers of colour to show through. Note some parts of the fur are almost scribbled and don't have to be as smoothly layered as other project drawings.

Refine any areas that need attention. You may need to adjust the eyes now that all the fur colours are layered on his face. Perhaps make them more shadowed at the top, so they appear round. I have added strokes of White to feature his eyebrows.

Use Cocoa and Ivory Black to draw in a shadowed area underneath Cato, so that he appears to be sitting on something. I chose these two colours because they subtly blend with Cato's fur.

Finally, add White to the grooves created for his whiskers. Make sure the pencil is very sharp, then gently fill in the grooves. Work from the inside outwards and let the pencil lighten at the tips of the whiskers. Be careful not to press too hard, otherwise the point will break off, and don't allow the pencil to stray out of the groove.

You now have a lovely pet portrait and are ready to practise with your own pet!

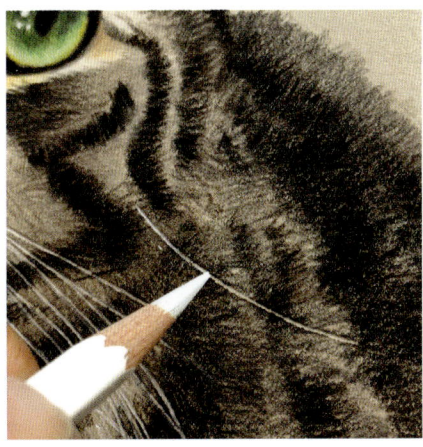

ABOVE *Take a sharp White pencil and gently fill in the grooves you created with the embossing tool.*

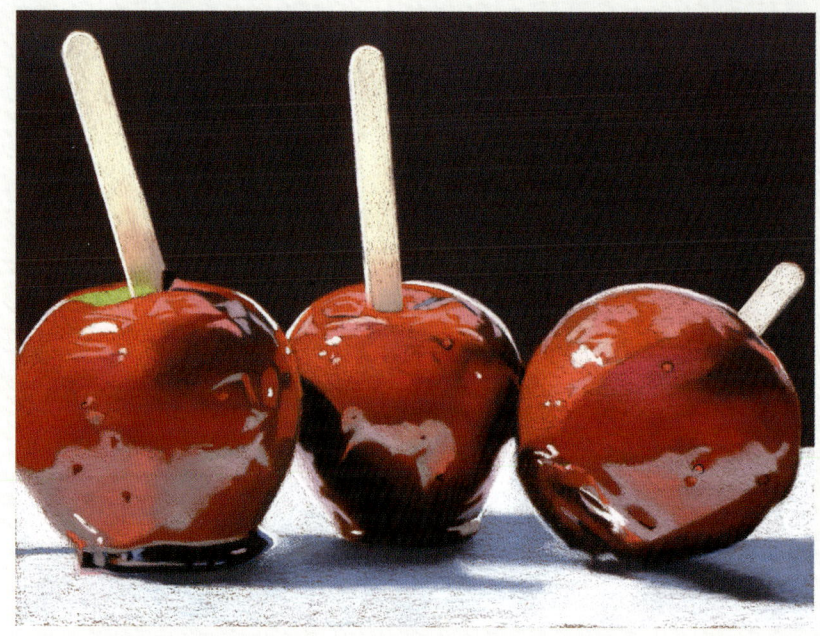

Toffee Apples

In this project we will learn how to combine coloured pencil with solvent to create a more painterly effect. Solvent melts the wax binder in the pencil, eliminating pencil strokes and smoothing out the surface of the drawing. This technique also helps make the layering of colours much quicker.

PENCILS USED: PRISMACOLOR AND CARAN D'ACHE LUMINANCE

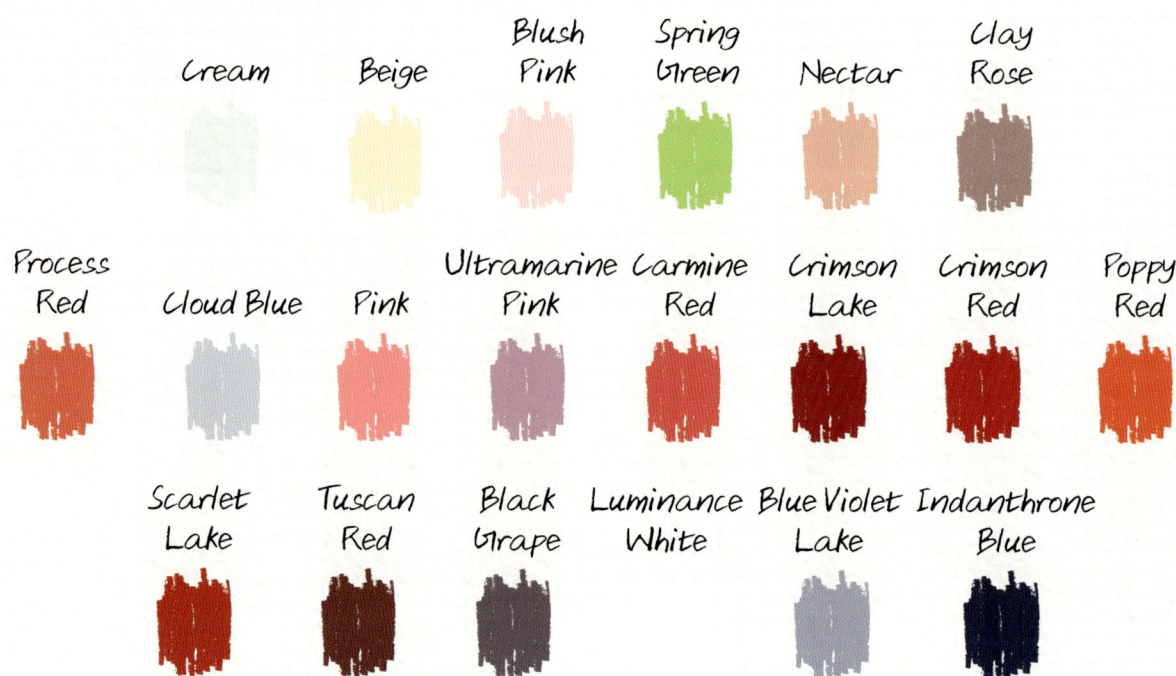

Cream Beige Blush Pink Spring Green Nectar Clay Rose

Process Red Cloud Blue Pink Ultramarine Pink Carmine Red Crimson Lake Crimson Red Poppy Red

Scarlet Lake Tuscan Red Black Grape Luminance White Blue Violet Lake Indanthrone Blue

OTHER MATERIALS NEEDED

- Odourless mineral spirits or turpentine
- ¼in (6mm) soft flat synthetic paintbrush
- Optional: ½in (12mm) soft flat brush or soft round brush
- Good-quality kitchen paper

CHOOSING THE RIGHT MATERIALS

The best pencils to use with solvent are those that have a soft wax base and blend more easily than harder pencils. Practise with different brands to determine which will work best for your type of drawing application.

Choosing the right paper is also a factor. I like a sturdy paper or board that will withstand layers of colour and solvent, and won't buckle or disintegrate when solvent is added. I often choose a sanded paper surface because the rough tooth holds the pencil, blends and builds colour quickly, but keep in mind it will also wear down the pencils faster. For this project I chose a warm red-toned sanded board, as the red background complements the apples so I could allow it to show through in some areas.

A word of warning when using solvent: even though it is considered odourless or natural, all solvents release some toxins into the air. We will only use a small amount of solvent for this project, but be sure to work in a well-ventilated area. Odourless mineral spirits and natural turpentine are the safest to use.

ADVANTAGES OF USING SOLVENT

Adding a little solvent to a layer of coloured pencil with a soft bristle brush will break down the wax binder and allow you to move pigment around the paper. Solvent fuses the colour into the paper and the layers of pencil become thick and opaque. After it dries, you can apply more layers of coloured pencils and solvent if needed. I enjoy this technique because I can create rich, vivid colours and make my drawing look more like a painting. It also means I can apply the coloured pencil more quickly and less evenly because I will smooth it out at a later stage.

Tip

It's a good idea to practise working with solvent and coloured pencil on a scrap of paper first to understand the results.

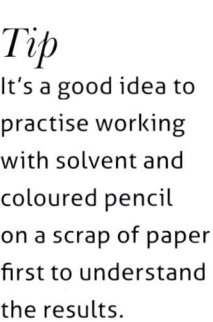

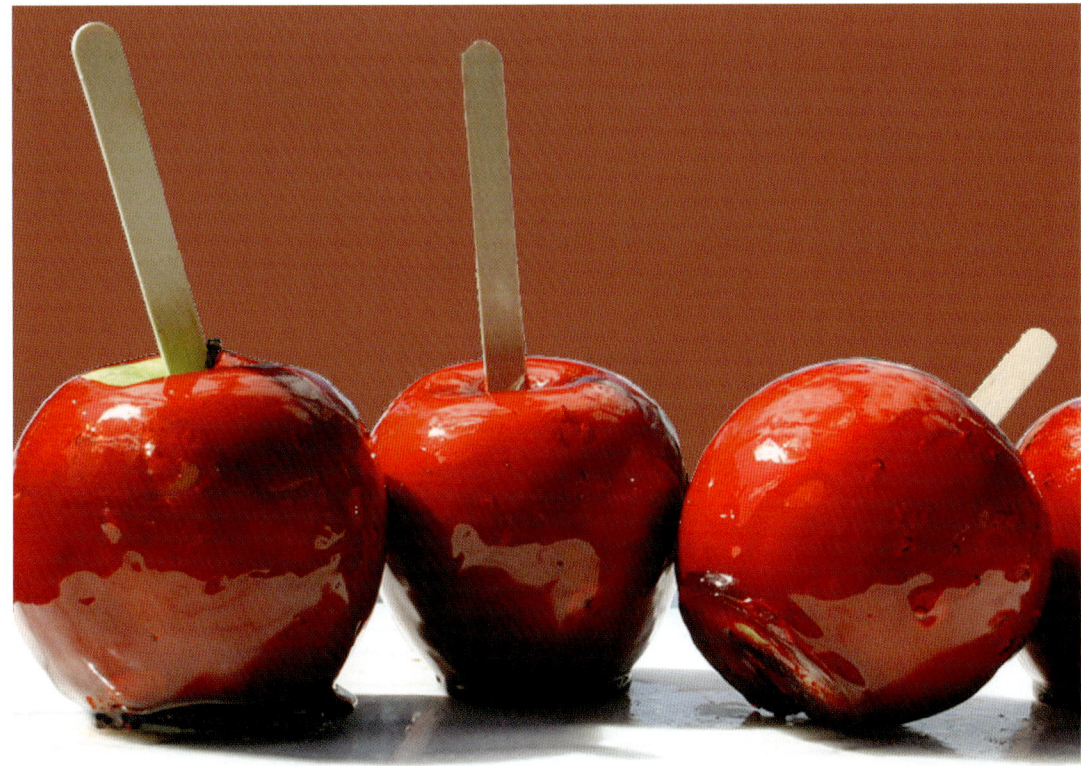

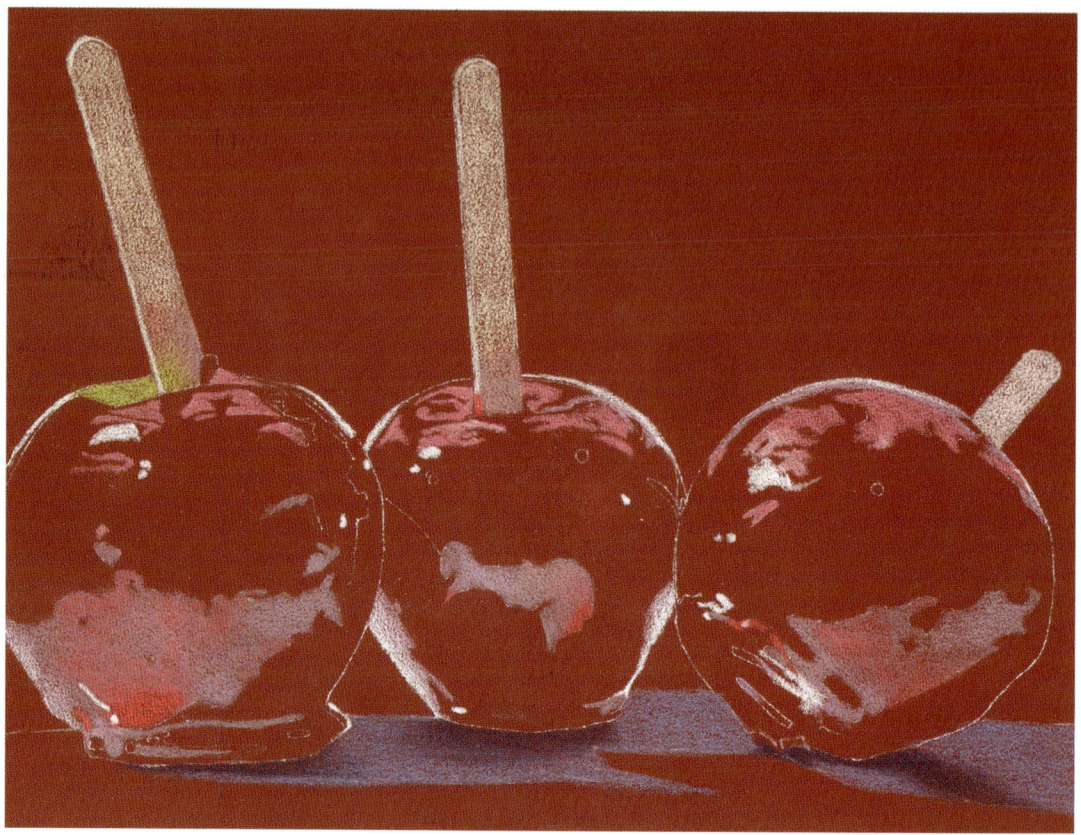

STAGE 1

I have drawn my outlines using a white erasable pencil so they will show on the red-toned paper. Sanded paper helps the pencil to blend and layer much easier but it will wear down the pencils faster. I test my colours on a scrap of the same coloured paper I am working on, as colours will appear different on a dark-toned surface such as this red.

Colouring the toffee apples will be similar to the Glass Bottles project (see pages 230–5), as we will be drawing shapes that are reflected in the apples. But as these shapes are opaque, rather than transparent, we will also round them with tonal values. And remember, you don't have to be very particular when laying down colour, because the solvent will smooth everything out later.

I begin by drawing the white highlights in the apples, where the light is hitting the fruit's shiny surfaces. Colour the reflections at the top of the apples with Blush Pink, Pink and Ultramarine Pink. For the larger reflections on the lower half of the apples, use Clay Rose and Ultramarine Pink, Blush Pink and Carmine Red.

Tip
Sanded paper is a good choice when you want to lay down colour quickly.

Now work on the sticks. First, apply Cream where the light is catching the side edges of the left and middle sticks. Add a bit of Carmine Red to the bottom side edge of the middle stick. Colour all three sticks with Beige but as you near the bottom use Nectar, Clay Rose and Spring Green on the left stick, as shown. The bottom of the middle stick is coloured with Nectar and Clay Rose and use just Beige on the right stick. For the shadowed area under the apples, use Blue Violet Lake and Black Grape.

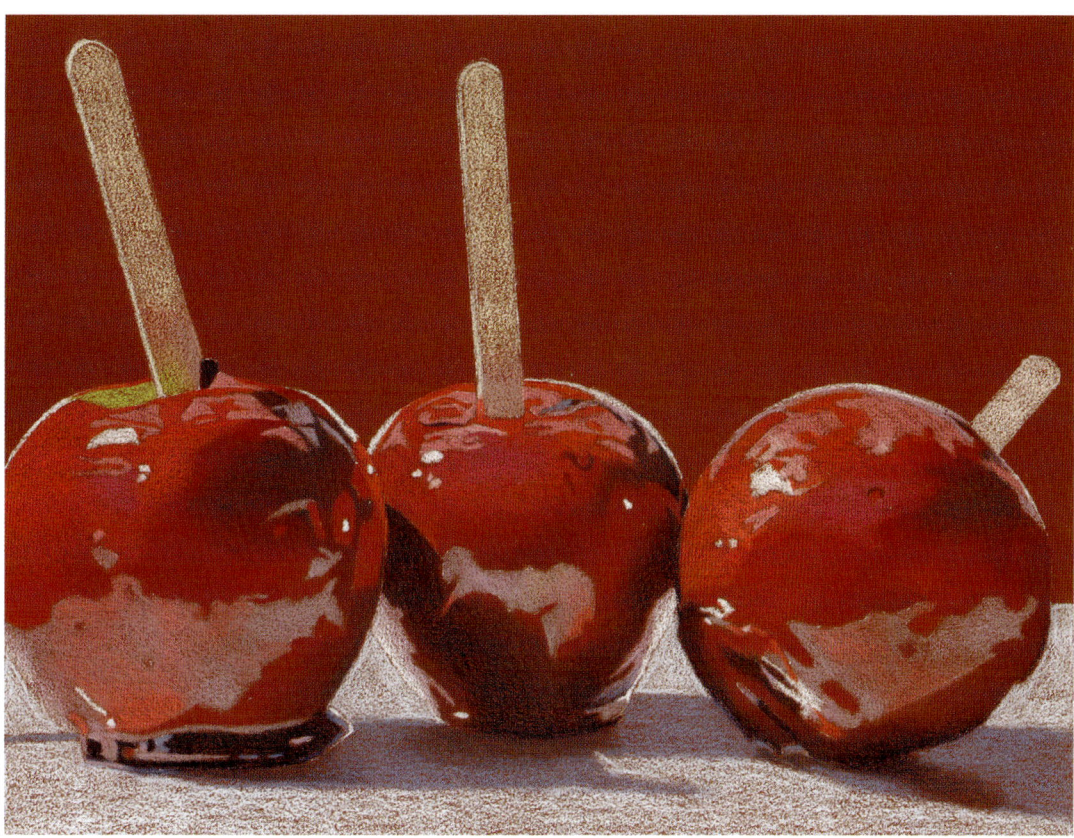

STAGE 2

Now the reflections are drawn, you can add red tones to the apples around
the reflected shapes using the picture as a guide. You'll notice that the red-
coloured pencils are softer and crumble more easily than other coloured
pencils. We will be blending edges of colours placed side by side into one
another in order to have a soft transition of tones. There isn't much layering
here, more placing colours next to one another.

We will use Poppy Red, Scarlet Lake, Crimson Red, Crimson Lake,
Process Red, Tuscan Red, Black Grape and Indanthrone Blue to add
colour to the rest of the apples. Apply Poppy Red to the lightest areas.
Use Scarlet Lake, Crimson Red and Crimson Lake for areas that turn
into shadow. Add Tuscan Red, Black Grape and Indanthrone Blue to
the dark shadowed areas between the apples and at their bases. Use the
dark pink colour of Process Red for accent.

Add or readjust colours in any of the reflections drawn in stage 1, then
carefully blend their edges into the red colours you have just applied.

Complete the surface on which the apples sit by applying Luminance
White to the lighter areas between the fruit, then add Cloud Blue and
a little Luminance White around the shadows.

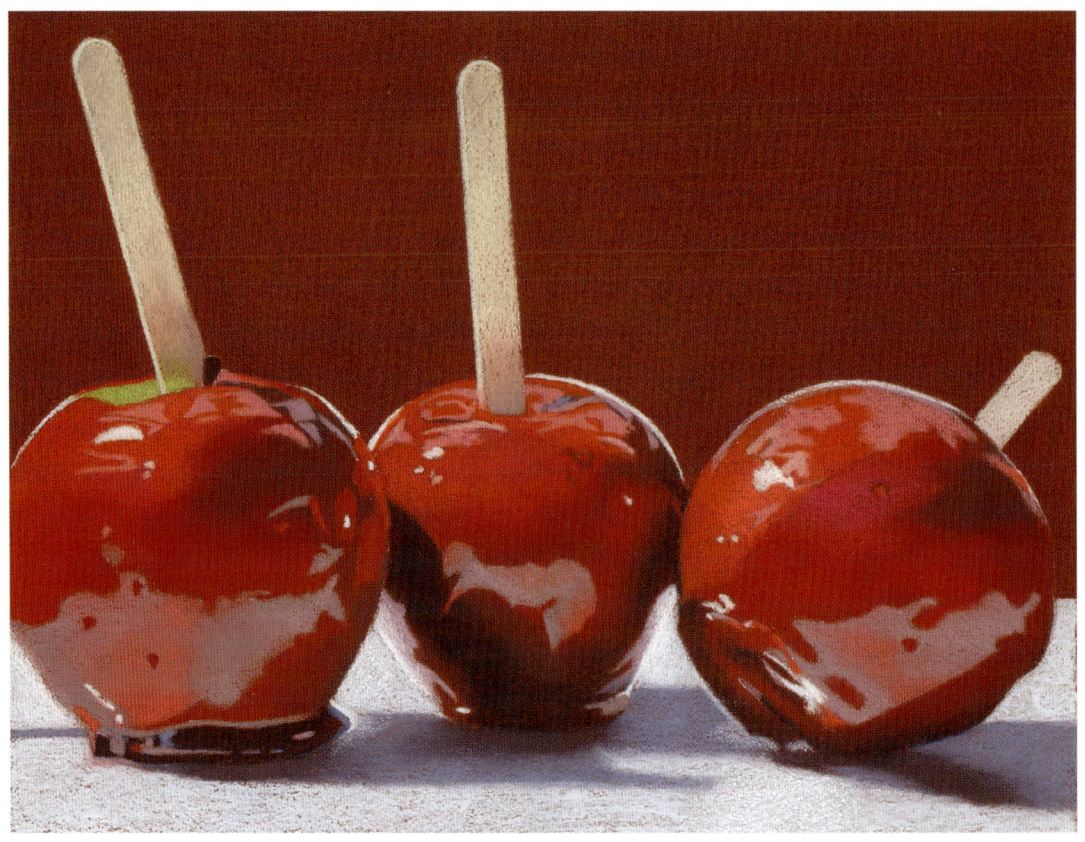

STAGE 3

All the colour is in place, so we can start adding the solvent. Dip your brush in solvent and lightly blot on kitchen paper before applying it to the paper. You want the brush to be damp but not overly wet to avoid it creating a puddle on the paper. Lightly brush very small areas of colour, staying within areas of similar colour, and be careful not to brush colours into the white areas. Notice how the solvent begins to melt the pencil and make it move around like paint.

Lights and darks should be done separately and with a clean or separate brush. Take the same coloured pencil as the area you are working on and draw into the solvent area while it is still damp. This will build a bright and opaque layer of colour. The tip of the pencil may start to mush from the solvent, so clean it with kitchen paper, then lightly wipe away any crumbs of colour with a soft brush.

Take the damp brush and go over each colour again, smoothing it out and blending it with the solvent. I sometimes blend with my fingertips too. If the solvent area is too wet to add more pencil, let it dry for a few minutes. Solvent stays moist for about ten minutes.

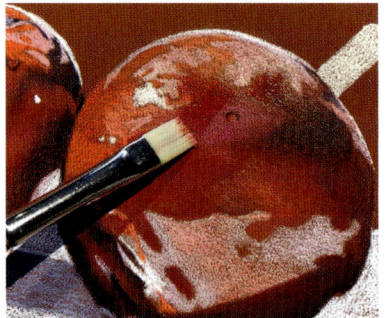

LEFT *Add solvent to the drawing by lightly brushing areas of colour with a damp brush.*

Blend the surface with solvent using two brushes for the light and dark areas or clean your brush well in between working the different areas. Notice how the Cloud Blue area is a little more difficult to get smooth, as you are blending a very light colour into the dark-toned paper surface. You can also add lighter colours over darker colours while the solvent is wet or after it has dried. For instance, I have put Crimson Lake over the darkest areas blended with Tuscan Red, Black Grape and Indanthrone to lighten them a little and give them a red glow.

Add a layer of Black Grape to the background, but don't worry about applying it evenly, as it will be covered with solvent in stage 4. I chose a dark-toned background to make the apples stand out.

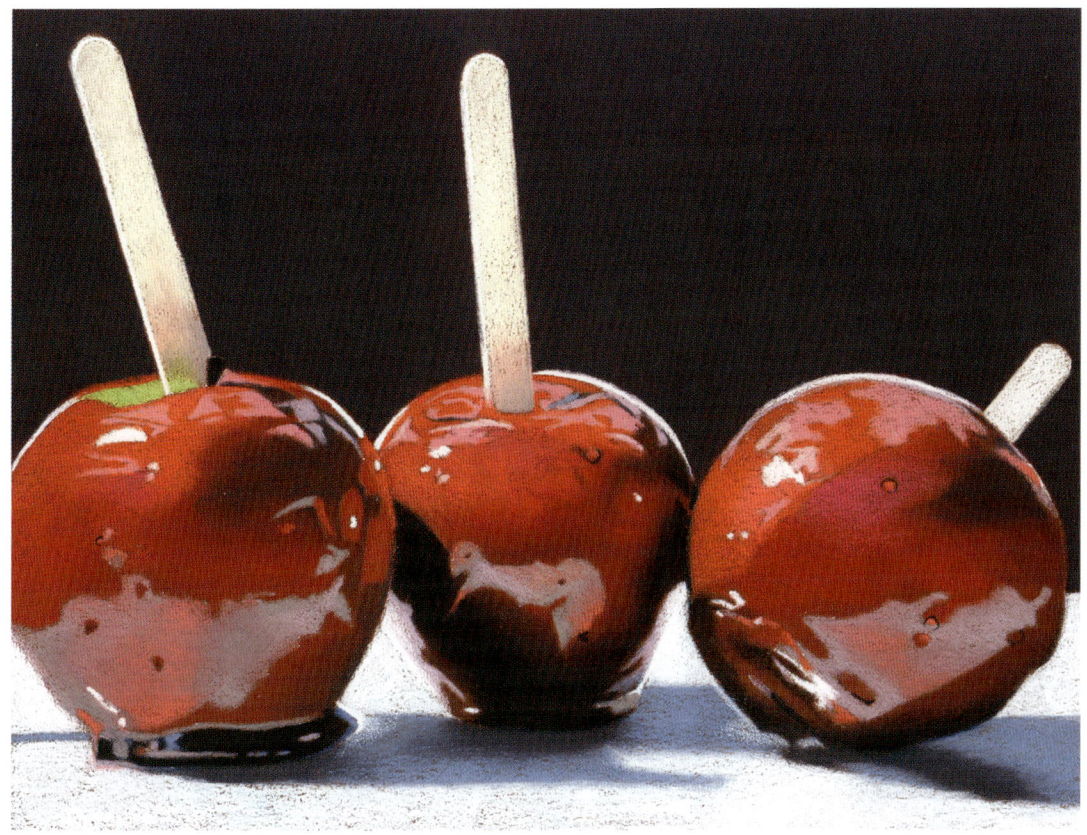

STAGE 4

Now you can add solvent to the background, working on small areas at a time with a flat brush (I like to use a ¼in/6mm soft flat brush for this), perhaps using a ½in (12mm) brush to smooth larger areas. Apply solvent as you did in stage 3, making sure the brush is damp but not overly wet. Use strokes in different directions to even out the background. After applying solvent to an area, add more Black Grape and smooth out again with the brush. If it gets too wet or pencil colour starts to move around, let it dry for a few minutes and go back over it. You can also add more solvent after the background is dry and rework it with the brush and the pencil.

To finish, accentuate the large reflections in the apples with an outline of Tuscan Red, then reapply any colours where needed.

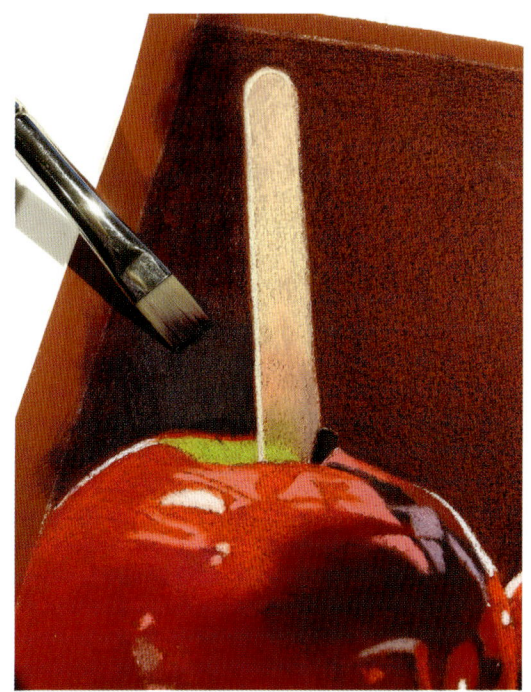

RIGHT *Apply solvent to the background base colour, working small areas at a time. I have added more Black Grape pencil and am smoothing it out with the brush.*

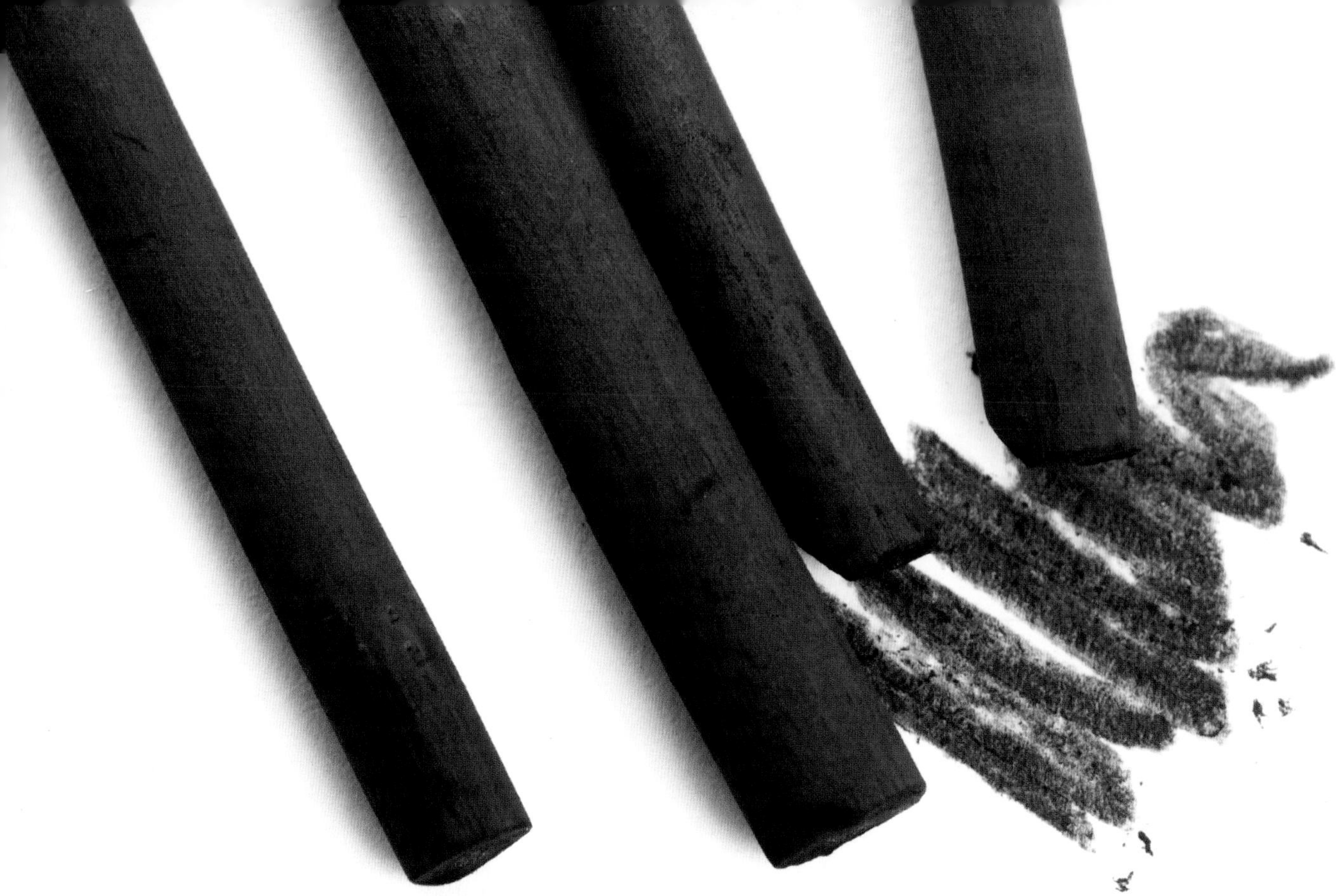

CHARCOAL

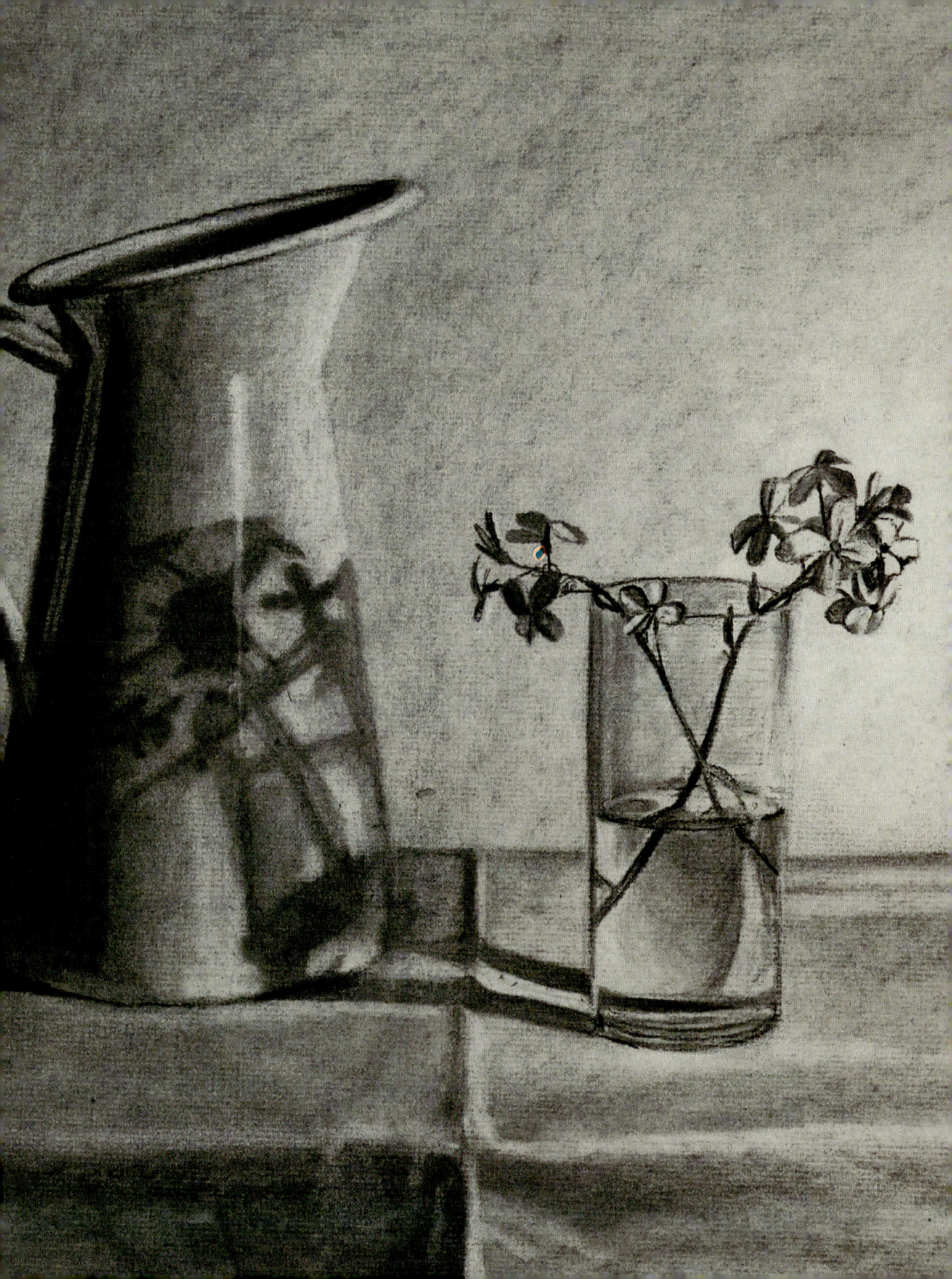

Introduction

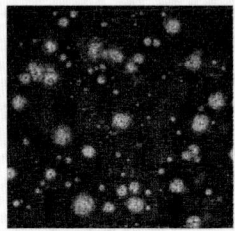

Humans have been using charcoal to create art for at least 30,000 years and its appeal is stronger now than it ever has been before, so what is it about the medium that makes its allure so enduring?

For me, there is something wonderfully tactile and elementally simple about a stick of charcoal. In its purest form, it is nothing more than a piece of wood with the impurities burned out of it. What remains is a beautifully dark, lightweight stick that sits comfortably in the hand. When you pick up a piece of charcoal, you feel compelled to draw with it, and this is when you can discover the rich velvety marks that it leaves – marks that can be smudged, smeared and easily erased to produce an array of different effects.

Artists love using charcoal because it is so soft that it feels like it is dissolving onto the paper. It is possible to produce thick lines and large areas of shading extremely rapidly, which encourages an expressive and carefree form of art that makes it particularly well-suited to working on a large scale. For those who prefer working on a smaller scale, and who value subtlety, it is a medium that enables very fine gradations of tone, and it can be reworked repeatedly as the image evolves or to correct mistakes.

Aesthetically, there is the captivating and somewhat glamorous charm of monochrome. There is a timeless, nostalgic quality to black-and-white images that makes them look great anywhere and explains why they never go out of fashion.

In short, charcoal is an incredibly versatile and forgiving medium, capable of producing stunning results. Within this chapter, I aim to provide a comprehensive overview of the subject. As you work through the tutorials, you will gain a 'virtual toolbox' of knowledge, techniques, skills and terminology that will empower you to take your own project ideas from the concept stage all the way through to a finished piece of artwork. You will also find information on how to preserve your finished artwork to ensure it stays looking good for years to come.

First, I will explain the difference between the product types and teach you the techniques to get the most out of them. I have included some fundamental knowledge and skills that are common to all representational art, including the basics of observational drawing, perspective and composition. As such, the tutorials are suitable for people entirely new to art, but they are also suited to more experienced artists wanting to gain a greater depth of understanding of charcoal as a medium.

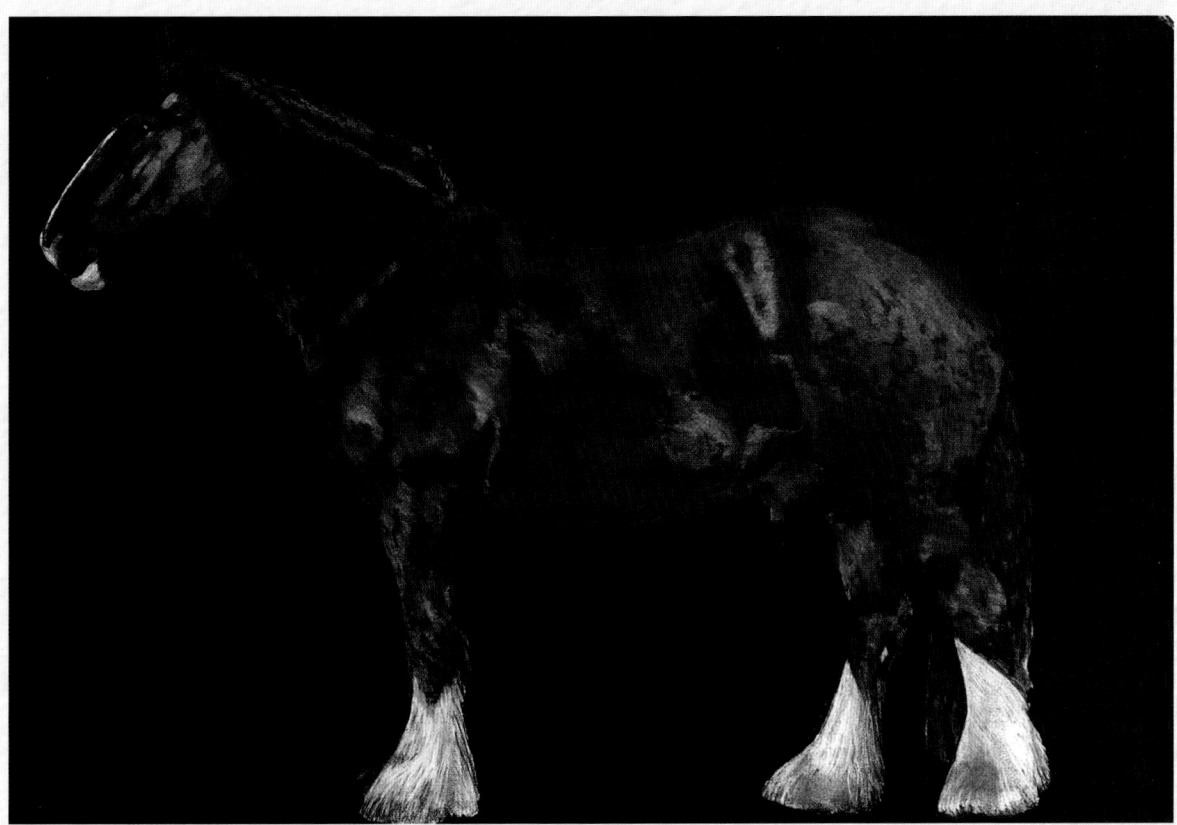

On a final but important note, you should not lose sight of the fact that the materials, tools, techniques and equipment are just one aspect of what you can use to create works of art. The most important element is you as the creative force behind the work. There is no need to slavishly mimic my style of work – that's not the aim here. The aim is to provide you with the foundations from which to develop your own style. The key to this is to grasp the basics through the tutorials and then to experiment; in that way, you will develop your own unique artistic approach.

Happy drawing!

Materials and Equipment

One of the most appealing things about charcoal drawing is you need only a sheet of paper and stick of charcoal to create wonderful results. However, other equipment can help you push the boundaries of your work and make life easier for you. You can experiment with using different charcoal, paper and tools to learn what best suits you, but here are some basics to get you started.

Charcoal

One of the most important things to understand is that natural charcoal and compressed charcoal are different – and there are pros and cons to both of them.

NATURAL CHARCOAL

Traditionally, artists use natural charcoal, the cheapest and most commonly available form. It is generally made from willow, grapevine or linden wood. What you can purchase locally will depend on where you live, but they all produce similar results. Throughout, I will use 'natural charcoal' as the generic term for all three versions.

Brittle and powdery by nature, when you start drawing with natural charcoal you will find it virtually dissolving onto the surface of the paper, essentially leaving a trail of loose particles that form a matt black or dark grey mark. It is easy to move these particles from one part of your drawing to another and to blend, grade and even out tonal areas. Because it is so soft, natural charcoal requires no effort to apply and you can fill large areas of tone quickly. Another key quality is how easily it can be erased to reveal the original surface. It is a great material for expressive and atmospheric work.

However, these same qualities that make natural charcoal so appealing to work with also impose some limitations. Its soft and brittle nature means thin sections break easily and it is impossible to maintain a sharp point. This makes it difficult to draw fine detail. It is also hard to produce really dark blacks: because of its powdery nature, only

BELOW *Natural charcoal is usually available in pencil-length sticks ⅛–⅜in (3–10mm) thick, but you can also buy chunky sticks at 1in (25mm) thick.*

BELOW *Compressed charcoal is available in pencil and block form. There can be significant differences in the quality of products, so try different brands to discover the ones you prefer.*

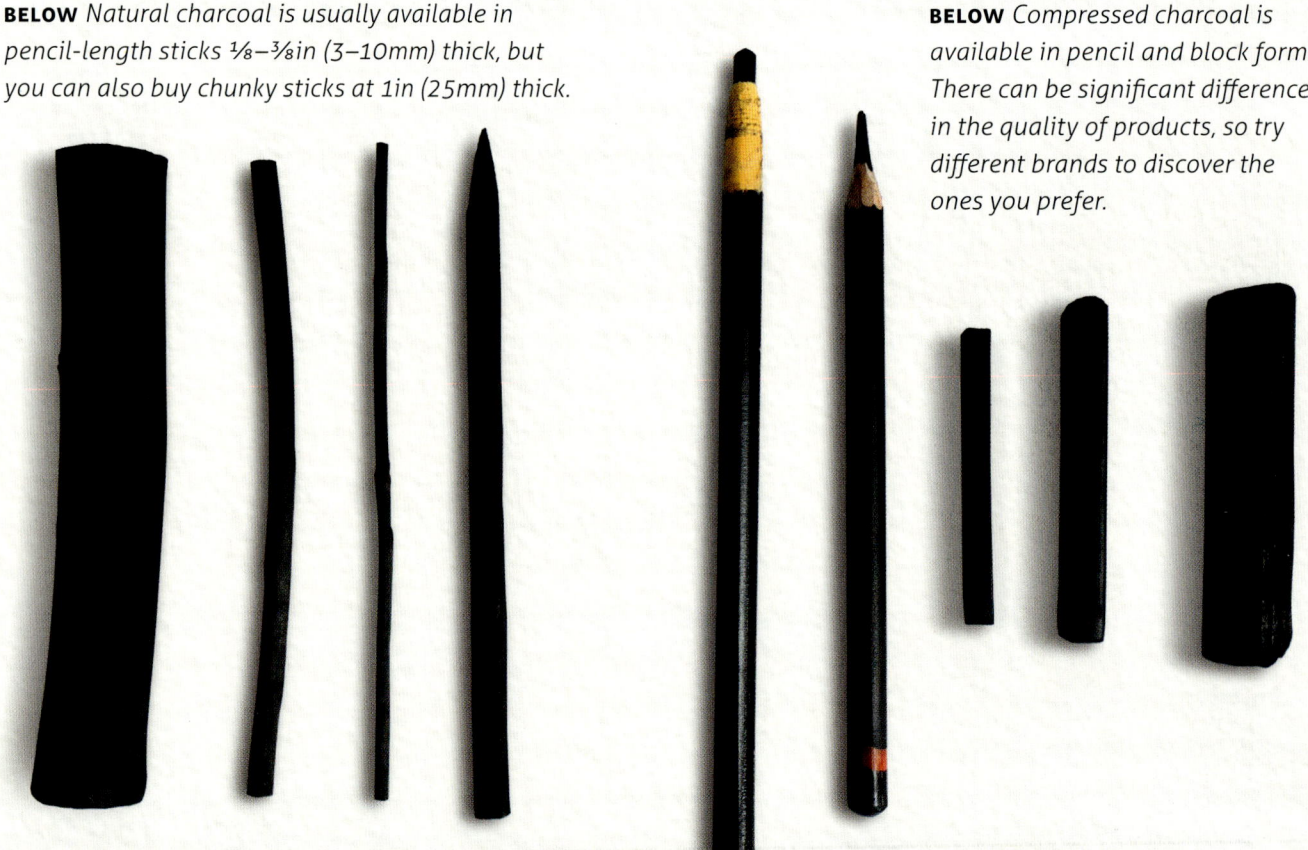

a certain amount of the material sticks to the drawing surface, so the best you can hope for is a dark grey. These are not problems if your artwork plays to the strengths of the medium, but if you want darker tones and finer detail, you will need to use compressed charcoal.

COMPRESSED CHARCOAL

Binders such as wax, gum or a resin are added to the charcoal particles in compressed charcoal. These binders enable manufacturers to control the hardness or softness of the material as well as regulate the grey scale value (see page 258), enabling them to produce very dark blacks or a graduated range of greys. In pencil form, you can sharpen compressed charcoal to a point for fine detail. In block form, you can achieve broad sweeps of tone and lines of uniform width.

Because it is designed to adhere to the drawing surface more effectively than natural charcoal, compressed charcoal is useful if you want to get really dark tones or if you want to work in layers without losing your underdrawing. However, the flip side is that it is more difficult to erase if you make a mistake or if you want to reveal your drawing surface.

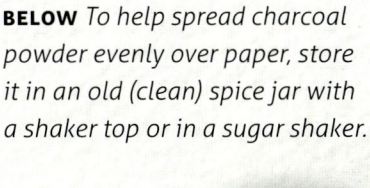

BELOW *To help spread charcoal powder evenly over paper, store it in an old (clean) spice jar with a shaker top or in a sugar shaker.*

Following the same HB scale used for graphite pencils, all compressed charcoal pencils are on the B scale: a higher B number indicates progressive blackness – or softness. But some compressed charcoal pencils are graded as 'soft', 'medium' and 'hard' or 'dark', 'medium' and 'light'.

CHARCOAL POWDER

Artist's charcoal powder is natural charcoal ground to a fine powder and is used to create even tones or mixed with oil or other binders to produce a paint. You can create a similar effect with natural charcoal sticks, but powder produces more consistent results. Buy charcoal powder manufactured for the art market – it does not contain gritty particles that could damage paper.

WHITE CHARCOAL

White 'charcoal' is not really charcoal but is designed for using with charcoal to create highlights. White charcoal is handled much like compressed charcoal.

Paper

The drawing surface is the foundation of an artwork and is as important as the drawing materials. For most charcoal

drawings, a good-quality drawing paper, such as heavyweight cartridge paper, is fine but there are factors to consider.

If the brightness and whiteness of the paper is important, look for 'high-white' or 'ultra-white' paper. You can also choose papers in a range of colours, earth tones and mid-tones. These tend to be marketed for use with pastels, but they are equally suitable for charcoal.

The unique properties of natural charcoal require a paper that traps the fine particles. This is known as 'tooth'. A paper with good tooth holds more charcoal, so you can build up darker tones; too little tooth and the charcoal will not stick to the paper, making it difficult to get good results. The quality of tooth is less critical when using compressed charcoal: the binding agents help the medium stick to the paper.

The texture affects the drawing: smooth paper allows for finer detail, but rough paper is great for creating grainy effects and soft edges. Art paper is sold in three categories of texture: hot pressed, cold pressed (or 'NOT') and rough. Hot pressed paper is the smoothest, rough paper has the most texture, and cold pressed is between the two.

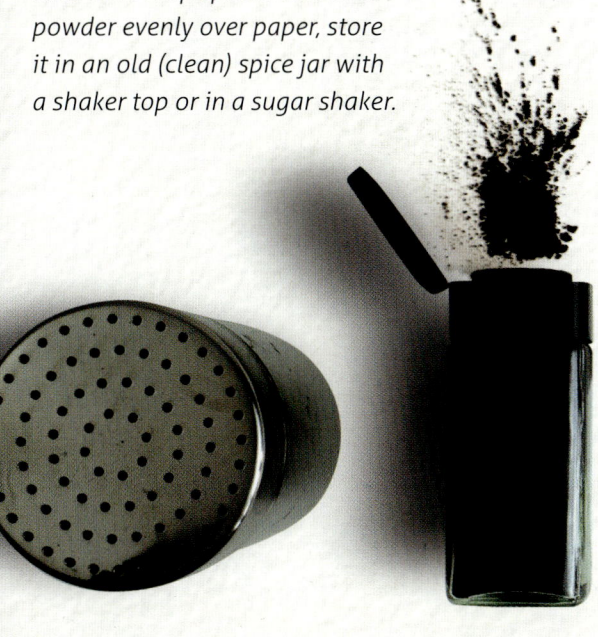

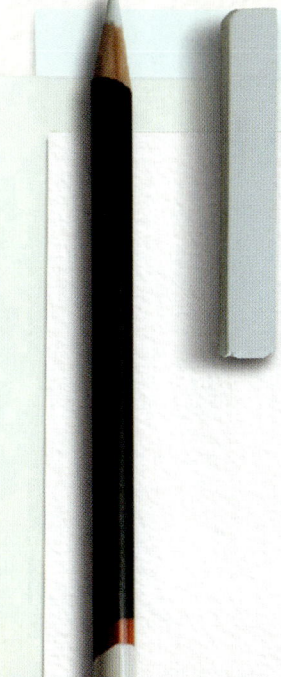

LEFT *White charcoal is sold in pencil or block form.*

Not all 'white' papers are equally white. When you compare them together, you can see the variations.

Other useful equipment

ERASERS

A collection of erasers of various shapes and degrees of hardness is useful not only for erasing but also for blending and smearing. However, you can achieve a great deal with just a standard block or kneaded eraser and a pencil eraser.

A hard block eraser is good for revealing the white of the paper or for cutting through compressed charcoal. A soft kneaded eraser is used with natural charcoal for fine detail, making delicate adjustments to tonal values and lifting charcoal particles from the paper. You need to work it between your fingers until it is soft and tacky, then you can shape it to suit a particular drawing task.

Pencil erasers allow for accuracy and fine detail. Those in a stick form work like a mechanical pencil but dispense a long, thin eraser. They can be more comfortable to hold than other erasers and come in a range of thicknesses.

An electric eraser rotates the eraser element at high speed, which is ideal for revealing the original surface. A less expensive but surprisingly effective option is the eraser at the top of a pencil.

BLENDING AND LIGHTENING TOOLS

You can use a paper-based blending tool to smudge and smear loose charcoal particles around the paper or to subtly remove areas of charcoal to lighten tone. A paper stump is formed from reconstituted paper fibres, whereas a tortillon is made from a single piece of paper rolled tightly. Both are inexpensive, produce similar results and come in a range of sizes. Some are pointed at both ends so you can use either end. In this chapter, 'blending stump' is used as a generic term for both.

A soft cloth is useful for lightening areas of tone. Traditionally, chamois leather is used, but an excellent alternative is bamboo kitchen cloth. You can also use tissue paper and kitchen paper towels.

SHARPENING TOOLS

Compressed charcoal pencils will need sharpening. Ordinary pencil sharpeners will do the job but cut away a lot of the charcoal with the wood. You can use a craft knife instead to carefully carve away the wood, leaving about ⅜in (10mm) of the compressed charcoal revealed. This will allow you to use the side of the pencil lead to cover broader areas of tone.

You can also use a sanding block to put a point on any natural charcoal or compressed charcoal, but a sheet of any medium-grit sandpaper is suitable too.

FIXATIVES

Charcoal drawings are susceptible to smudges and marks when handled or stored. Spraying a drawing with a fixative will glue loose particles to the image so they don't rub off. It also helps screen the image against damage from sunlight.

Apply a 'working' fixative as the work progresses to enable a layering of charcoal that produces darker tones, to avoid the

BELOW *Erasers (from left to right): two block erasers and a kneaded eraser (top), an electric eraser, super-fine pencil eraser and a pencil eraser.*

BELOW *Blending tools (from top to bottom): two tortillons, two paper stumps and a bamboo cloth (folded into a pad).*

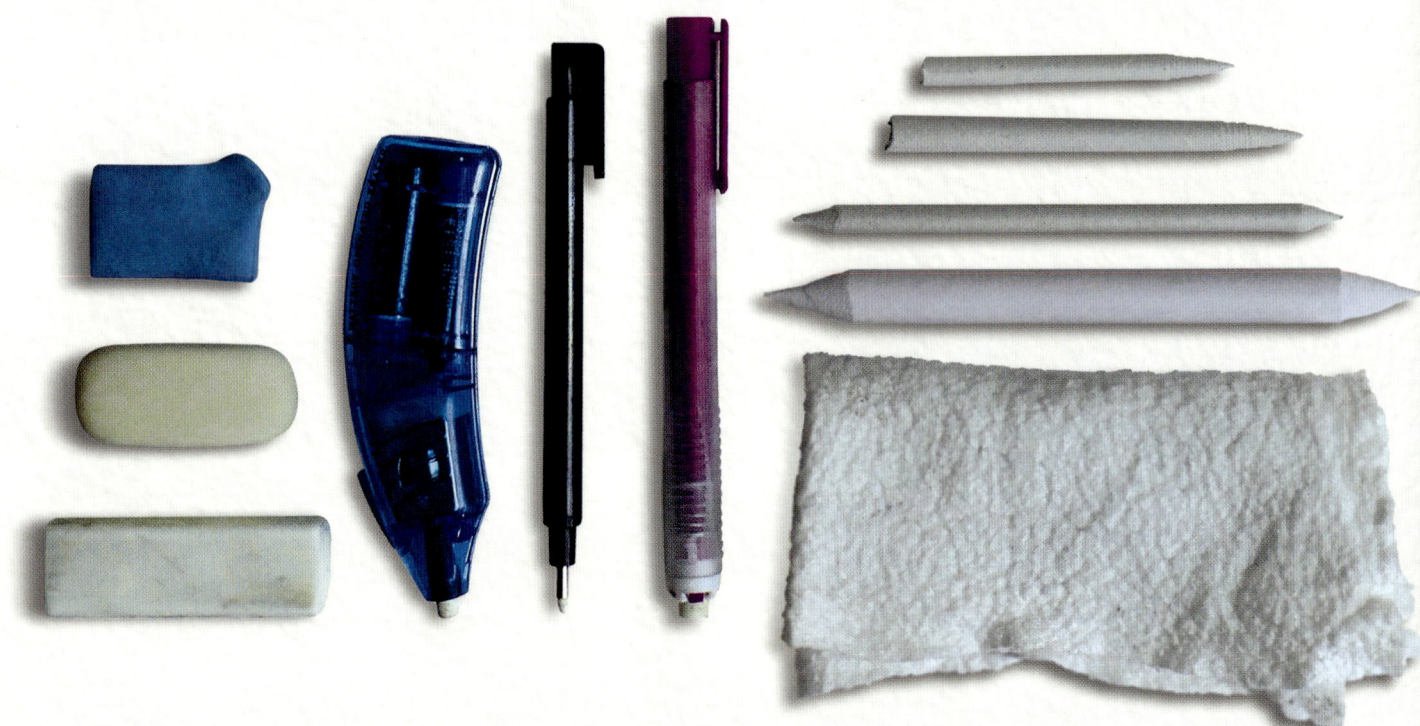

smudging of lines as you work or to protect the work between drawing sessions. Apply a 'final' fixative at the end of the process.

Fixatives can slightly affect the tonal values of the drawing. To minimize this, you should follow the fixing process properly (see Focus On Preserving Your Work, pages 288–9).

PAINTBRUSHES

A mixture of artist's paintbrushes (their quality doesn't matter) is useful for applying charcoal powder, softening edges and creating highlights. Have a range from short, stiff paintbrushes for brushing charcoal from the paper to long, thin, soft paintbrushes suitable for making subtle changes to tonal appearance.

MAHLSTICK

A mahlstick is useful for working in the centre part of a large drawing. It has a padded end that rests on the drawing board, and you rest the wrist of your drawing hand on the stick as you work.

It will help you to maintain fine control as well as keep your hand away from the surface of the work, preventing smudges and smears. You can purchase one in an art shop or online.

Studio equipment

You do not need to have a fully equipped art studio to make ambitious art but there are a few items that you should consider investing in if you plan to do a lot.

DRAWING BOARD

Choose a board that will not warp, is not too heavy and has a smooth surface. A good-quality piece of plyboard or MDF will do. The bigger the board, the thicker it needs to be to prevent warping. Look for a wood thickness of between ¼in (6mm) for a small board to ⅝in (15mm) for a large drawing board.

Seal the wood, especially if it is MDF, with acrylic varnish to protect its surface from water damage when cleaning off the

charcoal. You will also need clips, pins or brown paper gummed tape to secure the paper to the board.

EASEL

You may want an easel. For example, if you enjoy observational drawing, it will let you view your work and subject on the same plane and make visual comparisons more easily. It will also allow you to step back from your work to see it at a distance. What you select will depend on the size of your work, how portable the easel needs to be and if you will want to use it outdoors.

LIGHT

For still-life and portrait drawing, you will need a light that you can angle to a desired height and direction. It will give you a consistent single light source that does not change, like sunlight does, throughout the day. You can also use it to adjust the shadows in your composition. As well as lighting the subject matter, you may need to light your work area too.

BELOW *Sharpening tools (from left to right): a disposable craft knife, a sanding blocking and three pencil sharpeners, one of which stores the shavings.*

BELOW *The end of a mahlstick is padded to protect the work.*

BELOW *Paintbrushes (from left to right): short, stiff brush to remove charcoal, long, soft brush to soften edges, fan brush to create foliage, watercolour wash brush to apply charcoal powder.*

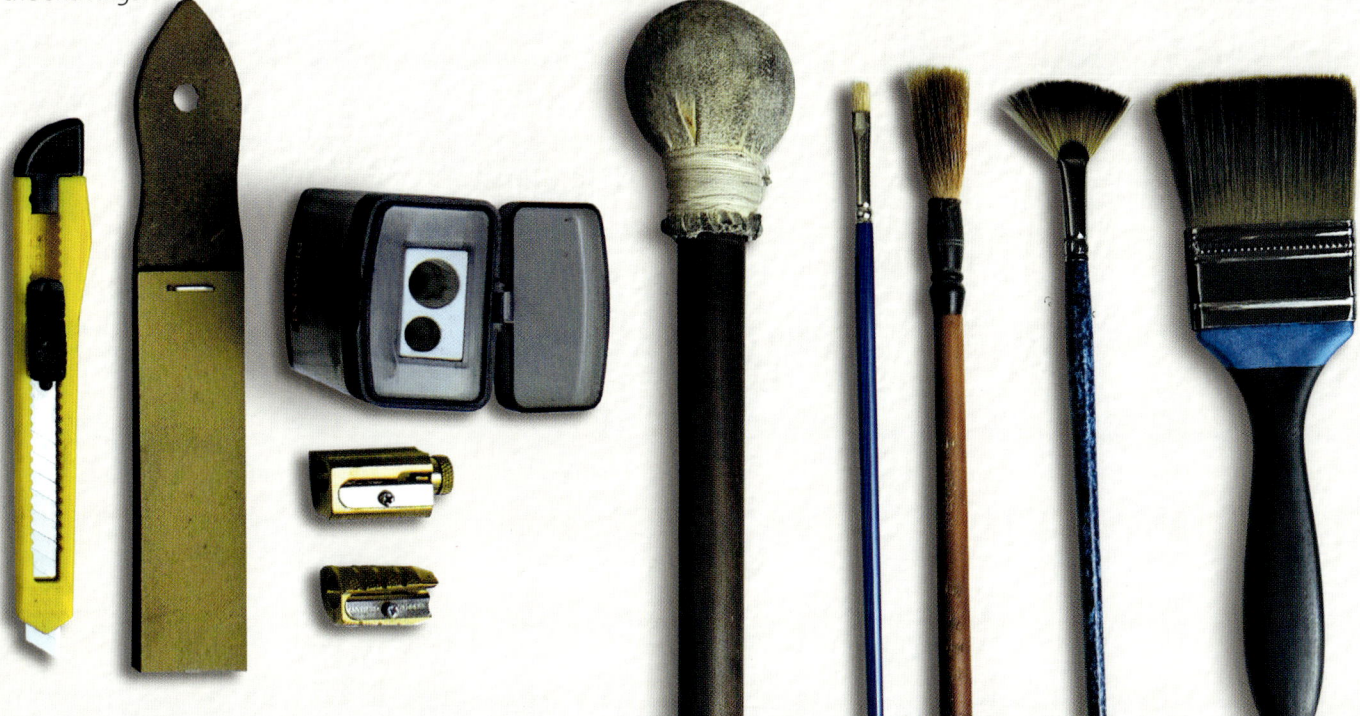

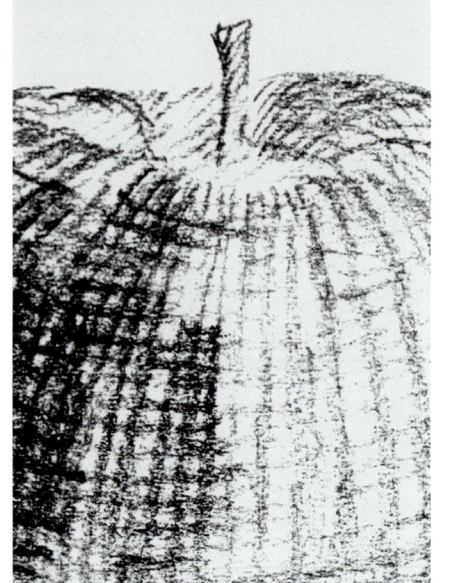

Lines and Shading

When applying charcoal to a surface, you can draw lines or areas of shading. Here is a look at these two basic methods, focusing on how to create different line widths, how to hold your charcoal and adjust the pressure you apply, and the different techniques you can use to create shading.

Line width

When drawing a line with charcoal, you should consider its width. You can achieve different thicknesses of line simply by using a thicker or thinner piece of charcoal. However, you need to be aware that very thin natural charcoal breaks extremely easily. Although you can, to some degree, sharpen the tip of natural charcoal on a sanding block, it will become blunt again quickly and it will not be possible to press hard enough to get a dark line. Nevertheless, a really thin piece of charcoal can give you a consistent line that is less than ⅛in (3mm) wide, while a thick piece can give you a consistent line more than 1in (25mm) thick.

Likewise, with compressed charcoal, different-sized blocks produce different widths of lines, and compressed charcoal pencils can be sharpened to draw narrow lines. However, the medium is relatively soft compared with graphite pencils and will therefore require more regular sharpening to maintain their point.

Adjusting pressure

You can regulate the amount of charcoal on the paper, and therefore how light or dark it is, by adjusting the pressure as you draw. Changing the way you hold the charcoal in your hand will help you control the amount of pressure being applied. A standard pencil hold with a compressed charcoal pencil allows good control for fine detail (**A**). A firm holding position allows charcoal – whether natural or compressed – to be pressed hard into the paper for darker lines or shading (**B**). A lighter hold will produce lighter lines or areas of shading (**C**).

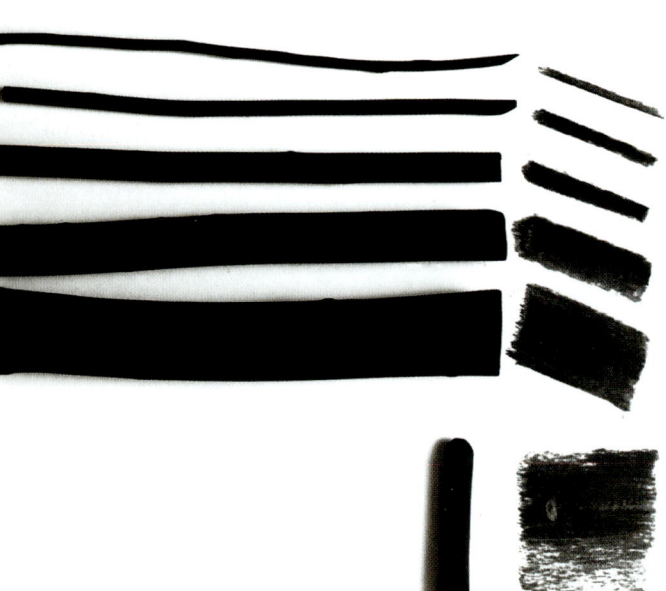

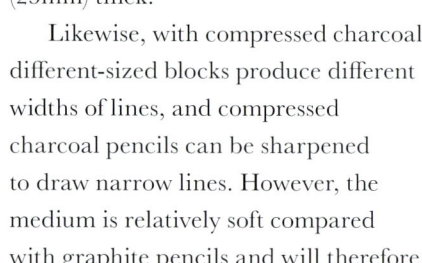

ABOVE *Different thicknesses of charcoal produce lines in different widths (above, top). A piece of charcoal can be dragged on its side to produce a wide line or to block in large areas (above).*

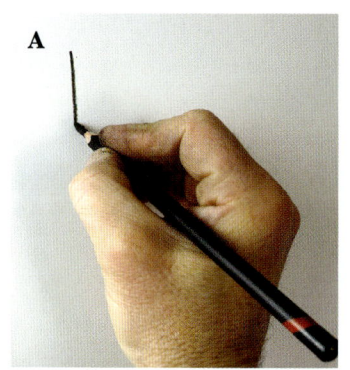

A

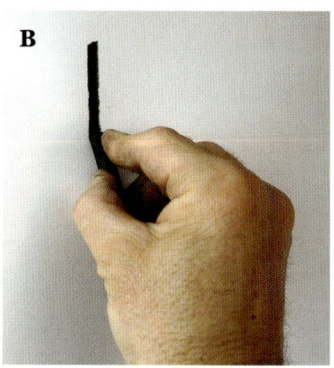

B

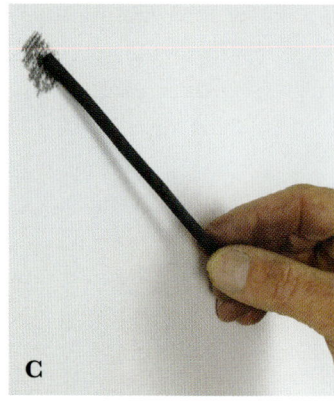

C

D

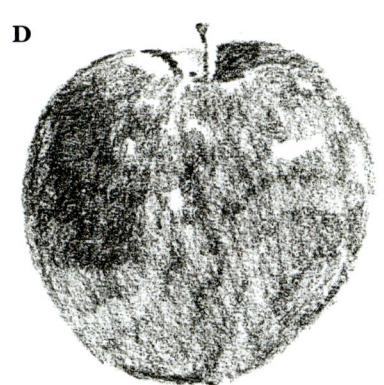

E

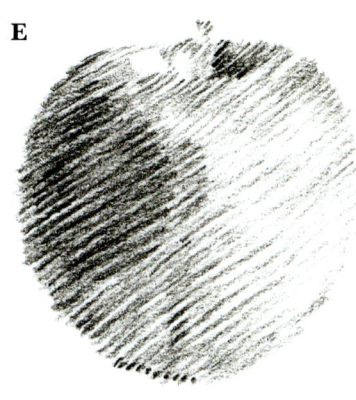

H

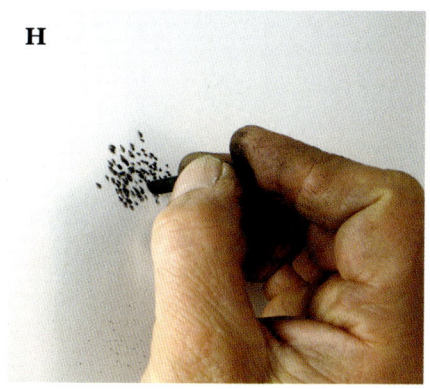

F

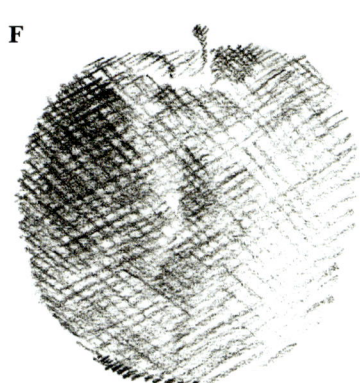

I

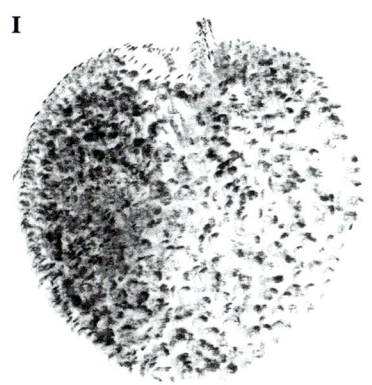

Shading

You can fill areas of paper with value (see page 258) by shading them, basically by drawing lots of lines. You can then leave the lines visible to achieve a certain finish or effect, or blend them together for a more even finish. The method you choose will depend on your personal preferences and individual drawing style.

Basic shading involves using a rapid, tight zigzag motion and regulating the pressure as you draw (**D**). You can add layers to further darken the values, such as on the left side of the apple.

HATCHING

In the same way, you can draw lots of parallel lines with white space between them. The more space between the lines, the lighter the value; the less space, the darker the value. When drawing lines going in only one direction, it is known as hatching (**E**). Adding an additional layer of lines at a 90-degree angle produces a darker value with a technique known as cross-hatching (**F**). A further development from this is the use of contoured hatching or cross-hatching to give the impression of volume (**G**).

STIPPLING

The technique of stippling requires you to hold the charcoal on its end and make marks in the manner of

G

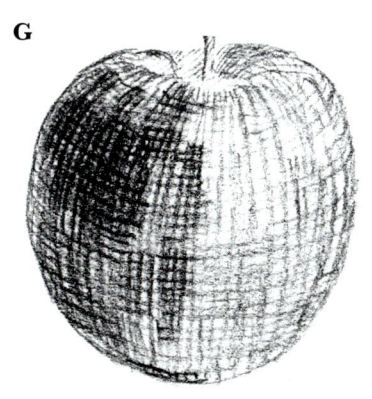

a woodpecker (**H**). As with previous methods, the value can be regulated through both the amount of pressure applied and the closeness of the marks (**I**). Some pieces of charcoal are better for stippling than others. Generally speaking, the softer the charcoal is the better, so try a few different pieces until you find one that works well for you.

The white of your paper is an important factor when regulating how light or dark your value appears. Light passes through the thin layer of

charcoal and bounces off the paper, so the more charcoal you add, the more of the white of the paper you block out and the darker your value appears.

You can also use the tiny peaks and troughs of textured paper (see page 253) to your advantage. By drawing lightly on the paper's surface, the peaks are dark and the troughs are light. When seen from a distance, the effect is like mixing black and white paint with a resultant shade of grey.

In the close-up below, you can see the charcoal is drawn on only the surface of paper. While more obvious on heavily textured papers such as this, the same applies to smoother papers.

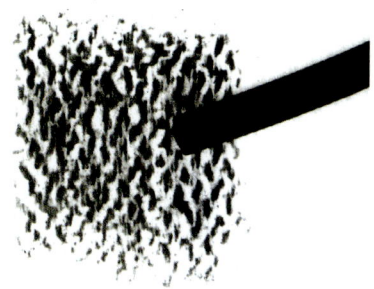

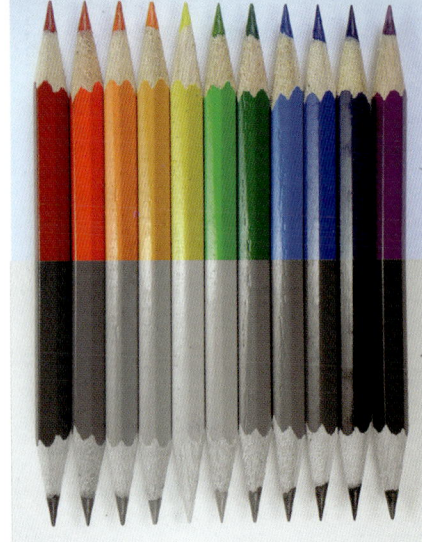

Understanding Tonal Values

The degree to which something is light or dark is referred to as its value or tonal value (or tone or shade). Values are important in monochrome mediums such as charcoal because you cannot use colour to differentiate one object or surface from another.

ABOVE *When converted to monochrome, reds and blues appear darker; yellows and greens, lighter.*

From colour to monochrome

When you look at an object, you normally sense relative areas of light, dark and colour. But when it comes to creating the illusion of three dimensions in charcoal drawings, you can transfer these areas only as dark and light onto your paper. However, colours don't translate to monochrome as you might expect, with some colours appearing darker while others look lighter (see above).

BELOW *From left to right, how you see in colour, how you see in monochrome and what you could draw with six steps of value.*

Values range

The difference between the lightest value and darkest value is known as the values range. When you look at things in the real world, you can discern a broad range of values – from a blinding light to an impenetrable dark. You can also distinguish subtle differences between values.

The range of values you can achieve is limited by the materials you use. You cannot go lighter than the lightness of your paper and you cannot go darker than your darkest drawing medium. This is why it is important to select your materials carefully to achieve the results you want.

LIMITED RANGE IN ART

It is difficult to accurately draw more than a few different shades of value. Most people can achieve around six distinct steps of values (plus an additional step darker with compressed charcoal).

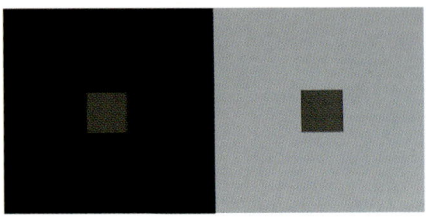

ABOVE *Looking at the two grey squares in the centre of the larger squares, notice how the left one looks lighter than the right – however, they are exactly the same shade of grey.*

This is fewer than you see. When you strip away the colour and reduce the number of tonal values you can draw with, the boundary of one object frequently appears to merge into another, resulting in a simplified image.

Simultaneous contrast

In a phenomenon known as simultaneous contrast, the way you perceive tonal values in an object is affected by its background. Two objects can have the same shade of grey, but one on a black background appears lighter while the other on a white background appears darker (see above). You can use this contrast to enhance the impression of light or dark in your drawings by adjusting the values in relation to one another.

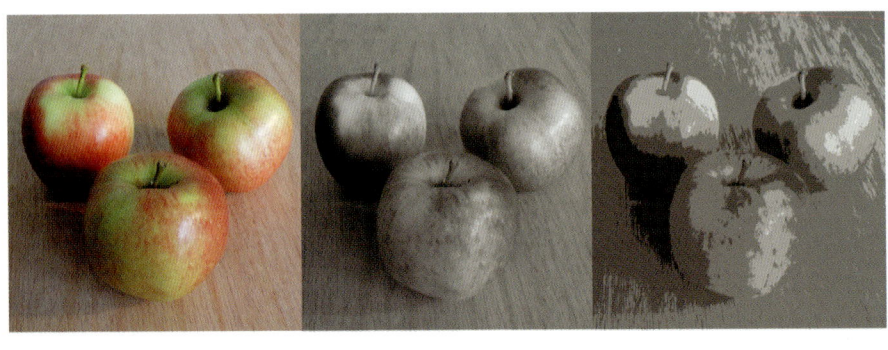

Light and Shadow

Being aware that rays of light often behave in surprising ways, and learning how to observe subtle variations of light and shadow will help you to draw more realistically.

Observing light

Light rays travel in straight lines from light sources before bouncing off surfaces to be perceived by you as relative areas of light and dark. The colour, material and texture of an object, as well as the angle from which you see it, all have a bearing on how you see light.

As an artist, it is not necessary to understand the physics in detail, but it is helpful to understand how light behaves. I will highlight a few observations to help you know what to look for.

THE TERMINATOR

Looking at the three objects (right), you will see that half of each object is facing the light source and the other half is in shade. There is a blurred but clear line dividing these two halves, which is referred to as the terminator. Everything on the shaded side gets progressively darker the further the surface turns away from the terminator. Everything gets progressively lighter from the terminator as the surface turns to face the light source more directly. This is most obvious in the octagonal object, with its distinct edges, but the same rules apply to the sphere and the cylinder, where the transition from dark to light is gradual.

SHADOWS

Notice that the taller the object, the longer the shadows and that the edges of the shadows become more blurred

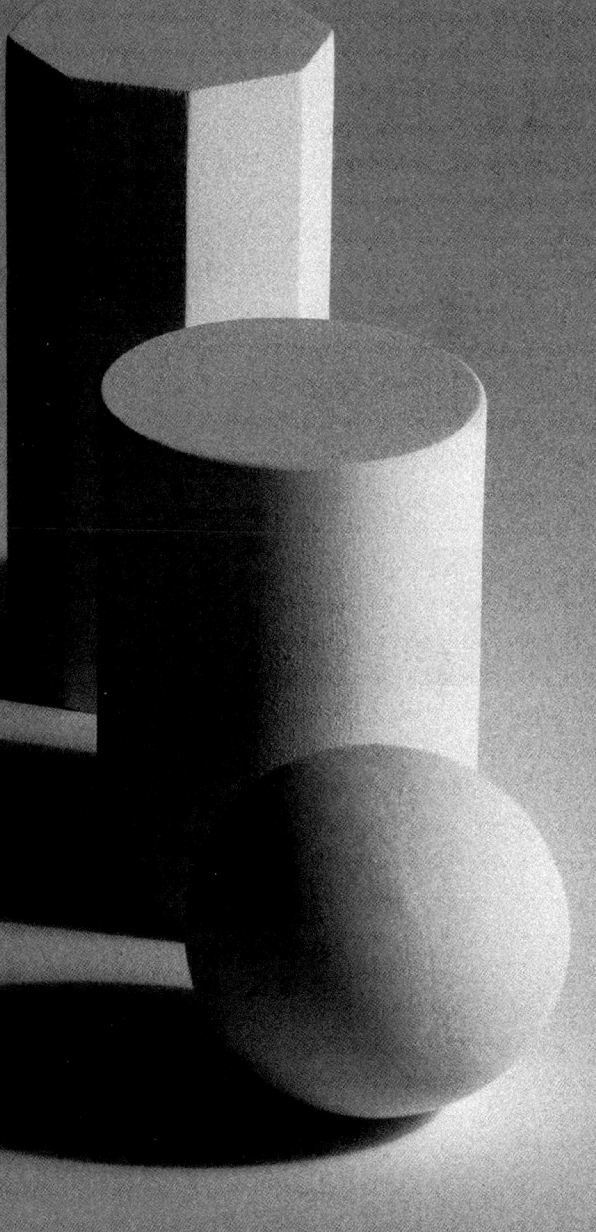

From top to bottom, an octagon, cylinder and sphere – highlighted by a light source from the right – cast shadows towards the left.

the further they are away from the object. This blurred edge is referred to as a penumbra. You should also see that the shadows thrown by the objects are not a uniform value. Parts of the shadow areas are lighter or darker than others.

REFLECTIVE LIGHT

Light is reflected onto objects from the surfaces around them and from objects onto surfaces around them. Looking at the sphere, you can see that parts of the rear edge are lighter than the shadow. This is because light is being reflected onto the rear of the sphere from the surfaces around it. Likewise, light is being bounced off the sphere onto the surface beneath it to make the surface appear lighter.

SIMULTANEOUS CONTRAST

Notice the simultaneous contrast on the top faces of the cylinder and the octagon. Even though they are an even value across the surface, they appear to be lighter when seen next to an adjoining dark face and darker against an adjoining lighter face.

Blending

A technique in charcoal drawing that is perhaps just as important as the charcoal itself, blending is used extensively to manipulate the charcoal.

ABOVE *Compressed charcoal is more firmly bonded to the paper, so it is not as easy to manipulate as natural charcoal. Blending it into the weave of the paper achieves a dark black. You can also see how blending can soften a hard edge.*

ABOVE *To produce a graduated transition from dark to light, adjust the pressure of the charcoal as you apply it to the paper, then blend the values together.*

Reasons for blending

When you blend charcoal, you are either working particles into the weave of the paper or lifting loose particles from the surface of the paper and depositing them elsewhere in the image. Once charcoal has been blended and effectively worked into the weave of

the paper, you can repeat the process to achieve darker values. However, blending is also useful for softening edges and creating even areas of shading. In addition, you can use it to remove hatching lines (see page 257) or underdrawing, to smooth the transition from an area of dark value to an area of lighter value, and to soften the boundaries between areas drawn in natural charcoal and those drawn with compressed charcoal.

How to blend

You can use a blending stump or a soft cloth to blend (see page 254). Blending stumps are ideal for working on more detailed areas, while a soft cloth is convenient for larger areas. To blend effectively with a blending stump, it is important to keep the side of the pointed end flat against the drawing paper so that you exert even pressure and maximize the area of the blending stump against the paper. Avoid using the sharp point unless you are trying to work into very tight corners. Papers with a good tooth produced for charcoal drawing tend to grip onto the particles, which is good for darker tonal values, but they can also be more difficult for producing even areas. Depending on the paper you use, you may need to be patient to achieve an even area of value – it may be necessary to work the charcoal into the paper from every conceivable direction.

When using compressed charcoal and natural charcoal in the same drawing, avoid contaminating areas of natural charcoal with compressed charcoal (unless you are deliberately blending them together). Either use different blending stumps or clean your stump between working on different areas.

Lightening values

If you need to lighten the values as you work, simply clean off the end of your blender with a piece of sandpaper and use the blender to lift off some of the charcoal from the paper, using the blending stump like you would a paintbrush to wipe away charcoal particles from the surface of the paper.

BELOW *Hold a blending stump almost horizontal to the surface to use the flat edge of the point for blending.*

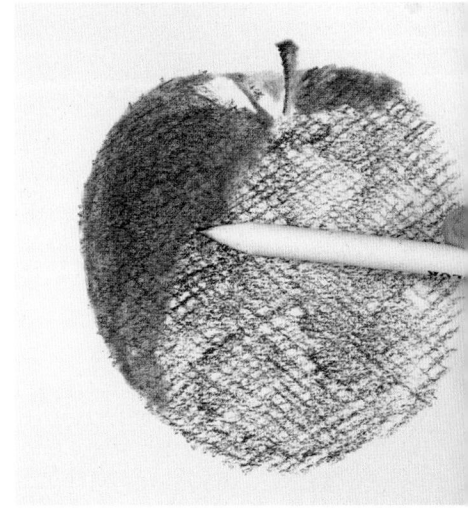

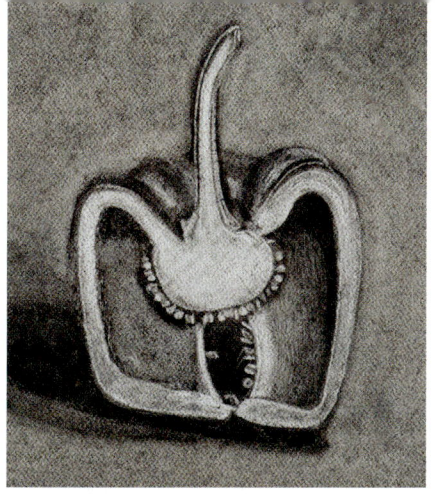

ABOVE *By using subtractive drawing techniques, this halved pepper was drawn in reverse.*

Subtractive Drawing

A technique known as subtractive drawing involves working from dark to light by removing charcoal from the paper. Instead of drawing with charcoal, you use erasers and other tools to 'draw' an image or reveal areas of lighter value.

Removing charcoal

You can use subtractive drawing if you want to create a lighter detail against a smooth and even background. You could simply draw a background around a lighter section and try to blend it in, but this is difficult to do without leaving obvious lines and marks around it. A better option is to create an even background by following the methods shown in Laying Down an Even Mid-tone (see page 262). It is important to understand that subtractive drawing is not a binary choice of charcoal or white paper. Just as with additive drawing, you can regulate the tonal value by adjusting the degree of pressure you apply. The only difference is that you are now letting light into the image rather than adding shading.

One caveat is that once applied, some of the charcoal particles will be ingrained into the weave of the paper, making it virtually impossible to get completely back to the original colour of your drawing surface. This means that if you want to keep any areas free of charcoal, you need to completely avoid drawing on them.

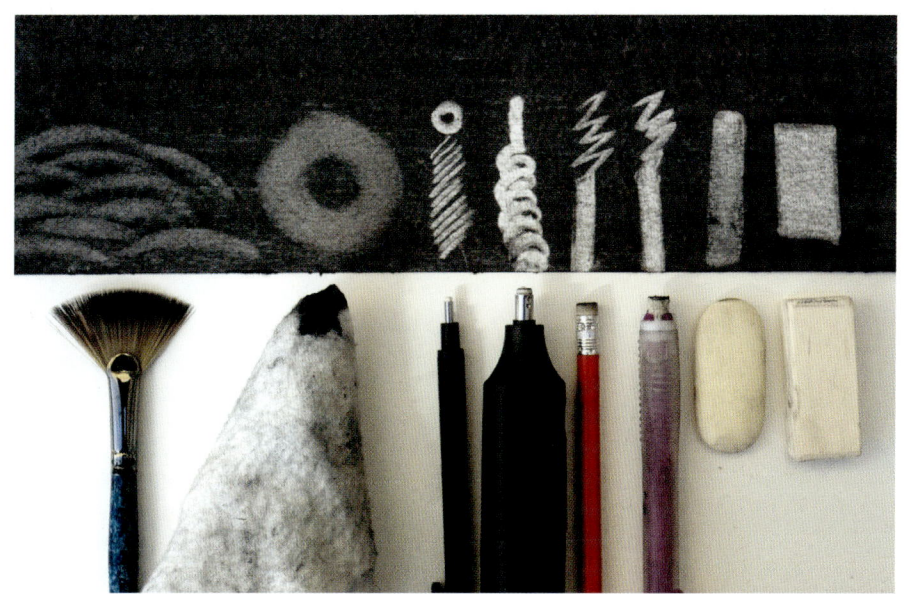

ABOVE *Tools for subtractive drawing include (from left to right): a fan brush, bamboo cloth, super-fine pencil eraser, electric eraser, pencil eraser, mechanical eraser, block eraser with rounded edges and square-edged block eraser.*

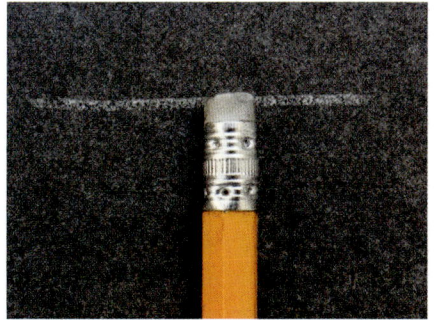

Tip

The eraser on a pencil is an excellent tool for subtractive drawing. You can simply draw with it holding it like a brush, and if you slice the rounded end off with a sharp knife and work it on the clean edge, you can achieve very narrow lines.

Tools and paper

The effectiveness of this technique depends on the paper you use. Ideally, you want to use a paper with a good tooth (see page 253) so that there is plenty of charcoal to subtract from. The most common method for subtractive drawing is to use erasers, but you can also use brushes, cloths, tissues and other tools to create a variety of effects.

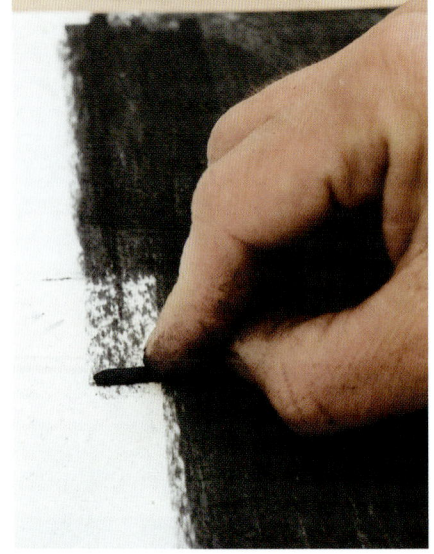

Laying Down an Even Mid-tone

In charcoal drawing, you will often need to begin by laying down an even mid-tone so that your entire sheet of paper is a nice even grey tone. The two methods for achieving an even mid-tone are described here.

ABOVE *When dragging a thin piece of charcoal to cover a large area, overlap each pass to ensure you cover all of the paper.*

Dragging charcoal

The first method involves dragging a stick of natural charcoal on its side all over the paper and then working it in with a soft cloth. The risk with this method is that any hard knots in the charcoal can scratch the paper, and these scratches will then be saturated with charcoal and show up as dark lines. This is a particular risk in drawings where you want even areas of value, such as in clear skies. One way of avoiding this is – counter-intuitively – to use thinner pieces of charcoal, which tend to be softer. Alternatively, a safer method is the second option of using charcoal powder.

Using charcoal powder

Rather than using a stick of charcoal, you can cover the paper with charcoal powder. However, it is usually a messy and dusty process, so begin by making sure you are dressed appropriately. You may want to work outside and wear an apron and vinyl gloves as well as a dust mask.

Lay your paper, attached to a drawing board, flat and begin by sprinkling some charcoal powder onto the paper. Using a container with a perforated lid (see page 253) will help you to spread it more evenly. The next step is to work the charcoal into the paper. If you have a broad paintbrush with soft bristles, such as a watercolour wash paintbrush, you can use it to brush it systematically into the paper from various different directions, spreading out the charcoal powder evenly across the paper (**A**). If you don't have a paintbrush, you can use a soft cloth – the results will be the same.

To use a soft cloth (see page 254), fold it into a pad and use it to work the charcoal powder into the paper (**B**). Again, try to work the powder into the paper from as many different directions as you can. Begin with a circular motion and then move to a criss-cross motion. Add more charcoal powder, if necessary, to get the value as dark as possible. Your paper will largely determine just how dark this is – every paper has its own saturation point.

Finish off by very gently wiping any residual loose particles off the paper (**C**). Now move the drawing board to your workspace, but make sure you are careful to avoid accidentally rubbing the surface of the paper.

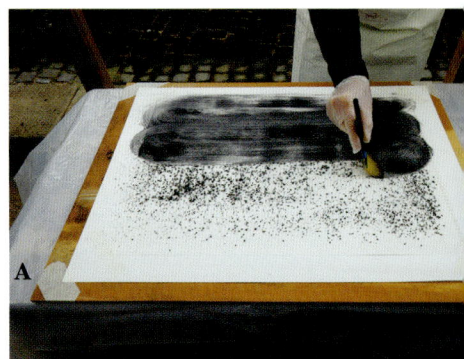

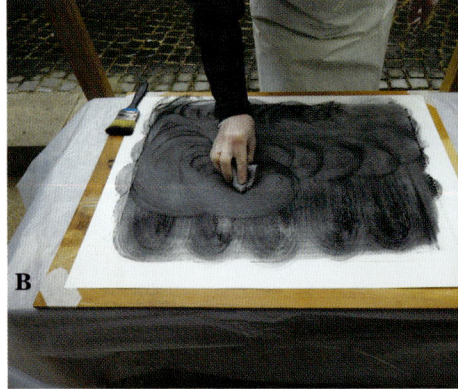

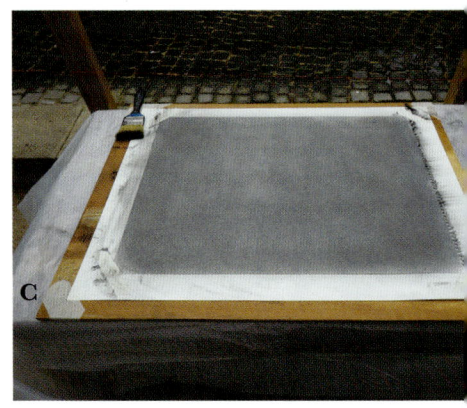

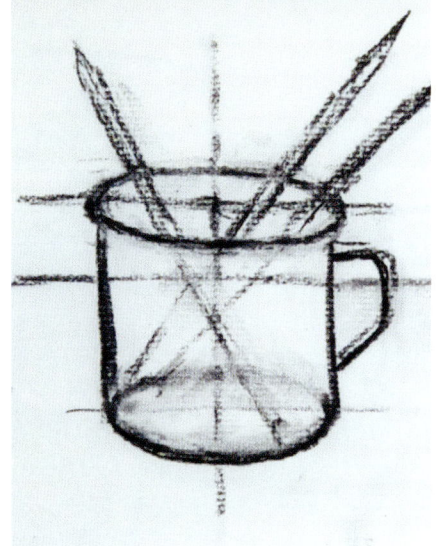

Observational Drawing Techniques

Drawing from life can be a challenging way of working but it is also incredibly rewarding. It frees you up from the constraints of working from reference material and can lead to a more expressive style.

Getting started

If you want to draw from life, it will help to understand the basic principles of observational drawing, a term referring to the process of converting what you see in front of you into a realistic drawing. Observational drawing involves a combination of sketching, sighting and measuring that is repeated as you progress through the drawing. It can be daunting for people new to the subject, but it is often easier than you might think, provided you do it systematically and follow some basic rules.

Before you start, you need to decide what you want to draw and what your composition will be. It will help greatly if you use a viewfinder, do some thumbnail sketches (see Composition, pages 268–269) or use a combination of both. Once you know which elements will be included in your picture, you can begin drawing.

Sketching

The term 'sketching' refers to the process of drawing rapidly and lightly without expecting everything to be in the right place immediately. Simply have a go at drawing it using your own judgement. Once you have the beginnings of an image emerging on paper, compare what you have

Tip

You can make your own viewfinder by cutting out a rectangle in a piece of mount board and attaching thin wire, dental floss or thread to make a grid, or purchase one from an art supply shop.

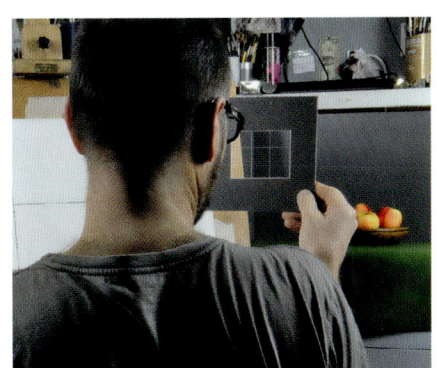

drawn to your subject matter and make adjustments until you have everything where you want it. As you become more confident that things are how you want them, firm up the lines by applying more pressure or by adding tone to define elements in the image.

Throughout this process you should use techniques known as sighting and measuring to help you get everything in the correct place.

BELOW *Sketching is a more intuitive process than measured drawing – it requires you to take a leap of faith and just start drawing. Practising often will build your confidence and skills.*

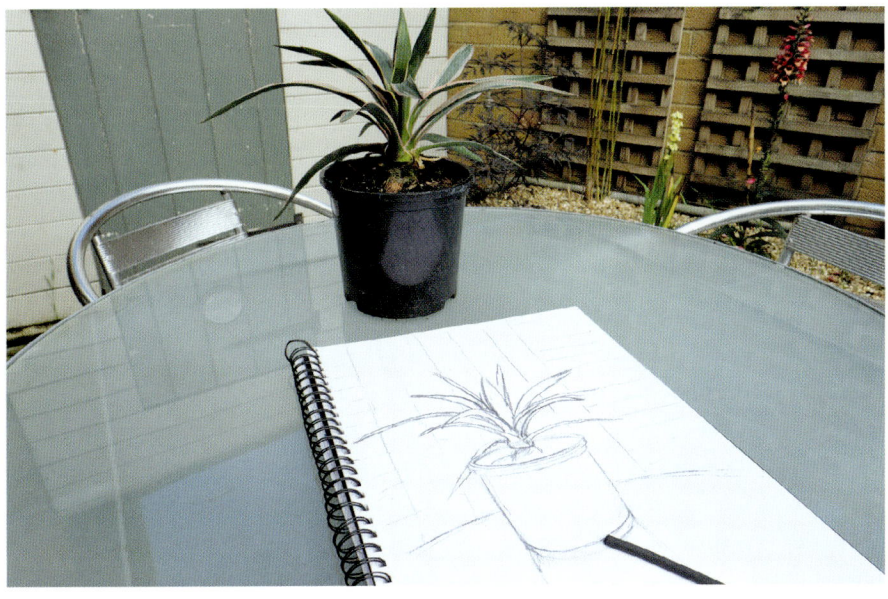

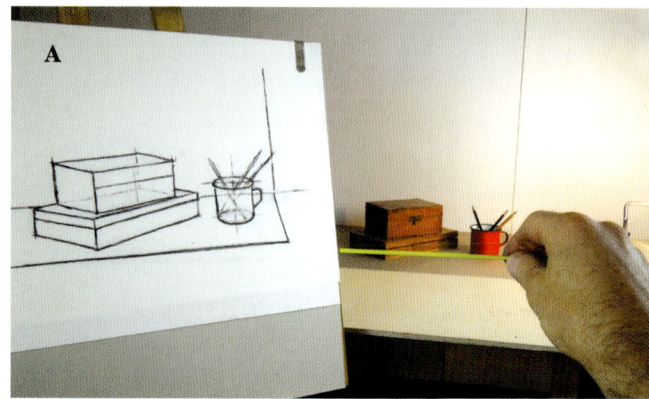

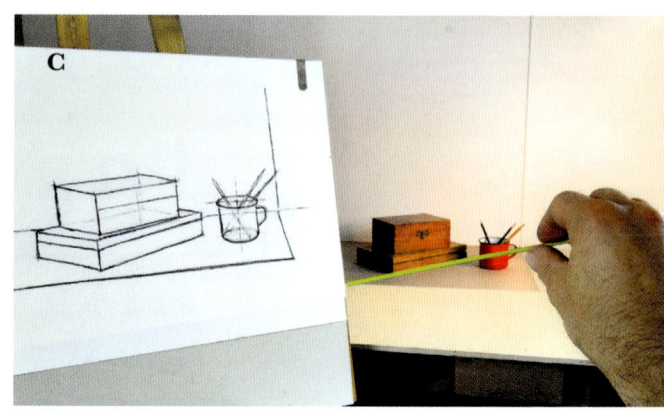

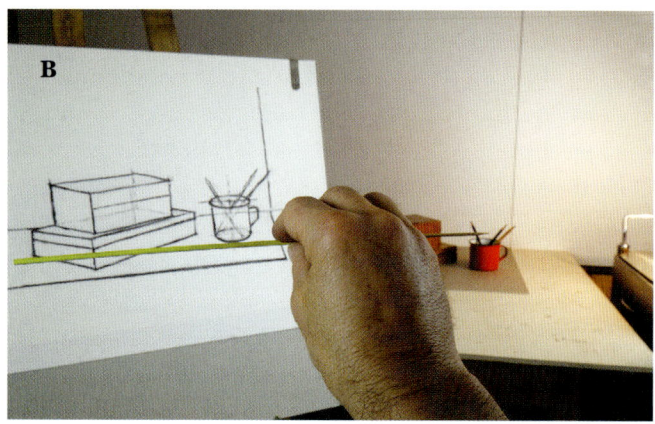

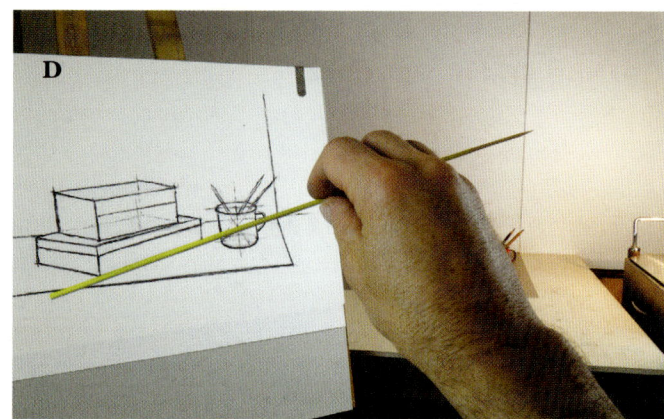

Sighting

An object with a straight edge is useful for sighting – a process in which you make vertical or horizontal comparisons of points or compare the angles in your subject matter against those in your drawing. A pencil works okay for sighting, but you may find it easier with something longer and thinner, such as a thin piece of dowel (wooden kebab skewers are perfect for this task).

HORIZONTAL SIGHTING

By holding the stick horizontally, in this example (**A**) you can see that the bottom left-hand corner of the lower wooden box is below the bottom of the cup.

By shifting the stick to the drawing (**B**), you can then check that it is correct and adjust it if necessary. Do the same to check the vertical alignment of the objects in the still life.

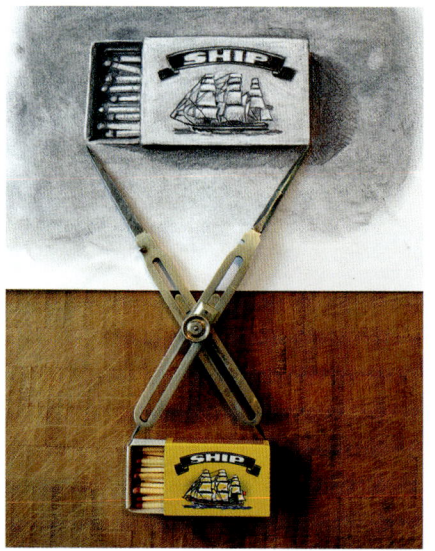

ANGLES AND INTERSECTIONS

You can use the same straight-edge tool to check angles and intersections. In this example, you can take a sighting along the bottom of the lower box to check that the angle of the box is correct (**C**). By holding your hand in the same position and turning around to the drawing (**D**), you can check that you have captured the angle correctly. You can also see that a line extended from the box towards the cup should intersect about halfway up the cup handle and check this at the same time.

Tip

You can use a proportional divider for measuring distances in observational drawing and when working from reference images. It allows you to accurately measure the distance between points in an object and transfer them to your drawing. You can draw on a scale of one to one or, by moving the pivot point, you can scale up or down.

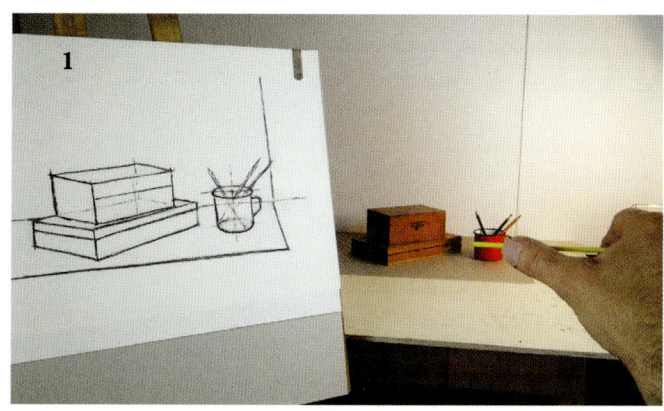

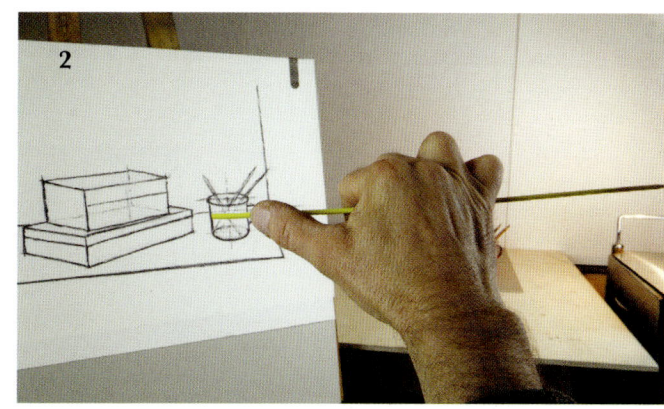

Comparative measuring

You can confirm the relative distance between points by measuring and comparing them. The simplest method is called comparative measuring and can be achieved using the same pencil or straight-edge tool you use for sighting. As the term suggests, it is a case of measuring a distance and then comparing it against other distances in your drawing. In this way, you can determine whether it is longer, shorter or about the same.

Once you have measured a distance, you might be tempted to just transfer your measurement directly to your paper. However, drawings tend to be drawn to a different scale, so many artists use the measurement to make a broad judgement.

So, for example, when measuring the width of the cup (**1**) and then comparing it to other elements in the still life, you can see that the width of the cup is almost exactly the same measurement as the height of the top box and that two times the cup's measurement is slightly longer than the side of the same box.

You can then turn to your drawing (**2**) and measure the width of the cup in your drawing. Whatever the actual measurement is, use it to make sure the other measured elements conform to the same proportions as those in the still life. In other words, as in the still life, the width of the cup in the drawing should be almost exactly the same as the height of the top box in the drawing, with the side of the box being slightly under two times the cup's measurement.

Being consistent

Repeat this sketching, sighting and measuring cycle until you have everything where you want it.

It is important to note that you must measure from exactly the same point every time, otherwise your measurements will be inaccurate. Sit or stand in the same position every time you take a measurement, and stretch your arm out to arm's length. If you try holding your arm halfway outstretched, it will be difficult to ensure that you maintain exactly the same distance from your eye each time. If sitting, it is advisable to use a chair with a back rather than a stool. This way you can press the small of your back into the chair back, forcing you to adopt the same upright position every time. To avoid the risk of your chair being moved or of you failing to stand in exactly the same place, you can mark the position of the chair legs or your feet with tape or some other marker.

Sketching, sighting and measuring, done systematically and with careful observation, can result in a surprising degree of accuracy, so don't give up too quickly if you're initially finding it a little challenging to master. Like all skills, it just needs a little practice.

Negative space

Not only should you concentrate on the objects in the drawing but also on the space between them. Sometimes you can be concentrating so hard on individual elements that you could fail to pay enough attention to how accurately they sit in relation to one another. To avoid making this mistake, it is good practice to look at the negative space between objects.

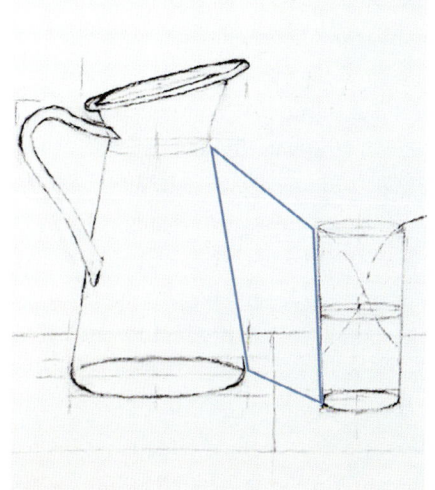

ABOVE *When attempting to place objects correctly in relation to one another, it helps to look at the negative space between them as shapes.*

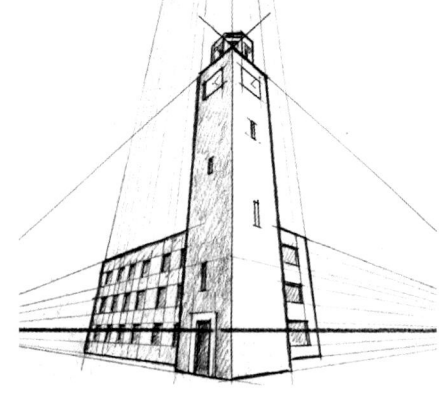

Perspective

There are two key observations in perspective – a set of rules for creating the illusion of depth in a drawing – that will help you to draw things more realistically.

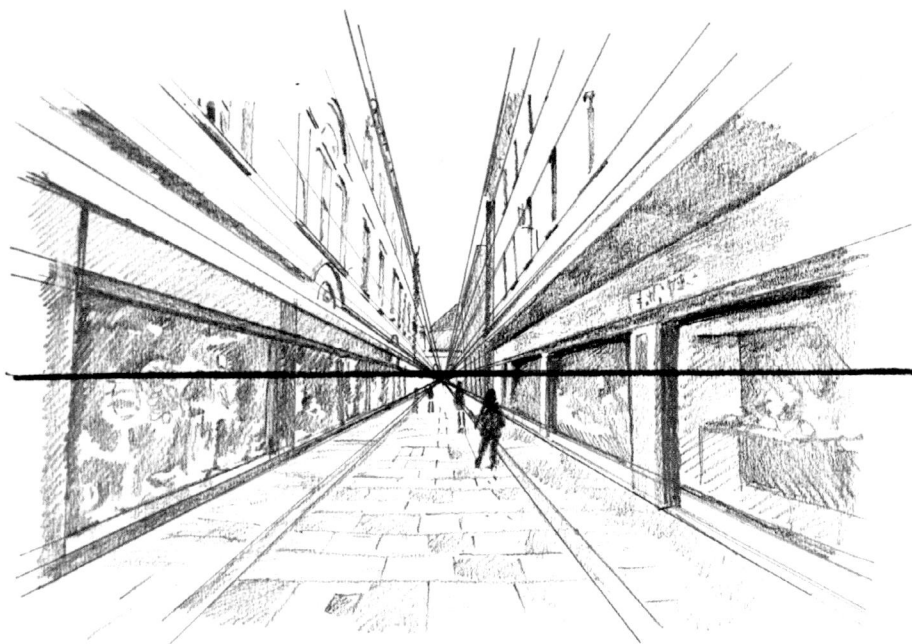

Linear perspective

The first observation is that all objects appear smaller the further away they are from the viewing point, including natural features such as clouds and waves. However, this rule is most obvious in objects with straight sides or linear features and equally spaced objects of identical size, such as telegraph poles and fence posts. This attribute is called diminution, and the method we use to take it into account is called linear perspective. This is because if you extend imaginary lines along points of equal height and alignment, they converge on the horizon line at points we call vanishing points. The horizon line is not the topographical horizon you can see but at the level of your line of sight when

ABOVE *A street scene shows how lines converge at a single point in one-point perspective.*

BELOW *The oblique angle in this building is formed by two-point perspective.*

looking straight ahead. Once you work out the location of these points, you can use them to accurately place other elements in your drawings.

ONE-POINT PERSPECTIVE

Straight lines converge to meet at a single point at eye level in one-point perspective. Using a single point is appropriate when the front of objects, such as buildings, is directly facing the viewer or when looking down a long road, for example, or railway tracks.

TWO-POINT PERSPECTIVE

In two-point perspective, there are two points along the horizon line. This style is suitable when objects such as buildings are not flat-on but placed at an angle to the viewer. You don't need to draw physical lines to them, but use your understanding of perspective to project imaginary lines from your objects to the horizon line, and then judge whether they meet in about the right place. Be aware that vanishing points may be off the paper to the left or right of your drawing area.

THREE-POINT PERSPECTIVE

Just as objects appear smaller in the distance, the same is true as you look up or down upon them. The most obvious example of this is when you look up at a skyscraper, but it applies to all objects. Generally speaking, it is enough just to take this knowledge into account when you sketch out shapes, but for greater accuracy you can add an additional vanishing point directly above or below your viewing position in what is termed three-point perspective.

RIGHT *The viewer is looking up in this three-point perspective drawing, in which the vertical lines converge towards the top.*

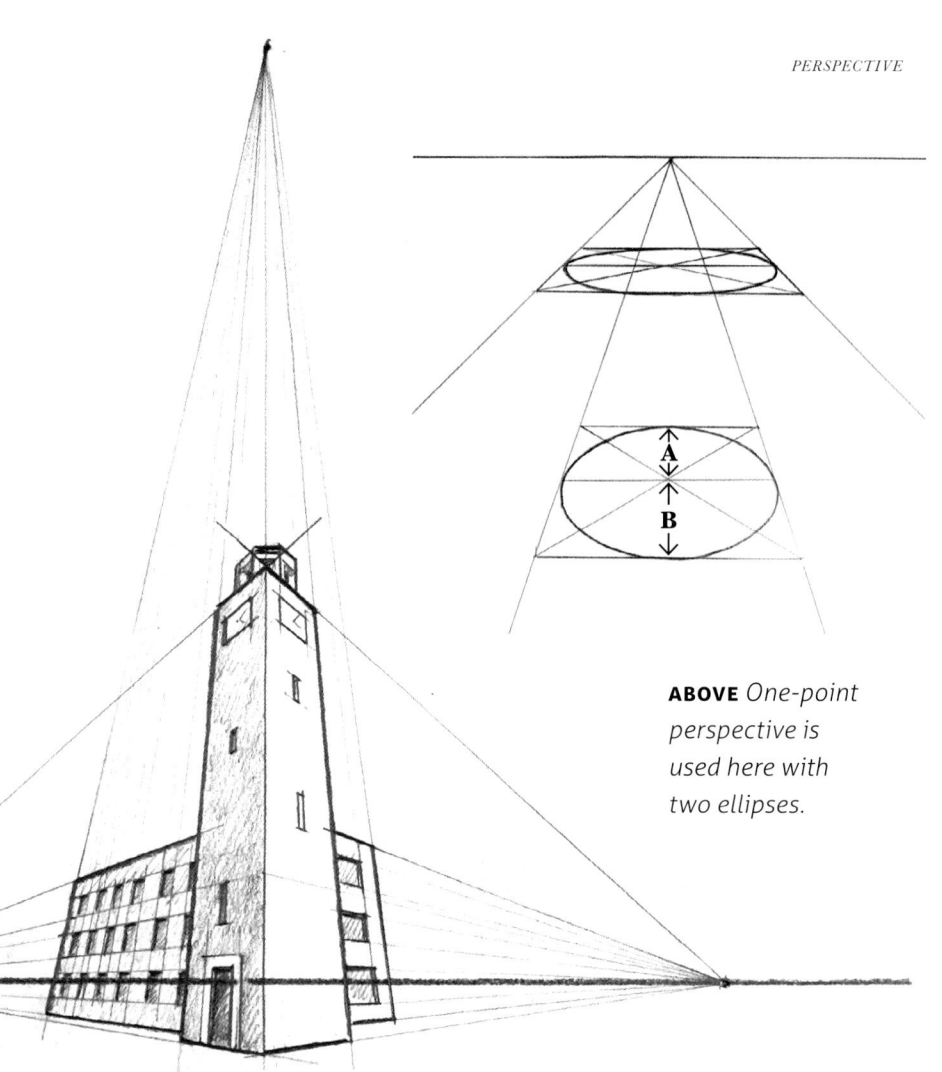

ABOVE *One-point perspective is used here with two ellipses.*

ELLIPSES

Ellipses feature regularly in objects in still lifes and other drawings, such as vases and bowls of fruit, so it is worth taking a few minutes to register the following two key points. The first is that the depth of an ellipse increases and becomes increasingly circular as you move away from the horizon line (see top right). The second is that line A (in the back) is always shorter than line B (in the front).

Atmospheric perspective

The second key observation on perspective is referred to as atmospheric perspective, which is also known as aerial perspective. It refers to the phenomenon that objects appear less clearly defined the further away they are from the viewing point. This is because air in the atmosphere is not completely transparent.

BELOW *In atmospheric perspective, features become increasingly faint and indistinct the further they are away from the viewer.*

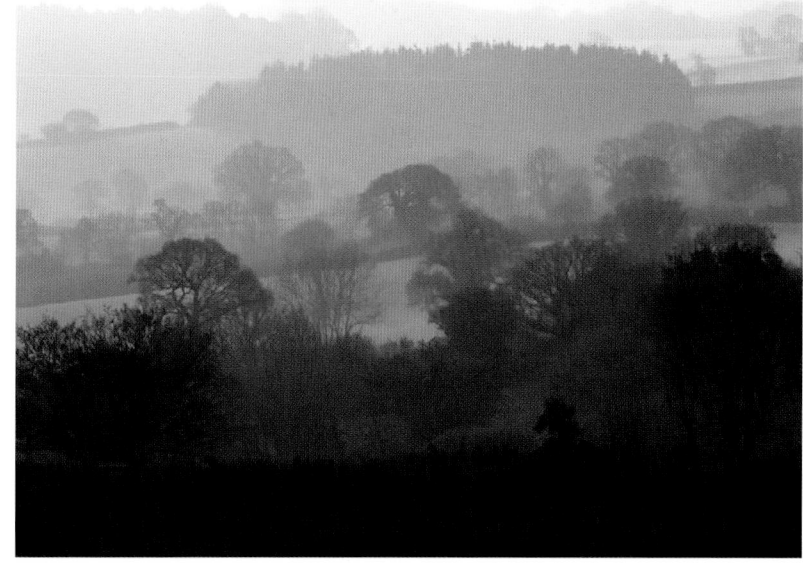

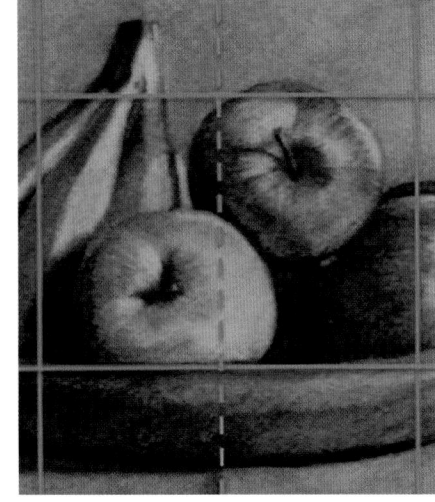

Composition

The term composition describes the way in which we place the elements within our drawings to produce the overall effect we want. In most cases, this means attempting to create something that is pleasing to the eye, but it can be used to emphasize scale or to draw attention to certain features within an image.

What is composition?

Simply type the words 'composition in art' into an Internet search engine and you will find a flood of theories, ideas and opinions. Needless to say, composition can be a contentious subject and it is largely subjective. Ultimately, you will need to use your own intuition – if it looks right to you, then it probably is right.

Even so, it is important to consider the following composition factors before you start a drawing, whether you use charcoal or another medium.

CROPPING

The first factor is something you are probably familiar with from cropping photographs on your home computer or smartphone. The principle is exactly the same in drawing: it is a case of deciding which part of the image you want to keep and which part you want to discard.

THE RULE OF THIRDS

Many artists frequently use the rule of thirds and it is recommended for being simple and effective. To apply this rule, you just need to mark out lines horizontally and vertically at points a third along the height and width of your paper (see opposite, top right). The idea is that you place key elements, such as horizon lines or the main features of your drawing, on the lines or on the points where the lines intersect. This can help you to ensure balance in your drawing and assist you in leaving enough space around your subject matter.

If you don't want to actually draw them on the paper, you can put marks outside the drawing area to show you where they are.

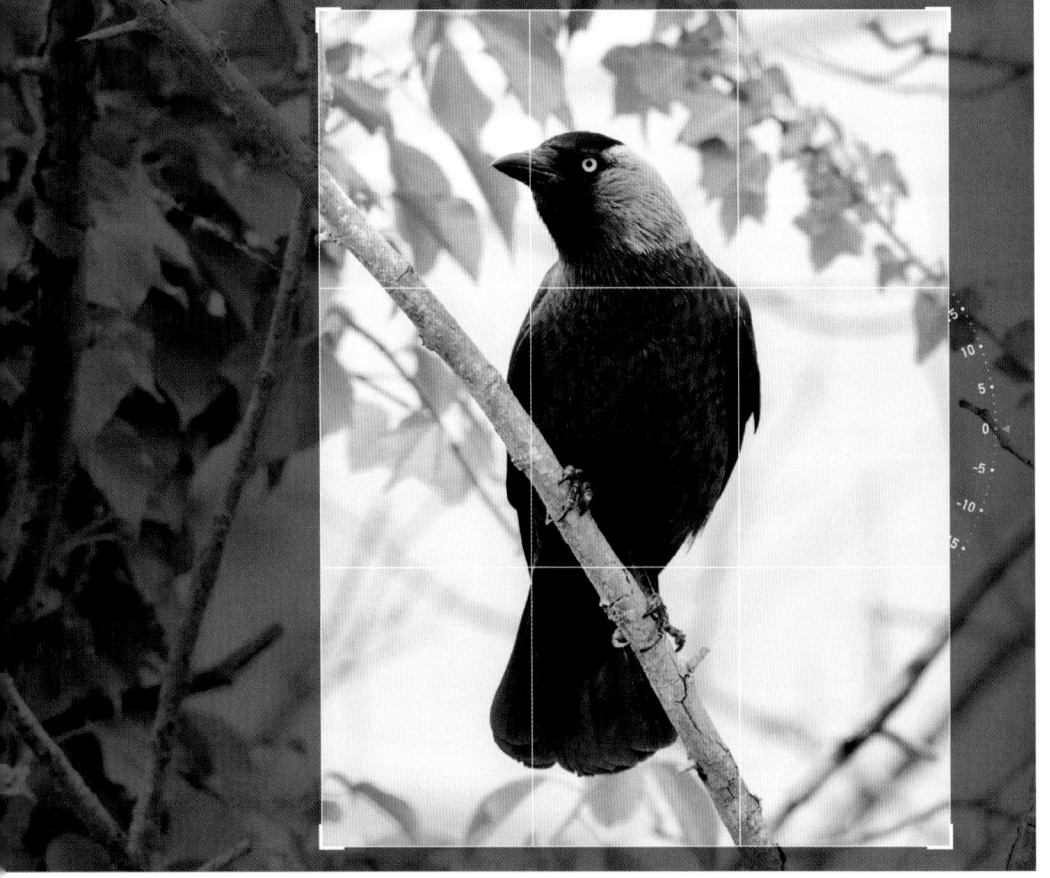

LEFT *A reference image can be cropped on basic computer editing software to help you decide the final shape of the drawing. Here, it is cropped from a square to a portrait format, placing the focus on the bird in the centre (within the four points of the rule of thirds grid).*

LEADING LINES

Leading lines are features that draw your gaze from the front of your image towards something you want the viewer's attention to see. Typical leading lines include fence lines (see below) or train tracks, but they could be any linear feature that achieves this aim.

AREA OF FOCUS

A typical photographer's trick is to make the background out of focus so that your attention is drawn to an area in the image that is in sharp focus. This is a technique you can apply just as effectively in drawing.

CREATING DEPTH

The illusion of depth is a factor you can control in your drawings by following the rules of perspective (see pages 266–7).

BACKGROUND

Consider carefully how your background will affect the subject matter in front of it. Emphasizing the contrast between light and dark or the simplification of a distracting background can help to draw attention to the main subject matter.

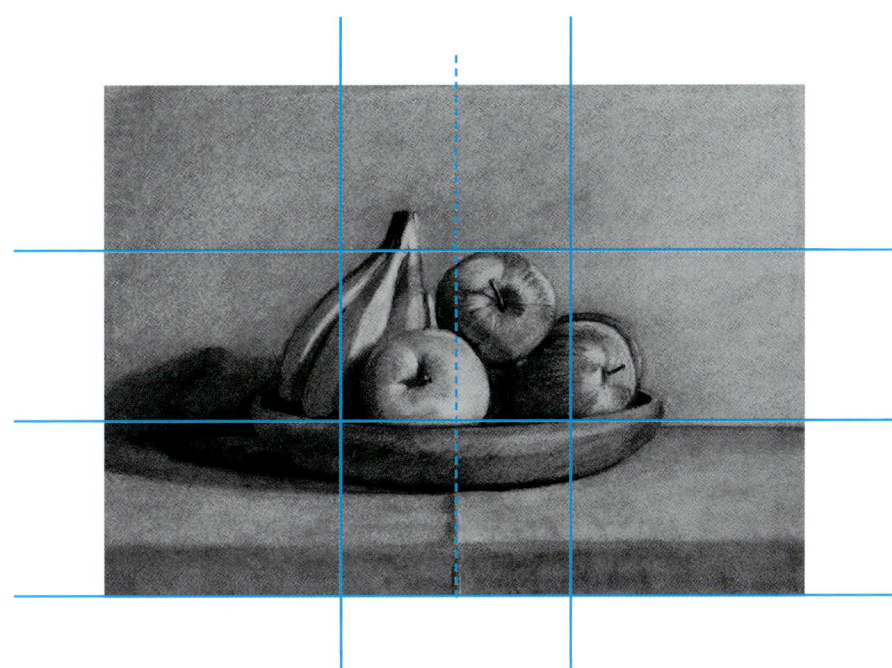

ABOVE *In this simple still-life image, notice how the objects are placed centrally to provide symmetry and balance while the back edge of the tablecloth is placed on the lower horizontal line of the rule of thirds grid.*

BELOW *The lines of the fence posts and the narrow road help to draw your focus into the image and towards the unusual cloud formation.*

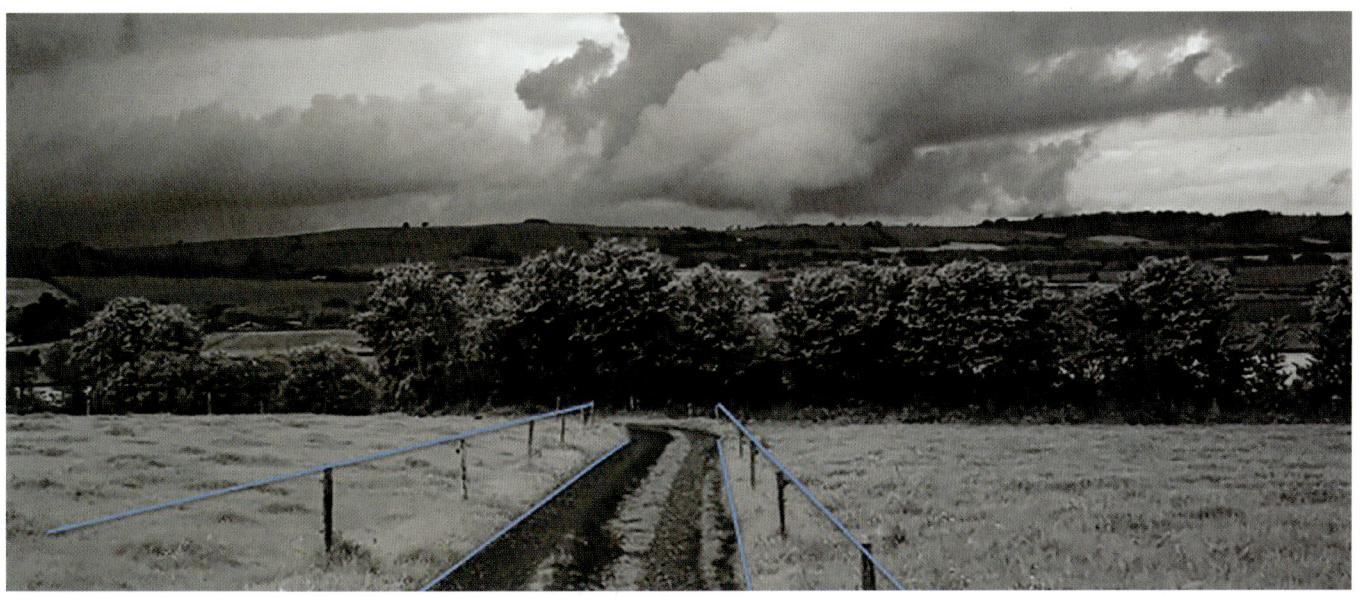

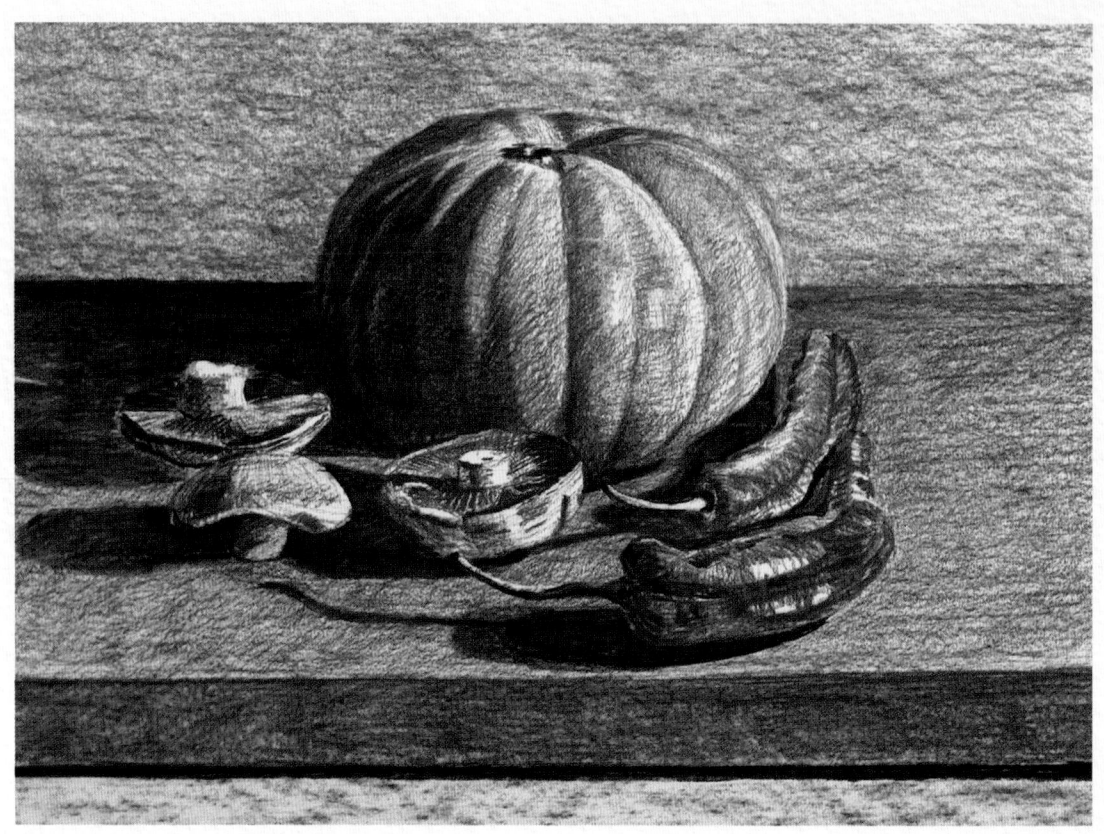

Vegetables Still Life

For our first tutorial, you will discover the drawing characteristics of natural charcoal as you draw a simple still life. You won't be using any blending techniques, so the lines of your drawing will remain visible. Vegetables offer a good range of interesting natural forms, but when starting out it's best to avoid those with overly complicated surface textures.

YOU WILL NEED
a sheet of good-quality heavyweight cartridge paper with a reasonable tooth • several thin to medium-thick natural charcoal sticks • if you have them, a viewfinder and a sanding block

The still life has been a favourite genre in art for centuries. For the viewer, it provides a meditative contemplation on a scene that is often composed of ordinary and everyday objects. From the artist's perspective, it is relatively easy to set up using items from around the home and to compose it to be aesthetically pleasing.

More importantly, a still life allows the artist to set up a scene that will remain static throughout the drawing process. This means the light source can be controlled to produce highlights and shadows that will not shift, and it's ideal for practising observational drawing (see pages 263–5). Beyond this, the subject matter is only limited by the imagination, so it can be as simple or complex as you like.

Although this will be a challenging exercise, it is intended to help you get a feeling for natural charcoal as a drawing material. There are two key aims: for you to practise the application of natural charcoal in a controlled manner and for you to learn to progressively build up layers of darker tonal value until you get them to where they need to be.

For this reason, I would ideally like you to try and complete the exercise without using erasers. However, if you do accidentally add too much and go too dark, then simply wipe away the problem area and rework it.

Setting up

Try to place your vegetables in a pleasing way that sits nicely within your chosen format – in this case, a landscape-oriented rectangle. Think about the various composition factors (see pages 268–9) as you arrange the elements, as well as the negative space (see page 265) between them. If you have a chopping board or something else to place the objects on, you can also include it in your composition.

You should use a suitable single light source, such as an angle lamp (see page 255). Set it up to shine light from one side, slightly to the front and pointing down to throw distinct shadows. Try to take these shadows into account as you arrange the still life and make sure you think of them as part of your composition.

BELOW *When composing a still life, thumbnail sketches are a great way to try out a few ideas to see what looks best. Drawn loosely and rapidly, they will help you to get into the right mindset before starting your main drawing. They will also help you to place your initial lines on the paper more confidently.*

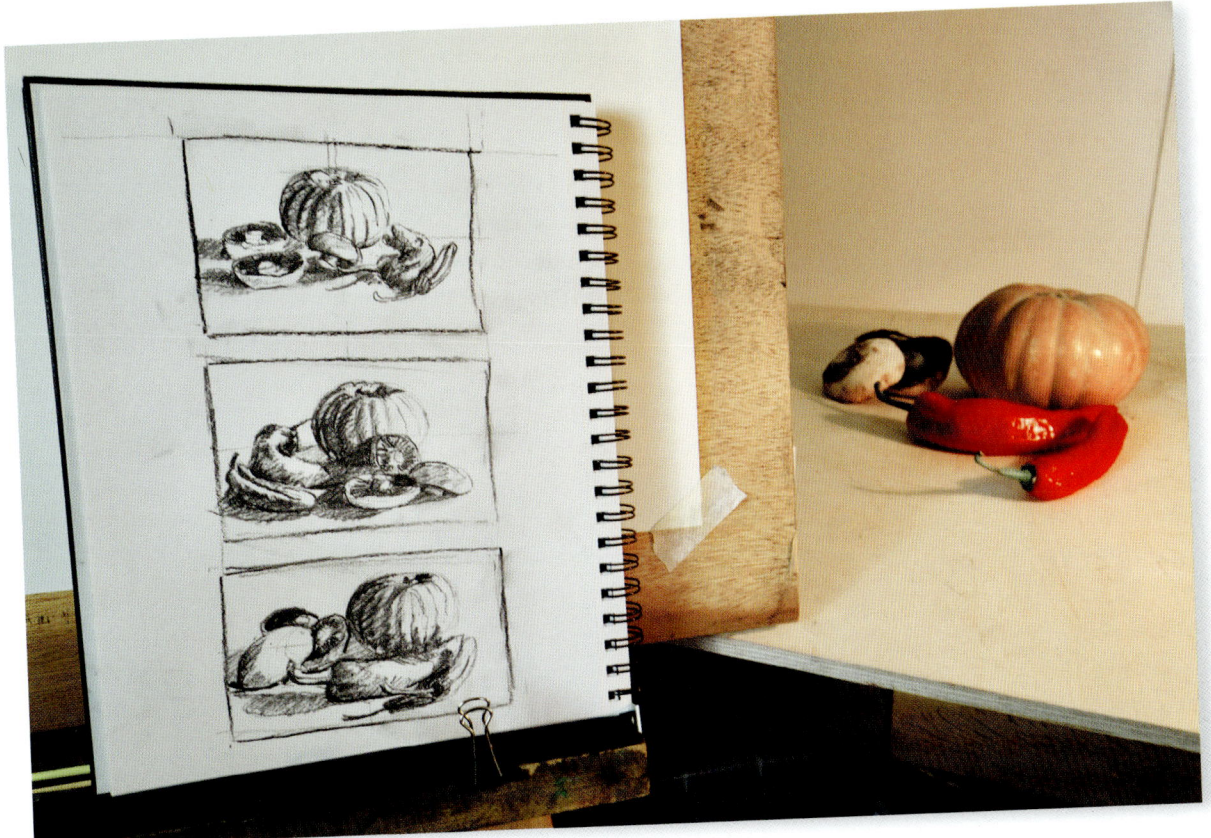

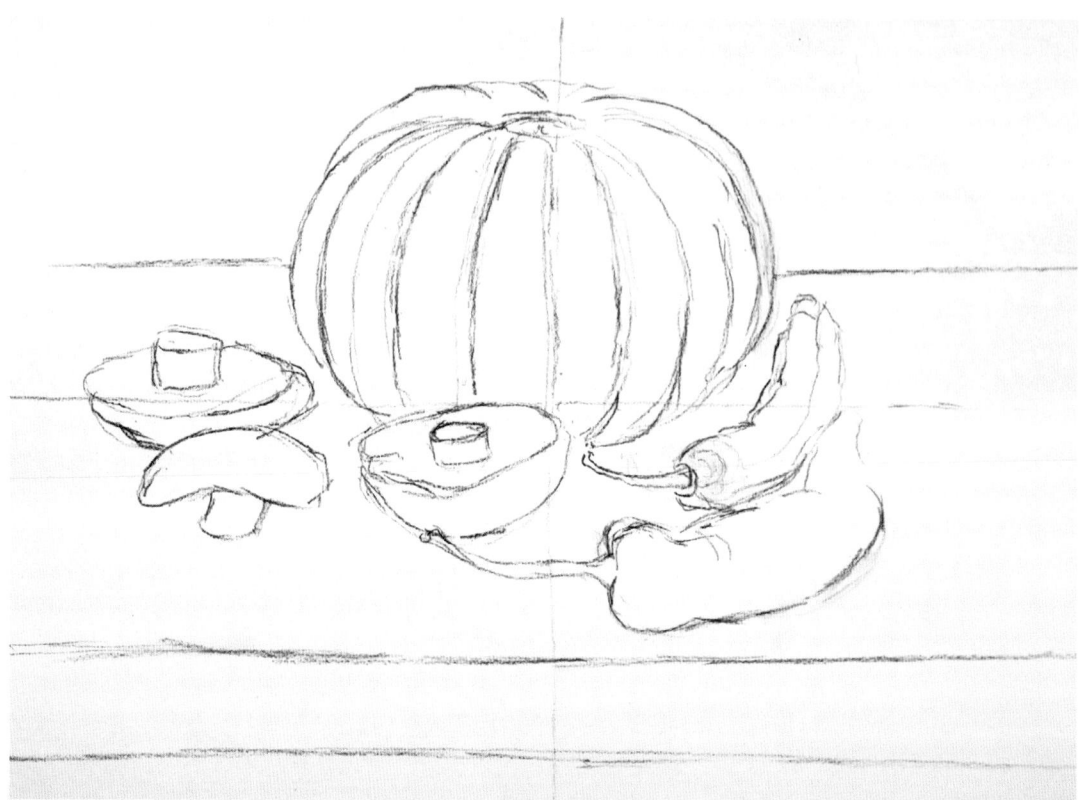

STAGE 1

To start, you should sketch out the main elements in the drawing. Take a long piece of thin charcoal – around ⅛in (3mm) diameter is ideal – and rub the edge off one end, using a sanding block or the side of your paper, to produce a slight point. Try to maintain this point throughout the sketching phase.

Lightly mark out a cross in the middle of your paper and then look carefully at your objects to decide where the centre of your composition is. You can use a viewfinder (see page 263), if you have one, to help you identify this point. In this case, the vertical centreline runs straight down the middle of the pumpkin and the bottom of the pumpkin comes down slightly below the horizontal centreline.

The pumpkin is the most prominent element of the drawing, so we will start with it. This stage is all about shape, so start by sketching in the basic outline shape quickly and loosely and, most importantly, very, very softly until you feel confident that it's about right. You can then add a little more pressure to define its final position. With the pumpkin in place, use it as your reference for everything else in terms of position and scale.

Now begin to draw in the remaining vegetables, working in order of those that are easiest to place accurately first. While doing this, continually look at the negative spaces (see page 265) between them to help you place them correctly on the paper.

When everything is where it needs to be, you can continue to define the lines a little more heavily until you have all of the main shapes in place.

Tip
If you don't have a sanding block or sanding paper, you can use a corner of your drawing paper, outside the drawing area, to hone the shape of your charcoal. You can either remove sharp edges to get a softer mark or sharpen the end to get a thinner, darker line.

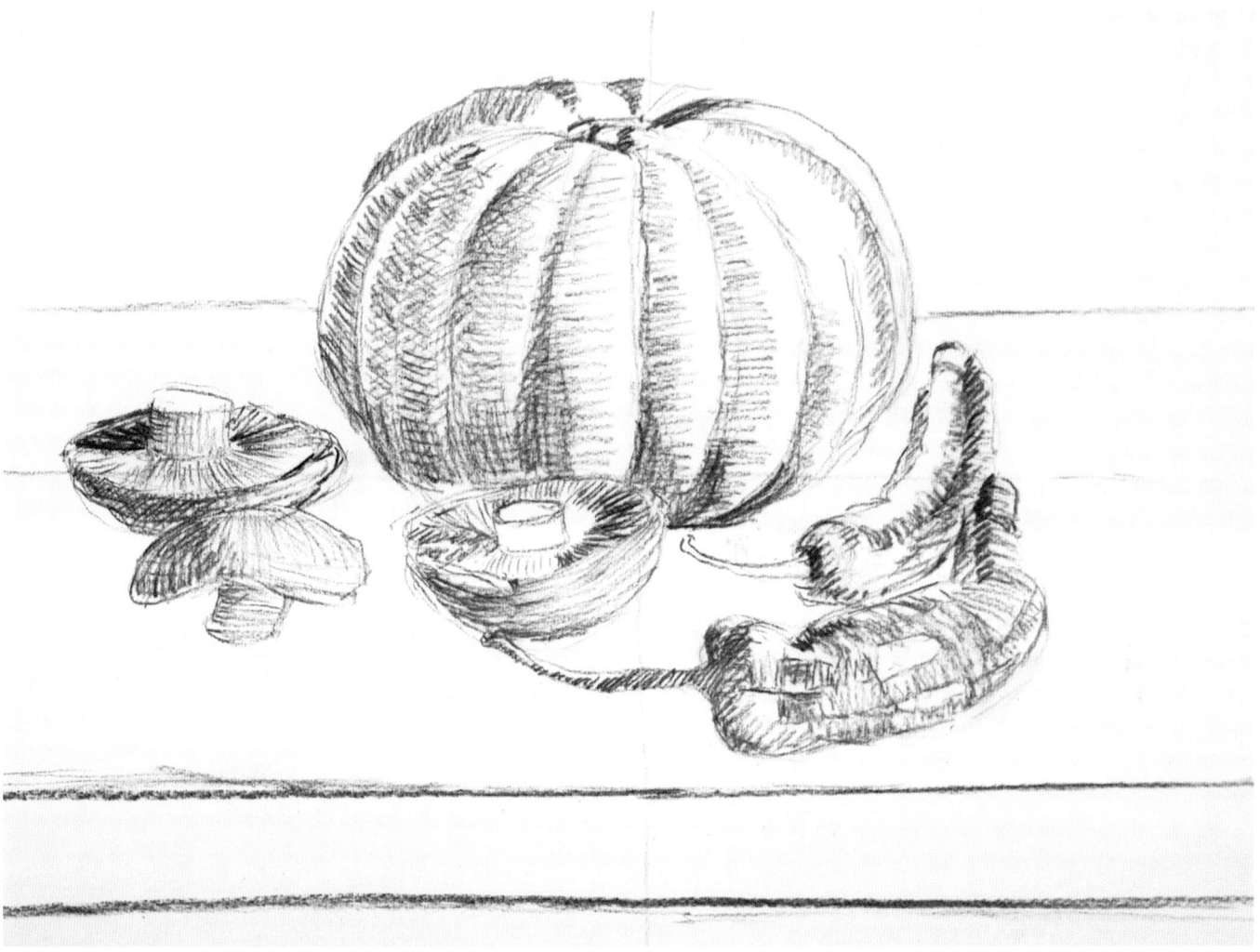

STAGE 2

Having previously focused on the shapes of the objects in relation to one another, you should now shift your observational focus to look at how the light falls on them to produce highlights and shadows, revealing their form.

Begin shading where you see it is required, using hatching and cross-hatching marks (see page 257), but be careful you don't go too dark. You are not trying to get the tonal values absolutely correct at this point – all you want to do is to map out where the light and dark areas are in relation to one another. Once everything has been given some tonal value, it will be easier to see which elements need to go darker.

Because you will not be using blending techniques in this drawing, the lines will remain visible. Try to contour the lines to reflect the form of the objects, which will really help give them a sense of volume.

You may think that the drawing looks a bit scruffy and clunky at this point, because it's difficult to control charcoal and the lines will be uneven, but stick with it. You will add layer upon layer of lines until they merge to form an evenly textured surface.

As in the previous stage, try to maintain a moderate point on your charcoal. Build the drawing up slowly and keep reminding yourself that you can always go darker but not lighter (remember that one of the challenges for this exercise is not to use erasers).

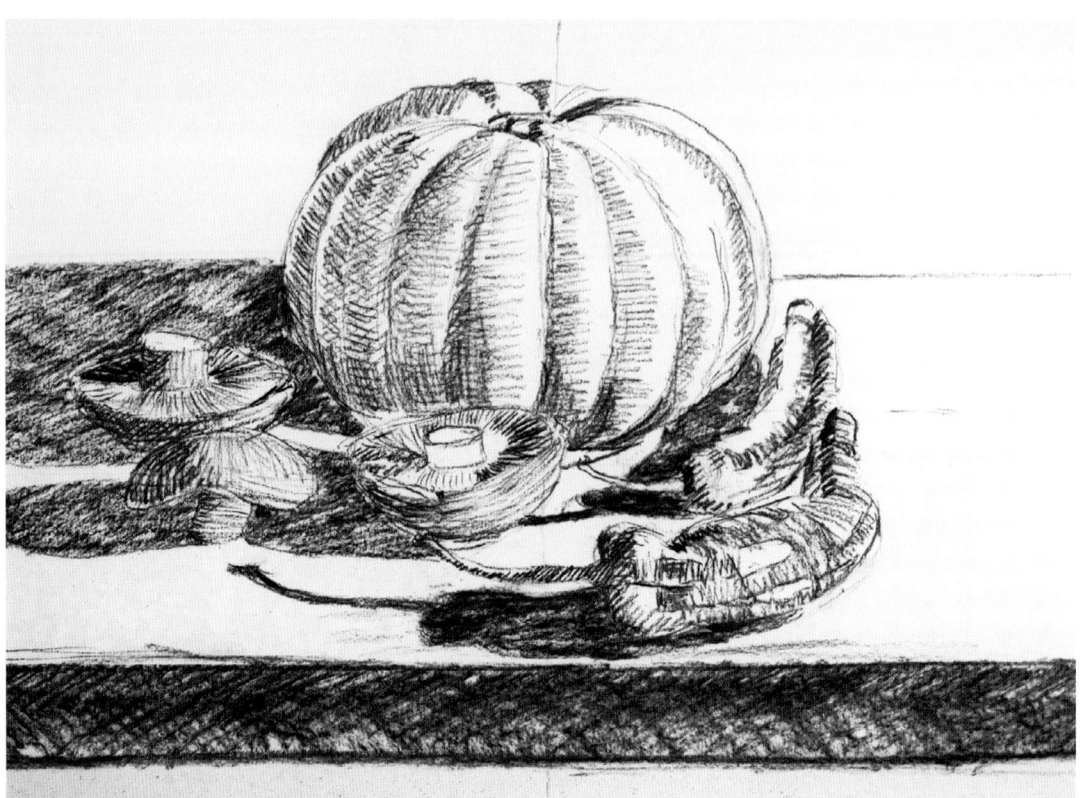

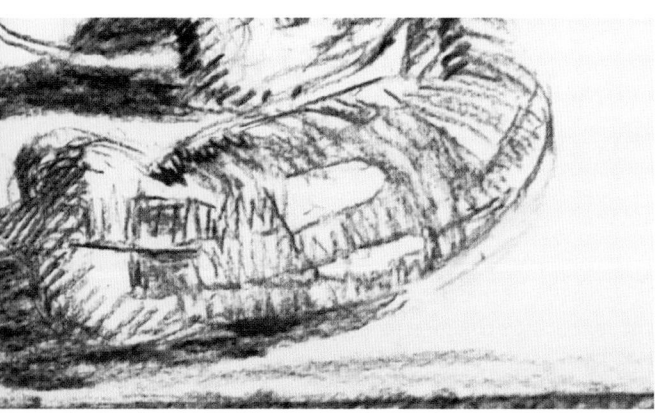

ABOVE *Draw a light line around areas you want to keep as highlights, as you can just see here on the side of the pepper. This will help you to avoid accidentally drawing over them.*

STAGE 3

In this stage, you will be adding the shadows cast by the vegetables. As mentioned earlier, the shadows are an important element in your composition, and they also help to give the objects a sense of mass. Notice how before this stage the vegetables appeared to be floating in space, but the shadows now make it clear that they are firmly sitting on the chopping board.

When you draw out the shapes of the shadows, look carefully at the shapes in relation to everything around them, exactly as you did when drawing the actual vegetables. Remember, too, to check the negative spaces as you draw. Notice that not all areas of shadow are of equal value – some areas are distinctly darker than others.

Once you are happy that the shadow shapes are captured accurately, start hatching them in. Just as in the previous stage, avoid going too dark too early, as you want to leave yourself at least another step of value to go darker later on. Really concentrate on controlling the pressure applied to the charcoal, but allow the drawing end to become blunt so that a greater surface area of charcoal is in contact with the paper. Concentrate, too, on trying to keep your hatching lines parallel.

Hatch in the shaded front edge of the chopping board. This helps to indicate that the vegetables are sitting on a solid object. It will also provide a sense of depth by visually pulling the front edge towards you.

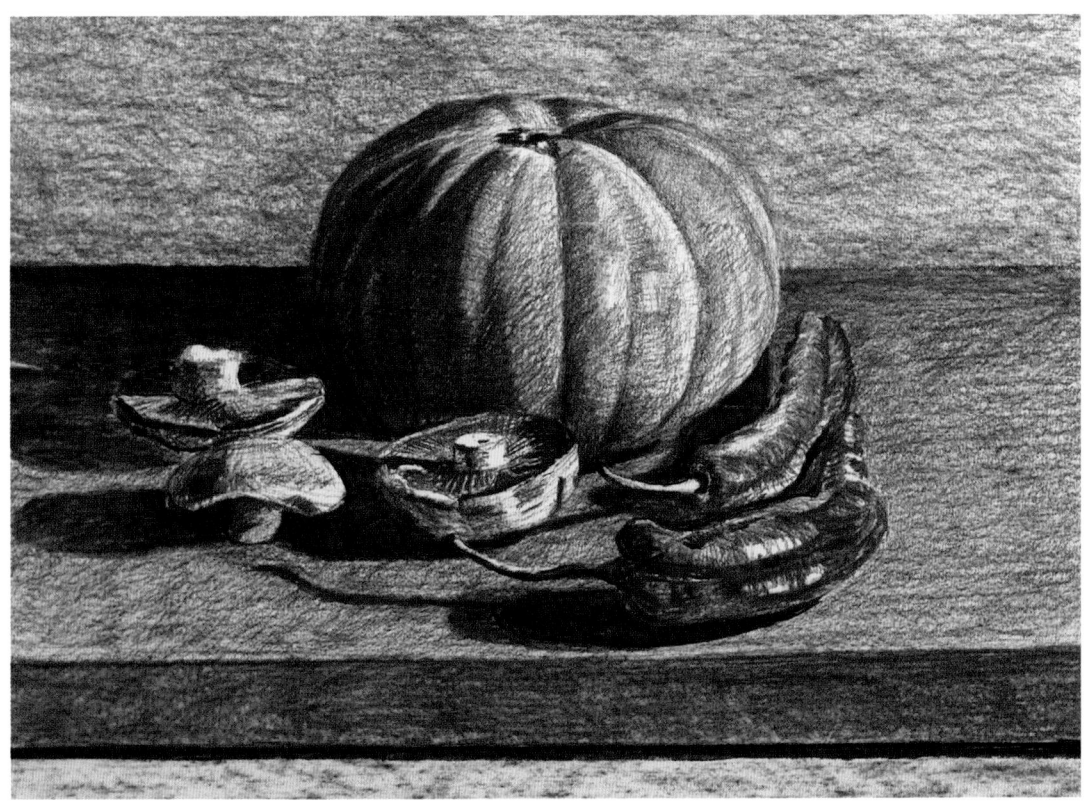

STAGE 4

Slowly, slowly build up the tone on the vegetables while continuing to follow the contours of the shapes, but avoid applying your darkest darks just yet. Keep looking really carefully to compare values across the drawing and start defining the extents of your highlights. Try to avoid drawing over the areas you identify as your highlights, because you want the white of the paper to show through in these areas.

In this case, the most obvious highlights are on the peppers. Not only is their red colour quite dark when viewed in monochrome, the surface is also shiny and reflects a lot of light.

For the flat surfaces, try to maintain parallel lines in your hatching and ensure that you apply a uniform thickness of charcoal. Draw the lines in several different directions until they produce a textured but reasonably even tone.

Look carefully to observe the difference in values transition between the hard edges and the more gradual transition of the rounded forms. Remember how the light fell across the three objects in Light and Shadows (see page 259) and observe how the same principles apply to the objects in the still life.

Finally, when you feel you are just about there, look carefully to identify your darkest darks and draw them in with some firm pressure. Look particularly closely at your shadow areas and identify variances in tonal value. As with the highlights, you should use your darkest values sparingly, but note how much they help in improving the illusion of three dimensions.

BELOW *Build the image gradually by adding tone to all of the surfaces and constantly asking yourself if the area you are shading is lighter or darker than the area adjoining it.*

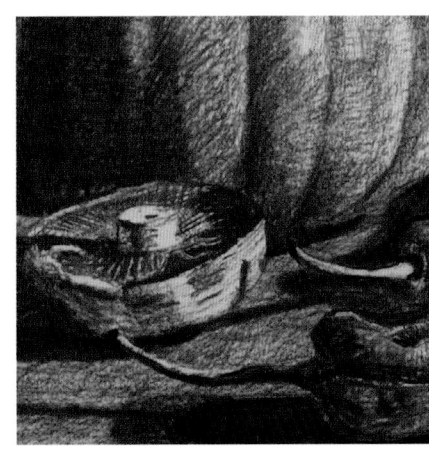

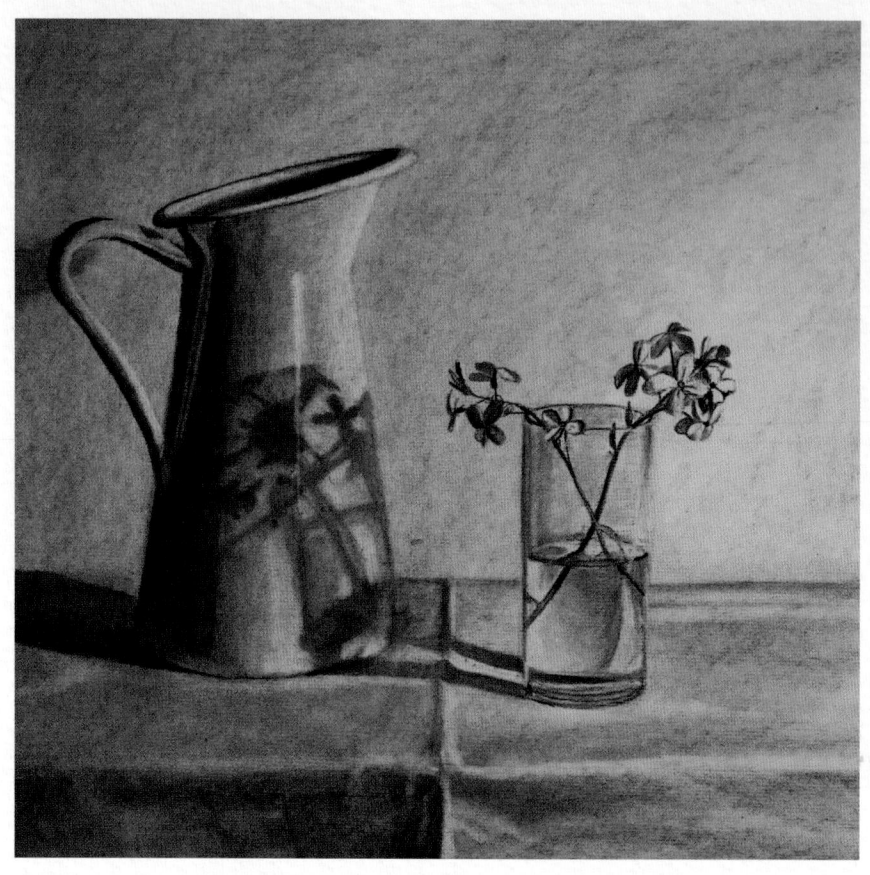

Still Life with Water Jug and Plants

Here is a tutorial aimed at adding blending and measuring to your range of skills, helping you to produce a more sophisticated still-life drawing.

YOU WILL NEED

a sheet of good-quality heavyweight cartridge paper or charcoal paper
• several natural charcoal sticks in different thicknesses • blending stumps
• a soft cloth • erasers – a kneaded eraser will probably suffice but a super-fine
pencil eraser will be useful in the latter stages

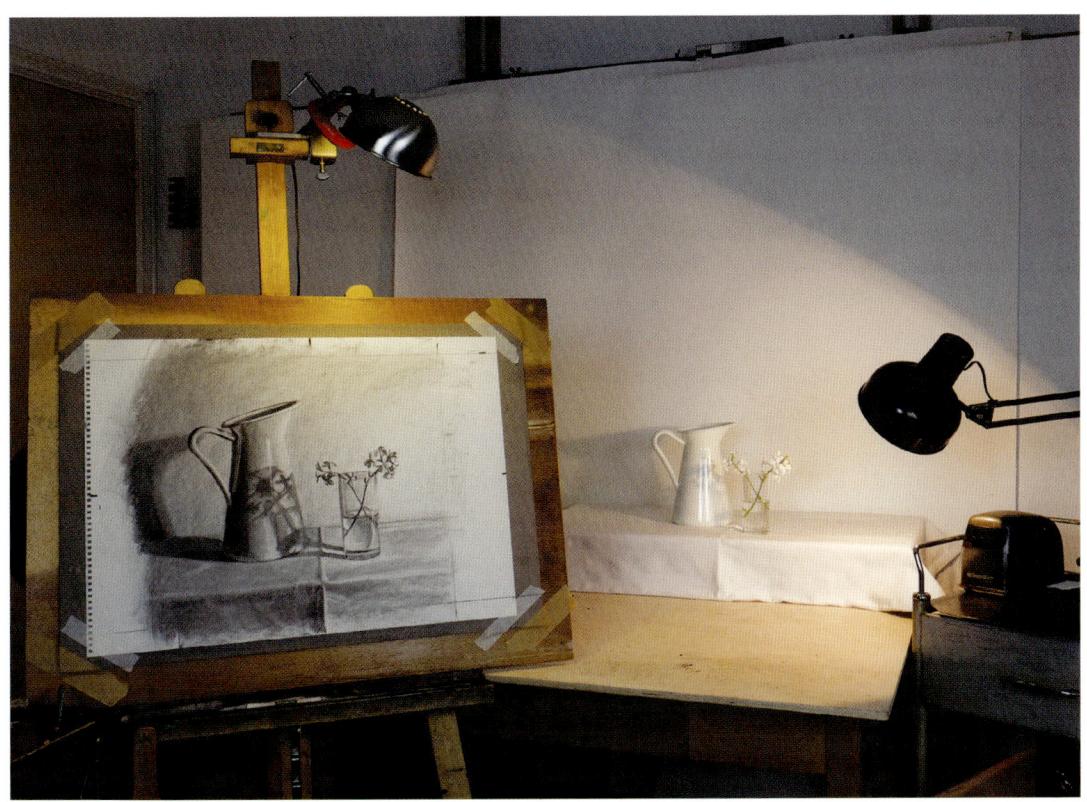

The first tutorial focused on the importance of having precise control of your charcoal and erasers as well as a gradual approach to get to the tonal value you want. This tutorial will introduce you to working both positively and negatively as well as how to use blending as a method of graduating transitions from lighter to darker areas of value. You will be removing the hatching lines in your shaded areas to enhance the impression of realism.

You will also be tackling a couple of ellipses and practising comparative measuring to ensure that everything is in the correct place before you start shading.

Setting up your still life

When you select items for this still life, choose two or three elliptical objects. A couple of flowers in a glass or vase will add some additional challenge and interest, but you could use a plant in a flowerpot if you prefer. Because bright colours can be distracting when you are trying to make monochrome value judgements, try to include objects that have a neutral colour. The tablecloth provides another element of interest – note how the light falls across its surface, creating shadows and highlights in the folds of the material.

For this set-up, you should use two lights: one to provide a single light source to illuminate the still life and another attached to the easel to illuminate the drawing. When positioning the light over the drawing, make sure you angle it carefully to avoid throwing a secondary light source across the still life.

When composing your still life, try to keep it simple. Have a few different objects to hand and try them out to see what works best. In this scene, the rule of thirds (see page 268) was used as a compositional guide. The back of the tablecloth, for example, lies on a horizontal line about one third up from the bottom of the picture. The jug and the glass of flowers are placed on either side of the crease in the tablecloth, which lies centrally to provide some balance. If you choose to draw flowers, try to select ones that are not too complex.

Now that you have set up your still life, take some time to just sit and observe it for a while. Notice where the light and shadow form soft or hard edges and squint to determine where your lightest and darkest areas of value lie.

Tip

There are some pros and cons to what you use for securing your paper to a drawing board. Pins leave holes behind that can show through when you later draw over them. Clips are great if you have a drawing board that is matched in size to your paper because they are clean, easy and reusable without damaging the paper – however, you can't lay the board flat. Tape is fine for most work, as long as you remember to keep the tape out of your drawing area and use a suitably low-tack tape.

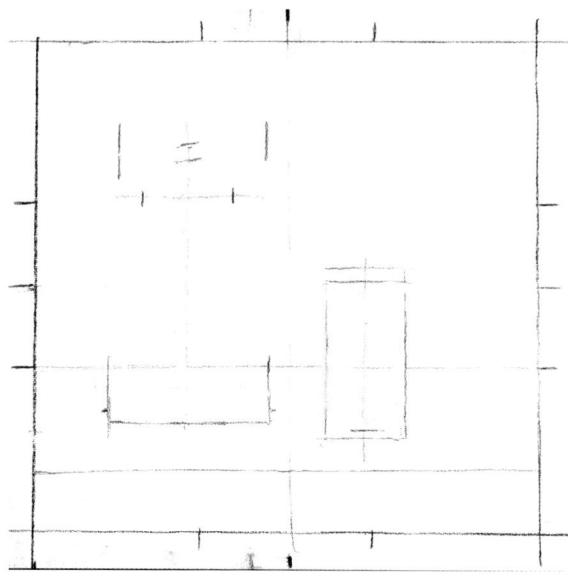

STAGE 1

Begin by marking out the extent of your drawing area. Mark out the centre lines and the position of the rule of thirds lines just outside the drawing area to help you place things compositionally. Using a viewfinder will help you to decide on a format: a square format works well with this piece, so it is marked out within the rectangular piece of paper.

With a thin piece of charcoal and pressing lightly, use observational drawing techniques (see pages 263–5) to compare and measure elements in your composition, such as identifying the left and right as well as lower and higher extents of key points in your objects. Check your measurements and angles from different points and adjust them as necessary to gradually increase the accuracy. As you become confident that the marks are correct, mark them in more clearly.

It is worth investing some time into this stage, because the further you get into the drawing, the harder it will be to rectify mistakes. You can substitute the carpenters' mantra of 'Measure twice, cut once' with 'Measure twice, draw once'!

STAGE 2

With the key points marked out accurately, you can tackle the ellipses and complex shape of the jug handle.

You can't see the full ellipse at the base of the jug, but draw it in roughly to estimate where the rear portion of the ellipse lies. Doing so will help you to draw the front portion correctly. Remember that due to perspective (see pages 266–7) the front half of an ellipse will always have a more pronounced curve than the rear. The glass, although close to you, also follows the rules of perspective in that the ellipse becomes more pronounced (more oval) the further it is below your horizon line (which is above the glass). It conforms to the rules of three-point perspective, too: because you are looking down on the glass, the lines converge slightly towards the base of the glass.

Turning your attention to where the jug handle joins the jug, measure from the base of the jug to the bottom of the handle. From this point, measure the width of the handle and mark it on the paper. Do the same for the upper part of the handle, where it joins the jug. Now measure and mark where the left and upper extents of the handle lie to form a corner where the handle curves. Sketch in the shape of the handle and adjust it, if necessary. (The handle here was drawn too low and had to be erased and adjusted accordingly.)

Draw in the upper part of the jug, treating it like any other ellipse.

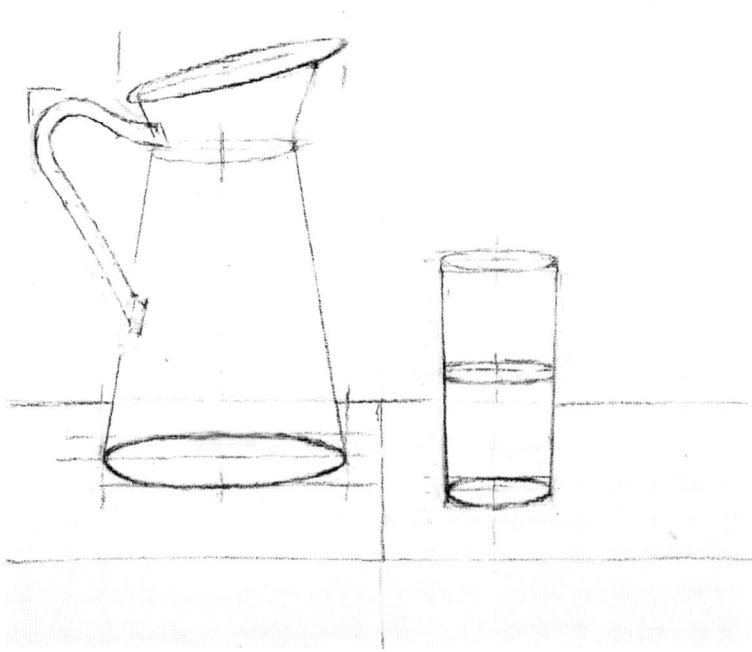

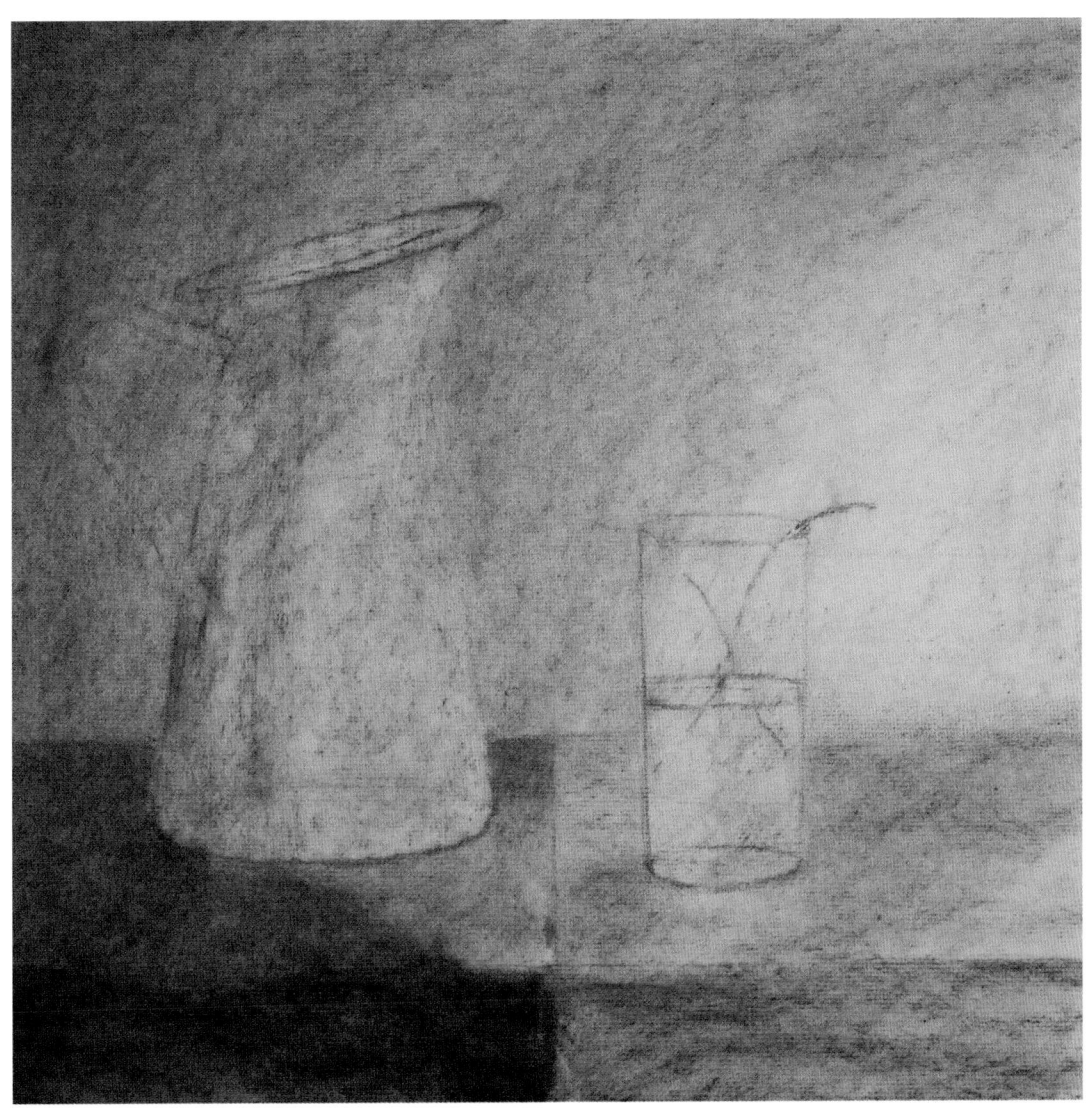

Tip

When looking closely at the still life, you may pick out areas where adjoining values are the same. For example, look closely at the right-hand edge of the jug and you will see it is very close to the background value. In such cases, you can simply draw your charcoal straight over the boundary between the two.

STAGE 3

In this stage, you should be ready to block in the main areas of shading – without focusing on the detail. Although there's an indication of the flower stalks, for example, the flower heads have not been added. Start by looking very carefully to identify where the main areas of values are, and how light or dark they are relative to the adjoining areas.

Close one eye and squint the other to help identify how light falls across the whole area of the composition rather than just individual parts of it. You should see how the light is significantly brighter where it is closest to the light source and that it becomes significantly darker on the left-hand side of the drawing, where the light drops off.

Apply a layer of natural charcoal by hatching in or dragging, and then use a blending stump to work the charcoal into the paper. Repeat, applying layers of charcoal and working them in with a blending stump to build up dark areas. Remember that it is a case of building up the layers gradually. When you use the blending stump, work it from various different angles. This stage can be hard work and it may take some time to blend out the hatching marks, but persevere until you get it to where you want it. If you go too far and add too much, you can lighten those areas with a soft cloth or an eraser.

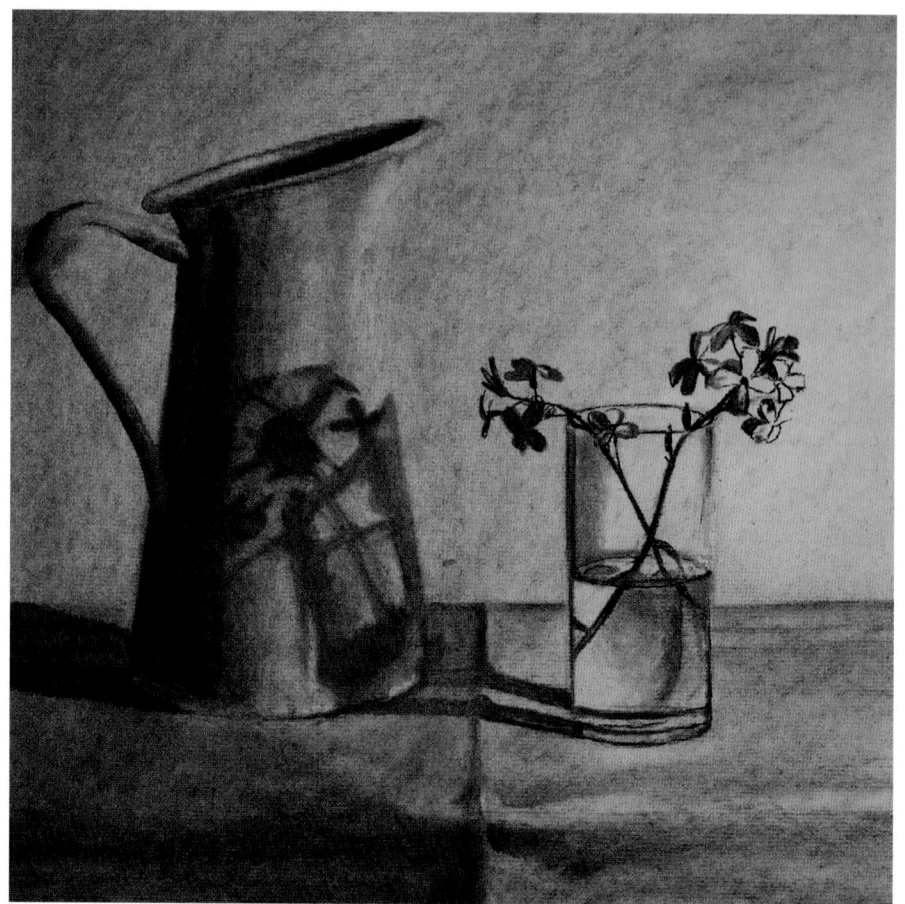

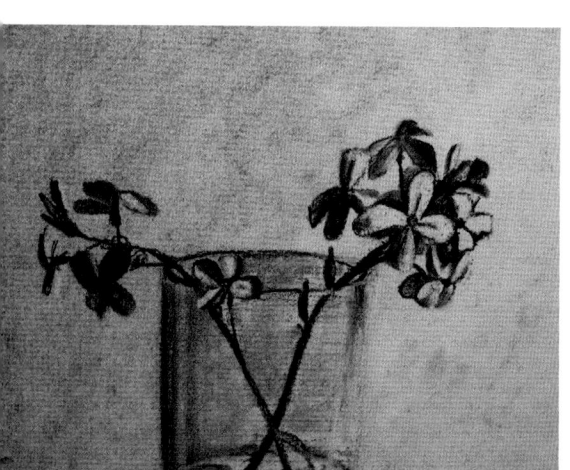

ABOVE *When drawing the flowers, after first getting the stalks drawn in correctly, identify the centre points of each flower head before attempting the petals. You may not need anything more than simple suggestions of light and shadow to give shape to the petals on your own flowers.*

STAGE 4

With your main areas of value blocked in, you can now start defining the forms of the objects and adding detail. Begin with the jug. As mentioned in the last stage, the right-hand edge of the jug is very close in value to the background but the form turns away from the light source to become relatively darker on its left-hand edge. Notice the line of the penumbra (see page 259), where the value is significantly darker to the left and lighter to the right, and the graduated transition that tells us that the jug has a curved form. However, the shadow is darkest inside the jug on the right-hand side, where it is most shielded from the light source, and it becomes lighter on the left-hand side. Add charcoal and blend it in with a motion following the contours of the jug. Spend some time getting this right before you tackle the shadows of the flowers.

When working on the transparent glass and the water, try to imagine this area as a two-dimensional pattern of light and dark rather than a complex three-dimensional object – try really hard to just draw what you see. For the flowers, you will need to use a thin piece of charcoal and keep it honed to a relatively sharp point. Start with the stalks to get the positioning of the flower heads correct and then draw in the petals.

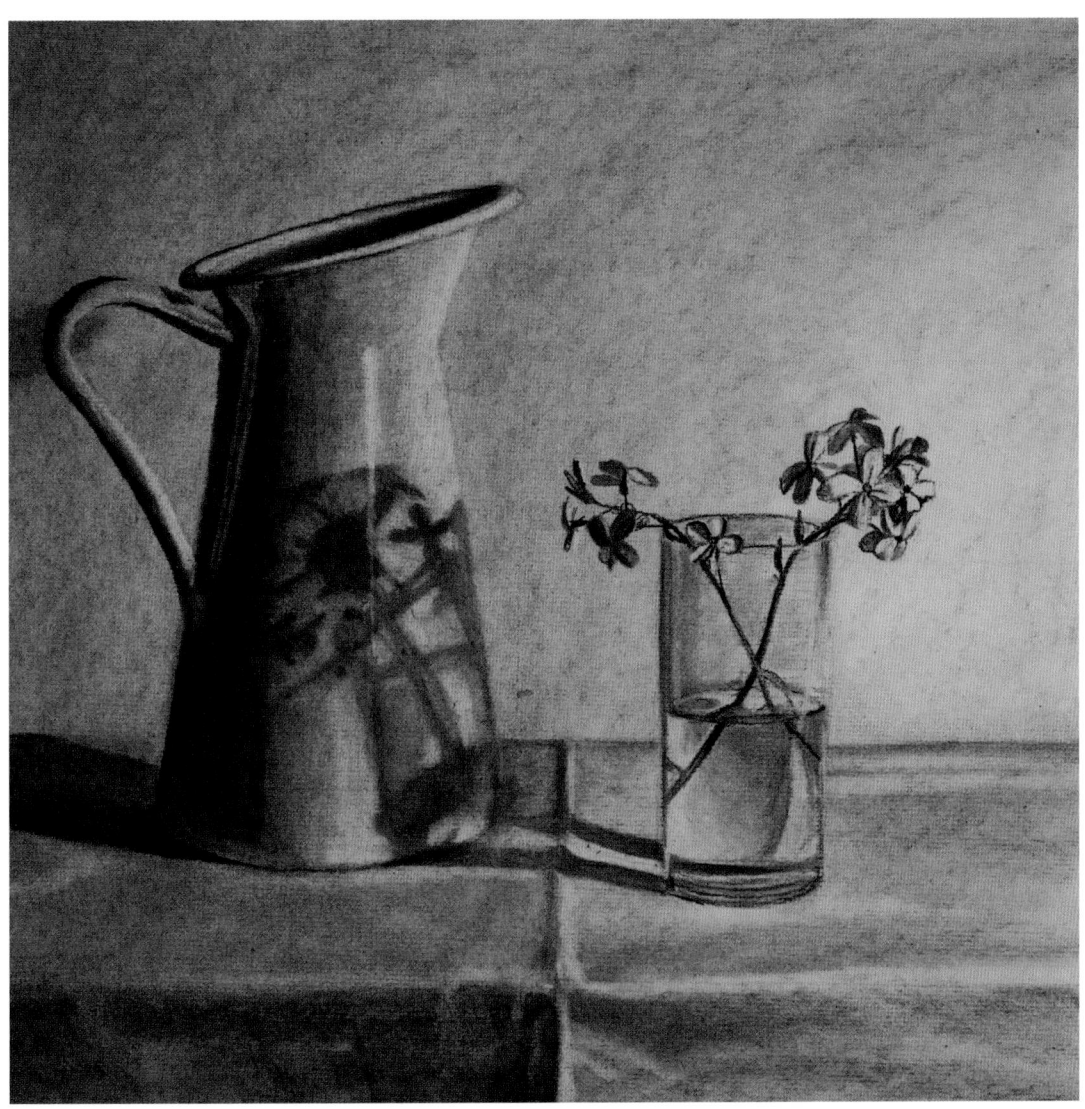

STAGE 5

Having held off the temptation to use erasers to lighten areas of value up until now, the next step is to switch mindset and work subtractively to add highlights. The key areas in this drawing are along the right-hand edge of the jug, which is very slightly lighter than the background, so very gently remove charcoal from the top surface of the paper along that edge. There is also a strong highlight on the surface of the jug facing the viewing position. The jug is metal painted white, and the highlight is correspondingly quite clearly defined. Likewise, with the jug handle and the rim of the jug mouth and the area on the left-hand side of the jug, where the light bouncing off the handle is reflected onto the shadow side of the jug.

A soft cloth is a good tool for lightening areas of the tablecloth, such as the front edge and the creases. Finally, use a very narrow eraser to lighten the petals facing the light source. Now tweak anything else required to complete the drawing.

Tip

When you think you've finished, avoid the temptation to fix the drawing and disassemble the still life immediately. It is good practice to leave a drawing in position for a while – ideally overnight – so that you can look at it with fresh eyes after you've had a break. You will often notice small errors, omissions or areas for improvement that you simply missed when you were engrossed in the drawing process.

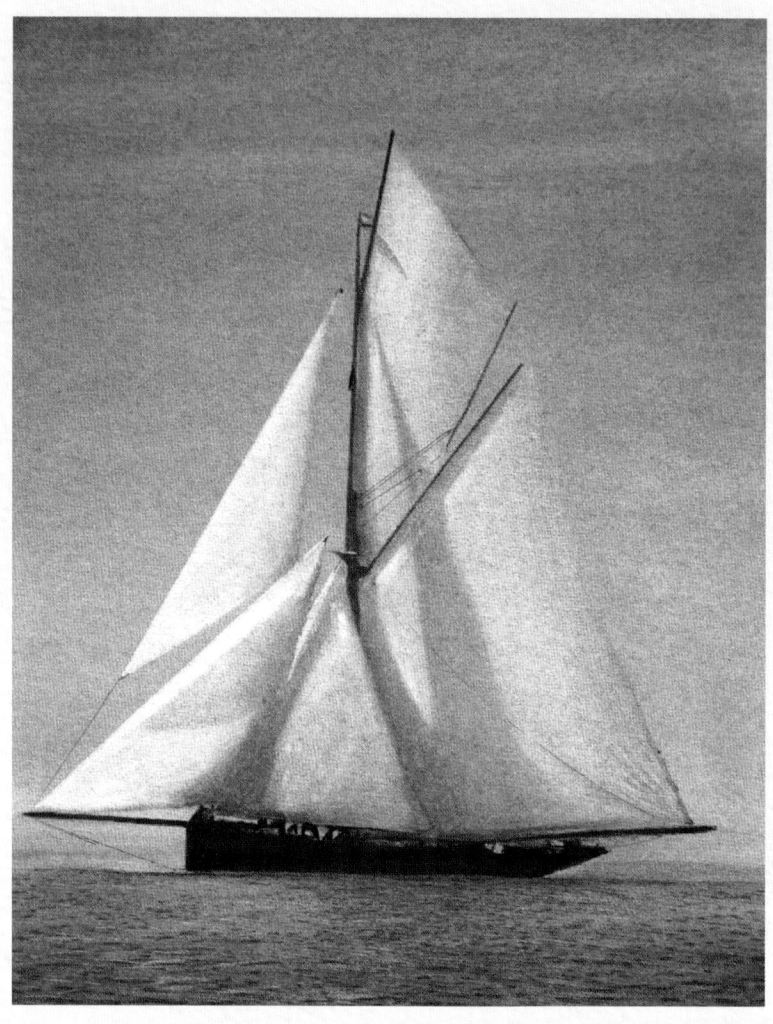

Sailing Ship

*Combining compressed charcoal together with natural charcoal
can produce beautiful results, which will be the focus in this tutorial.*

YOU WILL NEED

*a sheet of good-quality heavyweight cartridge paper • a fine-line black pen or sharp waxy pencil
• tracing paper (optional) • a ruler or other straight edge • a good-quality compressed charcoal
pencil • medium-thick natural charcoal sticks • charcoal powder • a soft cloth • a kneaded eraser
• a pencil eraser • blending stumps • a mahlstick or wooden battens (see page 287)*

The reference material for this artwork is an old photograph of a 19th-century racing yacht. It is such a special image that I decided to try to recreate it in charcoal. In doing so, I realized that it is an excellent image for teaching key lessons in charcoal drawing – which is why it frequently makes an appearance when I am running workshops or drawing demonstrations.

What I love about this piece is that it's actually quite simple to produce, but there are a couple of stages when something magical happens: first when you blend the waves to create a watery effect, and again when you reveal the white of the sails by removing charcoal with subtractive drawing (see page 261). When people first see this image, they often assume that I've used a white pigment to do the areas of lighter tone, but these are merely areas of exposed white paper. They help to hold elements in the drawing together visually and add to the sense of simplicity and tranquillity in the image.

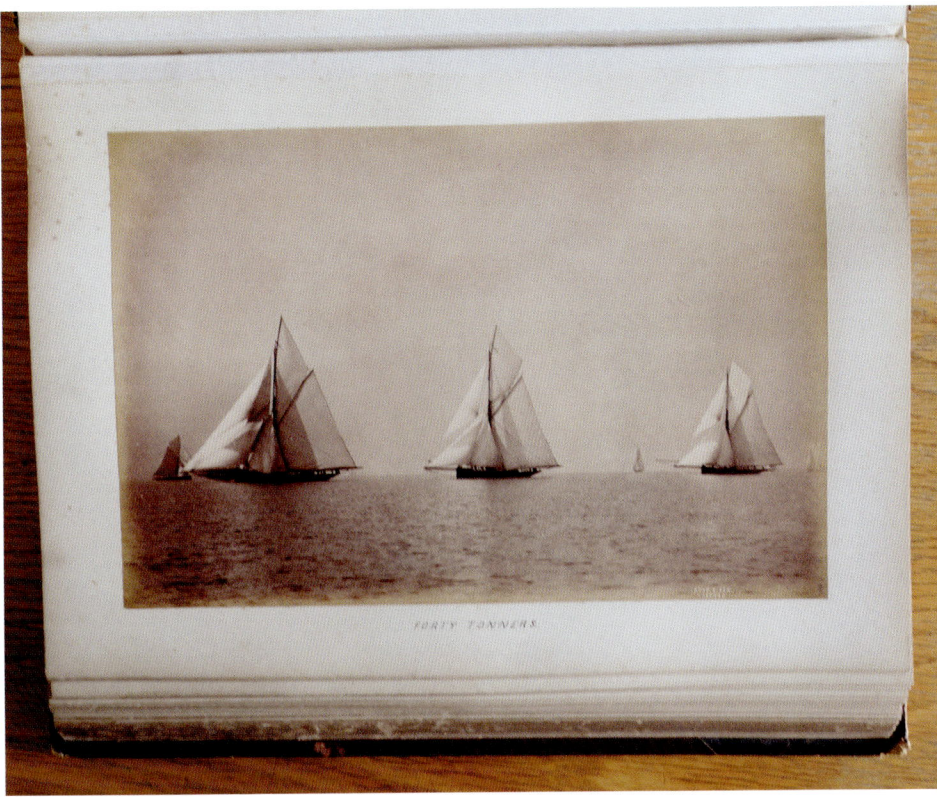

Scaling up the boat

There are three yachts in the original photograph, but I decided to concentrate on just one for the drawing – the yacht in the centre. I used a camera to take a digital copy and then cropped the image on my computer. From this, I produced a scaled-up image from which I could trace my initial outline. If you don't have a computer but do have access to a photocopier, you can use it instead to enlarge the image. Or if neither is available, you can use the grid system (see page 305) or proportional dividers (see page 264) to sketch out an enlarged boat.

Once you have an enlarged image, you can copy the outline onto tracing paper, first by positioning the tracing paper over the ship and tracing it with a pencil, and then rubbing charcoal onto the opposite side of the tracing paper where the pencil lines show through. Now you can position the tracing paper, with pencil marks facing up, over your drawing paper where you want the boat to be placed and draw over the pencil marks with your pencil once again. By using a coloured pencil, it will be easier to see where you have already traced over the original pencil marks.

ABOVE *Picture plates found in old books can provide interesting reference material for a charcoal drawing. Sepia and black-and-white illustrations make it easier to ascertain the tonal values.*

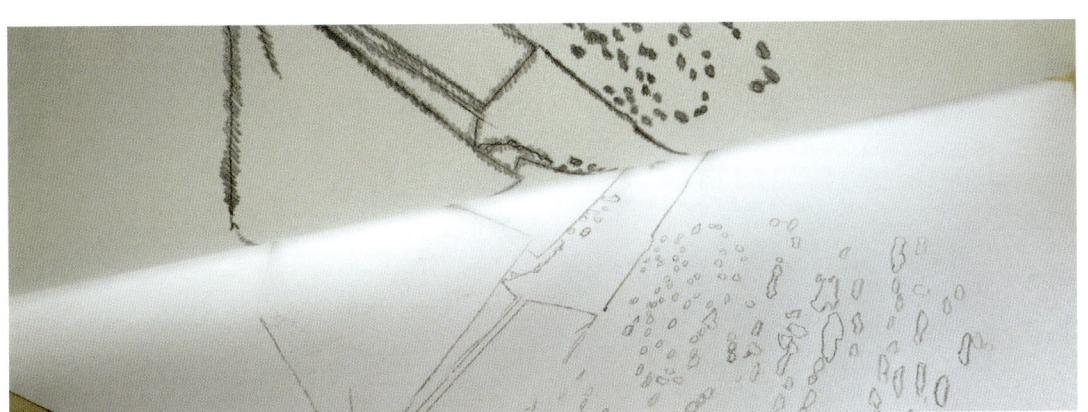

LEFT *When using tracing paper to transfer an image onto your drawing surface, remember the image will be reversed (flipped horizontally). Make sure you take this into account when you make your compositional decisions.*

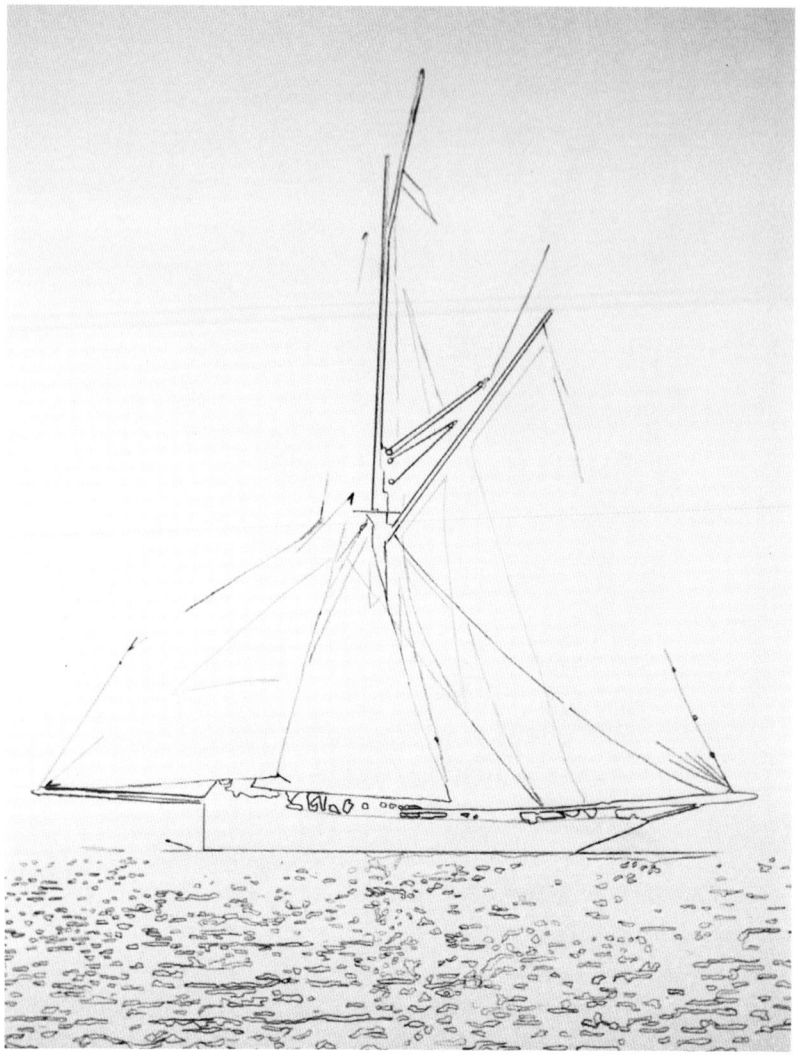

STAGE 1

Begin by tracing or marking out the outline of the boat with a thin black pen or sharp, waxy pencil. If you are using tracing paper, position it over the charcoal paper and tape or otherwise secure it in place to the drawing board to avoid marking the drawing paper.

You can use a ruler or other straight edge to get the mast and spars (thin long poles) absolutely straight. Instead of drawing the curves of the sails by moving your hand from your wrist, use your arm as a pivot point to draw the slight curves. However, note that you should not mark the line for the sails all the way around: the areas where the sails meet the sky on the right-hand side are close in value to the greys in the sky, so these areas will bleed into each other. Where the sails at the front of the ship meet the sky on the left-hand side, the tonal delineation will be light, so you will be marking out these lines later with an eraser. Regardless, you do need to make sure that you mark the start and end points of the sails to act as a guide for when you will be drawing them in.

It is a good idea to also include some of the rigging at this stage, because it will be difficult to add it later on, and the thin pen you used for marking the outline is more suitable for this task.

As you start to mark in the waves, remember that waves conform to the rules of perspective (see pages 266–7), so the waves at the front will be larger and more spaced out than those in the distance. Notice how the reflection of the ship in the water is darker in the centre section, so add more waves here to increase the density.

Tip

You can trace out the waves at this stage, as I have done here, or you can skip this laborious process and mark them in directly with compressed charcoal during the next stage. They don't need to be placed exactly to create the illusion of water and should look fine as long as you remember that waves conform to the rules of perspective.

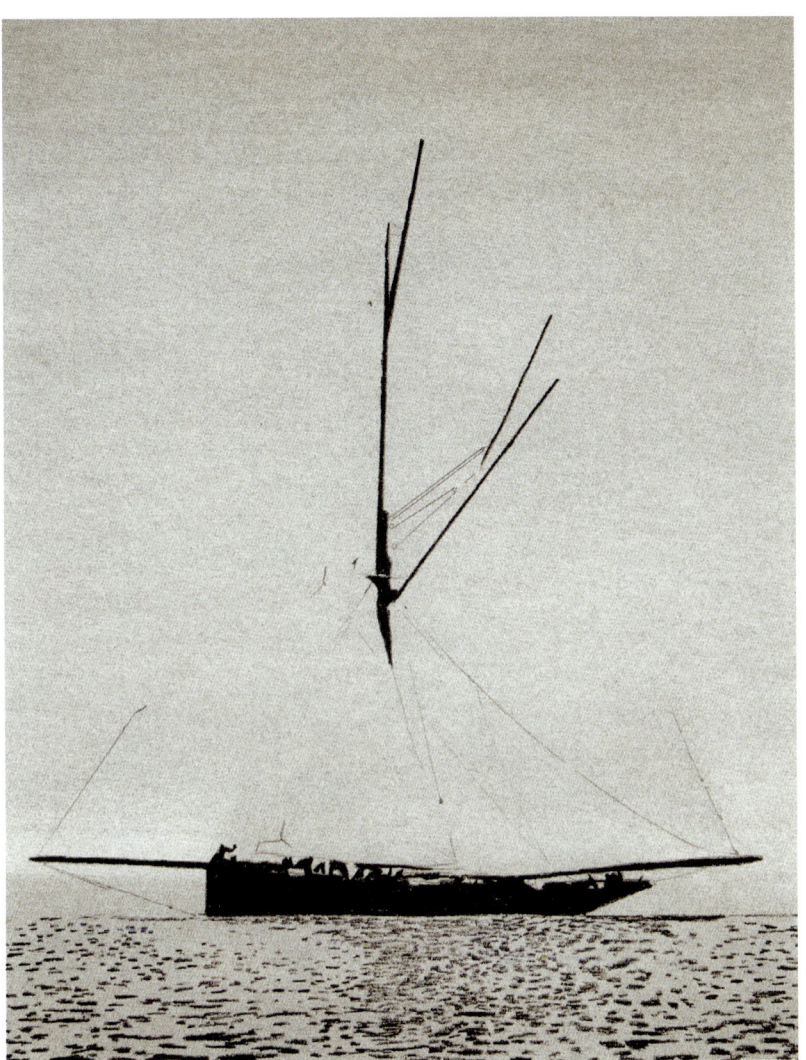

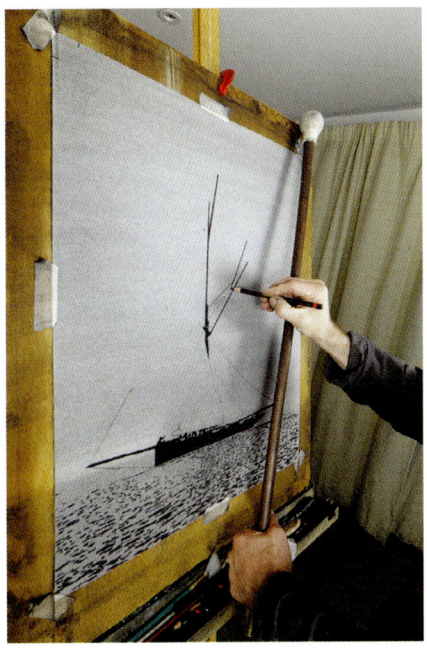

Tip

I'm using a homemade mahlstick, made from an old walking stick. I've padded out the end so it is wide enough to rest against the board without the walking stick touching the drawing. By holding it steady, my drawing hand can rest on it for support, allowing for more controlled drawing and preventing smudges.

STAGE 2

You now need to add a light grey background to your drawing. To do this, lay your drawing flat and cover the whole image in charcoal powder before working it into the grain of the drawing paper with a soft cloth (see page 262). Your aim is to create a nice and even tone. However, the horizon line should be ever so slightly lighter to create the impression of a slight sea mist – use a clean portion of the cloth to wipe away a little charcoal in this area, but only where you know the sails of the ship will not obscure the horizon.

Using a sharpened compressed charcoal pencil, carefully shade in the silhouette of the hull and the mast and spars. Keep sharpening the pencil as often as necessary to maintain nice sharp lines on the mast and spars. During this step, you will need to be careful to avoid accidentally smudging the grey background, so I suggest using something to lean on. The ideal tool for this is a mahlstick (see page 255).

Now start shading in the ripples on the water as solid shapes – don't attempt to draw them as three-dimensional forms yet, just as dark shapes.

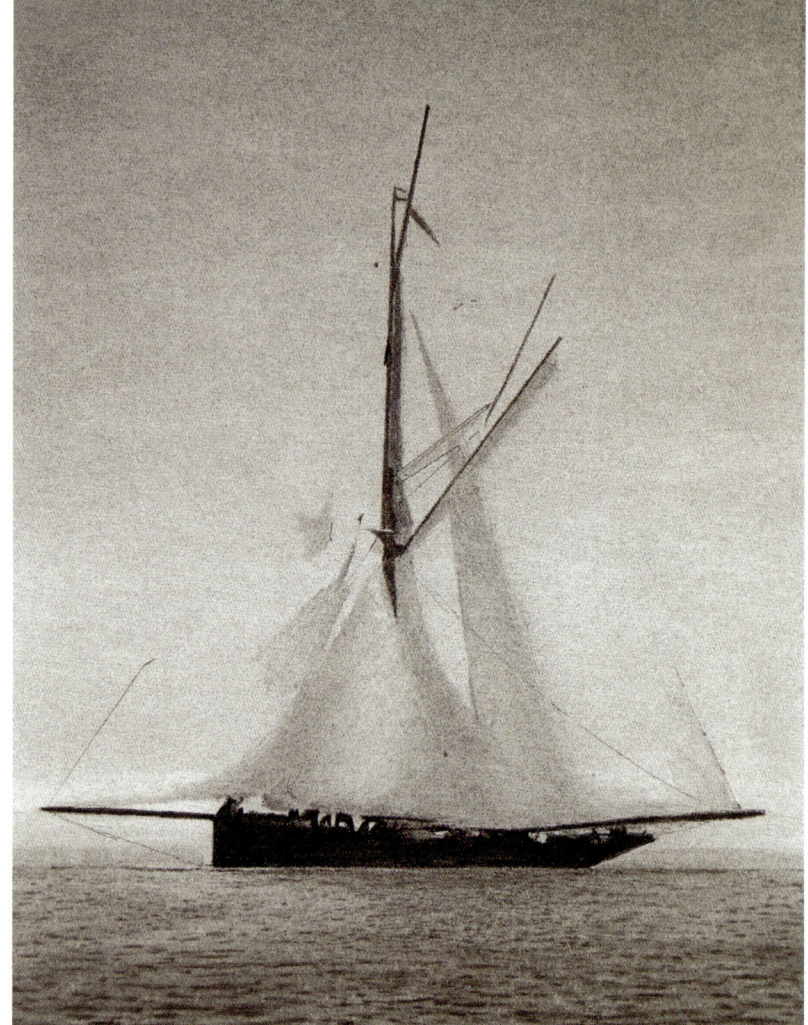

BELOW *When blending the waves, ensure that you move the paper stump horizontally, going in the same direction as the waves.*

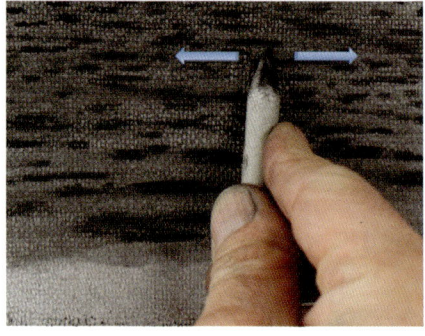

STAGE 3

The waves drawn in as dark shapes in the previous stage have hard edges that now need softening so they appear more watery against the lighter background. Rub the blender vigorously from side to side, and try to keep your movements parallel to the horizon to accentuate the linear pattern of the waves.

Notice that when you use the blender, it will pick up some of the compressed charcoal and carry it across the paper, so the areas you've drawn become a bit lighter and the light grey background becomes a bit darker. This is exactly what you want. You can see now why it was important to use a good-quality compressed charcoal pencil that adheres well to the paper.

Now look carefully at the sails and determine where you need to add tonal value. Choose a long piece of natural charcoal and prepare the drawing end by flattening it against a piece of scrap paper or a sanding block. Hold it right at the end to minimize the amount of pressure you apply and very gently start adding value, being careful not add too much too soon. As you do this, you will probably have to move to different positions around your artwork to draw from the right angle. It is not absolutely necessary, but if it helps to use the mahlstick, you can do so.

Using a blending stump, gently blend in the charcoal you've added to remove the drawing marks and work the charcoal into the grain of the paper. Ideally, you should use a different blending stump from the one you used to blend the darker compressed charcoal or you should clean your blending stump before using it.

STAGE 4

You are now at the exciting part where you use subtractive drawing and wiping to reveal the white of the sails. For this stage, you will need erasers and a clean soft cloth. If you are working upright, lay the work flat again and clear some space around the drawing. You will need a piece of batten or other long thin strip of wood or metal to act as a ruler to get your lines straight, and you will also need a way of keeping your ruler off the drawing paper. My preferred method is to use three pieces of batten (see inset, below). The arrangement will allow you to keep the ruler about 1in (25mm) off the paper. Select an eraser that you can run along your ruler to produce a neat line. If you have a stick eraser, it would be ideal, but a standard pencil eraser at the end of a graphite pencil works well too.

Align the straight edge carefully with the marks on your drawing, making sure you allow for the width of the eraser. Lean forward to ensure that your eyes are directly above the line you are drawing and erase along the line, being careful to keep the eraser straight all the way along. You can now use other erasers and the cloth to gently reveal the white paper in the areas where the light is falling directly on the sails. Try to avoid using erasers with square edges – if necessary, rub the eraser edge on a piece of coarse-textured cloth to soften the edges, because this will help you to make a smooth transition between different areas of tonal value.

The final step is to lightly erase along the top of some of the waves to enhance the illusion of three dimensions, and your drawing is complete.

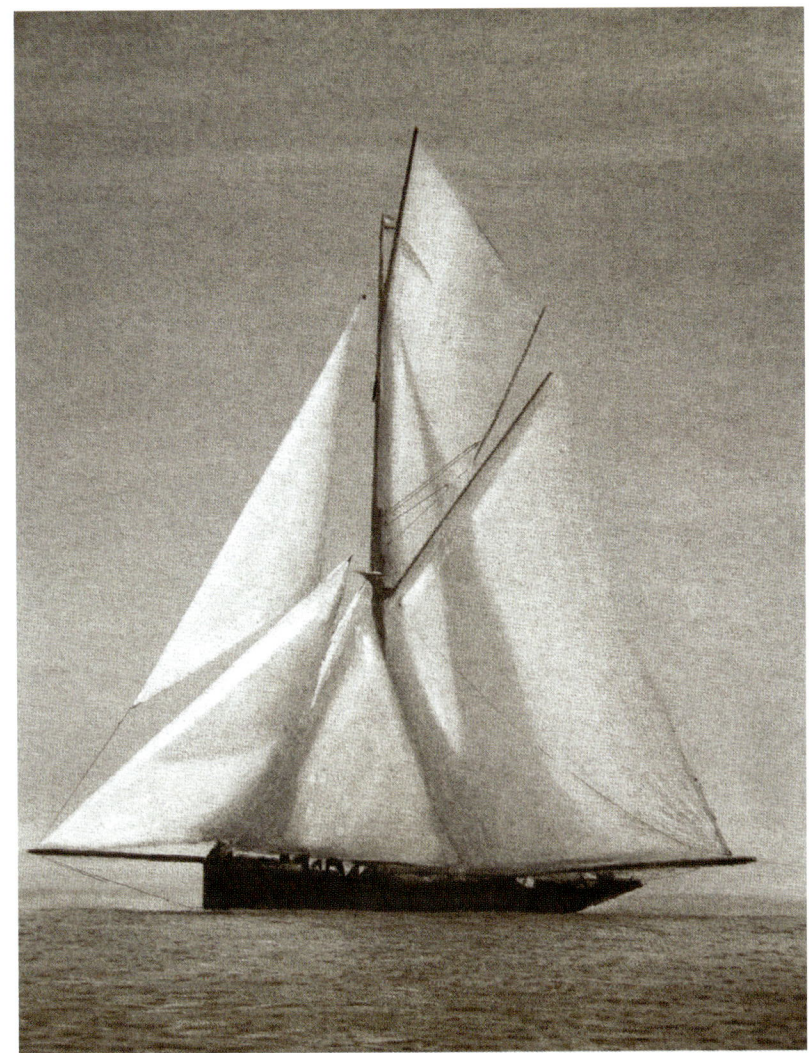

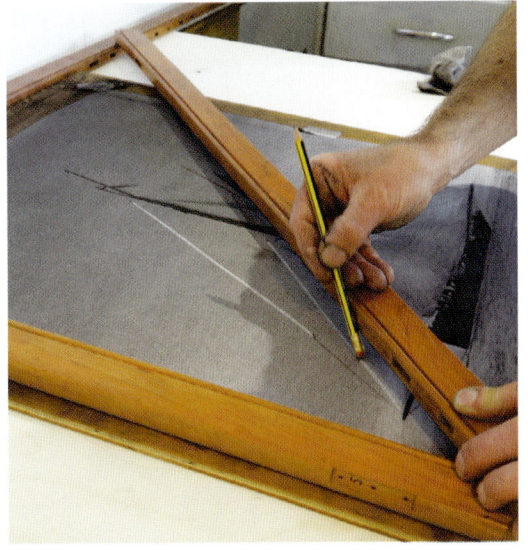

LEFT *Two pieces of batten placed along the edges of the work support the third batten (being used as a ruler) above the drawing to prevent smudging it.*

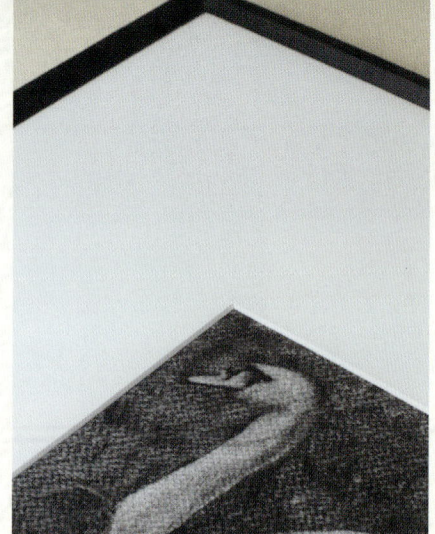

ABOVE *A mount board sits between the charcoal drawing and a layer of glass held by the frame, thereby protecting the charcoal.*

Spray fixatives

When choosing a fixative, make sure you read the product description carefully. If you want your work to last for many years, you should choose one that is specifically of archival quality and specially designed to preserve the work for a long time.

Preserving Your Work

The uniquely delicate properties of charcoal mean that you need to think carefully about how to preserve your work for the future. The normal practice is first to 'fix' the image using fixative sprays and then to frame the image behind glass. However, if you are not ready to frame your work just yet, you will need to know the best way to store it.

Before applying a fixative, be sure that the work is completely finished (with a signature if you are including one). Then make sure there are no obvious loose particles or flecks of eraser on the paper. Using a light from the side can help you see any problem areas. If necessary, tap the easel or drawing board or use a small brush to very carefully remove any debris.

Modern fixatives are less noxious than they used to be, but I strongly recommend you take measures to avoid inhaling the fumes as you spray. Work outdoors if you can, but if this is not practical, spray it in a well-ventilated space. If you need to protect the floor, make sure you place old newspapers or something similar around the area where you will be spraying.

Now, keeping your drawing taped or clipped to your drawing board to stop the paper flapping around and dislodging loose charcoal particles, move it to your spraying area. Lay it flat, or at a slight angle, but not upright.

RIGHT *Hold the spray can perpendicular to the drawing and let the fixative mist drift onto it from a distance.*

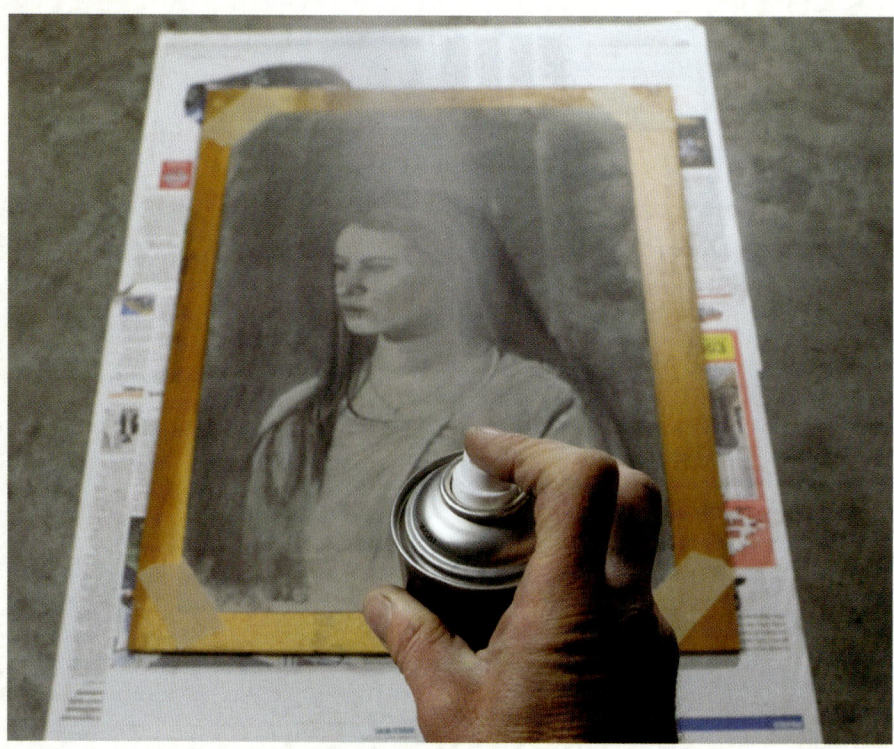

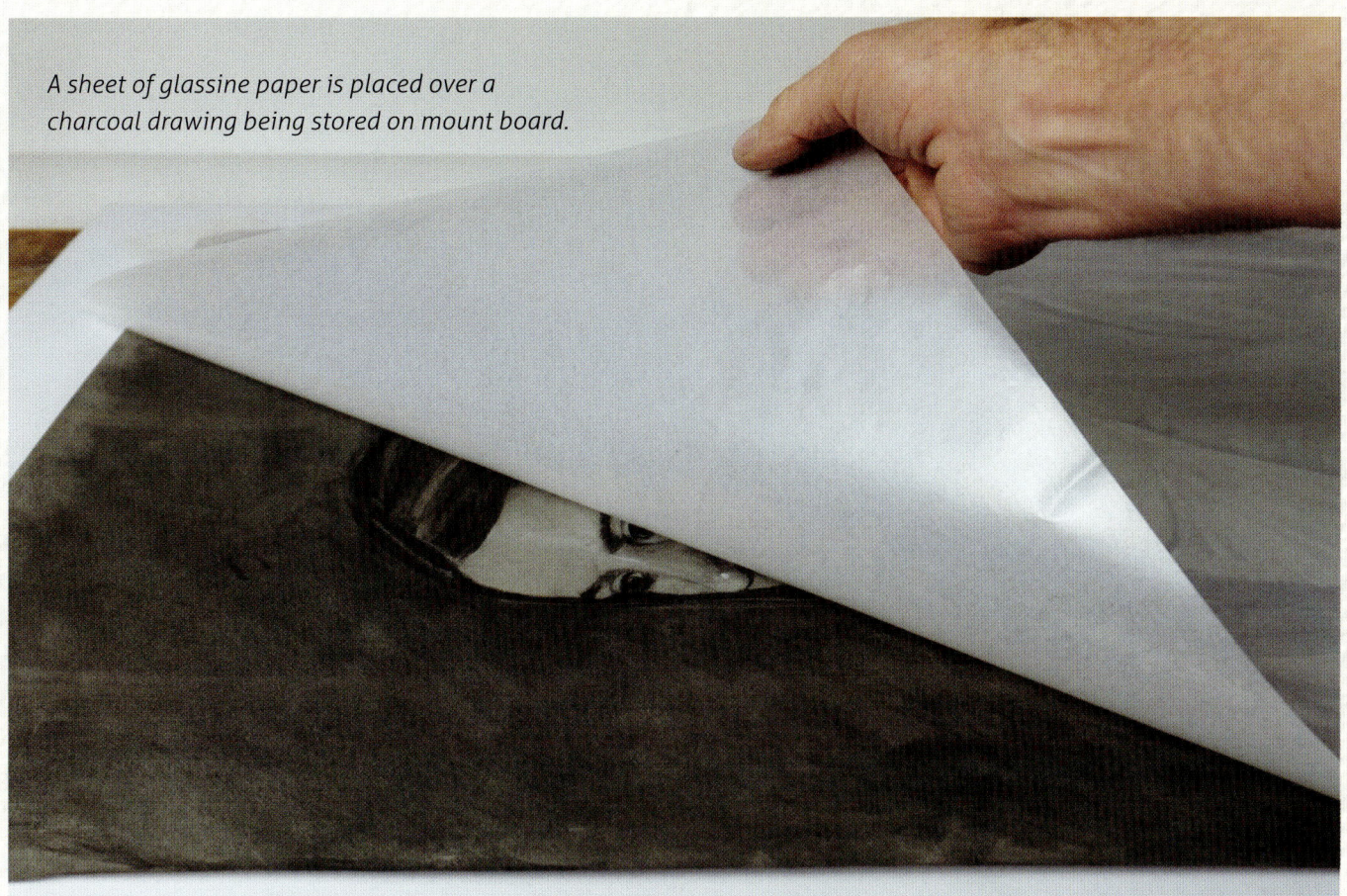

A sheet of glassine paper is placed over a charcoal drawing being stored on mount board.

The golden rule when applying a fixative is that several light layers are always better than one heavy one. The spray will be pressurized when it comes out of the can, so if you hold it too close to the paper, there is a risk that it will blow away some of your charcoal details. Another risk is that you might saturate the drawing paper with too much of the liquid spray, which can reduce definition.

The first stage, therefore, is to create a light mist of the fixative from a distance and allow it to fall gently onto the drawing paper. Start in one corner and work in a criss-cross pattern to ensure the whole area of the paper is covered. Be patient and let it dry for at least 10 minutes before spraying the next layer. In the second pass, do the same but at right angles to the direction you just sprayed.

Once the first couple of layers have dried, you can go a little closer, but you should never hold the can closer than about 12in (30cm) from the paper. Allow the drawing to dry for at least half an hour before proceeding to framing or storing the artwork.

Framing

The best way to preserve your work is to place it behind a sheet of glass. It is important, however, that the charcoal itself does not actually touch the glass, so the conventional method is to place the work behind a piece of mount board with a window cut out of it. Together with the choice of frame, this mount board should be considered an integral part of the design of the finished artwork and can greatly enhance its appearance.

I recommend you use the services of a professional framer. Although more expensive, a professional is appropriately skilled and equipped to do a good job and can provide excellent advice on how to present your work in the best possible way.

Storing your work

If you do not plan to frame your work immediately, you should still apply a fixative, but once it is dry, tape it flat to a piece of mount board or foam board before laying a sheet of glassine paper over the top of it. Glassine paper has an antistatic quality and is very smooth, so there is less risk that areas of the image will be rubbed away. As with every product you use to frame or store your images, it should be of archival quality – in other words, pH neutral and acid free.

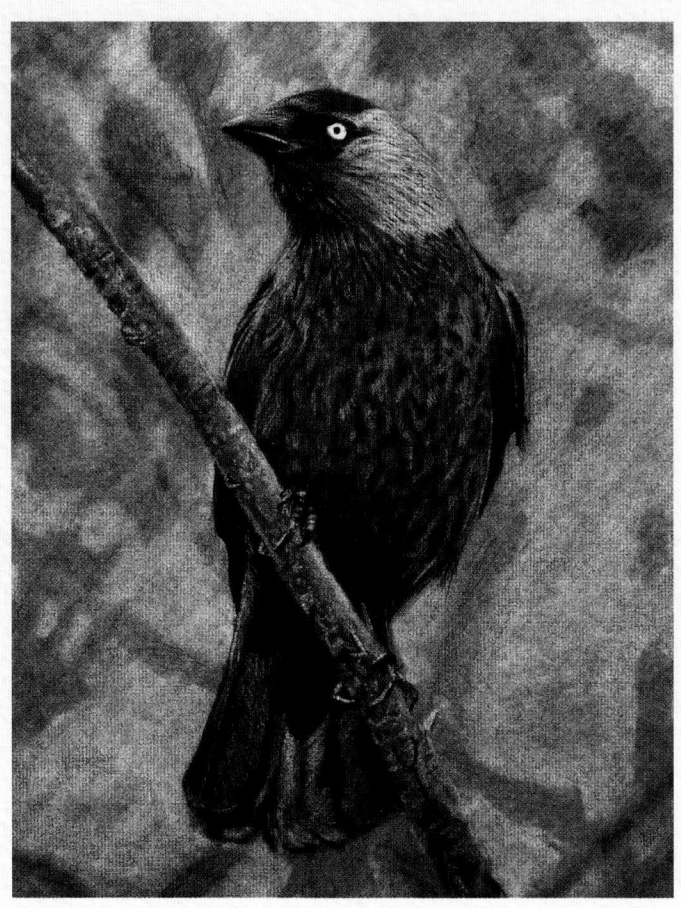

Jackdaw

*Birds are delightful creatures to draw – and their feathery coats
present us with some nice drawing challenges. In this tutorial you will
discover that it is relatively easy to achieve effective results by
using some simple techniques and basic equipment.*

YOU WILL NEED

a good-quality heavyweight cartridge paper • a good-quality compressed charcoal pencil
• some thin to medium-thick natural charcoal sticks • a kneaded eraser • blending stumps
• a soft cloth (optional) • a super-fine pencil eraser or the eraser on a standard graphite pencil

With a relatively small number of techniques you can tackle just about any subject matter. In the Sailing Ship tutorial (see pages 282–7), the technique of combining compressed charcoal with natural charcoal successfully created the effect of ripples on water. In this tutorial, you will be using the same fundamental technique but will take the process a little further to achieve the effect of feathers.

The quality of your compressed charcoal pencil can make a big difference to the results you get, and this is particularly true for this project. Make sure you choose one that will adhere well to paper, because you don't want the marks to be smudged too easily when you start blending.

BELOW *The background in the reference photograph is already blurred, but I blurred it even more in the drawing to focus on the bird. The leaves are suggested but not drawn in as dark and detailed.*

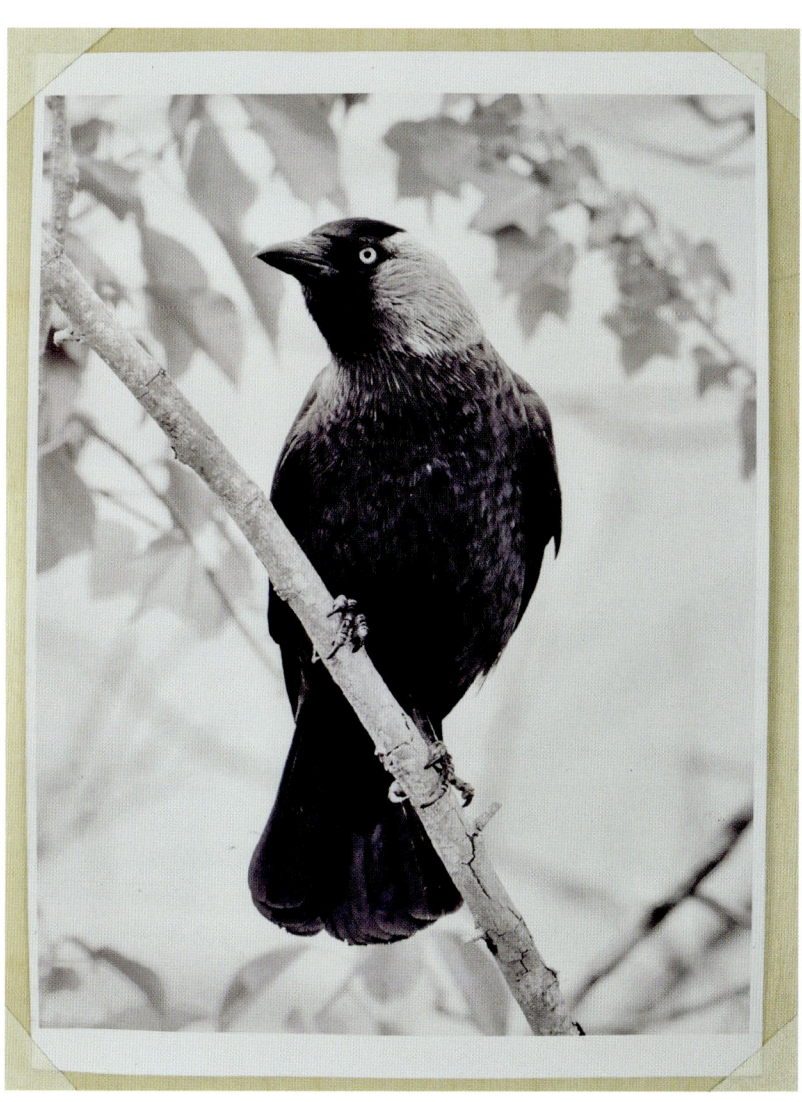

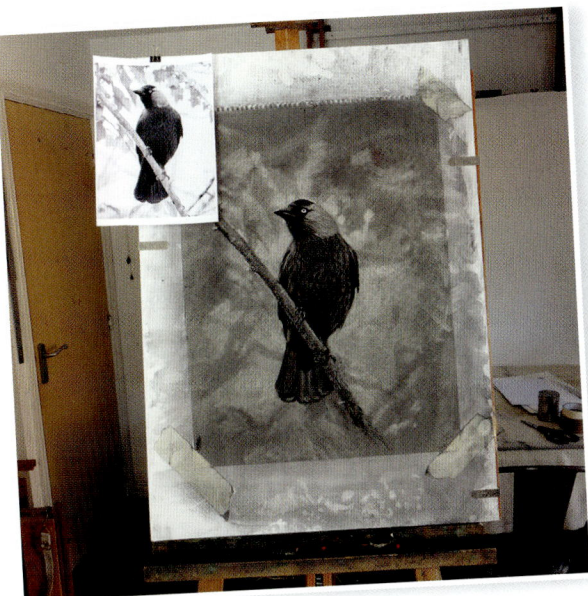

Tip
When drawing from a source material such as a photograph, it helps to clip it to your drawing board for ease of reference when adding the final details.

Choosing your source

I wanted to draw a jackdaw as I felt that its monochrome plumage and grey neck feathers would work well in charcoal. Jackdaws are also one of my favourite breeds of bird and occasionally visit my garden, so I decided to try to capture something I could work with on my camera. Having placed some bird food in a tree opposite a window, I patiently waited and was eventually rewarded with a visit from this fine specimen. If you struggle to produce your own source image, you could look for an image online. Try to find one that shows a good amount of detail in the feathers, so you can practise the techniques set out in this tutorial.

One of the goals of this piece is to create a contrast between the detailed bird and simple background. Take a few moments to compose your artwork. Here, the bird is in the centre with an even amount of space all around it, and the diagonal branch it is clinging to provides a nice dynamic element to the composition.

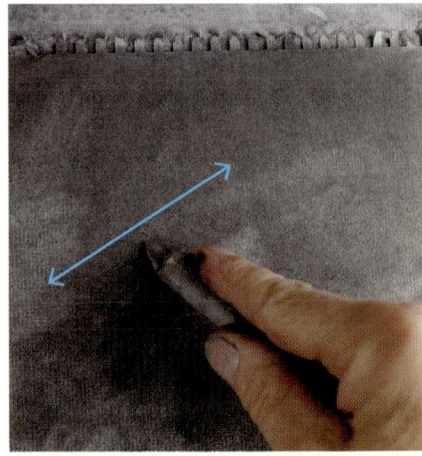

ABOVE *When blurring a background, it helps to use a large blending stump, using long strokes while pressing it hard.*

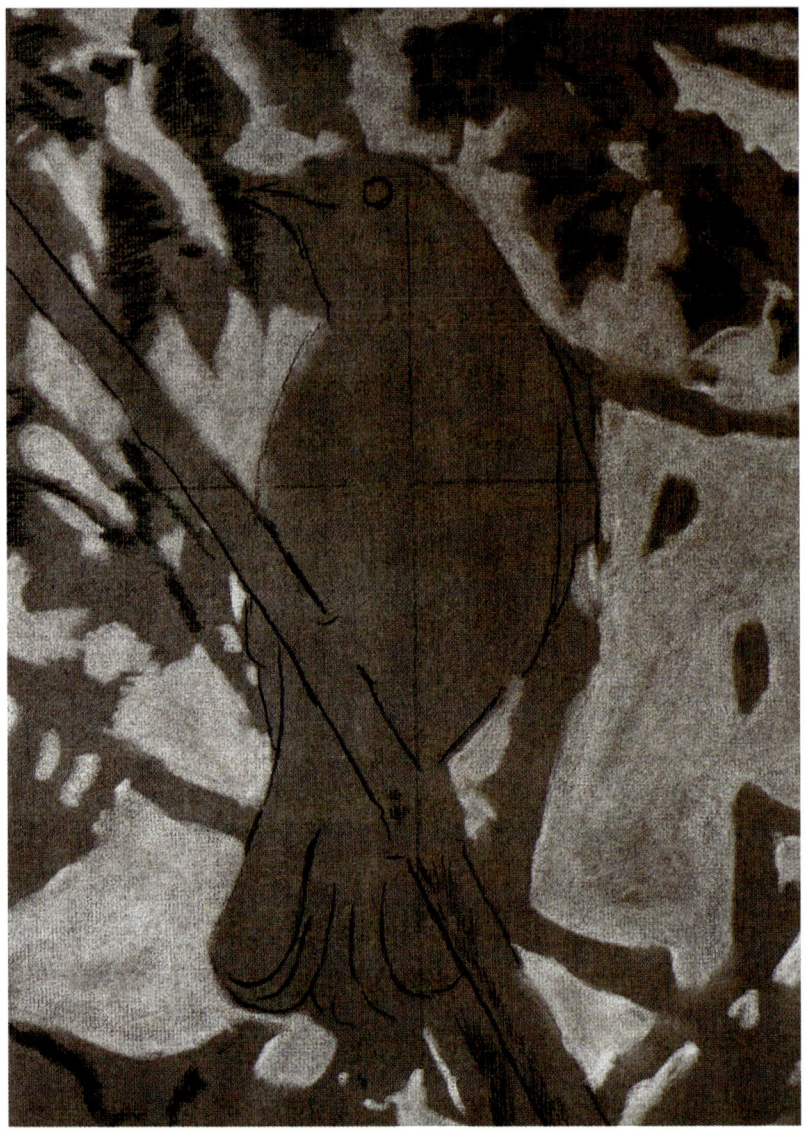

STAGE 1

The first step is to prepare your drawing paper. Using charcoal powder, if you have it or, failing that, a stick of natural charcoal held on its side, cover the whole sheet of paper with charcoal (see page 262). Now you can work it into the paper until you have a reasonably even grey mid-tone all over.

Once your mid-tone layer is ready, use a piece of thin natural charcoal to draw the outline of the bird as well as the leaves and branches in the background. Using an eraser, gently remove the lighter areas of the background. Using an eraser

with rounded edges is the most effective way to create the impression that the background is slightly out of focus and blurred. If necessary, you can further soften the edges and remove any marks with a soft cloth, but don't go too light too soon. Don't cut all the way back to the white of the paper, but do remove enough to break up the large expanse of grey.

The next step is to identify where your background needs to be slightly darker than the mid-tone and add natural charcoal where necessary. Note that you don't need to do anything to the bird at this stage.

STAGE 2

You can now blend in the background with a blending stump so that it further softens the edges, which will increase the illusion of the background being out of focus. Use broad strokes from side to side and have confidence to press quite hard so that the darker areas become lighter and the lighter areas become darker. You can adjust the background again later on after the bird is draw in – at which time you will better see how well the two elements of the drawing work against one another – so there's no need to spend too long on this step.

The next step is to draw in a layer of darks with a sharpened compressed charcoal pencil. As you do this, keep referring back to the source image and take your time to draw as accurately as possible, because once compressed charcoal is applied, it is more difficult to go back.

Drawing on the surface of the paper and carefully leaving areas untouched where you want your lighter values, start shading in the clearly defined darker feathers on the bird. While doing this, try to make your marks in the direction of the feathers, which will help enhance the illusion of reality in the finished drawing. Bear in mind that these areas will go darker when you work the compressed charcoal into the paper during the blending process, so don't go too dark too soon; you can always add more later. Because you are working in the centre of a piece of work you may find it helps to draw accurately if you use a mahlstick (see page 255) or a suitable alternative during this phase.

Once you judge that you've added enough compressed charcoal to the bird, move on to the main branch that the bird is sitting on and continue using the compressed charcoal pencil to add some detail. Again, avoid adding any compressed charcoal to the background to keep the foreground and background quite distinct from one another.

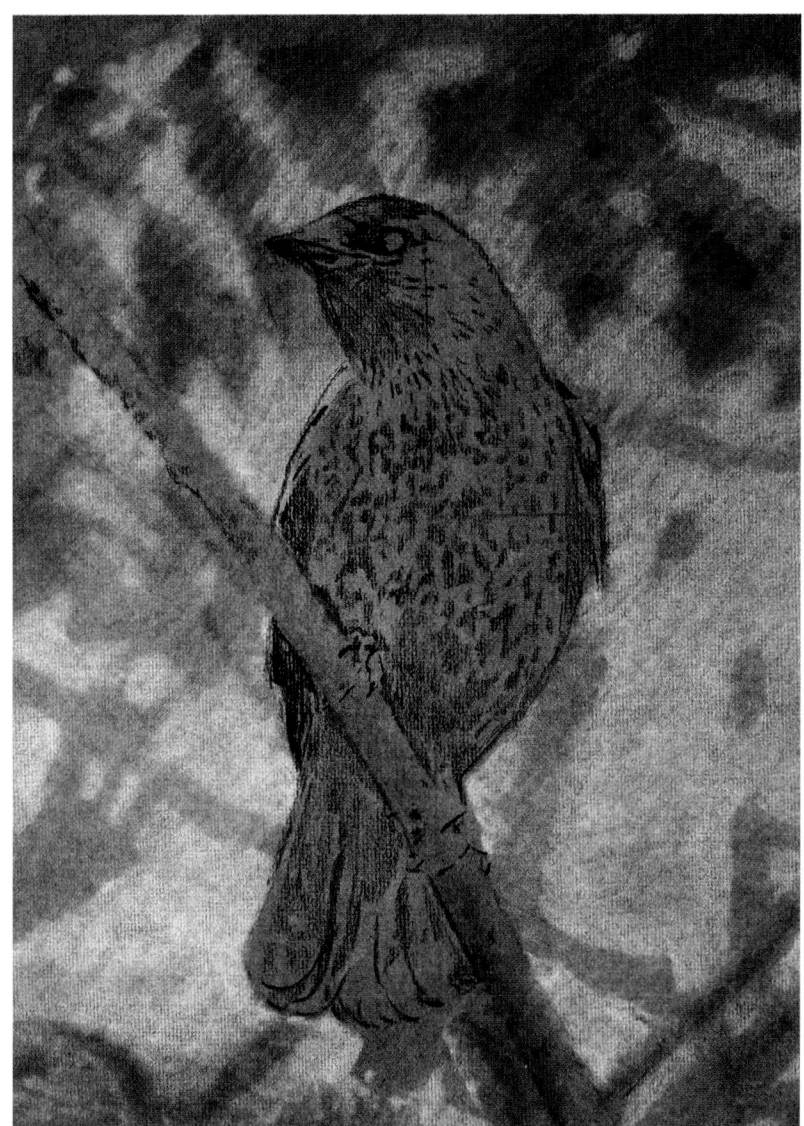

Tip

For images with plenty of fine detail, such as the feathers on this bird, it is better to work on a scale larger than life size, which lessens the limitations of your tools and materials when drawing on a small scale.

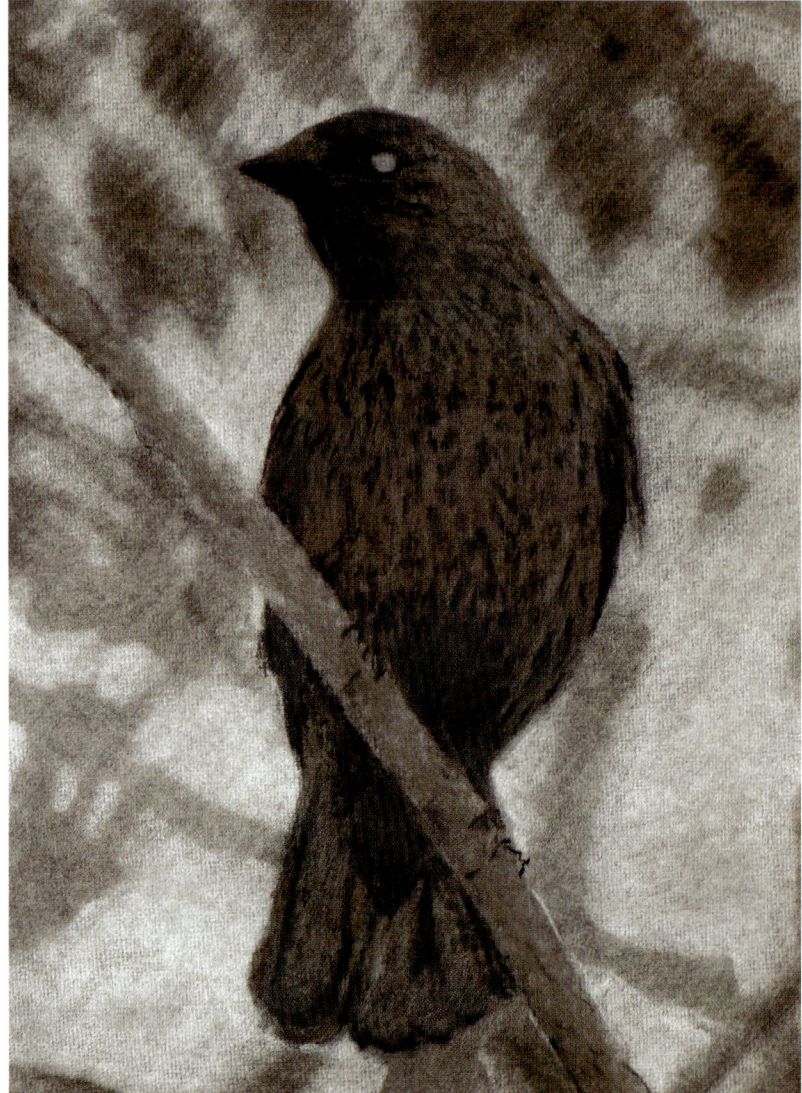

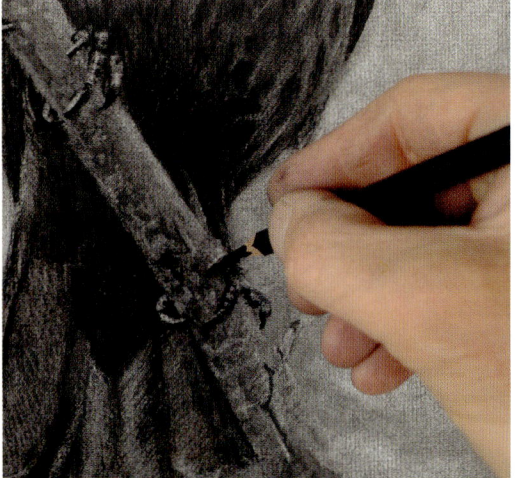

ABOVE *You can define the feet by drawing with a sharpened compressed charcoal pencil, but don't be tempted to draw a black line around every claw or to make them the same value throughout – like every other part of the image, they are a mixture of highlights and shadows.*

STAGE 3

At this point, you can blend in the compressed charcoal marked in the previous stage and add any additional compressed charcoal as required to get your darkest darks to the values you want. Using a small to medium-sized blending stump, work the compressed charcoal into the paper in a motion that contours the form of the bird. Try to be reasonably neat around the edges of the bird – however, you will have the opportunity to tidy these areas up later on.

The next stage is to work subtractively (by removing charcoal) to add detail, but for this to work effectively, you need to add plenty of natural charcoal on the paper to have something to subtract from. Using a reasonably thin piece of natural charcoal, cover the entire area of the bird – with the exception of the eye – with charcoal, working it into the weave of the paper.

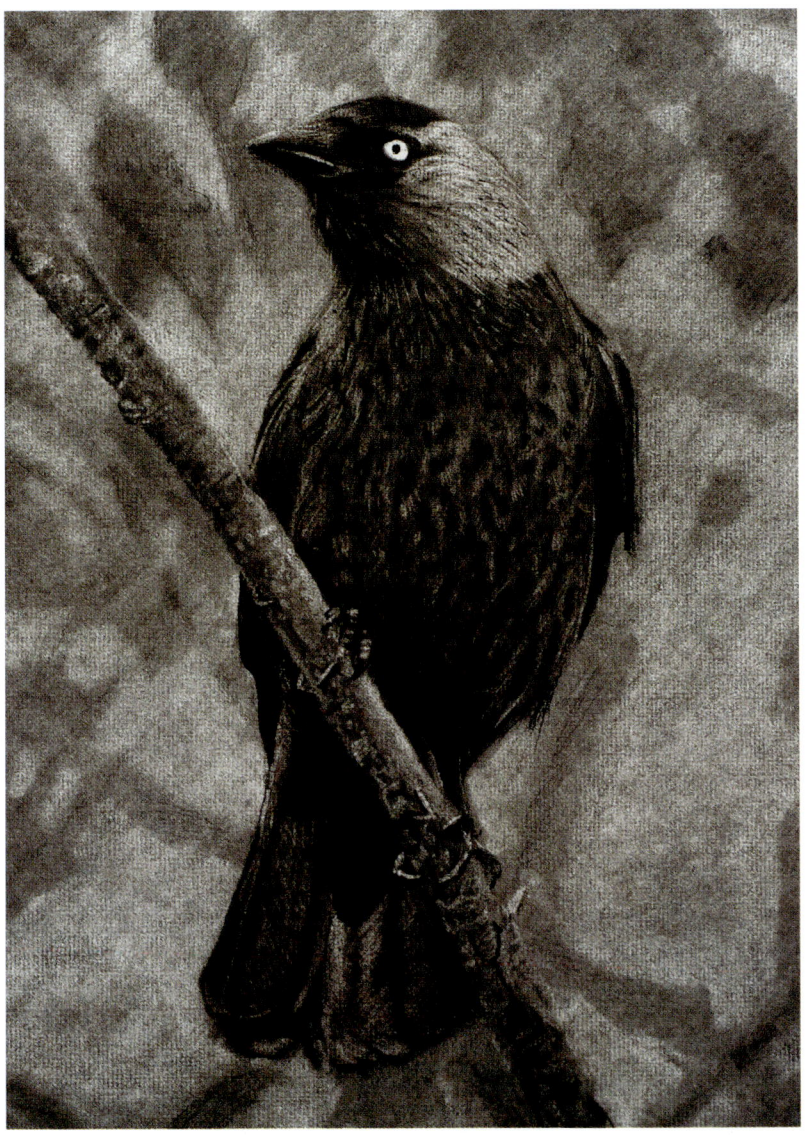

STAGE 4

You are now in a position to add detail with subtractive drawing. For the first part of this stage, it is best to use a kneaded eraser. You should avoid rubbing all the way back to the white of the paper, and kneaded erasers are better at this task because they are softer than other erasers and there is less chance of removing too much medium by accident.

Your aim is to lighten the value slightly in the right places and simulate the texture of feathers. You also want to enhance the impression of a three-dimensional form by adding highlights and shadows. For the lightest highlights, you will find a super-fine pencil eraser is convenient for applying more pressure and replicating the very fine feathers around the back of the head, the beak and the tail feathers, helping to show their transparency. A key point is that you don't need to draw in every detail of every feather. An occasional fine light or dark line here or there will be enough to suggest the illusion of feathers. You should also use a super-fine pencil eraser to work in some detail on the branch and the bird's claws. You can add any darker detail with a finely sharpened pencil.

The final touch is to draw in the eye. Clearly defining an eye always helps when drawing animals. Begin by erasing the white portion of the eye to expose as much of the white of the paper as you can. You will inevitably produce a slightly blurred edge when doing this, so you should then re-emphasize a sharp edge of contrast around the eye using a sharpened compressed charcoal pencil. Finally, add the black pupil.

Tip

For the areas where you need to produce a fine highlight, you will need to form a narrow erasing edge with which to make your marks. The best way to do this is to pinch the end of a kneaded eraser to form a ridge rather than a point. This is because a point will not be strong enough to rub away the medium.

Alternatively, you can shape the eraser at the end of a standard graphite pencil using a sharp knife to form a narrow edge.

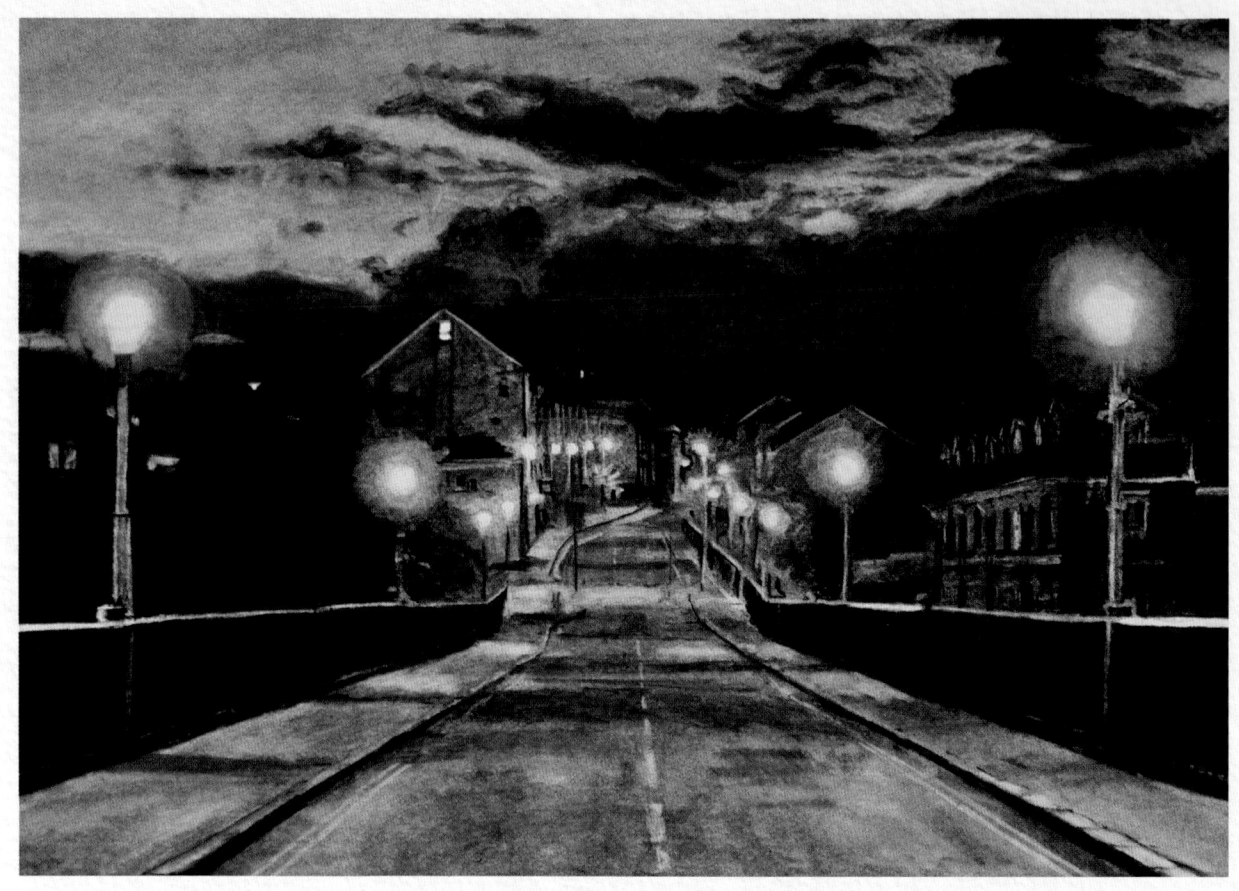

Chiaroscuro Night Scene

This tutorial will require you to use the widest possible values range to produce a night scene with bright highlights and deep shadows.

YOU WILL NEED

a sheet of good-quality heavyweight bright white cartridge paper • some thin to medium-thick natural charcoal sticks • compressed charcoal in block and pencil form • blending stumps • a soft cloth • various erasers, including a super-fine pencil eraser

'Chiaroscuro' is an Italian word that literally means 'light and dark'. Artists use it as a term to describe scenes that have a very strong contrast between light and dark – in particular in scenes where some of the detail is lost into the shadows. As a technique, it came to prominence in the Renaissance period of the 14th–16th centuries, when it was often used in figurative or still-life paintings, but it can be applied to any genre.

For this tutorial, you will be producing a street scene with street lights against a dynamic background of dark clouds. The view is of the Iron Bridge in my home city of Exeter, England. The old lanterns on the bridge have been converted to electricity since it was built in 1834, but otherwise it is a scene that has changed very little in nearly 200 years.

Your aim is to make the lights look like they are shining brightly, so choose a sheet of paper that is a nice bright white. You also want to achieve some deep black darks, so you will be using compressed charcoal to achieve these.

BELOW *To get the main elements in the photograph, such as the bridge, street lights and clouds, onto paper, you can trace them (see page 283) or use observational drawing techniques (see pages 263–5).*

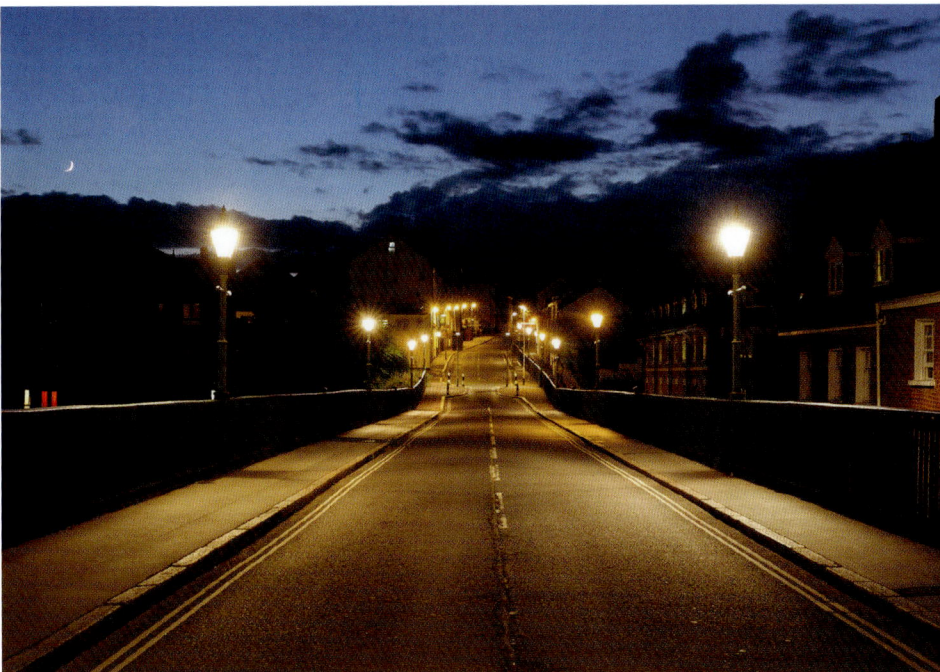

ABOVE *The original photograph before being cropped, converted to monochrome and adjusted to enhance the contrast slightly.*

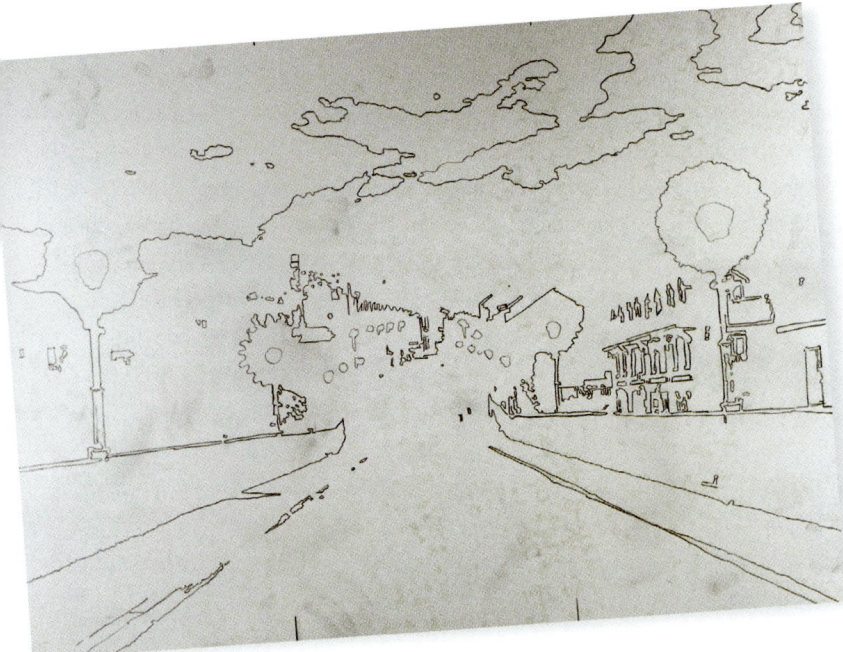

Choosing an image

If you want to work from your own reference material, choose a nice sharp photograph. Night-time photography takes some effort to get good results. Before heading outdoors, check both the weather forecast and phase of the moon, which can have an impact on the photograph. Generally speaking, a current digital camera will produce better results than a smartphone. Both should have a setting for shooting at night that defaults to a slow shutter speed, which means you will have a blurred image if you try to take your shot by hand. For a good crisp image, it is critical that the camera is absolutely still throughout the shot. Ideally, use a camera tripod, or place the camera on something static. Use a timer setting or remote shutter release so that you do not touch the camera at all while the image is being taken.

You should think about the composition (see pages 268–9), especially if you plan to take your own photograph, or how you want to crop the image. I placed the point at which the road disappears into the horizon at the centre of the piece to provide symmetry and balance. Notice that the road conforms to single-point perspective (see page 266) and that the lights get smaller in accordance with diminution.

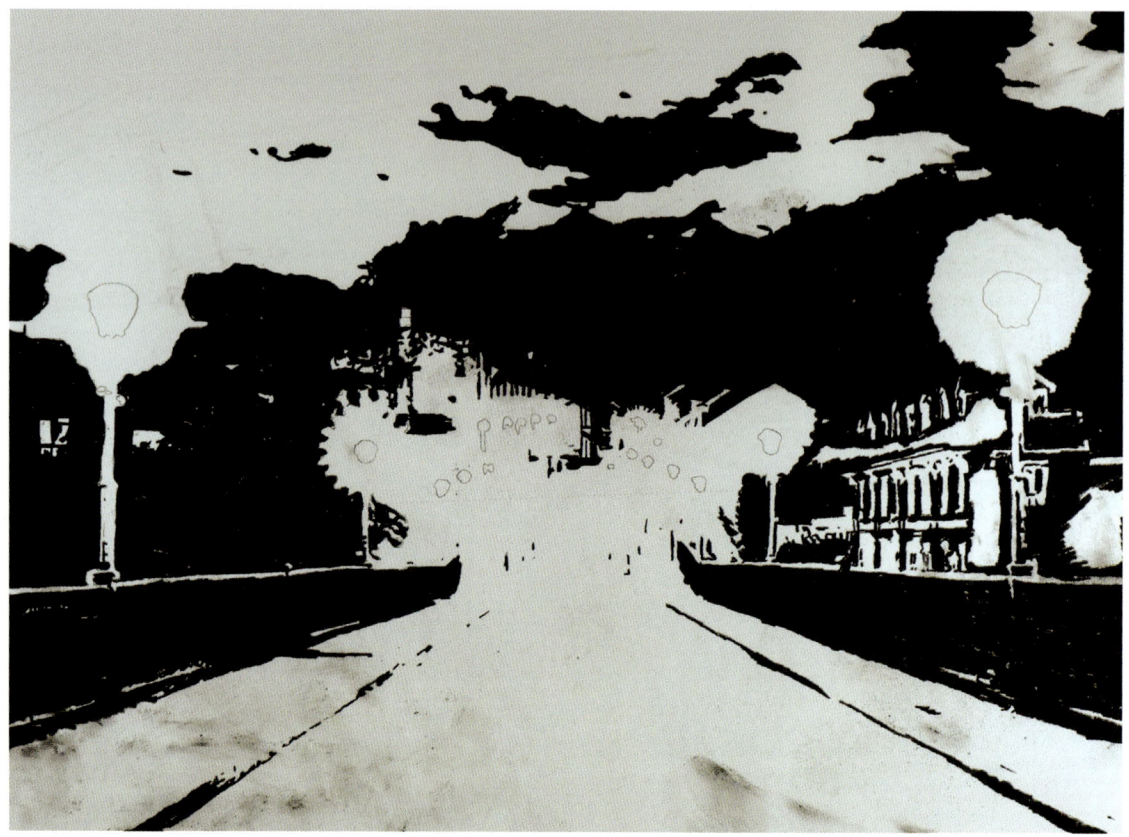

STAGE 1

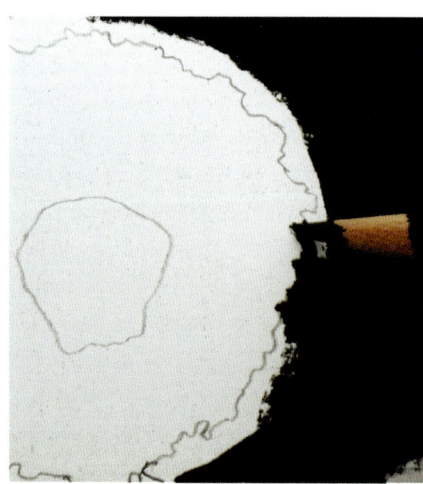

ABOVE *Because compressed charcoal pencils are more expensive than blocks of compressed charcoal, use the pencils to outline the shapes and the blocks to fill in the larger areas.*

To give the impression that the street lights are shining, you should avoid getting any charcoal into the areas of your lightest lights, so use a graphite pencil to mark the areas you want to keep free of charcoal. Even with this precaution, charcoal dust will still settle on the surface of these areas as you work. However, you don't need to be overly concerned – as long as you do not rub the particles into the weave of the paper, you can blow them away or erase them at the end of the drawing process.

Again using a graphite pencil, mark off everywhere you want your darkest darks to be. Now fill these areas in with compressed charcoal and then blend it into the paper using your fingers or a blending stump. In this stage, you are applying the principle of blocking in value at the start of a drawing without worrying about trying to get the detailed values correct – these will be adjusted later. Normally, you would only apply compressed charcoal where you want your darkest darks, because it is harder to lighten areas drawn with compressed charcoal than areas drawn with natural charcoal. In this piece, however, you want the dark clouds to be virtually silhouetted against the sky and the outline of the buildings to be virtually outlined against the dark clouds. This will require some subtle adjustments later on, but for now just get the material on the paper.

Notice that I have accidentally smudged some compressed charcoal onto the paper in the foreground while I worked on the upper section (I could have avoided this by using a mahlstick, see page 255). I plan to cover this area with natural charcoal, so I will work over it later on – and using an eraser at this point could make it worse.

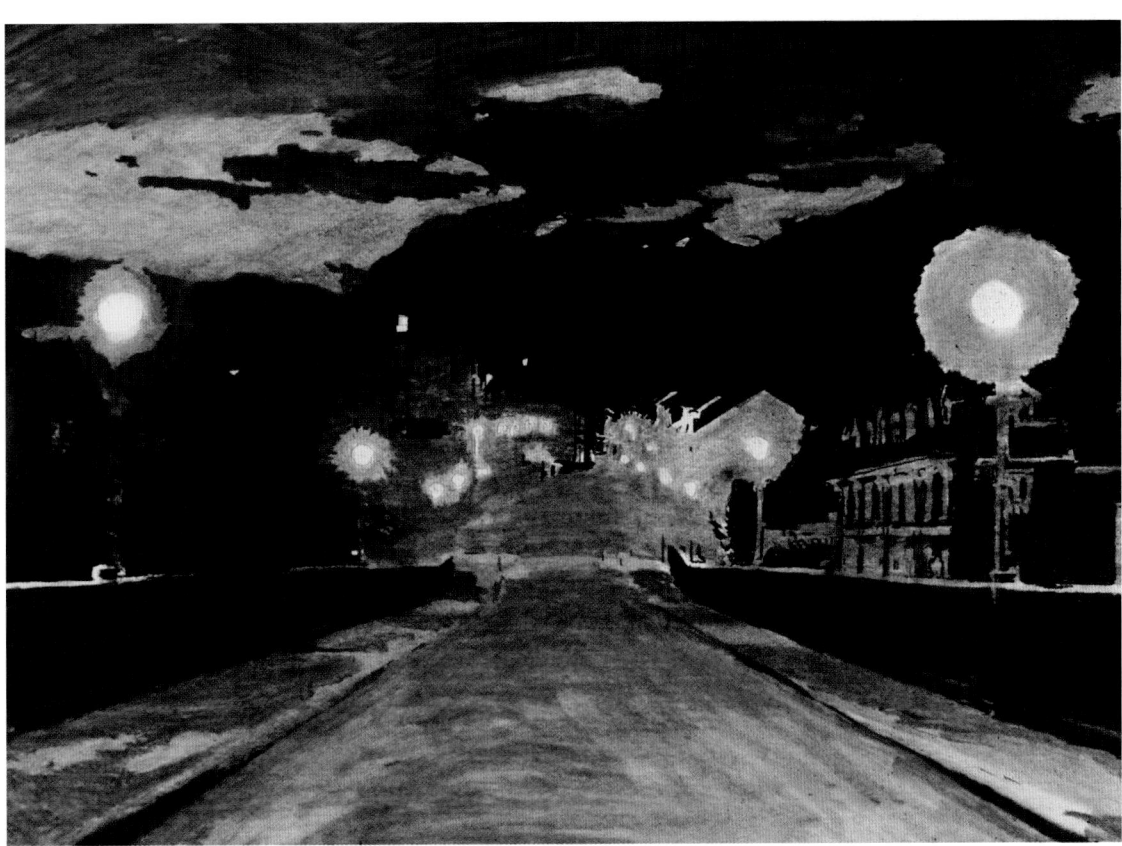

STAGE 2

The aim in this stage is to block in the main areas of value, which means getting plenty of natural charcoal (and only natural charcoal) onto your paper so that you have enough to subtract from later. Starting with the areas around the street lights, draw up to the pencil lines, leaving the lightest lights completely free of charcoal. These areas are now more obvious, so there should be less risk of accidentally drawing over them. Get into the habit of layering on charcoal and then blending it in until you are close to the value where you want it to be. You can adjust it later on by going lighter or darker, so it is not critical to get it absolutely correct at this stage. However, the closer you are, the easier it will be to make more subtle values judgements when you start drawing in the detail.

Make sure you apply plenty of natural charcoal to the area of the sky. It may look light in relation to the darker elements in front of it, but the sky is still dark when compared to your lightest lights.

Remember that the sky is generally lighter closer to the horizon, so don't hold back from applying plenty of medium at the top of the image. You will have lots of loose charcoal sitting on the surface of the paper that you can work in and manipulate in the next stage.

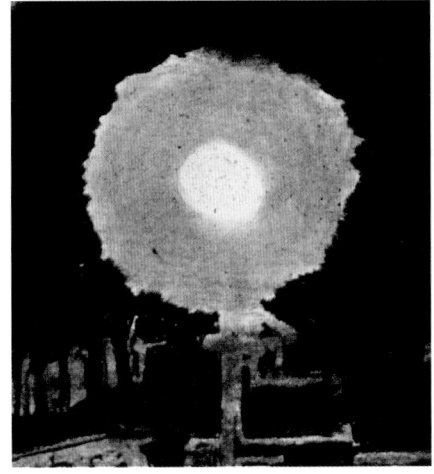

Tip
Remember the principle of simultaneous contrast (see page 258) – you can make lights appear lighter by increasing the relative darkness of the things around them.

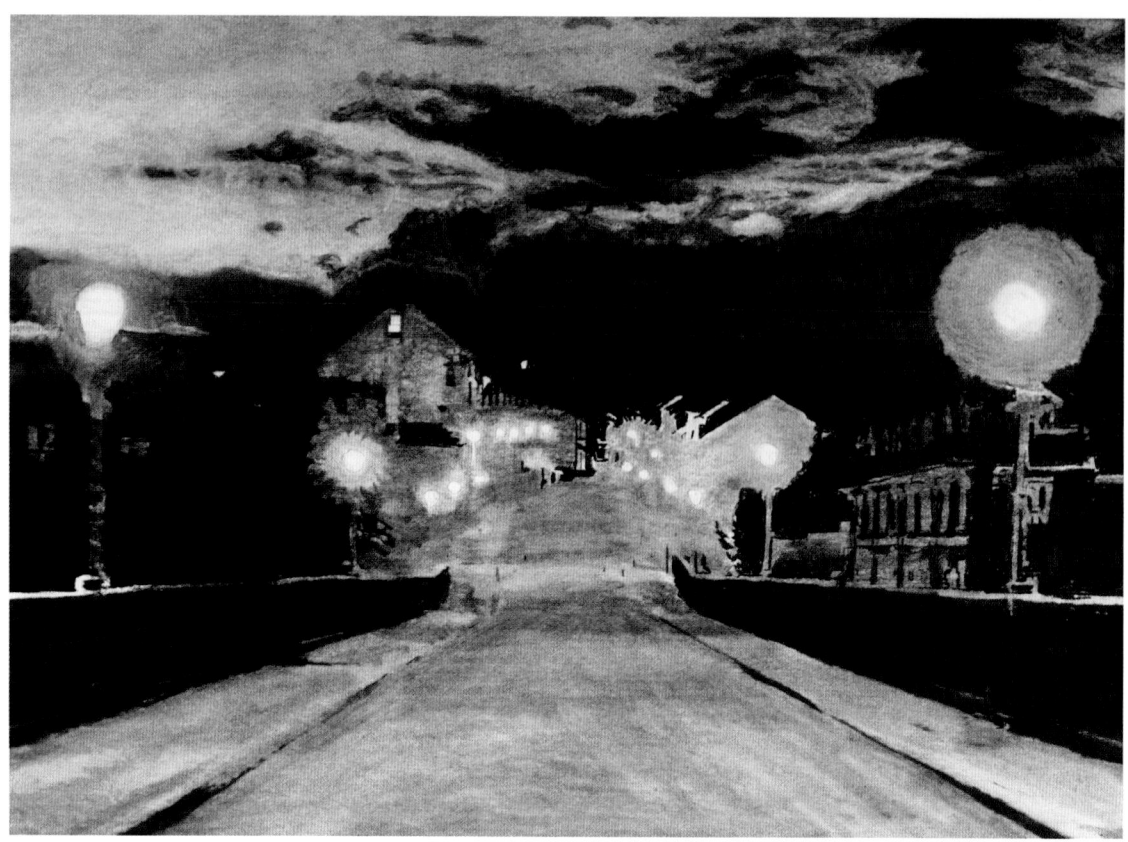

STAGE 3

This stage is fiddly and will take some time to get right, but it is fun and satisfying. It is all about getting the sky to look right. You should always try to work from the back forwards so that you are adding visual layers. At a glance, the clouds just look like a mass of black shapes against the sky, but if you look closely, they are quite transparent and wispy in parts. You will also notice that the buildings on the skyline are just about silhouetted against the mass of dark cloud in the centre of the image.

Start by blending in the natural charcoal you added in the upper part of the sky during the last stage. Blend it into the paper with a soft cloth folded into a pad, using a circular motion and simply working over the top of the compressed charcoal cloud masses, until the lighter areas of the sky are nice and even, and slightly lighter in the lower part.

Use a blending stump to soften the edges of the clouds by using a small circular motion that lifts some of the medium away and deposits it on the surface of the paper. If you need to lighten larger areas, use a soft cloth wrapped around your finger and press hard to wipe the medium away. For the smaller clouds, you can use a blending stump to 'draw' using compressed charcoal lifted away from other parts. You can also use erasers and thin pieces of natural charcoal to lighten or darken your tonal values as necessary. Finish this stage by lightening the sky behind the buildings very slightly with a soft cloth.

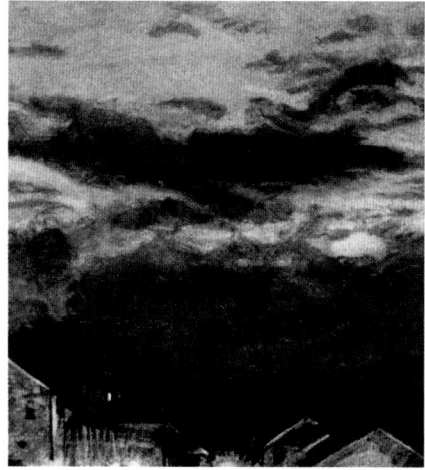

Tip

Bear in mind that clouds conform to both linear and atmospheric perspective (see page 267), so not only do they get smaller towards a vanishing point but they will also be less clearly defined.

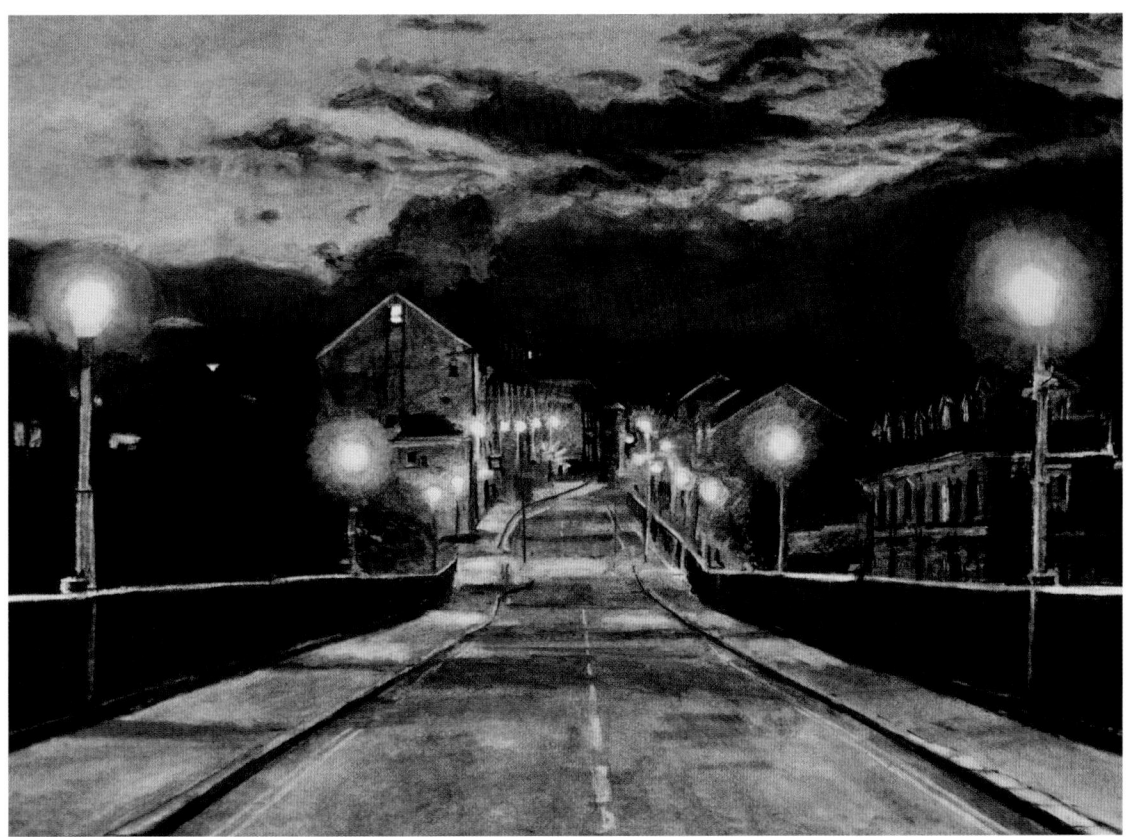

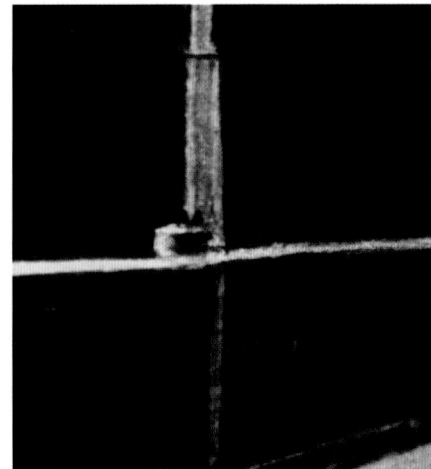

Tip
When drawing highlights, such as on the lightest parts of the railings, you can emphasize the apparent glow by drawing the lighter line a little wider than it actually is.

STAGE 4

The final stage is about adding detail, refining tonal values and sharpening up the drawing. Just as before, start at the back and work forwards. Begin by drawing in the silhouettes of the buildings on the horizon using a compressed charcoal pencil. Now use natural charcoal to draw in detail, such as the posts of the street lights, the shadow areas thrown across the road, the flagstones and the glow around the street lights.

Once you feel you have taken the additive drawing as far as you can, switch to subtractive drawing using erasers. A super-fine pencil eraser will allow you to draw in the lines on the road and the highlights on the rails. You can also use it to very lightly draw vertical lines in the railing on either side of the road. You don't have to draw every single one of them, and they only need to be hinted at – they should provide enough of a visual clue so that people can tell what it is.

The final stage is to erase any medium that is lodged on the lightest lights in the centre of your street lights. A mechanical eraser is useful here, but use whatever you have.

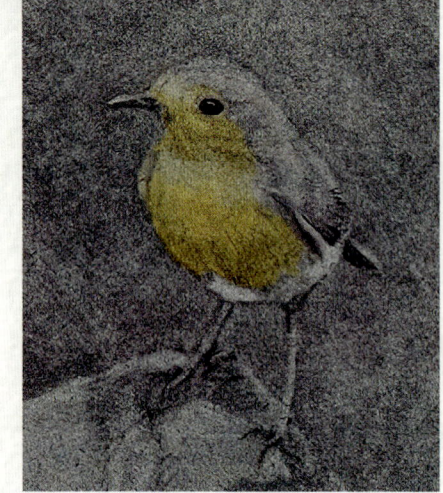

Advanced Techniques

After using charcoal on several drawings, it's time to experiment with some more advanced techniques. Every now and then you might be after a particular effect that is difficult to achieve through conventional charcoal drawing methods, so here are a few ideas that might help.

ABOVE *The colour reveal technique enables orange watercolour to subtly show through the charcoal layer on top in this picture of a robin.*

Masking

This is a technique used to temporarily cover a portion of your drawing surface so that you can avoid getting any charcoal on that part of the image while you work around it. You use masking to produce a sharp-edged transition from one value to another and, once masked, you can either add or subtract charcoal to lighten or darken the surrounding area – or to maintain the white of your paper. You can buy specialist masking tapes and masking fluids or you can simply lay a piece of card or paper over the top of an area and hold it firmly in place while you work.

MASKING TAPE

Tape is useful for masking straight lines such as when you might want to maintain a sharp white border around a drawing. To avoid tearing the paper you will need to use a low-tack tape or to reduce its tackiness by repeatedly pressing the tape down on a hard surface and lifting it off again.

MASKING FLUID

For curved or free-form areas, you can apply masking fluid with a paintbrush. Wait for it to dry completely before adding your charcoal. You will find it difficult to remove without wiping charcoal particles onto the paper as you rub it off. Fixing the charcoal first can help (see pages 268–9), but a better way is to lift the edge of the dried masking fluid with a sharp blade and then pull it off using a pair of tweezers.

Other advanced techniques

You can produce a range of effects, some of which involve combining charcoal with other mediums, while others involve unusual techniques. Most of these have been derived from creative thinking and experimentation, so I encourage you to experiment yourself. Not only is it fun, but you may also come up with something new and exciting.

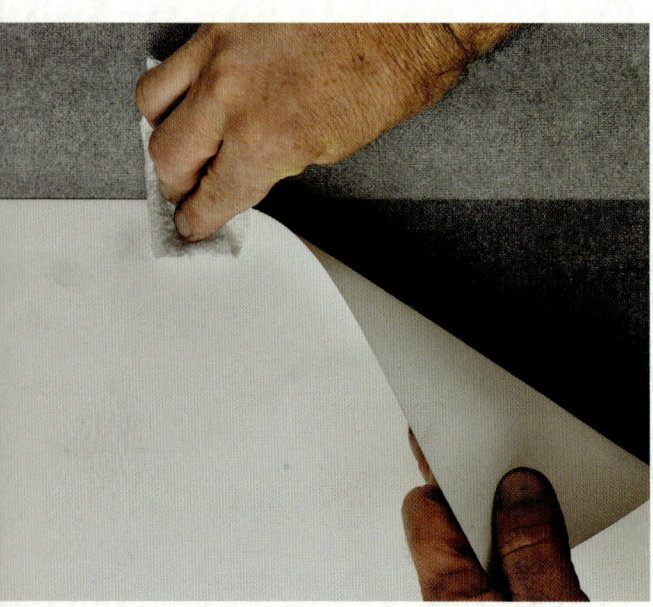

LEFT *Lightening a horizon line by laying a piece of card over a drawing and wiping along the edge with a clean cloth to remove charcoal.*

RIGHT *When using a pair of tweezers to pull off dried masking fluid from a complex shape, such as this star, work carefully around the edges towards the centre.*

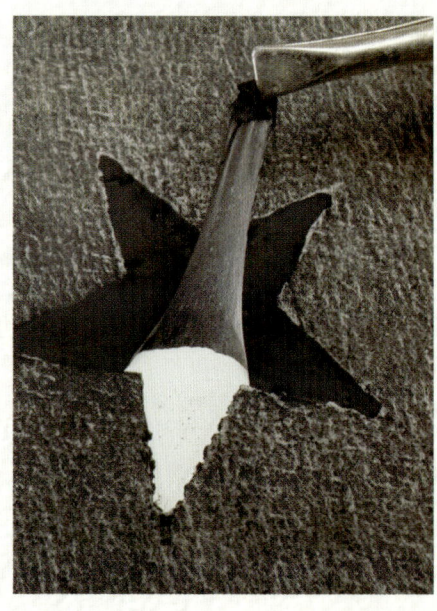

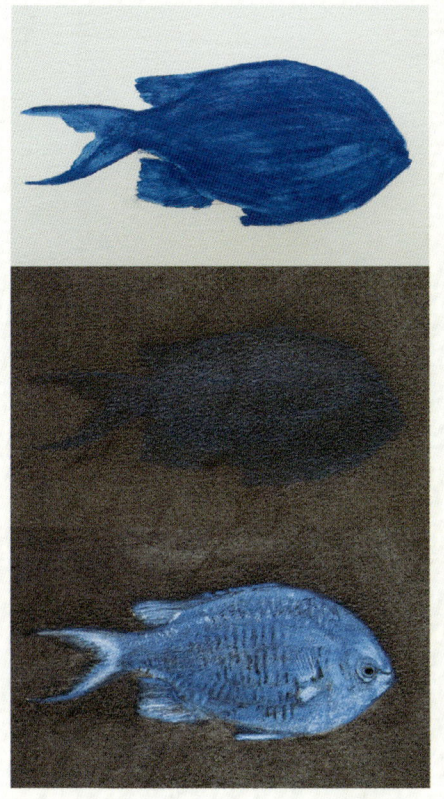

ABOVE *In colour reveal, the original colour (top) will not appear the same once the charcoal is applied (centre) and rubbed away through subtractive drawing (bottom).*

BELOW *These circles were created by a pen using the indentation technique. They appear in reverse in the charcoal on the drawing paper.*

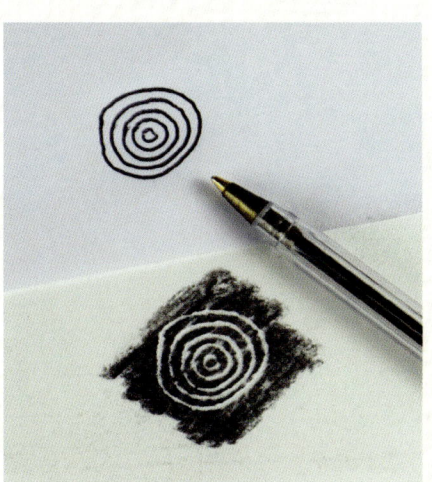

COLOUR REVEAL

You can add some colour to your charcoal drawing by combining it with watercolour paint. In colour reveal, for example, lay down a layer of watercolour paint in an even tone and let it dry completely before laying charcoal over the top of it. Now that the paper is prepared, use subtractive drawing to reveal the colour underneath. The beauty of this method is that the tone of the watercolour is regulated by the value of the charcoal. You can remove just some of the charcoal for a soft, subtle effect as in the robin (opposite page), or by erasing hard you can also remove some of the coloured pigment to allow light to reflect off the white paper, lending a sense of luminosity to the drawing, as in the blue fish (see left).

INDENTATION

Pressing hard into the drawing paper with a sharp object produces very fine grooves that are virtually invisible to the eye. However, when you draw over them with charcoal, they reveal

BELOW *Acetone dripped onto drawing paper covered in charcoal will form circles within the charcoal.*

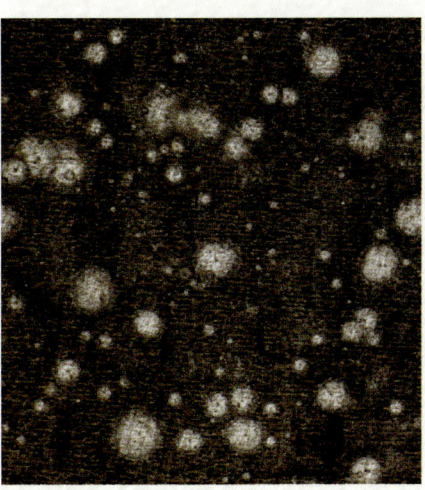

themselves as white lines. An effective method is to lay a piece of thin paper over the top and draw with a ballpoint pen, pressing very hard. Remember, however, that there is no reversing this process if you don't like the results.

ACETONE

When acetone (sold as nail varnish or nail polish remover) is dripped onto charcoal, it leaves small circular marks before evaporating quickly. Consider how you could use this effect in your own charcoal drawings and how you could apply it with different tools, such as flicking it with an old toothbrush.

REVERSE DETAILS

Another way to use masking tape is to create fine details in a drawing. Remove the tackiness completely before laying it gently on top of the area where you want to reveal the surface underneath. Once in place, use a pencil or pen to draw onto the tape, pressing down hard. Lifting the tape away will also lift off the charcoal underneath to reveal the fine detail.

BELOW *Lifting masking tape off the work with a design drawn on top reveals charcoal sticking to the tape and the reverse design left on the work.*

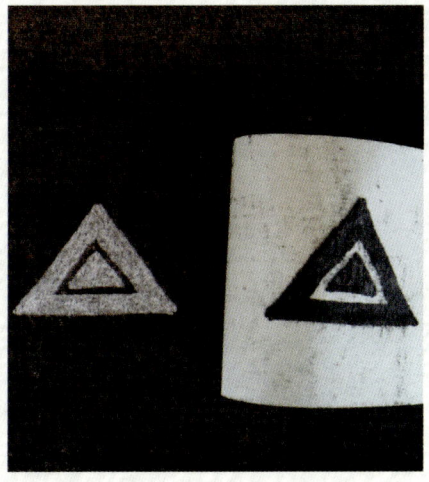

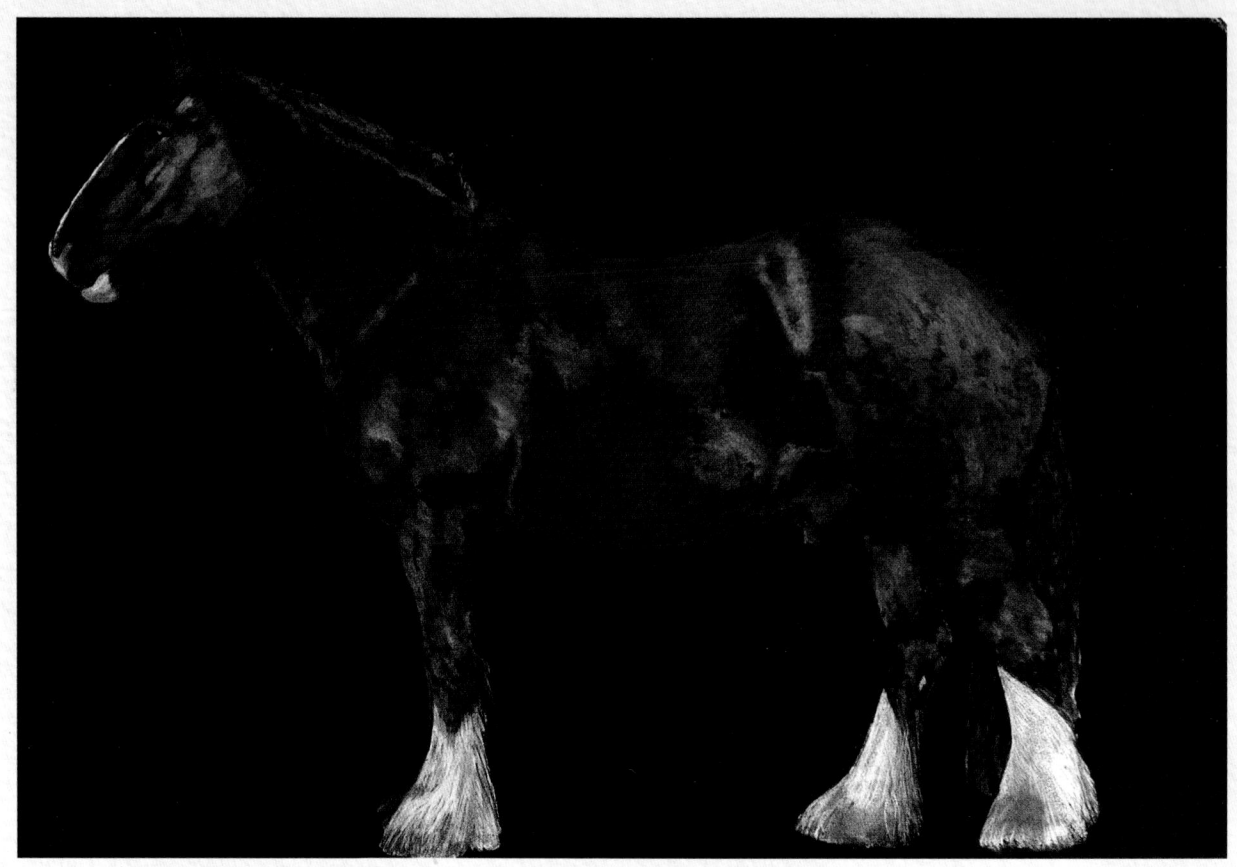

Shire Horse

*In this final tutorial, you will find I have scaled things up
with a suitable subject matter for the ultimate of challenges:
black against black.*

YOU WILL NEED
a large sheet of good-quality heavyweight cartridge paper
• several medium-thick natural charcoal sticks • a couple of compressed charcoal pencils
• a couple of compressed charcoal blocks • blending stumps • a ruler • a soft cloth

Trelawney is a shire horse owned by a school on the edge of Dartmoor National Park near my home in England. He is a massive 17 hands tall (about 5ft 6in/173cm), but he is so well socialized and gentle that he is a favourite with everyone he meets. I loved the sheen of his black coat and thought it would be interesting to place an image of him against a black background so that only the slight variations in value and texture indicate his form. Although it is not a true chiaroscuro charcoal drawing (see page 297), where there is a strong contrast in light and shade, it does borrow from the idea of allowing the edges of a form to merge into the background.

Scaling up with a grid

Trelawney is a very large horse, so I felt he deserved a large piece of paper. The largest standard size available in my local art shop is about 39 x 27in (100 x 70cm), but the principle of scaling up is exactly the same if you want to go even larger. In terms of composition, I placed the horse almost in the centre and left little border around him. This gives the visual suggestion that he is such a large horse he has to fill the whole frame of the image.

The photograph was taken on an overcast day, and I got one of the students to hold him steady while I took it. I removed the background on a computer to better illustrate the process, but this is not necessary and it doesn't matter if your photo has a background. The image was printed out on standard letter size (or A4) paper on my home printer, and then I drew a grid of squares on it using a fine line pen. I drew exactly the same number of squares on my drawing paper in the same format – in this case, ten wide by seven tall, but it could be applied to any shape piece of paper. The grid on the drawing paper was drawn using natural charcoal so that the lines could be erased where necessary as the drawing proceeded.

Use a ruler to measure and divide the lines equally across the photograph, or other reference material, and then create an equal number of squares on your drawing paper.

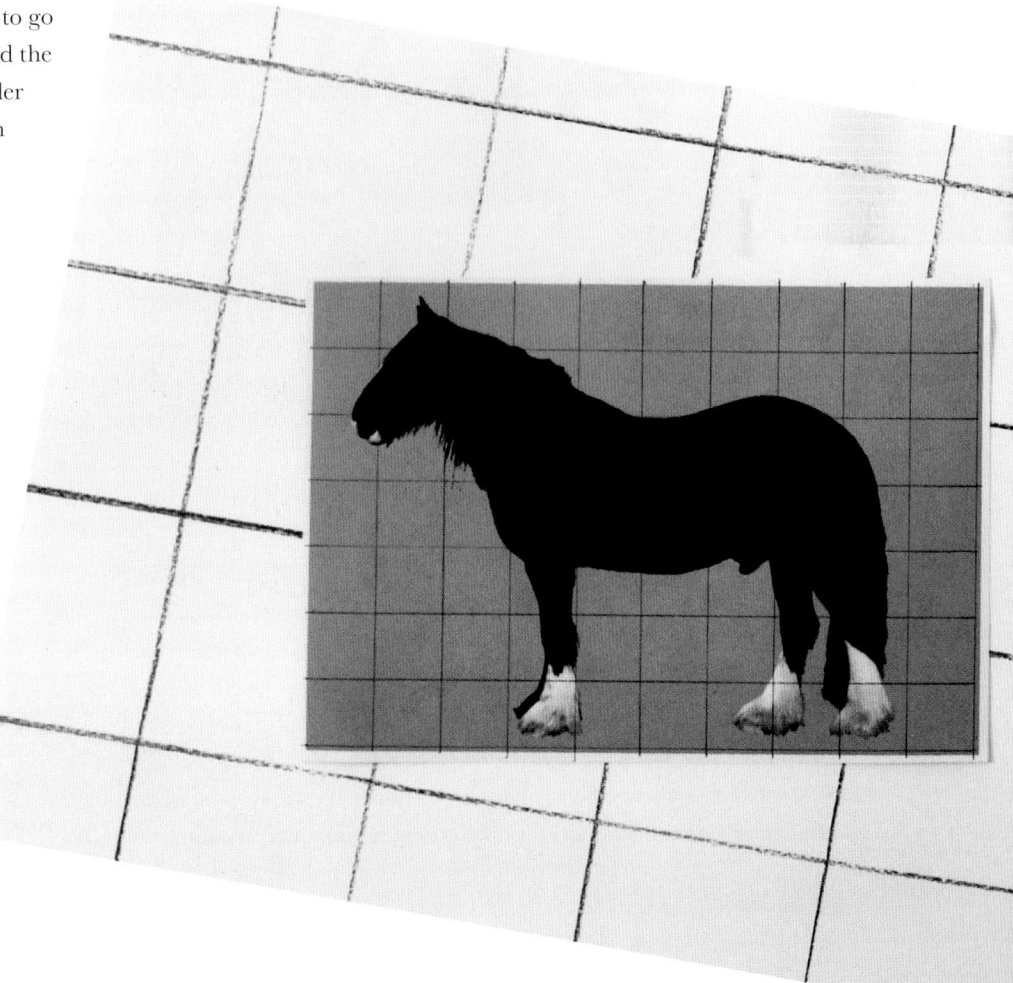

Tip

When you place such a large drawing on your easel, make sure you adjust it to a comfortable working height. You need to be able to reach the top part of the drawing as well as the bottom with the minimum of straining.

STAGE 1

Begin by marking out the outline of the
horse with a narrow piece of charcoal.
At this stage, don't worry about accidentally
smudging and smearing the charcoal lines.
Count along the squares on your paper
until you find the same location on your
reference image. Now look carefully at the
source photo and observe where the outline
intersects each square. Sketch in the lines.
If you don't think it's right, just wipe away
what you've drawn with a soft cloth and
start again.

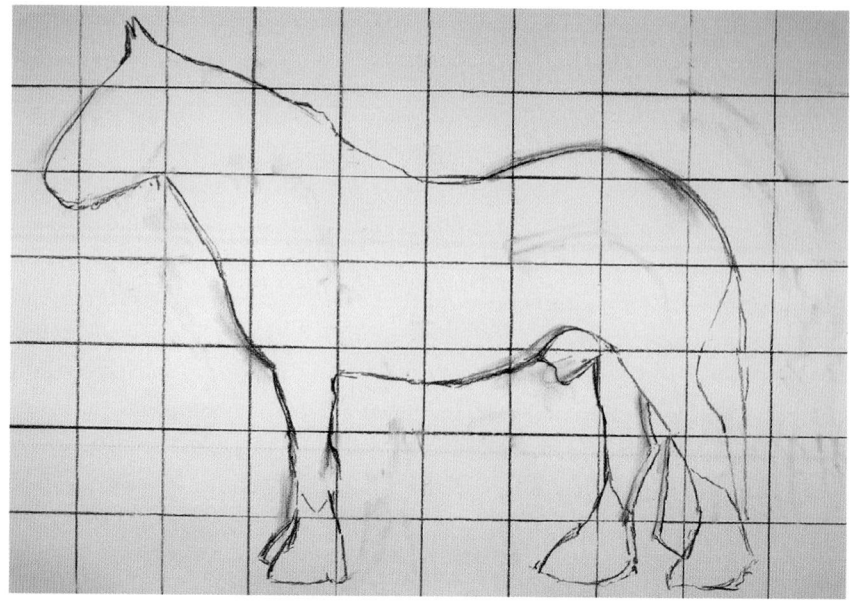

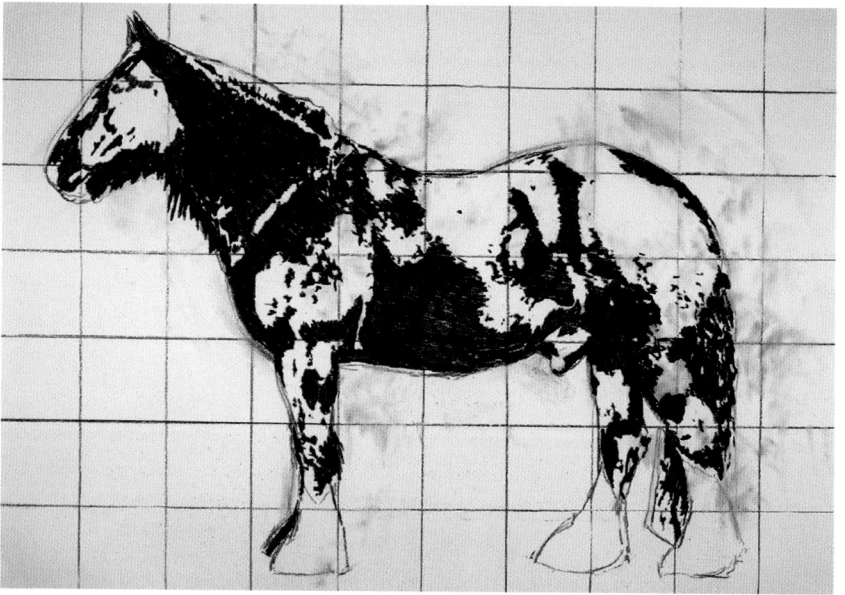

STAGE 2

Because you will be drawing the image in layers, it will look flat initially, but the
form will be revealed as you work through the drawing. Leave the black background
until last so that you don't accidentally smudge and smear it. Use a good-quality dark
compressed charcoal pencil or stick that adheres well to paper to draw in only the
darkest darks in the horse, making sure you refer to the grid to place the marks in
the correct place. You can use a rapid drawing action to get the marks on the paper,
because at the moment you don't need to be precise. Don't worry if the white crevices
of the paper texture show through – you will work the compressed charcoal into the
paper later on. Remember that the human eye can pick up very slight detail, so draw
your lines along the contours of the body. These marks will be almost imperceptible,
but they will help to create the illusion of volume.

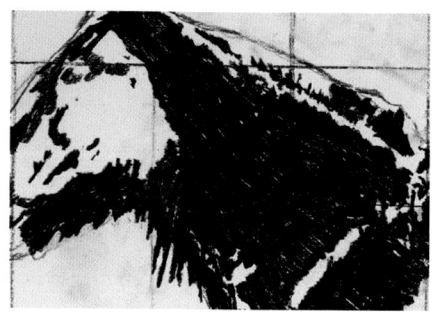

ABOVE *Notice that the drawing is
loose and rapid while aligned with
the form of the body – in this case,
running in the direction of the neck.*

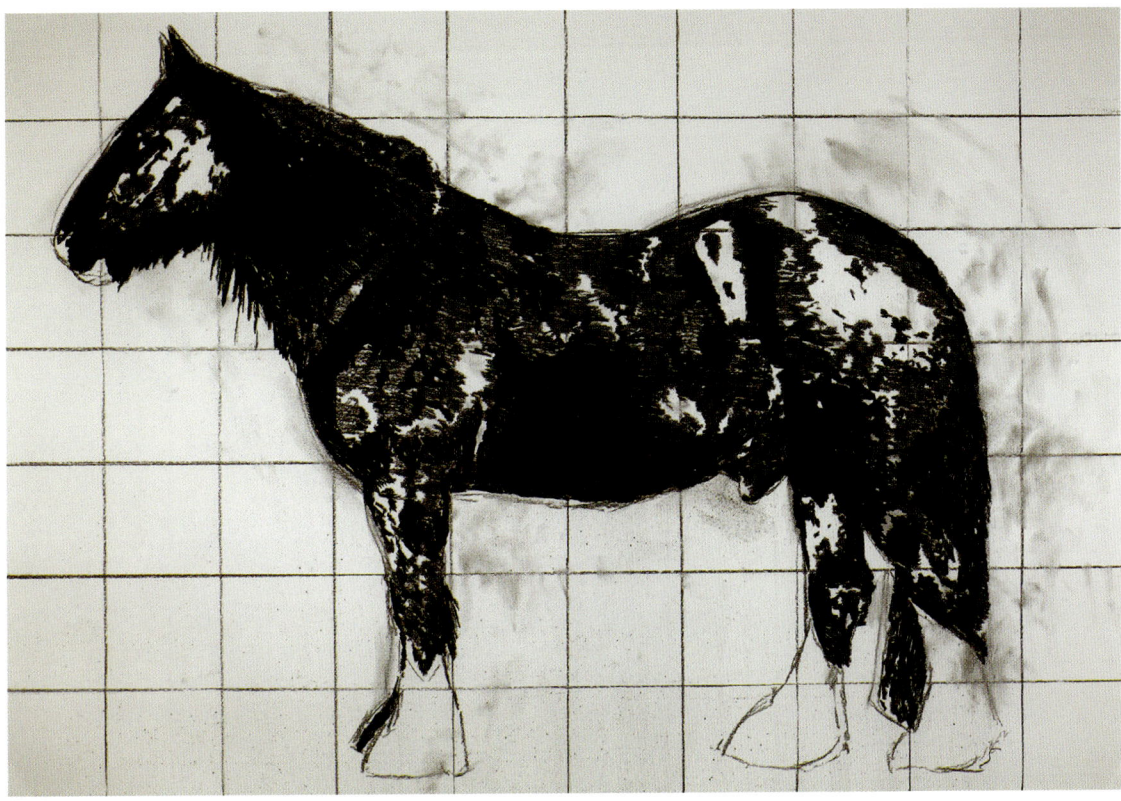

STAGE 3

Now use some natural charcoal to draw in where you judge the next layer of tonal value to be. You can draw right over the top of the compressed charcoal layer, because this will help to work it into the paper and add an additional layer of charcoal particle that will help to produce nice dark tones. Again, remember to work along the contours of the form of the horse, such as around the hindquarters and belly, to help give it a three-dimensional shape.

Use a medium thickness of natural charcoal for this stage, because you want something thick enough to take some firm pressure as you work the charcoal into the paper yet something narrow enough to attain a reasonable amount of detail. Try to really work the charcoal into the weave of the paper as you draw so that it doesn't get wiped away when you start working over this layer with blending stumps in the next stage.

Tip

You don't need to fill in the areas with a solid mass of medium. It is fine for the lighter lines to be visible within your shading lines. These will add subtle variations in tonal value.

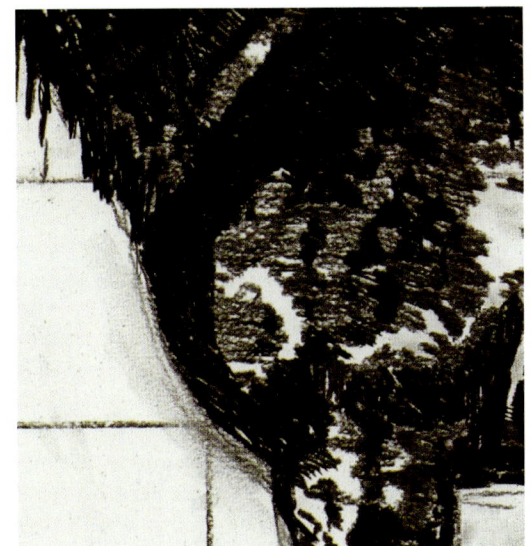

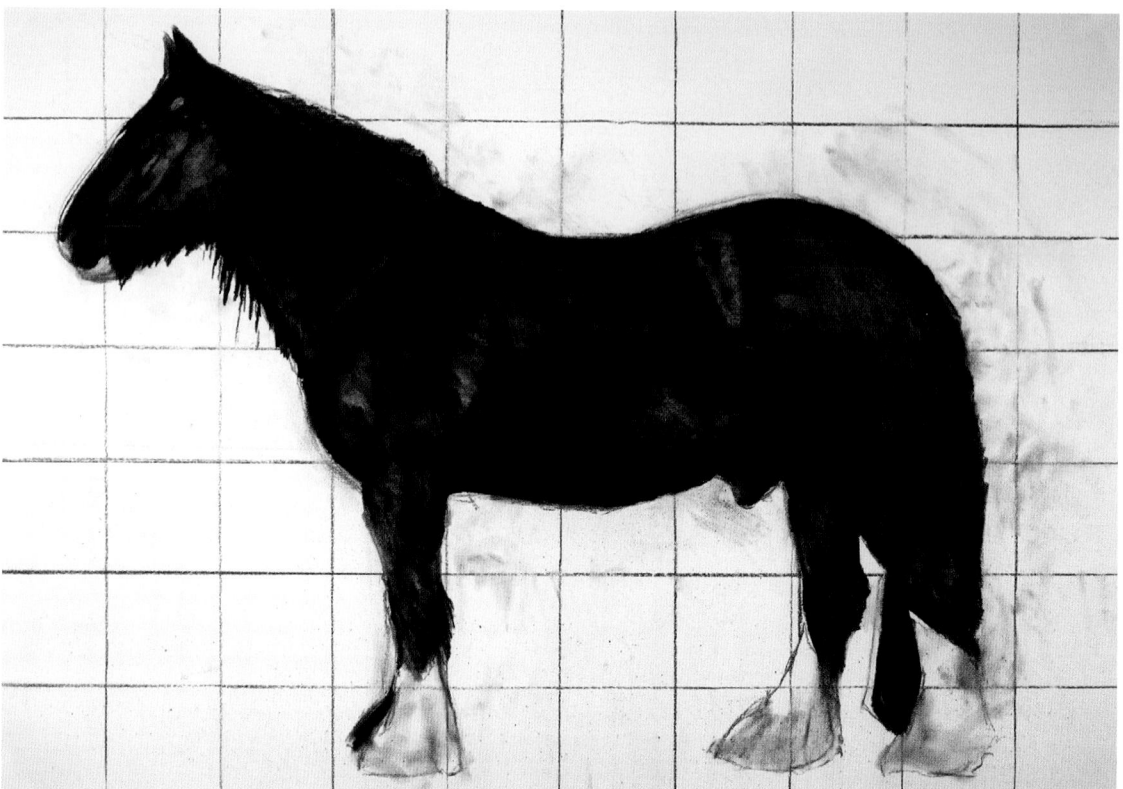

STAGE 4

It may look as if more charcoal has been added in the picture above, but in this stage all we do is blend what we've already put on the paper. Just like in the Sailing Ship tutorial (see pages 282–7), this is where blending makes the image look more real and less flat. Your aim is to turn three layers of tonal value into a wider range of values.

This process will require a leap of faith, because you will have spent a lot of time applying the first two layers. However, be bold – the more effort you put into this step, the more successful the results will be.

Using a blending stump, work vigorously across the compressed charcoal and natural charcoal to soften the edges and carry loose particles across the areas of paper that remain white – with the exception of the areas you want to remain white, which are on the feet and the head.

Just as when you were applying the charcoal, blend along the contours of the body. Use a large blending stump to work in a gestural motion across large areas, and smaller ones to soften the edges of particular areas. If your white areas require a little more charcoal, apply it, but gradually – there should be quite enough charcoal on the paper to carry across onto your lighter areas. You can now see why it was not necessary to be too precise when applying the first two layers.

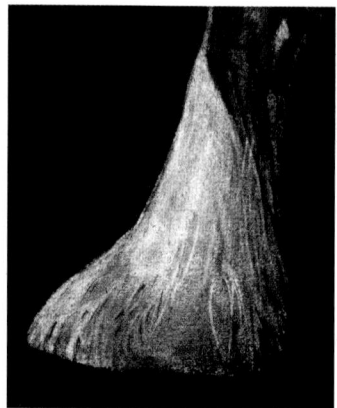

Tip
You don't need to draw every strand of hair to achieve a realistic impression. Just pick out a few that are either light against a dark background or dark against light and draw them in as finely as you can.

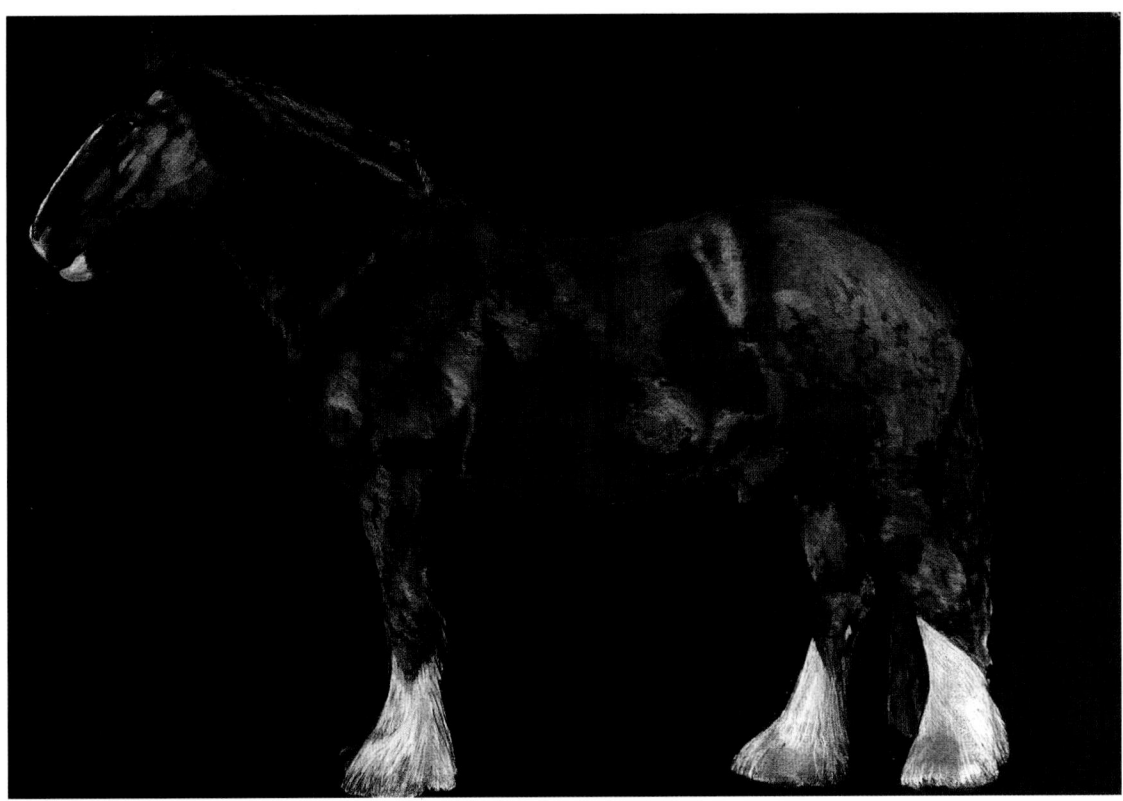

STAGE 5

In the final stage, you will be putting in your dark background and completing the feet and face. Using a broad stick of a really black compressed charcoal, draw around the shape of the horse before filling in the entire background. This process will probably create a lot of dust, so you may want to consider wearing a facemask or doing it outside. As when you worked the other areas of value, it is likely that the white of the paper will show through after your first pass, so you will need to work the compressed charcoal into the paper rigorously with a blending stump or your fingers.

The best way to achieve the white hair around the head and the hooves is with subtractive drawing (see page 261), but you will first need to darken the value of these areas with some blended-in natural charcoal so that you have something to subtract from.

As with the Jackdaw (see pages 290–5), one of the final steps is to sharpen up the eye, using your dark compressed charcoal pencil to get the darks and a pencil eraser for the highlight.

Considering the amount of charcoal used, it is a good idea to protect the final drawing behind glass (see pages 288–9). Doing so will also have the added benefits of adding to the illusion of depth and making your marks less visible.

Tip
Fingers can be effective blending tools, but first wash your hands well with soap to remove undesirable oils in the skin so they won't be worked into the paper. Or wear vinyl gloves to avoid getting your hands black.

Glossary

ACETATE A sheet of transparent film that is able to hold paint or ink.

ACRYLIC MEDIUM An additive that allows paint to flow more easily.

ACRYLIC RETARDER An additive to paint to slow down the drying time.

AERIAL PERSPECTIVE The effect of atmosphere on distant objects that makes them appear lighter in value and less defined the further they are away. Also known as atmospheric perspective.

ALLA PRIMA Technique of completing a painting in one go, before the paint dries.

ALLEGORICAL PAINTING A work that has hidden meanings within it.

ATMOSPHERIC PERSPECTIVE *see* AERIAL PERSPECTIVE.

BACKGROUND The plane of a drawing that is at the back of a scene, behind the foreground and middle ground.

BACKWASH When watercolour paint in one colour flows into another one that hasn't completely dried. Also known as a cauliflower.

BLEND To smooth out drawing marks to produce areas of even tonal value or a graduation from dark to light. Also, where two colours merge together on the paper smoothly.

BLOCKING IN The use of broad, rapid strokes to cover an area with colour as a basis for further development.

BODY Viscosity, or thickness of paint.

BURNISH Blend layers until pencil marks are smooth and none of the paper surface is showing through.

CALLIGRAPHIC Style of paint stroke that relies on rapid, expressive movement of the brush.

CARTRIDGE PAPER A high-quality type of heavyweight artist's paper used for illustration and drawing.

CAST SHADOW Shadow formed by an object upon another object.

CENTRELINE The lines running vertically and horizontally through the centre of your drawing area.

CHIAROSCURO Painting effect that strongly contrasts light and shadow, often with deep shadows that partially obscure the complete form of objects.

CLOISONNISM Style that encloses colours and shapes within a dark line.

COLOUR NOTE Small area of colour that usually contrasts with the larger areas of colour surrounding it.

COLOUR VALUE The relative lightness or darkness of a colour.

COLOUR WHEEL A visual device with different colours, showing the relationship between colours.

COMPLEMENTARY COLOURS A pair of colours from opposite sides of the colour wheel. They enhance each other when placed side by side and neutralize each other when mixed.

COMPOSITION The arrangement of shapes, lines, colours and textures within a painting.

CONTÉ CRAYON Drawing stick made out of compressed graphite and clay.

CONTOUR LINE Defines the outline or edges of a form as well as changes in planes within the form.

CONTRAST The difference between light and dark in a drawing; low contrast is when there is little difference and high contrast when the difference is great.

DRY-BRUSH TECHNIQUE Applying paint to a surface with little or no medium, so it looks as if it was drawn with chalk.

EARTH COLOURS Browns and muted colours.

FAT OVER LEAN The rule of using fatty paint (containing more linseed oil) over lean paint (containing less oil) in order to prevent cracking.

FIDDLING Adding unnecessary detail to a painting.

FIXATIVE A liquid spray similar to varnish that binds the pigment to the drawing surface for better preservation and to prevent smudging.

FLAT WASH A smooth, even layer of watercolour produced by moving your paintbrush in straight lines and slightly overlapping the line left by the previous brushstroke.

FOCAL POINT Area in the painting that first draws the viewer's eye through detail or contrast.

FORM An object's three-dimensional shape that takes into account its volume, thus its height, width and depth.

FOREGROUND The foremost plane of elements within an image lying in front of the middle ground.

FORMAT The shape and orientation of a drawing; landscape, portrait and square are commonly applied to artwork.

FROM LIFE Painting directly from a person, object or scene, as opposed to from photographs or drawings.

GESTURE LINE Otherwise known as the line of action, this is a fluid stroke that captures movement at a particular moment.

GOUACHE A heavily pigmented paint with characteristics of both watercolour and acrylic. It is diluted with water and is excellent for adding detail because it dries more opaque than watercolour.

GRADUATED WASH Where the paint becomes progressively lighter by adding more water to each band of colour.

GLASSINE PAPER A special paper used to protect artworks; it has a smooth surface that prevents abrasion.

GLAZE Thin transparent layer of paint used to modify an underlying colour.

GRAPHITE PENCIL A standard pencil with the 'lead' formed from graphite.

GRISAILLE Painting that is done in one colour, originally to emulate a sculpture. The word originates from the French word for grey.

GROUND Background colour that allows subsequent applications of paint to interact in a harmonious way.

HATCHING Groups of small parallel marks, which produce the effect of tone or density in a drawing.

HIGHLIGHTS The areas within an image that are the lightest lights.

HORIZON LINE A notional horizontal plane projecting at the artist's eye level.

HUE Pure pigment colour without black or white added.

IMPASTO Thick paint that remains raised and textured after drying. Derived from the Italian word for paste.

JUXTAPOSE Placing two or more objects side by side with the intention of comparing or contrasting elements.

LANDSCAPE A drawing depicting outdoor scenery; when applied to formats, it describes a rectangle with its longest length along the horizontal.

LAYERING Basic pencil technique that involves adding colours on top of one another using light pencil pressure.

LIMITED PALETTE Deliberately reducing the number of colours used to maintain harmony in the painting.

LINEAR PERSPECTIVE System for drawing objects that uses lines and vanishing points to determine how much an object's apparent size changes with distance.

LOCAL COLOUR The colour of an object itself, regardless of light or shade.

MASKING FLUID A rubbery solution that resists paint, thereby preserving white areas on your paper.

MATCHING MEASUREMENTS Technique of finding two identical distances in the subject which can be replicated in the painting.

MATT A surface that is non-reflective.

MEDIUM Any material with which drawing or painting marks are made.

MID-TONES Variations of tone that fall between the darkest and lightest.

MODELLING Achieving the appearance of three dimensions on a flat surface by shading or other marks.

MONOCHROME An image composed in black and white or shades of grey – lacking colour.

MOUNT BOARD A high-quality cardboard product used to create a surround for artwork when framing.

NEGATIVE SPACE Shapes around or between objects.

OPACITY The ability of a colour to obscure anything underneath; the opposite of transparent.

PALETTE A surface suitable for mixing paint; also used to describe the range of colours used by a particular artist.

PAN A small block of solid watercolour paint, which is reconstituted with water.

PANORAMA An elongated rectangle format that is longest along its horizontal length.

PAPER STUMP A useful little tool that looks like a pencil without the graphite and is made completely of compressed paper. It is used to blend and smudge coloured pencils on the paper, similar to using your finger to smudge but more precise.

PASSAGE OF PAINT An area of paint that has a certain style of brushwork, colour or rhythm.

PASTEL Pure pigment powder and binder in stick form, used like a crayon to add extra vibrancy.

PAYNE'S GREY A dark blue-grey used as a mixer in place of black, because it doesn't dirty the original hue.

PERSPECTIVE Techniques used to create the illusion of depth and spatial recession in drawing and painting. Aerial or atmospheric perspective is the illusion of distance in landscapes or seascapes by diminishing in colour, tone and size.

PIGMENT Natural or chemical coloured substance used in the making of coloured drawing media, such as paint, dyes, inks, etc.

PLEIN-AIR PAINTING French term for outdoor painting.

POSITIVE SPACE The physical space an object occupies.

PRIMARY COLOURS Red, yellow and blue – colours from which all others can be mixed.

PRIMING Applying a chalk solution to a canvas or other surface so that when it is dry, it forms an impermeable layer. Usually called gesso.

REFLECTED LIGHT Light bouncing off a surface into the shadow side of an object.

REGISTRATION Method of aligning a layer of colour so when it is printed it falls in the same position each time an impression is made.

RIGGER A fine, thin brush used for painting details.

RULE OF THIRDS Compositional concept of dividing the rectangle into thirds and placing major lines or subjects on these lines or junctions.

SATURATION The intensity of a particular colour (hue).

SCUMBLING Painting technique whereby a broken layer of colour is brushed over another so that patches of the colour beneath show through. Usually done with a stiff bristle brush.

SGRAFFITO Scratching back through wet paint to reveal underlying colours.

SHADING Adding medium within areas of a drawing to darken tonal values.

SOFTEN To make the boundaries between different elements within a drawing less defined through blending, smudging or smearing.

SOLVENT Clear liquid used to dilute and clean oil paints.

SPLATTERING Flicking paint from a loaded paintbrush or toothbrush to create a random texture.

STIPPLING A way of applying paint using a vertical stabbing motion.

STROKES Marks made with pencil, can vary in size, shape and width.

THUMBNAIL SKETCH A tiny, rapid sketch to assist in compositional decisions.

TINT A colour lightened with white.

TONAL PLAN A mental image of where the main light and dark areas of a painting will be.

TONAL VALUE (ALSO KNOWN AS TONE OR VALUE) Relative lightness or darkness of a colour.

TONE The lightness or darkness of a colour.

TONKING Applying paper to the surface of a wet painting to remove the paint.

TRANSPARENT PAINT Paints that allow light to travel through them and reflect back from the surface underneath. Suitable for glazing.

UNDERDRAWING An initial measured drawing or sketch to plot all of the elements in the correct position before adding tone or texture.

UNDERPAINTING Painting tonally in a single dilute colour to give a solid basis on which to apply colour.

VALUE Also referred to as tonal value, to describe the degree to which an area of shading is light or dark.

VANISHING POINT All parallel lines converge on this point, which sits on your horizon line.

VELATURA A glaze that contains an opaque paint such as white.

VIEWFINDER A device with a rectangular hole for viewing the subject.

WASH Dilute colour that can be easily spread over the canvas or paper.

WET-IN-WET Technique of applying wet paint on top of or into wet paint.

WET-ON-DRY Adding layers of paint on top of dry paint, to produce strong colours with defined edges.

Index

About the Artists

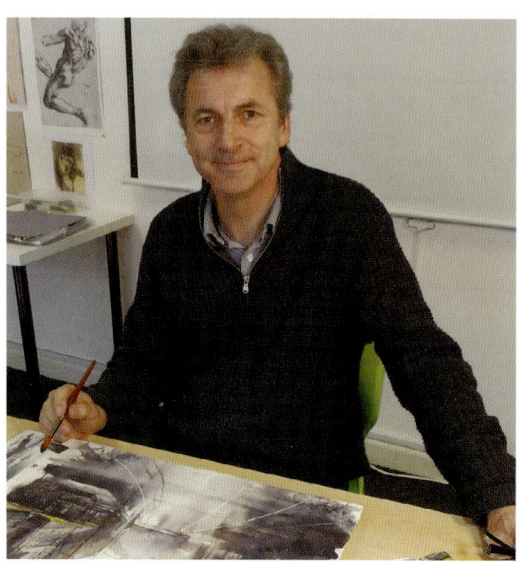

Paul Clark is a professional illustrator who has been teaching watercolour painting and drawing techniques for more than 25 years. Paul also runs his own successful design studio and art school in South East England. He has taught art to adults at several local colleges and education centres and continues to be involved in the local art scene, often judging art shows and exhibitions in and around Sussex.

'One of the greatest privileges for me, in teaching art, is to watch learners' individual styles develop and see the thrill they get from mastering new techniques,' says Paul.

Paul's ethos in teaching is that people learn better when working in a happy and relaxed atmosphere, so all his classes are open and fun, with a great emphasis on all artistic techniques being demonstrated.

www.artbypaulclark.co.uk

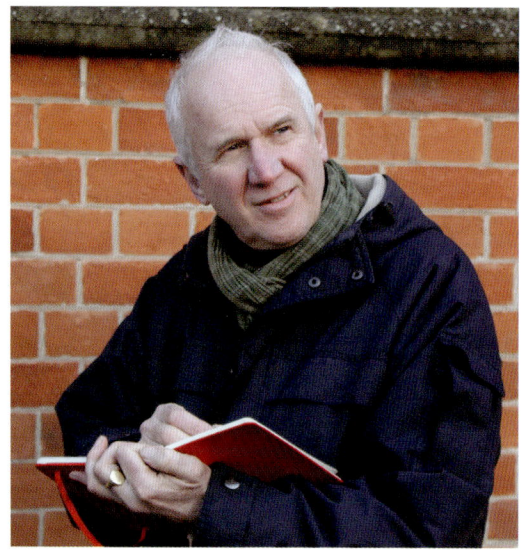

Adrian Burrows lives and works in South East England. He has a BA (Hons) in Graphic Design and is a qualified art teacher. Adrian divides his time between running a graphic design business and teaching art to adults. His love affair with acrylic paint is long standing.

'I think it is the designer in me that attracts me to acrylic paint,' he says. 'I love the fresh, flat quality of acrylics and how you can work on an already dry colour in the same sitting.'

Adrian believes that anyone can paint to an acceptable standard, as long as they have enthusiasm and a sincere desire to learn.

Norman Long BA MAFA studied at Blackpool and Fylde College, Newcastle University and the Pennsylvania Academy of Fine Arts. In addition to 13 solo shows, his work has featured in distinguished group exhibitions in the USA and throughout the UK, including the BP Portrait Award. He is a winner of the Royal Society of Portrait Painters' de Laszlo Award and Artist and Illustrator's Artist of the Year 2013.

A full-time artist and teacher since 1999, Norman says, 'I love that I can spend time alone in the studio, making discoveries, and then share them with enthusiastic students.' The independent Norman Long Studio School, based in Preston, was founded in 2012.

Norman lives in Lytham St Annes, North West England, with his American artist wife Lindsey and three budding artists: Boston, Jasper and Lennox Long.

www.normanlongartist.com

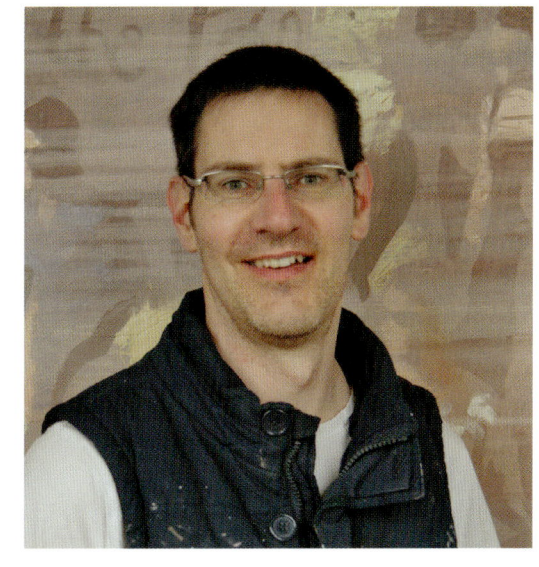

Kendra Ferreira has a bachelor of fine arts from Massachusetts College of Art and Design, Boston. She is a signature member of the Colored Pencil Society of America and has also earned a second signature status from CPSA in exploratory mediums with coloured pencil. Kendra's work has been included in many national and international art exhibitions and she is a recipient of numerous awards for her work.

Kendra has enjoyed teaching adult and teen art classes for over 20 years. She is the mother of three grown sons and lives in Bristol, Rhode Island, USA with her husband Paul and small dog Bandit. Besides coloured pencil, her interests are travelling, skiing, hiking and cooking.

www.kjfdesign.com

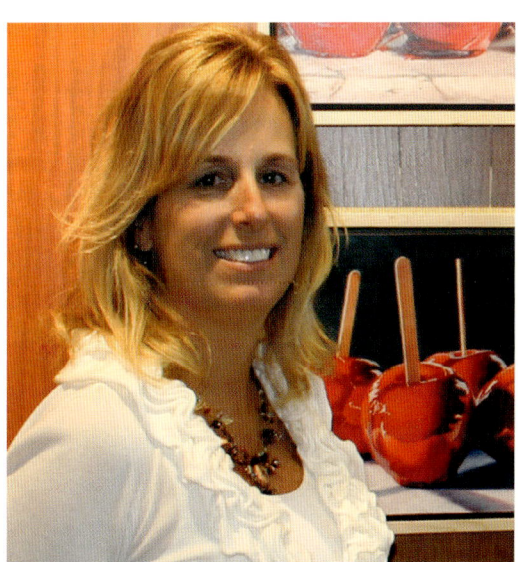

Richard Rochester studied Fine Art at Exeter College of Art and Design. Following his graduation, he served for 18 years in the British Army and the Royal Marines before returning to Exeter and his love of art. Richard works across a range of creative disciplines but is particularly inspired by charcoal.

Living near the coast and countryside of South West England has a strong influence on his art and he is possibly best known for his large-scale and immersive landscapes, as well as his work with the not-for-profit humanitarian endeavour 'Journey Through Conflict'. Beyond the studio Richard regularly delivers talks, demonstrations and workshops to art groups and societies. He is also an instructor with the online training organization Yodomo.

www.richardrochester.co.uk

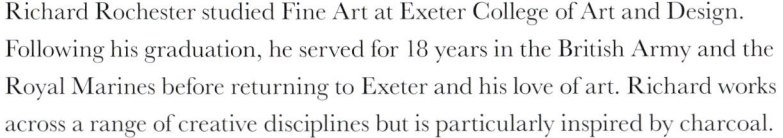

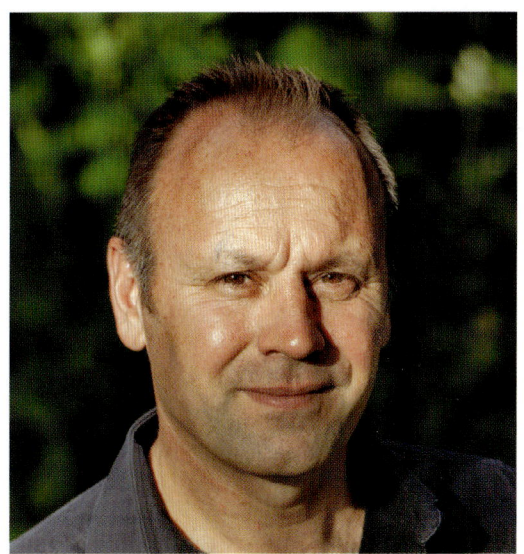

First published 2020 by
Guild of Master Craftsman Publications Ltd
Castle Place, 166 High Street, Lewes,
East Sussex BN7 1XU, UK

Text © Paul Clark, Adrian Burrows, Norman Long,
Kendra Ferreira, Richard Rochester, 2020
Copyright in the Work © GMC Publications Ltd, 2020.
Content taken from the series *Techniques and Tutorials for the
Complete Beginner*, previously published by GMC Publications.

ISBN 978 1 78494 586 2

A catalogue record for this book is available from the
British Library.

Publisher Jonathan Bailey
Production Jim Bulley and Jo Pallett
Commissioning & Senior Project Editor Dominique Page
Managing Art Editor Gilda Pacitti
Art Editor Rebecca Mothersole

Colour origination by GMC Reprographics
Printed and bound in China

To order a book, or to request a catalogue, contact:
GMC Publications Ltd, Castle Place, 166 High Street, Lewes, East Sussex, BN7 1XU, United Kingdom
Tel: +44 (0)1273 488005
www.gmcbooks.com

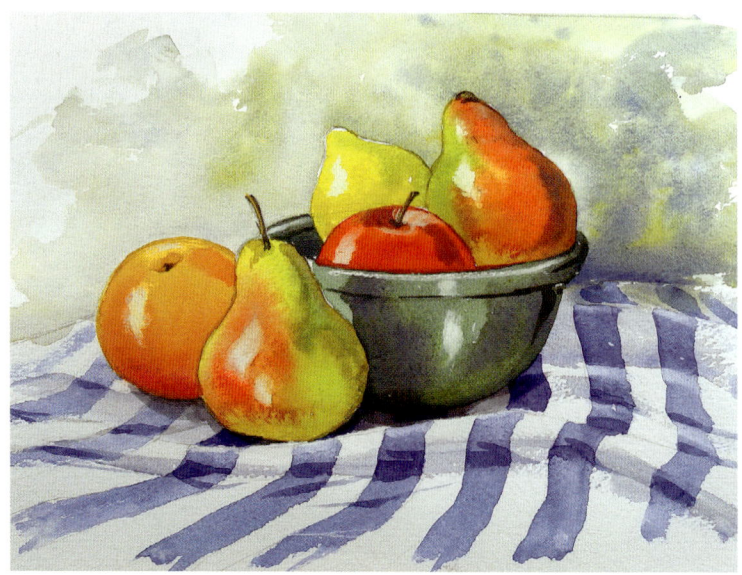